# merge

art . craft . design

GINGKO PRESS

# /Introduction

"My hand is the extension of the thinking process - the creative process. - Tadao Ando"

Emphasizing the idea of creating an artwork or a design through our 'hands' it is a joy for me to introduce to you MERGE; Art x Craft x Design - a book with over 80 interesting artists or designers using materials ranging from paper, wood, cloth and metal to create quirky pieces out of their works. Often leaving their audiences in awe and some times wondering how did they even thought of this?

The idea of this book started out when we noticed how intriguing and detailed some of these handcrafted works look which appealed to many out there. While further researching on all aspects, keeping in mind that has each project should be: wise usage of materials, handcrafted to its' maximum possibilities, interesting perspective and of course creative. It begin to show that there are many artist or designers who definitely takes pride in the idea of crafting their work plus their adventurous nature of dabbling with various materials, thus creating a work that is not only visually pleasing but also one with a process. We managed to also gather a few projects by strong recommendations from various artists that knew of projects that fit our theme perfectly.

In a generation where computer 'generated' designs are produced daily, it is works by such artistes that goes back to the basis of crafting and getting their hands all dirty. For them, the process of crafting a work is definitely time consuming and energy draining but we believe that the satisfaction is there. No, don't get us wrong, it is absolutely fine to use the computer as a tool in aid of a project, like even now? Though I wished the entire book was hand crafted, but if there was just 10% of the 'hands' involved, that would be good enough. MERGE; Art x Craft x Design is a book where others can gain inspiration from the featured works that has been carefully compiled for every creative person out there. So don't stop creating! I'd leave you with this quote which I hope will inspire you in some way or another, all the best in whatever season you are in, press on.

"A man who works with his hands is a laborer; a man who works with his hands and his brain is a craftsman; but a man who works with his hands and his brain and his heart is an artist.
- Louis Nizer"

# Contents

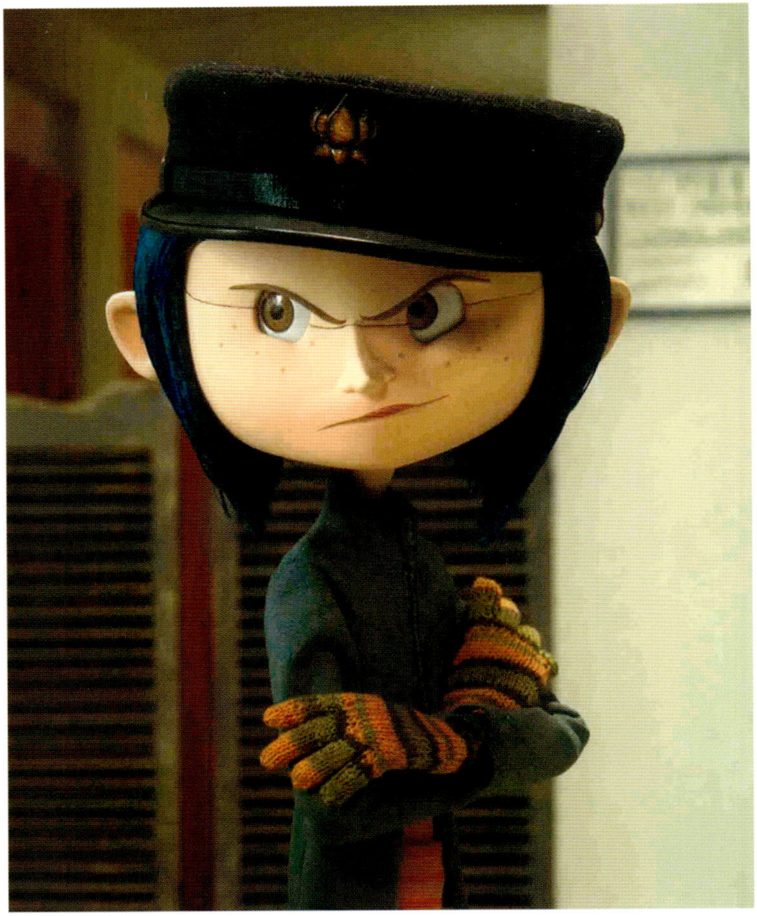

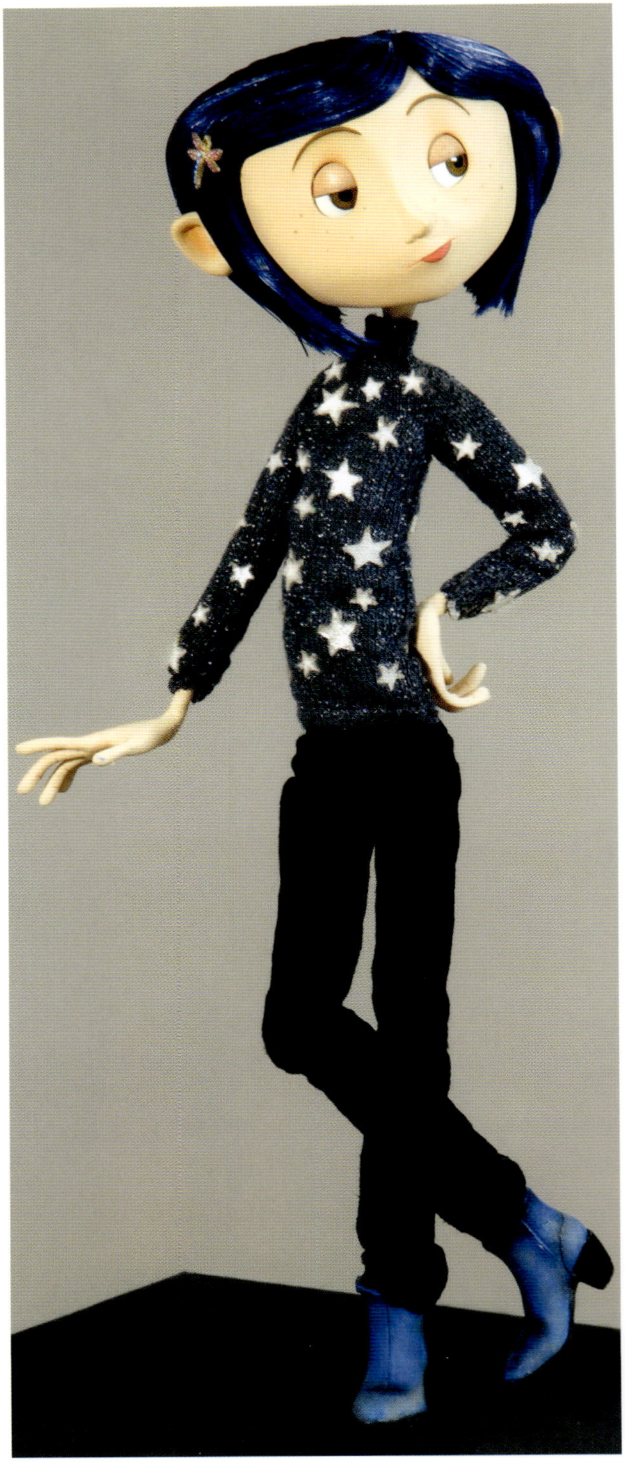

Coraline (voice by Dakota Fanning) finds Other Mother's (voiced by Teri Hatcher) snack treat to be distasteful in Henry Selick's stop-motion animated 3-D adventure CORALINE, from LAIKA Entertainment for release by Focus Features. 

# Althea Crome

www.bugknits.com

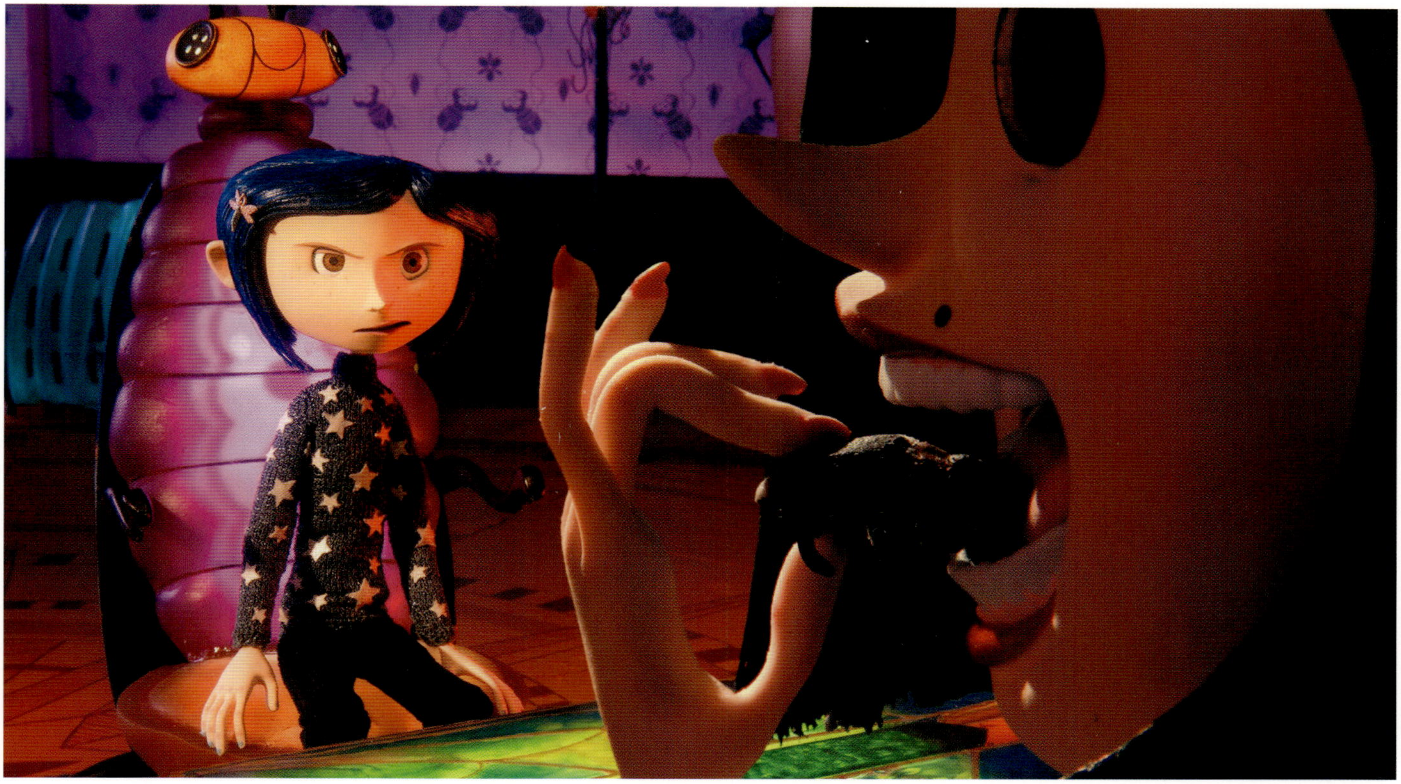

My work consists of extremely small knitted pieces that I like to call micro-3D soft sculptures. The tools I use, which I create myself, along with various magnifying lenses help me manipulate fine, carefully selected threads into my micro-3D soft sculptures. Working with these tools requires constant innovation and new techniques to allow me to translate my artistic vision into my technically challenging medium. In my work you will see tradition and innovation combining and merging in surprising ways. As a miniaturist I have learned the importance of proper scale, as a knitter I have come to respect the art of traditional technique and pattern design and as an artist I rejoice in adaptation, discovery and experimentation. Traditional formats and styles provide the basic framework for my pieces, and suggest a range of likely motifs; the manner in which these motifs are selected, adapted, altered and combined is then left to my own imagination and desire for innovation. Every one of my knitted miniatures is informed by rich artistic tradition, but none are mere replicas of existing patterns or styles. It is with a spirit of continued curiosity and a desire to create new and original pieces that I will continue to pursue my love of knitting within the limitless possibilities of this miniature scale. I began to explore micro-knitting as a medium for soft-sculpture and since then I have been pushing toward ever new technical and design challenges. Tough as it is to knit on such a small scale, the "bug-knit" scale has allowed me the freedom to create and experiment with designs which, on a larger scale, would be cumbersome and prohibitive. My success in developing commercial patterns and techniques for 1:12 scale gloves, socks and other garments and my ability to create specialized tools using surgical stainless steel, has inspired me to venture further into what I've come to think of as "extreme knitting" as a fine art. It is art that surprises and enchants while still communicating rich artistic content.

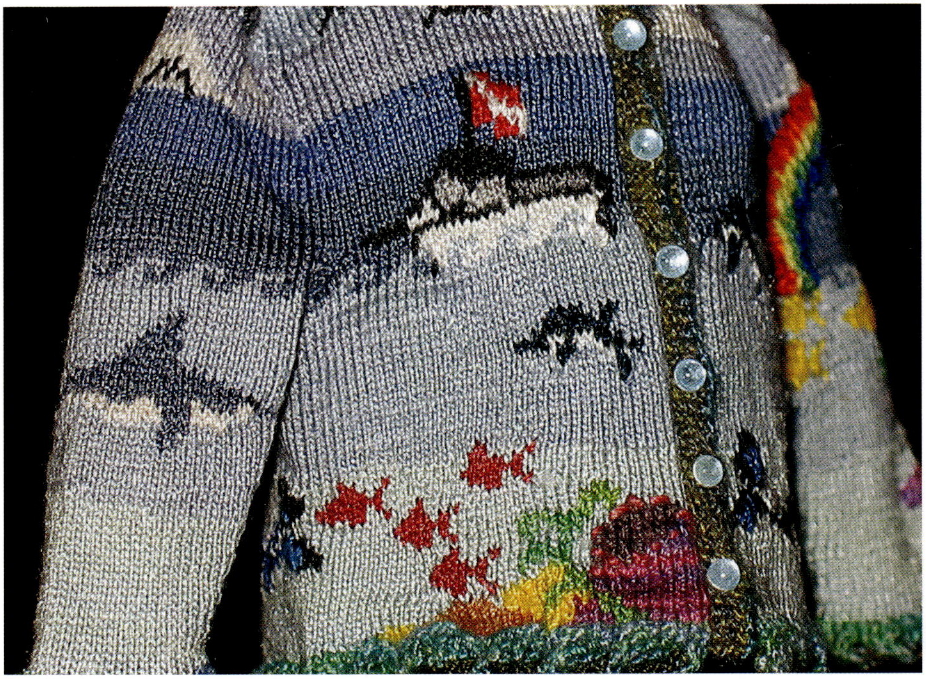

**Truth and Wisdom Kimono**
1 /12 scale 2 1/8" x 2 3/4" Silk thread and antique silk kimono fabric (lining) 2007

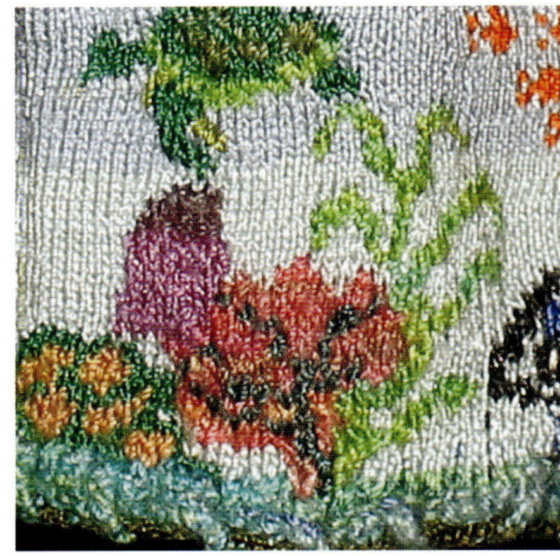

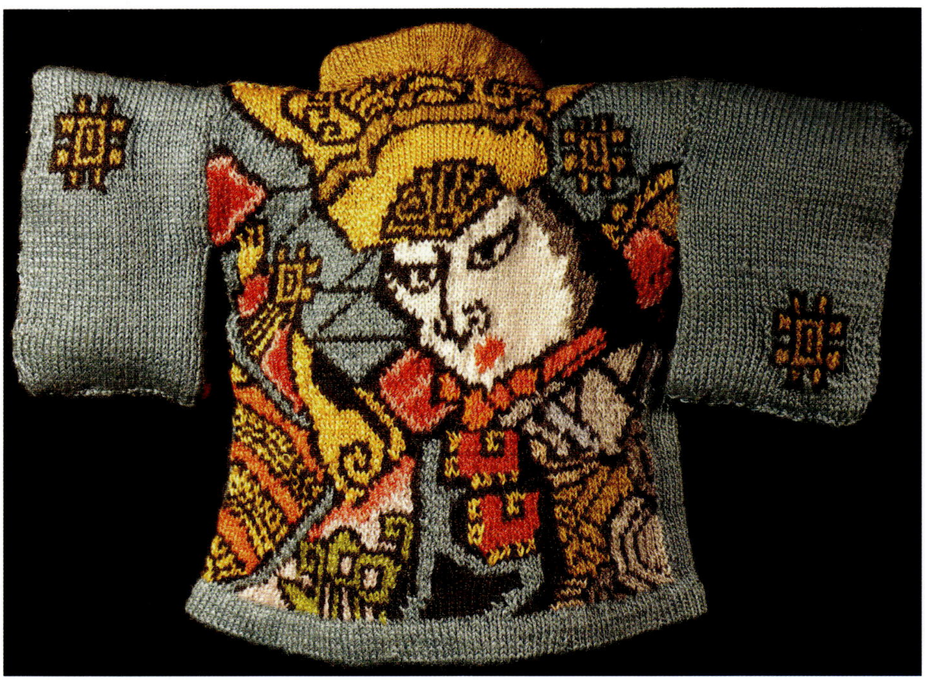

**Scuba Cardigan** 2" x 2 1/2"
Silk Thread 2007

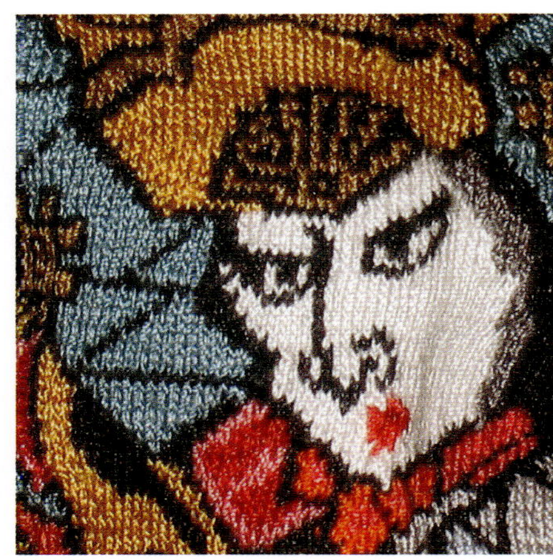

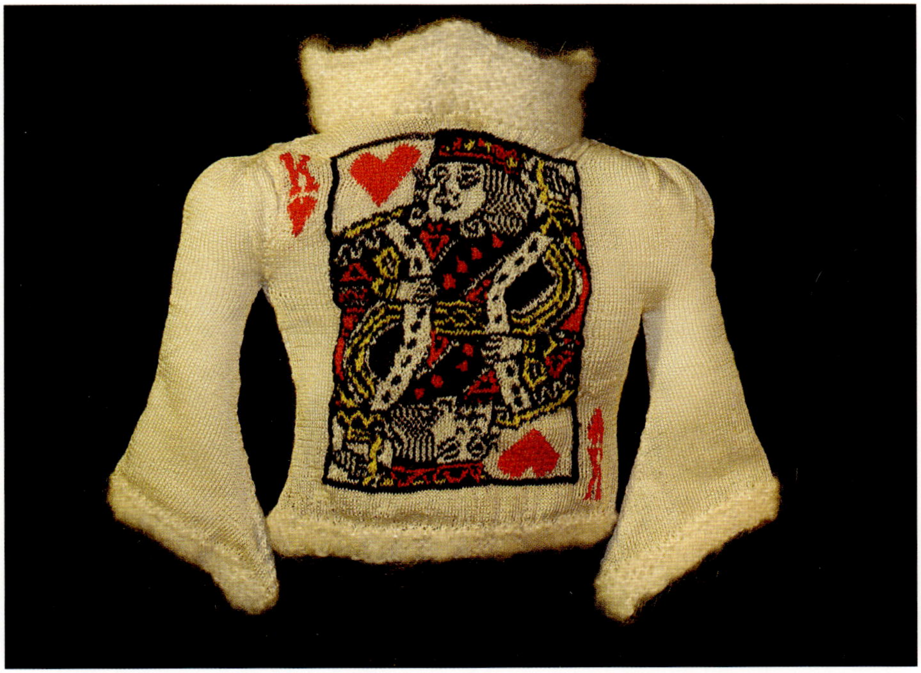

**King and Queen of Hearts**
3 3/8" x 2 3/8"
Silk Thread
2007

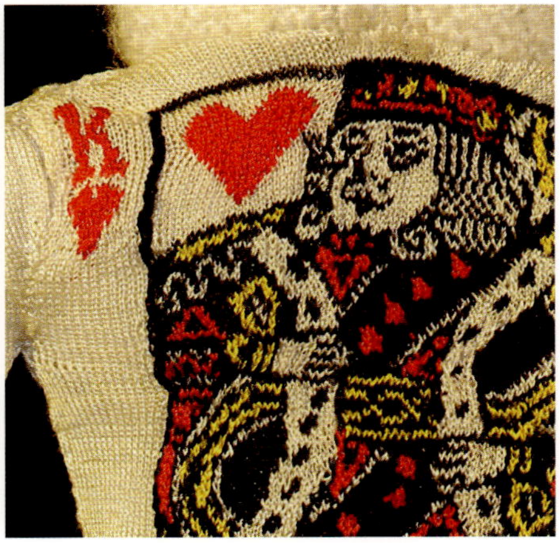

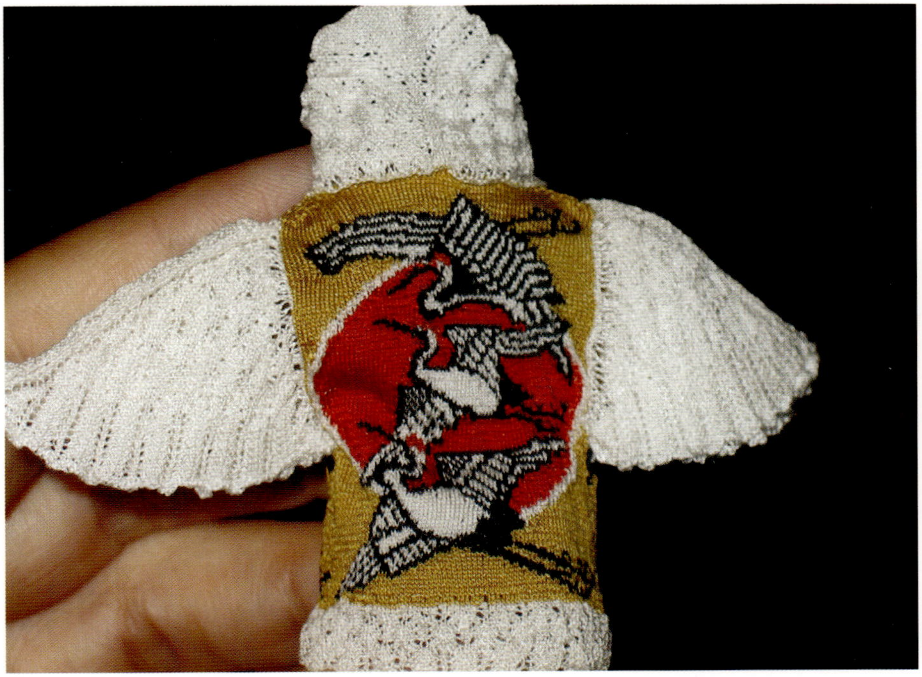

**Japanese Crane Sweater**
This cardigan is knit with very fine Japanese silk thread and contains approximately 40,000 individual stitches and took a little over two months to create.

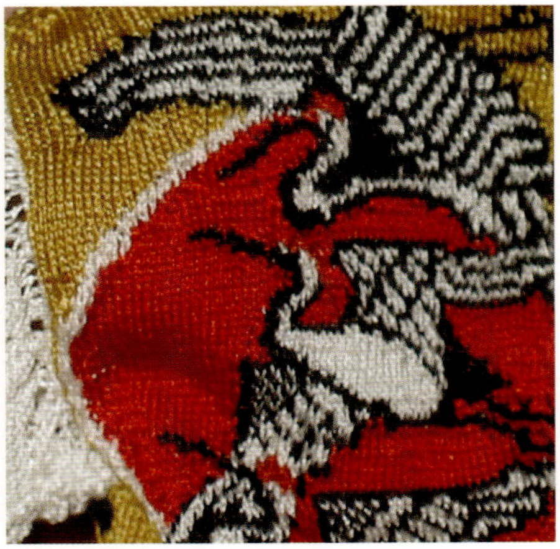

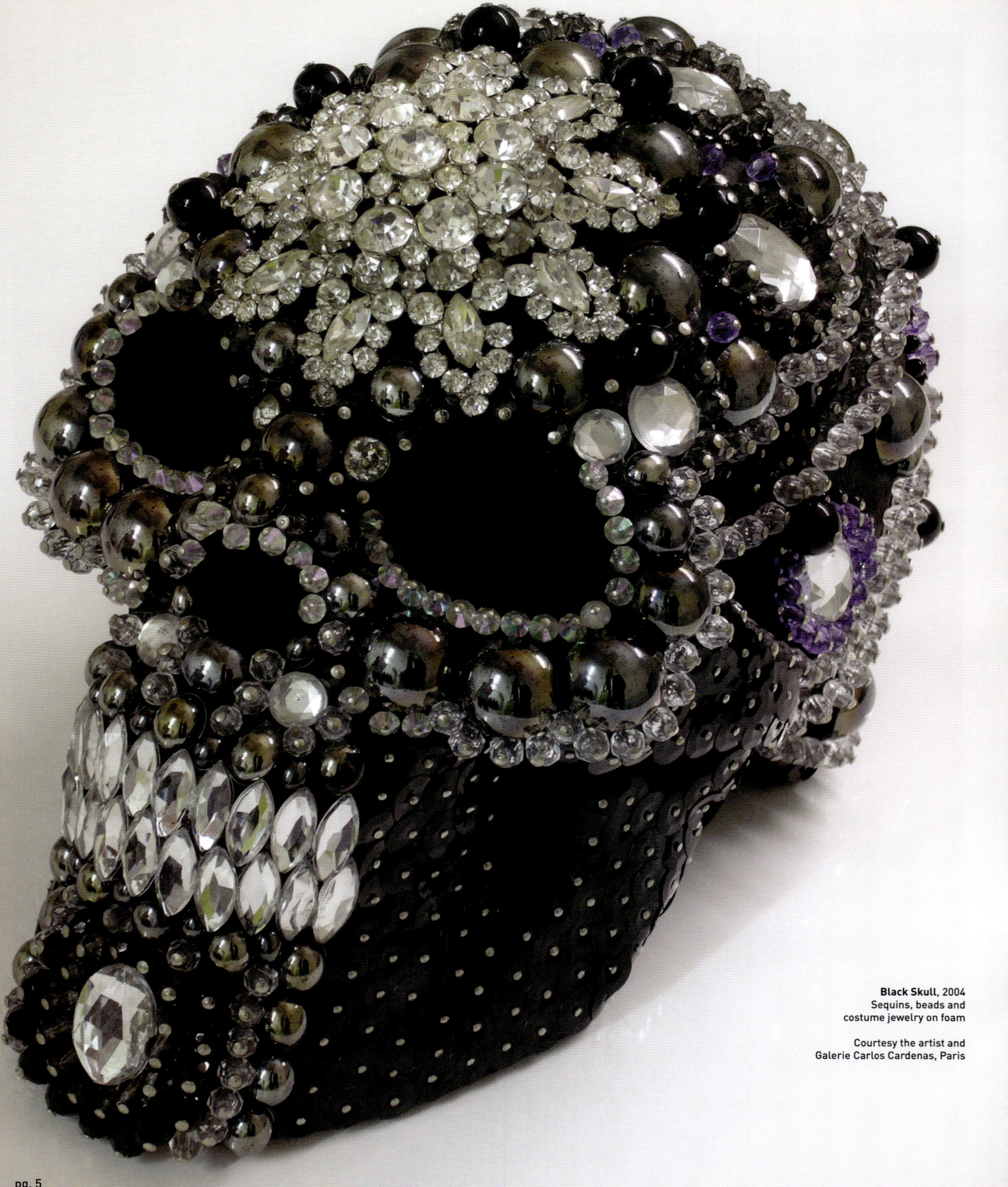

**Black Skull**, 2004
Sequins, beads and
costume jewelry on foam

Courtesy the artist and
Galerie Carlos Cardenas, Paris

# Amy Sarkisian

www.asark.com

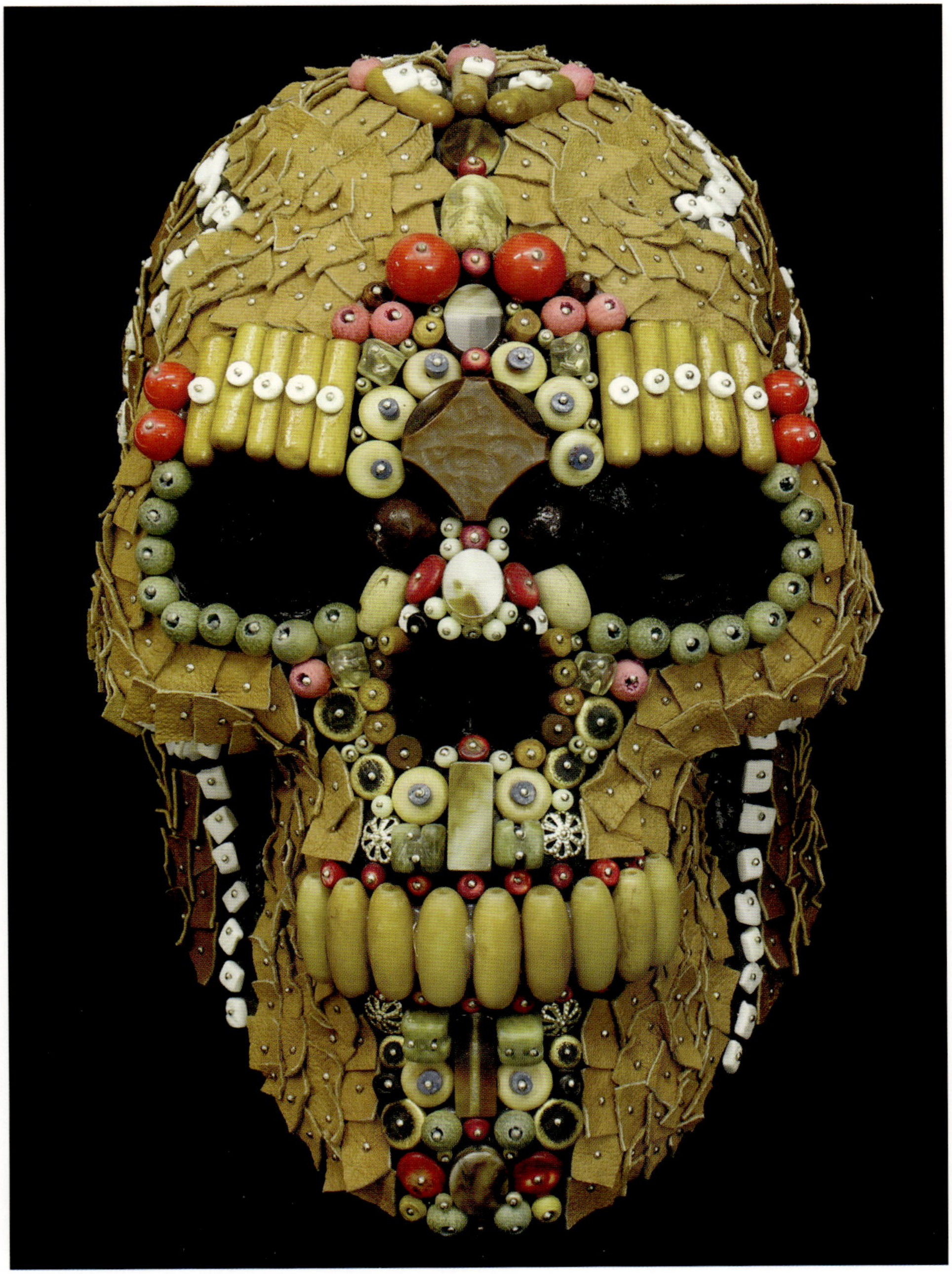

Amy Sarkisian received a BFA in sculpture from Kent State University in Ohio in 1994 and a MFA in sculpture from the University of California, Los Angeles in 1997.

After Amy graduated from UCLA she was able to rent a large studio and used half of it for a studio practice and the other half to curate art shows. It was called Studio 870 and was quite successful until she lost the space in 2000. That same year she was included in a group show at Roberts & Tilton Gallery in Los Angeles called Mysterious Prey. The show got a review and landed her work in a thumbnail image on the cover of Artforum. Amy continued to show steadily and was asked to do visiting lectures at Kent State University, Art Center School of Design and UCLA. In 2004 she was picked up by Atelier Cardenas Bellanger in Paris and Sister in Los Angeles. They are both still currently representing her work. In 2008 Amy was asked to join the Los Angeles Artists Pension Trust.

Other galleries Amy has shown with include Marella Arte Contemporanea in Milan, Milliken Gallery in Stockholm, Galleri S.E in Oslo, Anton Kern, Dietch Projects, Leo Koenig and the New Museum in New York, the London Institute, and several galleries in Los Angeles including, Marc Foxx, Suzanne Vielmetter, LACE, Angela Hanley Gallery, ACME, and the Mak Center.

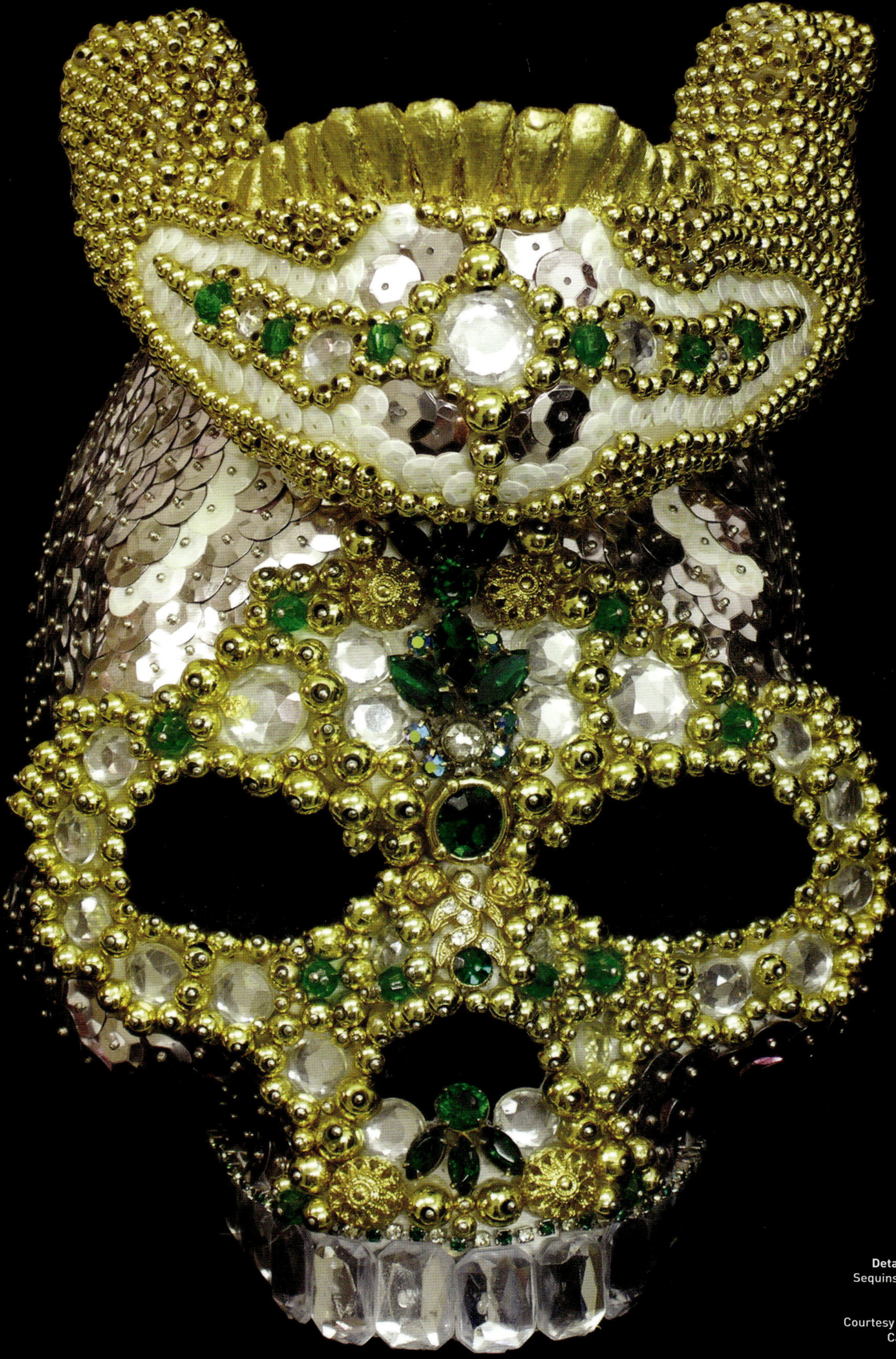

**Detached Jaw Skull**, 2004
Sequins, beads, and costume
jewelry on foam

Courtesy the artist and Galerie
Carlos Cardenas, Paris

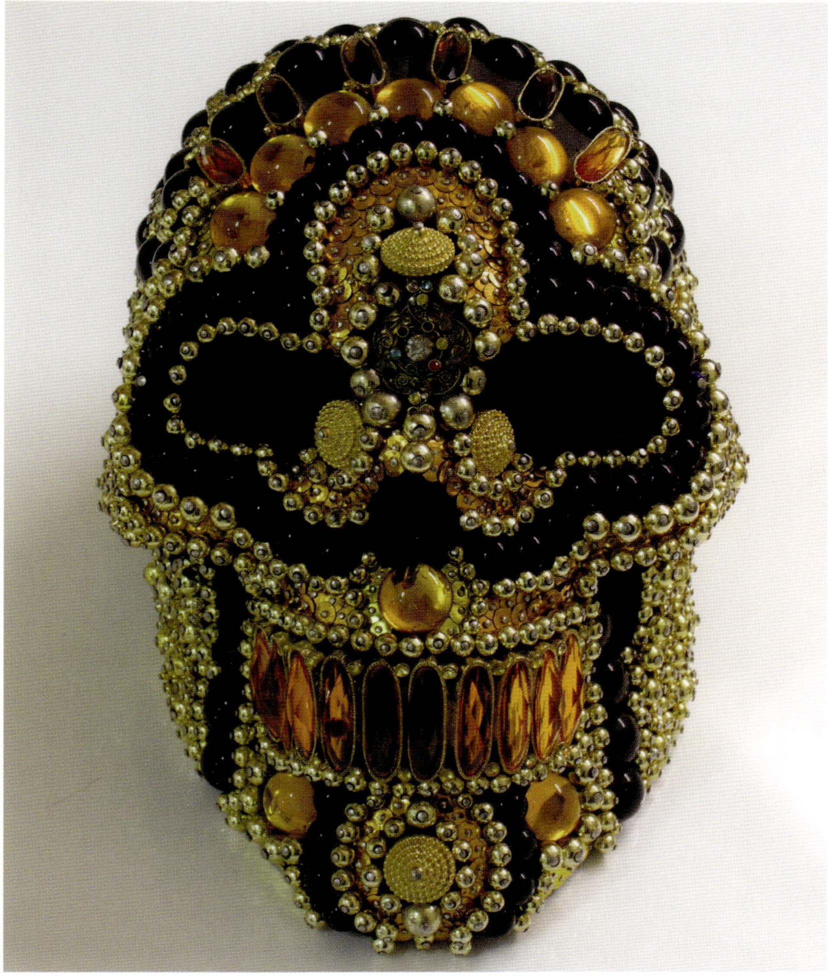

**Orange and Black Skull**, 2004
Beads and costume jewelry
on foam

Courtesy the artist and
Galerie Carlos Cardenas, Paris

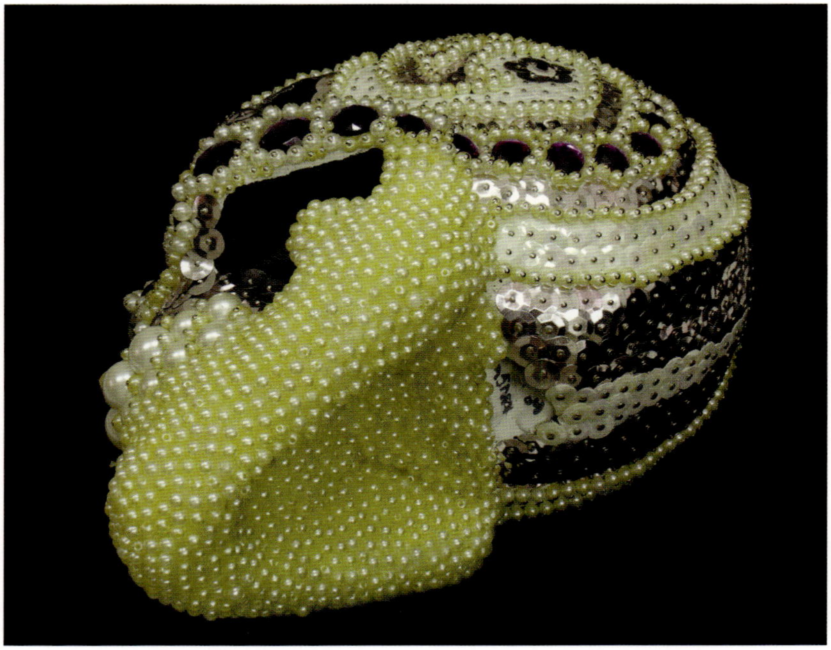

**White Pearl Skull**, 2004
Sequins, beads and costume
jewelry on foam

Courtesy the artist and Amélie
Bellanger Mathieu, Paris

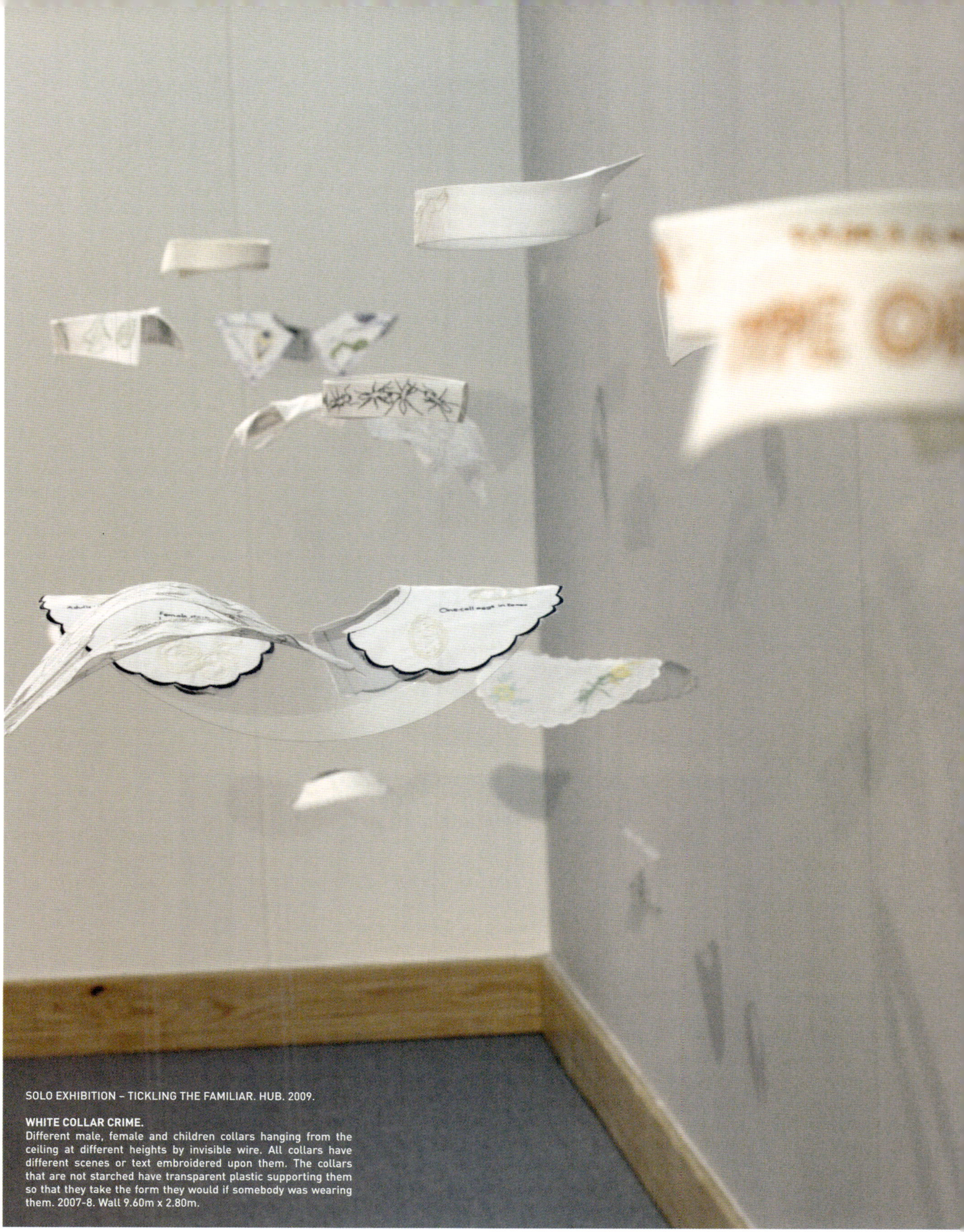

SOLO EXHIBITION – TICKLING THE FAMILIAR. HUB. 2009.

**WHITE COLLAR CRIME.**
Different male, female and children collars hanging from the ceiling at different heights by invisible wire. All collars have different scenes or text embroidered upon them. The collars that are not starched have transparent plastic supporting them so that they take the form they would if somebody was wearing them. 2007-8. Wall 9.60m x 2.80m.

# Anthea/Bush

www.antheabush.com

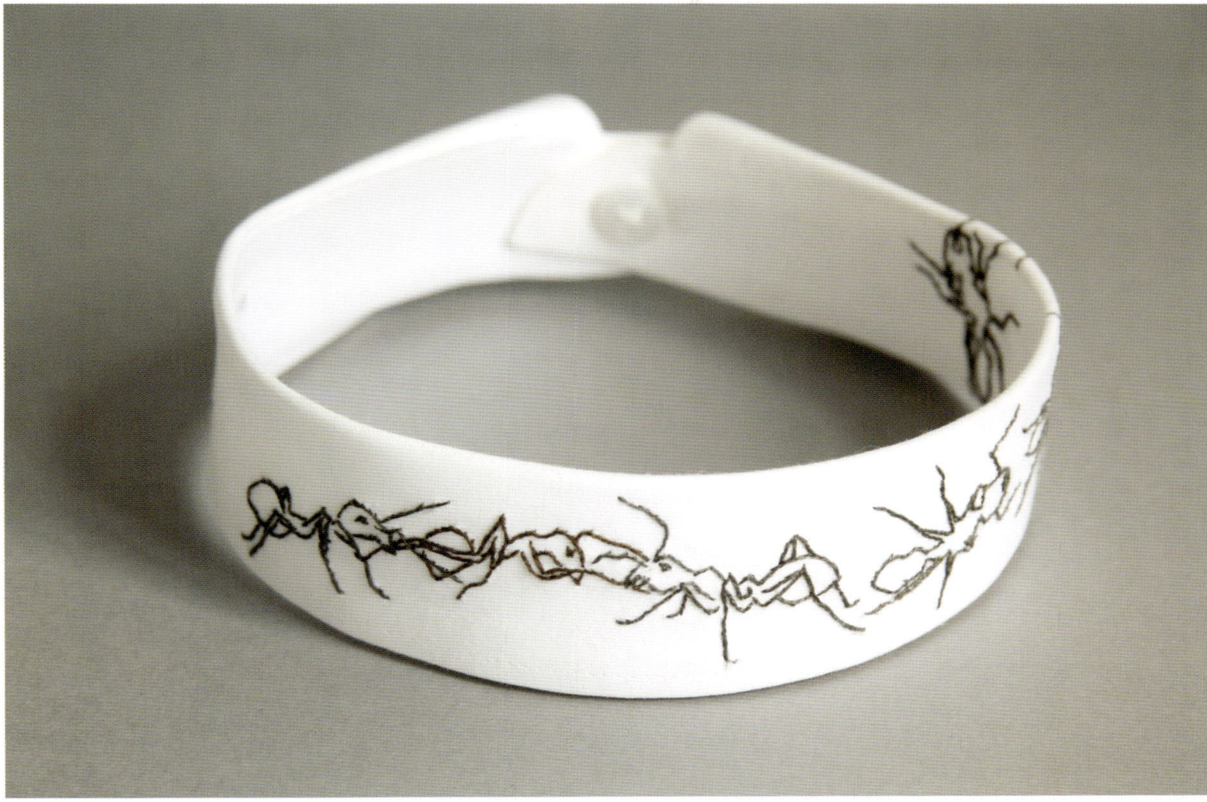

Anthea Bush is a visual artist who for the last 10 years has lived and worked in The Netherlands. Anthea Bush incorporates the role of fantasy and imagination and how these interact within our daily world and how these two aspects merge and separate from one another. She is interested in objects and images that are or have been in daily circulation, what and how they are used by individuals or collectively, to express their identity. In all her work the sensory feeling of touch is essential or the memory of that sensation, for example how shag pile carpet feels under the foot. She use personal experiences as a starting point and then develops them further. Since 2004 she has been developing a series of work based around the motorbike rider. She sees the motorbike rider as a character in her play. He changes, disappears and resurfaces. He represents different things he initially came in as reference to her childhood and from the memory of riding on her father's motorbike. Since then he has developed in different ways, he represents an alter ego, a superhero, and a form of identification as well as a way to remain anonymous, where the helmet is used both actually, and metaphorically, as a shield against the outside world. In 2007 there was a financial scandal at her part time job, which she used to develop the series 'White Collar Crime'. Clothing here used as a façade disguising an anti-hero; conventionally prim and proper external appearances concealing a darker underside - even predicting current worldwide circumstances - hinting at the possible discrepancy between the outer persona and what is really underneath.

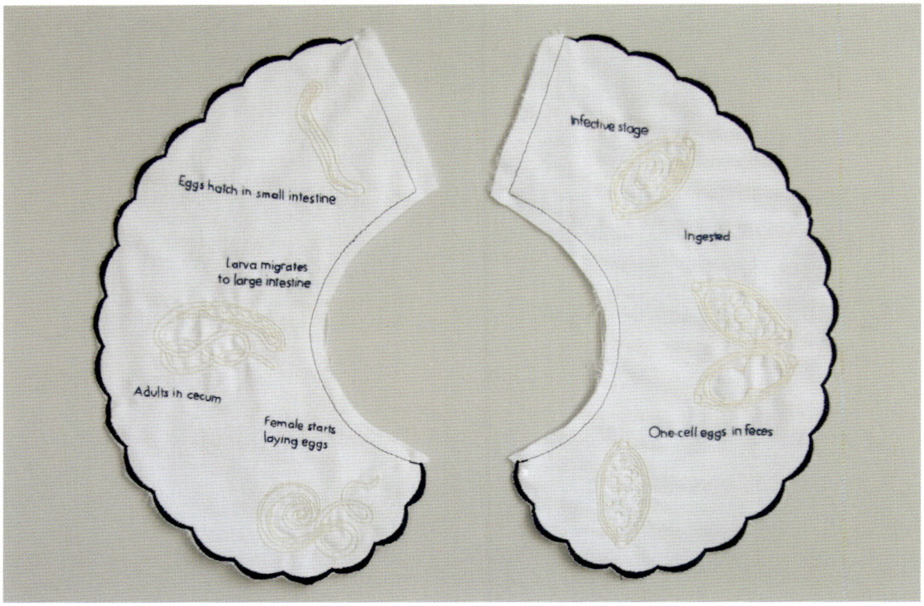


**WHITE COLLAR CRIME.** 2007. 46 x 55 cm.
White embroidered dogs on a female collar.

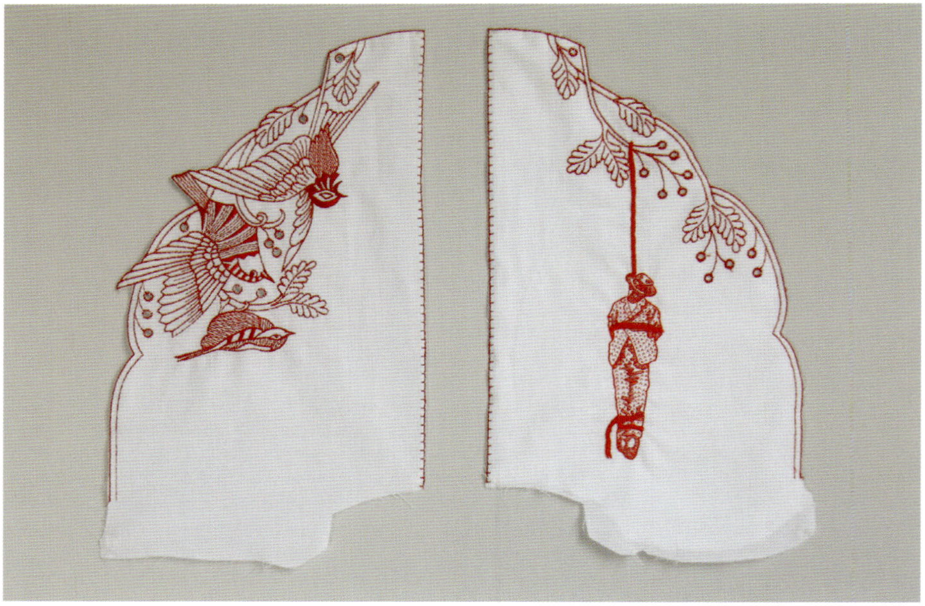

**WHITE COLLAR CRIME.** 2007. 46 x 52 cm.
Red embroidered birds and hanging man on a female collar.

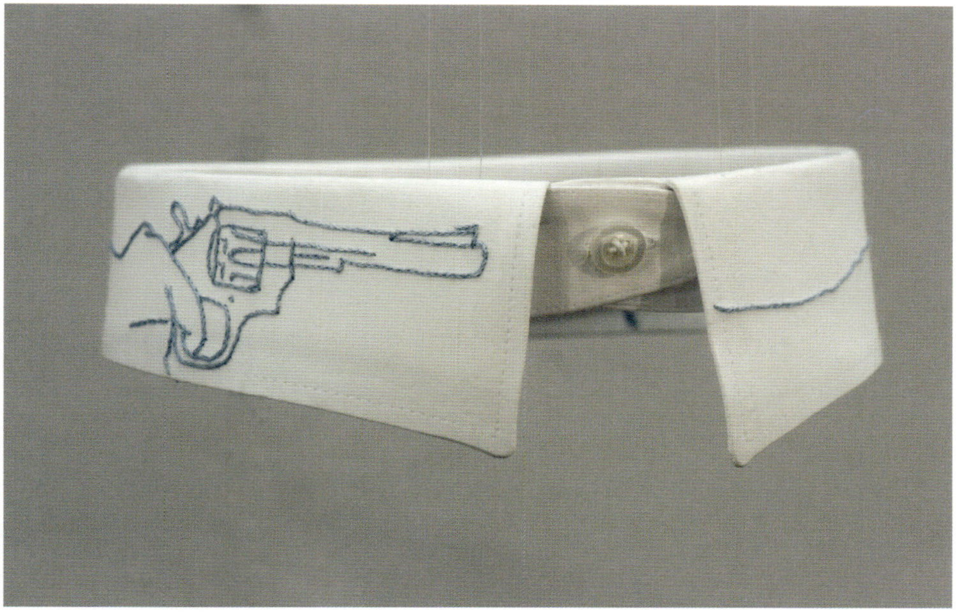

**WHITE COLLAR CRIME.** 2008. 7 x 16 x 17 cm.
Blue embroidered gun on a starched male collar.

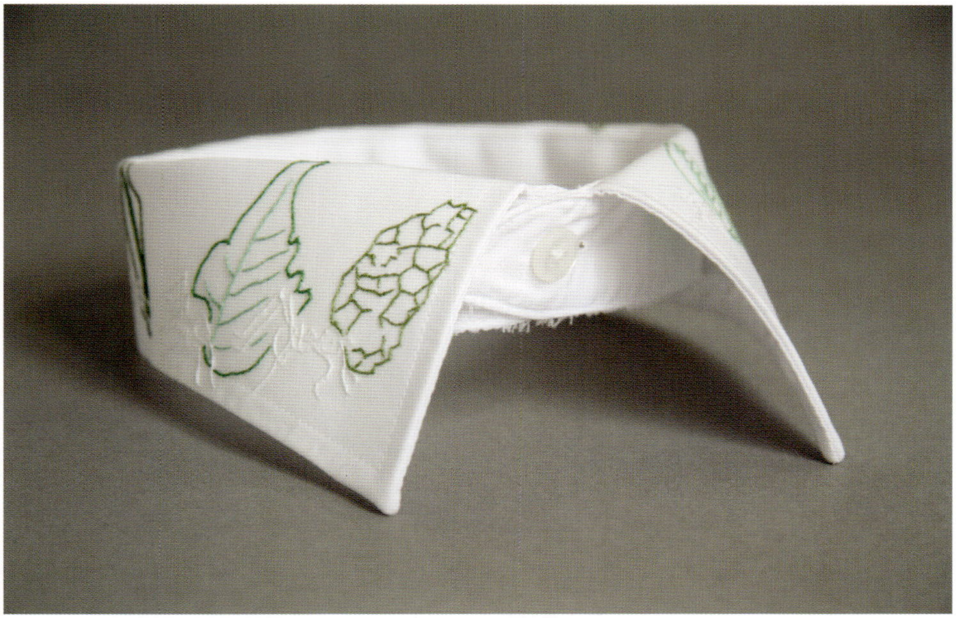

**WHITE COLLAR CRIME.** 2007. 8 x 15 x 17 cm.
White leaf-cutting ants embroidered on a starched male collar.

Carrosse antique

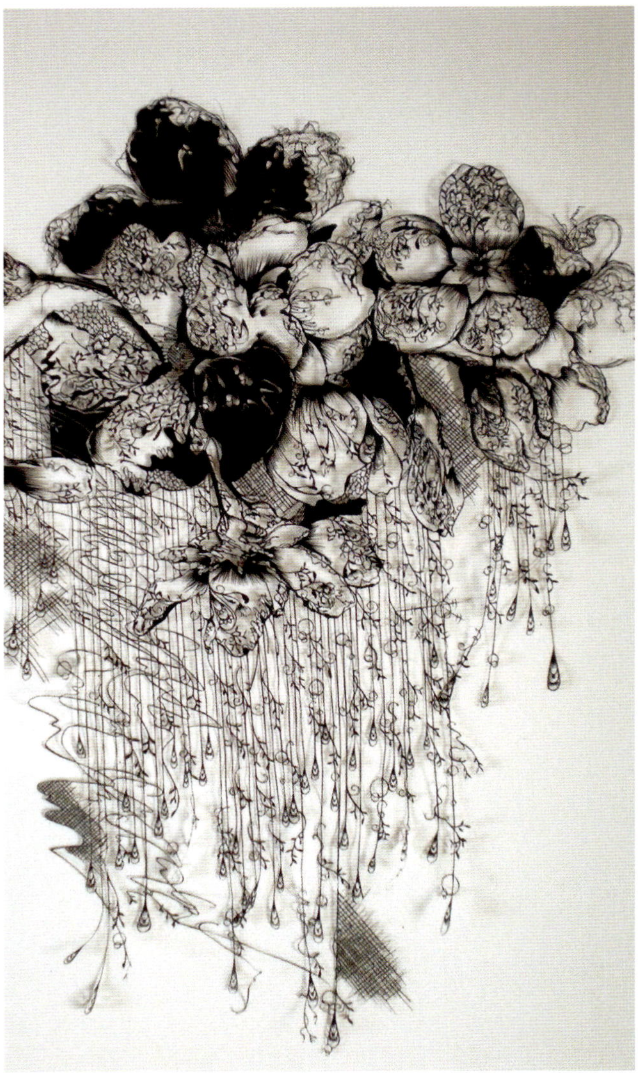

Fleur de serisiere

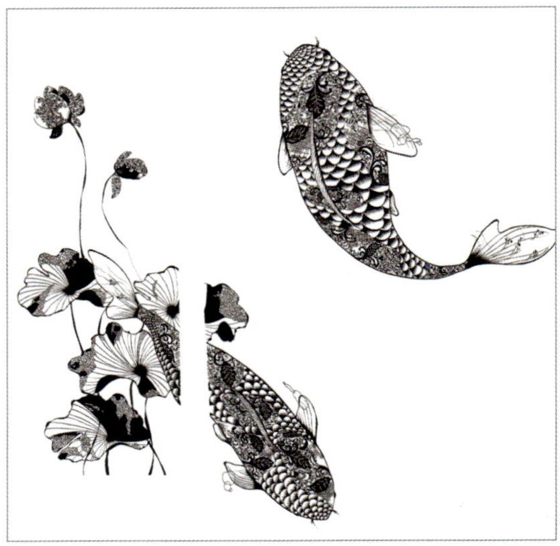

Carpes

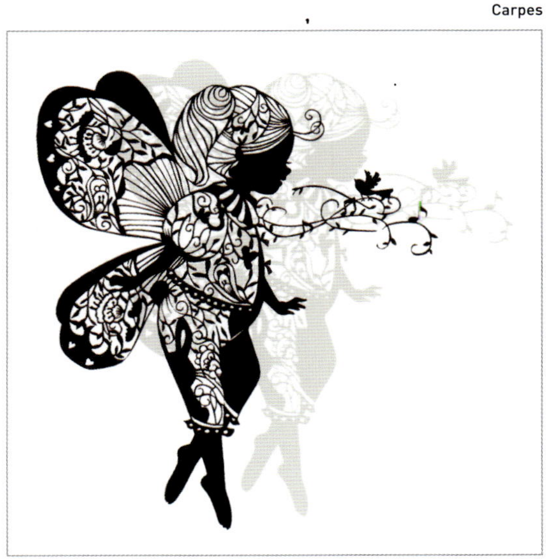

Fee de lapine

# Aoyama / Hina

www.hinaaoyama.com

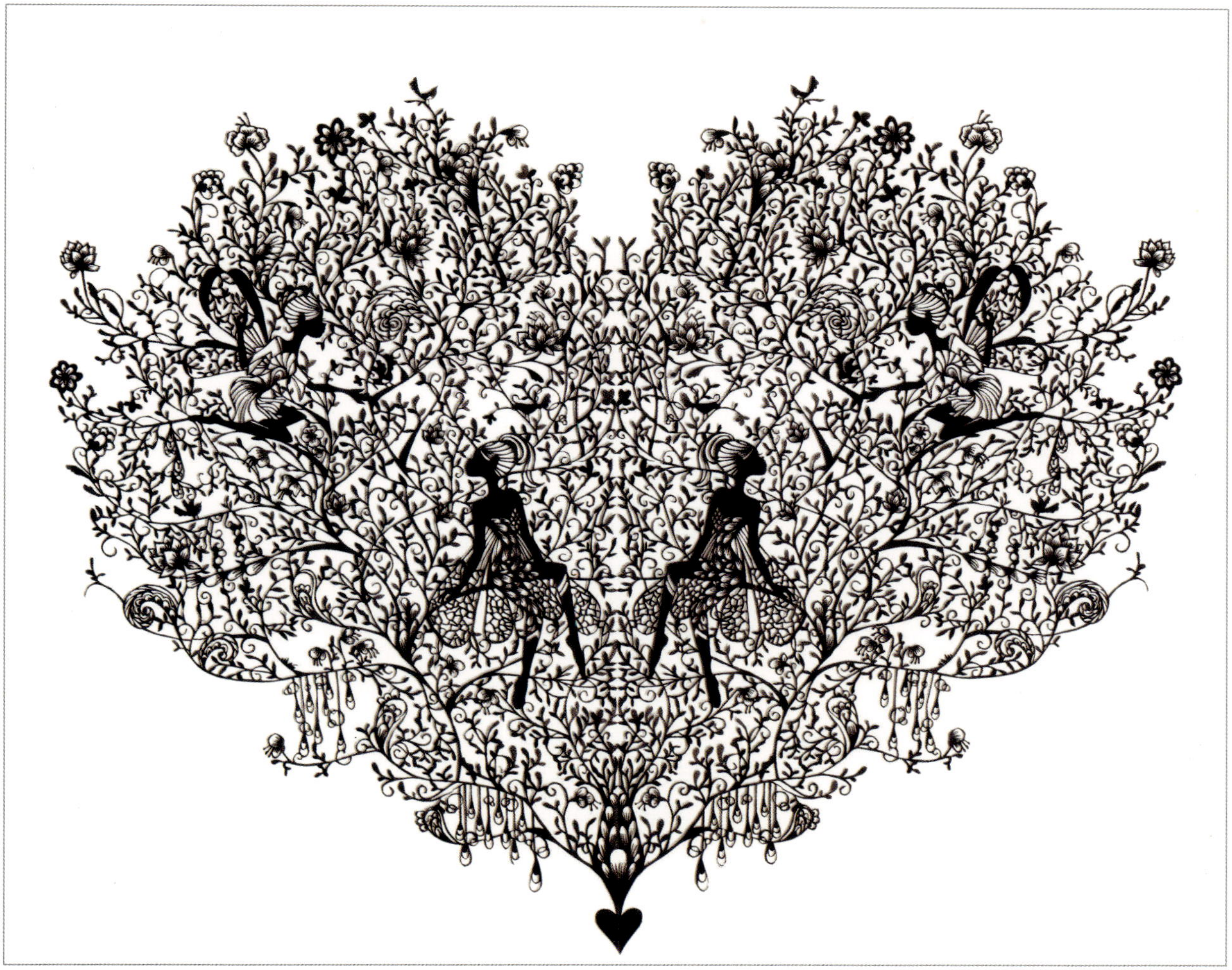

Foret harmonieuse les fees

Super fine lacy-paper-cutting artist and illustrator. Born 1970 in Yokohama, Japan. Started super fine Lacy-paper-cuttings since 2000 and currently lives and works in Ferney Volaire, France. They are super fine lacy-paper-cuttings done by a simple pair of scissors. Her passion is to create a finest cutoff beyond the level of the very time-consuming needle lace making. "I don't follow tradition but I am trying to create a mixture of the traditional and modern styles and to produce my own world through this super fine lacy-paper-cuttings technique."

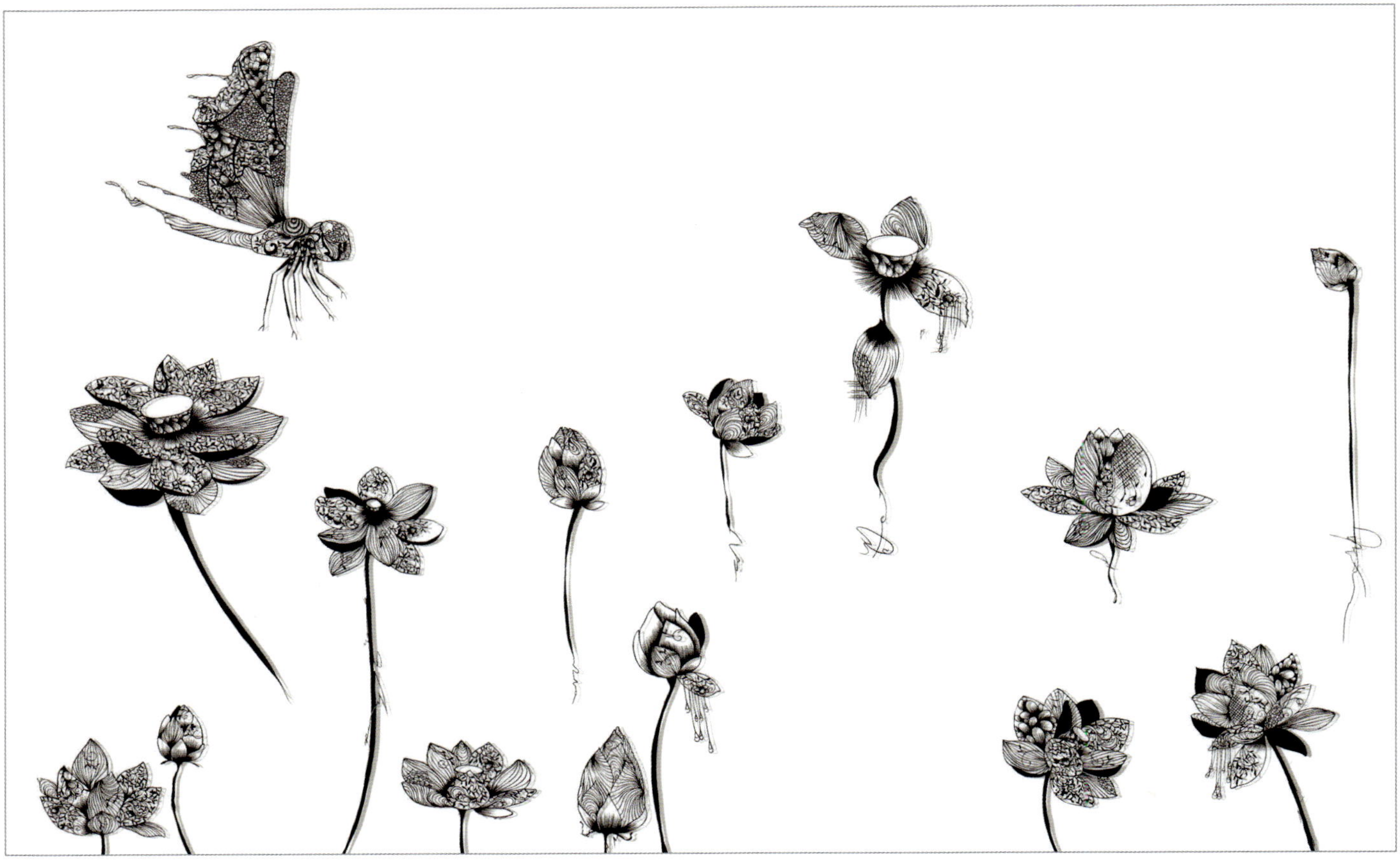

Lotus qui ne fane jamais

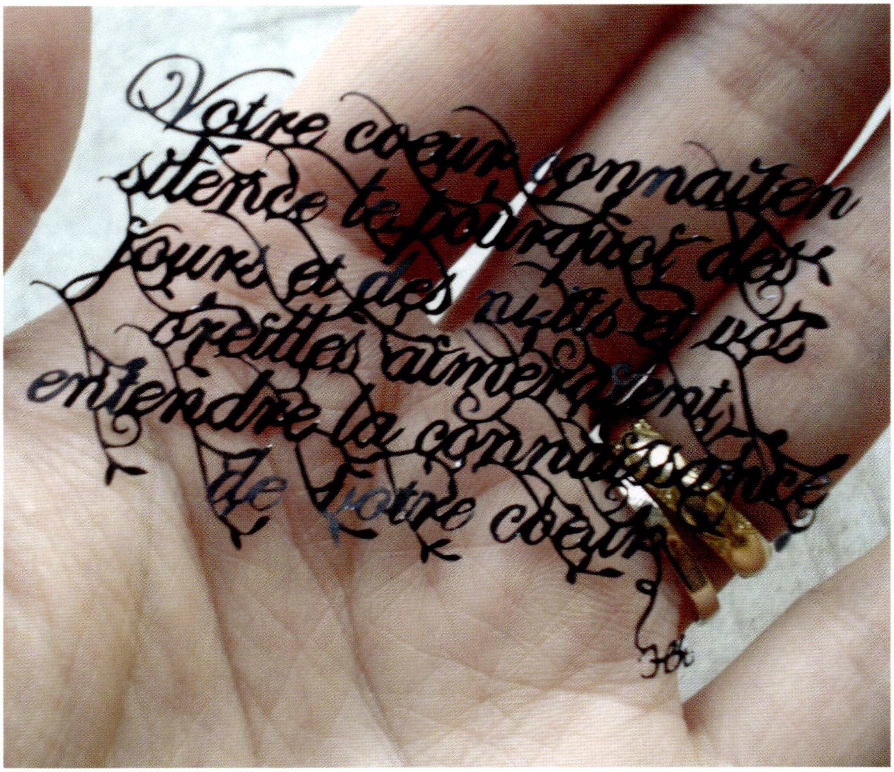


Petit Prance

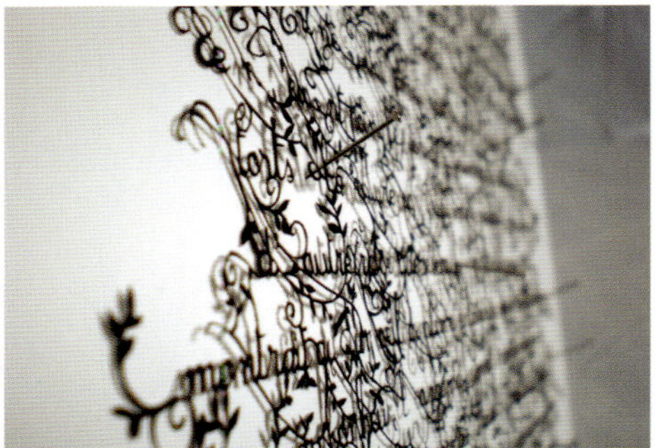

Voltaire

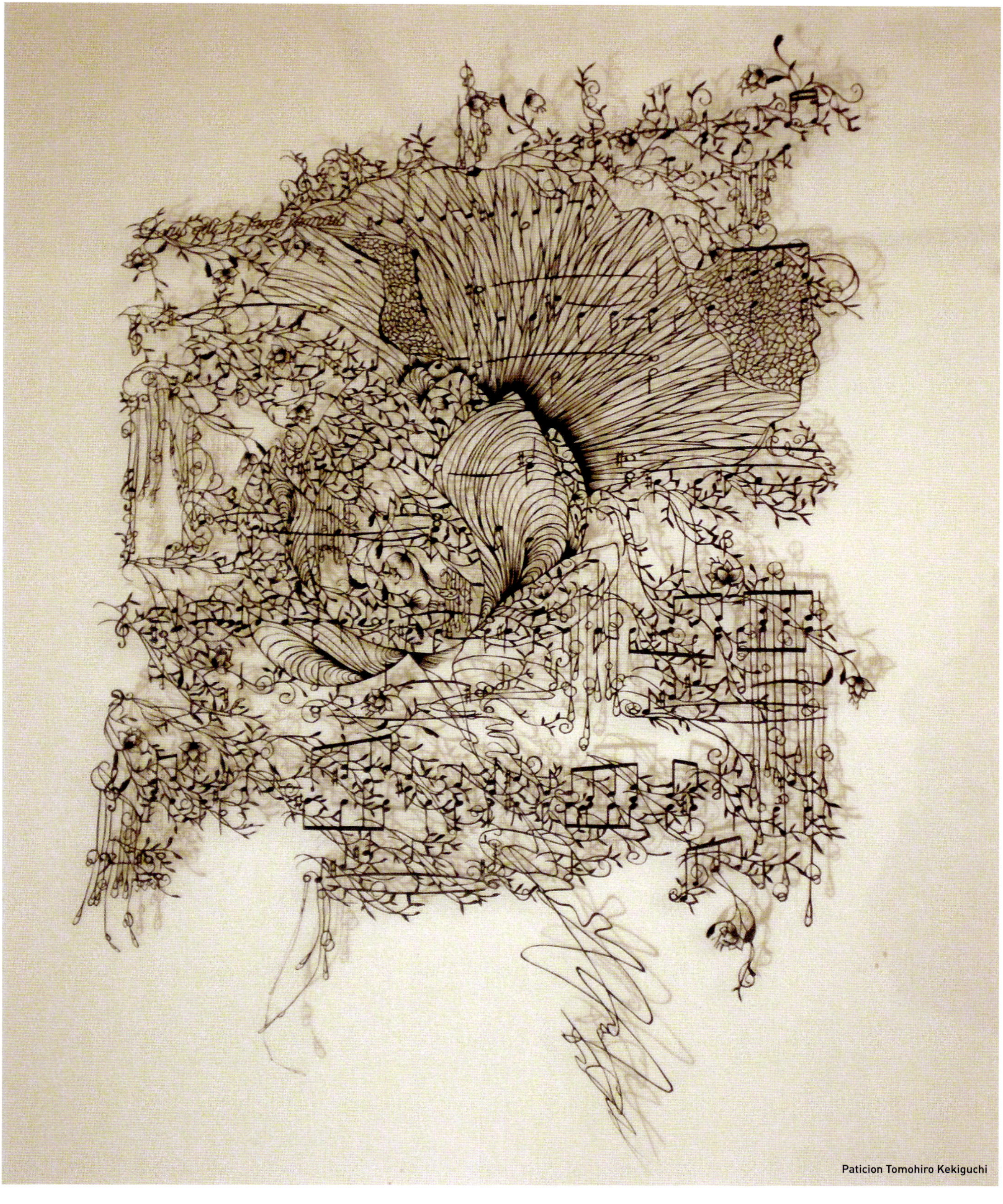

Paticion Tomohiro Kekiguchi

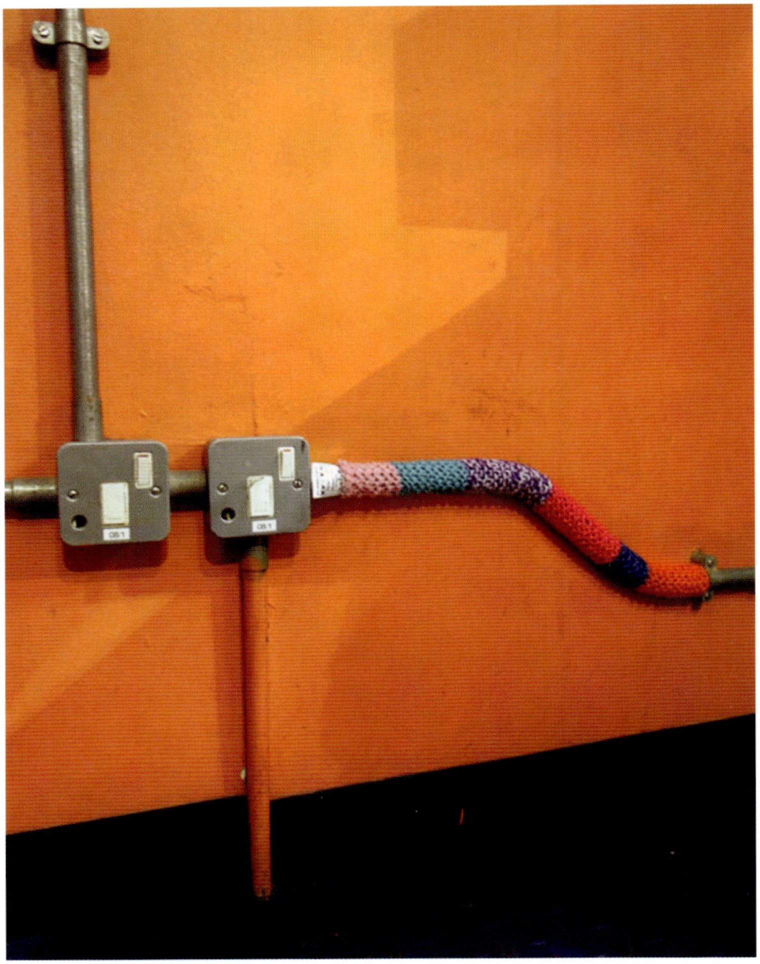

**Contact Theatre Residency 2009 (Manchester UK)**

Knitting and crochet, yarn fibres
During 2009 Artyarn were awarded the position of Artists In Residence at Manchester's Contact Theatre. Working with the unique architectural features of the Contact Theatre building, Artyarn made a series of knitting and crochet interventions in and around the building as the first part of their two part residency. During this time Artyarn also delivered a series of knitting and crochet skills workshops, encouraging workshop participants to explore the site and create their own yarn bombing pieces to place in and around the Contact Theatre building.

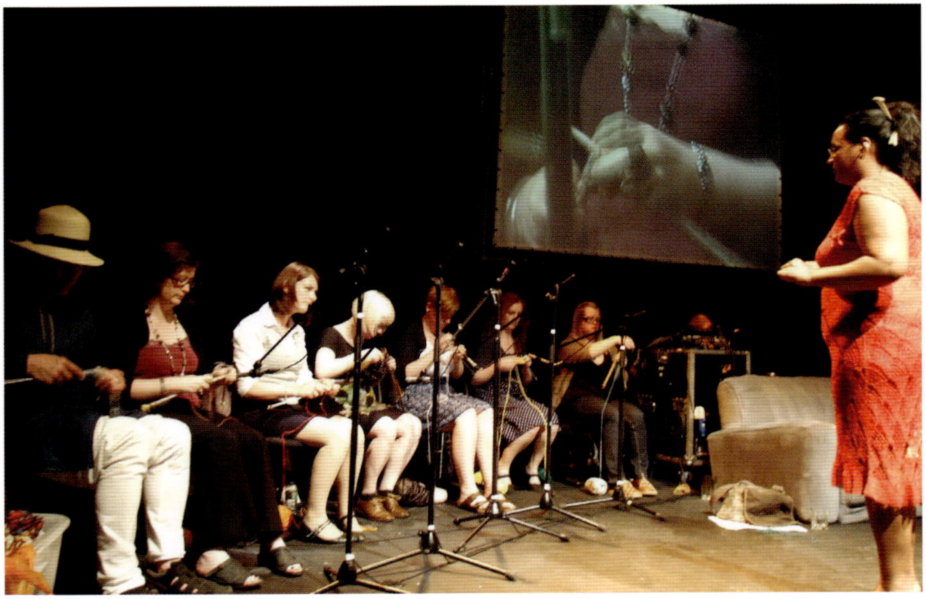

**The Knitting Orchestra (Manchester UK)**

Amplified knitting needles
The Knitting Orchestra gave their first performance as part of ArtYarn's 2009 artist in residency program at the Contact Theatre in Manchester UK, and was conducted by Anwen Lewis with sound production by Matt Wand. The Knitting orchestra is a curious experiment looking at all those parts between making a stitch, the rhythmic and gestural actions of knitting and crochet, and an investigation into the many varied yarns, needles and techniques that can be used in knitting and crochet activity. Through the ampflication of needles and hooks in action, Artyarn make public performances and produce recorded material to share their interest in the action of knitting and crochet.

# Art/Yarn

www.artyarn.org

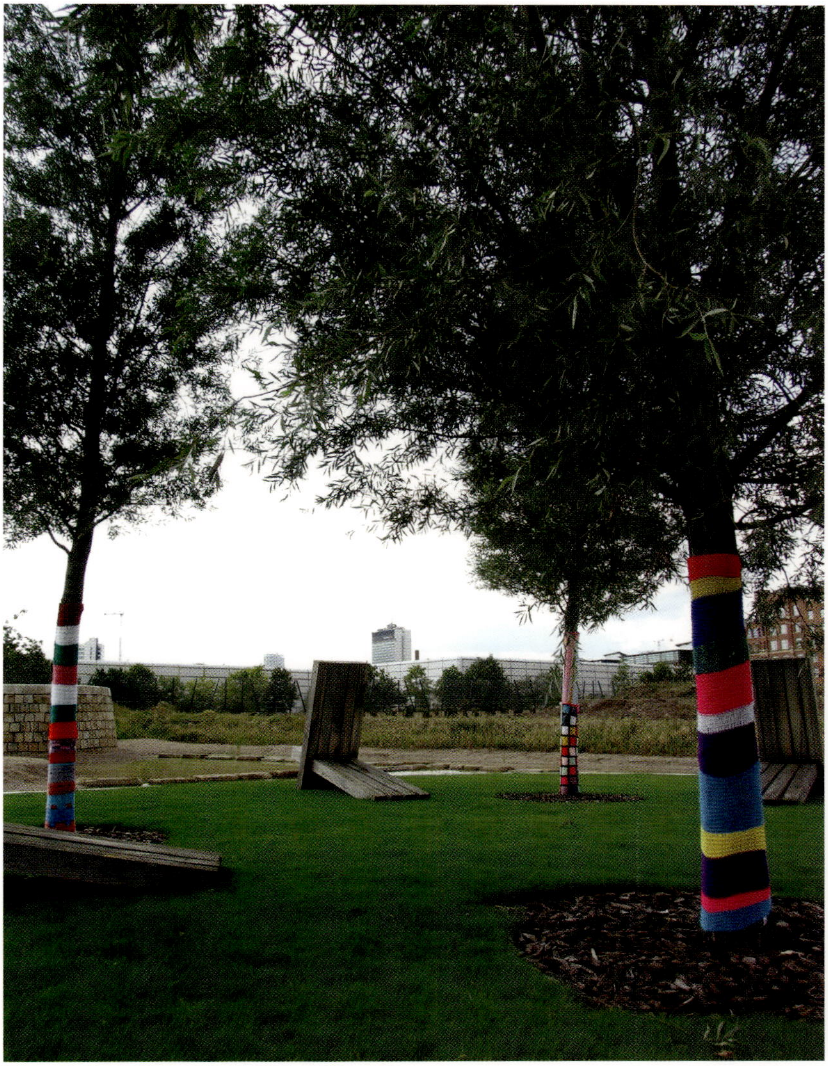

**New Islington Folk Festival 2008 (Manchester UK)**

Knitting and crochet, trees, yarn fibres
In the late summer of 2008 Artyarn made their first outdoor knitting and crochet installation on the site of the New Islington regeneration site in Manchester UK. On th 6th September 2008 New Islington was turned into a playground for Urban Folk. Alongside a mix of new urban and traditional folk art forms in Manchester's new community, Artyarn created an installation of 'Tree Cosies' that were placed around the festival site.

ArtYarn is a collaborative fibre arts project coordinated by visual artists Rachael Elwell and Sarah Hardacre. ArtYarn aim to use traditional knitting and crochet techniques in contemporary visual arts projects. And aspire to promote the diversity and versatility of knitting and crochet as a medium. Interested in the artistic, social and historical contexts of knitting and crochet, ArtYarn are focused on the tactility of hand processes. Enjoying the repetitive and often obsessive nature of this work, ArtYarn view knitting and crochet as an opportunity for individual creative expression and at the same time explore the medium as a way to make art accessible through participatory making and collaborative exchange.

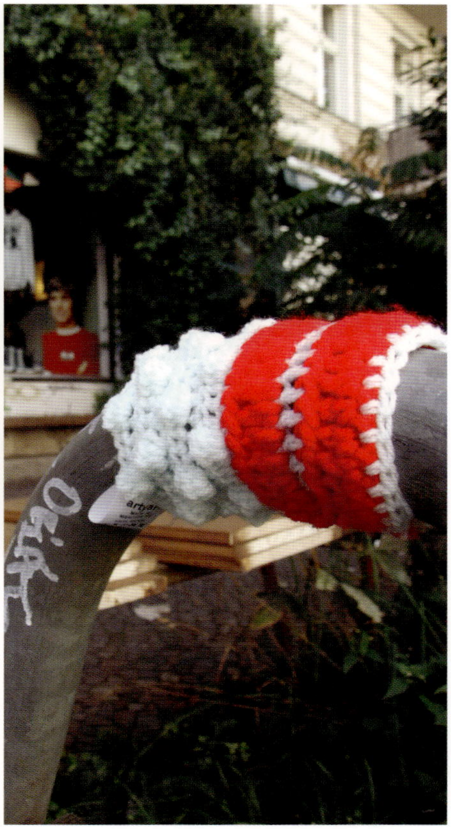

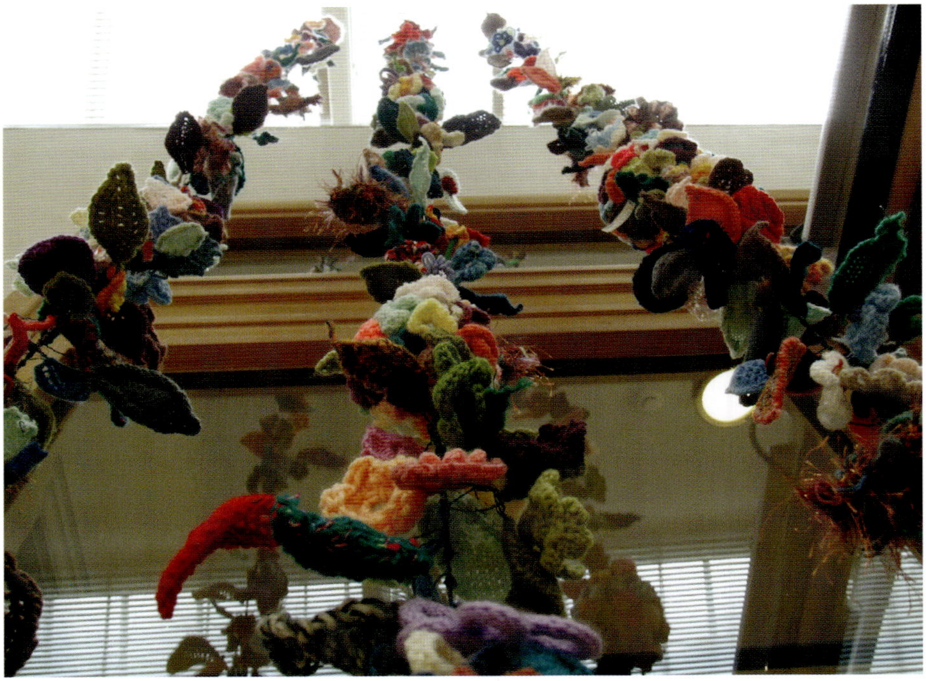

**Knitted Nature 2009**
**(Rohdale Touchstones Art Gallery, Rochdale UK)**

Knitting and crochet, yarn fibres
Knitted Nature is a commissioned community knitting and crochet project made by Artyarn and knitters and crocheters from around the world. Artyarn called out to a wider crafting community by inviting makers to knit and crochet flowers and leaves, and by delivering an open access workshop in April 2009. Artyarn used the collected wooly foliage to create an installation that is exhibited alongside the exhibition 'En Plain Air' at Rochdale Art Gallery. This installation is part of the UK(DIY) festival 2009. As part of the Knitted Nature project, Artyarn were also invited to create an our door installation in Broadfield park, Rochdale. The Orange Tree was inspired by a recent visit to Valencia, where orange groves sit beautifully amongst the inner city park areas creating a wonderful contrast to the city scape that surrounds them. Artyarn produced 100 crocheted balls that now sit within a tree in Broadfield park, situated opposite Touchstones Rochdale Art Gallery.

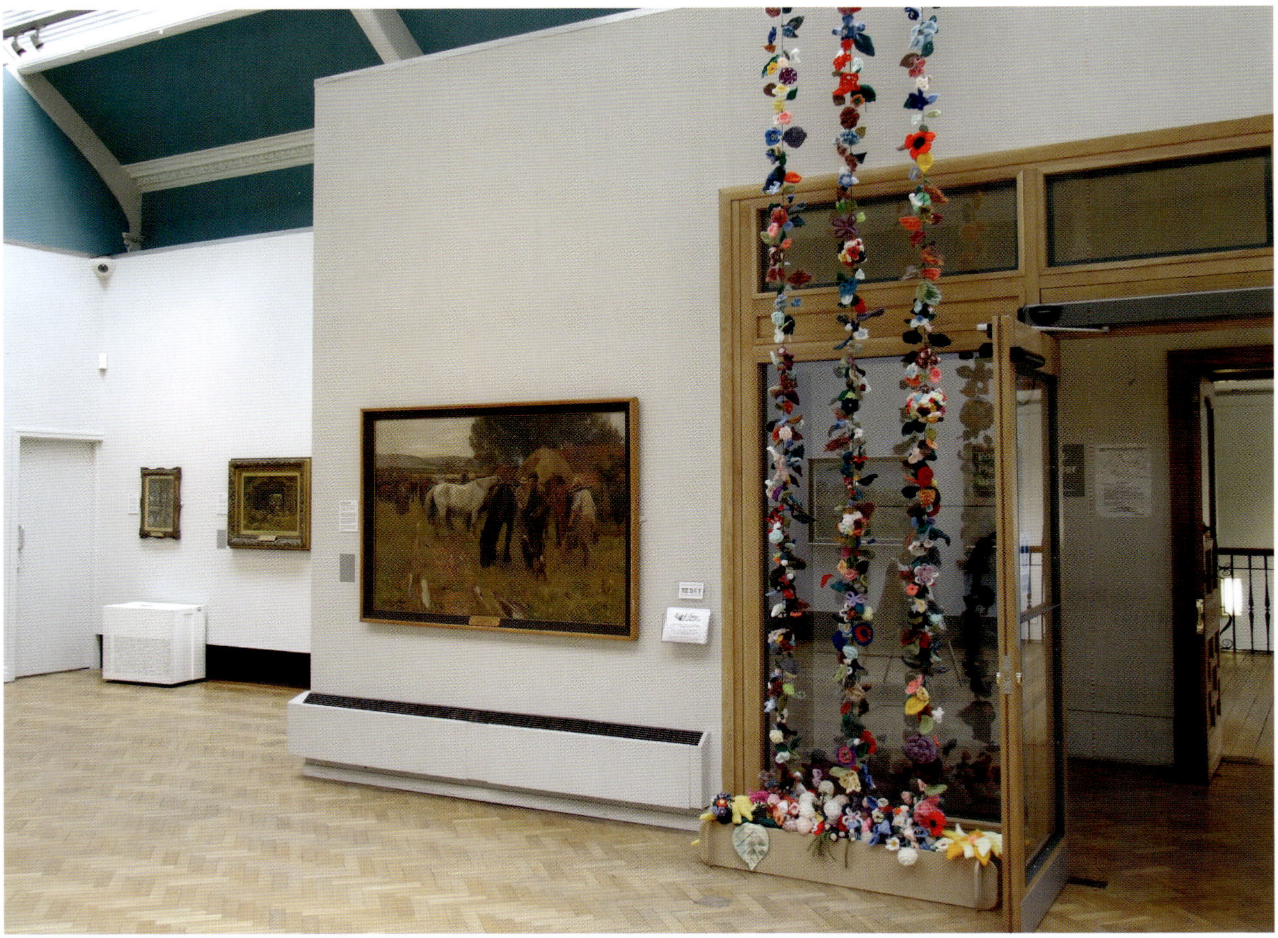

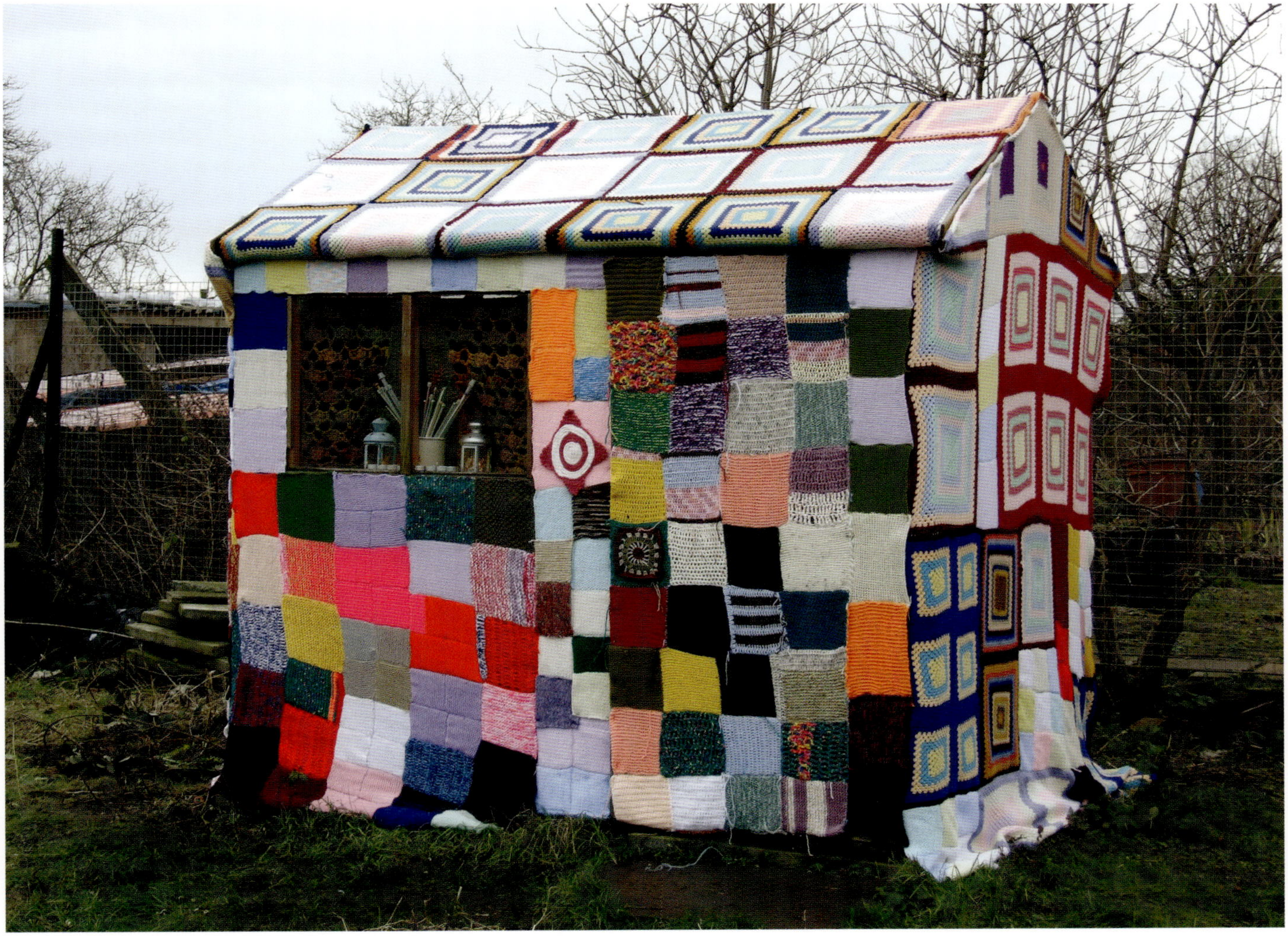

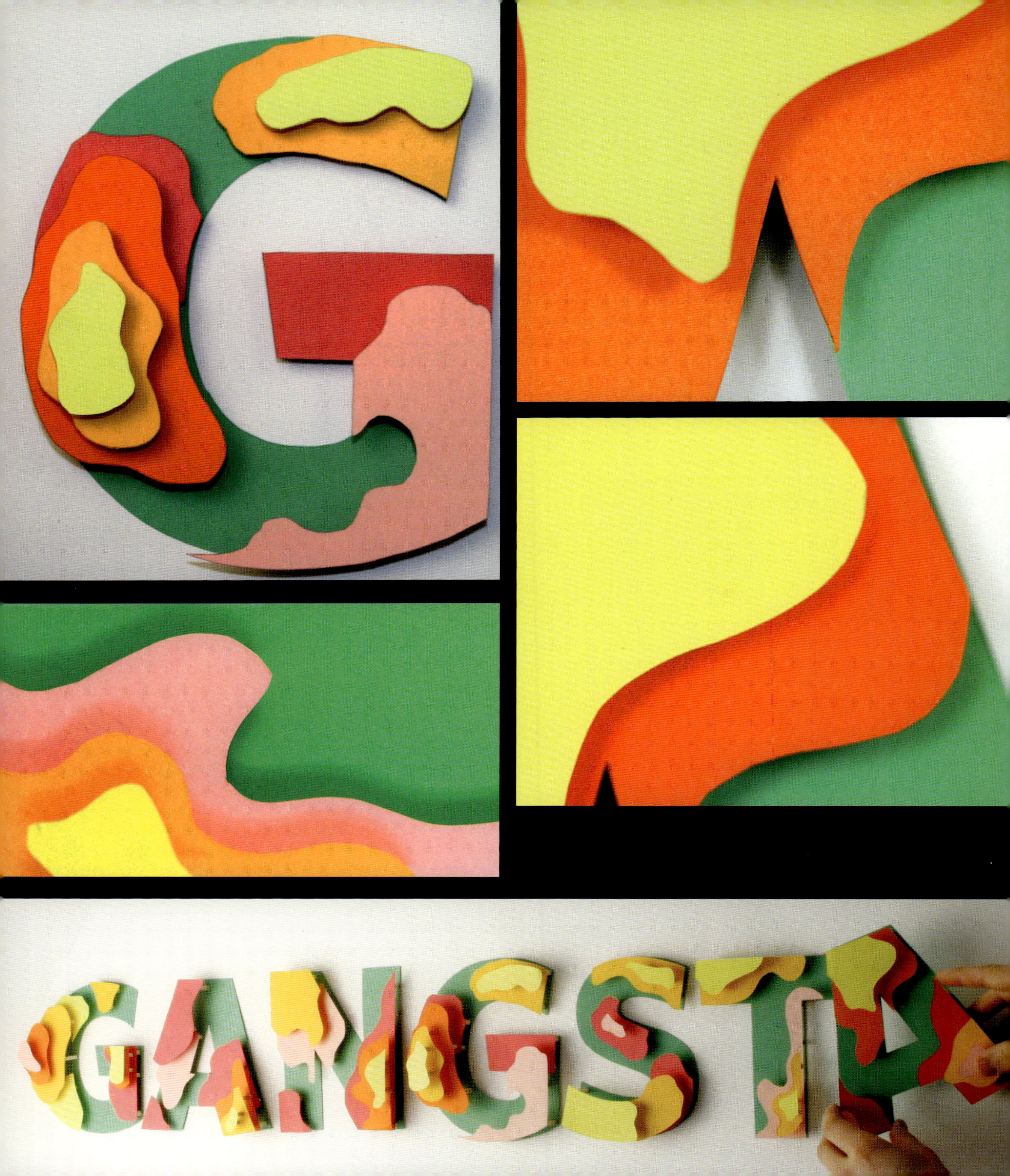
GANGSTA

# Atelier/Pariri

www.pariri.com

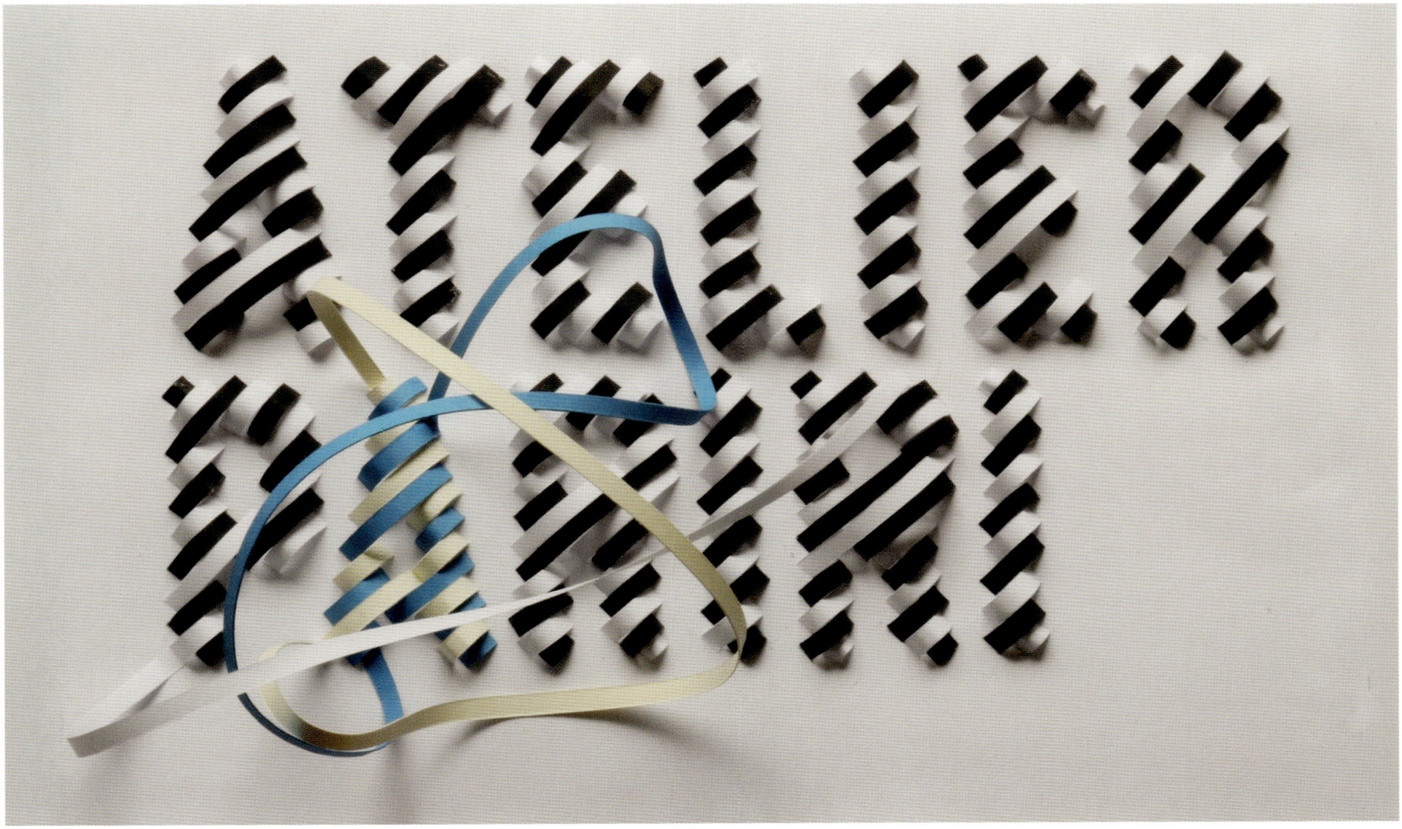

Personnal LetterPaper research. How to show geographic problematic in type.

Atelier Pariri, graphic design studio, was founded in 2008 by Jérôme Corgier, and grew quickly as Corgier welcomed collaborators Marie Holter in London, Lara Captan in Beirut, and most recently Emilie Prat, a second associate in Paris. The concept of Pariri is to create a network of multicultural exchanges, for the purposes of both professional projects and within the realm of graphic and artistic research. The members of Pariri work independently for the most part, taking on individual projects as they wish ; the loose structural skeleton of the studio kicks in as the members actively cultivate interaction by soliciting criticism and support from within their team of eight hands working under one label. Here the cross-cultural veins begin to flow, as each brings his or her singular and complex cultural tradition to the project. Each member's expertise derives from a unique visual culture, a distinct knowledge and education ; and the encounter made possible by the Pariri studio gives birth to a wealth of new concepts and languages. And yet, despite the cultural plurality of Pariri, the effect is rather opposite, that amidst the process of sharing and exploring, each artist may clarify and refine his or her own individual orientation within the culture of origin. The exchanges among Pariri members are largely remote, occurring through email, and via collaborative blog (Jarajaja). Within the bounds of the structure they've built, members of Pariri may question the communicative process. Their mutual engagement permits them to develop a unique visual language, to define the vocabulary of visual communication, to create a new visual reality through their projects, to pursue the new and the unpredictable that may result from the synthesis of their individual cultures.

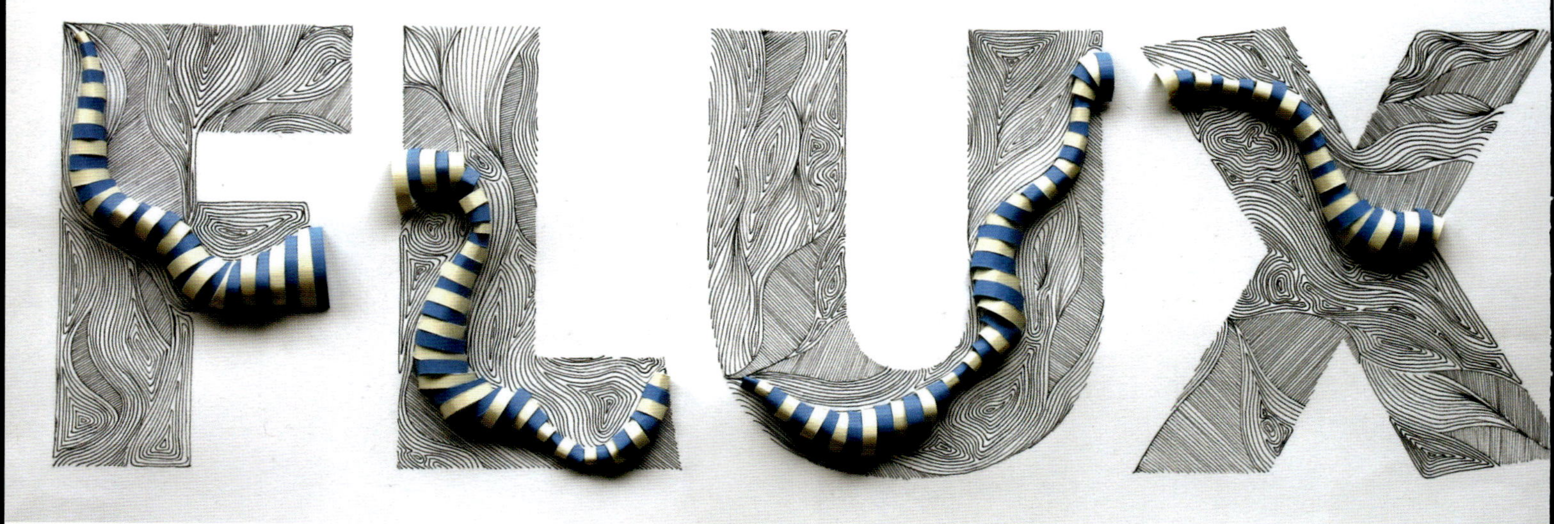


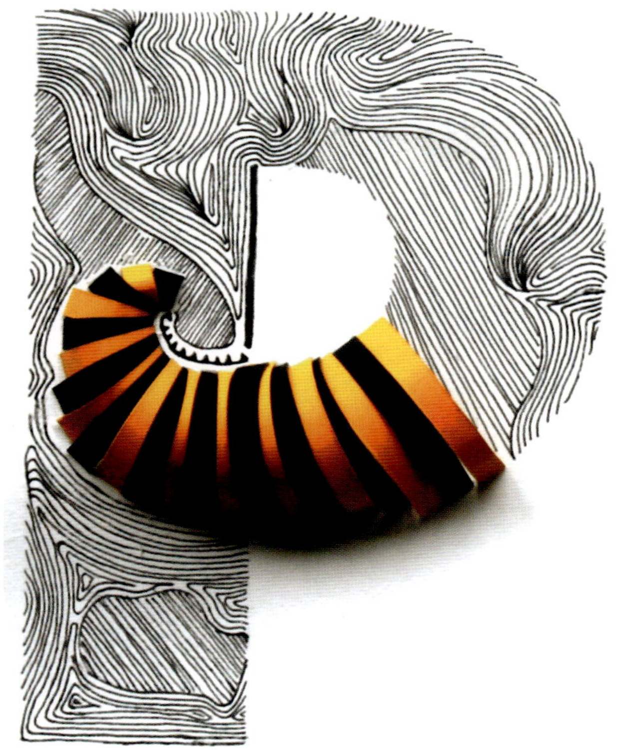


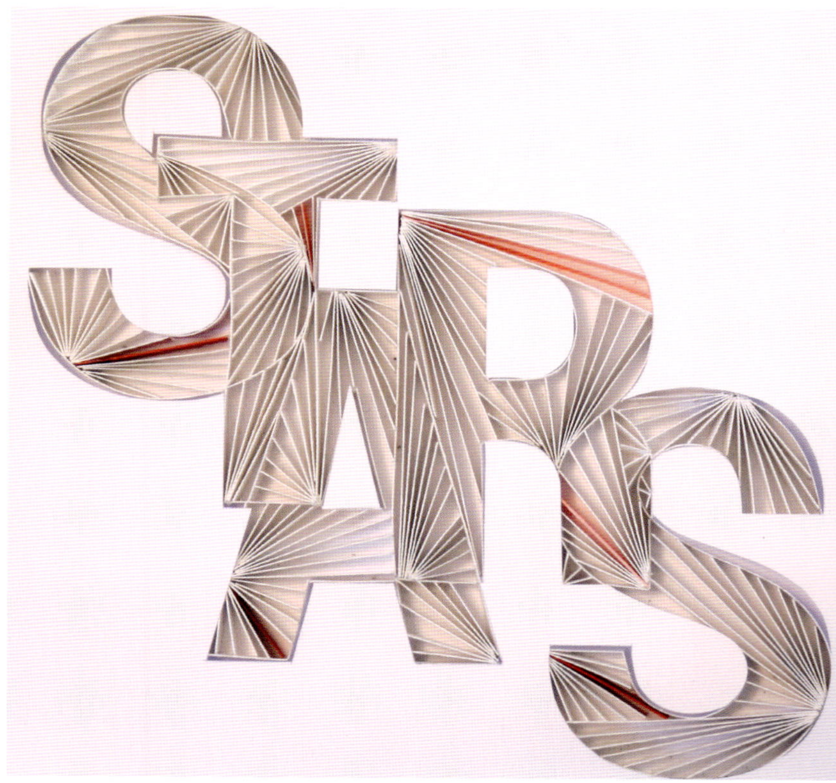

Second stage of flux researches in a letter. Paper.

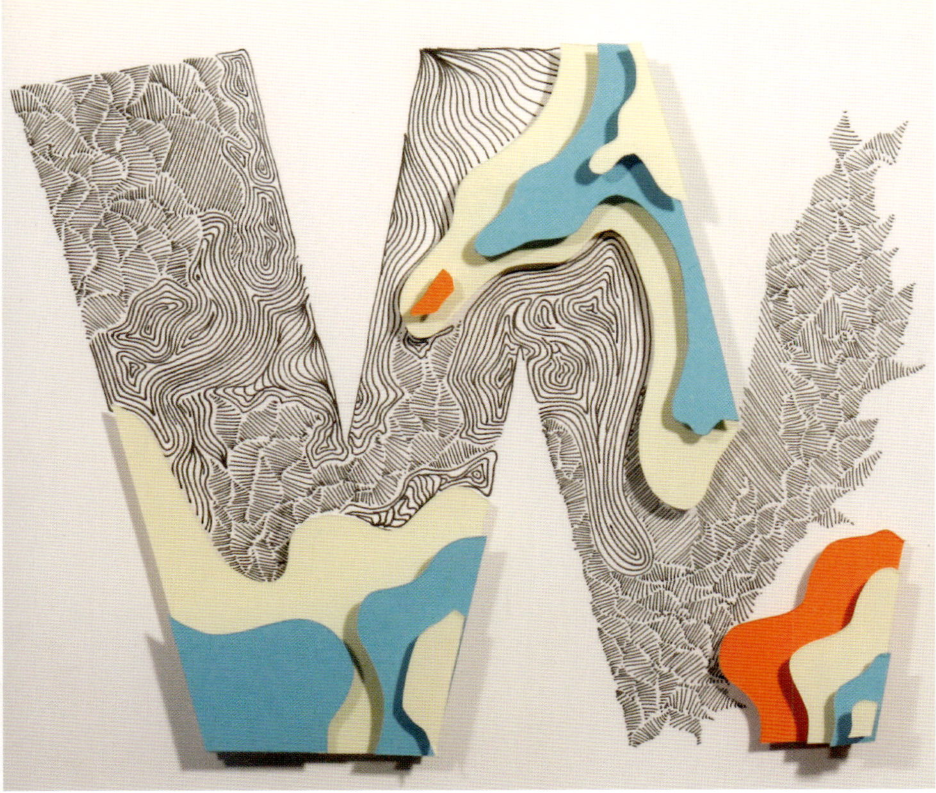

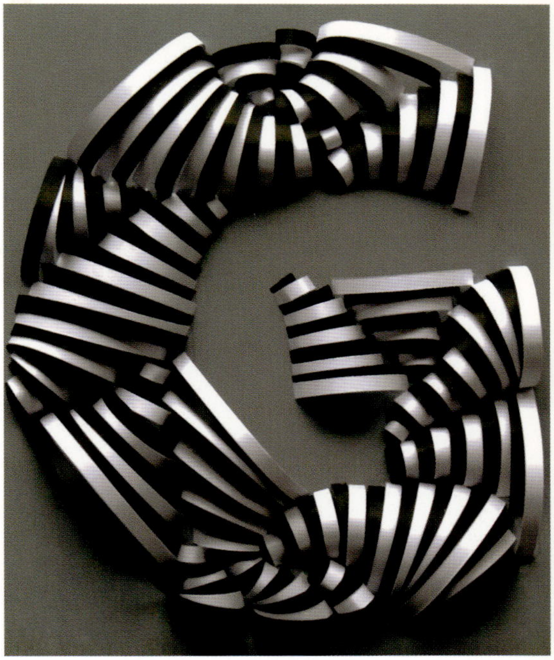

The movement of the paper is inspired by work of Lara Captan about the forms of arabic letters.

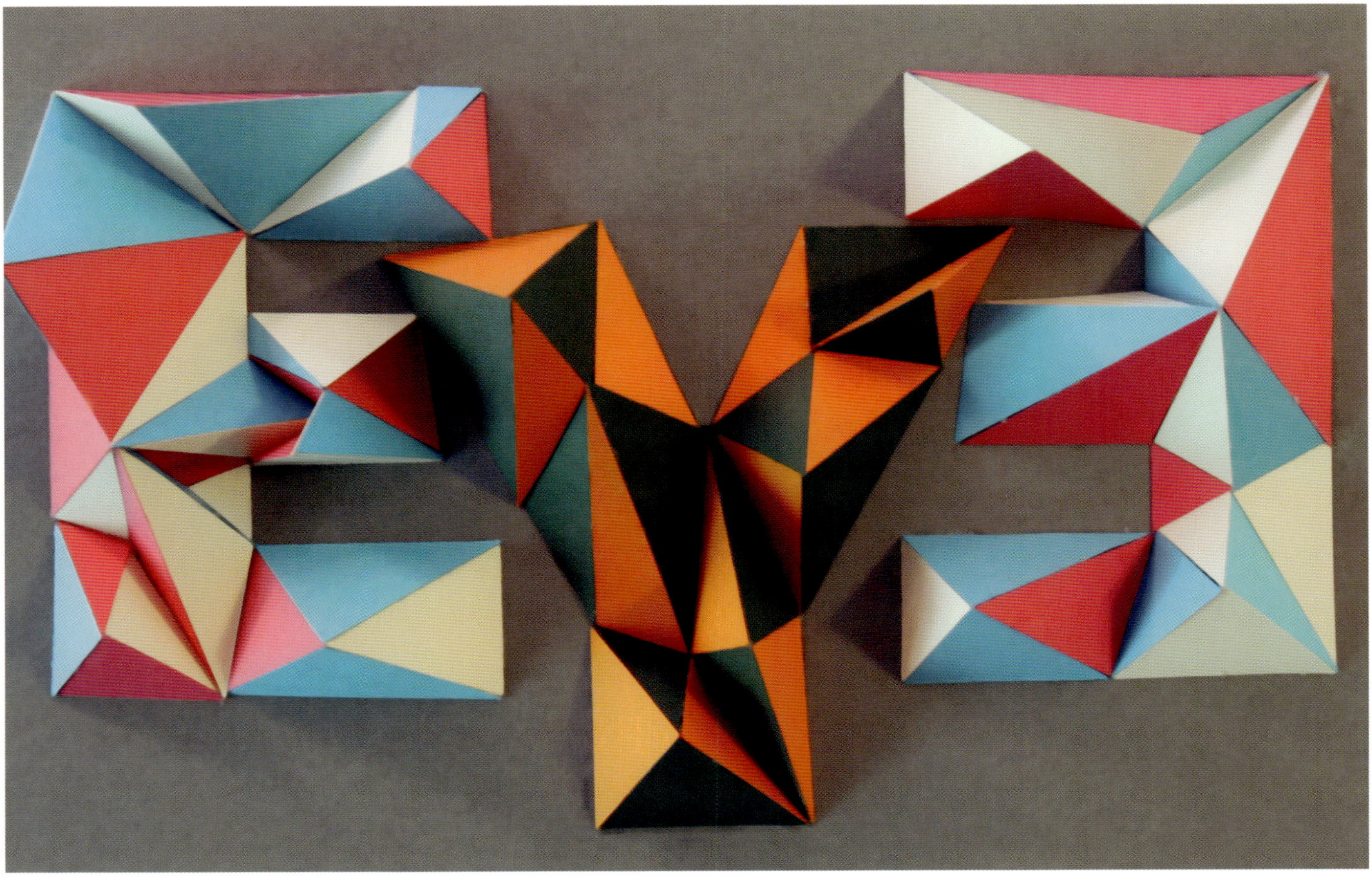

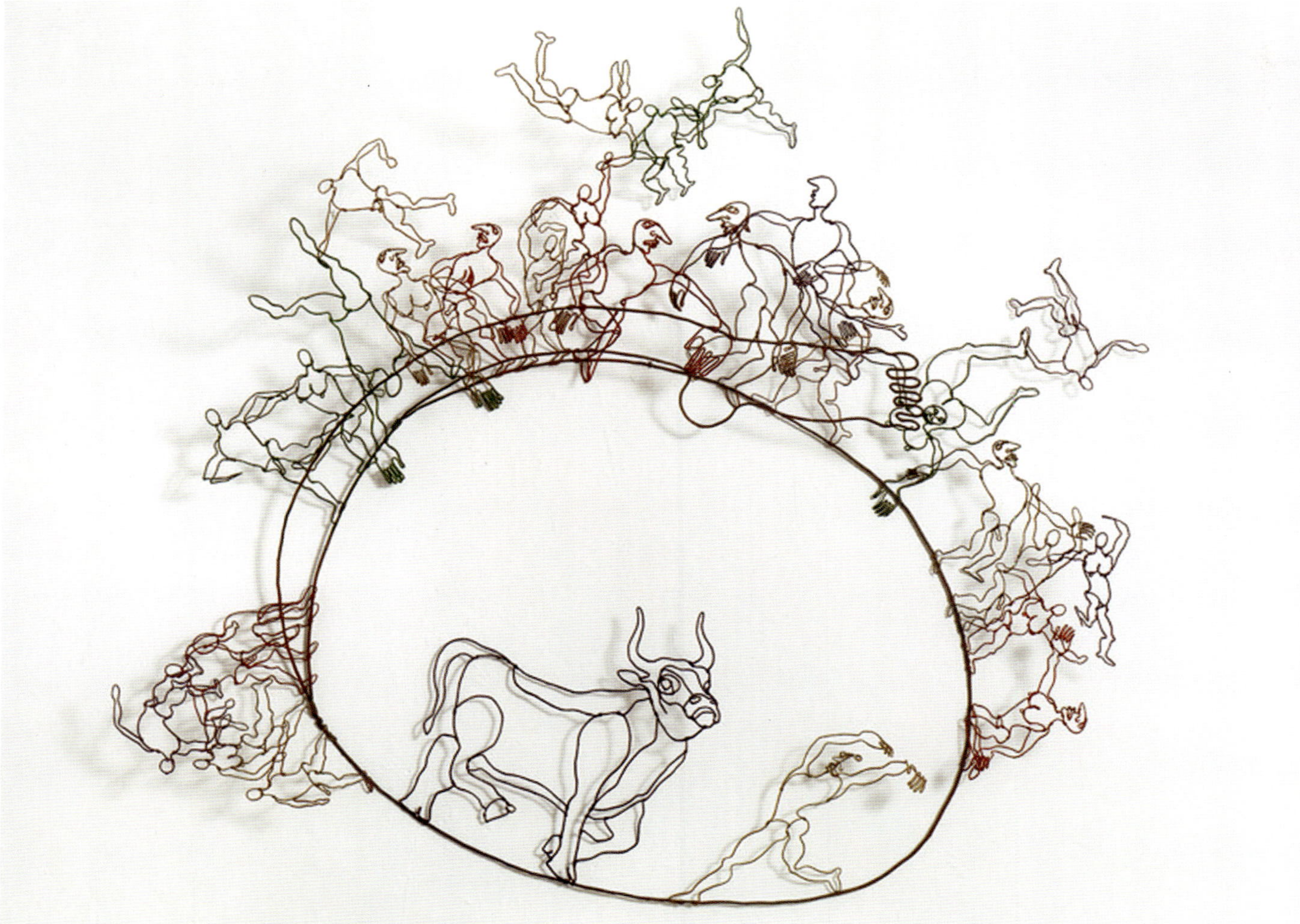

**Bread and games**
183x153x49cm

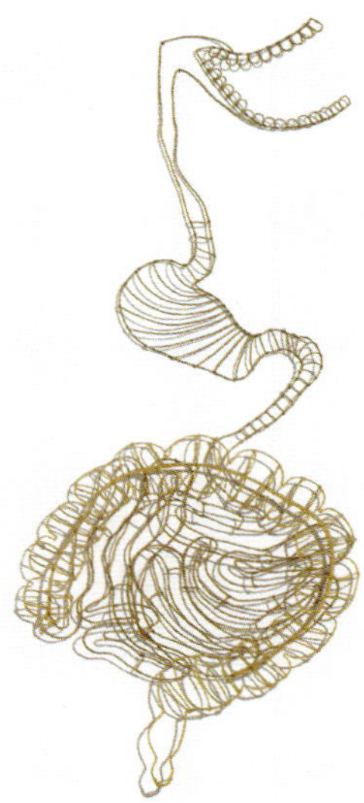

**Cloud of mentholated whipped cream**
183x74x13 cm

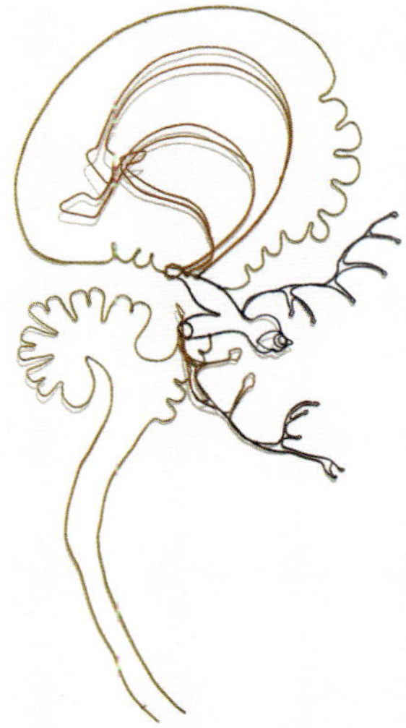

**Deep in the pool**
149x78x18 cm

# Béatrice/ De Domenico

www.myspace.com/beadedomenico

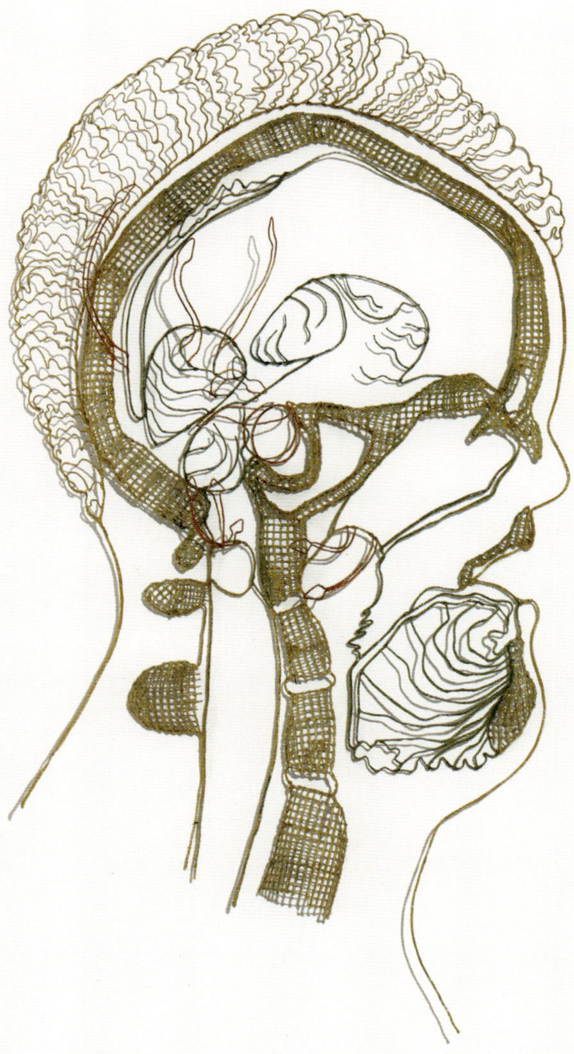

I began to use wire to realize a skeleton for my first sculptures. I covered them with resins, newspapers, grit until I obtained full, rich and classic sculptures. Then one day, I saw this thread which created a lively, nervous drawing with it's unstable shadow and I saw it was more alive than my standing sculpture. Thus i found the wall to be a support for this drawing in three dimension and it stabilized it. I came back to the resin because of it's fascinating and multiple possibilities. I coated this skeleton with a new skin defender that does not hide neither the light nor the breath while stressing the presence of this drawing. "This learned balance between poetry and drawing takes place here on held thread. Thread of iron, copper, brass or gold, nude thread or sheathed by resin. The creations of Béatrice De Domenico are not afraid of their shadows, they becon them. The light casts a twin who has it's importance, that of a duplicate of course brought on by the soul of the light reflected on the wall but more importantly because of its complicity with that which pretends to be the original. Shall we stick to one or the other ? After a good look could it not be a collusive and essential element of a "ménage à trois"? Is it white so as to participate in a strong revealing of the double, the creation of it's origin ? Having useful and necessary structural fonction for future sculptures these skeletons of twisted wire were flooted for a long time in the resin. Possibly because of their rich fullness and emptyness announcing their disappearance, the artist was obligated to take them into consideration. The soul of things and beings must be put forward and Béatrice was resolute to do this little by little. The imagination, the dexterity, the poetic vision of the artist did the rest. For the pleasure of those watching a multitude of new scenes emerging from the one and only creation, as everyone knows, because light draws the strings it is eternally new. Man needs to learn to look from all angles. Work of art or sentiment, same difference! Béatrice weaves her organic compositios of wire, lives and works in Nice." - Patrick Bertrand.

Photos by Francois Fernandez

**I have cobweb in my head**
179x105x22 cm

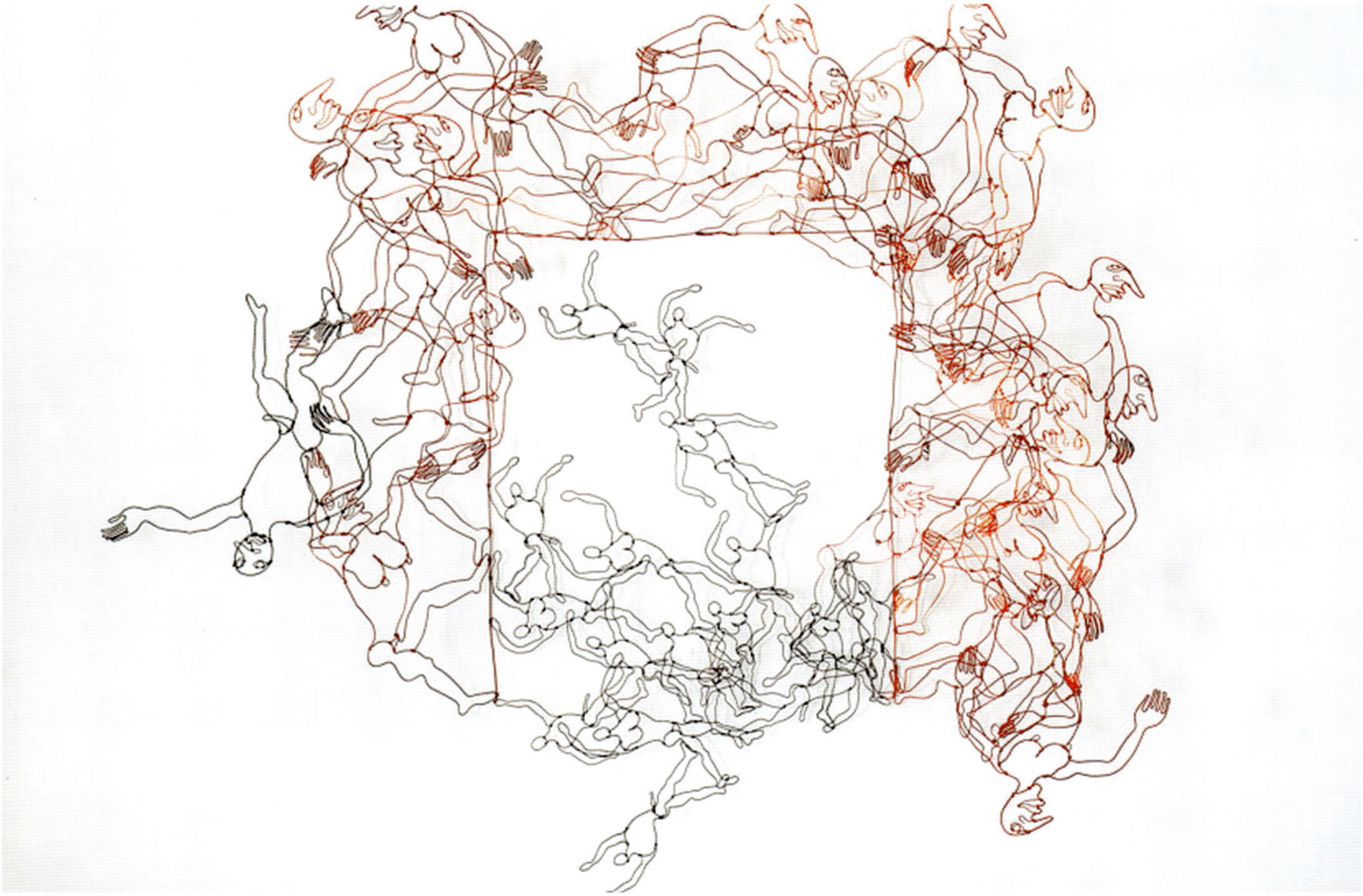

**Le 14 juillet**
160x175x49cm

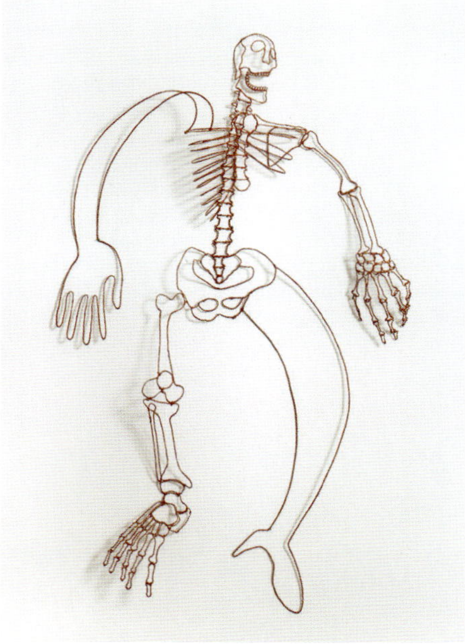

**Lazare**
181x96x29cm

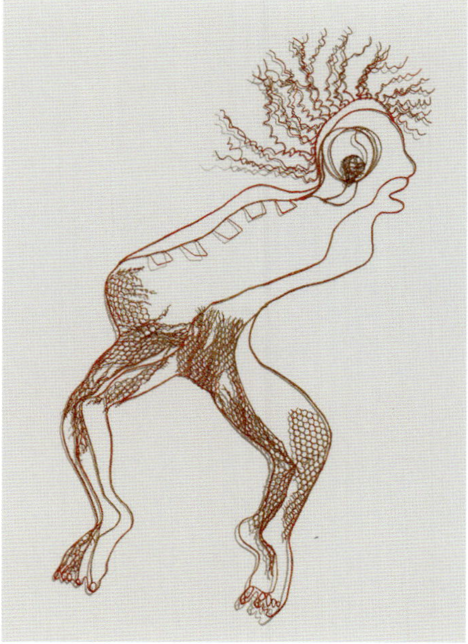

**The fairy electricity**
213x116x28cm

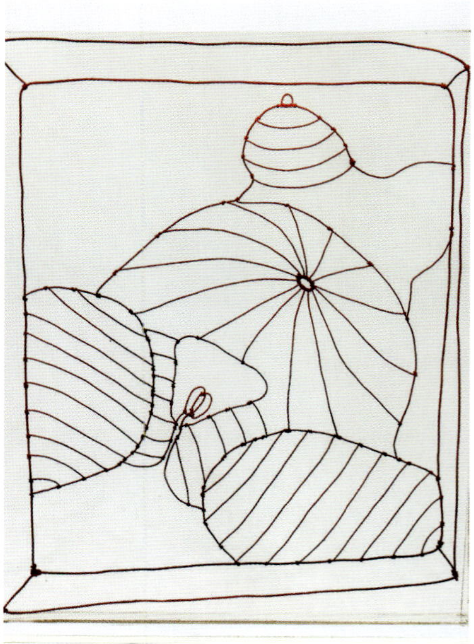

**The origin of the world**
54x61x7cm

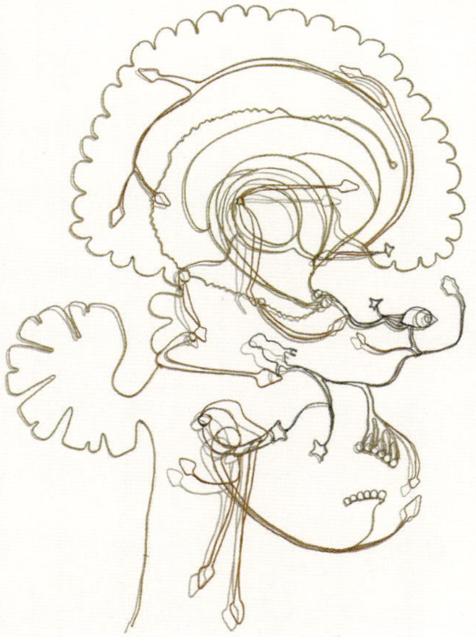

**Mister Freud**
201x135x27cm

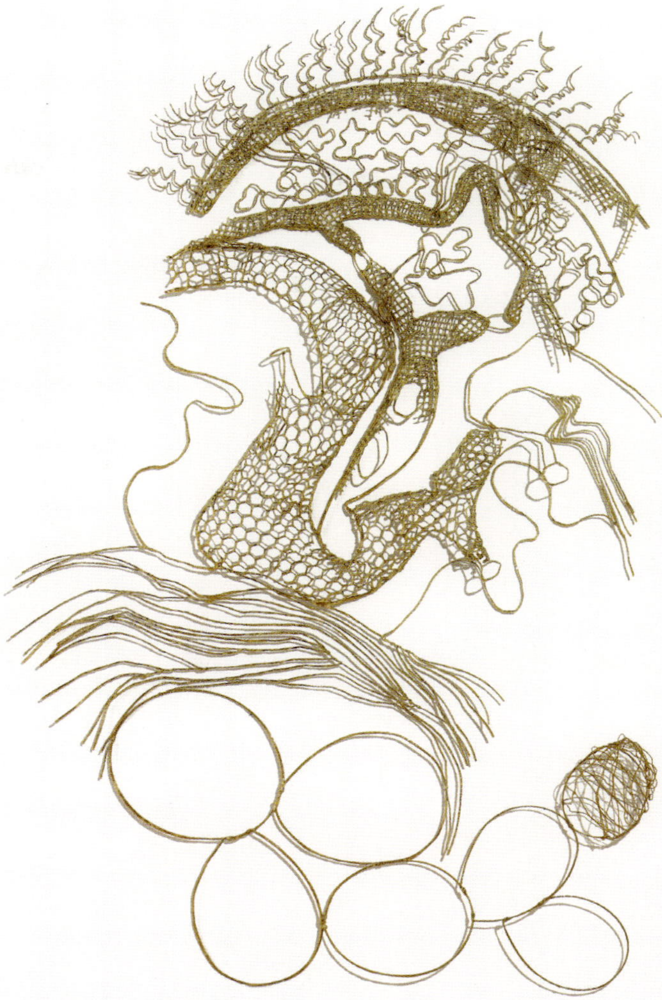

**Pollinisation**
210x134x23cm

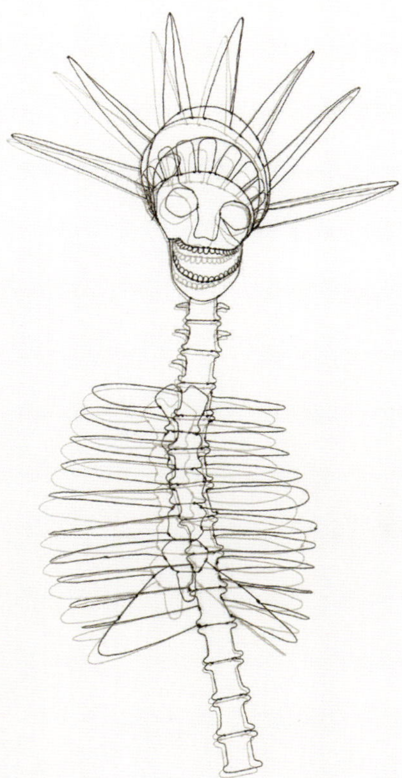

**The weapon of mass destruction**
162x95x45cm

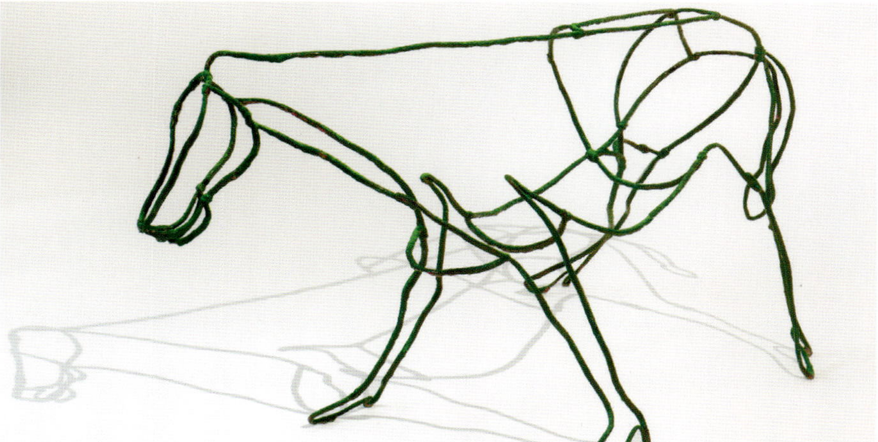

**Vegetarian but she cracks**
95x43x50 cm

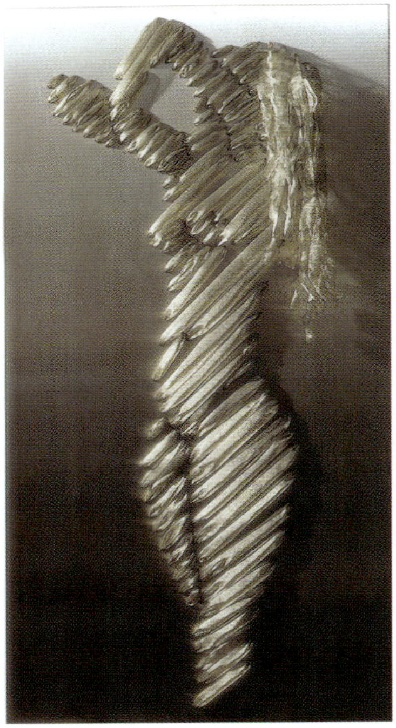

Steel Nude Study

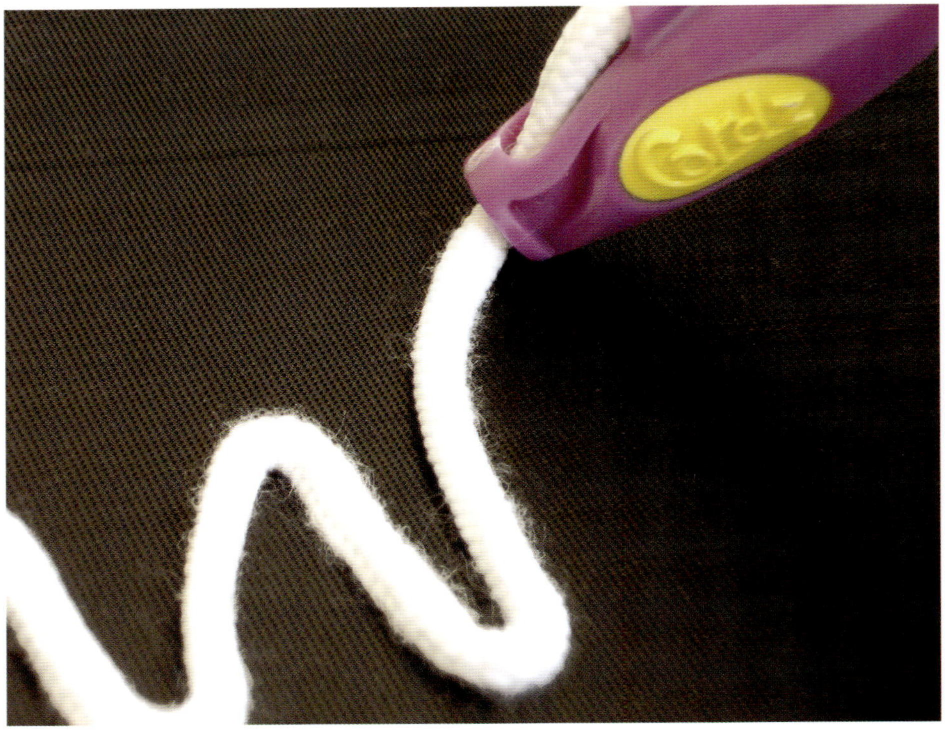


Cordz

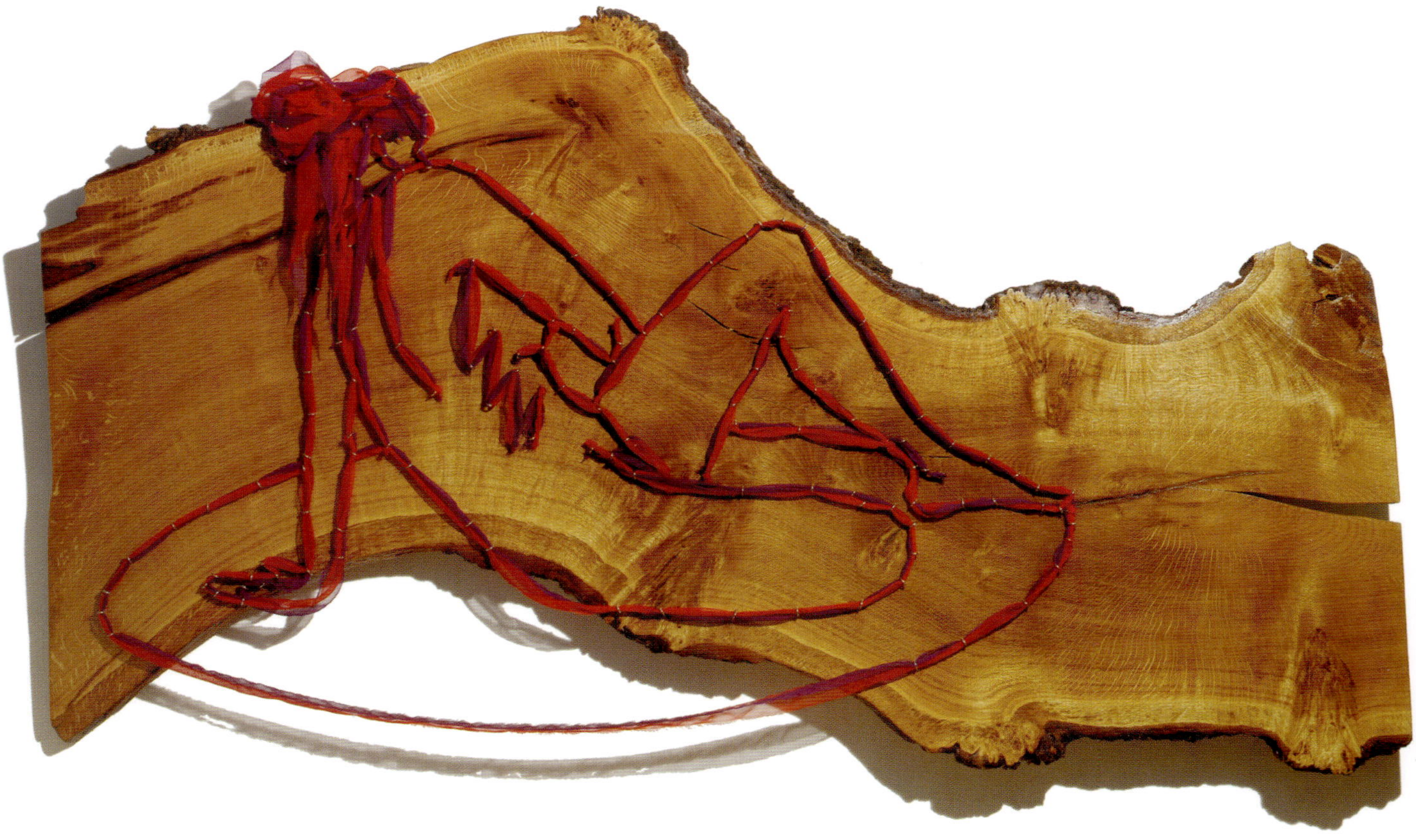

Figure Reclining Oak

# Benjamin Shine

www.benjaminshine.com

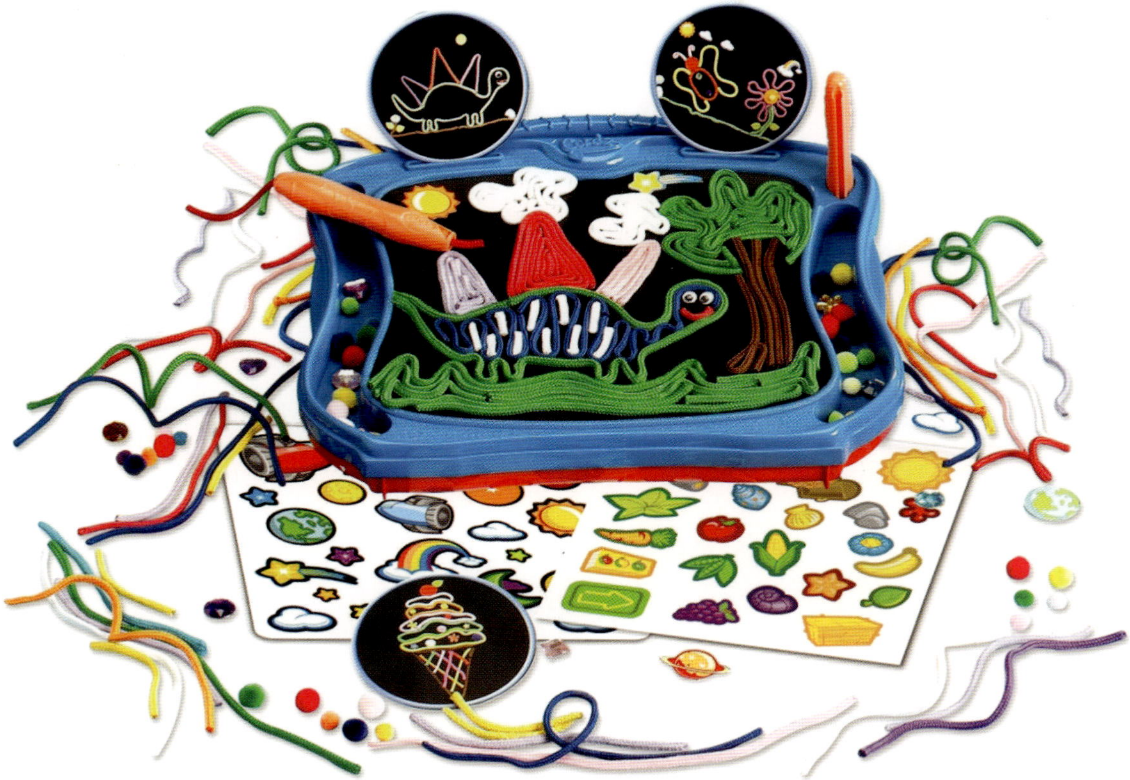

London-born, Benjamin Shine studied fashion design at The Surrey Institute of Art and Design and St Martins in London. Fashion, textiles and constructional ideas continue to inform Benjamin's style and broad creative vision, establishing a multi-disciplined design approach that strives for purposeful, memorable and timeless design through innovation and originality. Works range from commercial products and inventions to limited edition designs, fashion collaborations and commissioned artworks. To date, works include the award-winning SKOODY, which won Benjamin The Enterprising Young Brit Award 2004, presented by Gordon Brown, marking the first of his series of multi functional accessories. Benjamin has also collaborated with several fashion brands including Rohan and Schott NYC, for whom he was appointed to design an A/W 2005 menswear collection. Following his first exhibition of mixed-media artworks in 2003, Benjamin has continued to undertake new artwork projects and commissions, as well as being enlisted to design various corporate brands. Most notably, his fabric-portraits have generated a following of collectors including Baroness Thatcher, Sir Edmund Hillary and President Obama, with works exhibited in public locations including Deutsche Bank, Woburn Abbey, The New Zealand High Commission, Ligne Roset and the Museum of Arts and Design , New York. 2006 saw Benjamin invent CORDZ, a versatile and re-useable drawing product for children. The patented product is licensed to Flair Leisure Products PLC, in the UK and Mega Brands America in the US. CORDZ was awarded Top Creative Toy 2007 and recently won the acclaimed Red Dot Design Award 2009. Most recently Benjamin has been short-listed for an iconic public sculpture in Australia's capital city, Canberra. He has also recently won the prestigious Courvoisier Future 500 'One to Watch' title in the Art and Design category, in the UK. Benjamin's works have also been published in Lucy Siegle's book, 'To Die For' and 'The Eco-Travel Handbook' by Alastair Fuad-Luke.

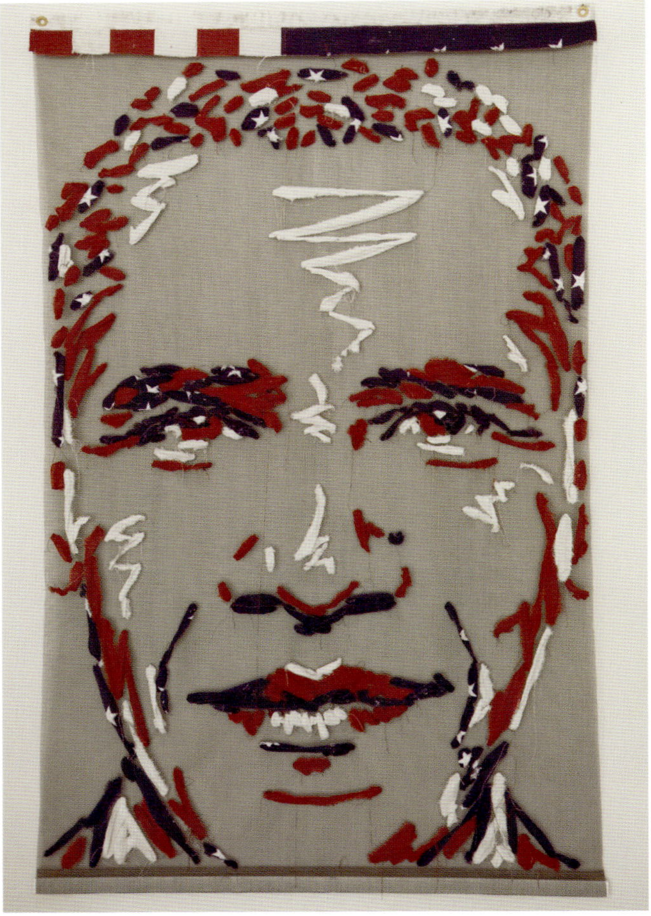

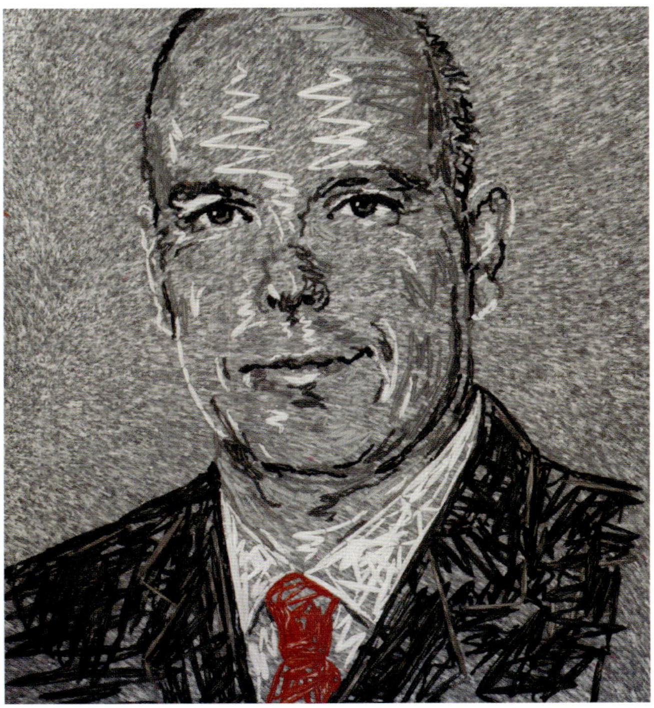

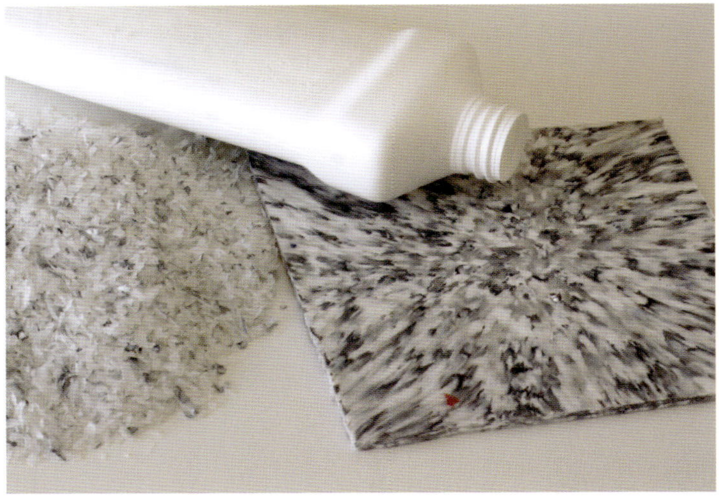

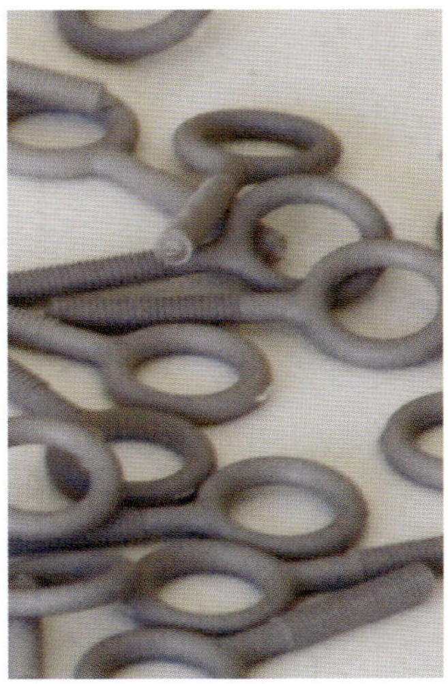

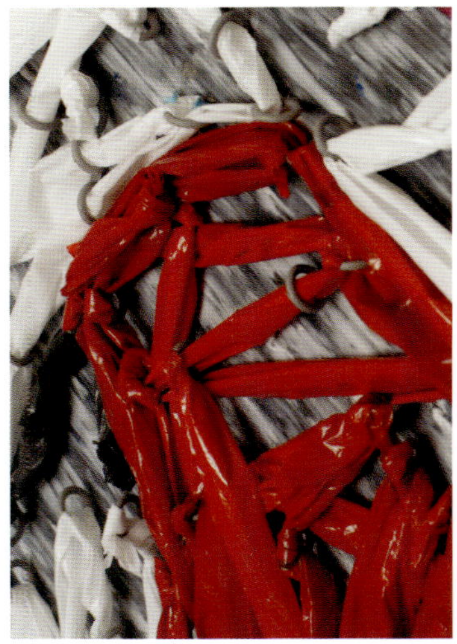

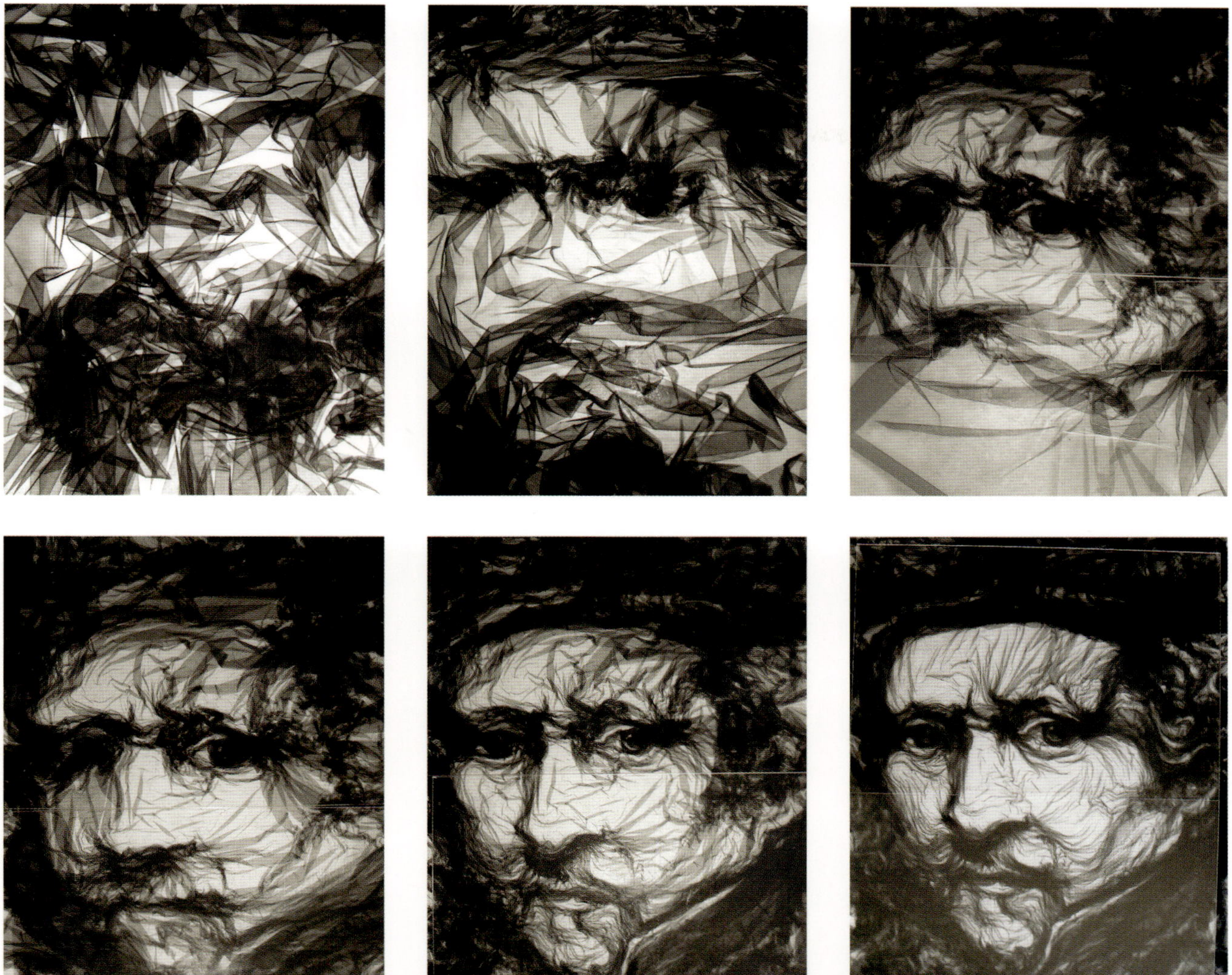

Light and Shade

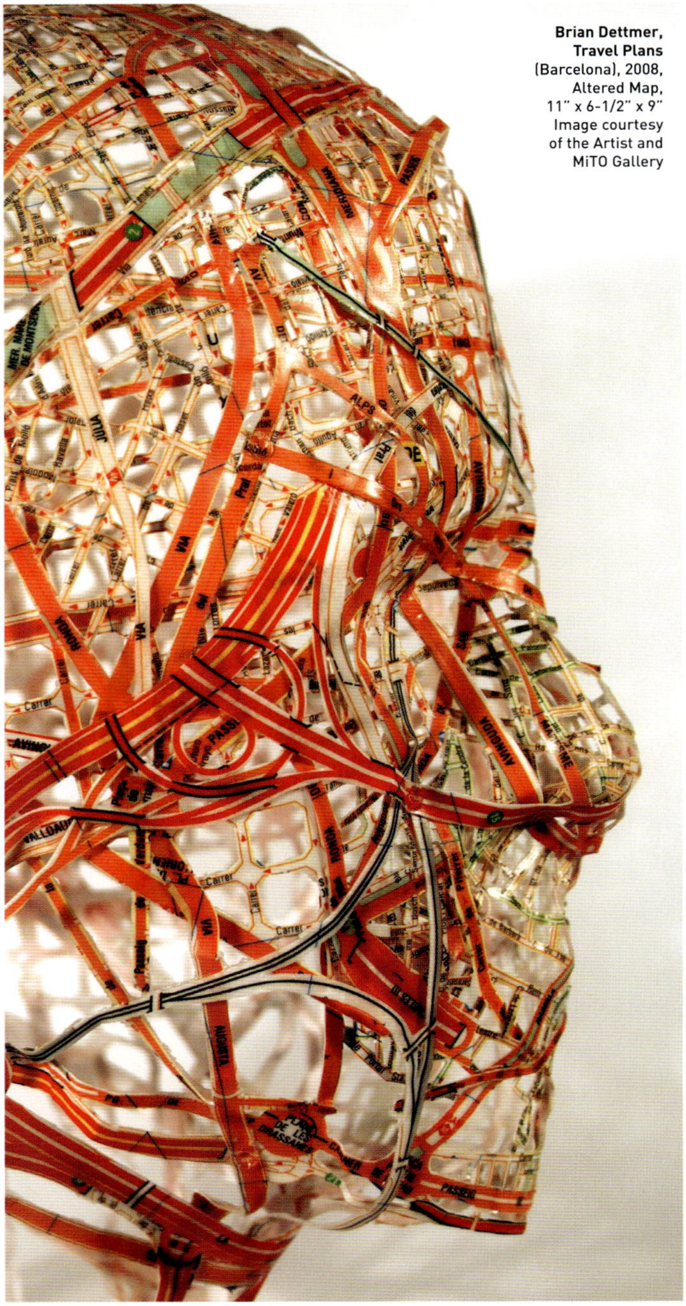

**Brian Dettmer, Travel Plans** (Barcelona), 2008, Altered Map, 11" x 6-1/2" x 9" Image courtesy of the Artist and MiTO Gallery

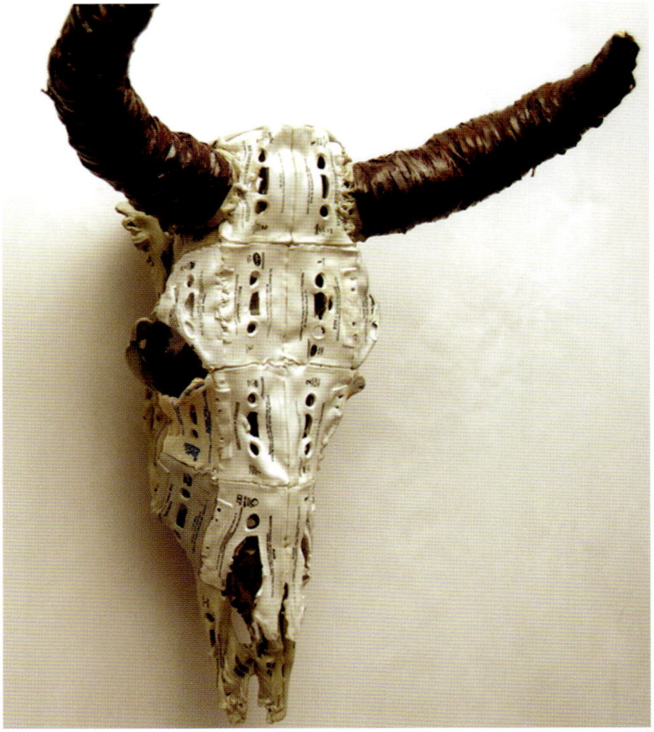

**Bull Skull**, 2007, Altered Cassette Tapes, 22" x 17-1/2" x 14-1/2"
Image courtesy of the Artist and MiTO Gallery

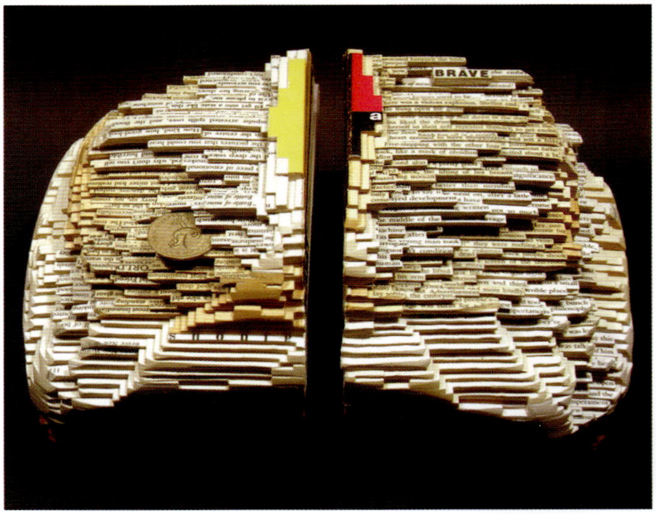


**Brave New World,** 2008, Altered Books, 5-3/4" x 11" x 8"
Image courtesy of the Artist and Toomey Tourell Fine Art

# Brian/Dettmer

www.briandettmer.com

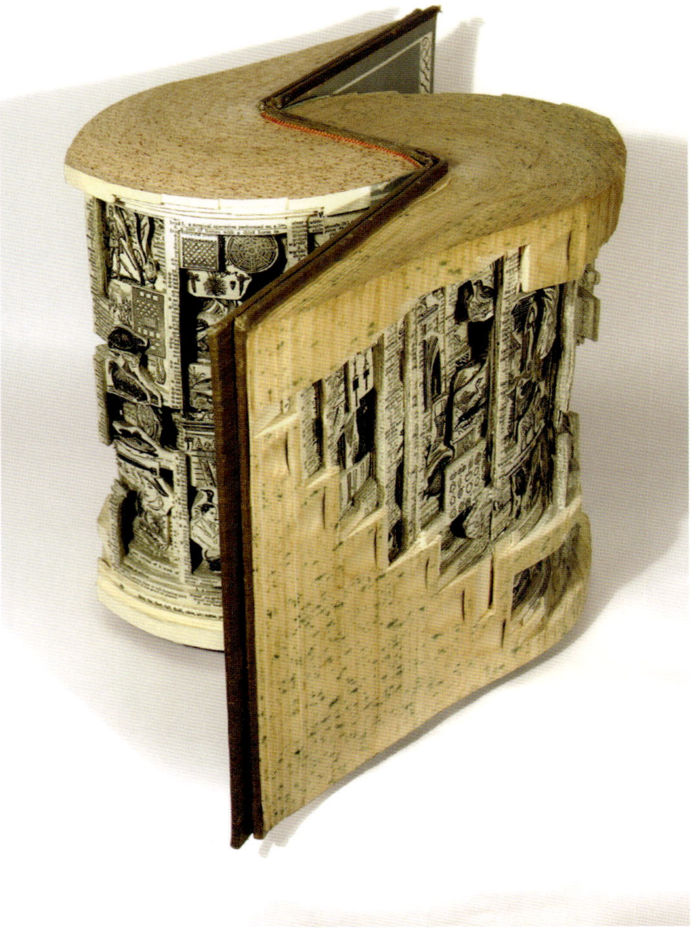

**Bull Skull (detail)**, 2007, Altered Cassette Tapes,
22" x 17-1/2" x 14-1/2"
Image courtesy of the Artist and MiTO Gallery

Dettmer is originally from Chicago, where he studied at Columbia College. He currently lives and works in Atlanta, GA.
Dettmer's work has been exhibited and collected throughout the United States, Mexico and Europe. He has had solo shows in New York, Chicago, San Francisco and has had projects exhibited in Mexico City, Berlin and London. He has been represented at several international art fairs including Bale Latina (Basel, Switzerland), Pulse (Miami), MACO (Mexico City), ARCO (Madrid), Scope (London, Miami), Art Chicago (Chicago) and many others.

The age of information in physical form is waning. As intangible routes thrive with quicker fluidity, material and history are being lost, slipping and eroding into the ether. Newer media swiftly flips forms, unrestricted by the weight of material and the responsibility of history. In the tangible world we are left with a frozen material but in the intangible world we may be left with nothing. History is lost as formats change from physical stability to digital distress. The richness and depth of the book is universally respected yet often undiscovered as the monopoly of the form and relevance of the information fades over time. The book's intended function has decreased and the form remains linear in a non-linear world. By altering physical forms of information and shifting preconceived functions, new and unexpected roles emerge. This is the area I currently operate in. Through meticulous excavation or concise alteration I edit or dissect communicative objects or systems such as books, maps, tapes and other media. The medium's role transforms. Its content is recontextualized and new meanings or interpretations emerge.

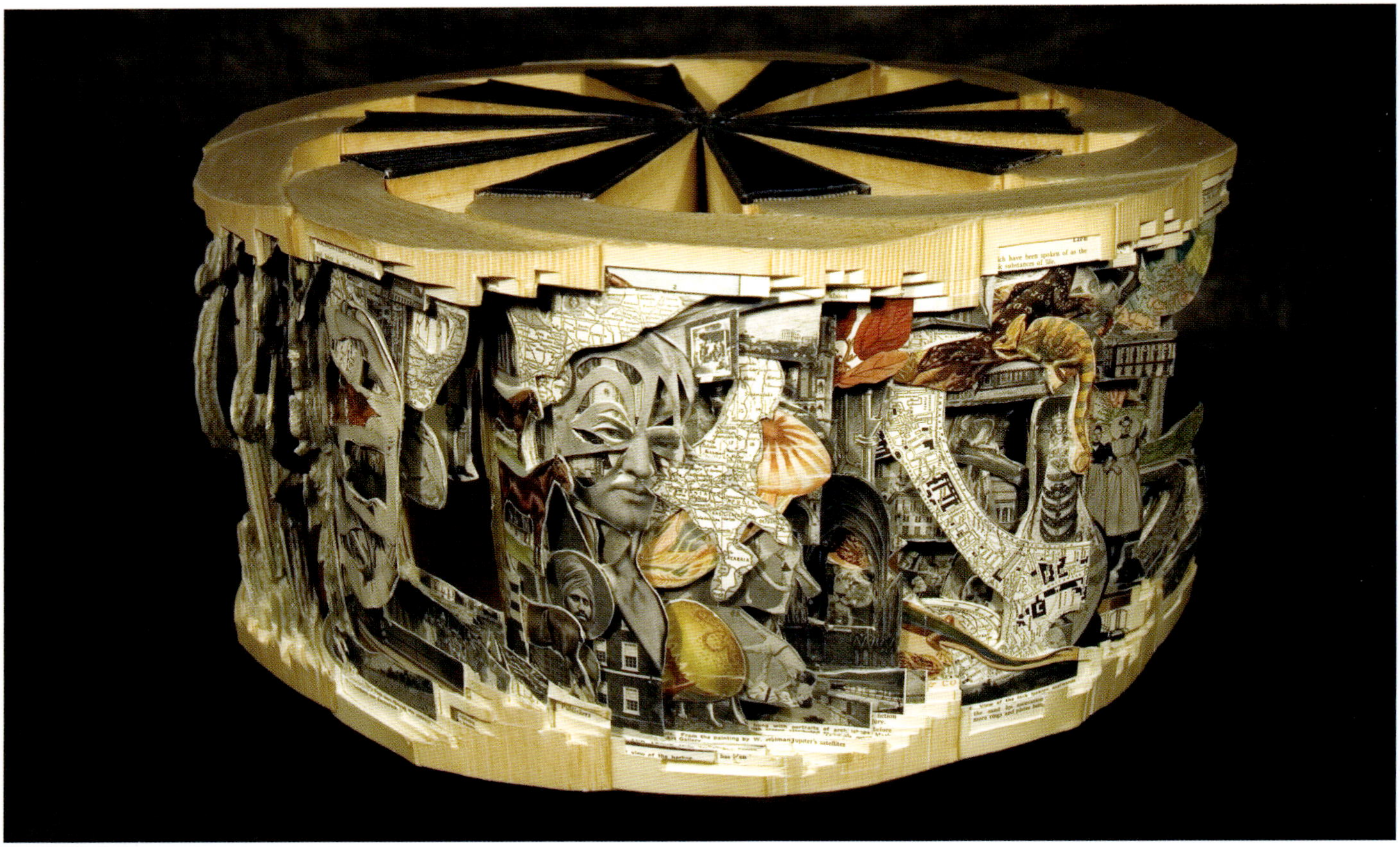

**Doubleday**, 2009,
Altered set of Vintage Encyclopedias, 10" x 19" x 19"
Image courtesy of the Artist and Toomey Tourell Fine Art

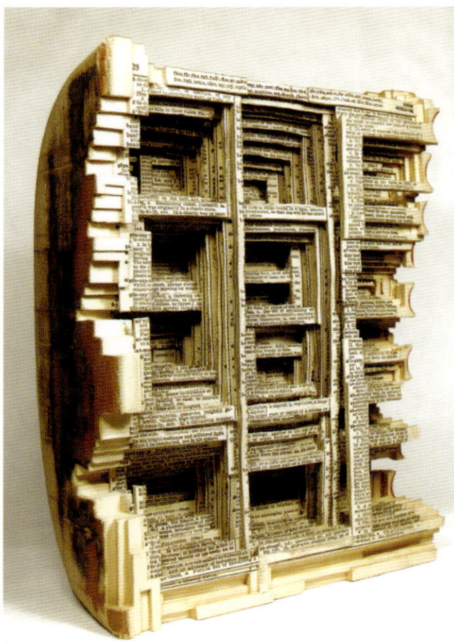

**Fate Far Fast Fall Final**, 2009,
Altered Book, 11" x 8-1/2" x 4-1/4"
Image courtesy of the Artist and Saltworks Gallery

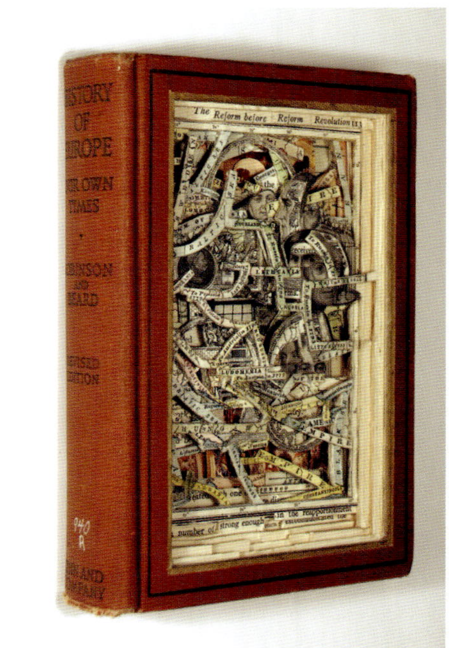

**History of Europe Our Own Times**, 2009,
Altered Book, 7-7/8" x 5-5/8" x 1-1/2"
Image courtesy of the Artist and Packer Schopf

**Explanation of Book Dissections**
In this work I begin with an existing book and seal its edges, creating an enclosed vessel full of unearthed potential. I cut into the surface of the book and dissect through it from the front. I work with knives, tweezers and surgical tools to carve one page at a time, exposing each layer while cutting around ideas and images of interest. Nothing inside the books is relocated or implanted, only removed. Images and ideas are revealed to expose alternate histories and memories. My work is a collaboration with the existing material and its past creators and the completed pieces expose new relationships of the book's internal elements exactly where they have been since their original conception.

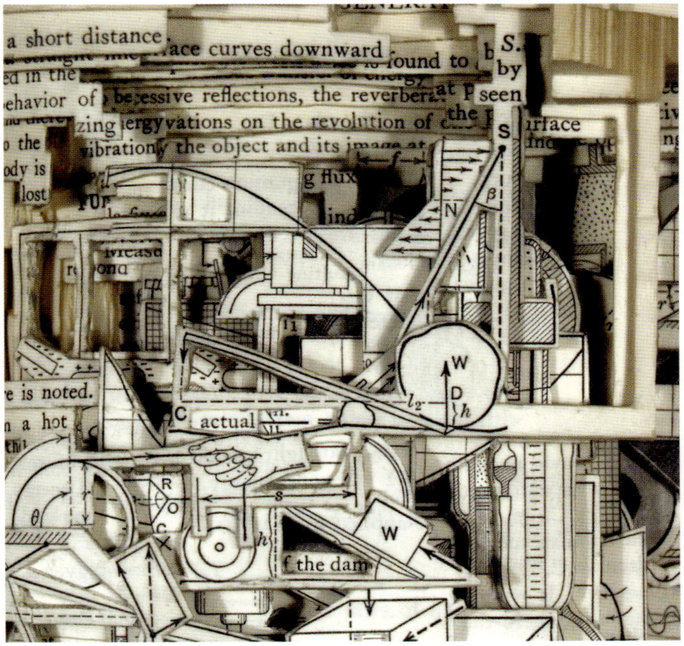


**Physics (detail)**, 2009,
Altered Book, 8-3/4" x 7-1/4" x 2"
Image courtesy of the Artist and Kinz + Tillou Fine Art

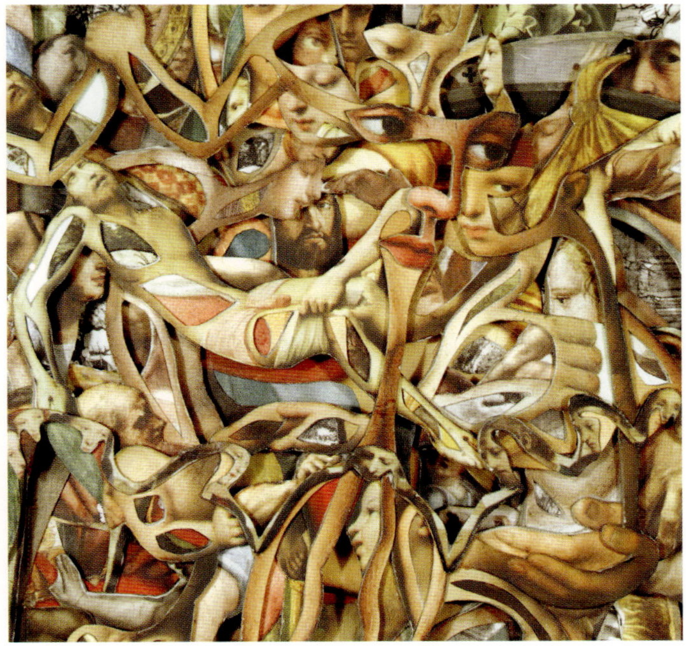

**Raphael (detail)**, 2008,
Altered Book, 15" x 11-1/2" x 2-1/2"
Image courtesy of the Artist and Kinz + Tillou Fine Art

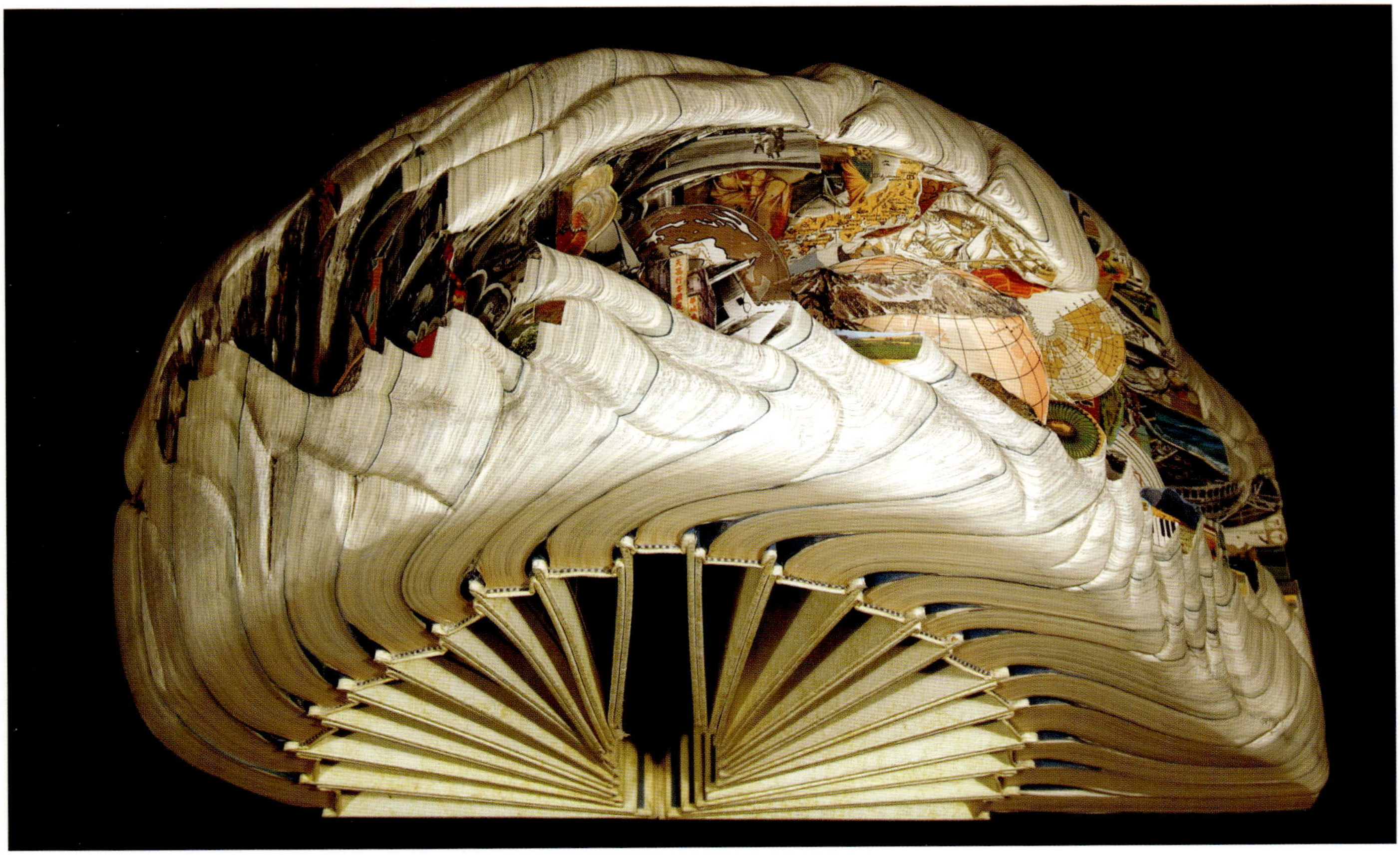

**New Books of Knowledge**, 2009,
Altered set of Vintage Encyclopedias, 16" x 26-1/2" x 10"
Image courtesy of the Artist and Packer Schopf

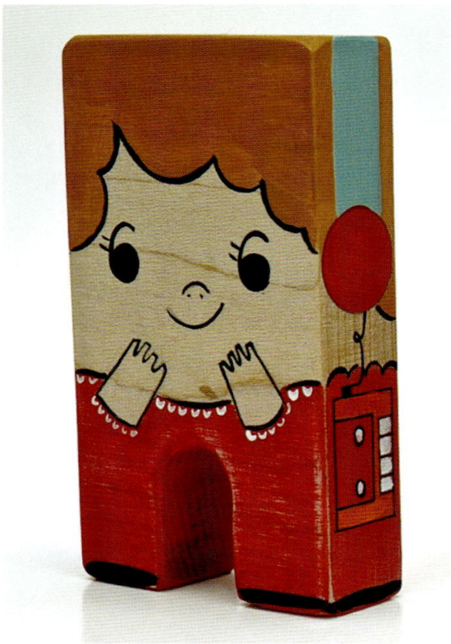
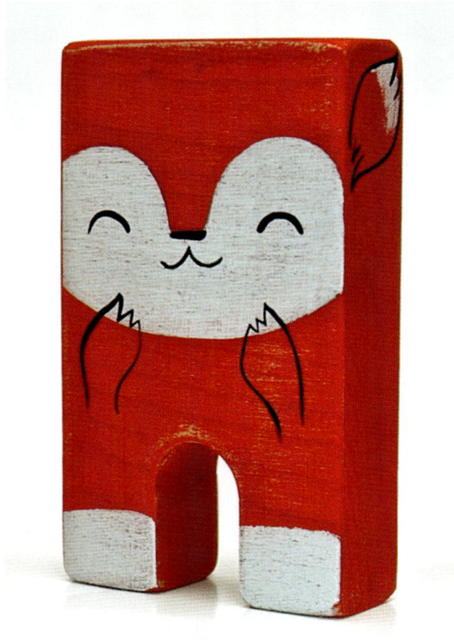
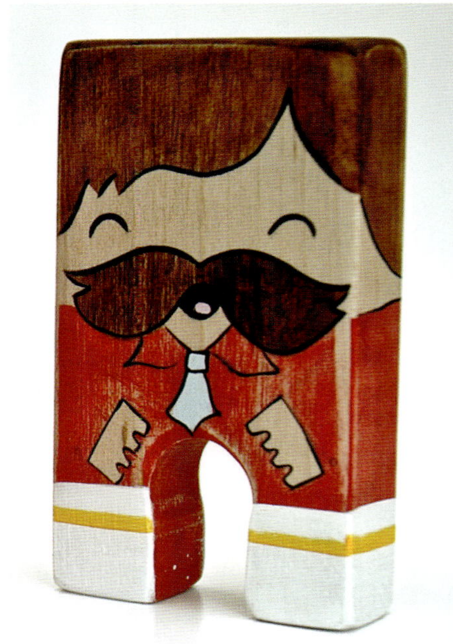
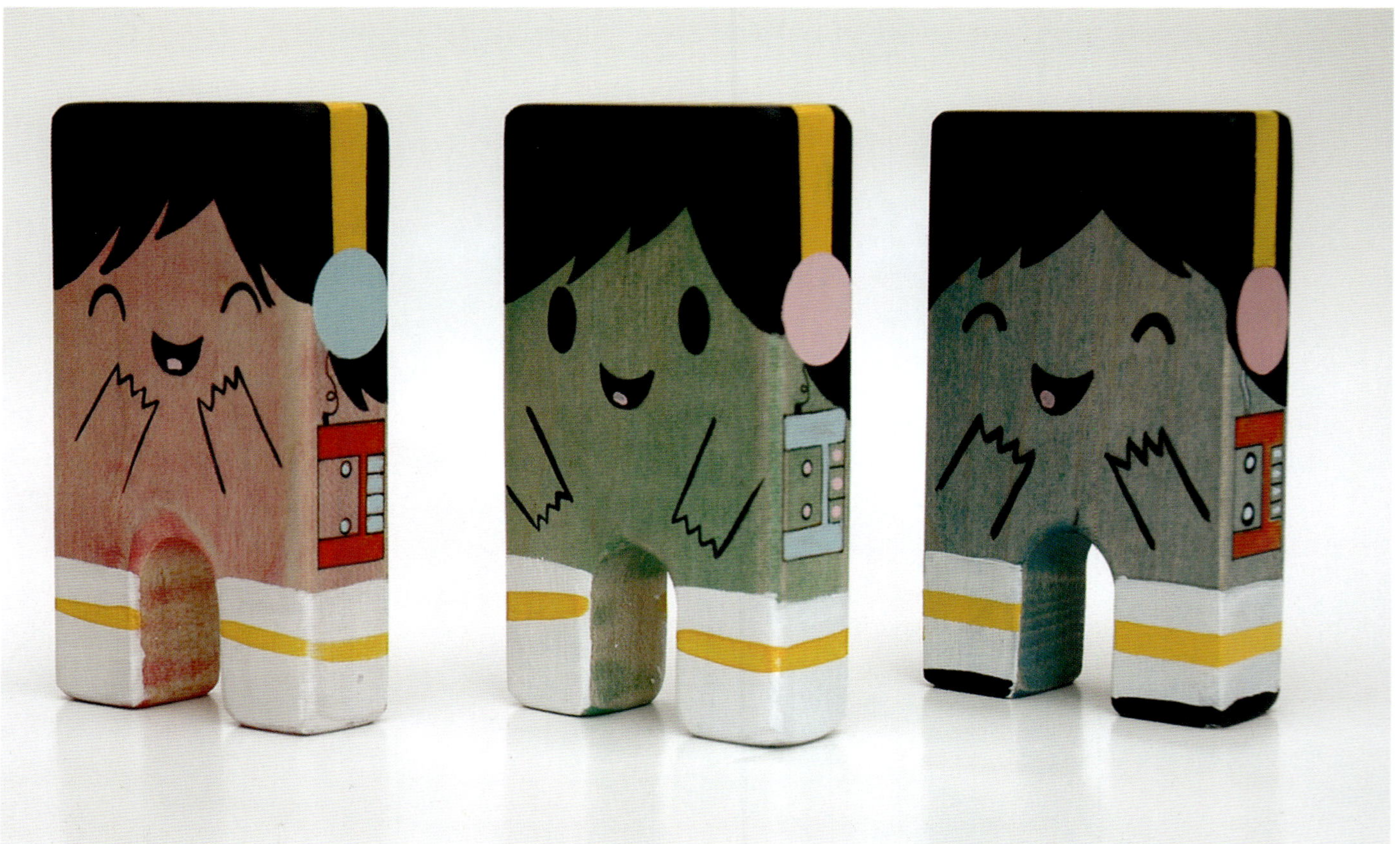

# Bubbles/Binsburry

www.bubblesbinsburry.com

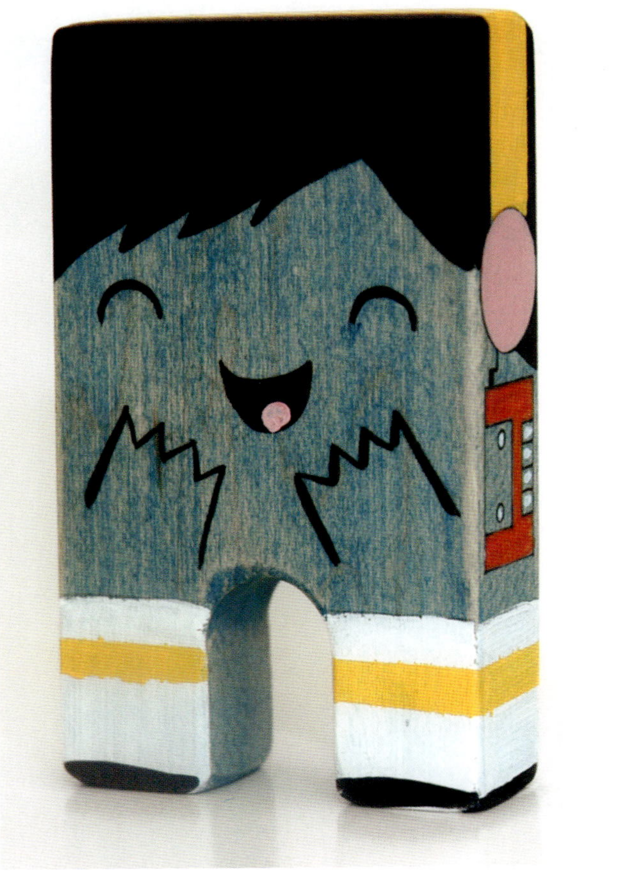

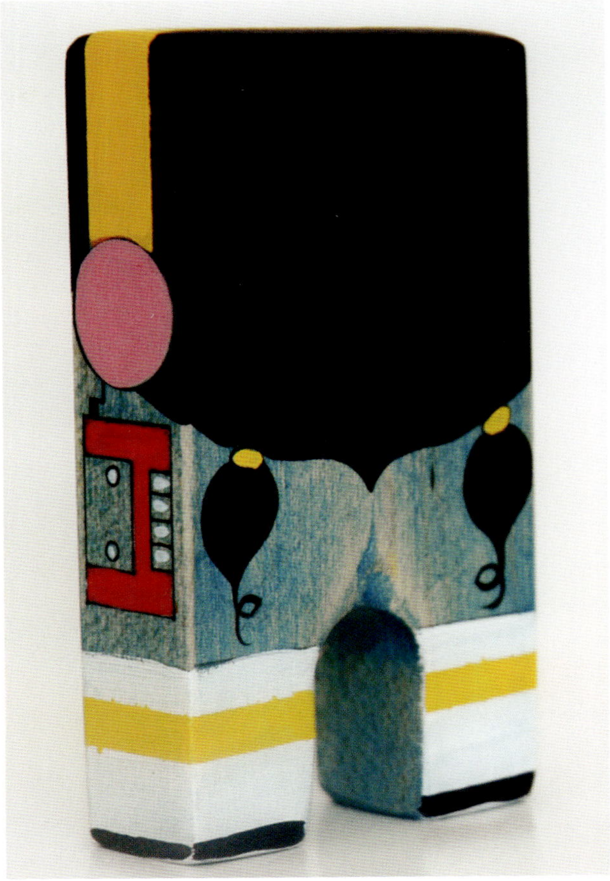

Bubblesbinsburry makes fun things for fun people. Just like you! Made up of a husband and wife team Kevin and Erin Stueber. We live in beautiful Milwaukee, WI USA with our two children Eli and Ruza. With Bubblesbinsburry we strive to make fun products that are free of sarcasm and irony. Something that can be enjoyed by people of all ages. We hope that our products bring some joy to the lives of our customers and to the people around them. Our wooden figures are made of 100% maple hardwood in our garage workshop. Once sanded to perfection they are painted by Erin's steady hand and then sealed with wax by my much less steady hand. All of the materials we use are totally nontoxic. Aesthetically, we strive to make our designs strong, simple and instantly recognizable as part of the Bubblesbinsburry universe. Our philosophy is that if a character design gets too complicated then it wasn't strong enough from the start. If we do it right, each character should be iconic.

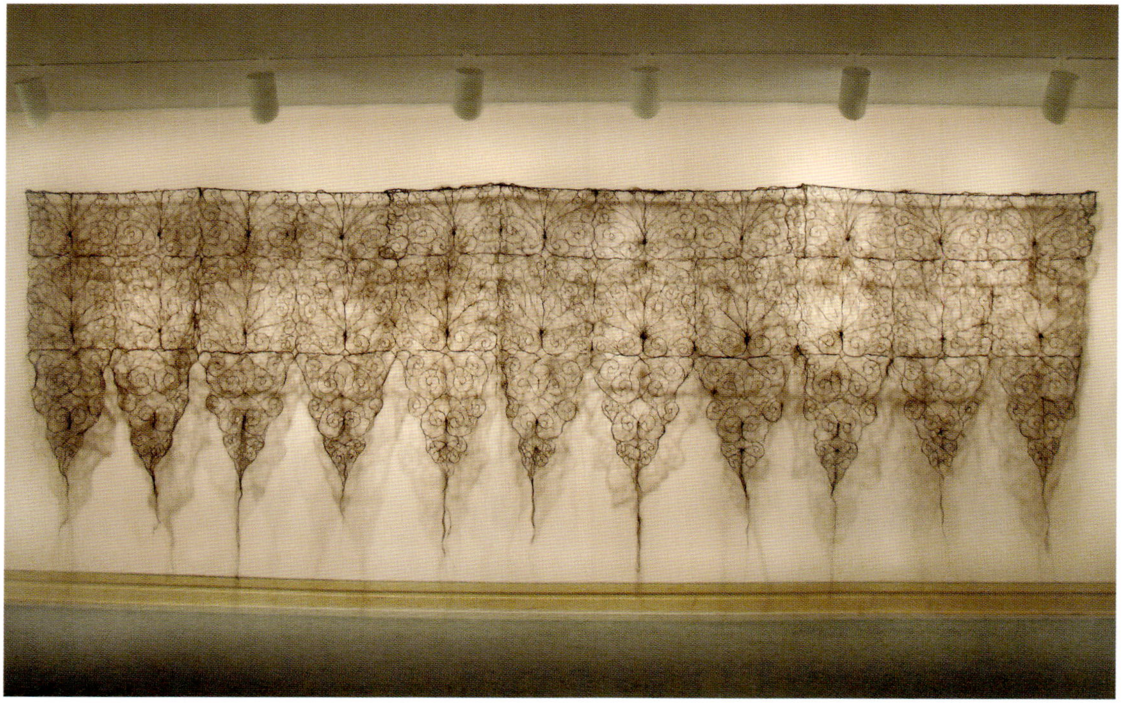

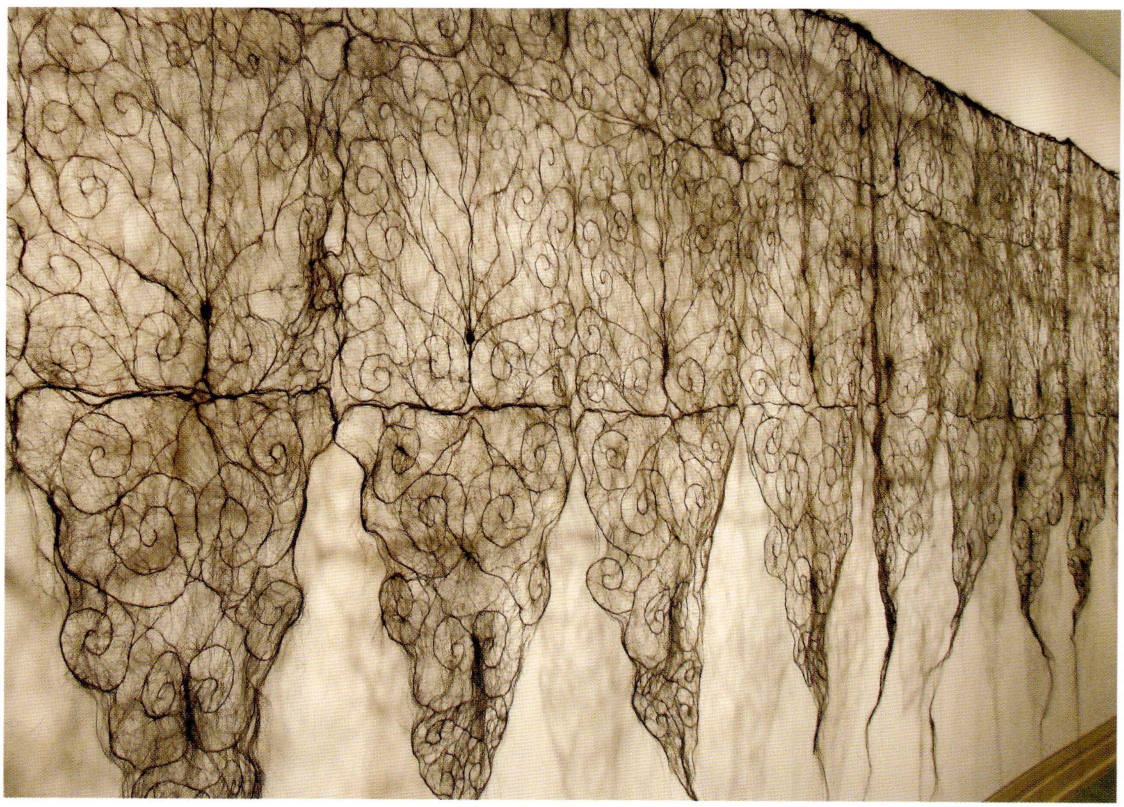

**Filigree #8.**
(installed at Jersey City Museum) Wire, artificial hair 7' x 30'. 2006

# Carson Fox

www.carsonfox.com

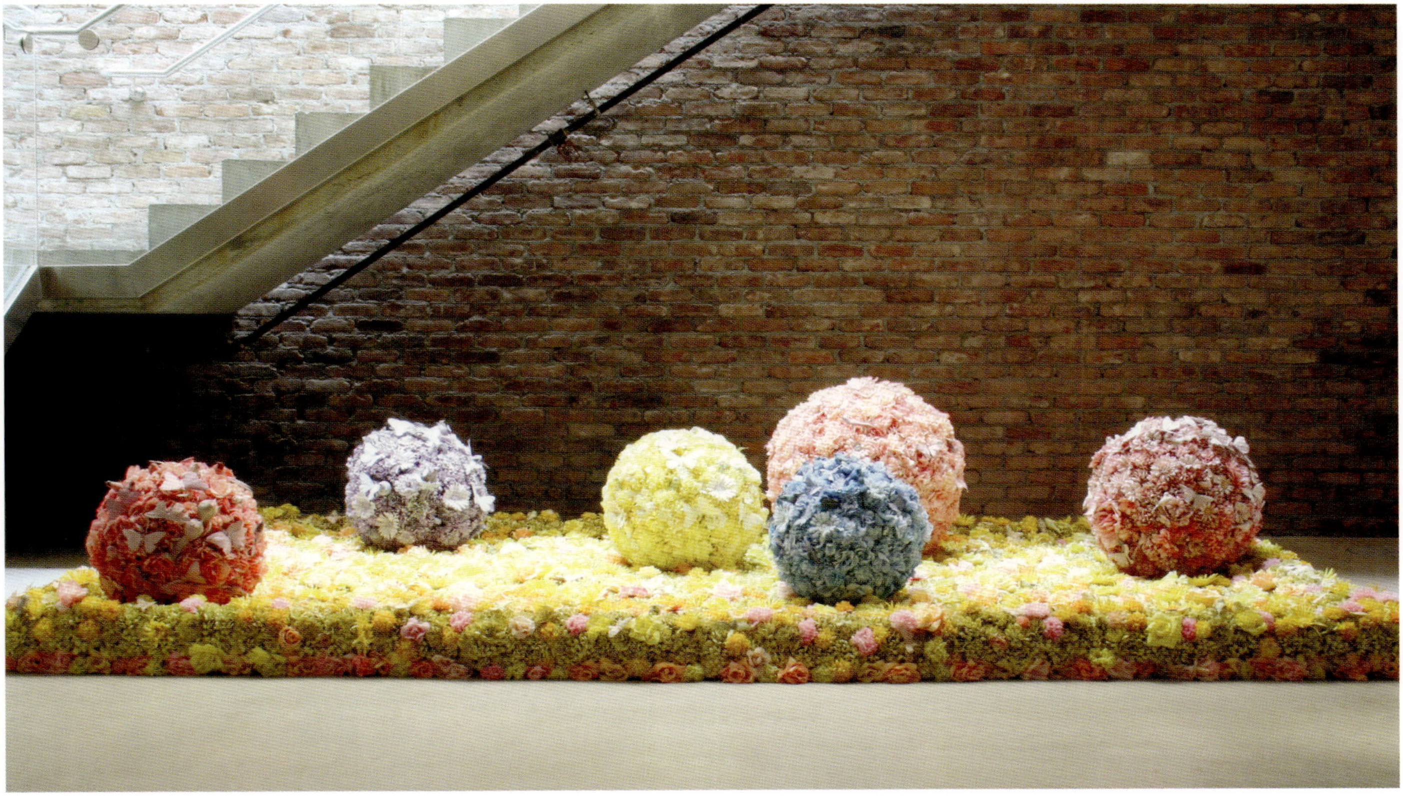

**Garden of Artificial Bliss and Joy.**
Artificial birds, butterflies, silk flowers, enamel, glitter
8' x 12'. 2005/6

American artist Carson Fox was born in Oxford, Mississippi, the small Southern hometown of William Faulkner. Named for novelist Carson McCullers, Carson's work is produced from a heritage of American Southern gothic tradition that relies heavily on the imprint that individual experience has on the artist. Carson Fox received her masters of fine arts from Mason Gross School of the Arts at Rutgers University and her BFA from University of Pennsylvania and the Pennsylvania Academy of the Fine Arts. Working across media, Fox produces prints, installation, and sculpture. Her work can be found in the permanent collections of The Museum of Arts and Design, The Royal Museum of Belgium, the Noyes Museum of Art, the Newark Public Library, the Jersey City Museum, the Morris Museum of Art, the Jane Voorhees Zimmerli Museum, the New Jersey State Museum, and the Pennsylvania Academy of the Fine Arts Museum. She has participated in solo and group exhibitions at the Boulder Museum of Contemporary Art, Boulder, Colorado, Claire Oliver Gallery, New York, O. K. Harris Gallery, New York, the National Museum of Wales, Cardiff, Wales, the Brunswiker Pavilion Kiel, Kiel, Germany, the Delaware Center for Contemporary Art, Wilmington, Delaware, and the Association Mouvment Art Contemporain, Chamalieres, France. Fox has received grants from the New Jersey Council on the Arts, the Barbara Deming Memorial Fund, and the Mid Atlantic Art Foundation, a Willem Emil Cresson Award, and a New Jersey Print and Paper Fellowship at the Rutgers Center for Innovative Print and Paper. Fox lives and works in Brooklyn, New York.

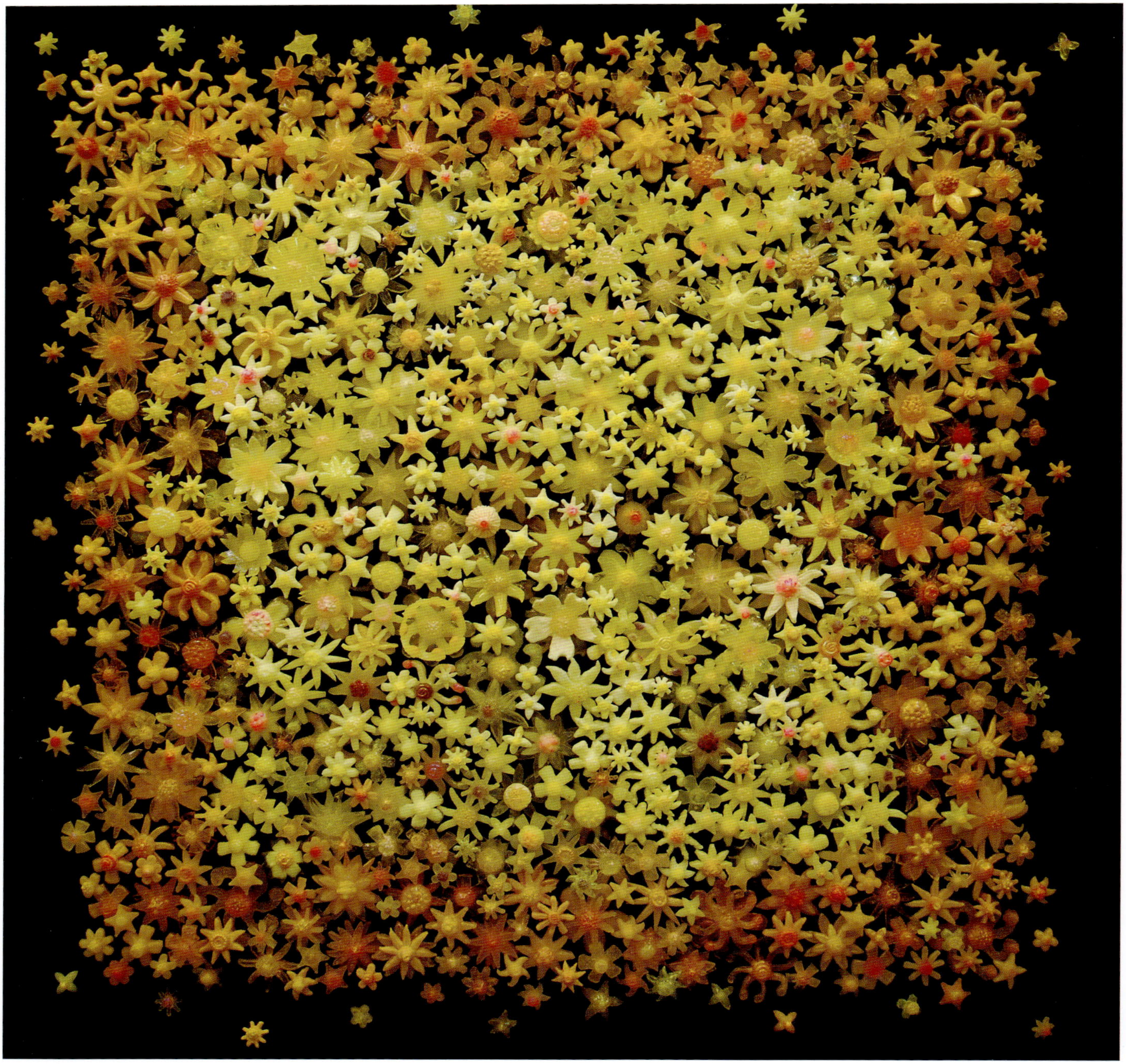

**Lemon Tangerine**
Cast resin, glue, pins
7' x 7'. 2007

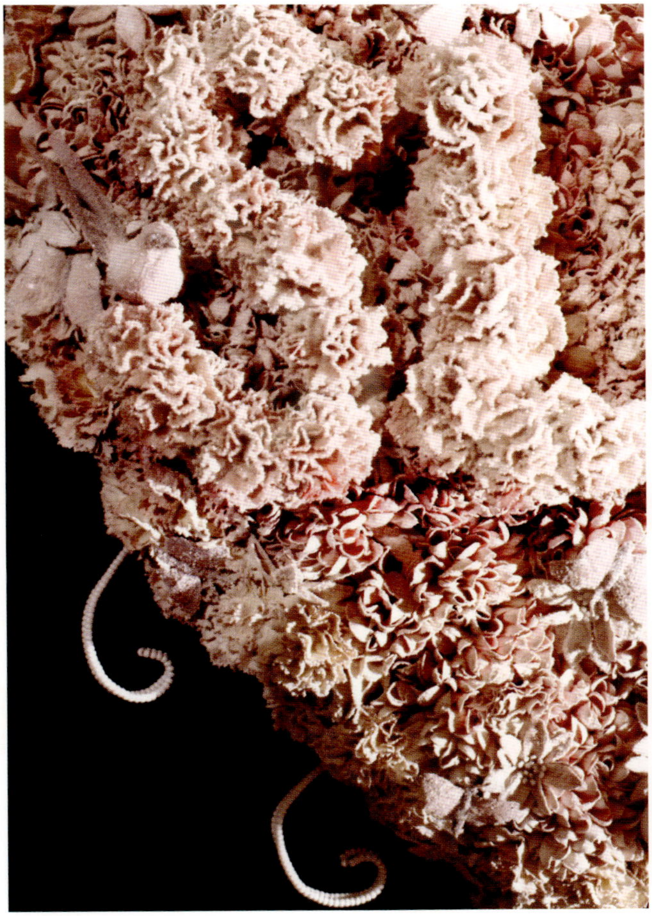

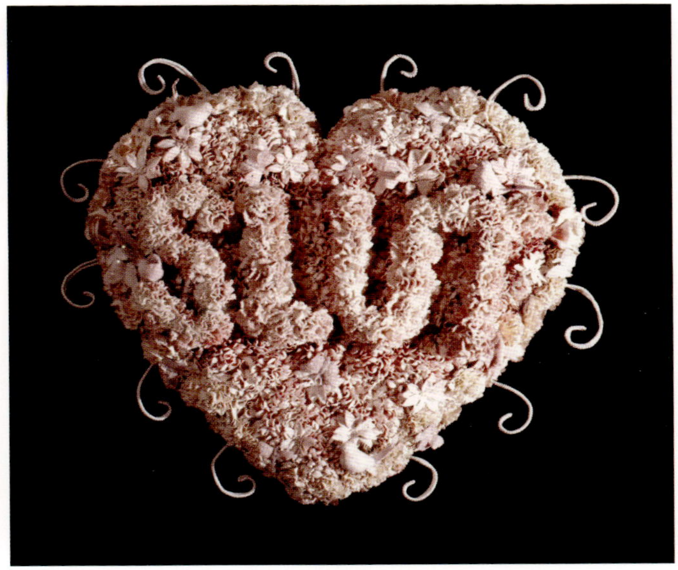


**Pink Slut.**
Mixed media
30w" x 32h" x 5 ½d ". 2004

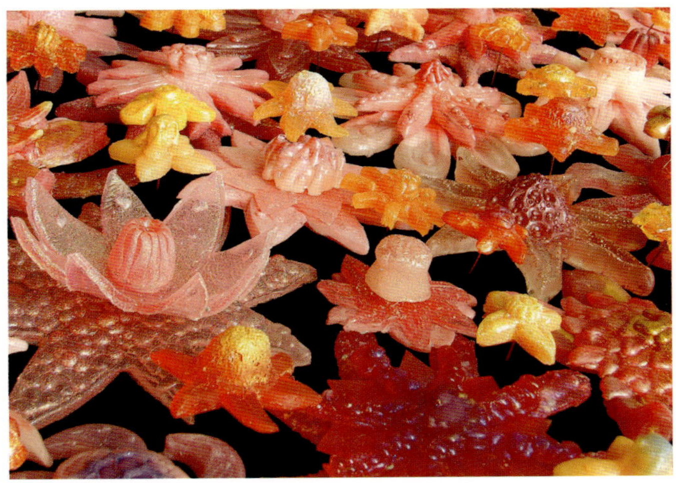

**September Snowflakes**
Cast resin

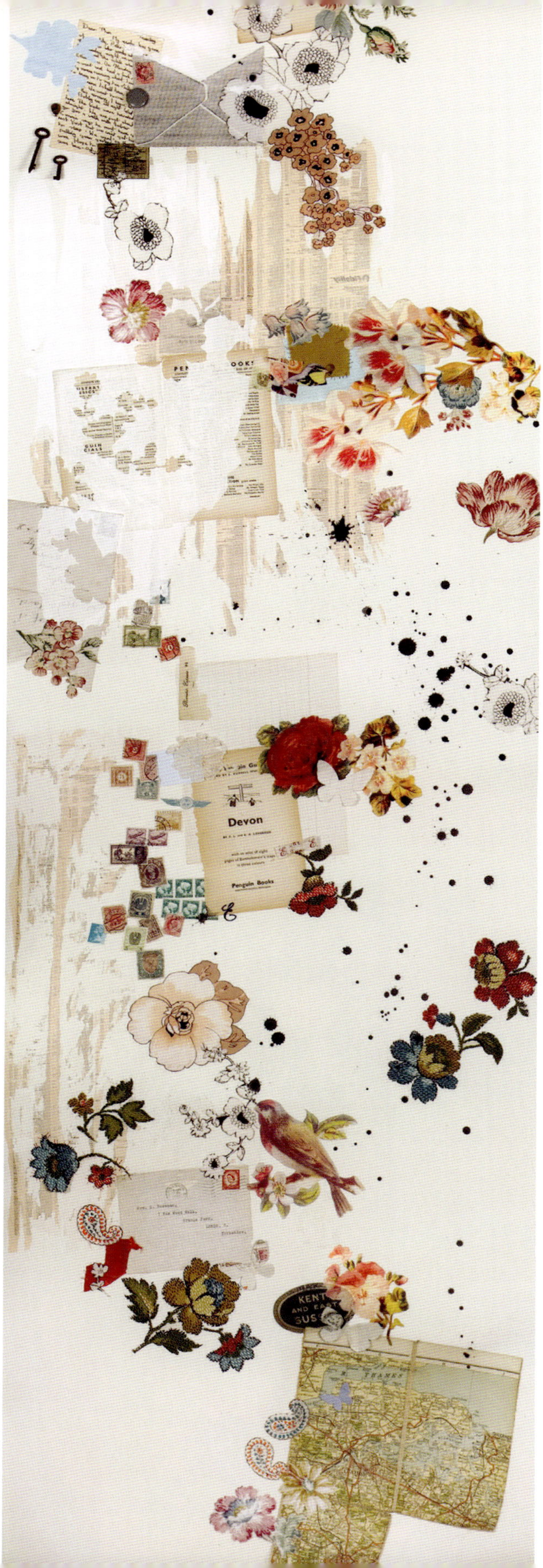

**Collection wall mural (vintage)**
Photographed from an original artwork and digitally reproduced as a scale print the Collection wall mural is a stunning trompe l'oeil twist on Catherine's signature collage wallpaper.
Roll length 52 cm x 6 m

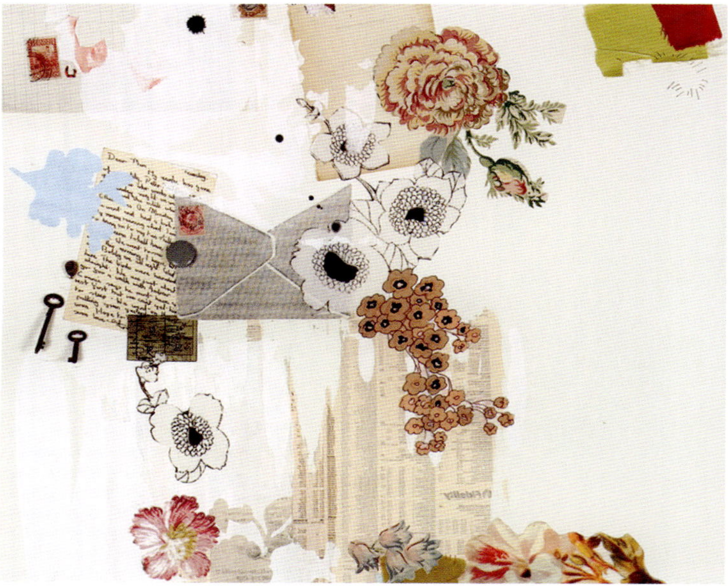

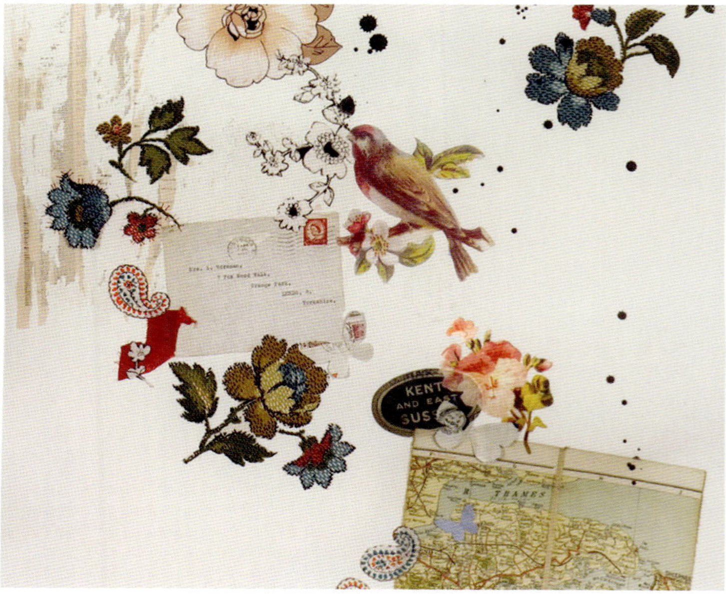

# Catherine Hammerton

www.catherinehammerton.com

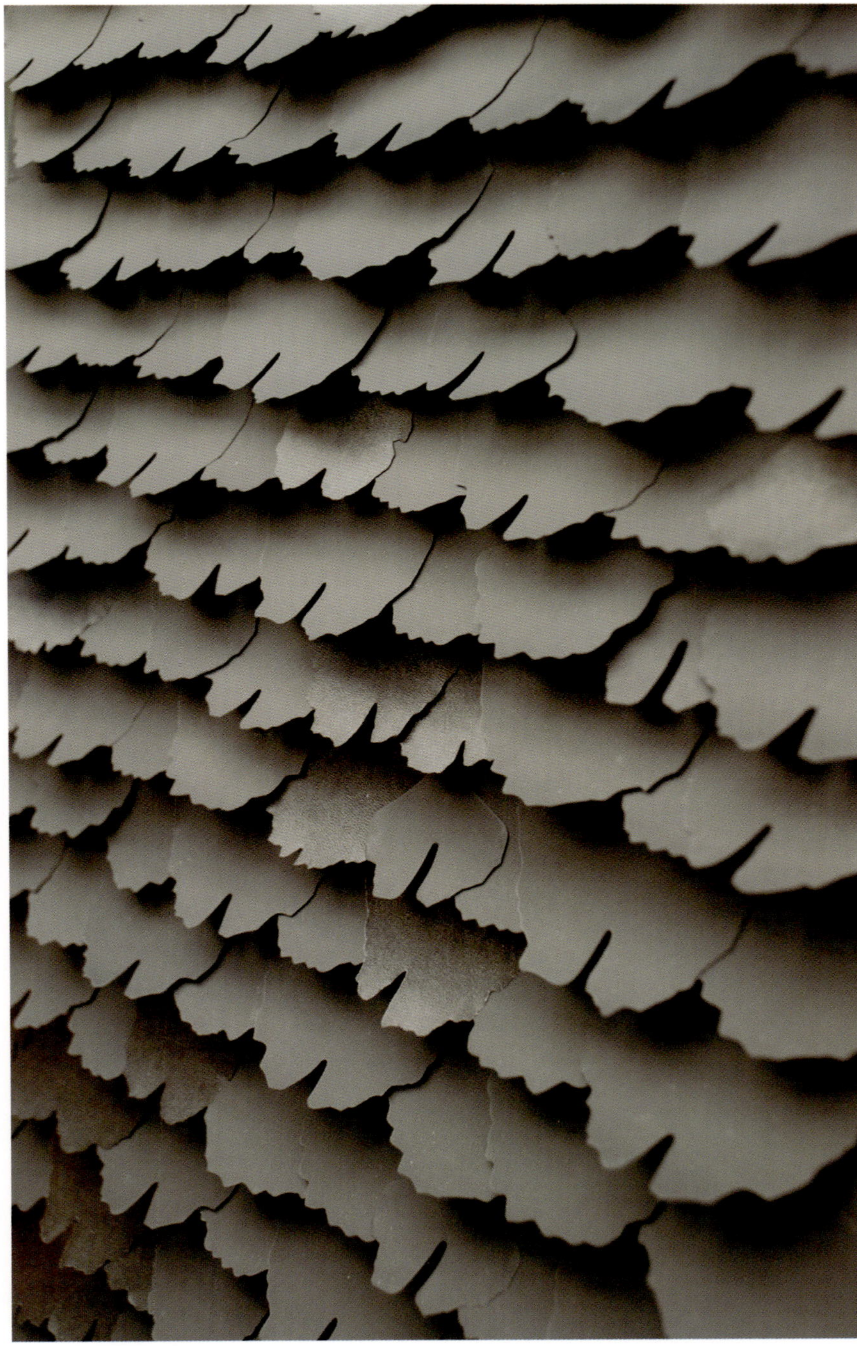

Graduated from the Royal College of Art, London, in 2005 with a Masters Degree in Mixed Media Textile Design. A London based Designer-Maker, her work is defined by its handmade aesthetic, utilising traditional silk screen printing and hand embroidery in tandem with cutting edge digital technology. Inspiration is eclectic, deriving from nature one season and military uniforms the next. Throughout there is an intuitive appreciation and approach to colour, texture and finish. The juxtaposition of these elements is channelled into the highly acclaimed "collection" of luxe interior products, which is of continuous improvement and expansion. Catherine's bespoke wallpaper service is likened to a Saville Row suit for the interior. Silkscreen printed and hand finished each panel is tailored to suit a client's individual need and aesthetic. Designs within the collection are currently made to order and priced per metre. Juxtaposing cutting edge technology with traditional hand finishing, Catherine uses only the finest fabrics and hides available for her soft furnishings. Hand-cut and embroidered, the range includes upholstery fabrics, throws and cushions all currently made in the uk.

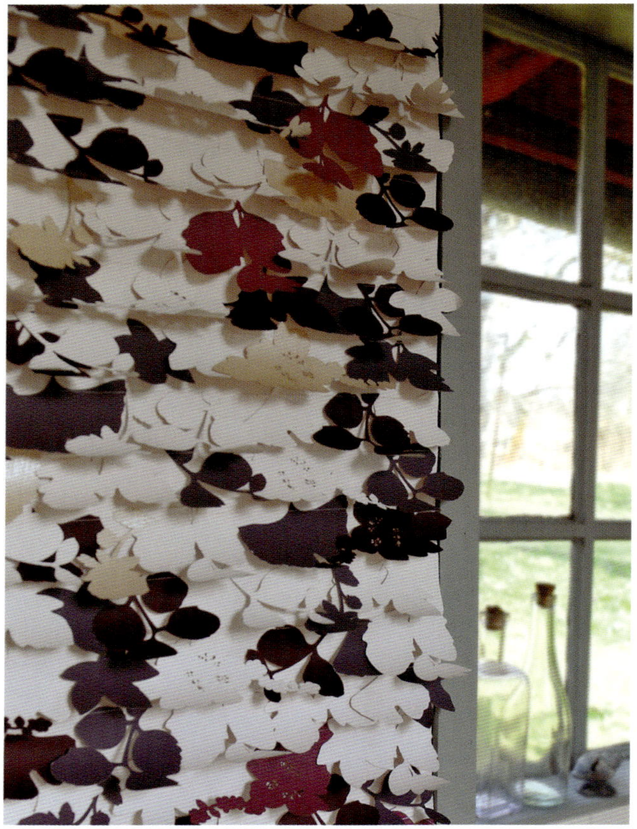

**Bramble wallpaper**
A wild foliage for walls, Bramble wallpaper is made from die cut flora shapes stitched to a traditional wallpaper base. It is colour matched to order and best suited to low traffic areas, due to its 3D textured surface.

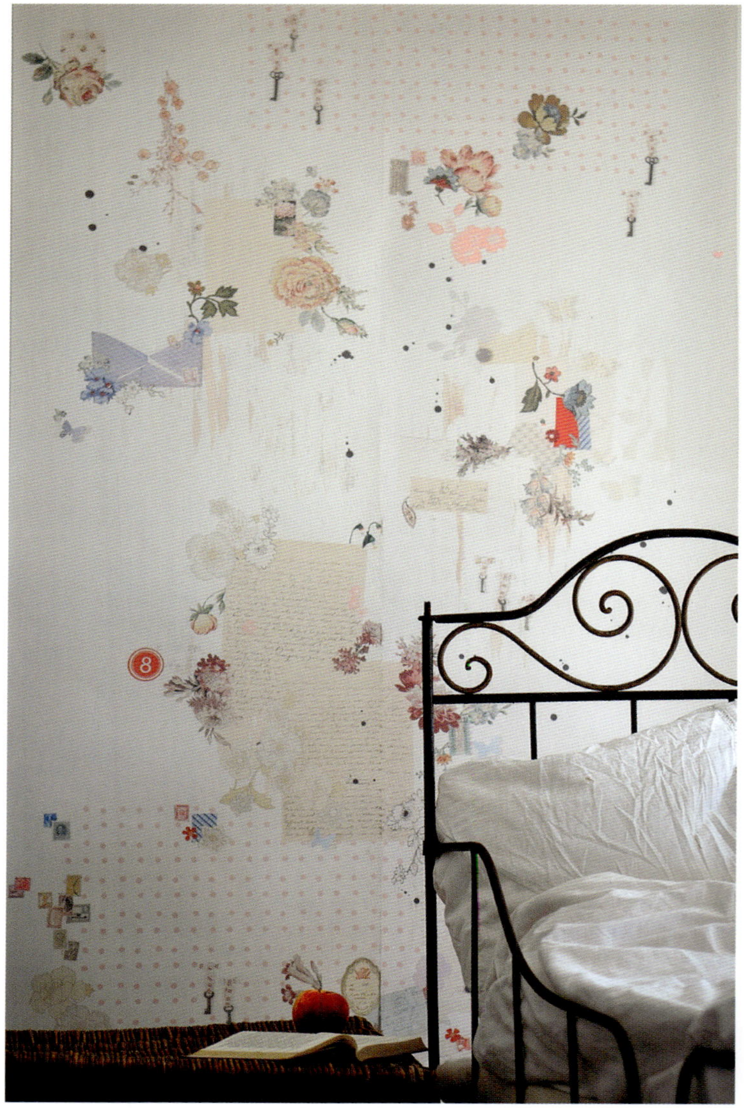


**Collection wall mural (lifestyle)**

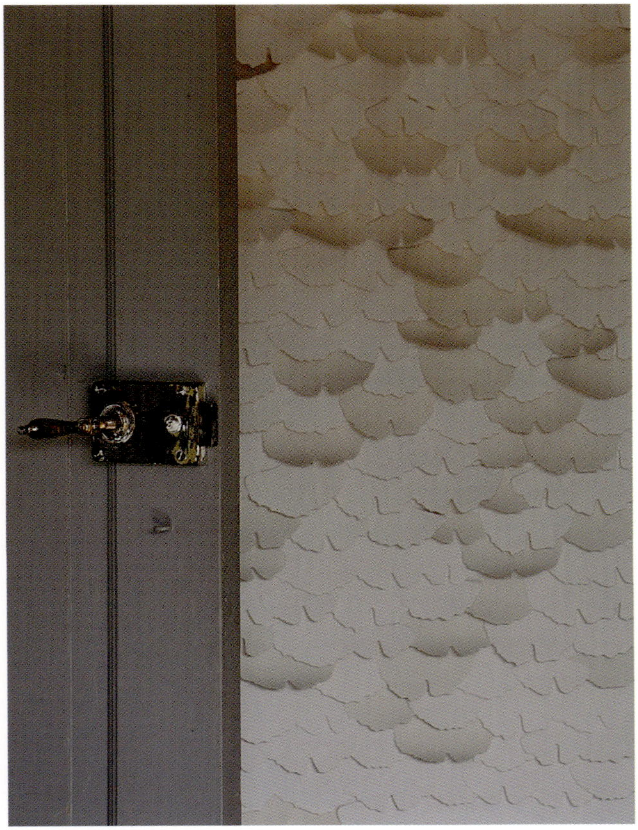

**Flutter wallpaper**
A striking ruffle of texture, Flutter wallpaper is hand made from die cut paper gingko leaves stitched to a traditional wallpaper base. It is colour matched to order best suited to low traffic areas, due to its 3D textured surface.

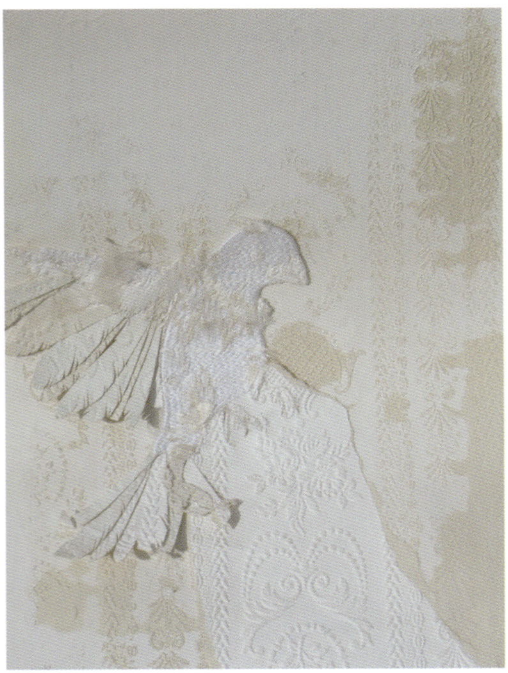

**Victorian Wallpaper**

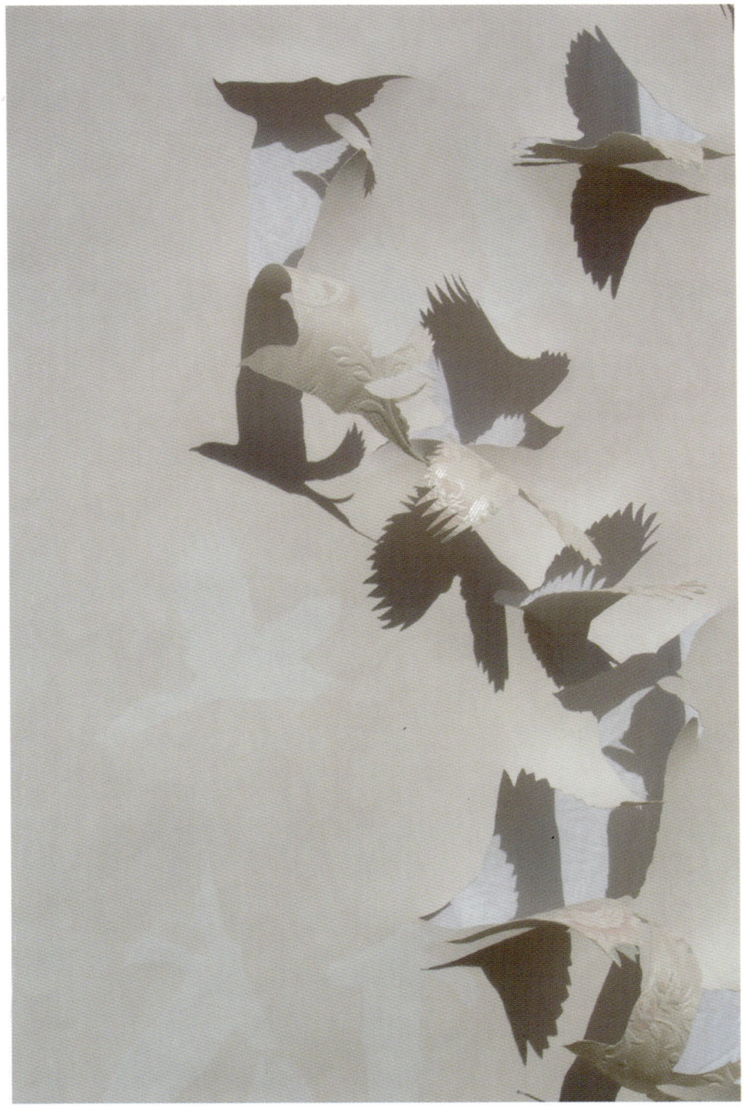

**Fly**
A wallpaper that also incorporates vintage wallpaper and is handcut with bird silhouettes.

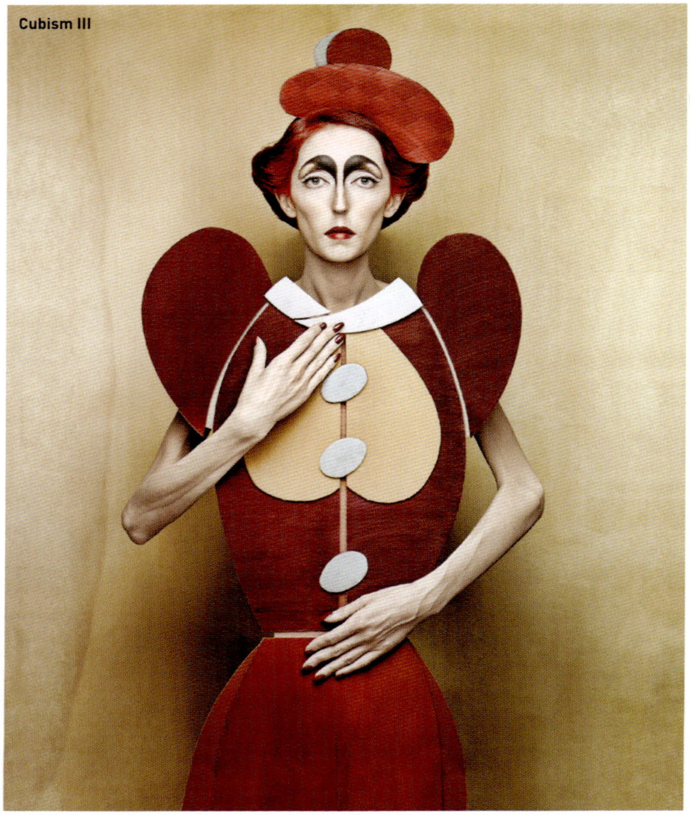
Cubism III

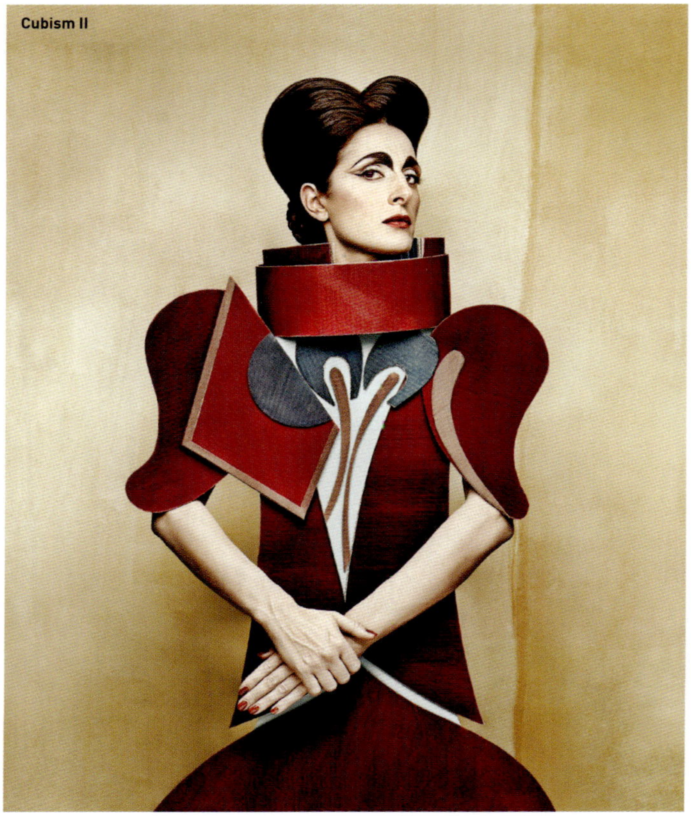
Cubism II

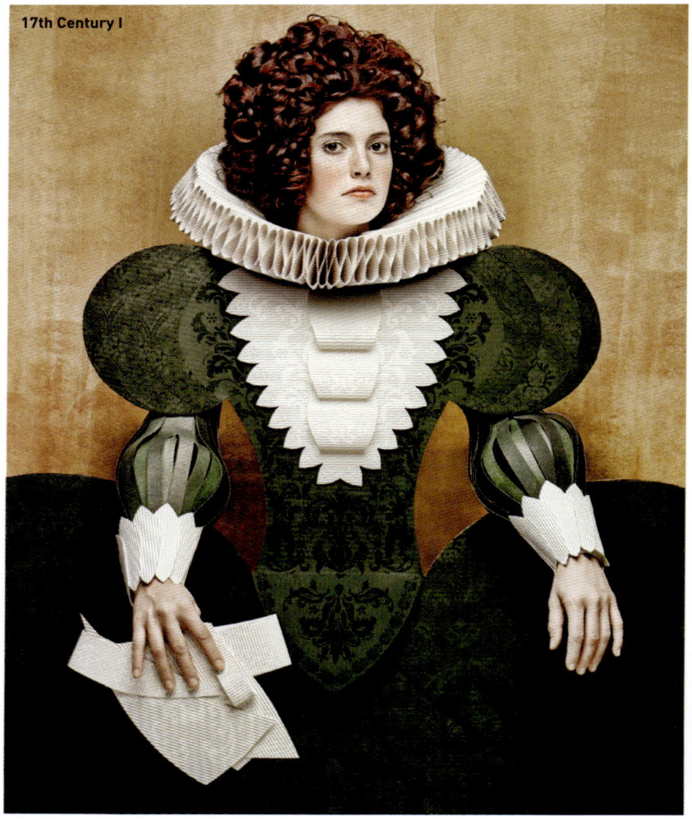
17th Century I

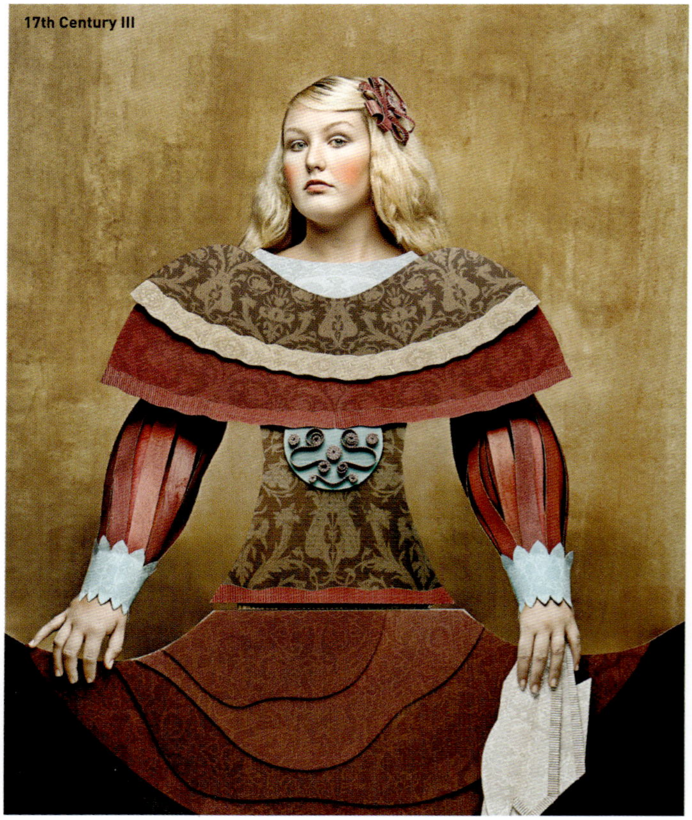
17th Century III

# Christian / Tagliavini

www.christiantagliavini.com

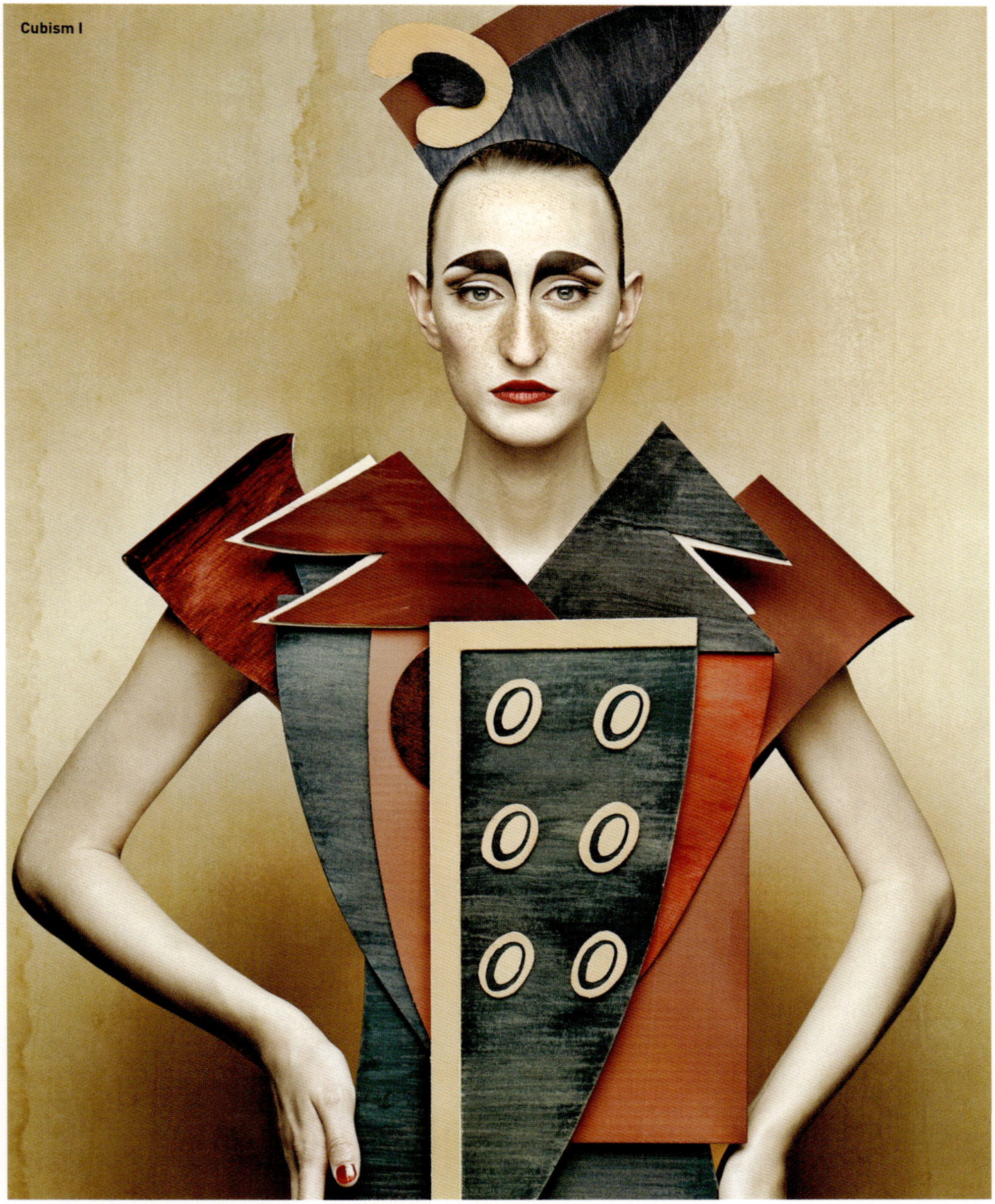


Dame di Cartone / Cardboard Ladies
Between two and three-dimensional perception, a gallery of nine unique portraits ranging from Cubism to 17th Century and Fifties-era. Neither paper dolls nor real women: just pensive, emerging figures. - 2008

1971 Swiss/Italian | I have lived and studied in Italy and Switzerland in the 80s. Technical education, creative evolution self-taught. Then, the crossroads: on one side, graphics. On the other side, photography. I start with the idea, then I search someone to impersonate it. I build up stories and dramatize them using photography and creativity as a skillful artifice being at the same time author, stage designer, costume designer, casting manager, director - and photographer. I draw inspiration from other photographers and artists: Luigi Ghirri is to me the greatest Italian photographer. His misty landscapes pierced with the winter light remind me of the places where I grew up. Erwin Olaf, creative, elegant, ironic: I consider him a flawless model of technique and style, a true perfectionist of the artificial image.

Photos by Christian Tagliavini

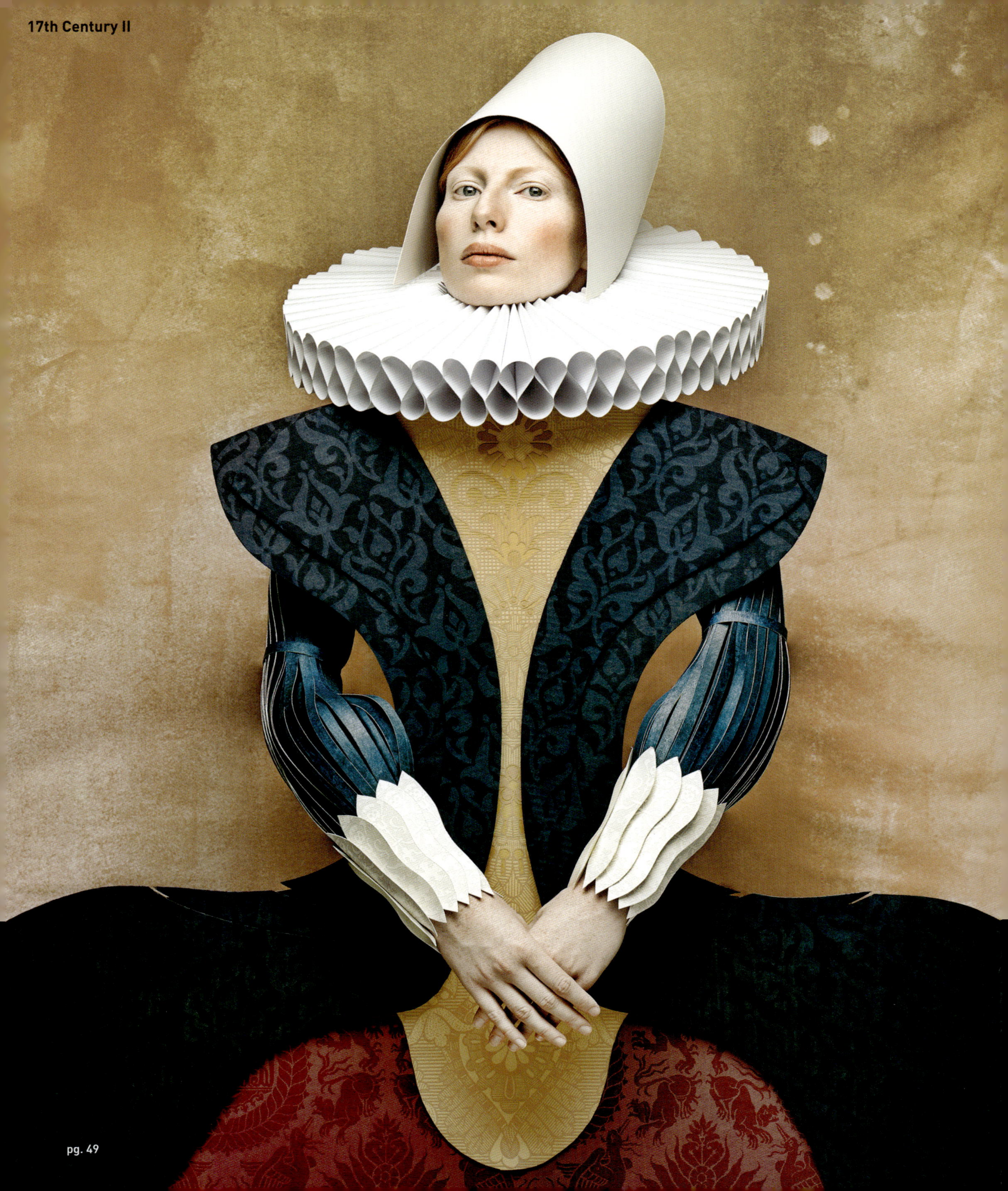

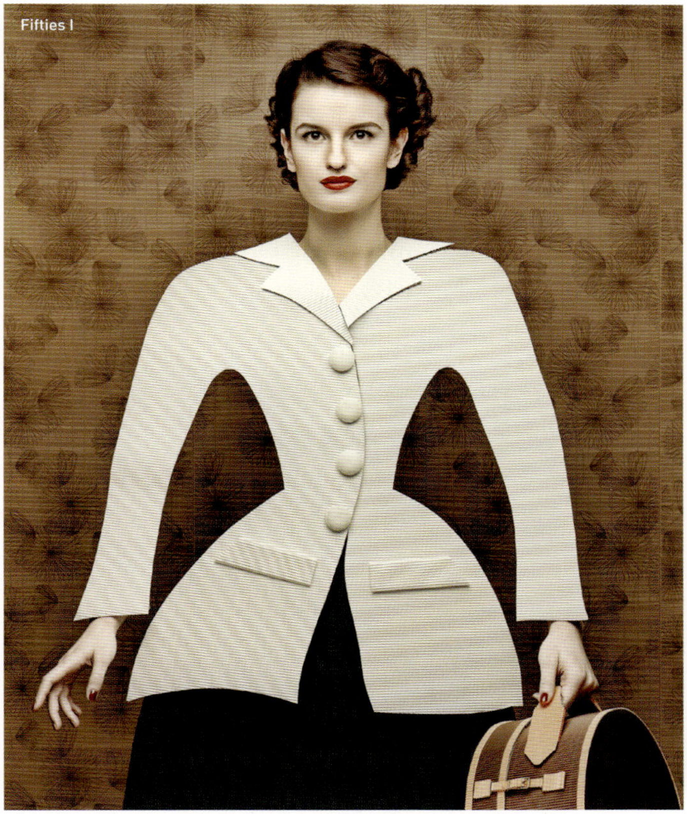
Fifties I

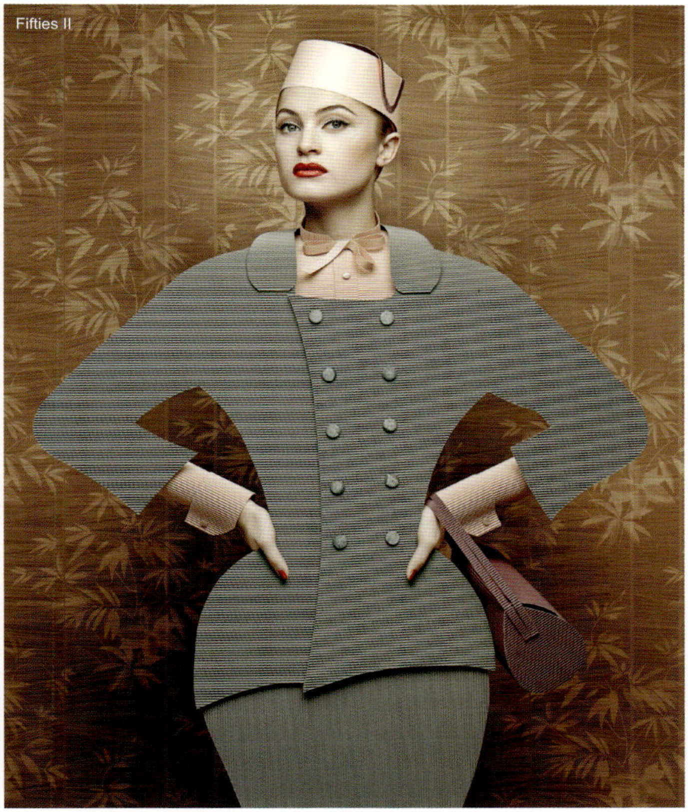
Fifties II

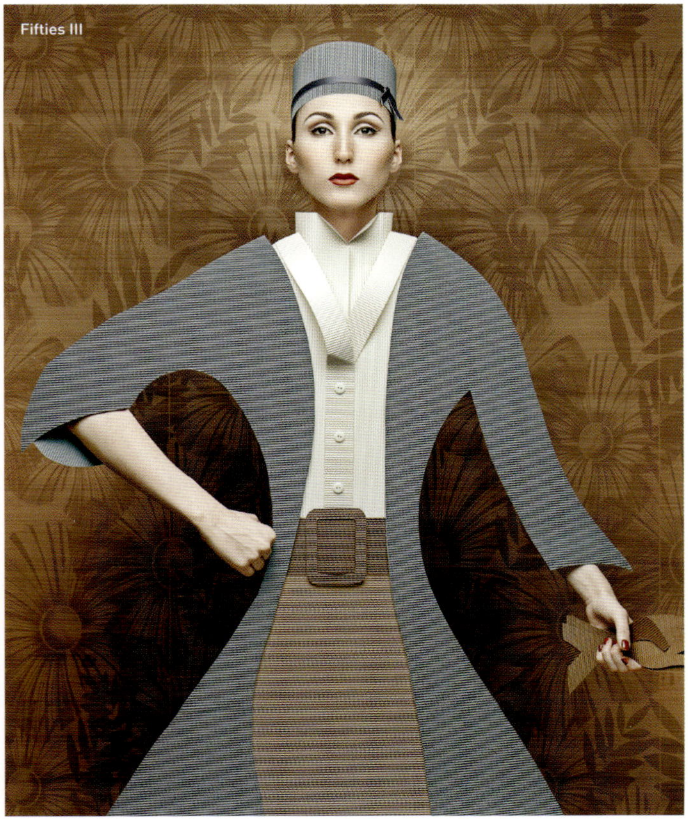
Fifties III

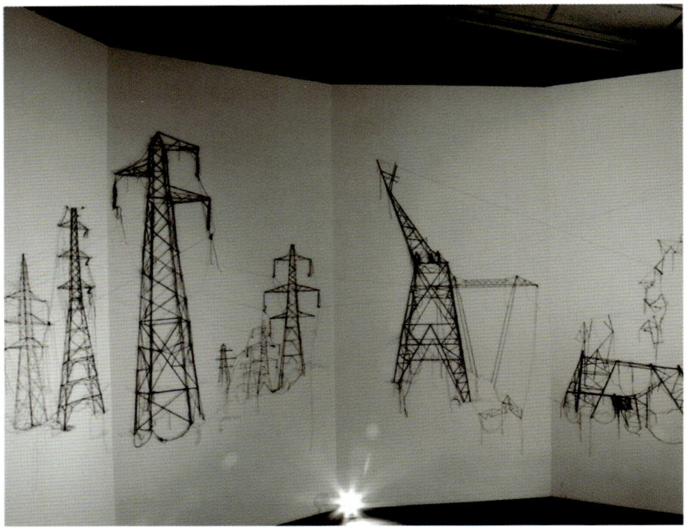

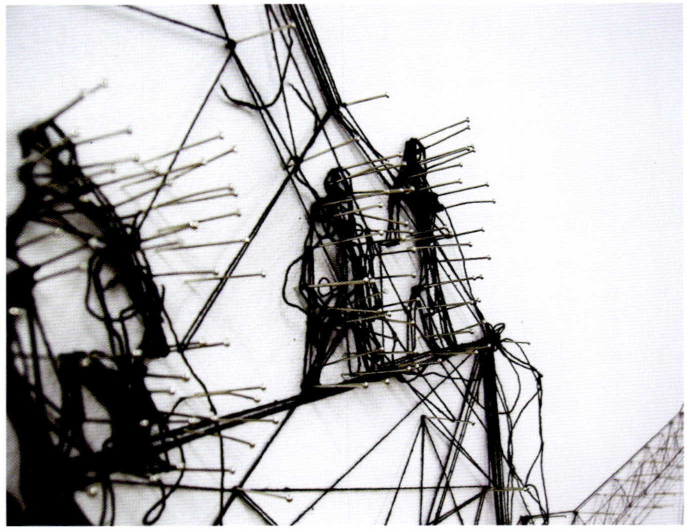

**Pins & Thread**
Pins and thread on panels
Myriad pins and lines of thread are given a new lease of life as floating linear structures. Each one plotted and measured accurately to depict the hated obtrusion of the electricity pylon which themselves are floating lines in space. Installed as at Graduate Show - 730 x 245 cm

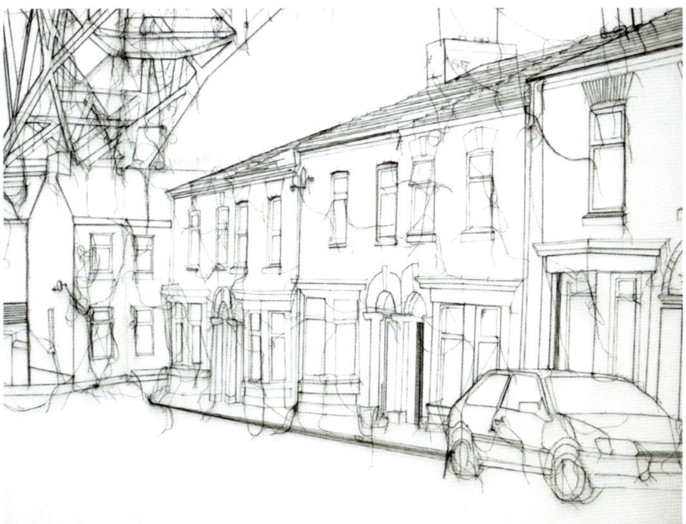

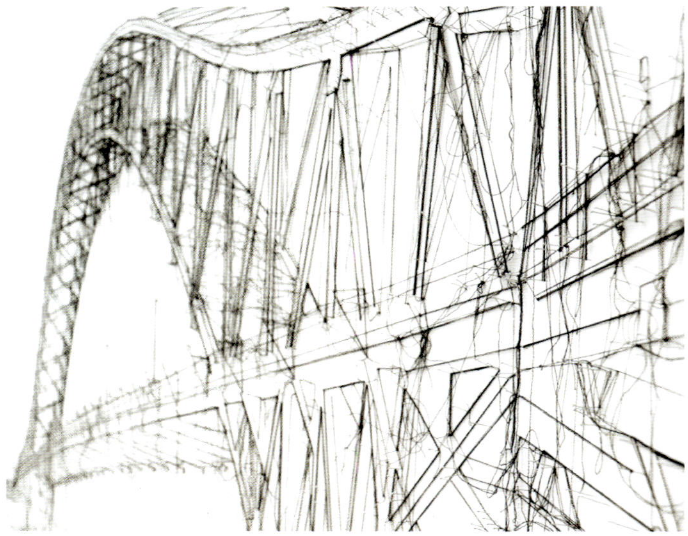

**Jubilee Bridge**
Pins and thread on panels
Commonplace industrial structures, architectural forms and bridges have always been a big source of inspiration for me and the Runcorn Widnes Bridge was no exception. Its dramatic scale, the repetitive nature of its structure and its intricacy all simultaneously intrigued me. The network of lines that I create by stretching lines of thread between accurately measured and plotted pins gives a unfamiliar 3-dimensional life to the drafted line. A simple drawing I feel would not give as much reality to the bridge. Installed as part of the Material Evidence exhibition in The Brindley, Runcorn - 365 x 245 cm

# Debbie Smyth

www.debbiesmyth.blogspot.com

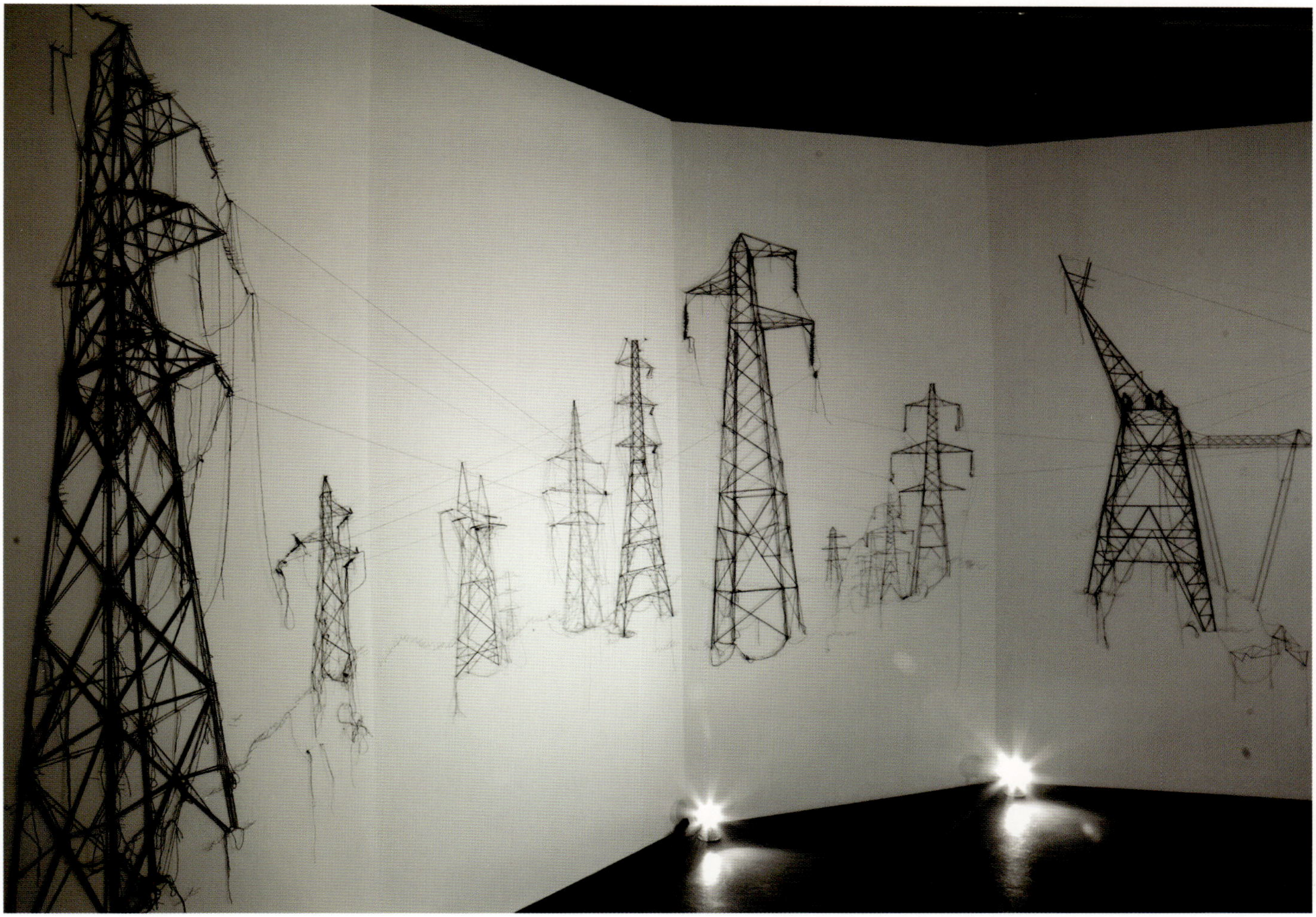

I am an artist with a workshop in Cheltenham. My playful yet sophisticated contemporary artworks are created by stretching a network of threads between accurately plotted pins. This diverse style developed through training at West Wales School of the Arts, where I gained a first class honours degree in Contemporary Textiles. Following this I began to establish my on practice; the past year has seen this grow and the work progress. My work has already been exhibited at New Designers 2008, Tent London 2008 and at various other galleries across the UK. For my degree show I created striking images of electricity pylons using a fine tableau of threads tensioned around steel pins. I feel it is this ability to take something static and boringly familiar and dramatise it with the simplest of materials that makes my work distinctive. My installation in The Brindley transforms the architectural icon, the Jubilee Bridge, in the same way. A simple drawing I feel would not give as much reality to the piece. Anchored to the panels whilst simultaneously floating in space; the piece plays with perspective and angles, similar to the intricacy of the bridge. It carries a narrative of construction as visibly loose threads are gradually tightened around pins to create the architectural forms or are simply left hanging free. As with all my work on first viewing, the matrix of lines creates confusion but it is this blurring of definition that draws the viewer in. On closer inspection the complexity of my works true nature is revealed. It has the ability to transfix and bewilder audiences, and this is the element of m work that I enjoy most.

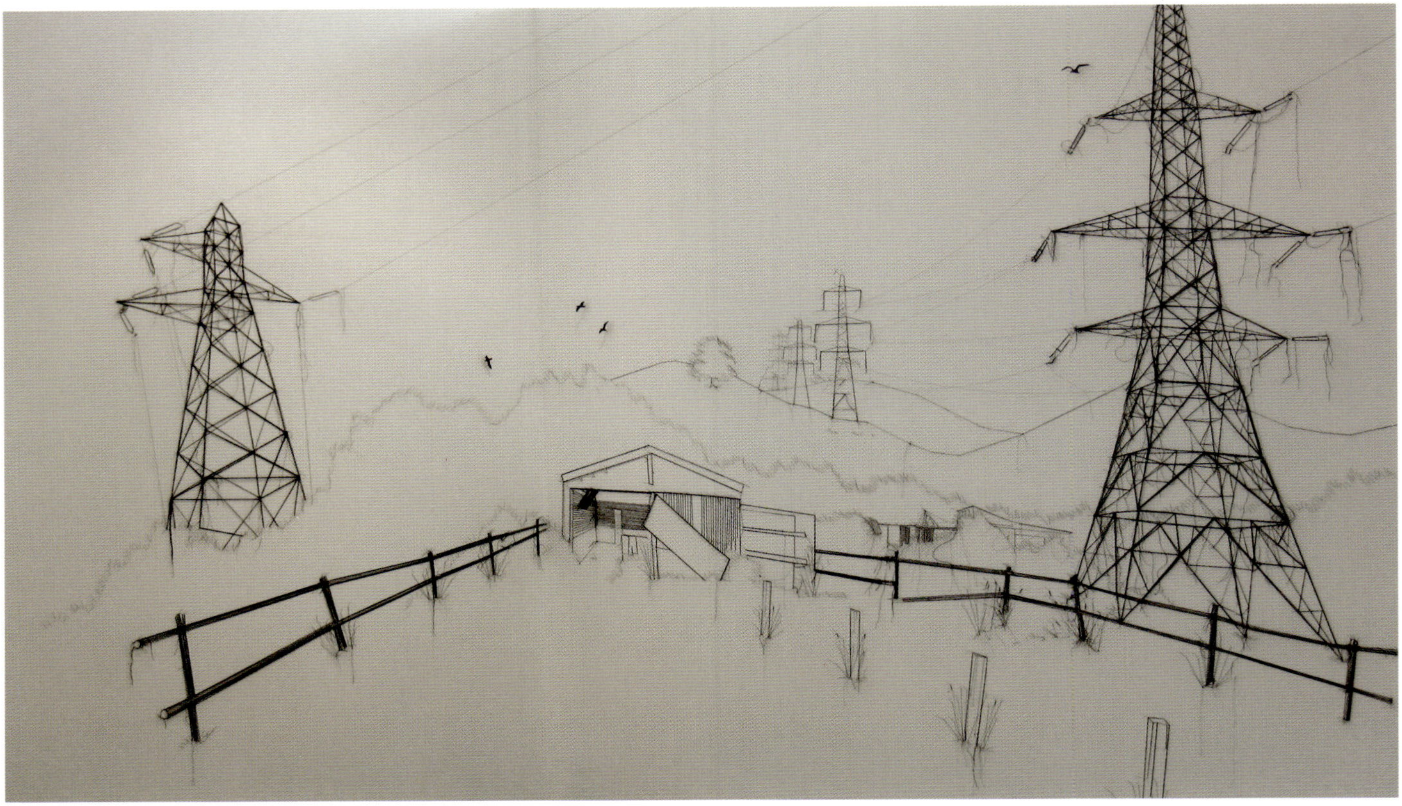

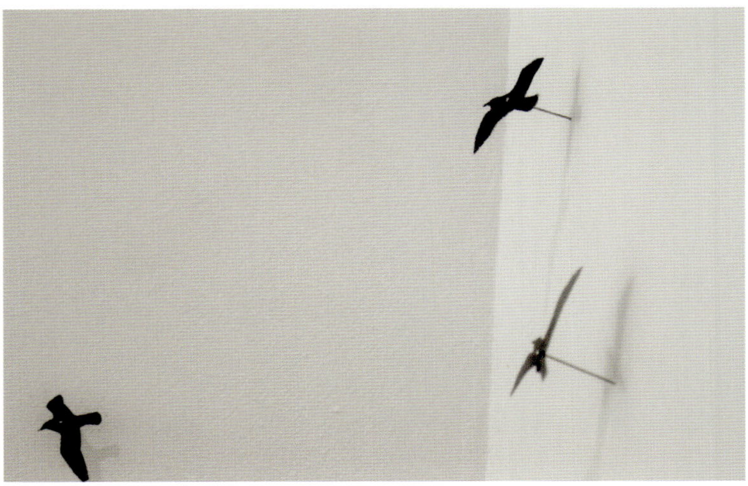

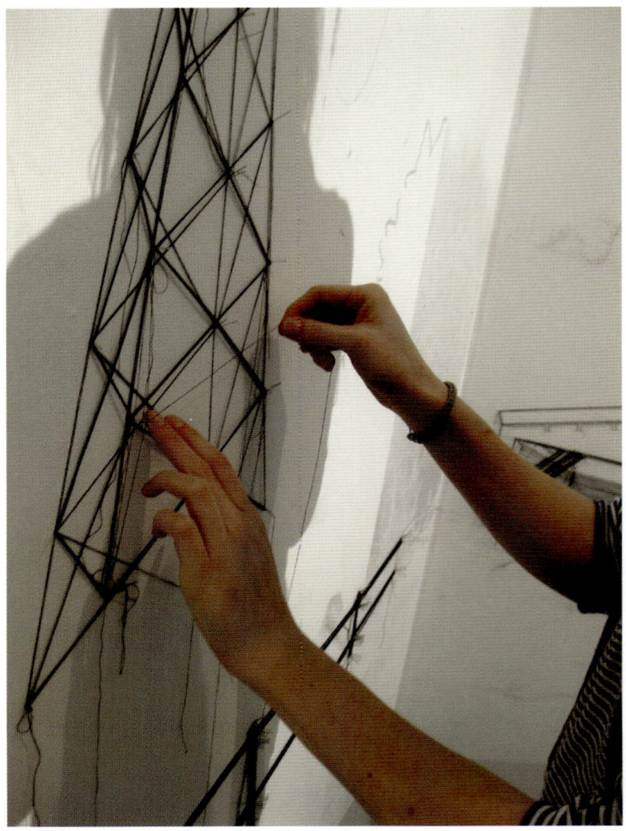

**Crafted Pylons**
Pins and thread on panels
Running on from my graduate show Pins & Thread, Crafted Pylons was an interesting addition to my pylon landscape. It provided the opportunity to develop the subject matter further and also the technique, as the piece was completed on site in the gallery during the exhibition setup week rather than being installed ready made. Installed as part of the Crafted exhibition in the Oriel Myrddin Gallery in Carmarthen, Wales - 365 x 245 cm

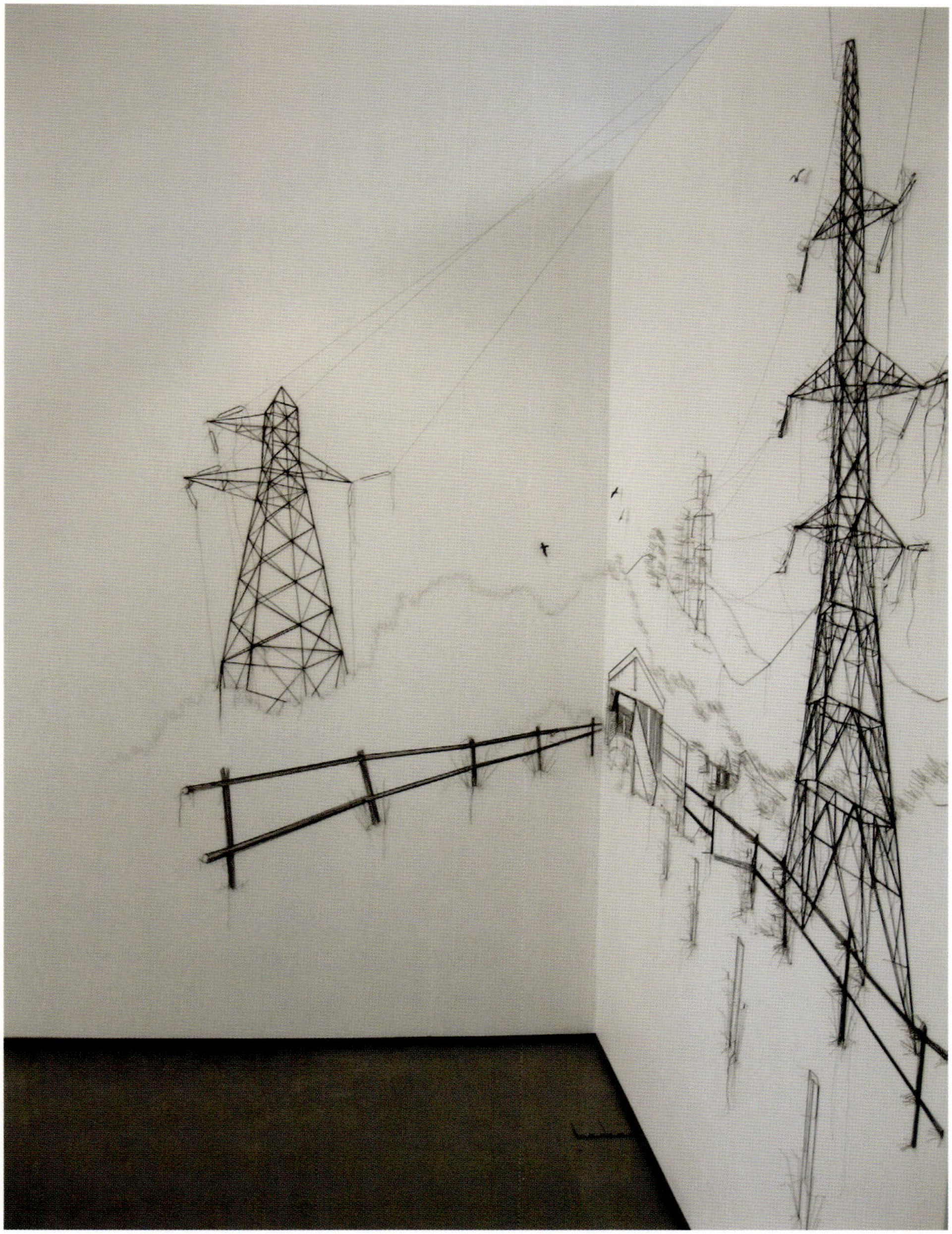

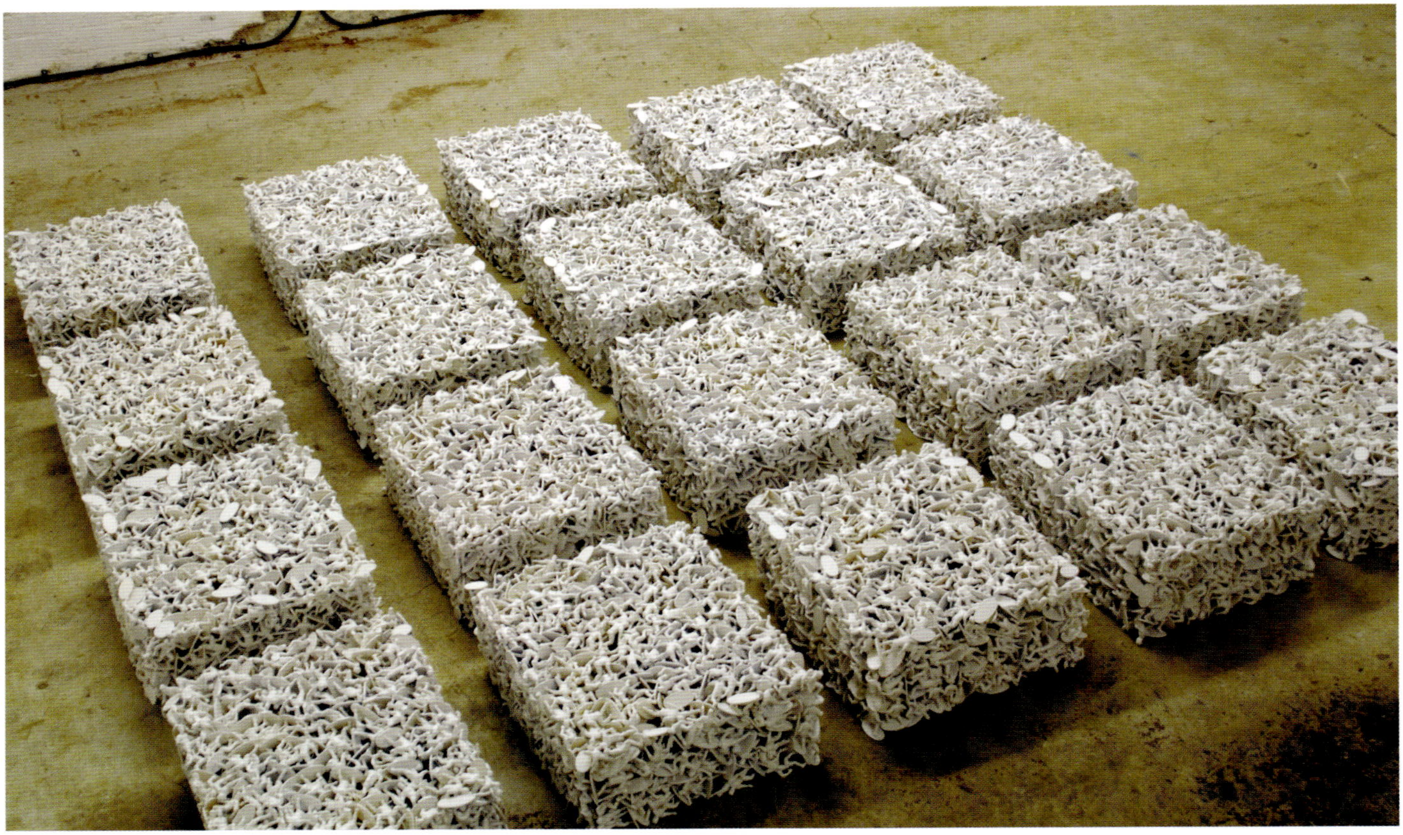

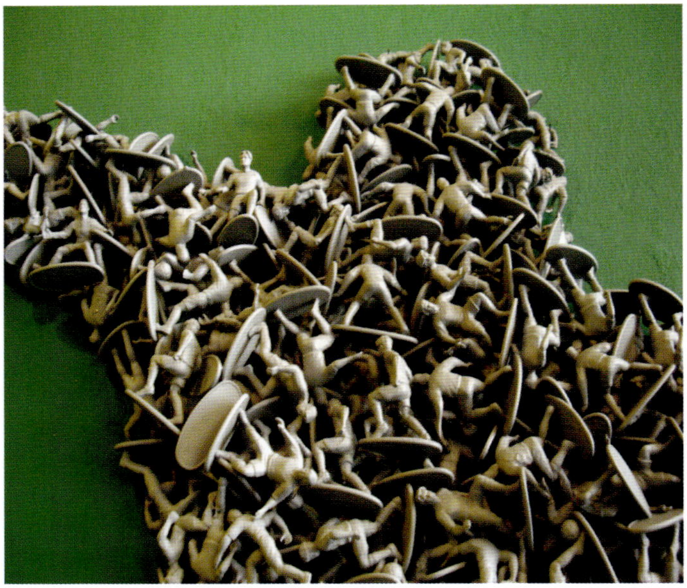

Nike project

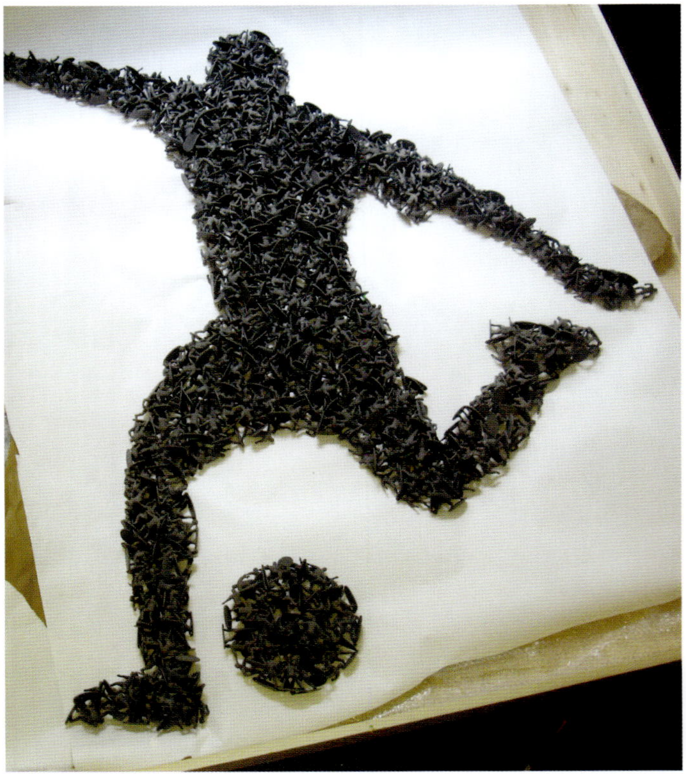

# Dominic Wilcox

www.dominicwilcox.com

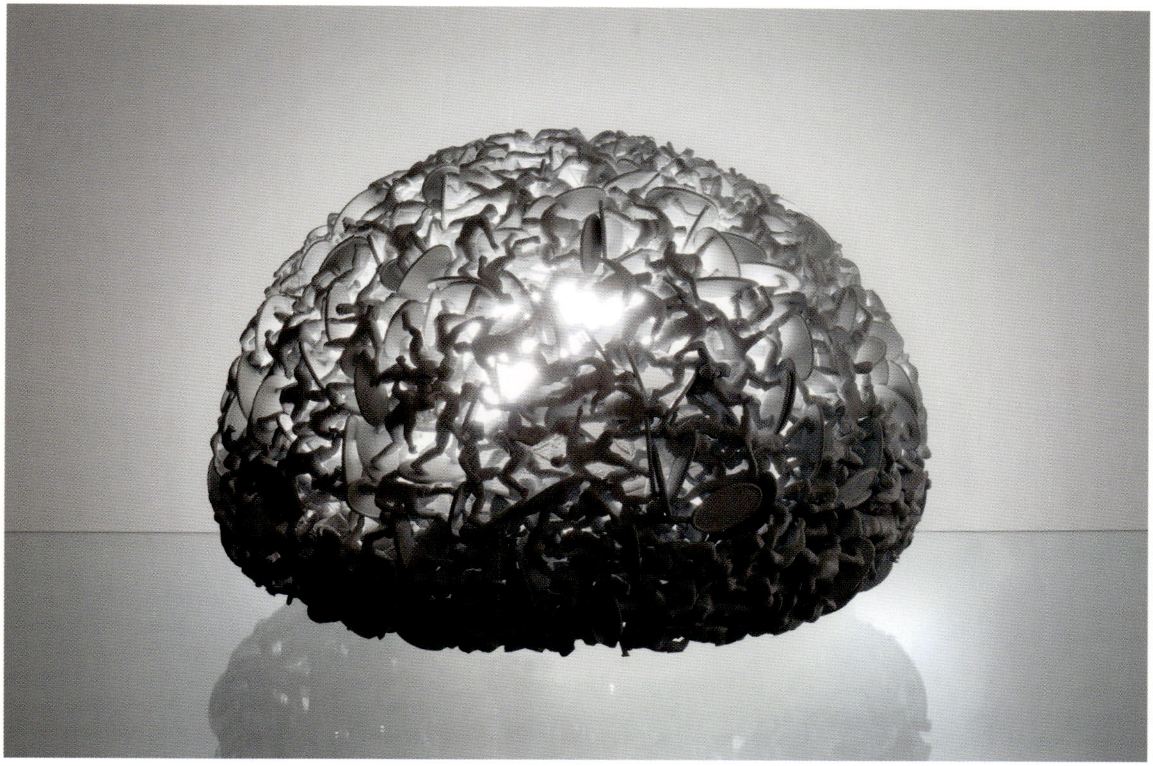

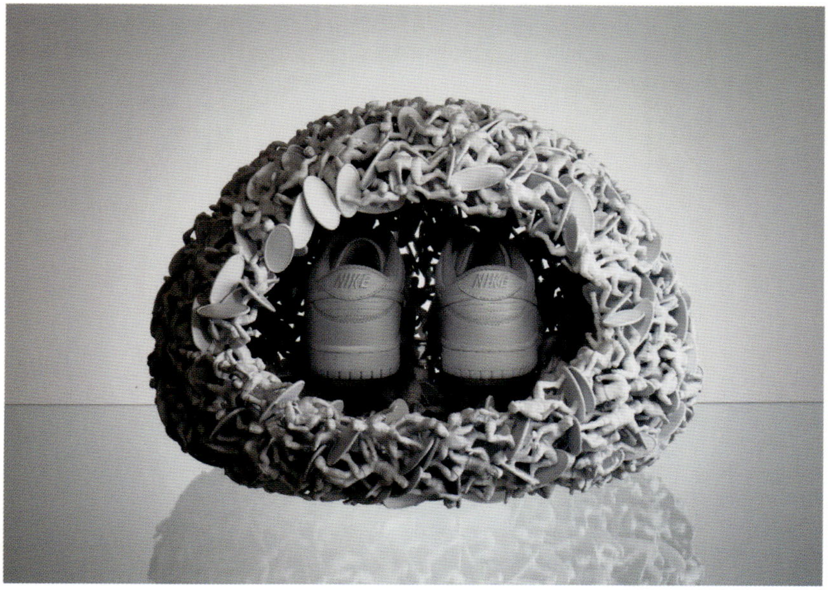


Dominic Wilcox is an artist who works within the territory of the 'everyday'. Everyday objects, environments, buildings, human interaction, no area of normality is out of reach. His work, which is usually layered with an ultra dry wit, places a spotlight on the banal, always adding a new, alternative perspective on things we take for granted. His work has been published and exhibited extensively around the world and he continues to develop his work in all fields of creativity.

**War Bowl**

A bowl made by melting model soldiers. There are two versions: the blue Battle of Waterloo, Half British Artillery, half French Infantry and the white 'English Civil War' War Bowl. 'The inspiration for the War Bowl came from a combination of ideas. I wanted to create a new material that would work on more levels than the usual qualities such as texture and functionality. My aim was to make a material that had a voice of it's own, not just a passive lifeless thing. I started with the idea of combining small objects in order to create something larger. I arrived at the idea of using toy soldiers as my ingredients. As found objects, they seemed to represent something of a paradox. On one hand they were a fun childhood toy that brought back happy memories and on the other, they were a representation of war with it's associated horrors. This is a contrast that I find slightly uneasy.'

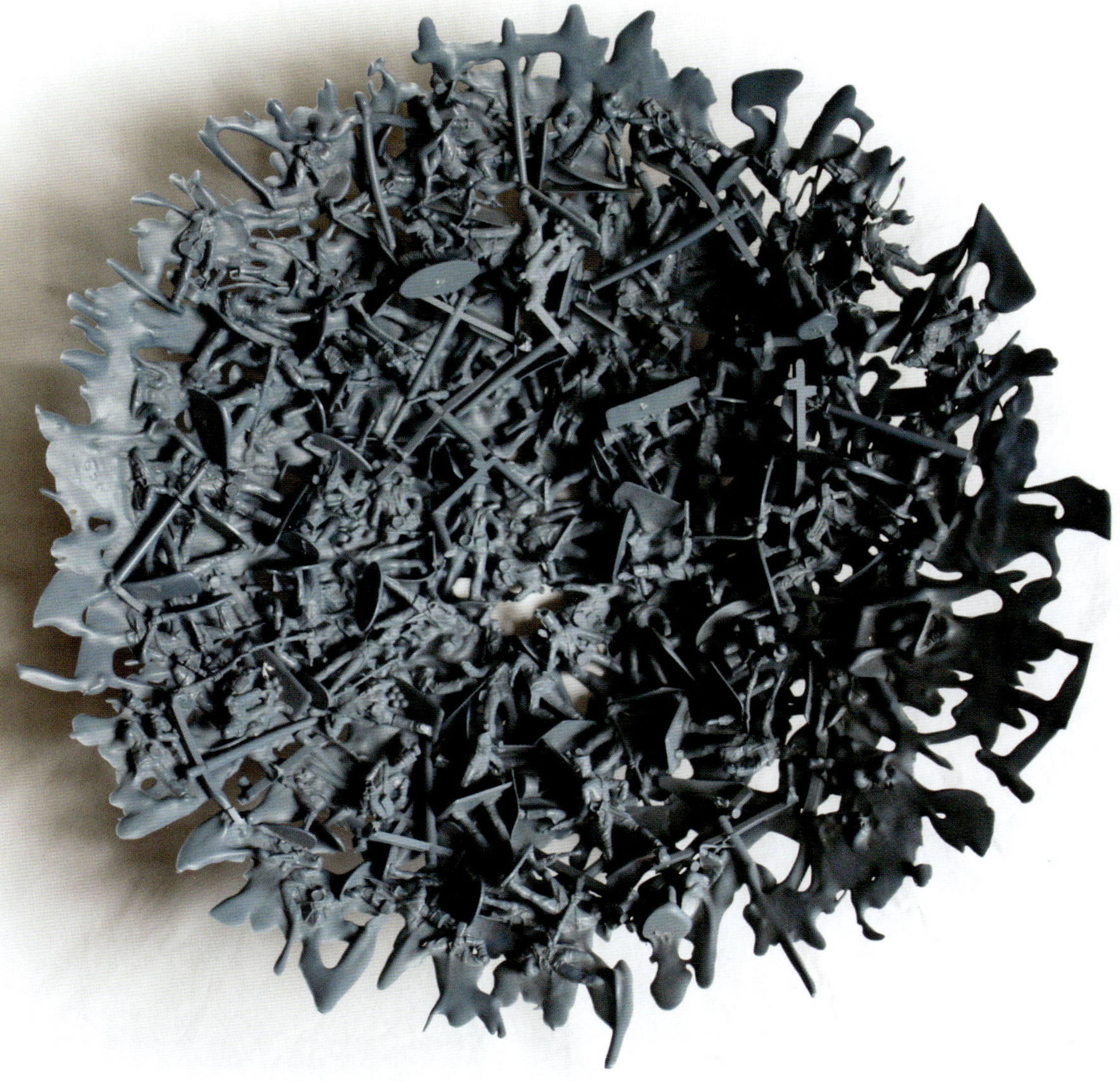

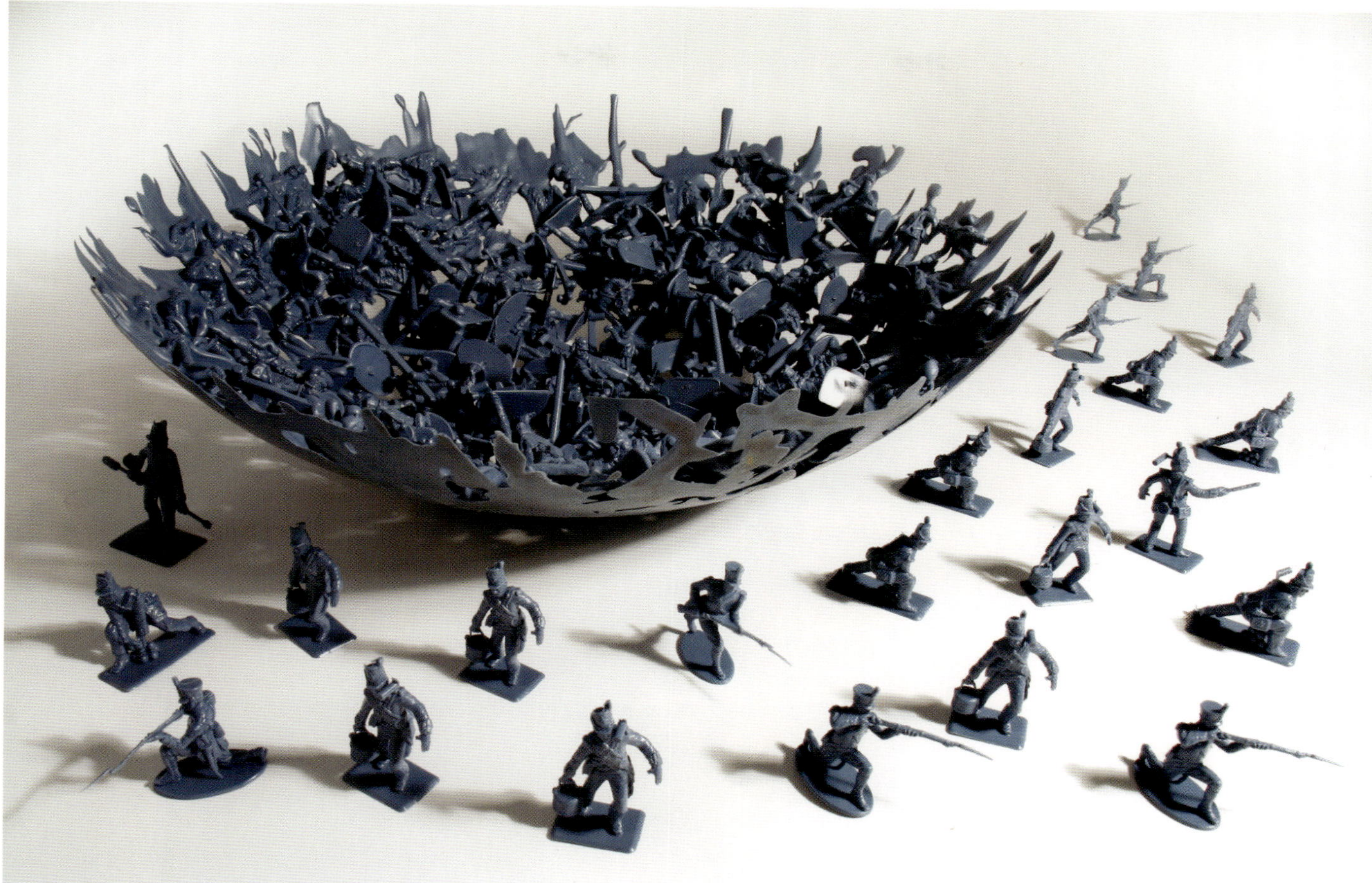

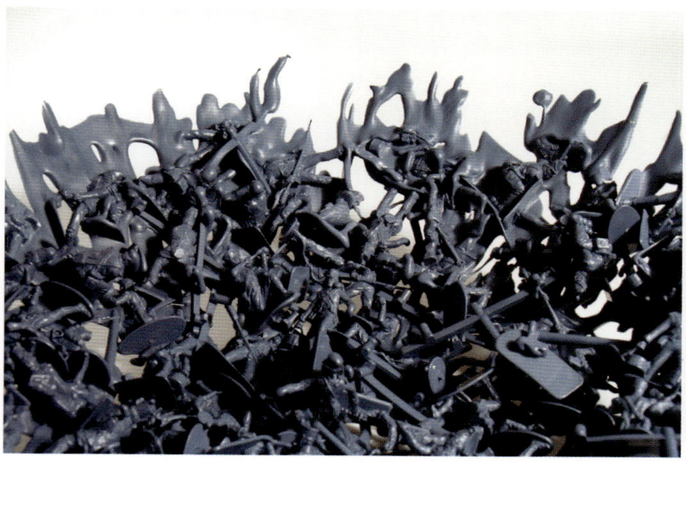

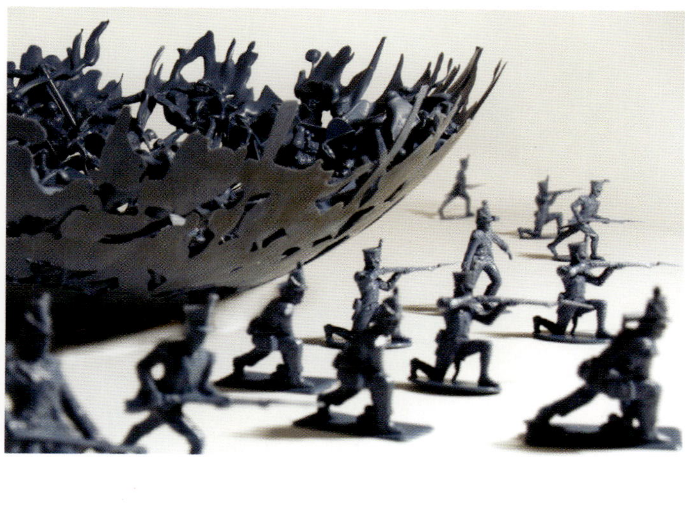

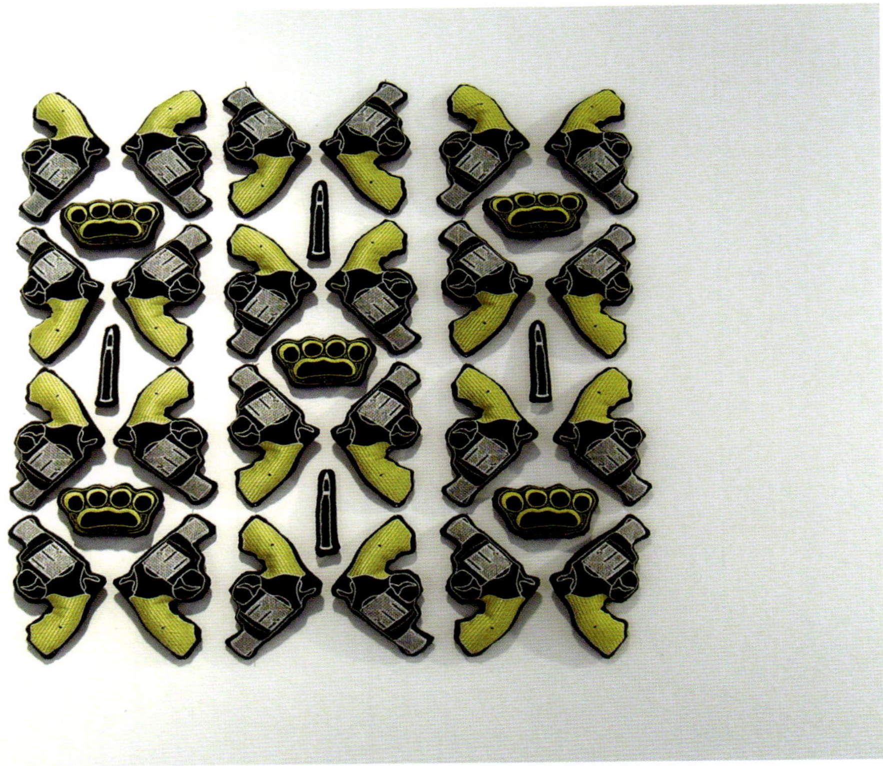

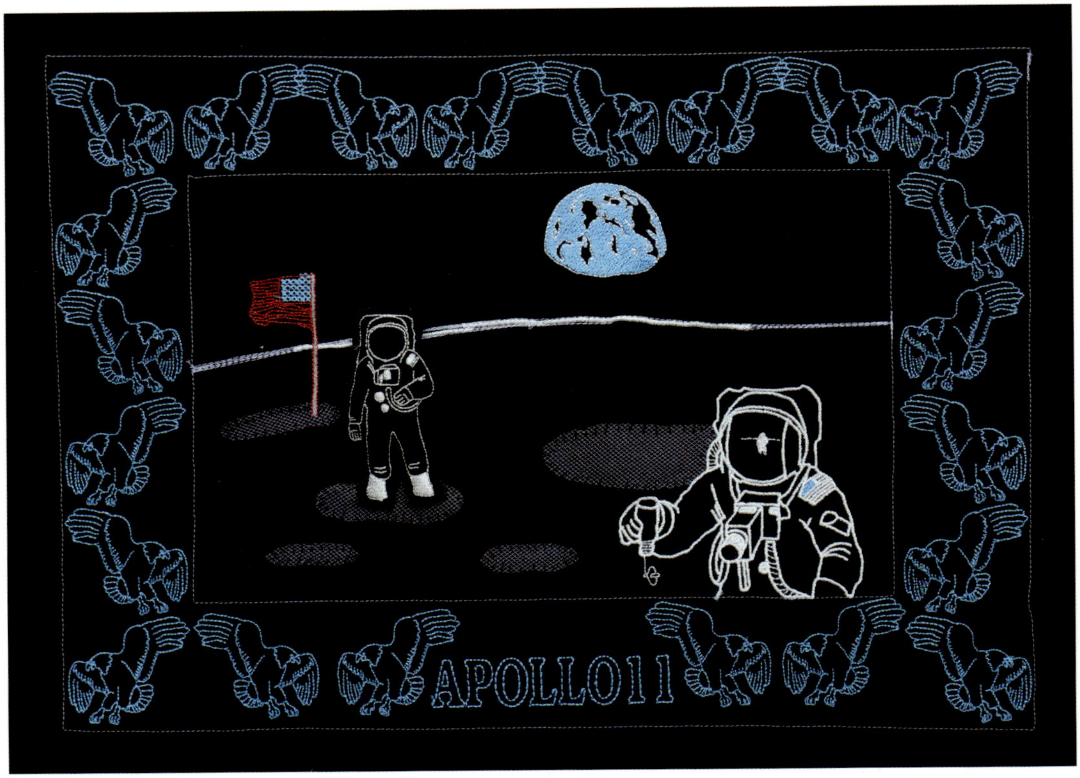
APOLLO11

# Dorothée Van Biesen

www.broderoll.wordpress.com

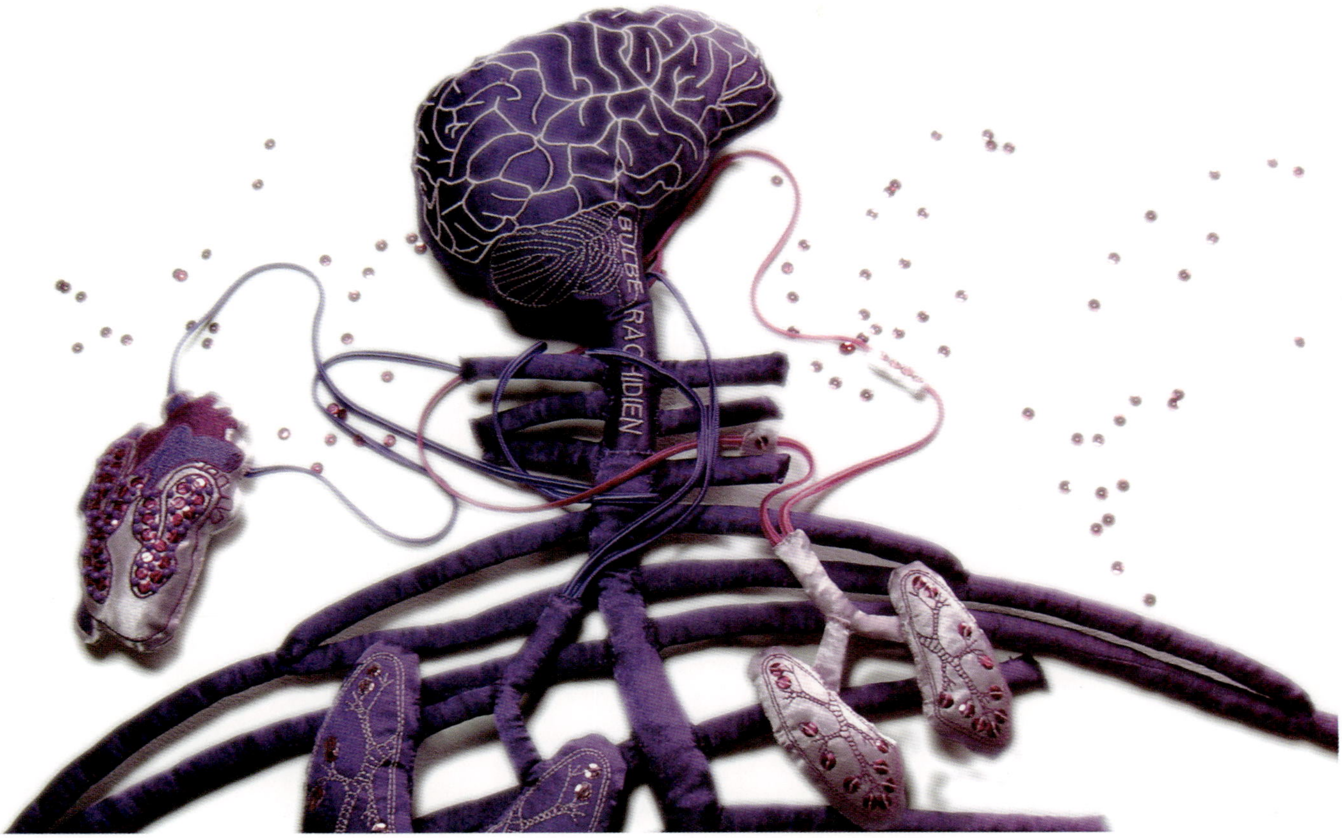


**Catacombs & Anatomy**
Materials used numerical embroidery, hand embroidery , cotton, satin, synthetic stuffing - 2009

Dorothée Van Biesen aka « Doro Brode & Roll » obtained her Arts Degree from The Royal Academy of Art in Brussels in 2002. She lives and works in Jemelle, Village in the Belgian countryside. Since 2004, to represent mankind's guts, Doro composes and questions the embroidery. Born from ancient traditions, with hijacked symbols and revived with numeric technology, Doro mixes bones, pearls, guns, satin, lungs and submarines to create supple sculptures to express mourning and its conventions, anatomy, the war and nature's disasters. Her work has always been evocative of mankind, particularly the various stages of the body, in the making or disintegrating. The body as a sexual asset, embellished, taken apart, venerated and commemorated. The use of embroidery allows a reflection on the textile language in itself. How to respect its history and tradition bearing in mind its "clichés" use. Doro exhibited her work as a sole artist and also as part of group exhibitions in Belgium, France, Quebec and Luxemburg.

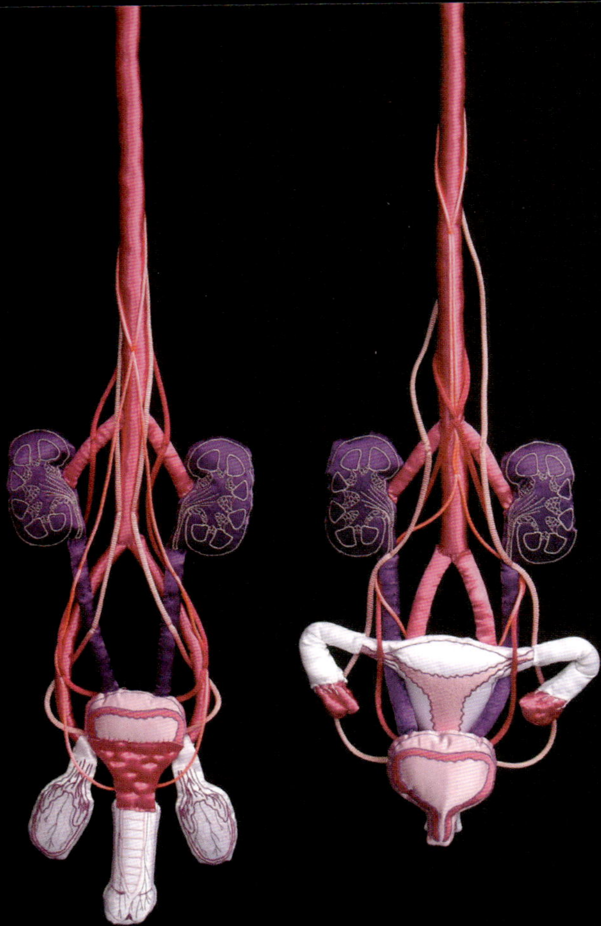

"Tribute to la specola" 1

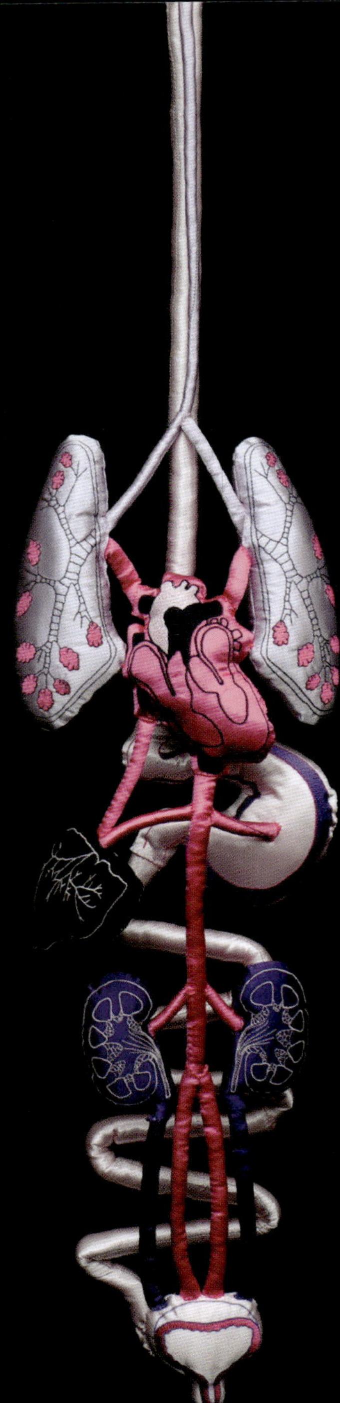

"Tribute to la

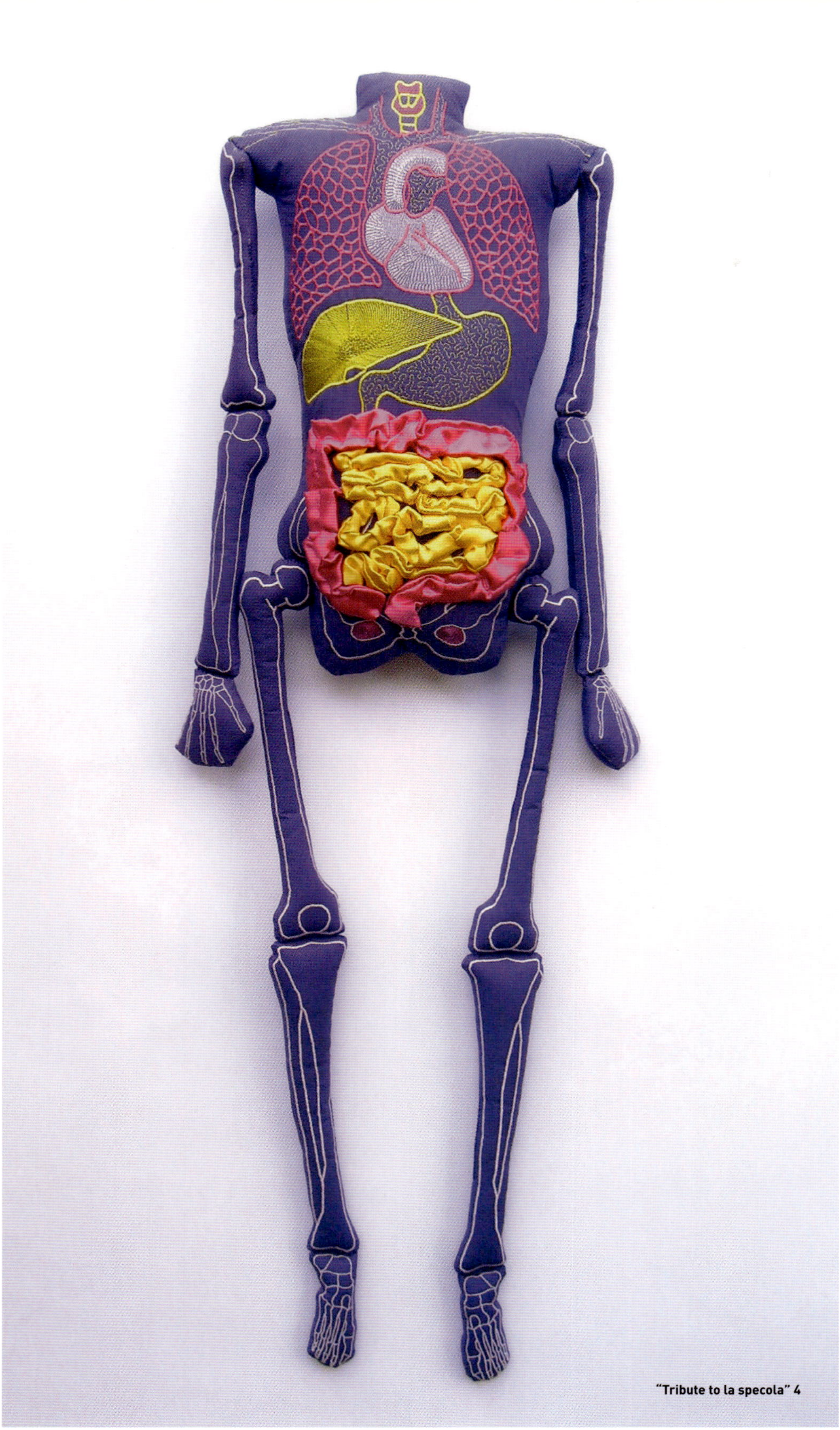

**"Tribute to la specola" 4**

Tribute to la Specola" an tribute to the anatomic waxes of "La specola Museum" in Florence. Materials used numerical embroidery, hand embroidery , cotton, satin, synthetic stuffing - 2009

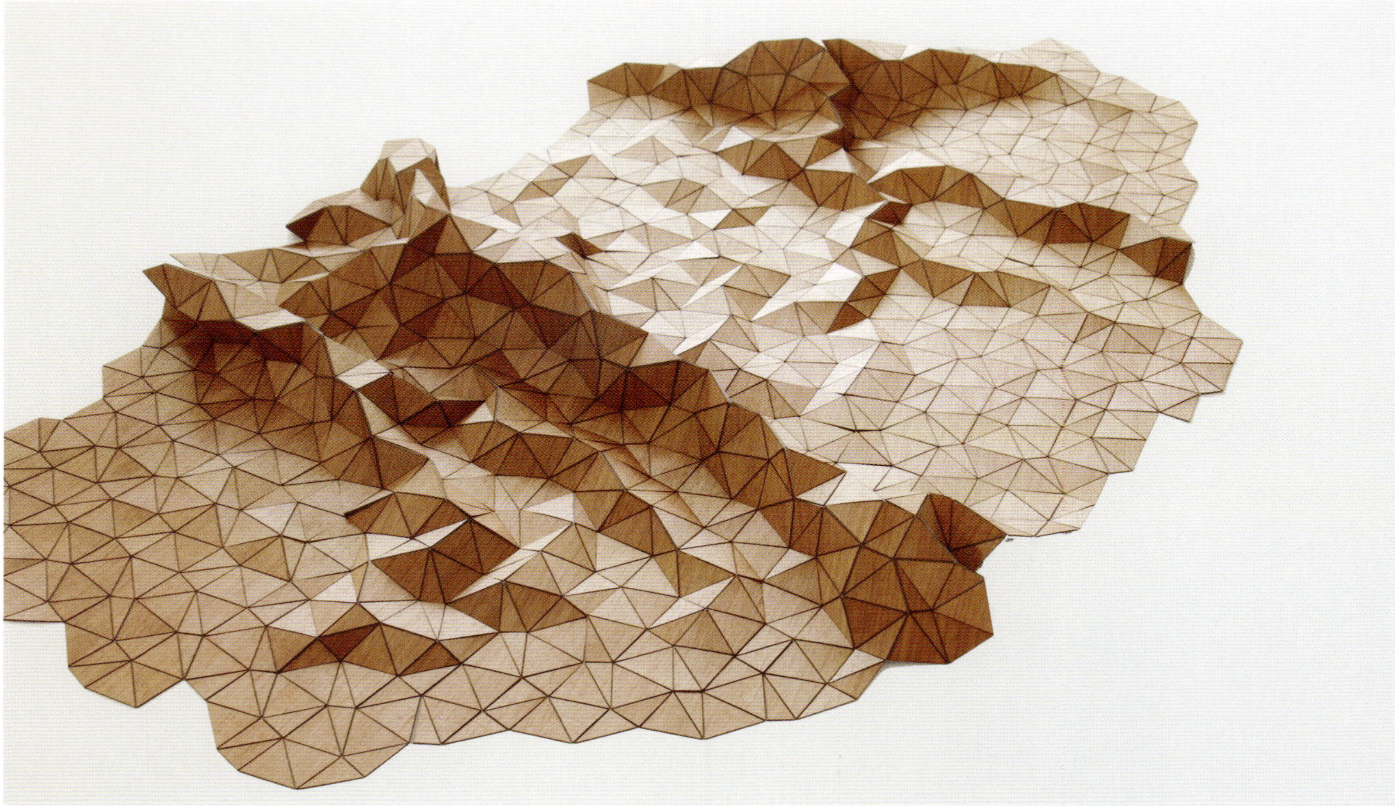

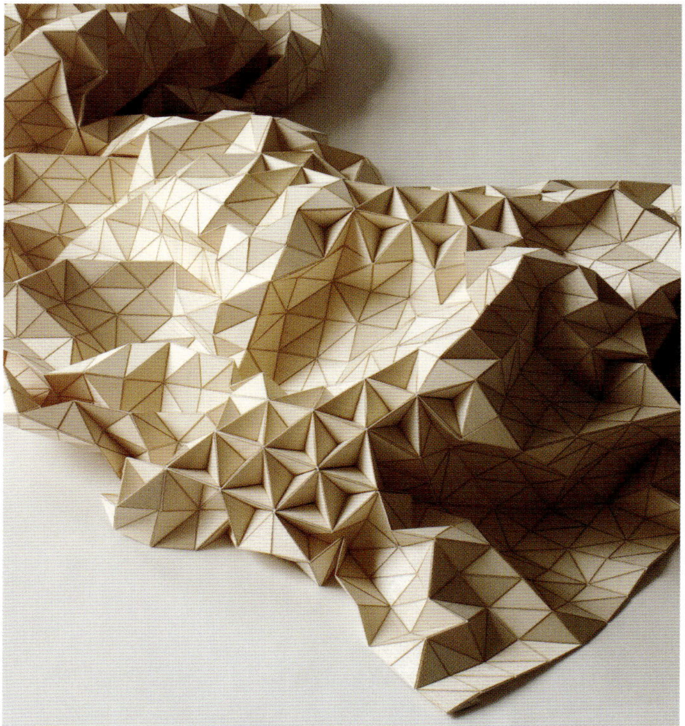

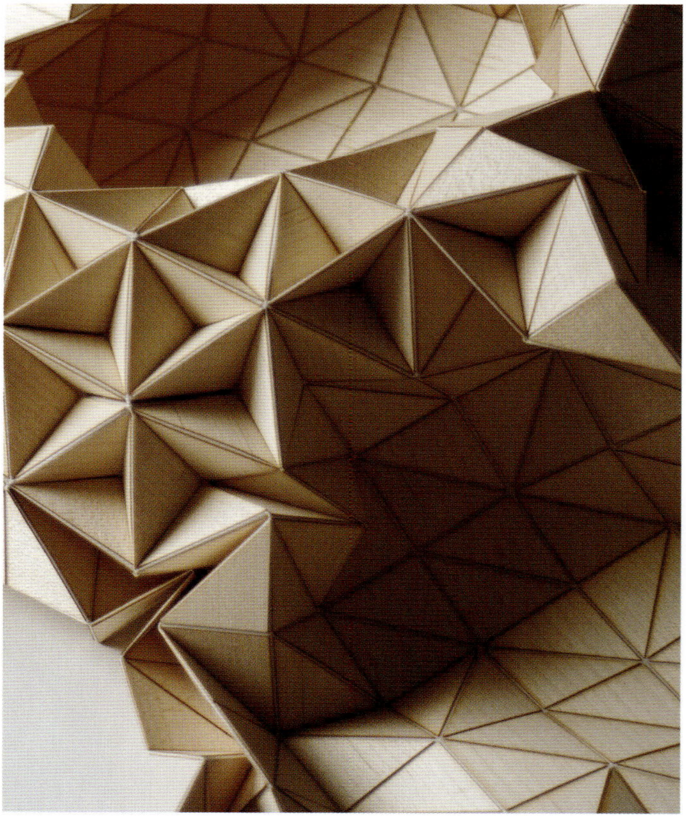

# Elisa/Strozyk

www.elisastrozyk.de

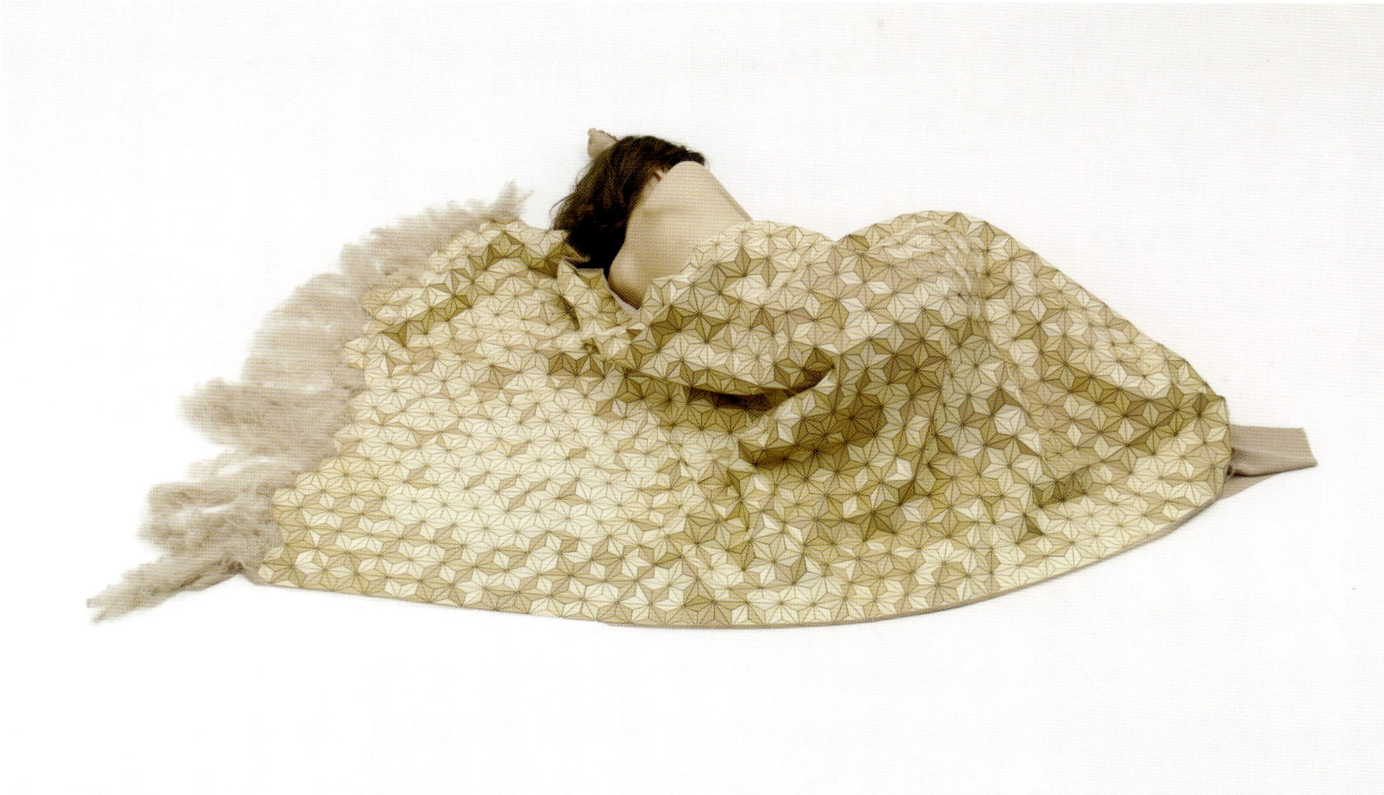

"**Wooden Textiles**" is an approach to responsible thinking concerning lifecycles of products. The outcome is a material that is half wood-half textile, between hard and soft, challenging what can be expected from a material or category. It looks and smells familiar but feels strange, as it is able to move and form in unexpected ways. From the perspective of a textile designer, I am researching ways to provide wood with textile properties in testing methods to make wood flexible and soft, or interweave textile elements. One of the processes to design a flexible wooden surface is its deconstruction into pieces, which are then attached to a textile base. The wood is cut by hand or laser cut, and all tiles are stuck by hand to compose a textile-like surface.

Elisa Strozyk graduated from the KHB in Berlin and Central Saint Martins in London. She has completed interior installations for the Circus Hotel and the Buffalo Shop in Berlin. Elisa had recently exhibited at the "Milan Furniture Fair" and "Tendence". Now she is setting up her own studio in Berlin.

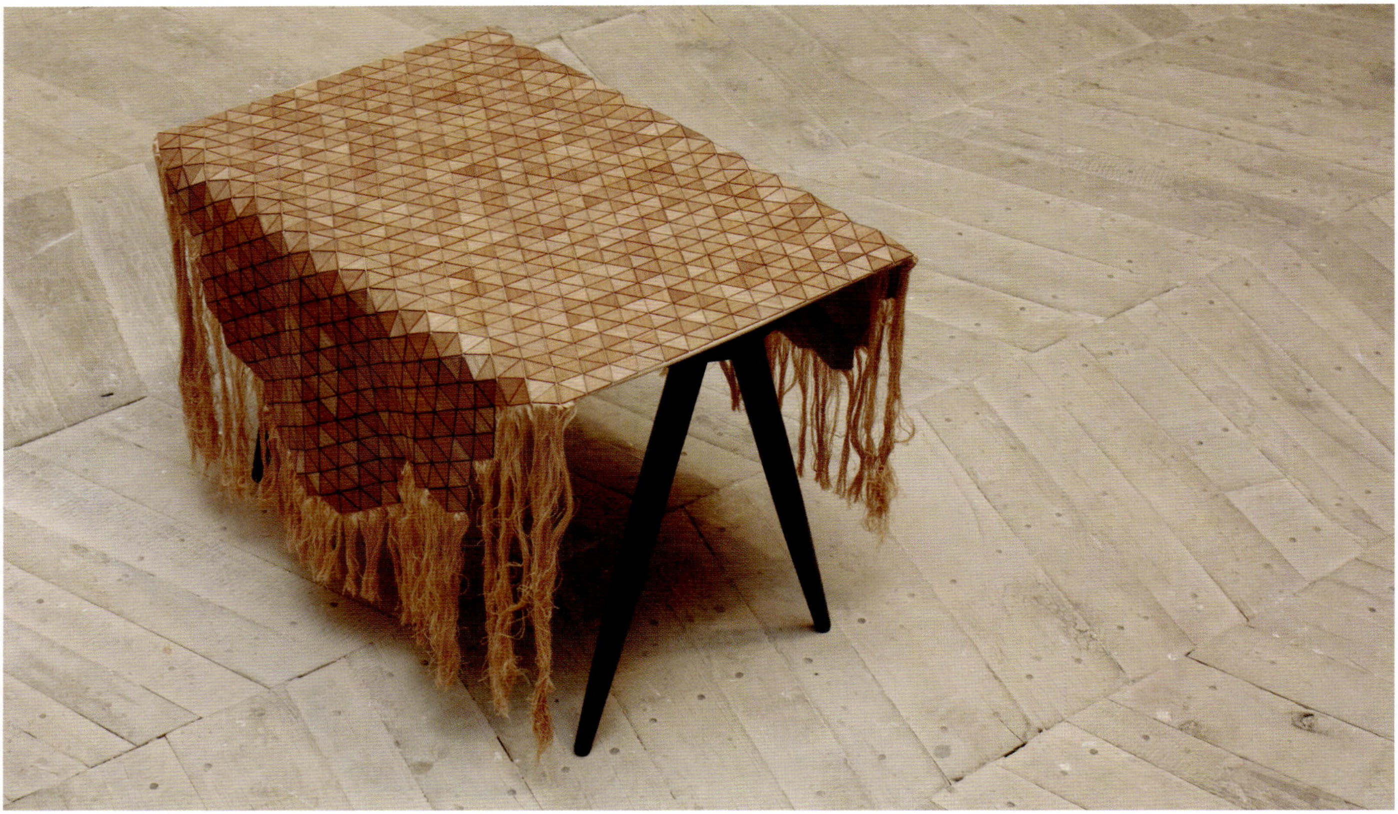

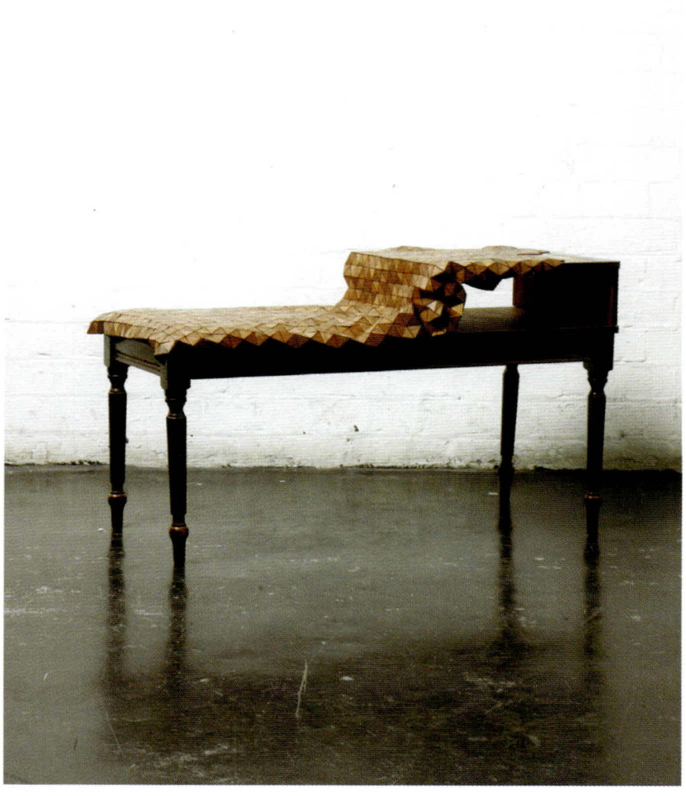

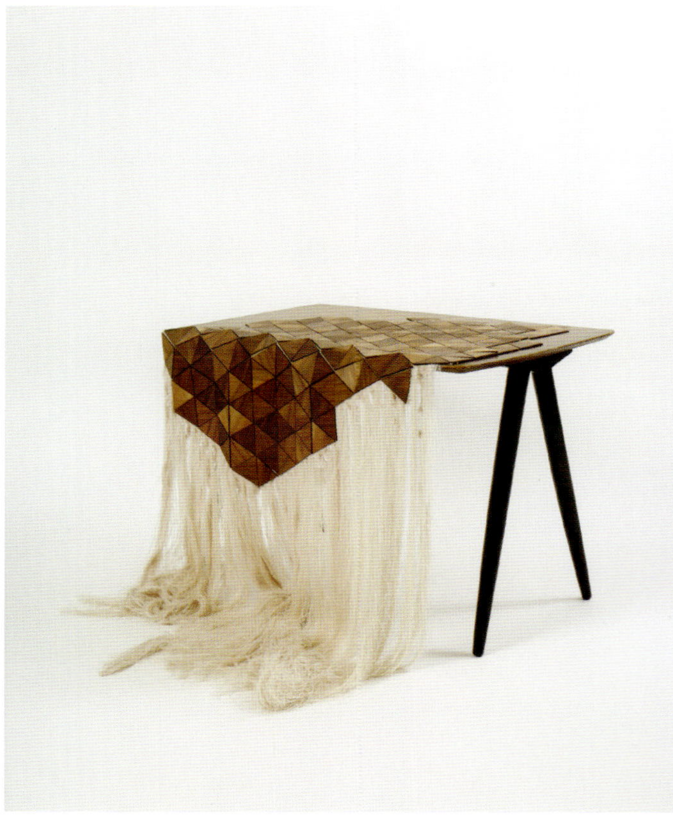

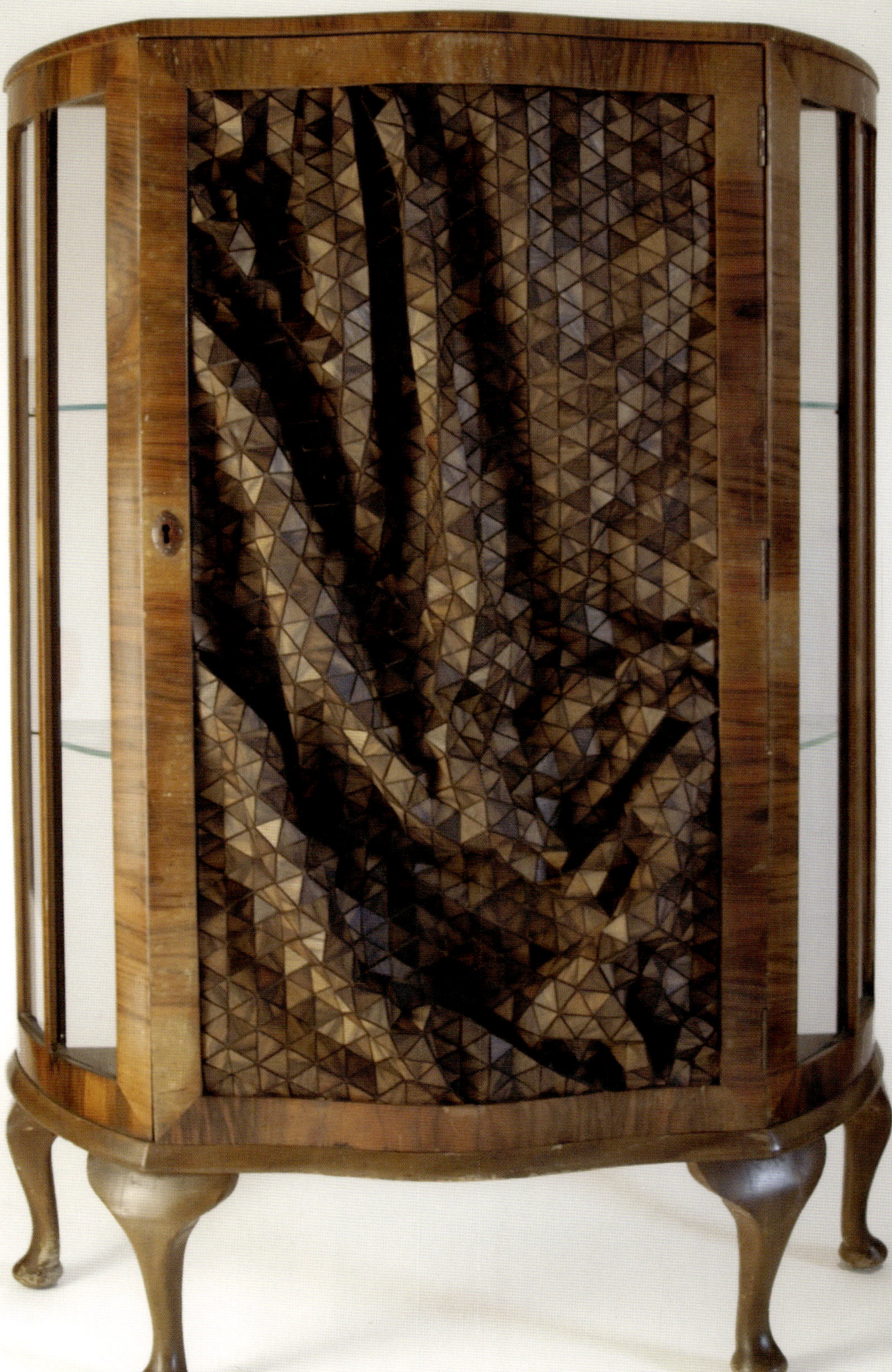

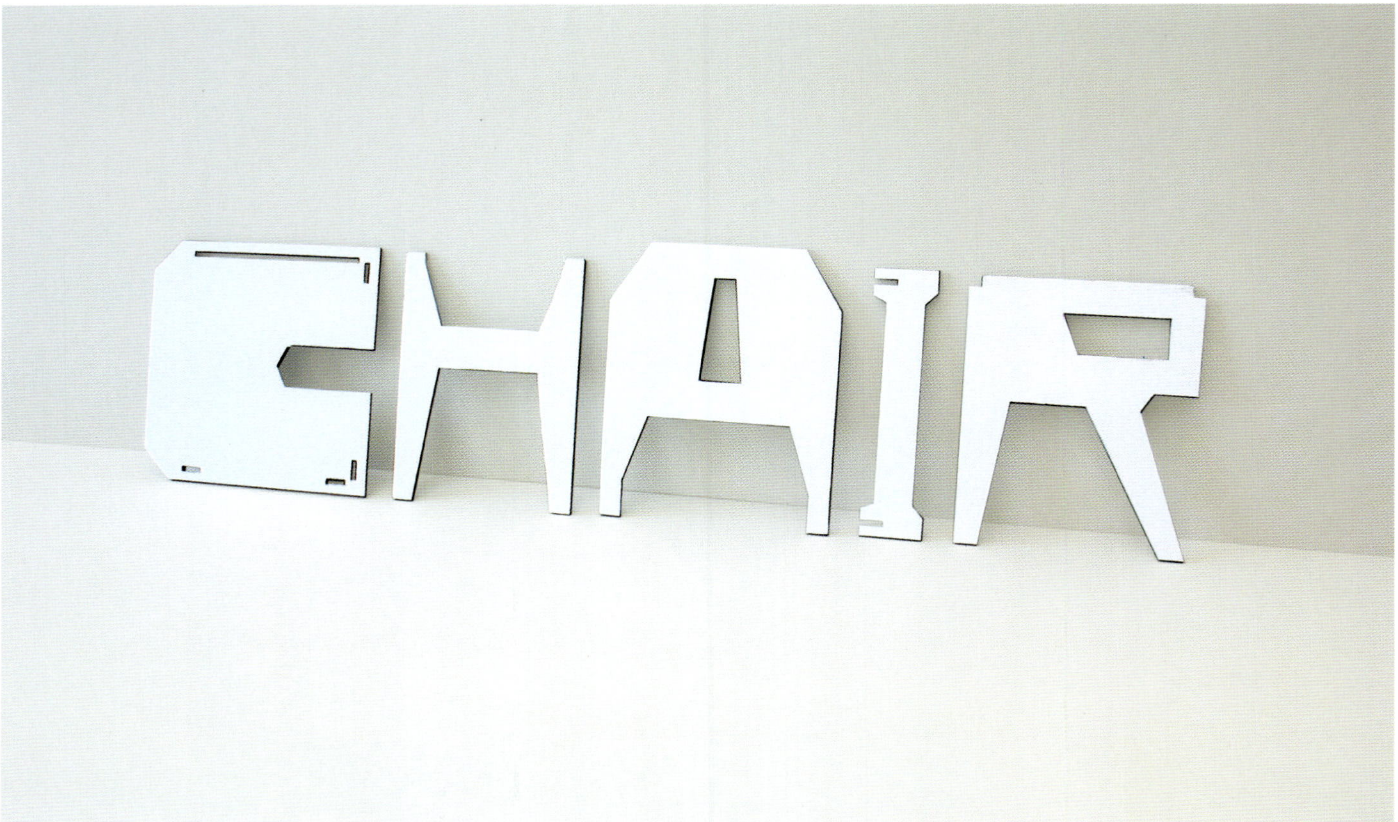


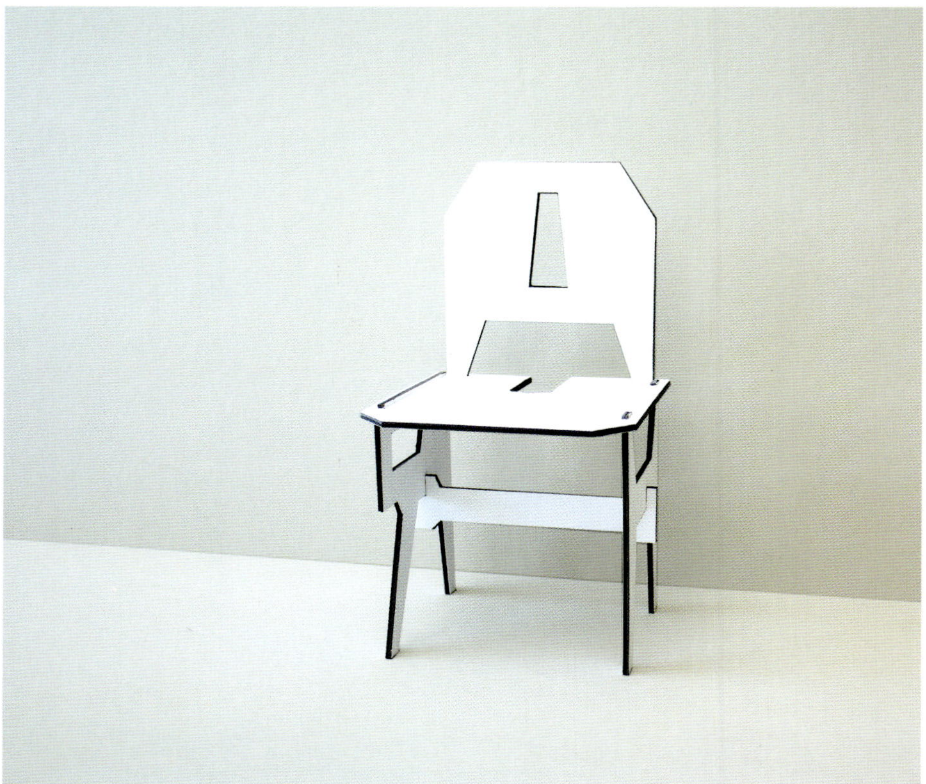

**Mission 2: Chair/Chair**
An inspiration from the American contemporary artist Joseph Kosuth, One and Three Chair. Instead of giving new definition, I redefined the concept of a chair by using alphabet. One is able to construct a chair by assembling the redesigned alphabets.

# Eric/Ku

www.ericku.org

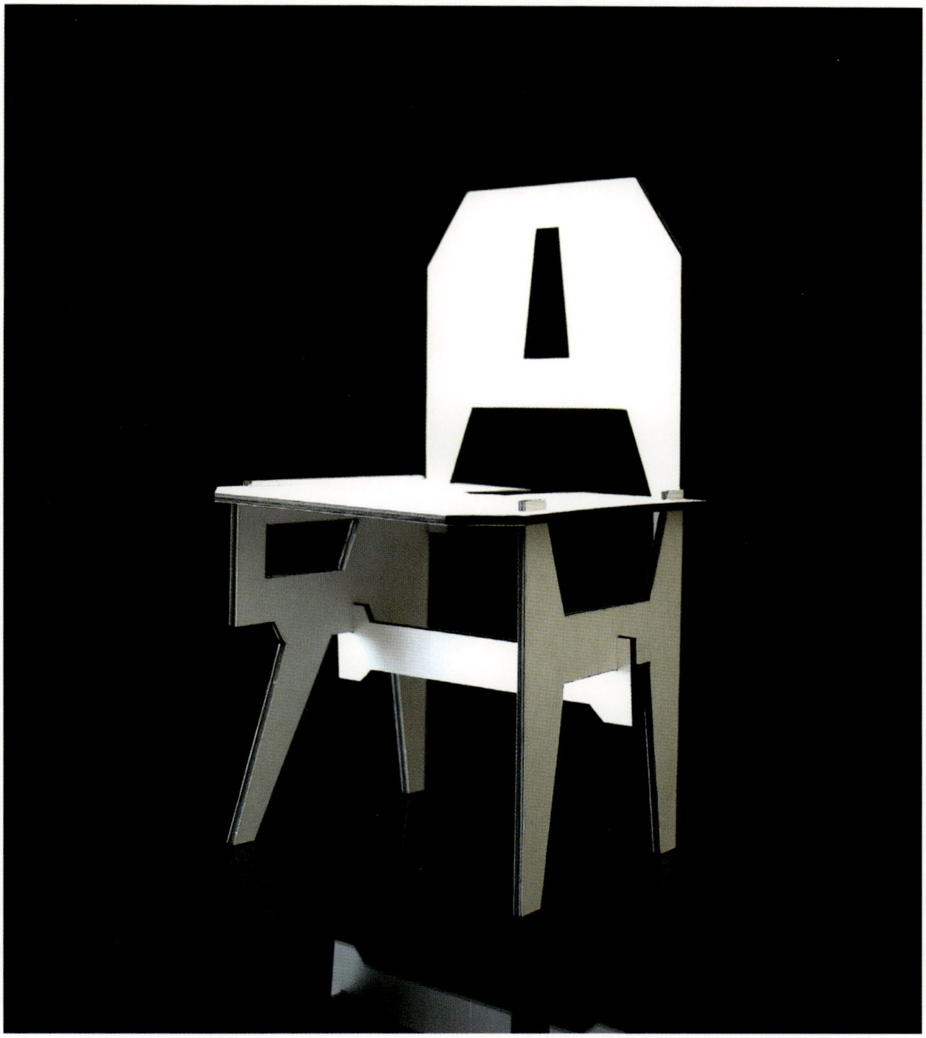

MISSION: REDEFINITION - It is a series of exercises; each exercise explore the idea of redefinition to a series of subjects thru the application of graphic design. To explore the idea of redefinition as it applies to graphic design, to rethink existing designed objects or graphic design formats in an unexpected way, and to attract attention.

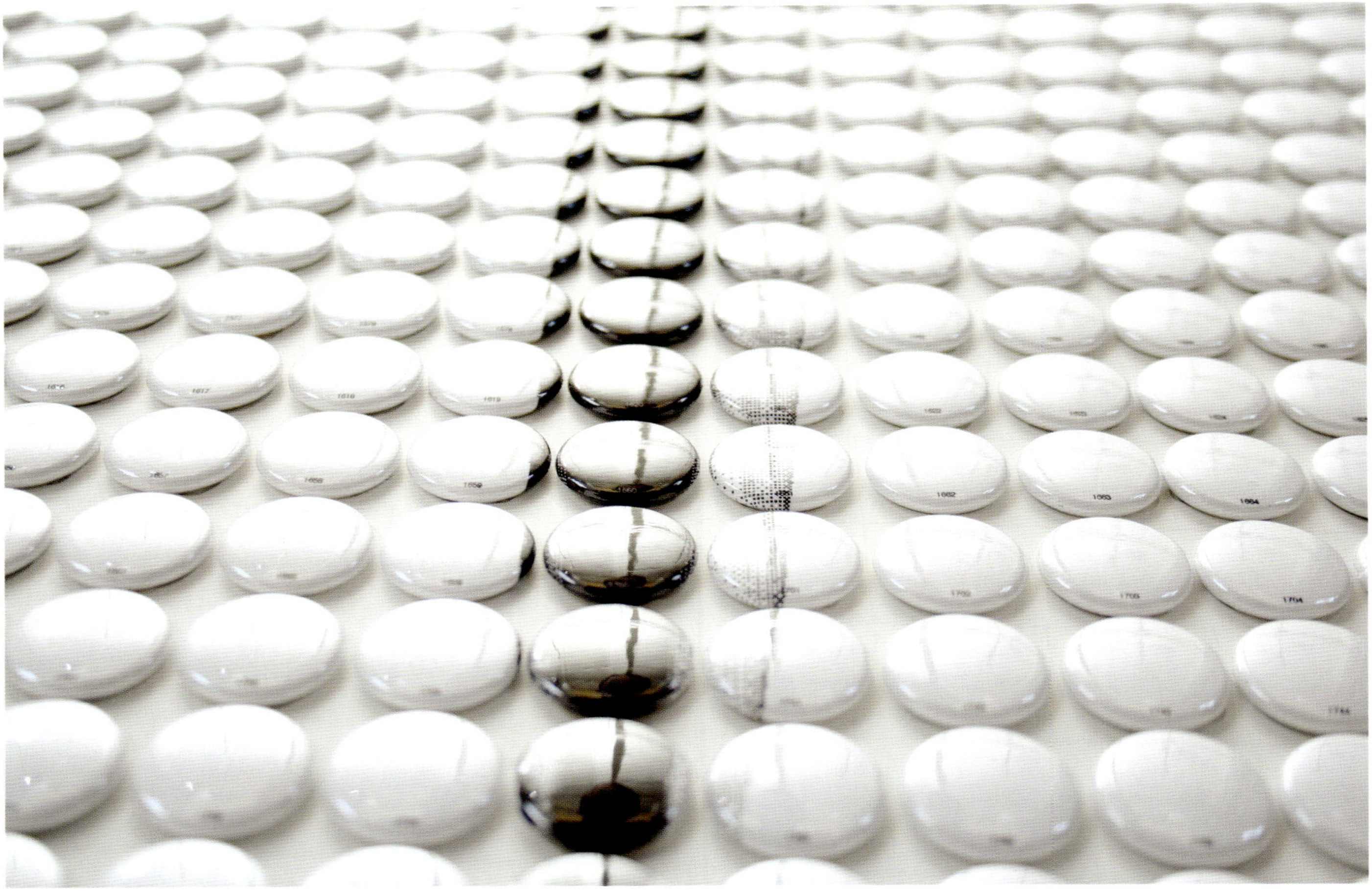
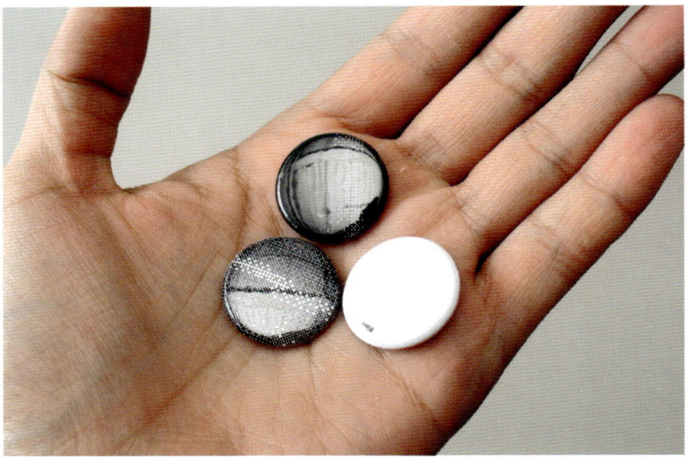
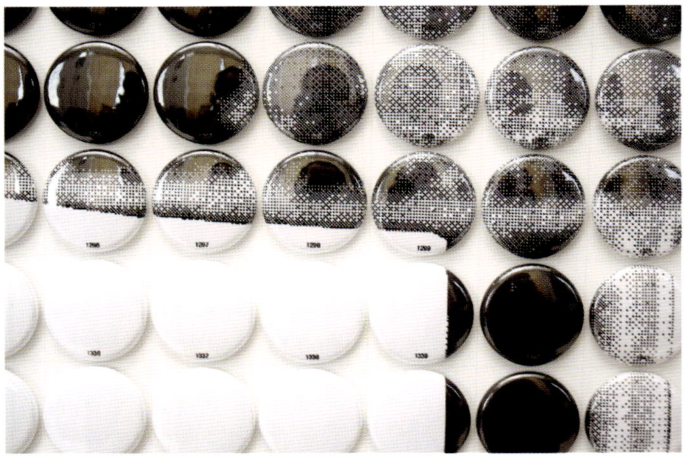

**Mission 6: Pin.s**
A pin creates by pins." This was the original concept. It is a push pin project created by 2200 of one-inch bottom pins. Each pin has a number and it is arranged by its numeral order.

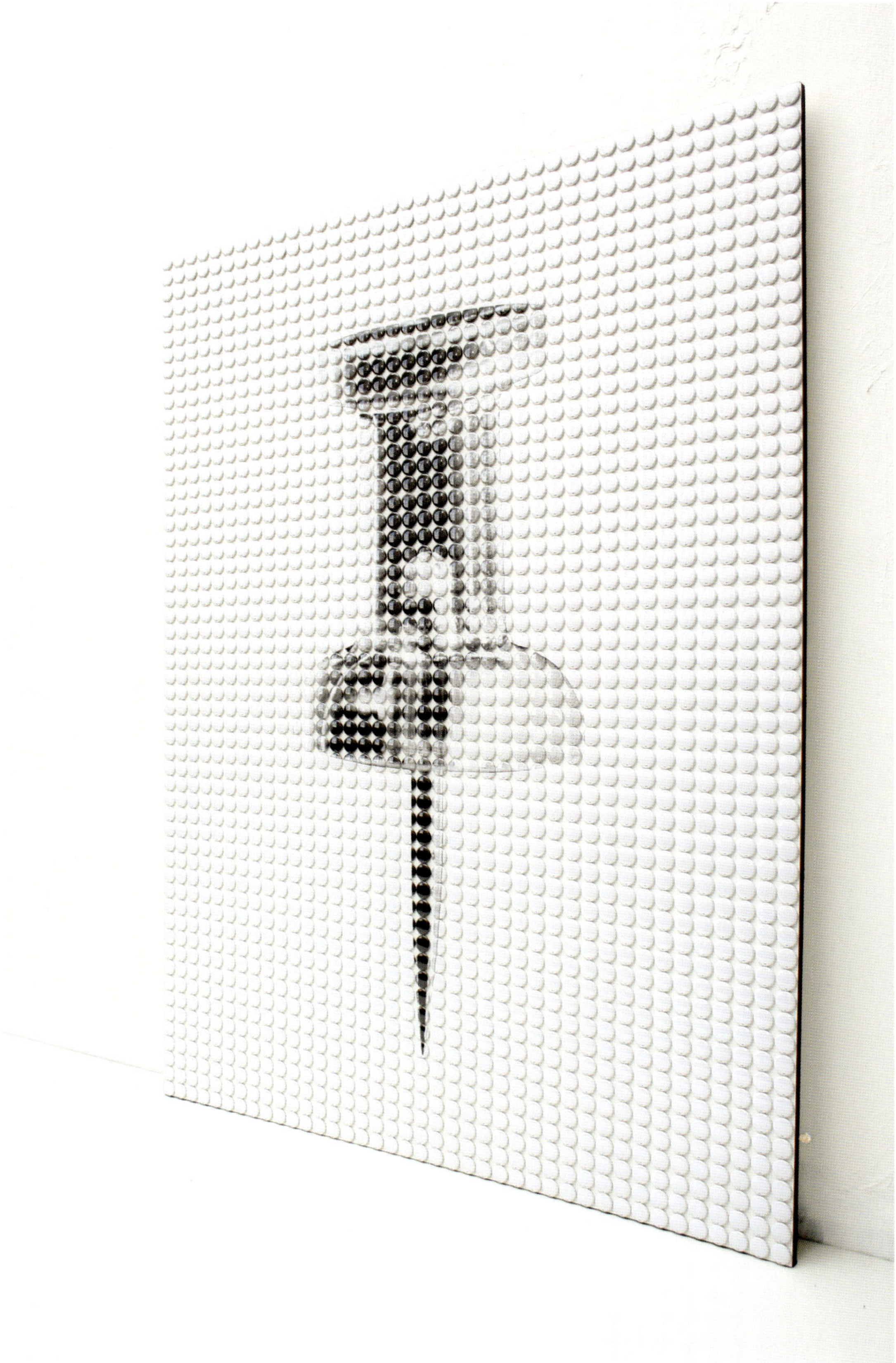

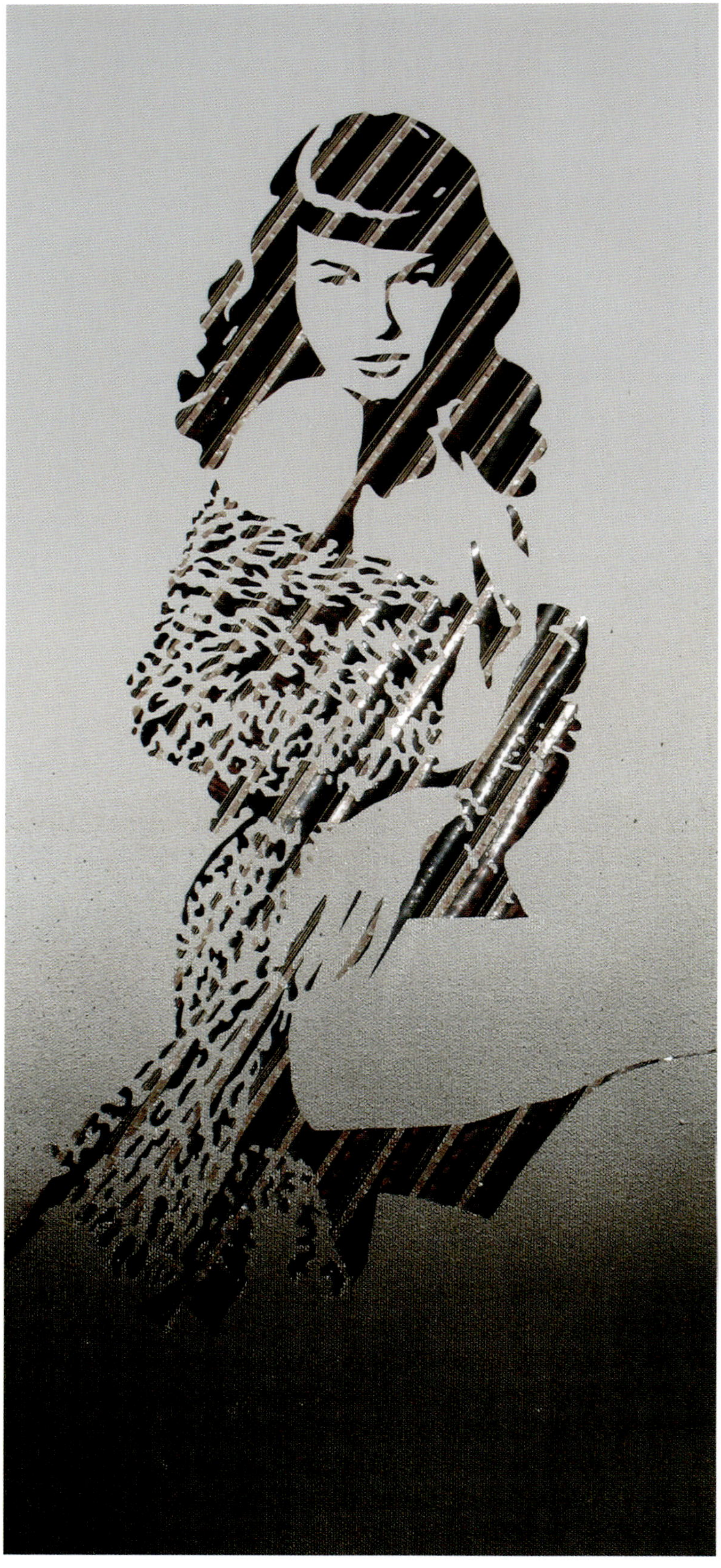

**Ghost in the Machine:**
**Betty Page**

# Erika Iris Simmons

www.iri5.com

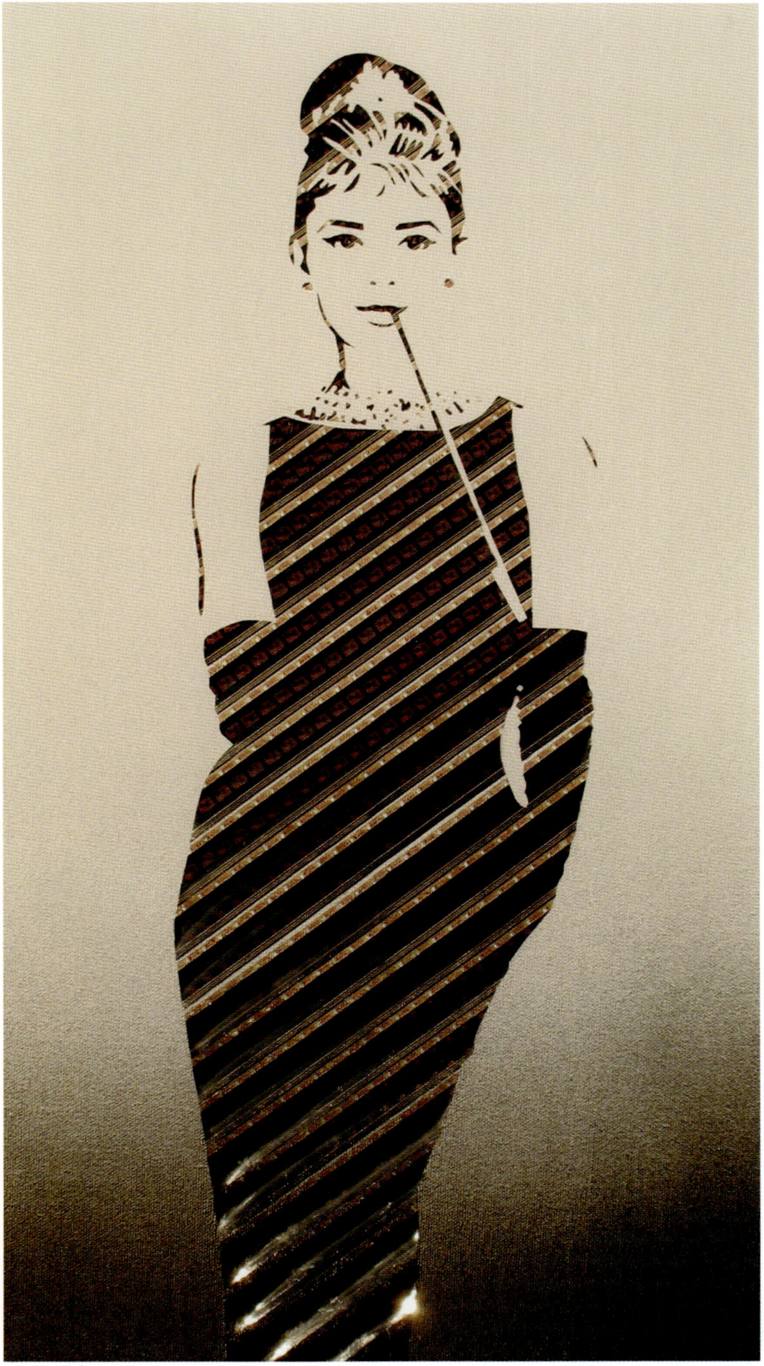

Ghost in the Machine:
Audrey Hepburn

iri5 is an imaginative painter and sculptor who is driven by an incredible passion for self-expression through art. Her works are often noted for their unique and innovative style that focuses on recycling found materials, such as old cassettes and used books. Her use of such a variety of techniques and materials make her work an excellent choice for a wide range of projects and purposes. iRI5's art has also been featured on major websites and in newspapers and magazines all over the world. In this series, Ghost in the Machine, I showcase a number of portraits of musicians made out of recycled cassette tape with original cassette. Also included are portraits made from old film and reels. The idea comes from a phrase (ironically) coined by philosopher Gilbert Ryle, a description of how your spirit lives in your body. I imagine we are all, like cassettes, thoughts wrapped up in awkward packaging.

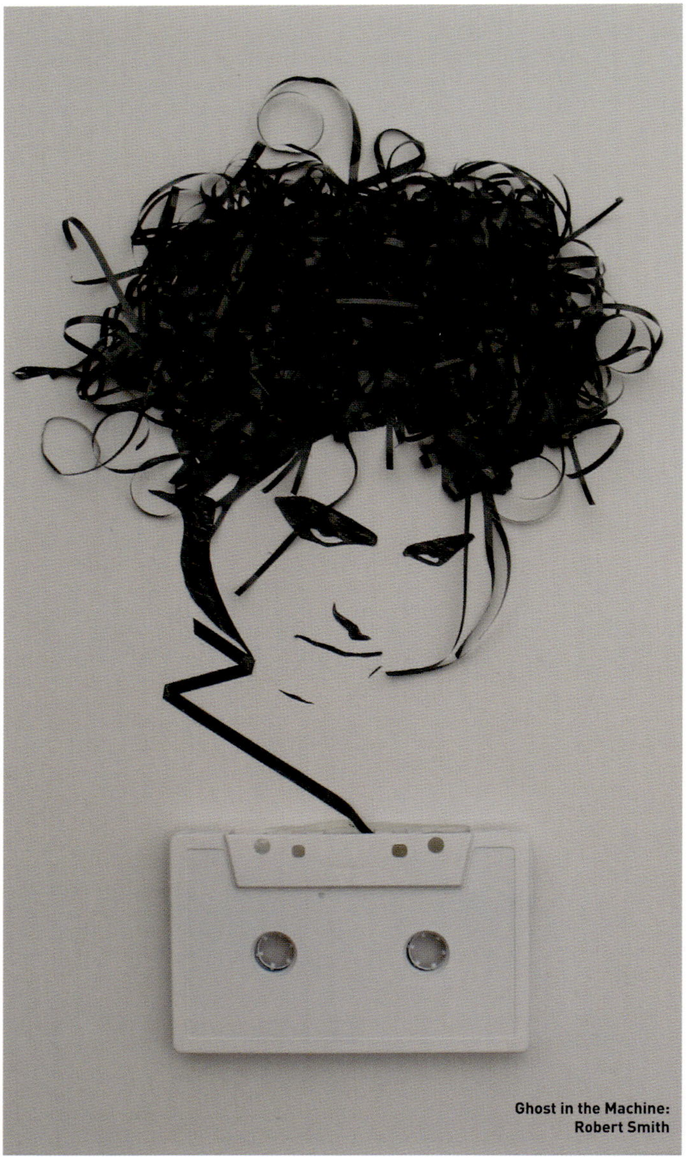

**Ghost in the Machine:**
**Robert Smith**

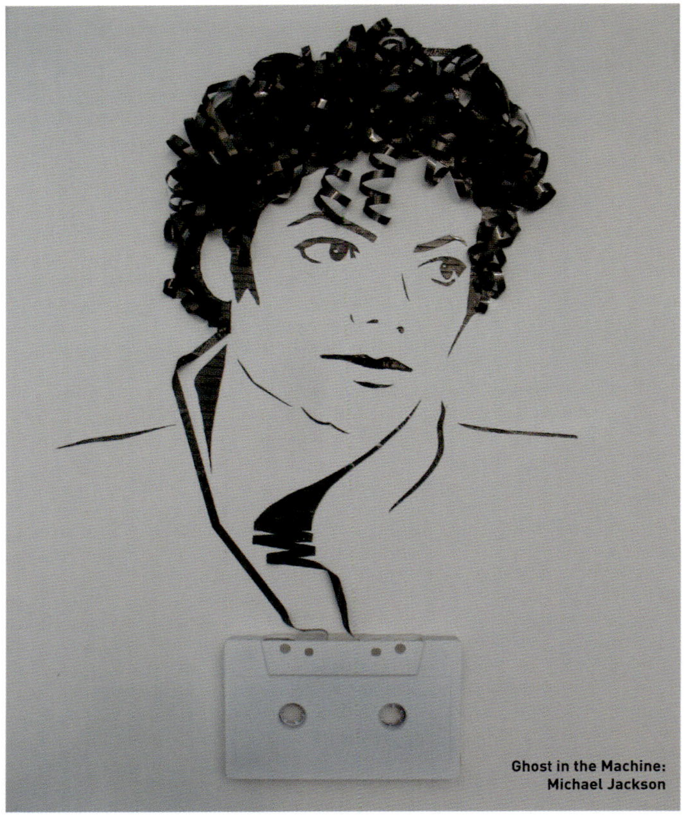

**Ghost in the Machine:**
**Michael Jackson**

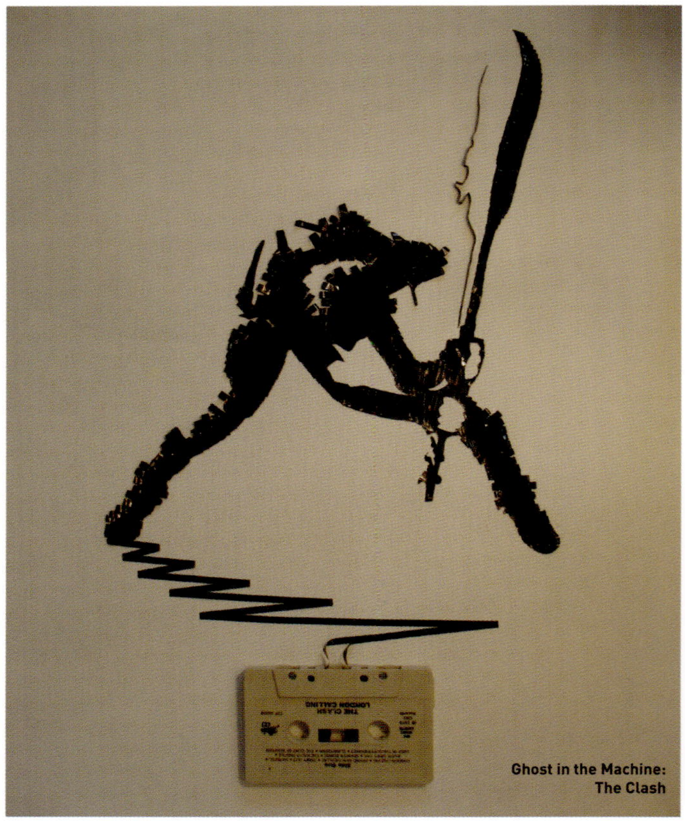

**Ghost in the Machine:**
**The Clash**

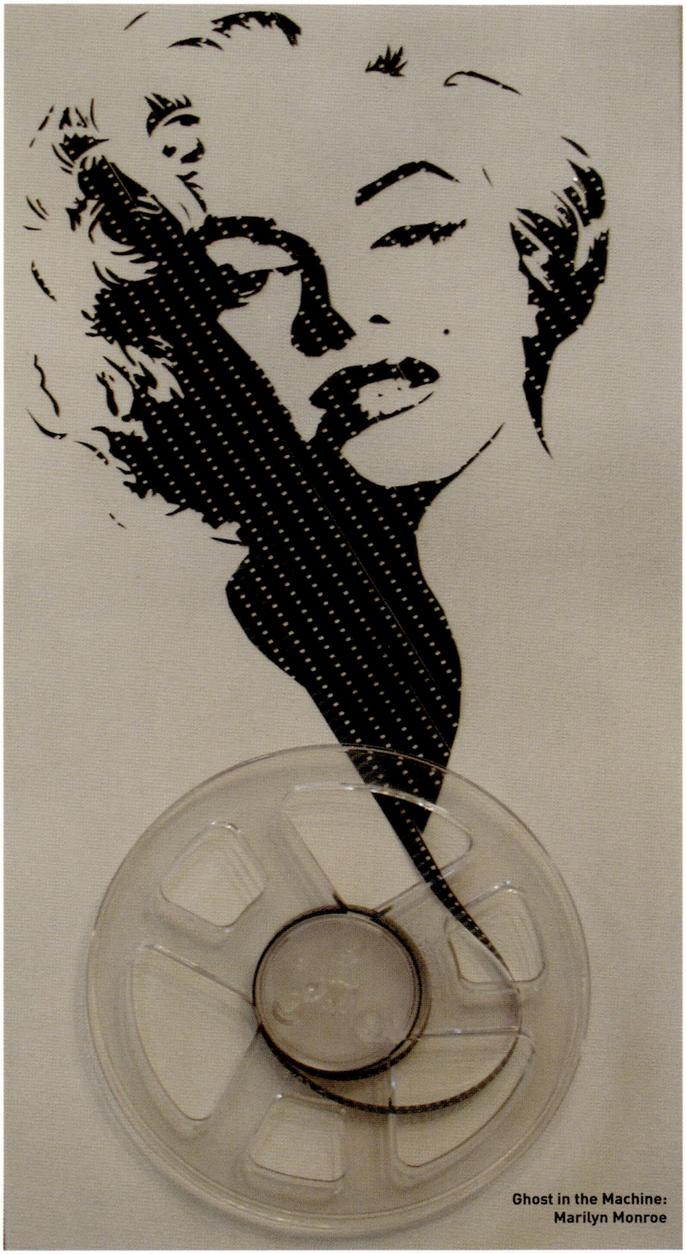
Ghost in the Machine:
Marilyn Monroe

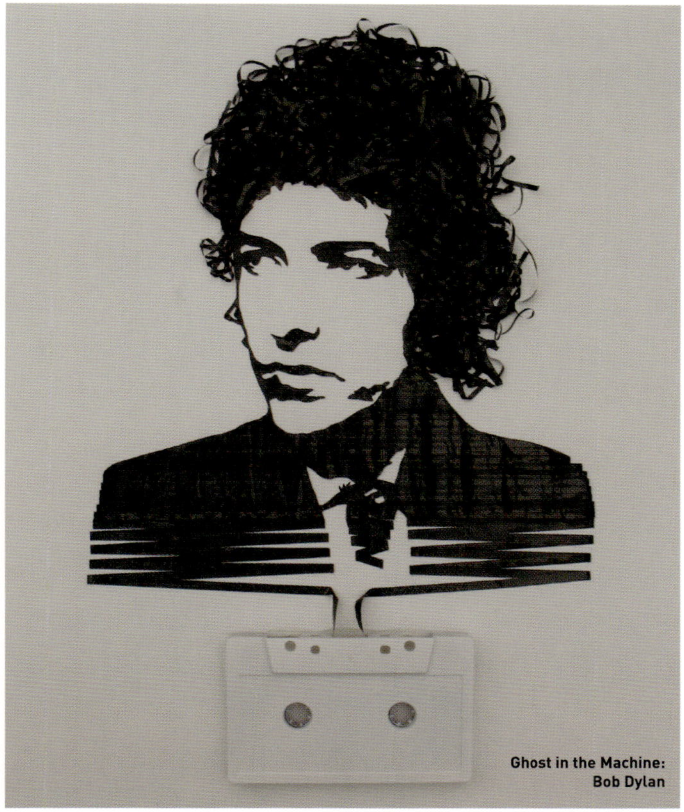
Ghost in the Machine:
Bob Dylan

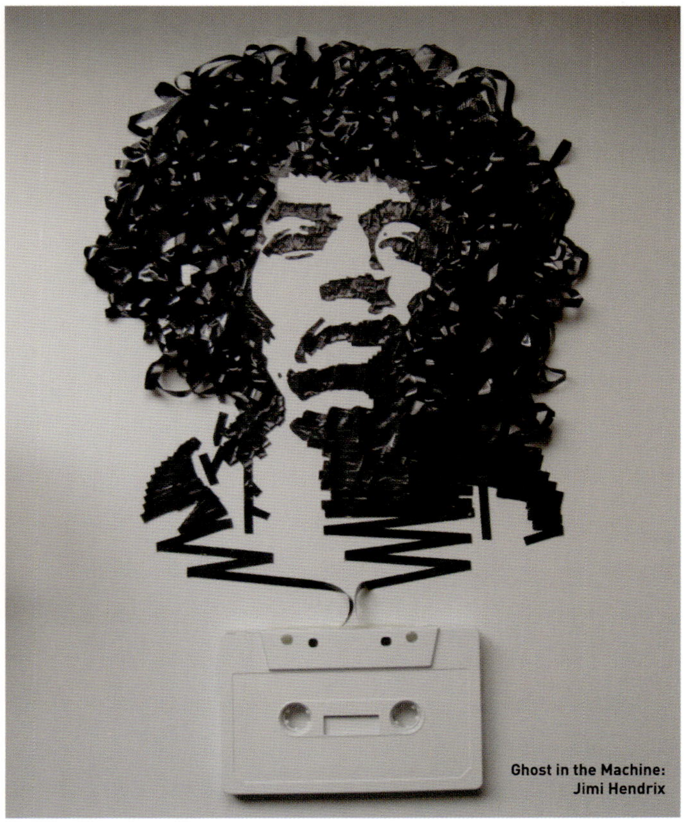
Ghost in the Machine:
Jimi Hendrix

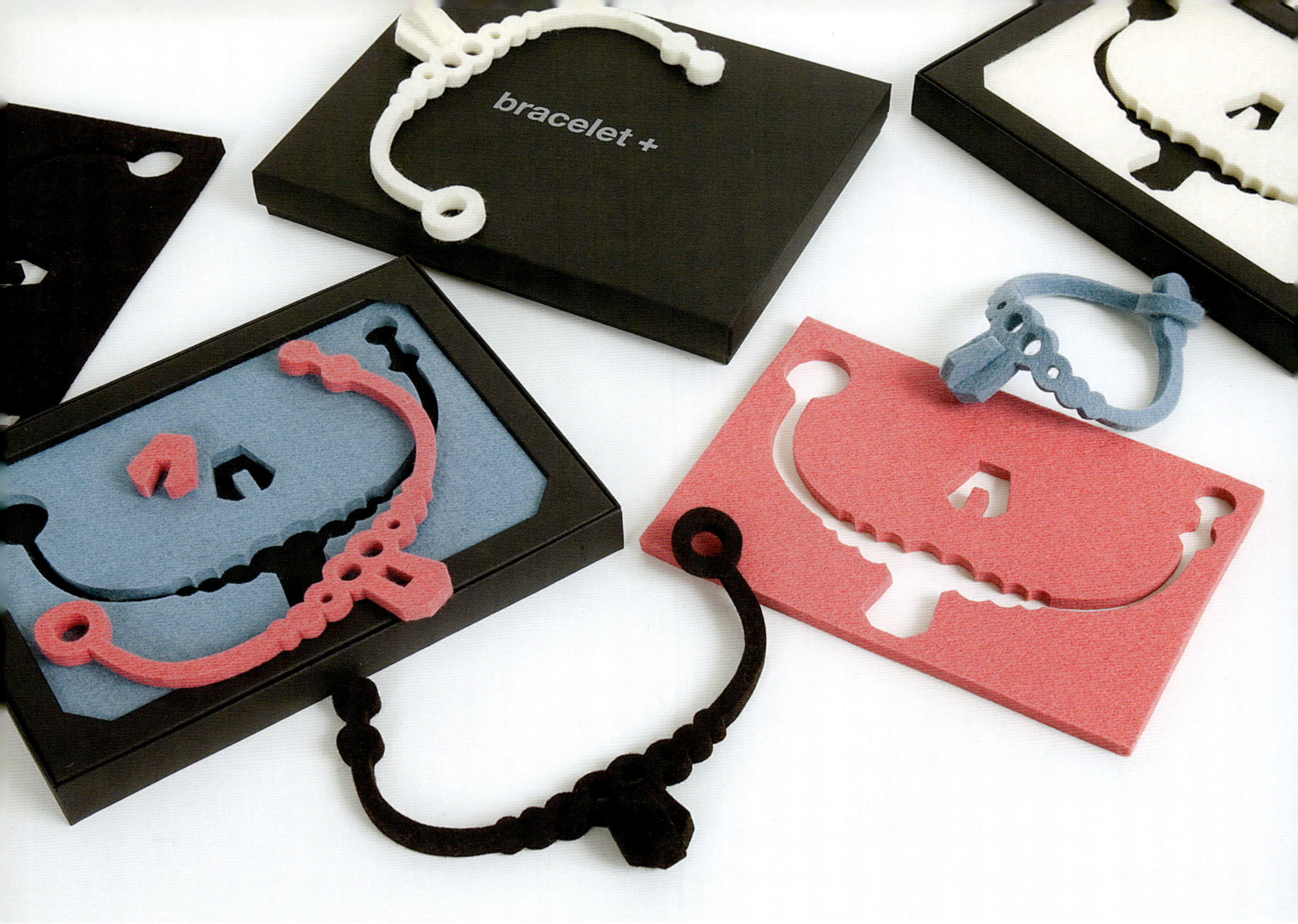


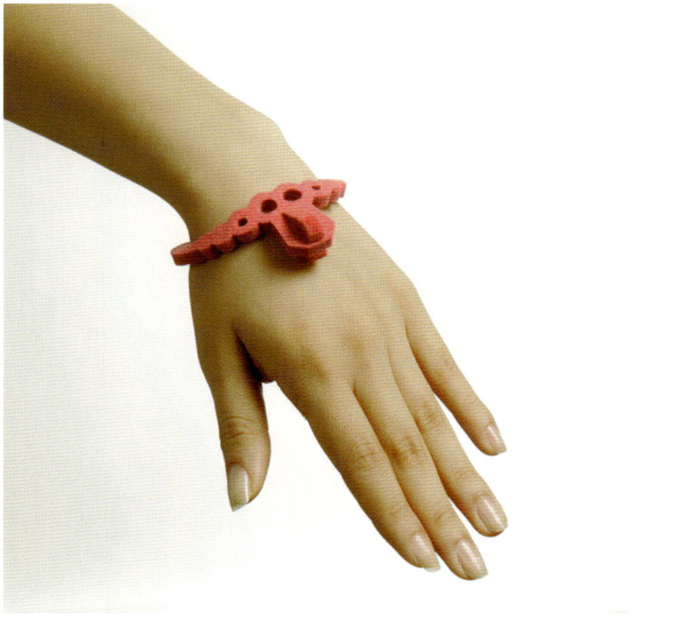

**Bracelet +**

# /Furnish

www.furnish.jp

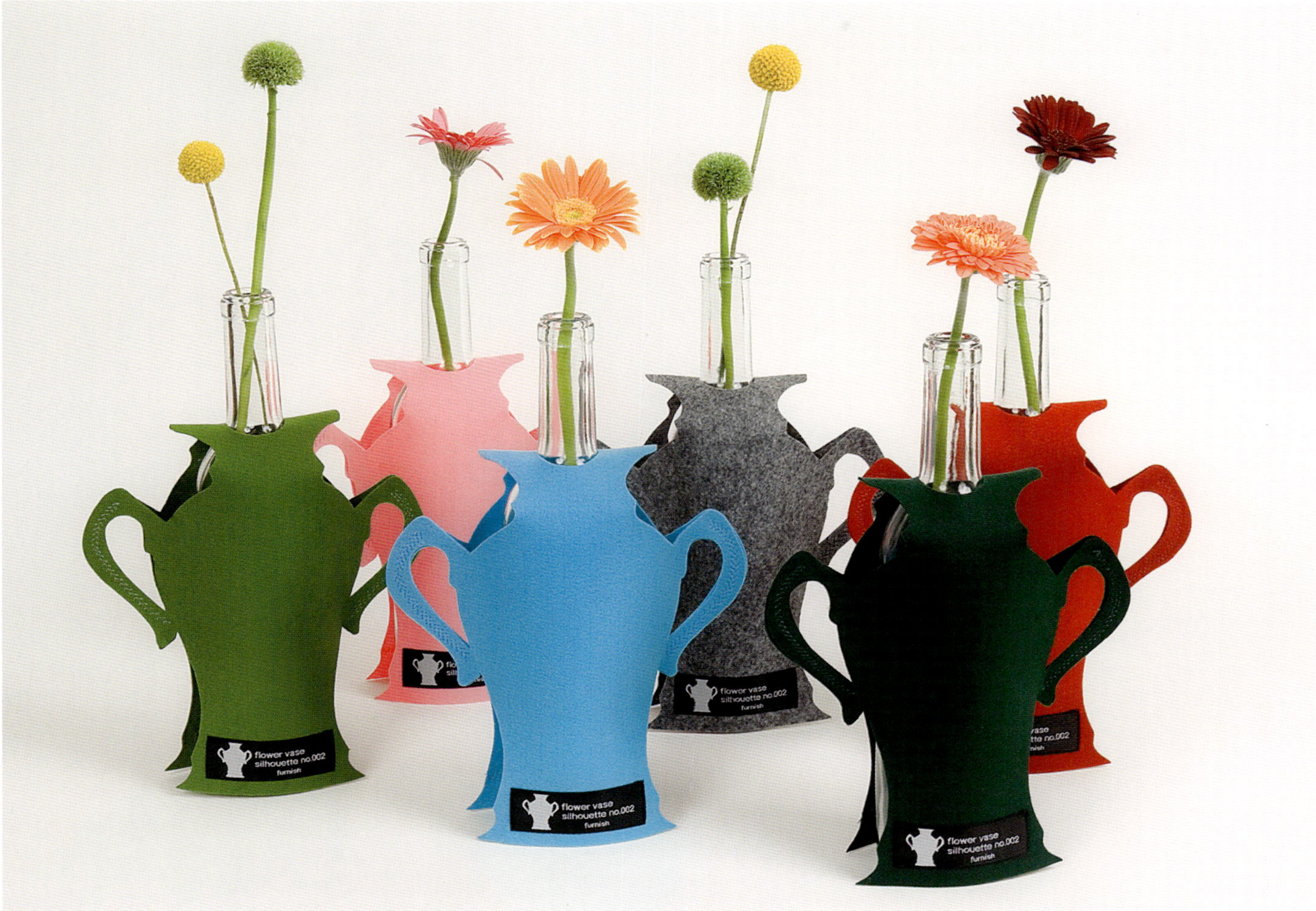


**Bottlevase**

Founded in 2005, furnish is a Tokyo-based designer unit consisting of Satoshi Yoshikawa and Bungo Komuro. Their collection is now gaining popularity not only in Japan, but also in Europe and in the U.S. The concept behind Furnish is to take an ordinary item and transform it to something that is not only practical, but fun to use. 80% fun factor combined with 20% self-expression (refers to the flexibility in the users' interpretation and arrangement of the product to best fit their way of life). All products produced by furnish are made in Japan - Furnish is based in Tokyo's Adachi-ward suburbs by utilizing traditional local manufacturers in the area for cutting and printing, others in Arakawa-ward for the package and through fabric manufactuers in Saitama Pref. All products are individually hand-made. For this reason, most products are not mass-produced and carefully made one step at a time. Furnish will continue to design and produce new products utilizing traditional Japanese techniques.

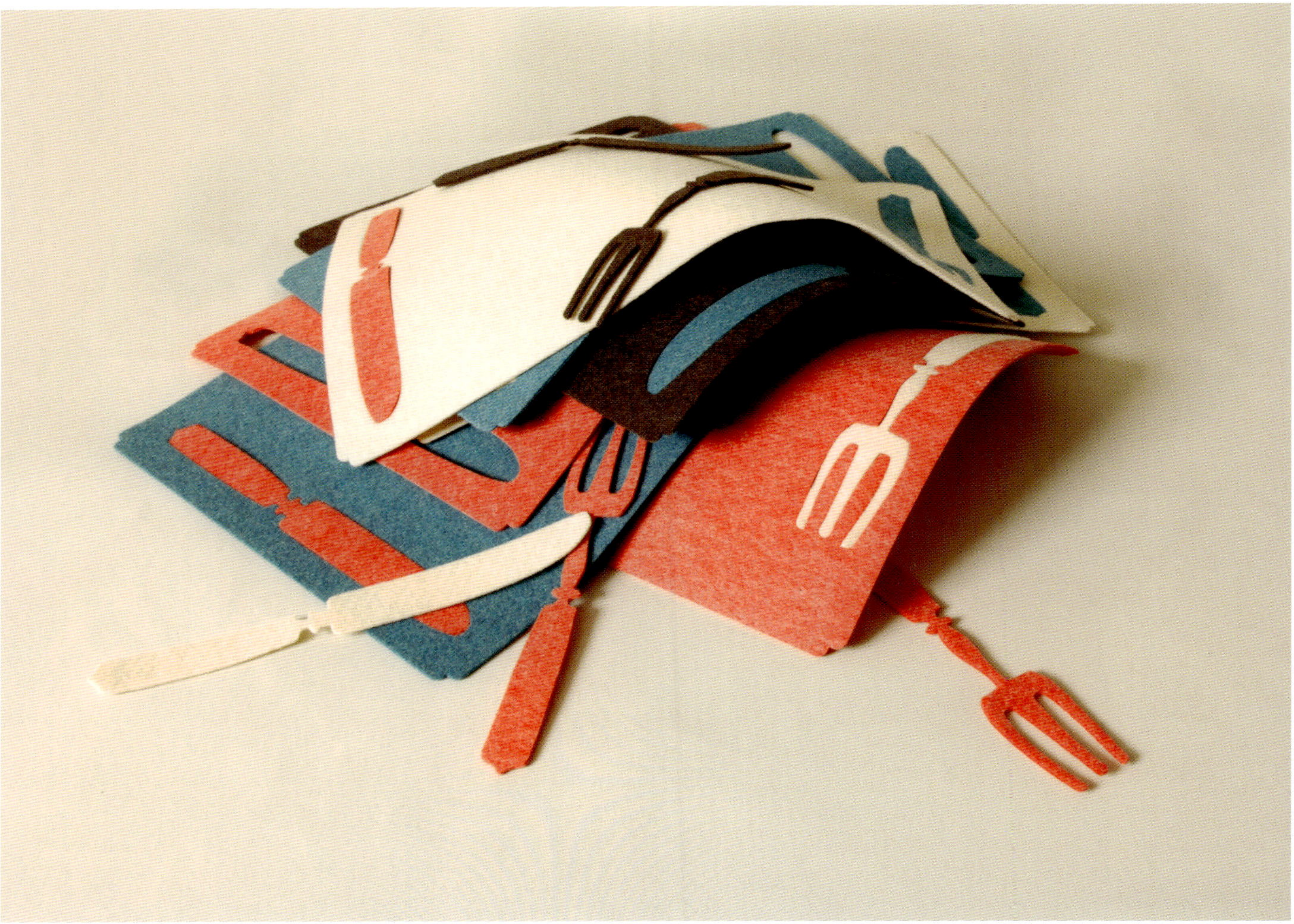

**Feltplacemat**

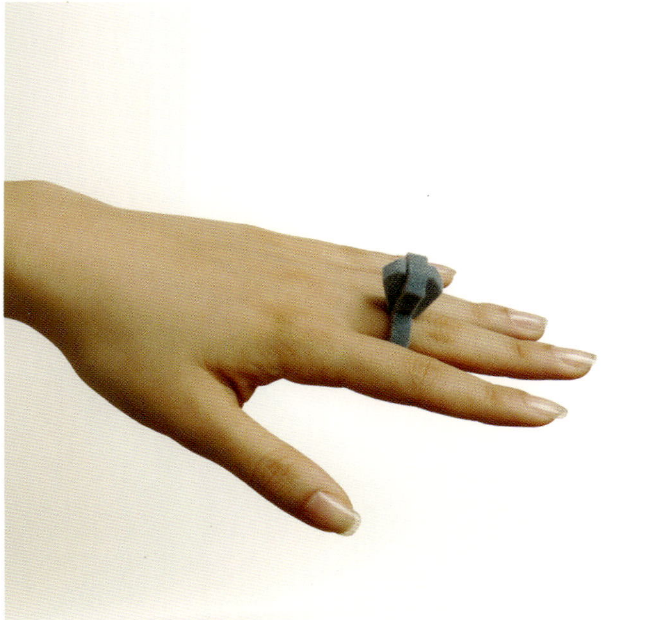

Ring +

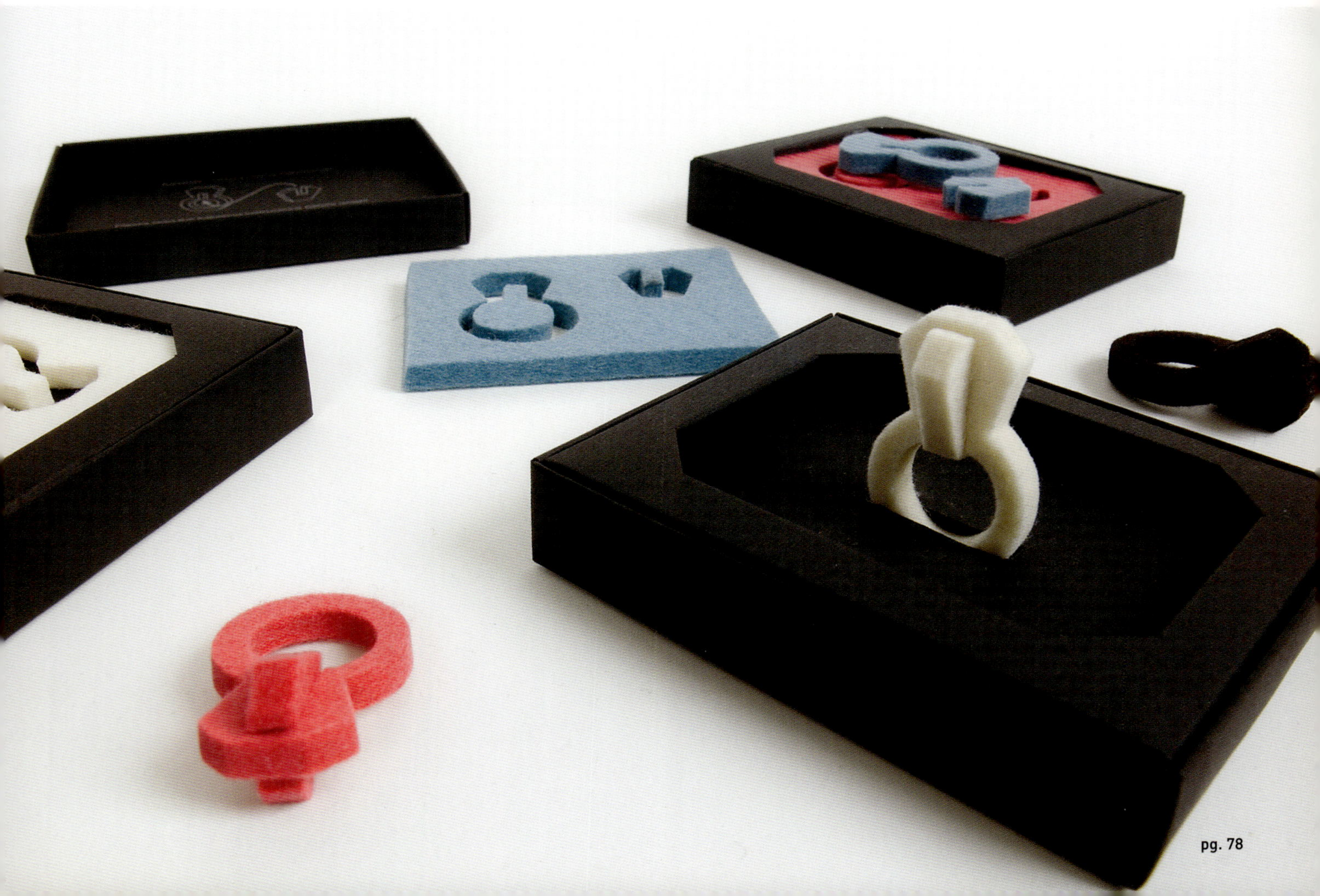

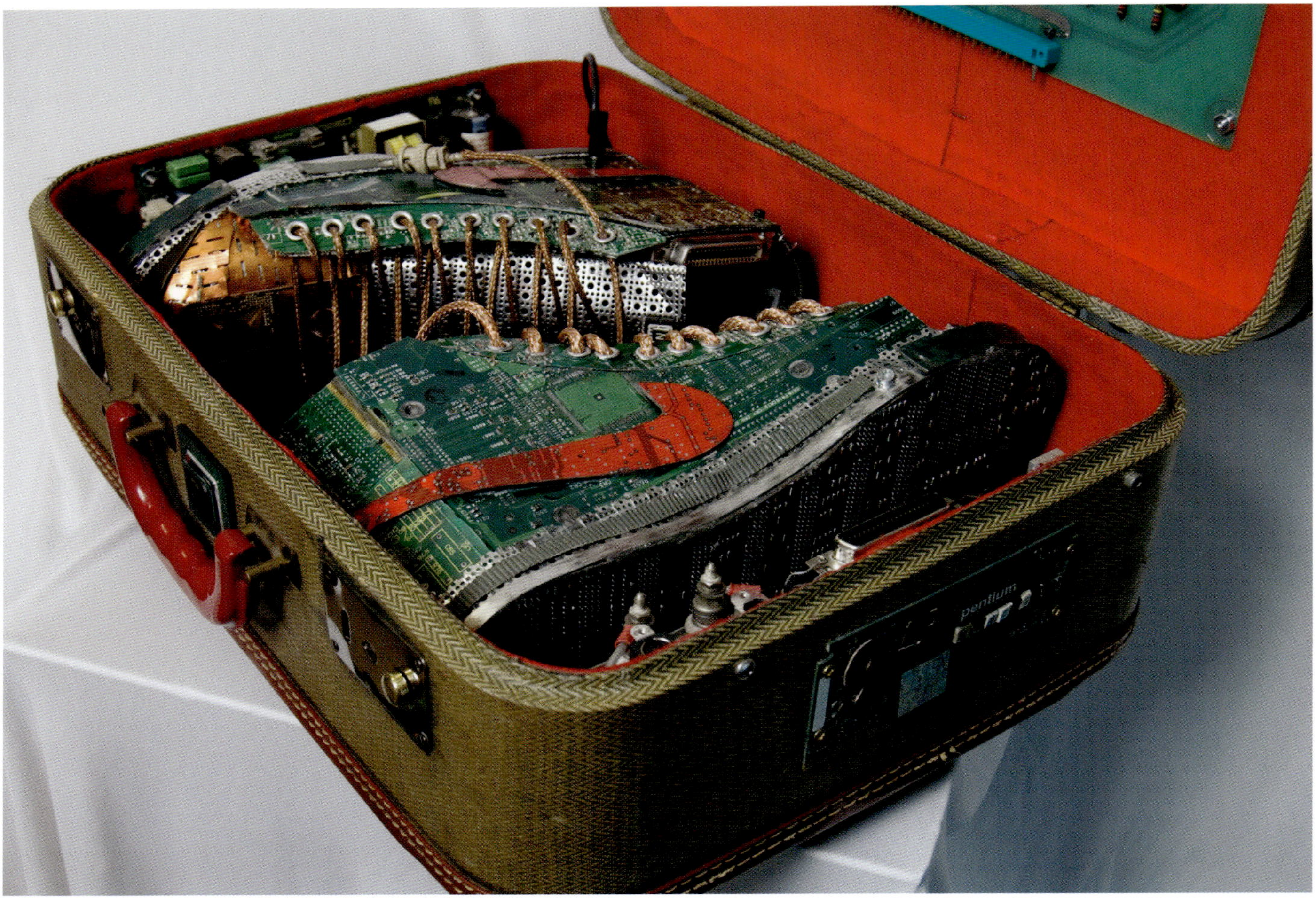


**Blazer Pentium 1.0**
This sculpture is part of a shoes series I'm currently working where I revisit some of my favorite classic sneakers silhouettes. With this piece I again tried to create a complete piece with both box and shoe notice some of the details, shoes lock down inside of box for easy portability, I also tied this piece around a theme,"Pentium", the name of Intel's chips. You will notice this repeated through out the shoes, and box.

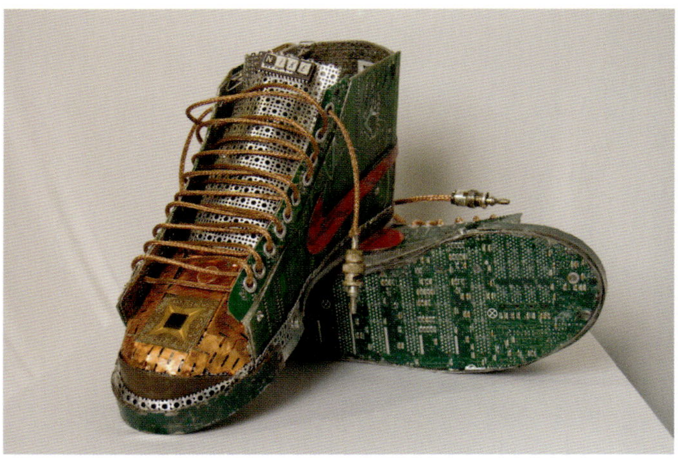

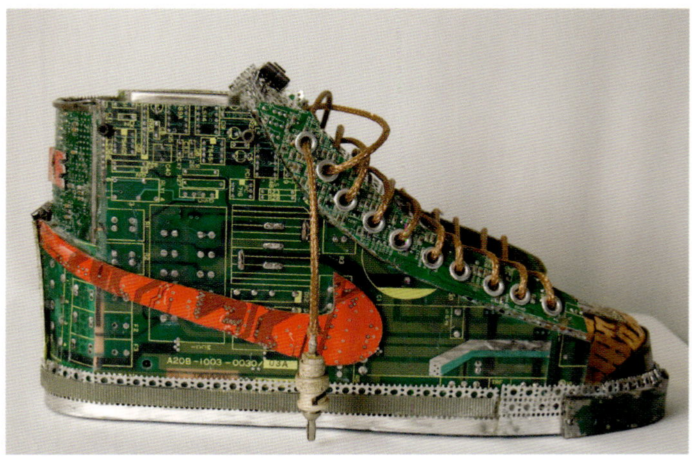

# Gabriel Dishaw

www.gabrieldishaw.com

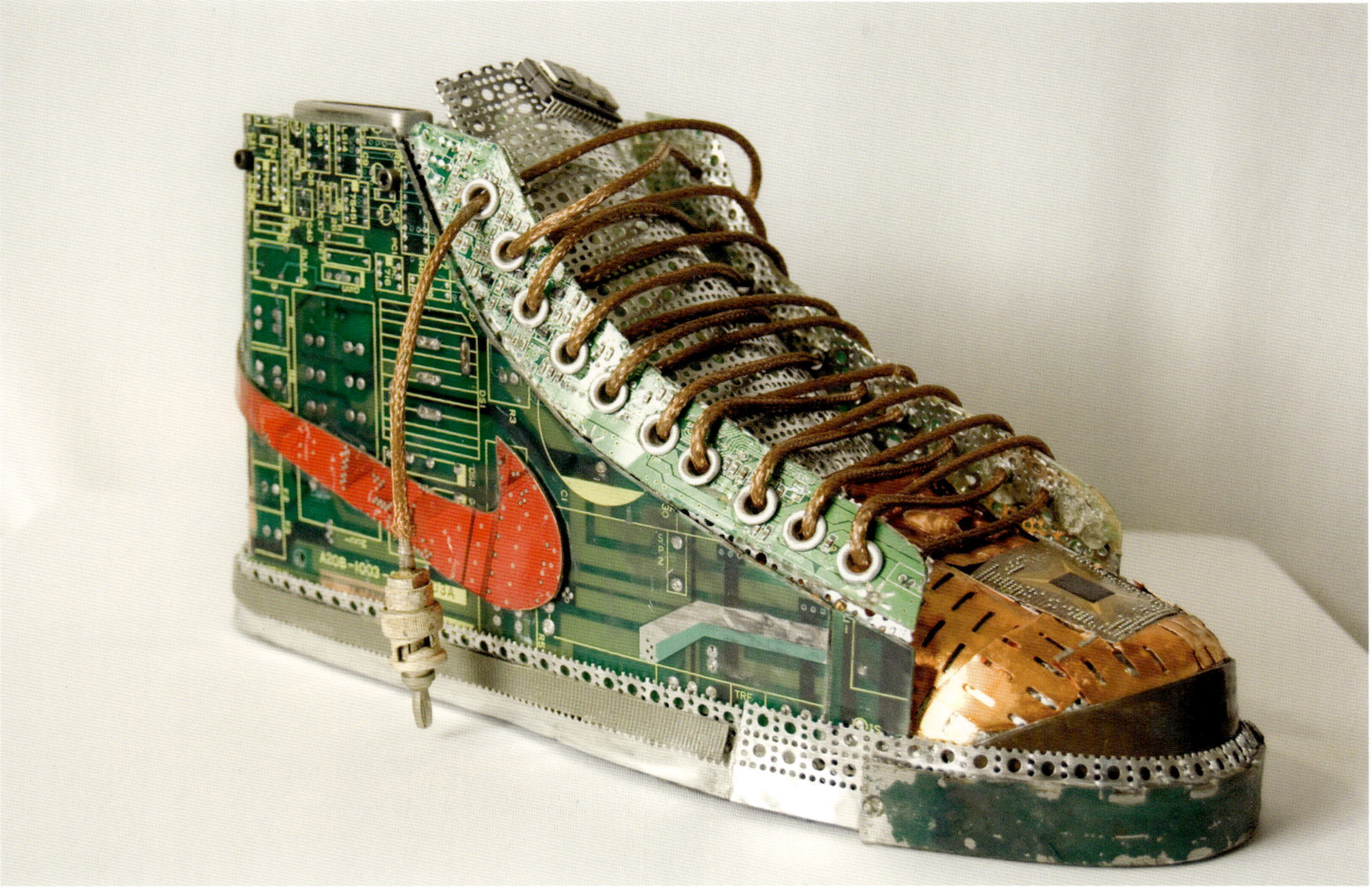

My passion for working with metal and mechanical objects has been crucial in the evolution of my art and freeing my imagination. It provides me an avenue to express myself in a way that both helps me and the environment. The metal has the ability to resonates the very fantasies and thought processes that I envision. Using found objects from typewriters, adding machines and old computers, I take the items people no longer have use for and I carefully disassembling these items and then reassemble these together using metal wire creating my Junk Art. I begin each sculpture with an idea of how can I take these found pieces of useless metal and insignificant objects and create something that everyone can understand and relate to. I find myself looking at ordinary mechanical items to see how I could turn that something, into something else not originally intended for that use. I started this process in my early teens and continued it through college and career after. My process has evolved over time and my pieces have gotten bigger in both idea and size.

**Junk Dunk**

This piece was a continuation of my previous piece JUNK DUNK I wanted to attempt this approach again, with a more refined and detailed outcome. I used very little wire and more glue to keep the piece more clean, and less bulky. I also added new details, a hinged tongue and nike logo's on both the tongue and back of the shoe. On previous models I used a real nike sole to build of off. With this piece I started from scratch and build the sole from circuit boards.

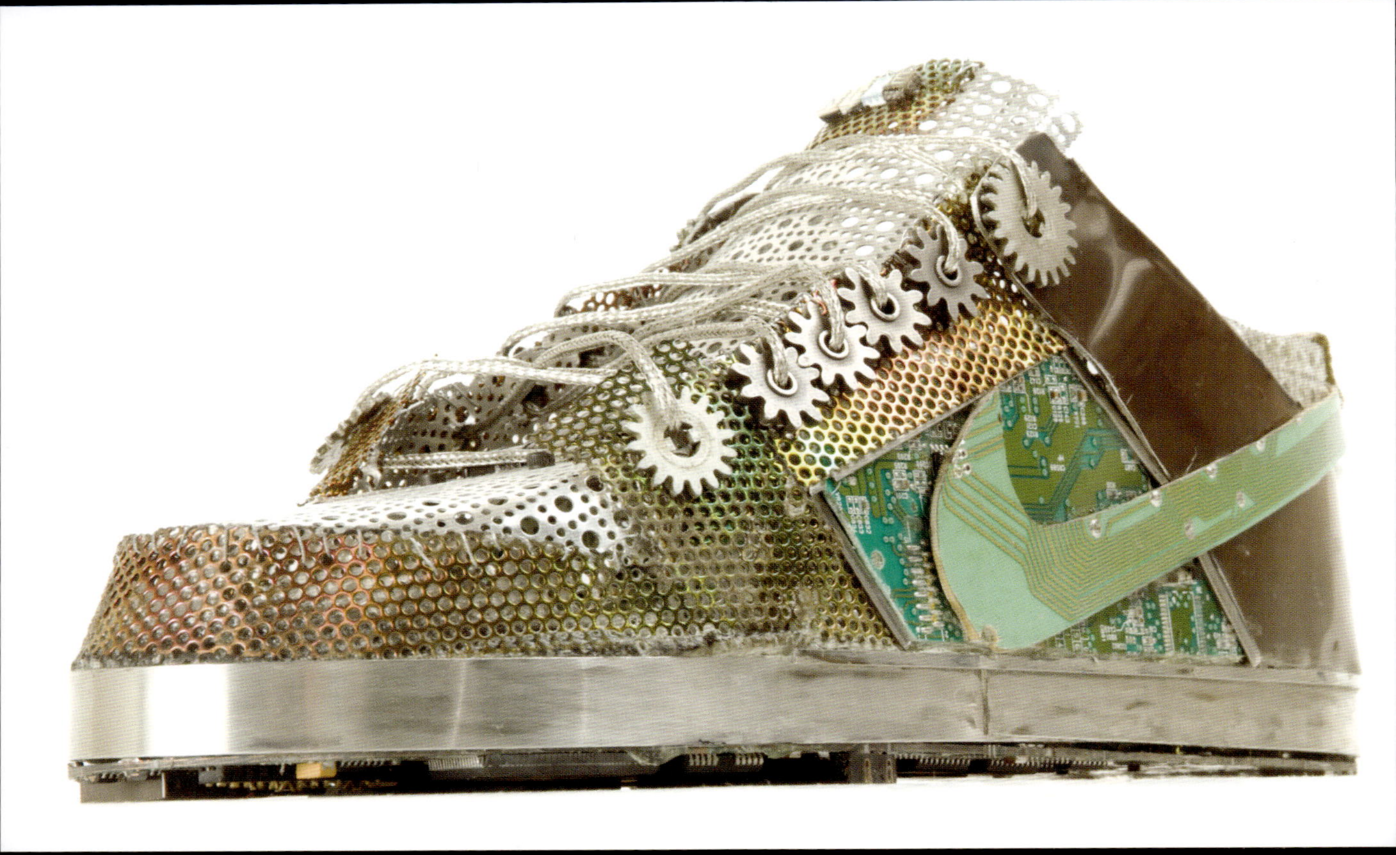

**Frankenstein Terminators**

This piece was inspired by my love of sneakers and, in particular, The High Terminator. I decided this time to do it right by making the entire package: from the shoes, to the shoe box, label, diagram and shoe tags. My theme on this piece is Frankenstein. You will notice the red felt is attached using staples like the skin of the great beast. This technique was also used to secure the metal sheet on the top of the box with the electricity logo.

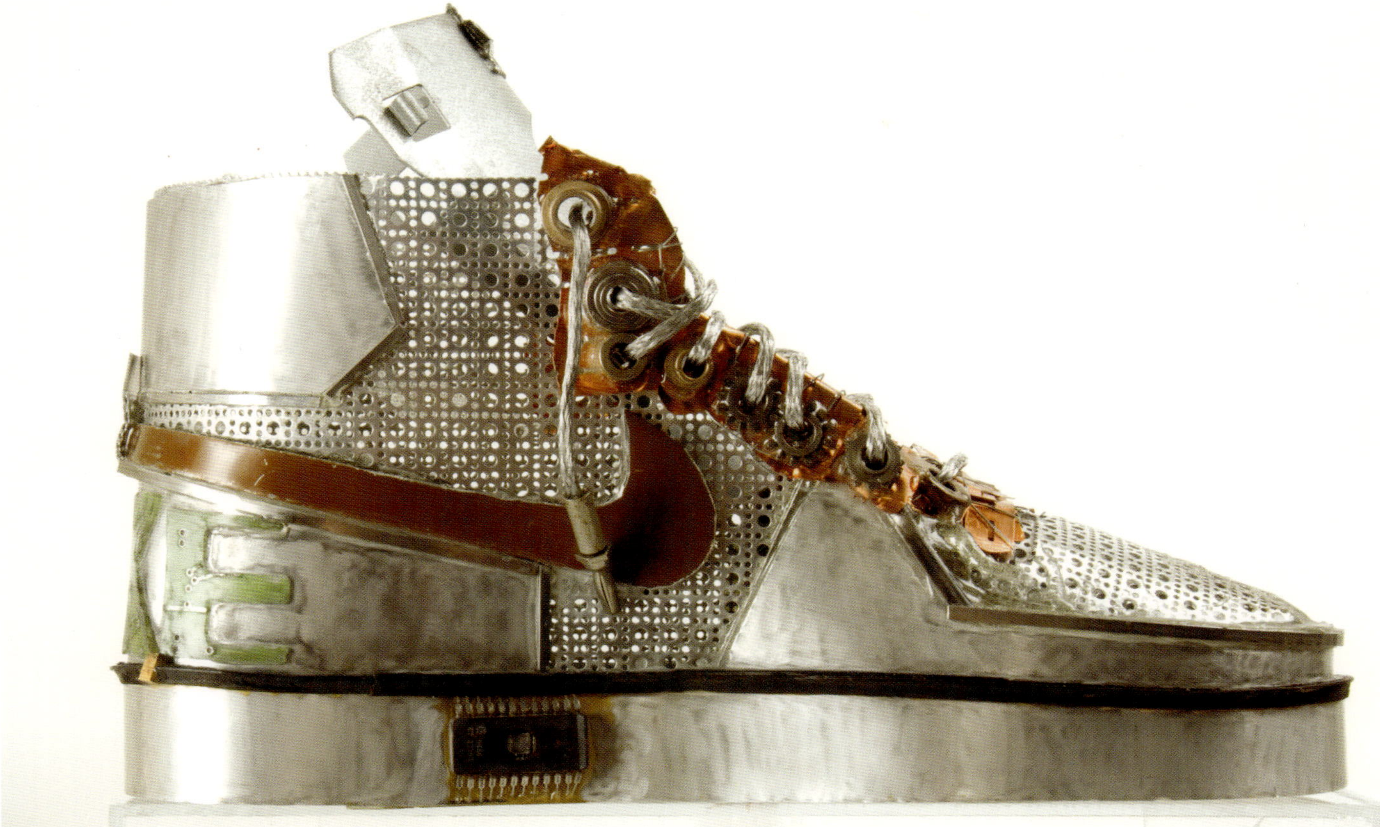

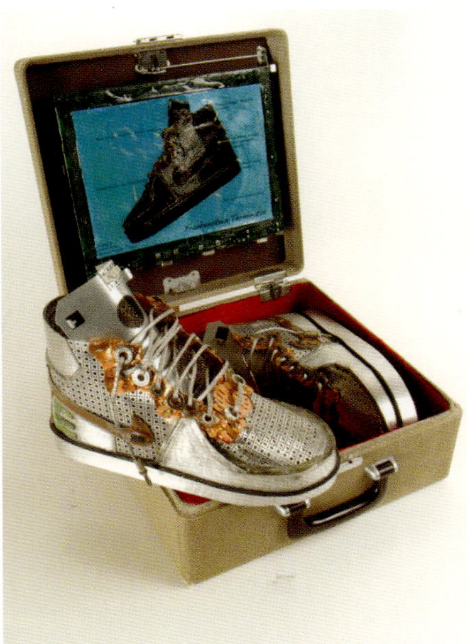

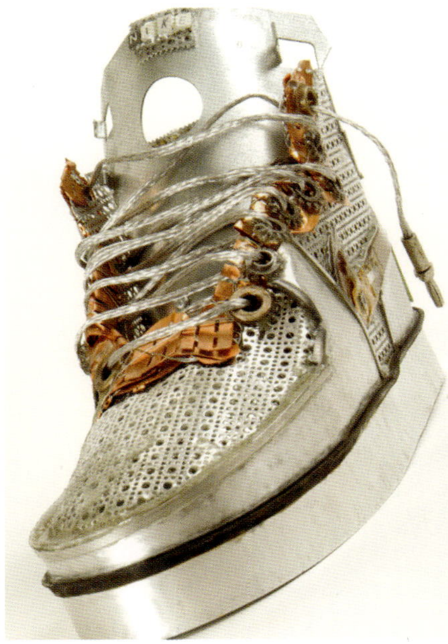

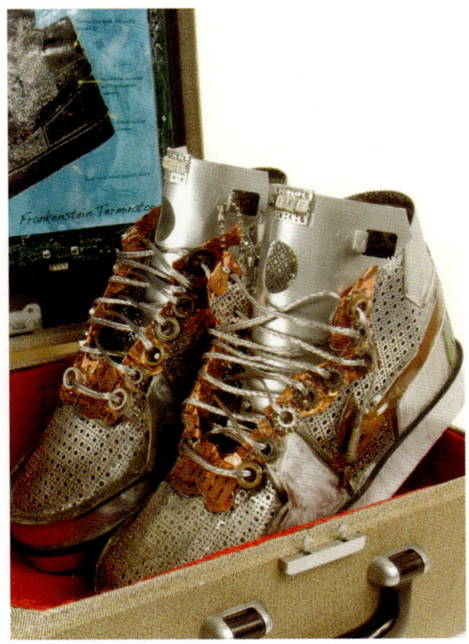

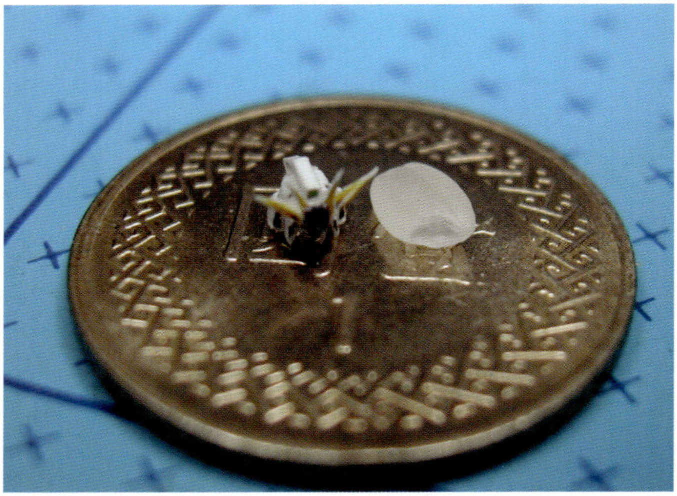

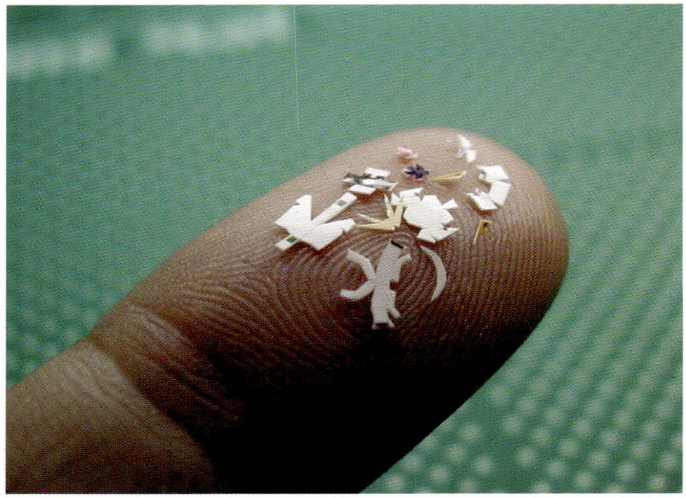

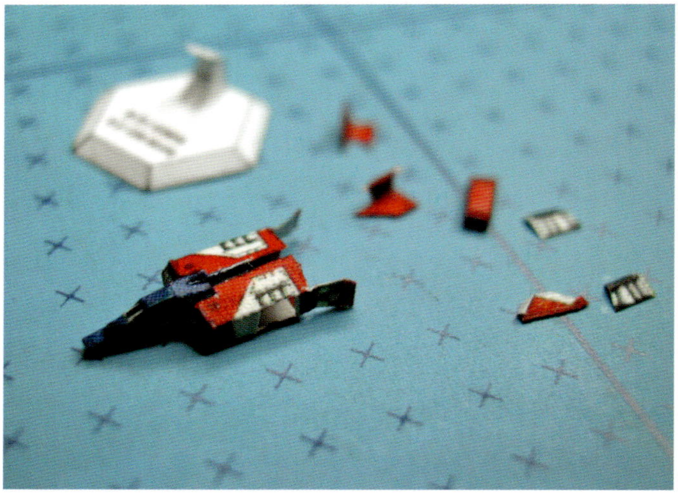

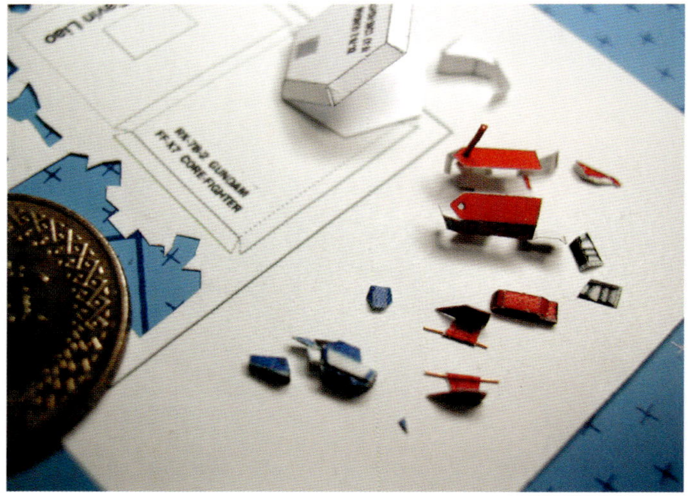
RX-78-2 GUNDAM
FF-X7 CORE FIGHTER

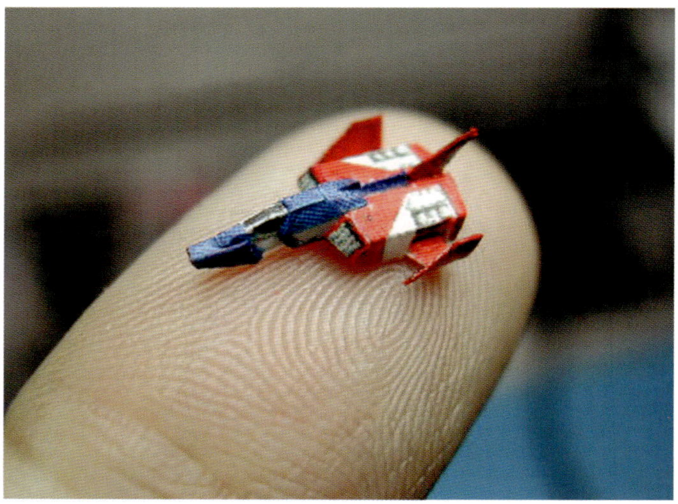

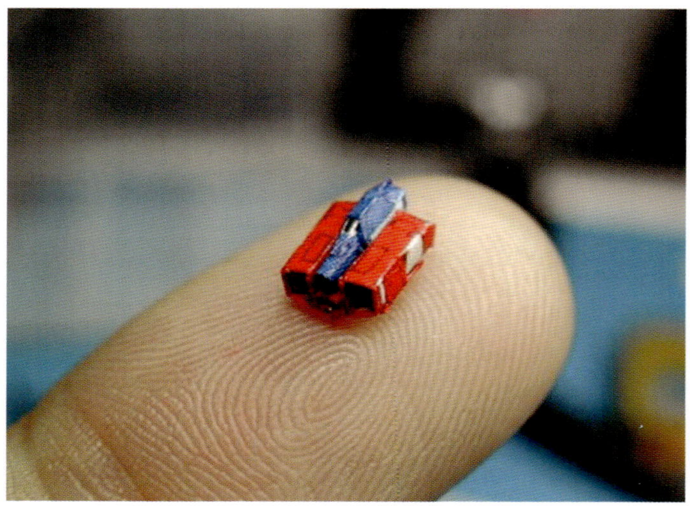

# Gavin Liao

www.cuber34.blogspot.com

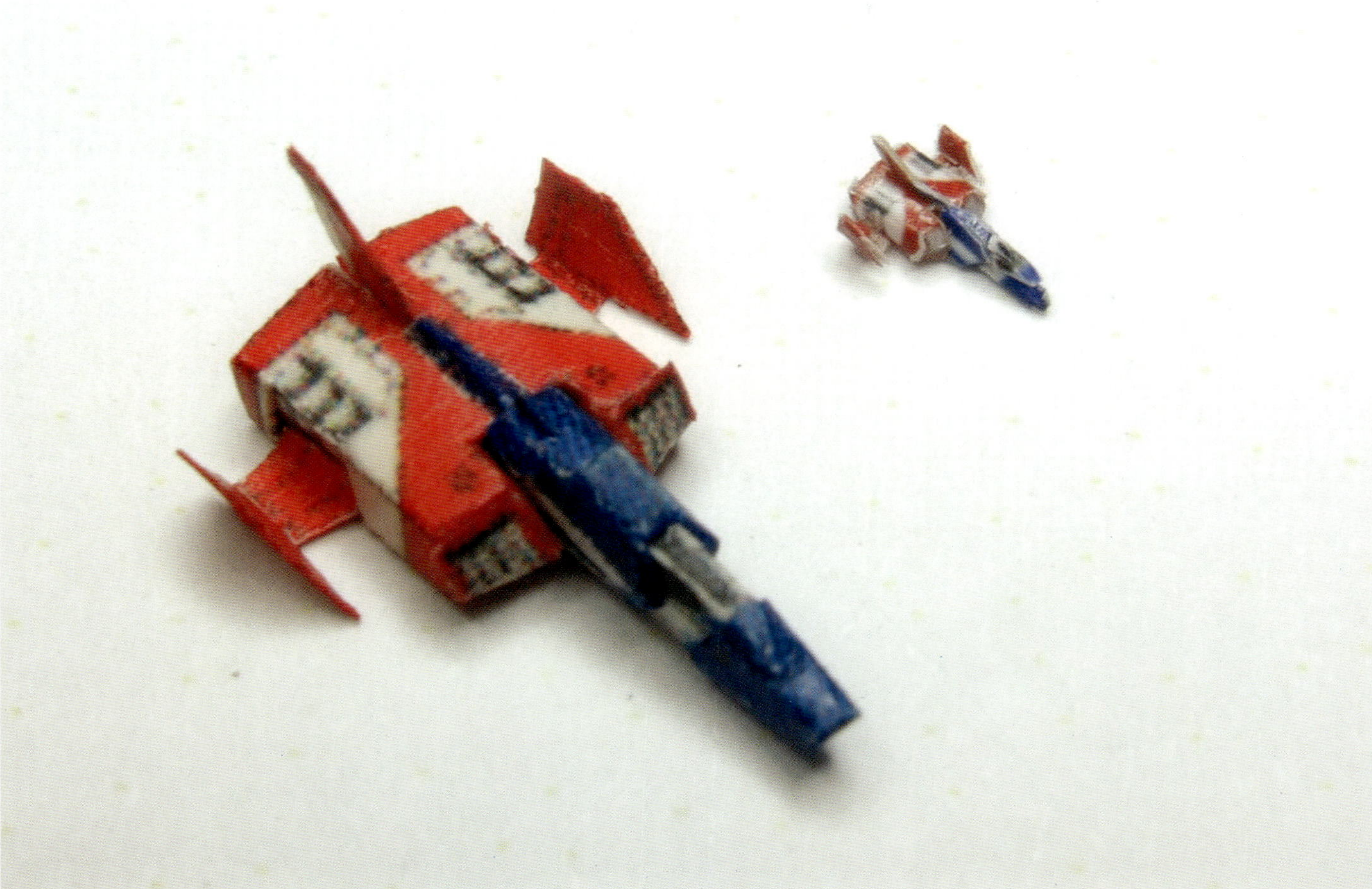

Taiwanese, cuber, paper sculptor, serious science fiction addition, miniature laboratory.

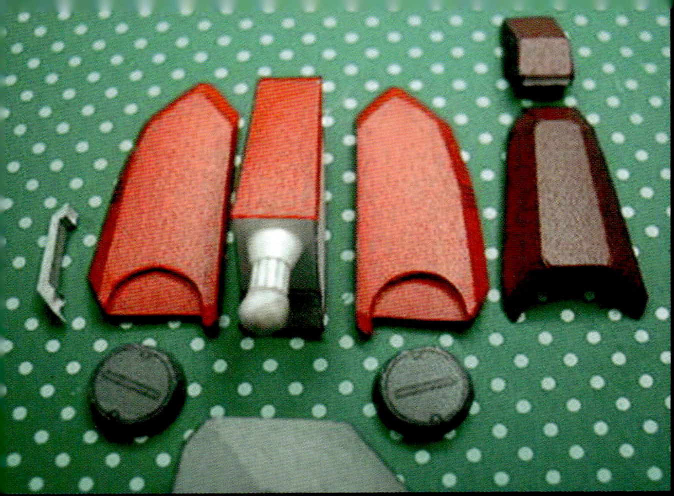
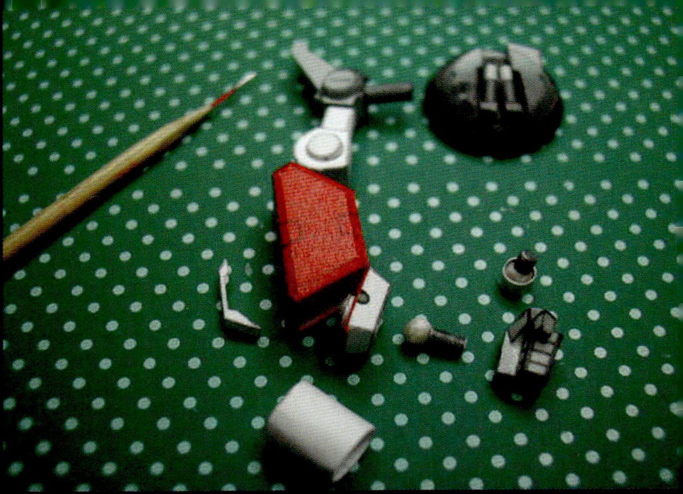
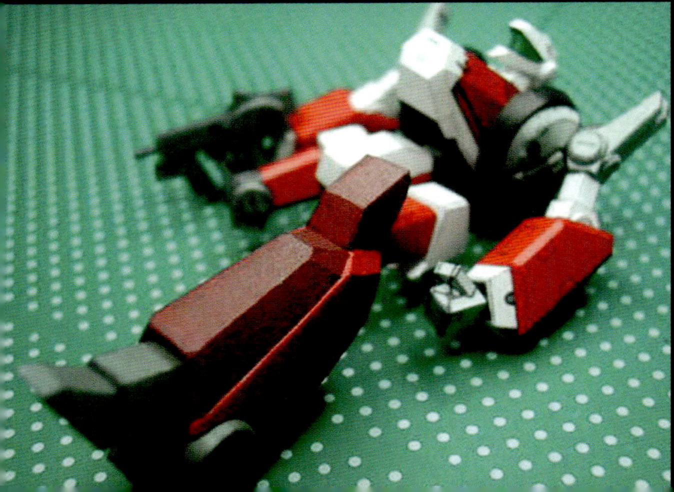
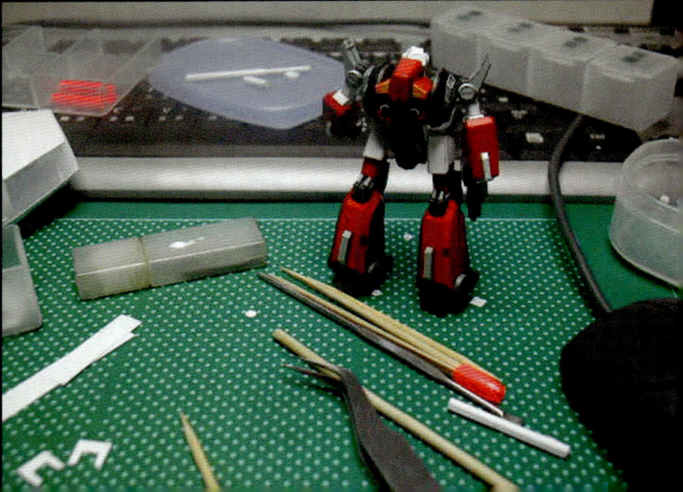

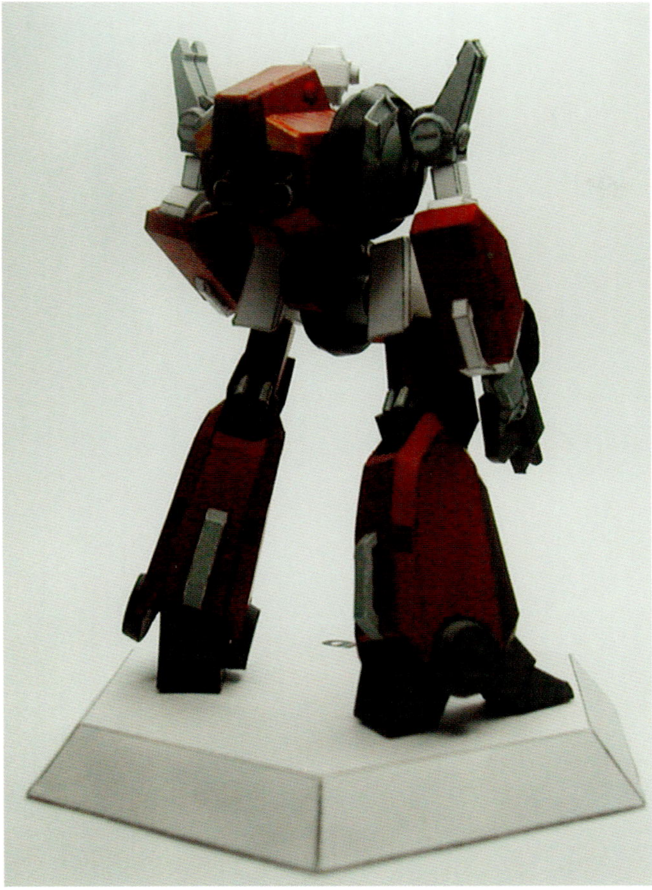

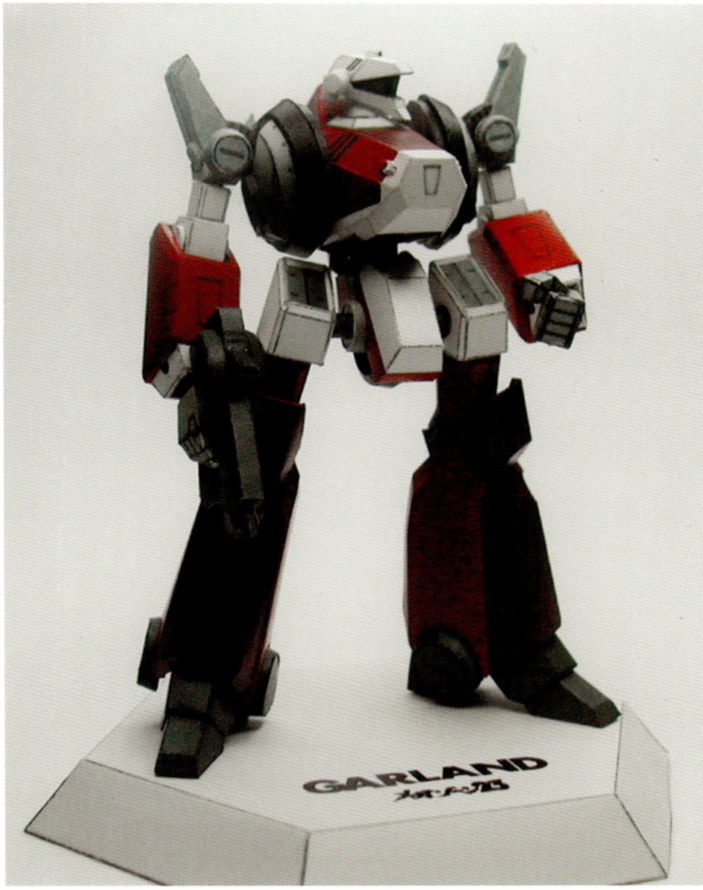
GARLAND

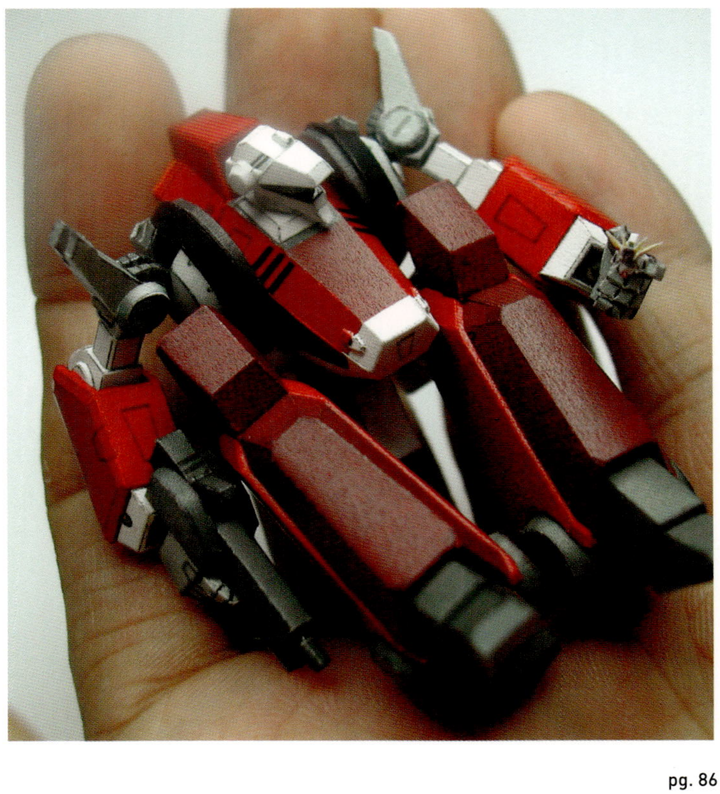

**Everything he lied was true**
2006, wood, 166 x 37.5 x 50 cm

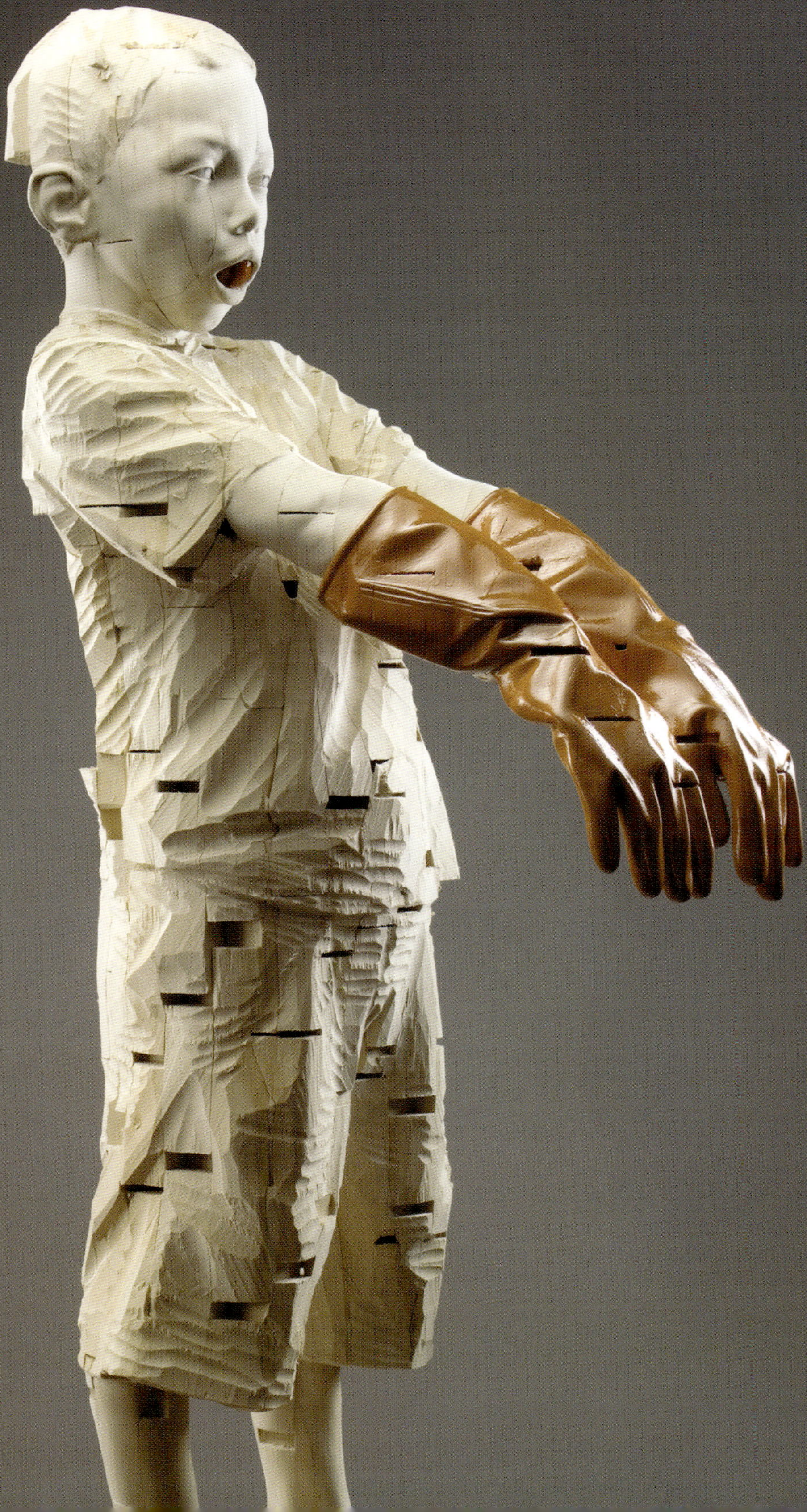

# Gehard Demetz

www.geharddemetz.com

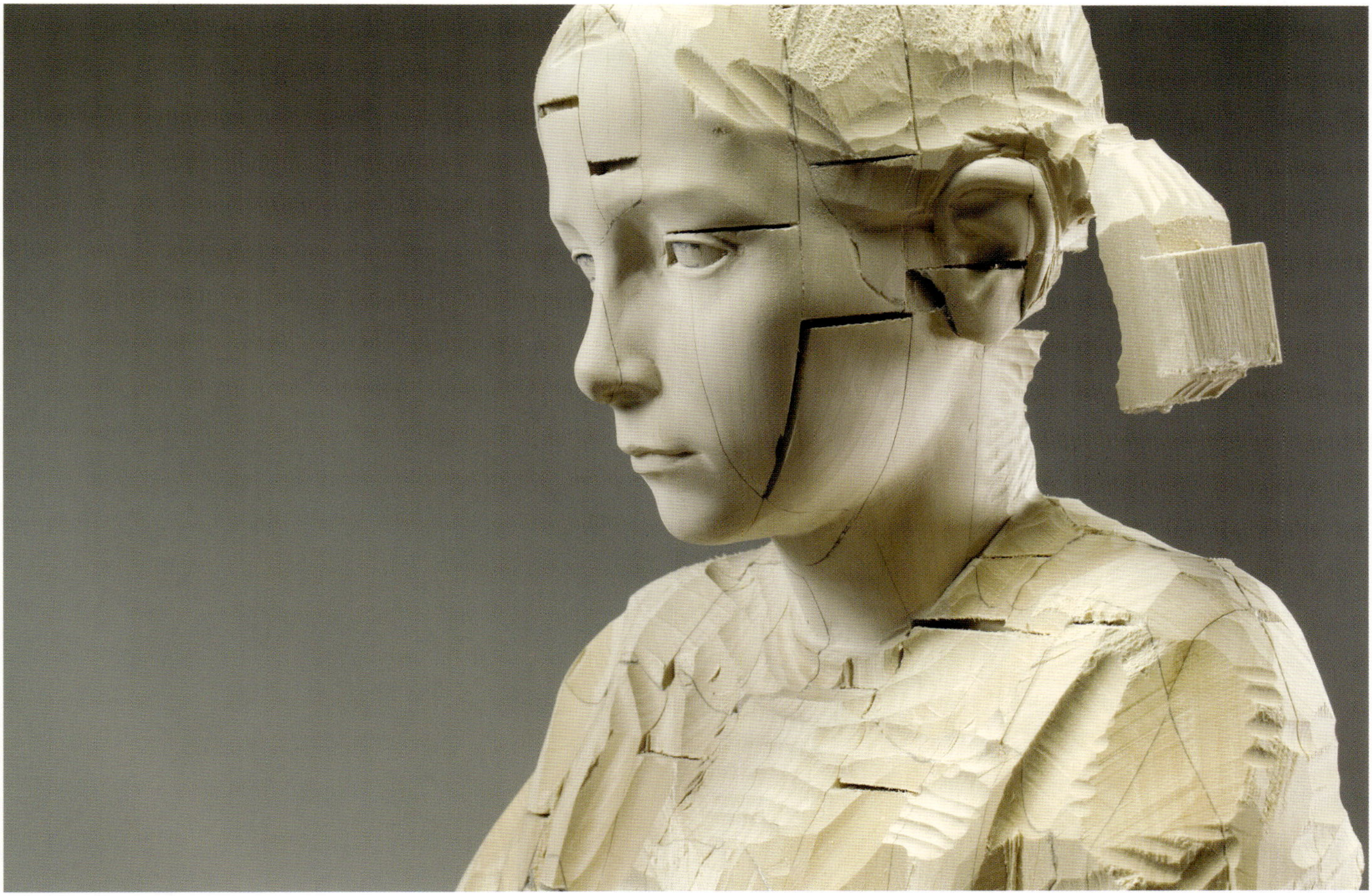

**Ragazza sinistra** 2005, wood, 138 x 38 x 32 cm

The Italian sculptor from South Tirol Gehard Demetz follows the ancient tradition of carving wood, tipical of the Gardena valley. Gehard Demetz choses not to work with a whole trunk of tree. His works are characterized by the assembly of small blocks of wood, that he pastes together leaving some spaces between one another. Then he sculpts the obtained wooden mass revealing his child figures. The whole work of the artist is characterized by the soft, smooth shapes of the front of the wooden figures paired with the fragmented and unfinished shapes of the back. Gehard Demetz's most original and poetic sculptures are related to the collective memory. The artist's aim is to create for the viewer a convincing and magic confrontation with our historical past, our roots, our childhood and the people we eventually grew up with, in order to become adults.

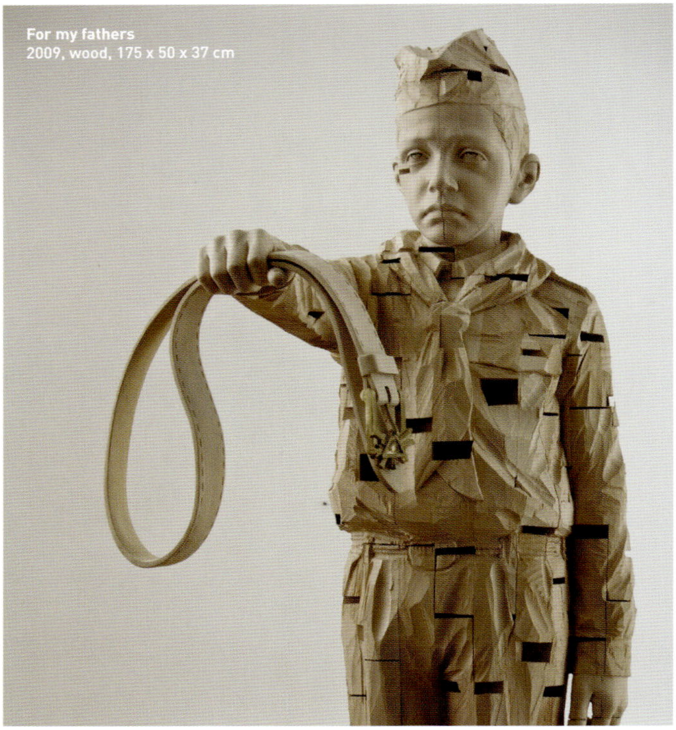

**For my fathers**
2009, wood, 175 x 50 x 37 cm

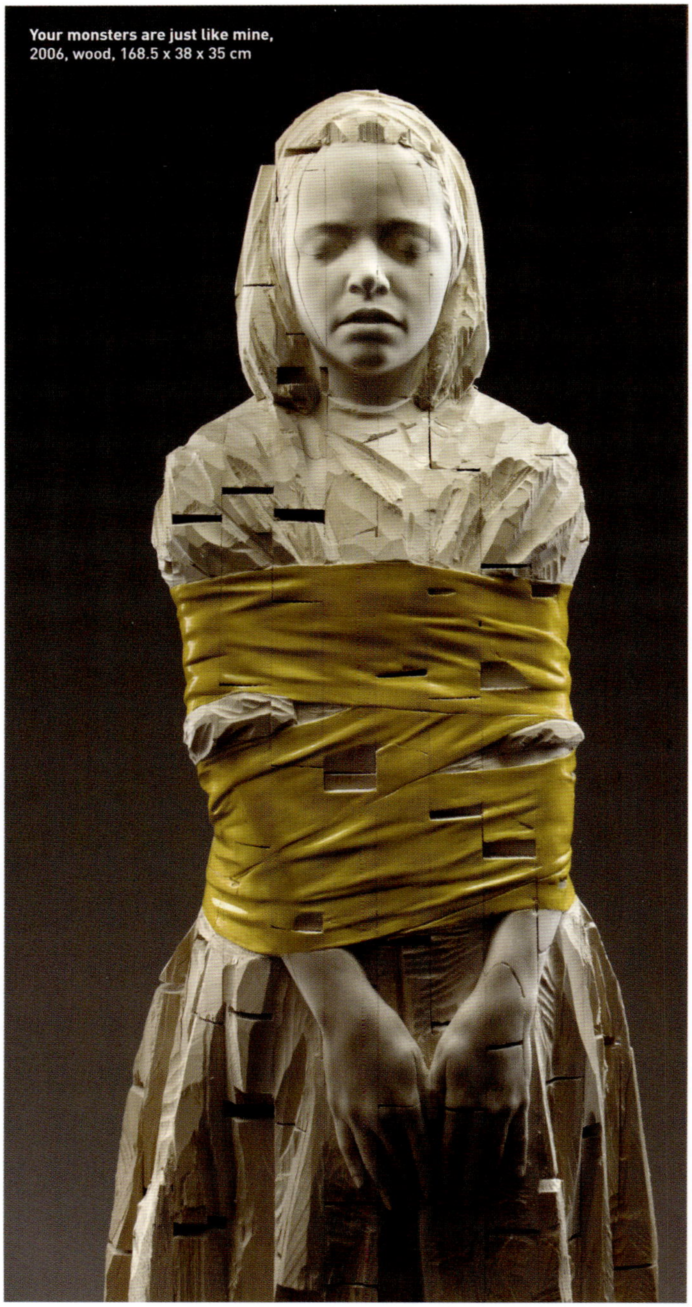

**Your monsters are just like mine,**
2006, wood, 168.5 x 38 x 35 cm

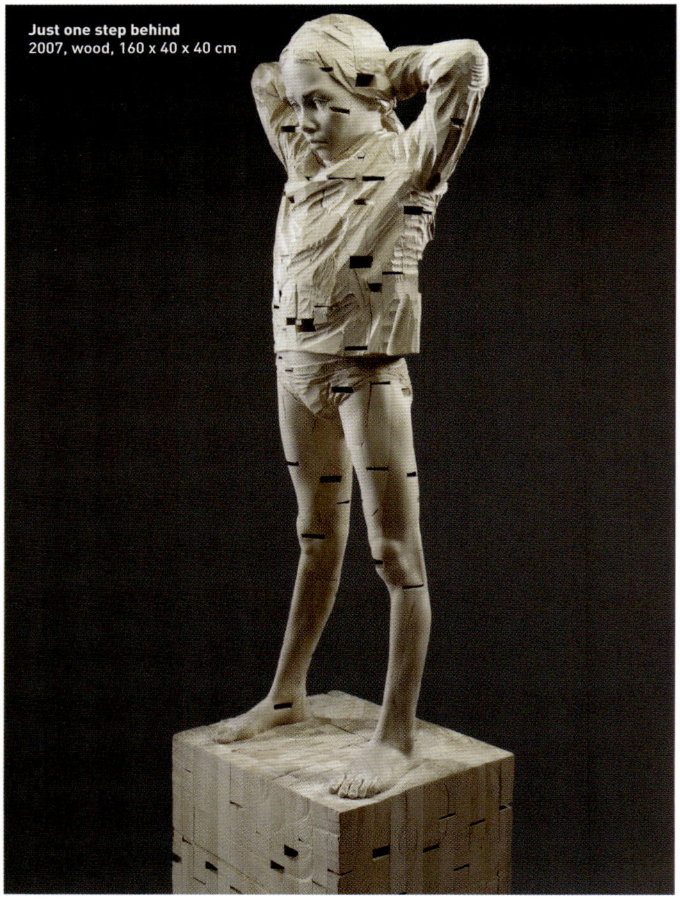

**Just one step behind**
2007, wood, 160 x 40 x 40 cm

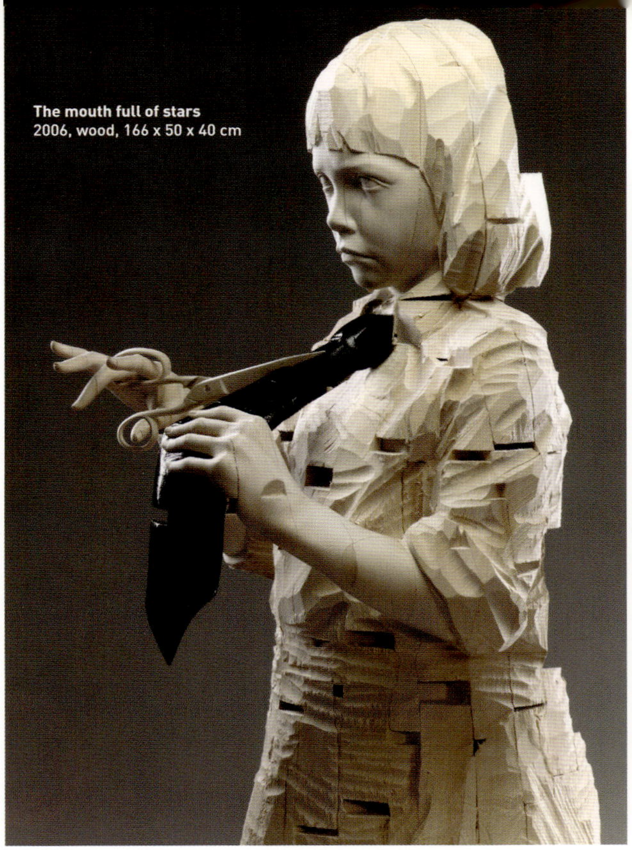

**The mouth full of stars**
2006, wood, 166 x 50 x 40 cm

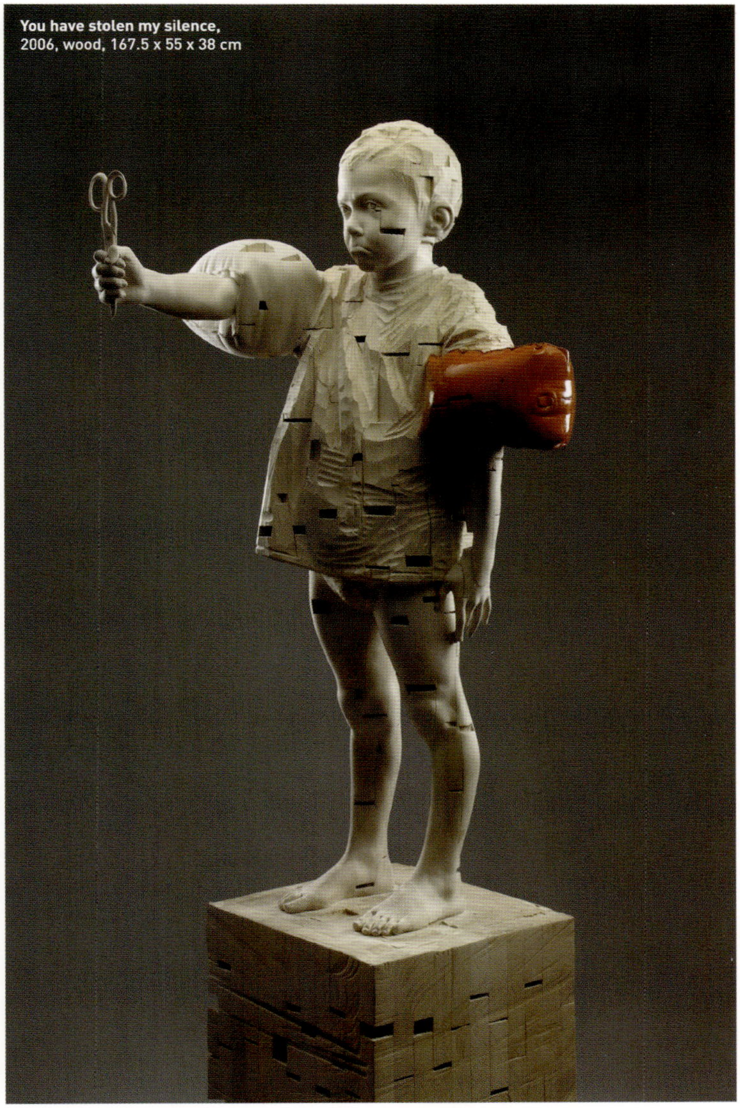

**You have stolen my silence,**
2006, wood, 167.5 x 55 x 38 cm

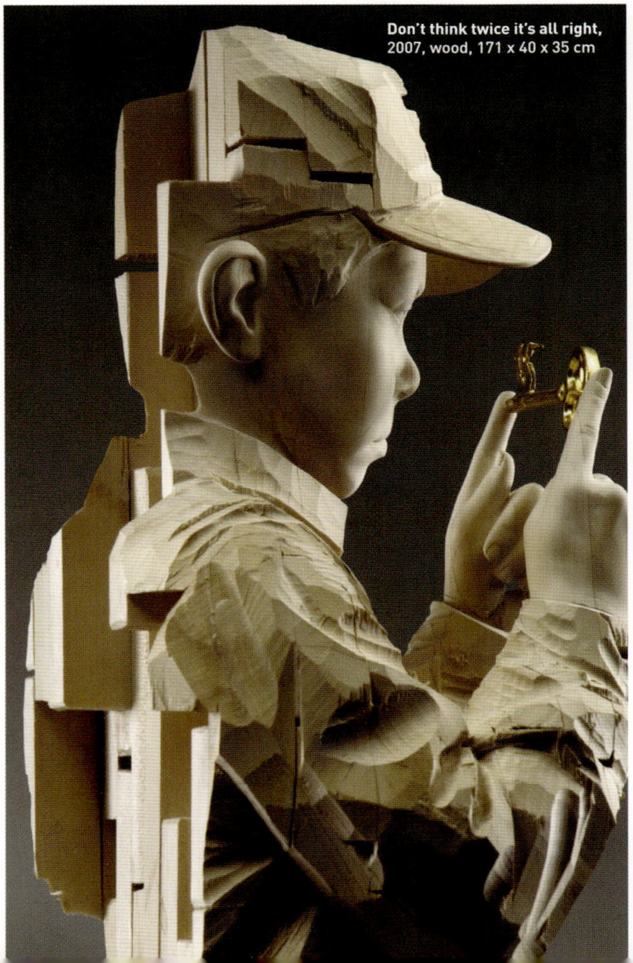

**Don't think twice it's all right,**
2007, wood, 171 x 40 x 35 cm

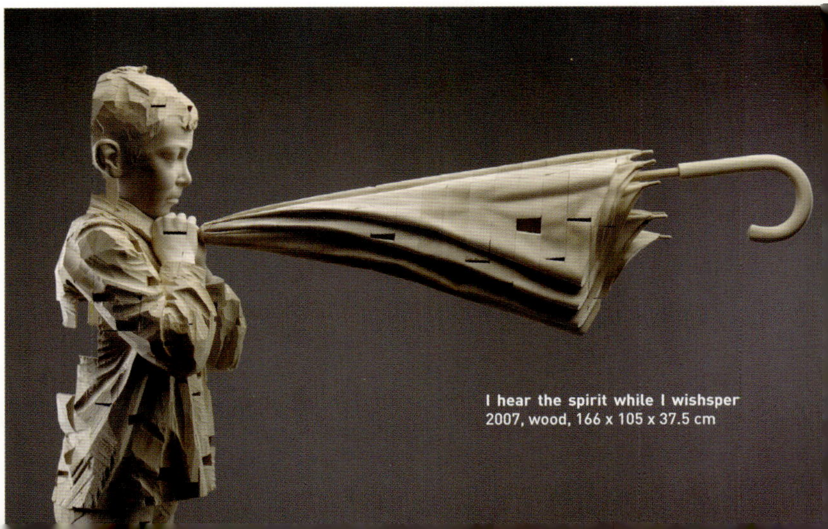

**I hear the spirit while I wishsper**
2007, wood, 166 x 105 x 37.5 cm

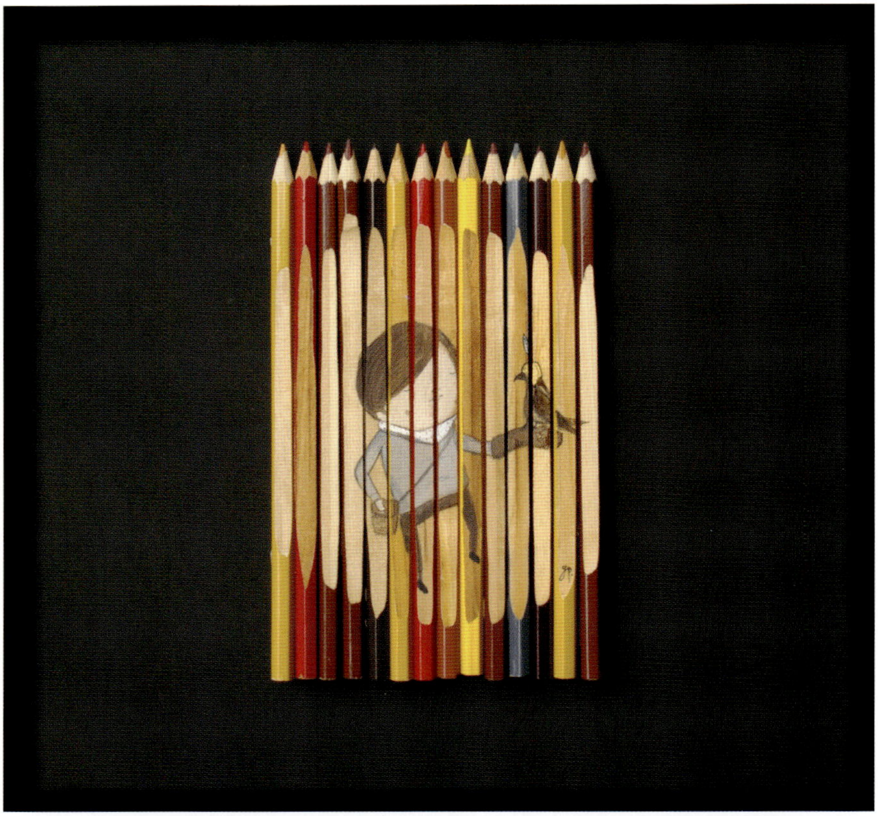

**Falconry**
12"x12"

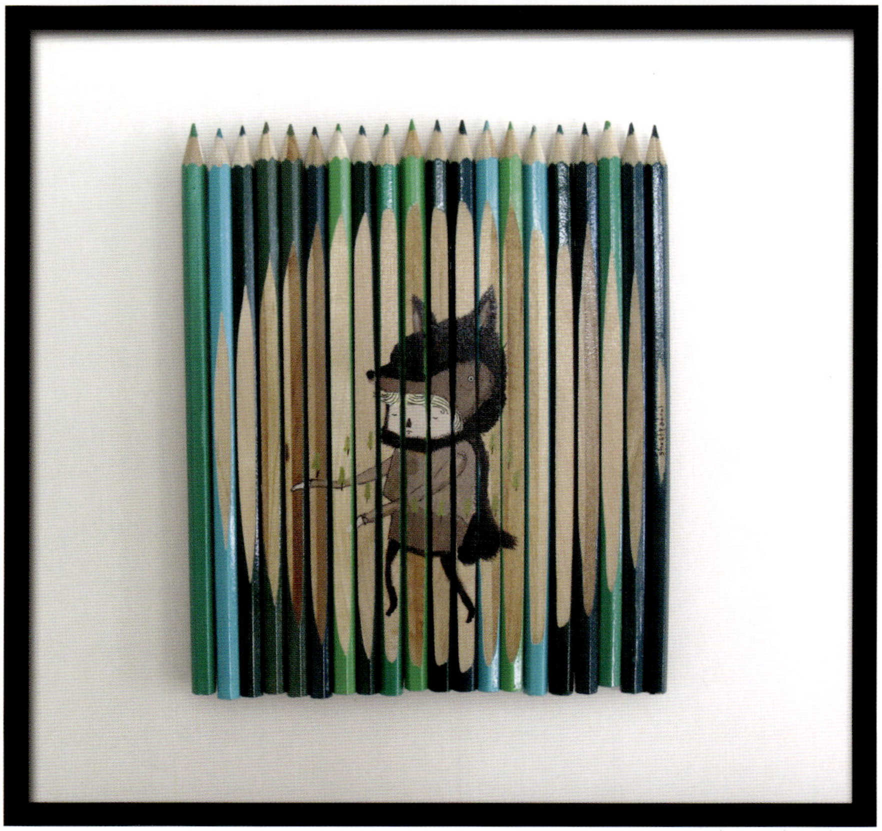

**Forest force field**
30 x 30 cm (framed)

# Ghost/Patrol

www.ghostpatrol.com

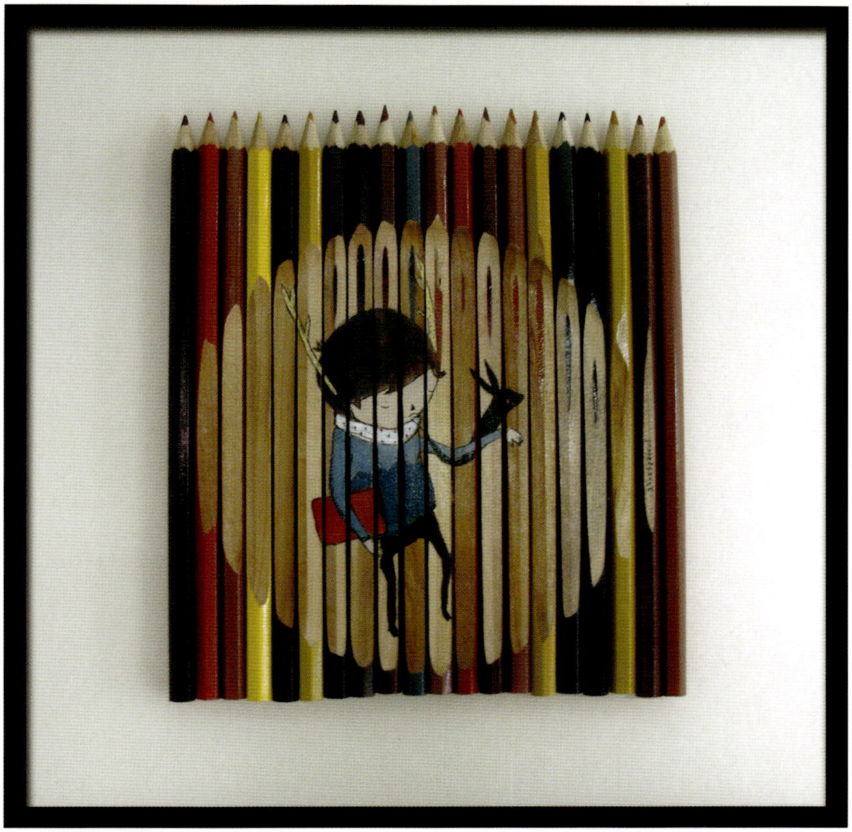

**After reading antler**
**30 x 30 cm (framed)**

Born In Hobart, Australia. Works and lives in Melbourne Australia. A self taught artist, Ghostpatrol has moved from the field of stencil art to exhibit his drawing based creations worldwide. He currently resides in Melbourne at his 'Mitten Fortress' studio. His work ranges form fine ink drawing, street-art, commissioned murals and soft sculpture. "You can't describe Ghostpatrol in one paragraph. Over a couple of years of the most regular contact I have had with any graffiti writer GP is as hard to truly understand now as on day one. Incredibly innovative and driven by creative impulses, with an infinite injection of energy, GP will always surprise. He sculpts, paints, draws and sews. GP works with whatever media he can find or afford to purchase including but not limited to spray cans, paper, pens, markers, wood, clay and so on. He has so many fingers in different creative pies he could be an octopus. He pen and ink drawings are delicate, rapidly produced and yet are meticulous in their detail and always bordering on the darker side of our nature. Conversely his large paste-ups are simple in design, but highly effective in capturing your attention.

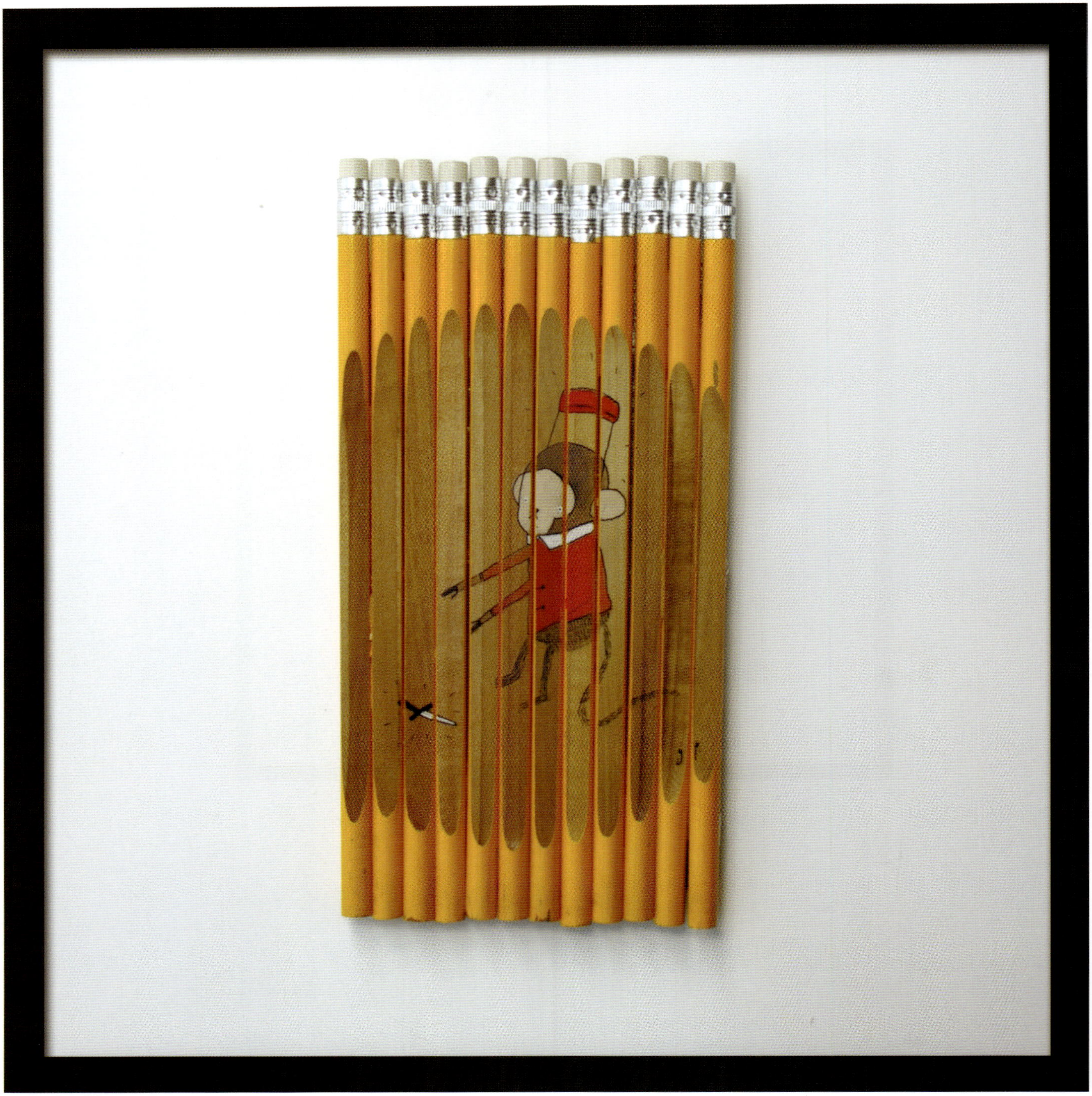

**Monkey knife fight pleasures**
12"x 12"

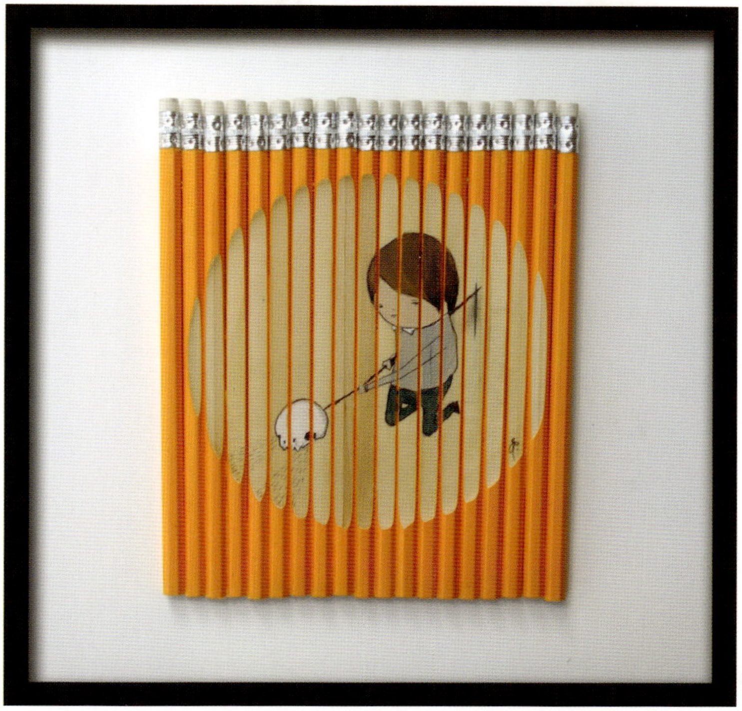

**Skeletor sprit**
12"x12"

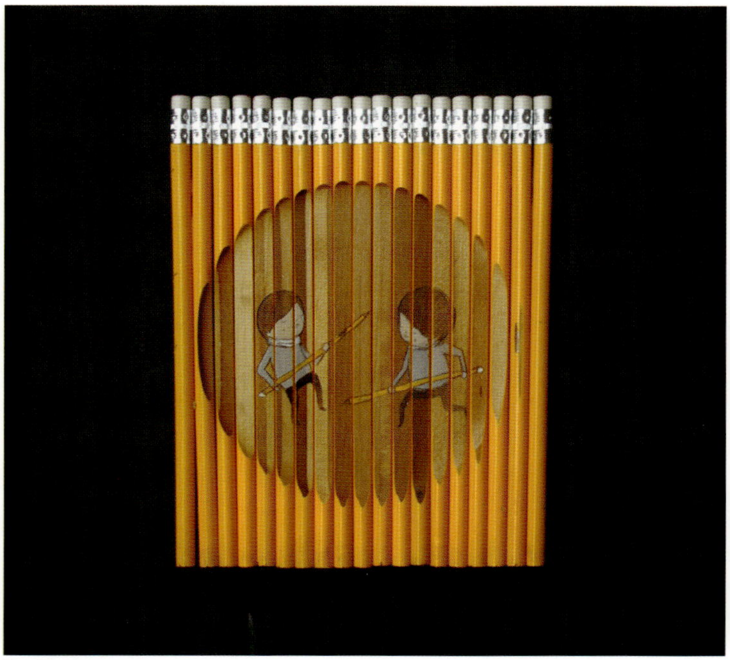

**Pencils war**
30 x 30 cm (framed)

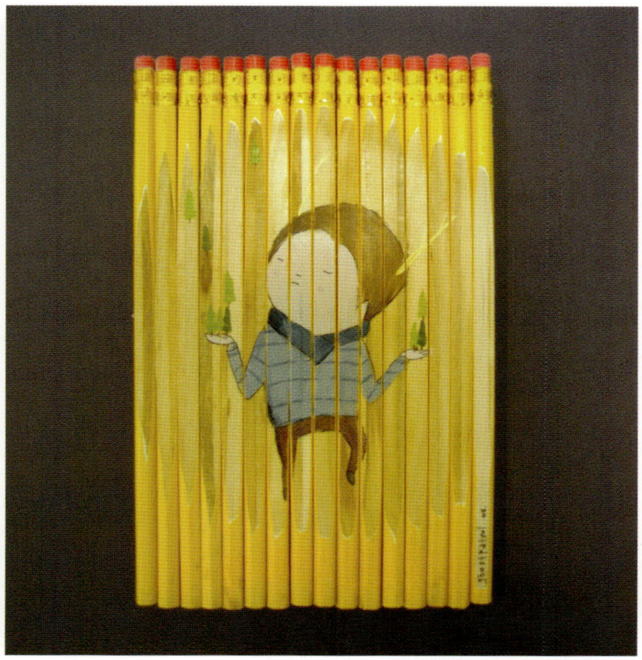

**Pencil pine; god amongst insects**
23 x 23 cm (framed)

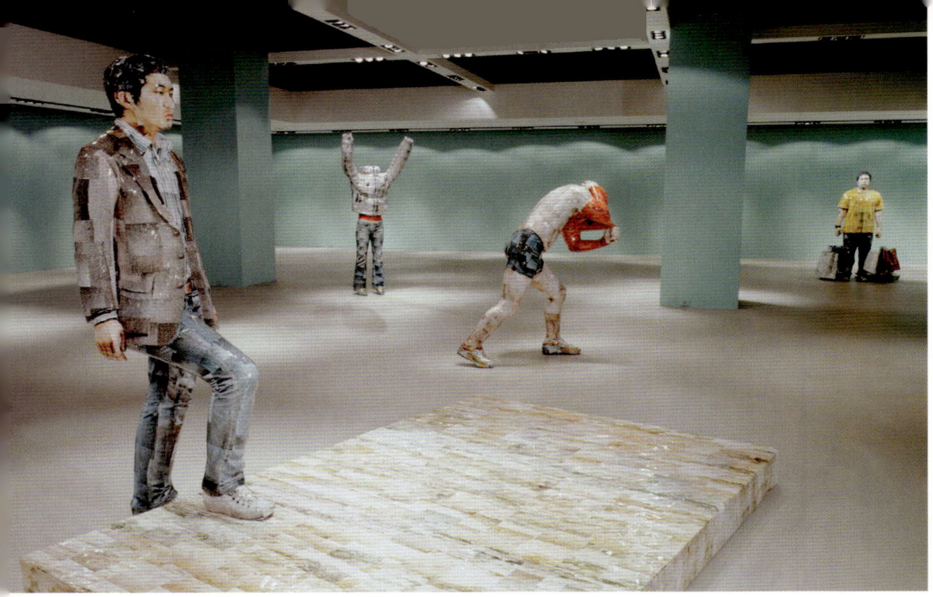

**Deodrant Type Series**
Installation view at Arario gallery
Cheon-an, Korea, 2006

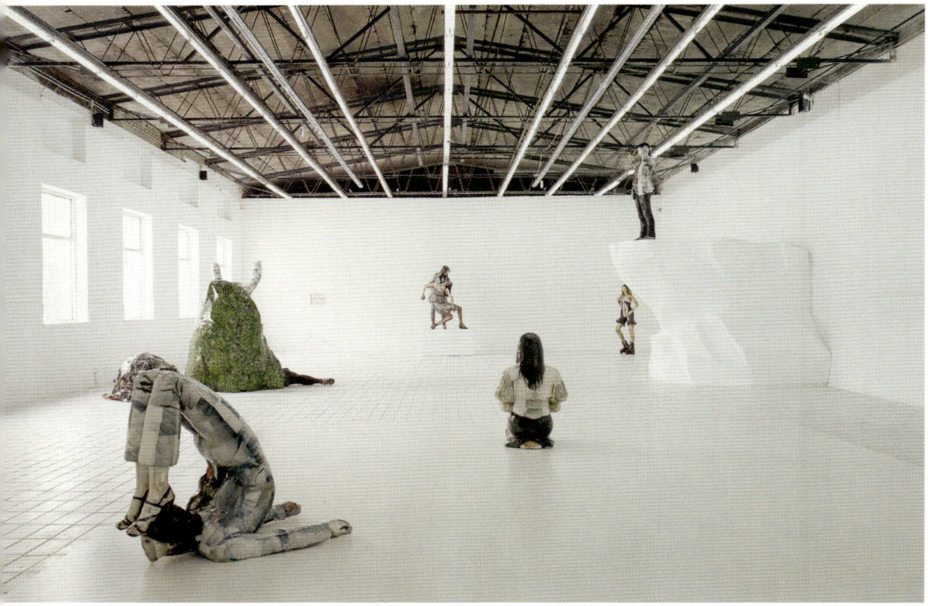

**Installation view at Arario gallery**
Beijing,China,2005

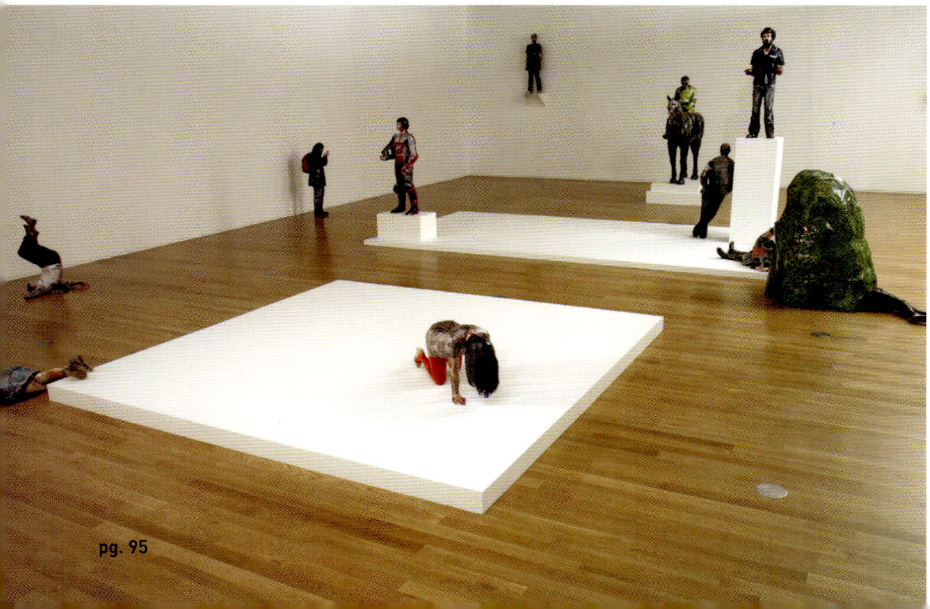

**Installation view at Manchester Art Gallery**
2008

# Gwon Osang

www.eosang.net

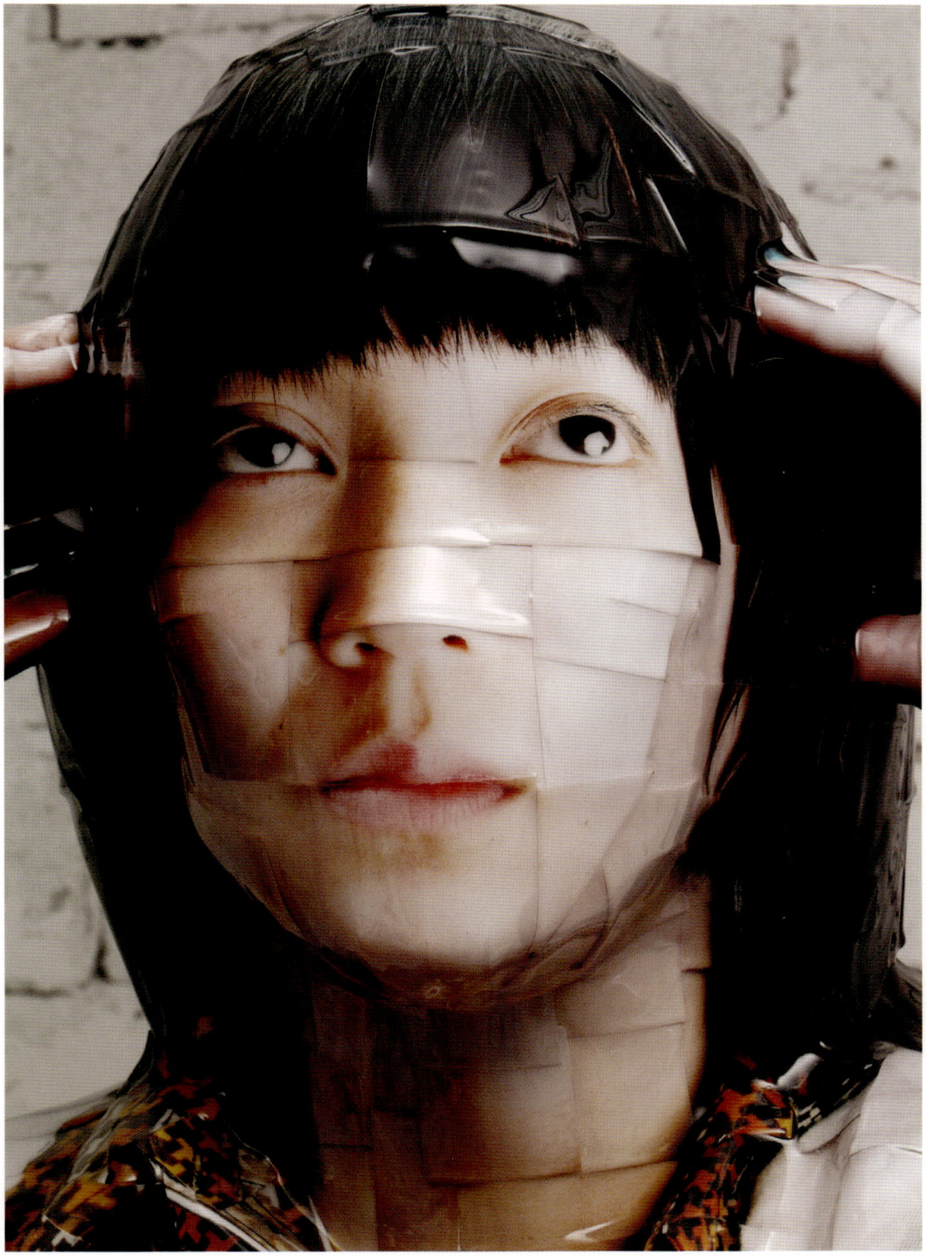

Osang Gwon (b. 1974) earned his MFA in sculpture from Hong-Ik University, Seoul (2004). He was one of the first Korean artists to achieve commercial success beyond the local Korean art scene that was once largely "second generation baby boomer" artists (those born in Korea in the early to mid 1970s).Gwon's work has been shown in solo and group exhibitions at galleries and museums throughout Asia, in addition to venues in the United Kingdom, Italy, Chile, the Netherlands, and Denmark. Osang Gwon developed and introduced his unique style of photo-sculpture while studying at Hong-Ilk University in Seoul, Korea. Called Deodorant Types, these life-size figures are pink foam shapes that have been covered with thousands of color photographs; Gwon meticulously shoots every inch of his sitter's clothing, skin and hair while also paying close attention to their facial expressions and postures. The artist primarily depicts the inhabitants of Seoul (where he continues to reside), raising issues of identity that are fundamentally tied to place. In the space of the exhibition, Deodorant Type form a peculiar landscape of vertical bodies, crouching and prostrate figures, some of which are placed directly on the floor and others atop pedestals - together they create new discourse and, as curator Eric C. Shiner states, forces us to "question the skin we are in." For Gwon's 2007 solo exhibition at the Manchester Art Gallery, he extended his practice to the United Kingdom by living, working and interacting with the residents of Manchester for a month. The resulting installation was a glossy multi-race mix of figures, some of which will be on view at Arario New York. It was around the time of this residency in Europe that Gwon was selected by the British piano rock band Keane to develop the artwork for their sophomore album, Perfect Symmetry - Gwon began by creating each band member as a Deodorant Type. This commission is one of the artist's most visible projects thus far.

**Control**
C-print, mixed media
77x74x43cm, 2007

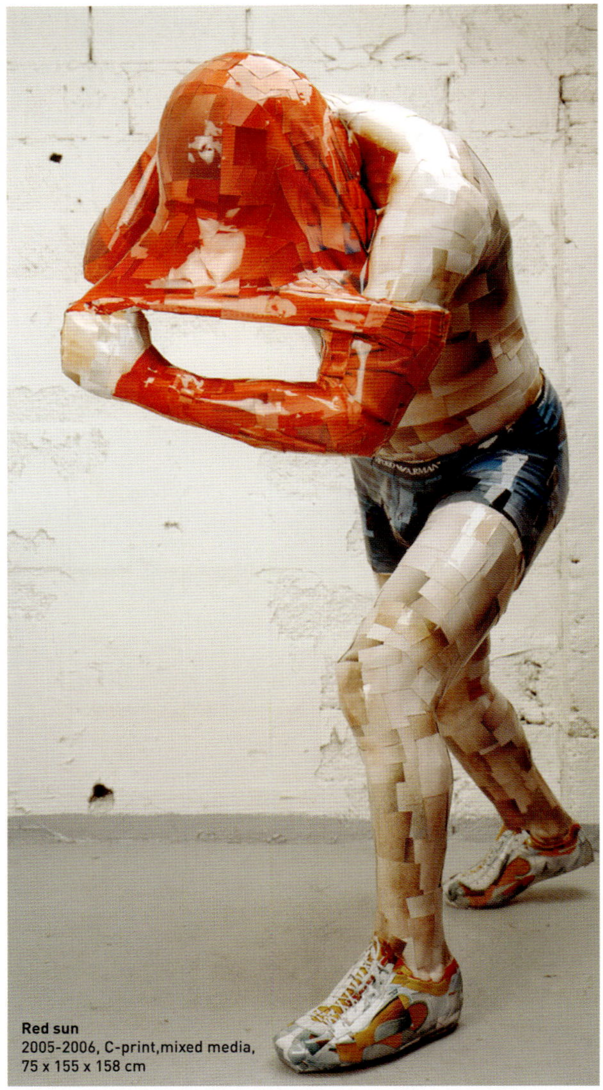

**Red sun**
2005-2006, C-print,mixed media,
75 x 155 x 158 cm

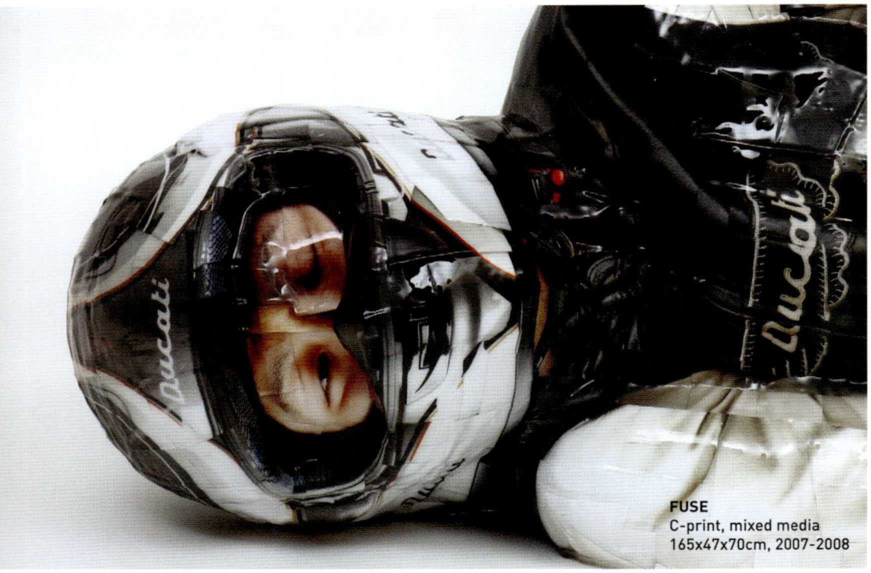


**FUSE**
C-print, mixed media
165x47x70cm, 2007-2008

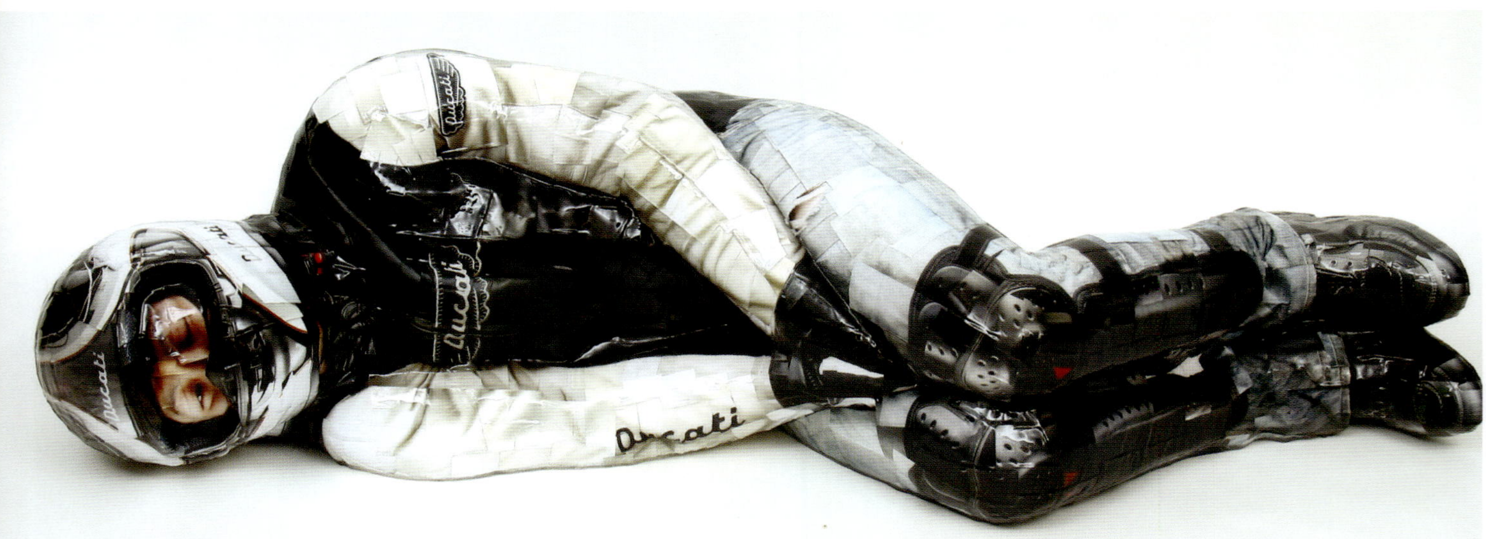

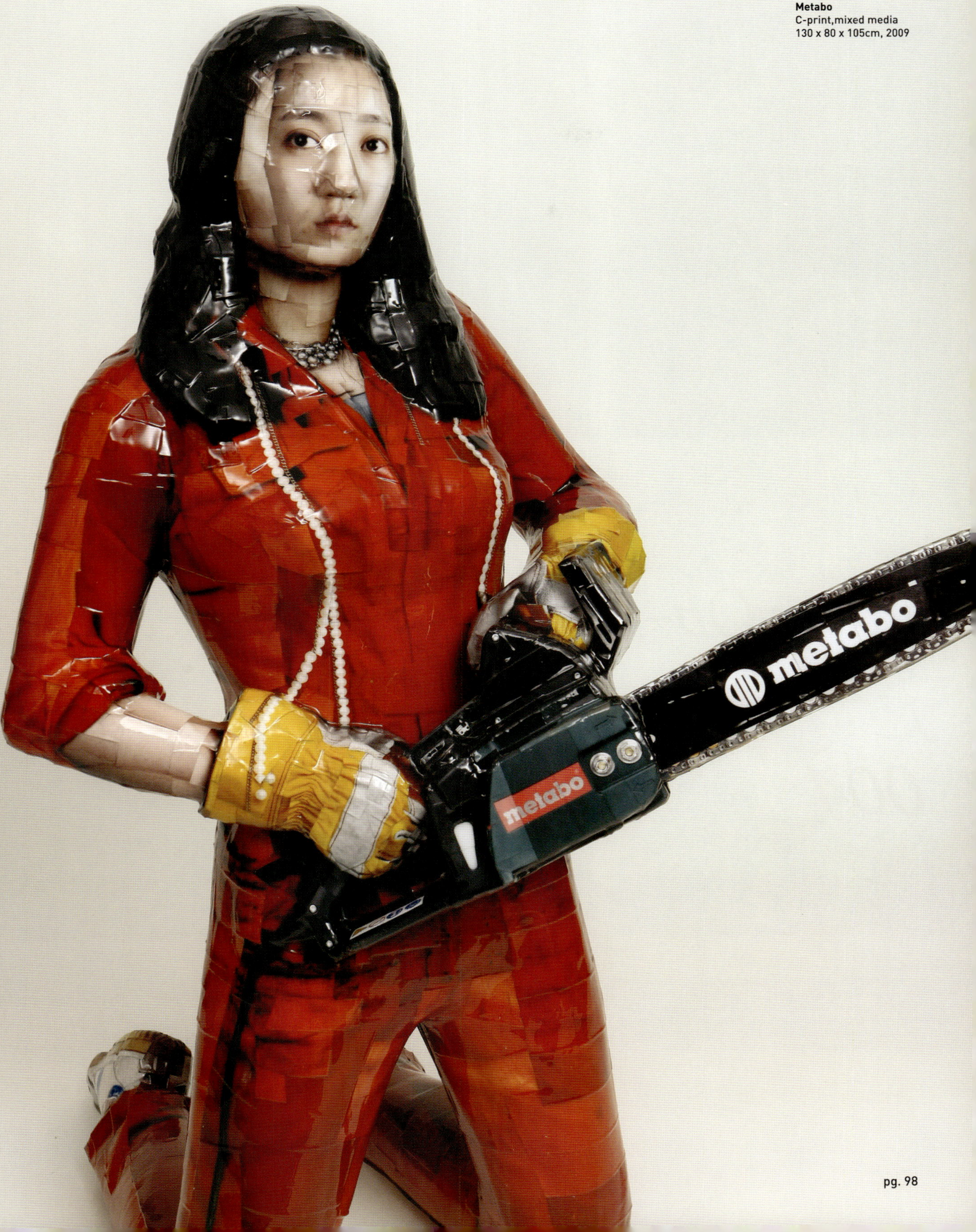


**Metabo**
C-print,mixed media
130 x 80 x 105cm, 2009

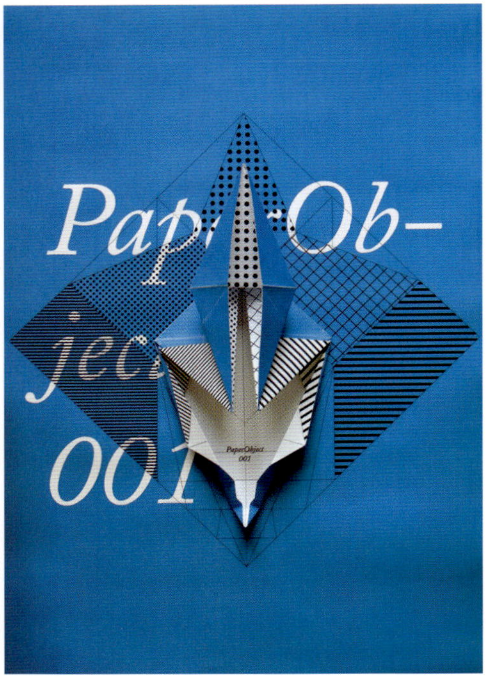

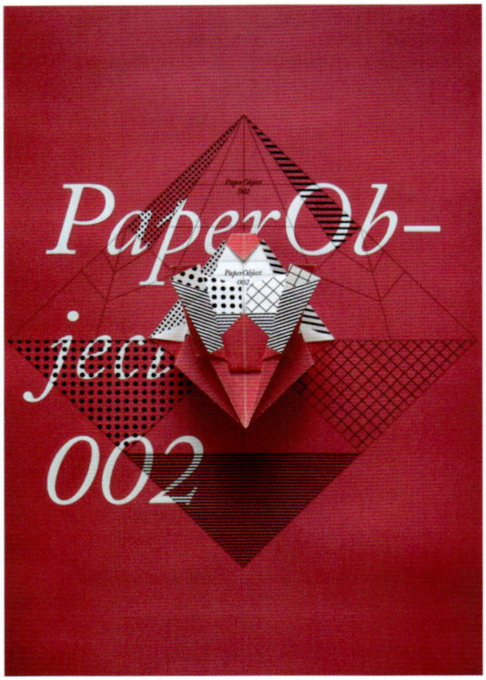

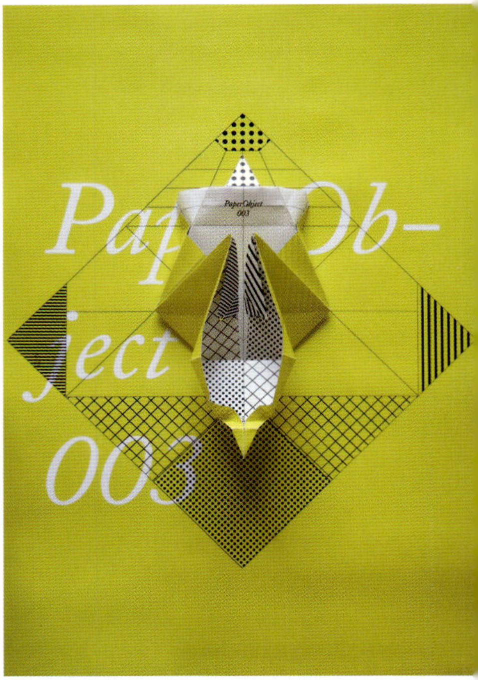

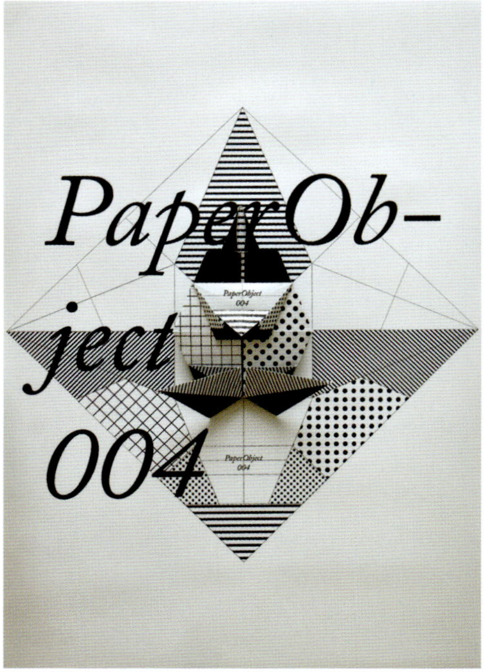

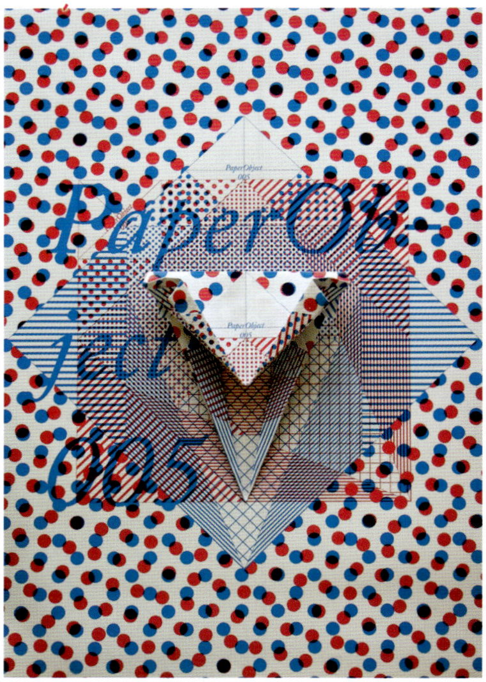

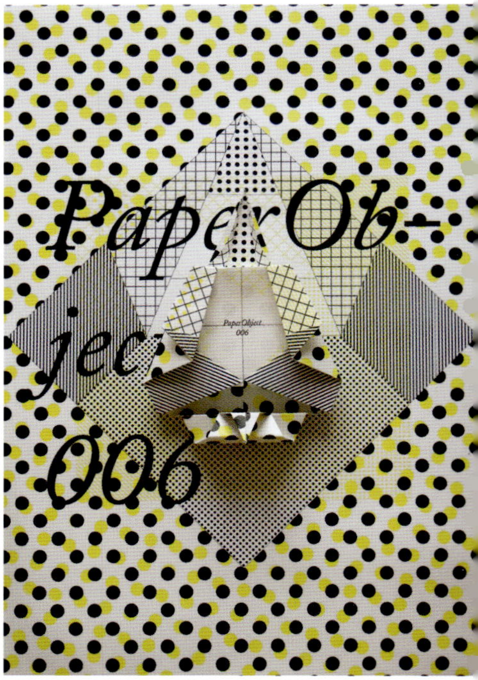


**Paper Objects**
This is a selfpromotional project. We really like the crafting feeling, the paper surfaces and the mix of the process ink. We love the culture of origami and with this project we personally tried to reinterpret the forms that arise from the paper. These are abstract forms and in the background you can see their structure. The light coming through the window and so it is a natural light, a daylight.

# Happy/Centro

www.happycentro.it

The study began in 1998, our city is Verona, the romantic city of Romeo and Juliet. In recent years we have worked with clients large and small, for local agencies and major international companies. Our approach to design is always the same: design a logo, an advertising page, a wall or direct a commercial is the same opportunity to deal with a problem. We have become quite good at solving problems. Mix complexity, order and fatigue is our formula for beauty. Always, in addition to the commissioned work, we spend plenty of energy in research and testing. Visual art, typography, graphic design, illustration, animation, film direction and music. We like contamination between creative disciplines and diversity in general. We do not like to redo twice what we are already able to do. It is tiring but satisfied. Happycentro are: Giuliano Garonzi, Roberto Solieri, Federico Galvani, Giulio Grigollo, Andrea Manzati and their photographer friend Federico Padovani.

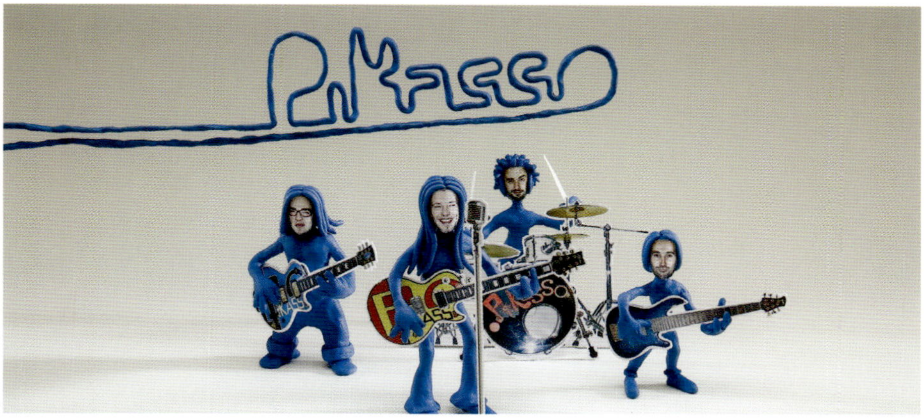

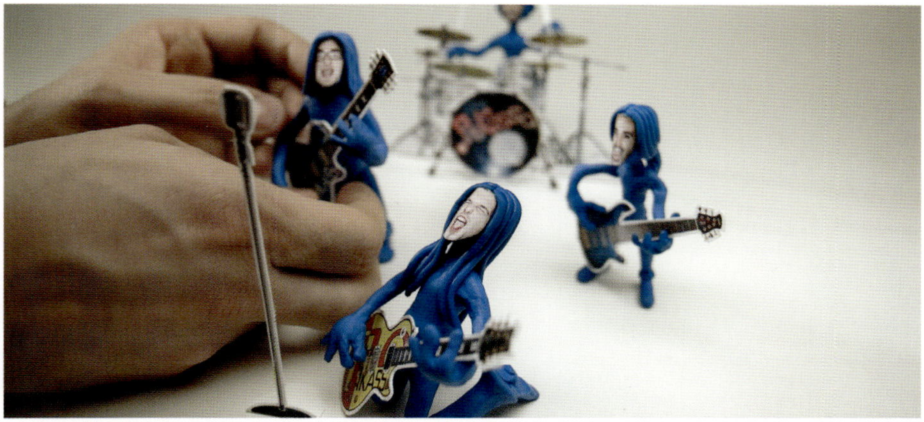

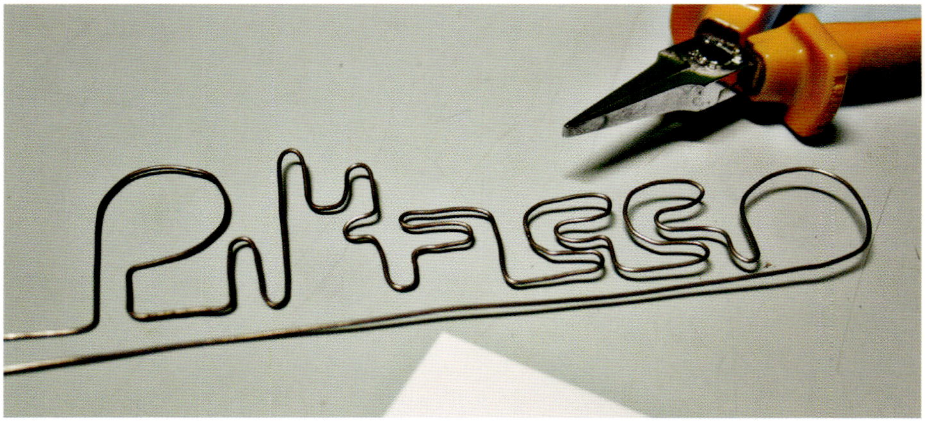

**Pikasso Pikalbum**
We designed the cover of the debut disc of this band of independent music from Rovereto. As always the music inspires us to produce artworks and this was one of those great moments when we feel artists seduced by the notes of other artists like us. We have chosen the clay material to construct the logo of theband and to create all the members on which we then stuck their faces printed.

**Photos by Federico Padovani.**

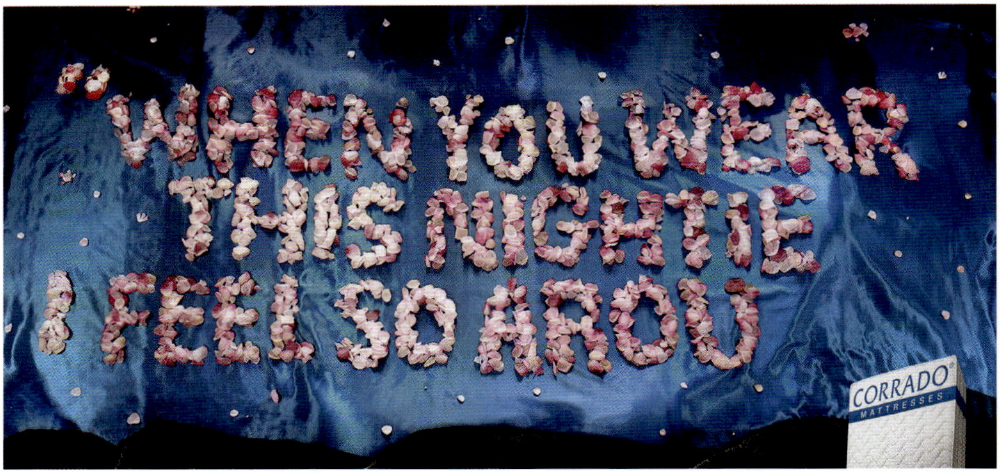


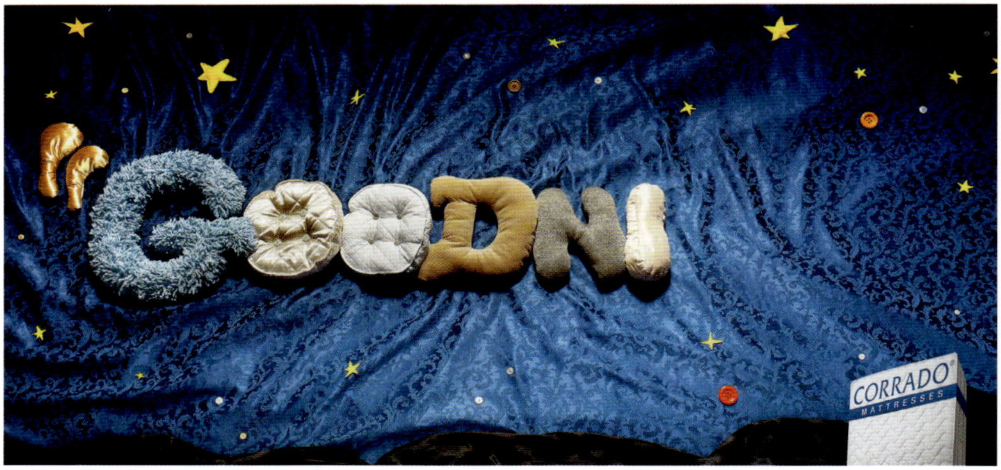


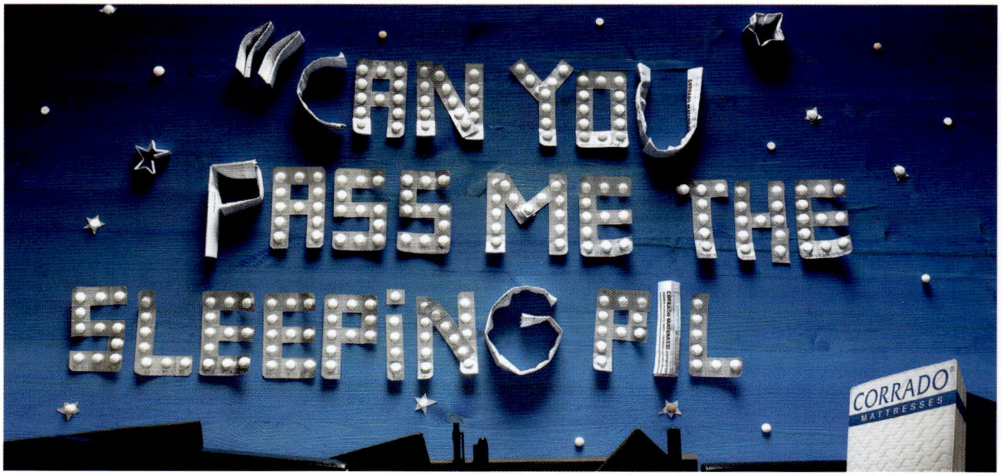


**Corrado Mattresses Sudden Sleep**
The goal of the campaign is to describe how irresistable the Corrado mattresses are. Once we lay down we don't even have the time to utter an entire frase before Morfeus gets the upper hand on us. We only have few days left to the deadline but we decide to continue developing all the layouts that will be carried out without any use of computer graphics what so ever. We want to work with objects, material and photography. This is the way that we have definited with Saatchi&Saatchi Milan.

Client: Corrado Mattresses
Advertising Agency: Saatchi&Saatchi, Milan, Italy
Creative Directors: Guido Cornara, Agostino Toscana
Deputy Creative Directors: Luca Pannese, Luca Lorenzini
Art Director: Luca Pannese
Copywriter: Luca Lorenzini
Art buyer: Rossana Coruzzi
Designer: Federico Galvani – Happycentro
Typographer: Andrea Manzati – Happycentro
Pillow Designer: Annamaria Gastaldelli
Photographer: Federico Padovani
Digital Artist: Marco Oliosi

ike Produit en Italie

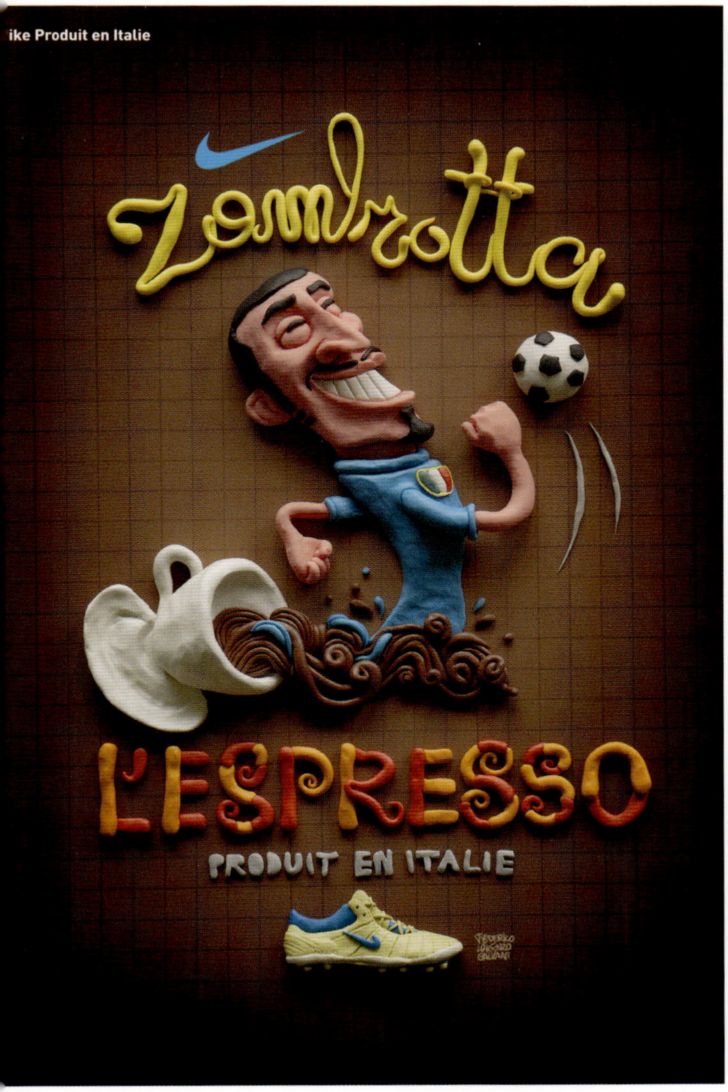


dits: Agency Wieden+Kennedy Amsterdam / CD Alvaro Sotomayor / AD Anders Stake / CW
lo Cavallone / Illustrators Federico Galvani, Giuliano Garonzi / Producer Andrew Koningen.

Nuovi Cedrini

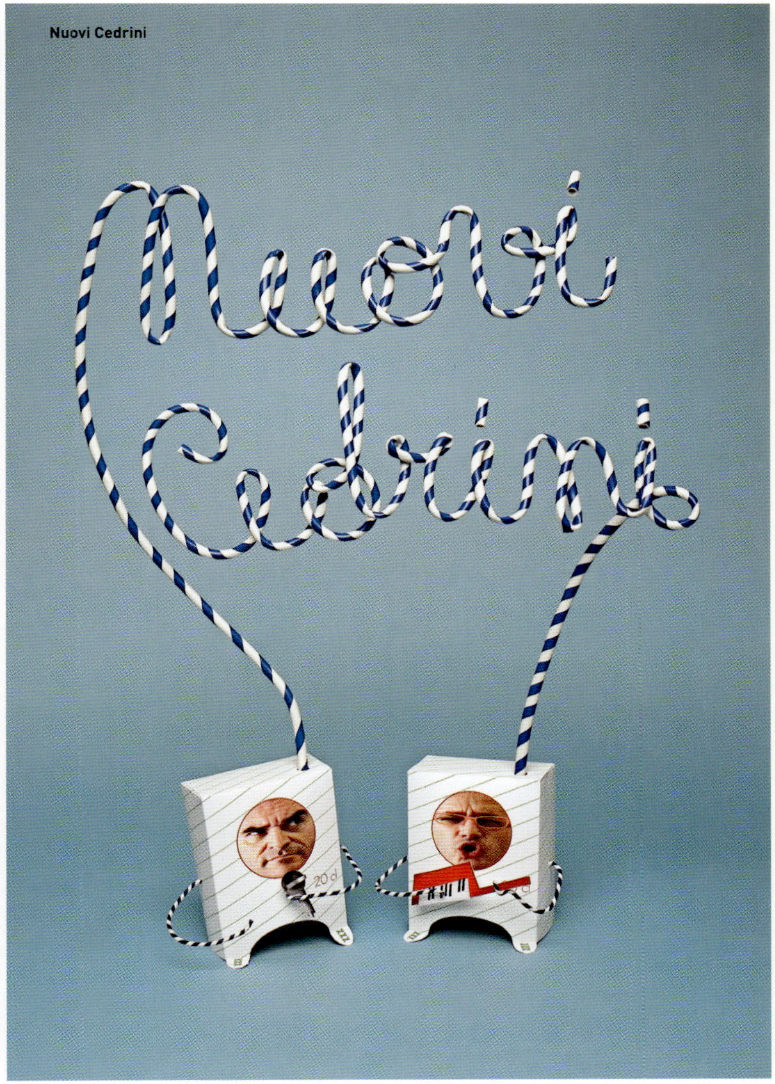


We designed a poster for a band called Nuovi Cedrini. "Nuovi Cedrini" sounds like "New Citrons" so we decided to redesign their logo and their silhouettes as lemon juice brick. Their music is really crazy. Now their look too! All the photo are made by Federico Padovani. It was a collective project in collaboration with the illustrator Andrea Rania for Scalacolore (Scalacolore is a Design Community based in Verona - Italy).

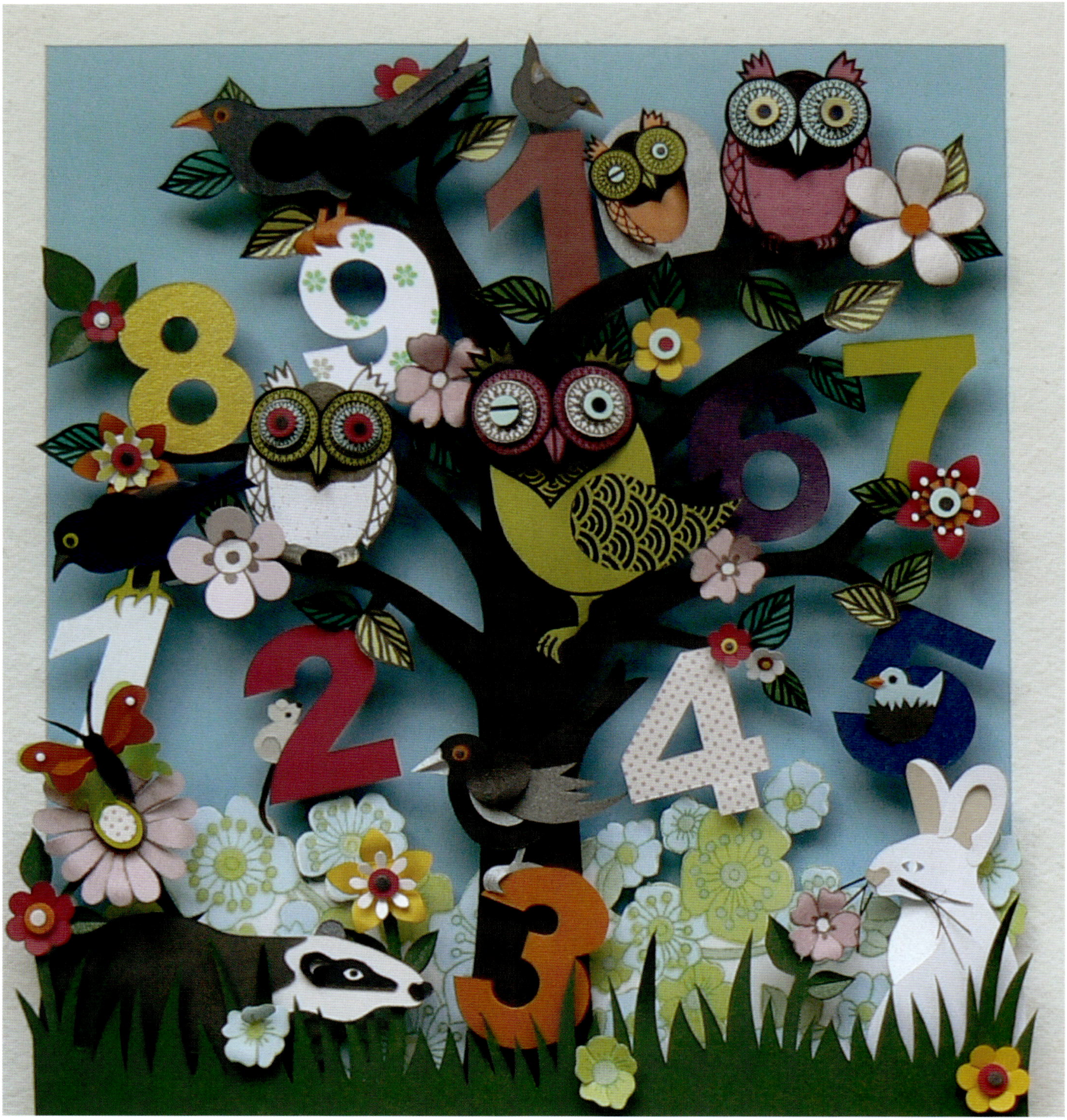

**The Number Tree**
Paper sculpture 240mm x 220mm
Creative Review 2009

# Helen Musselwhite

www.helenmusselwhite.com

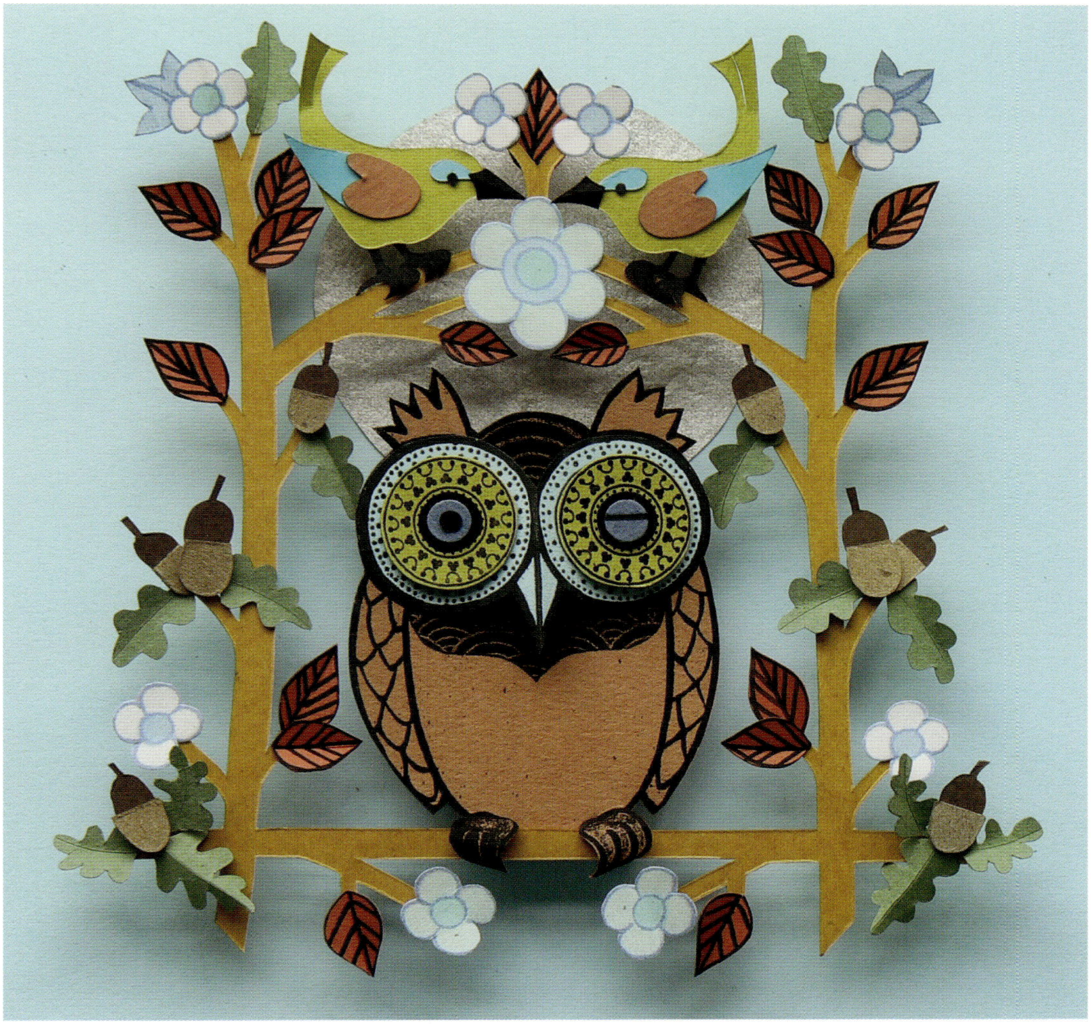

**Apple Owl Tree**
**Framed paper sculpture 255mm x 45mm**
**Private commission 2009**

By the use of bold colour, strong graphic line and familiar images I create highly individual and visually appealing pieces of art that make an instant impact. My work has a distinctive hand crafted quality that pays respect to all forms of mid century design, folk and ethnic art, as well as current and future trends. Each piece combines the hand cutting, folding and scoring of a wide range of papers and card that are further worked on to create patterned and textured surfaces. They are then used to build scenes in box frames which are often complex and consist of many layers. This process means that each item of work is truly individual with no two pieces the same. Influenced by the natural world each piece is manipulated to become an intriguing place, a glimpse into another world of fiction and fairytale. Every piece of work is handmade in my studio in the North West of the U.K.

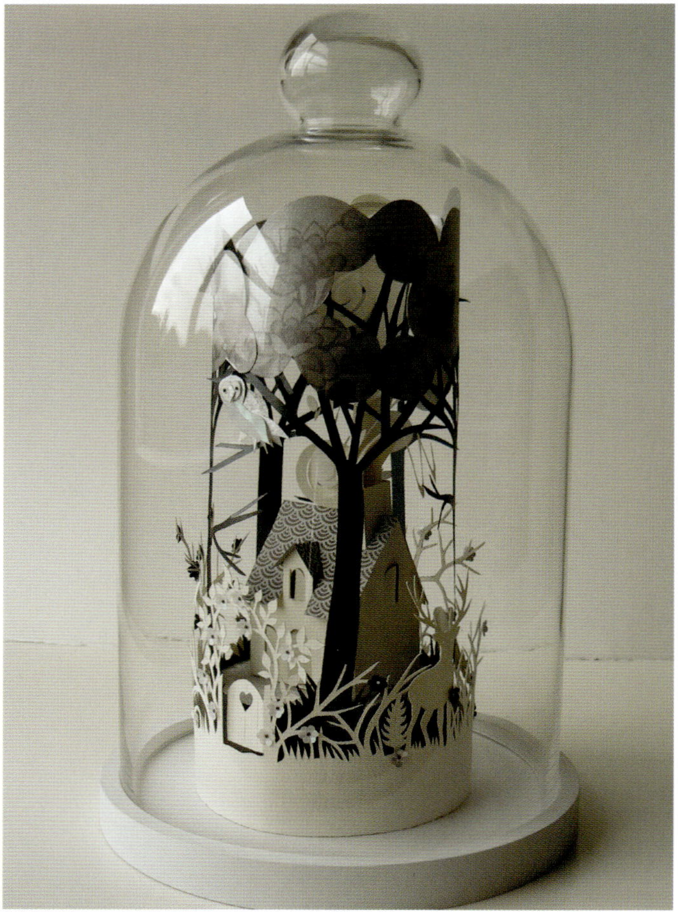

**Beauties Cottage**
Paper sculpture in glass bell Jar 440mm x 250mm
2009

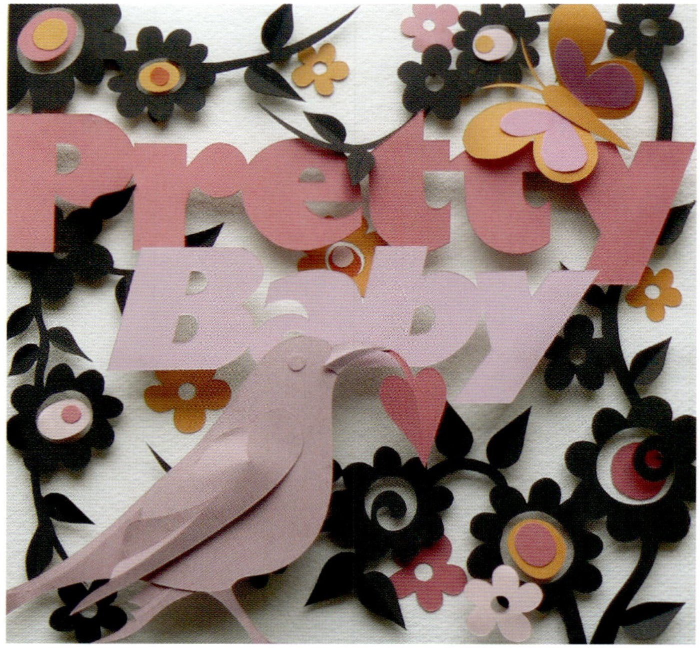


**Pretty Baby**
Framed paper sculpture 255mm x 45mm
2008

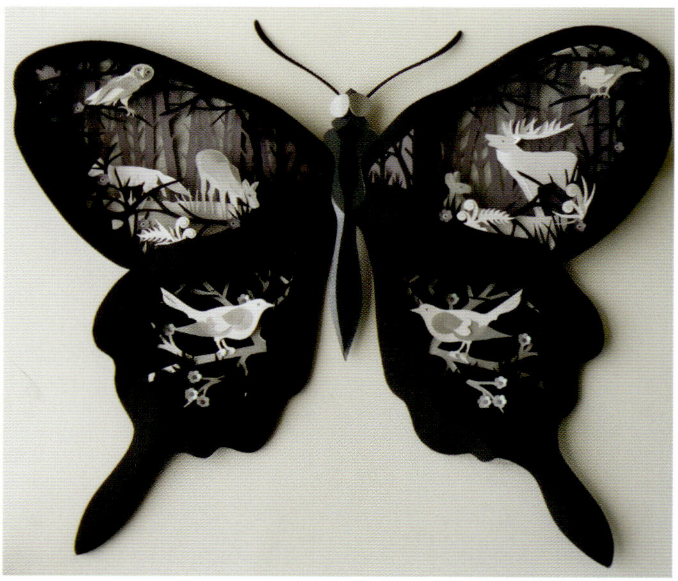

**Beauties Butterfly**
Framed paper sculpture 500mmsq x 45mm
2009

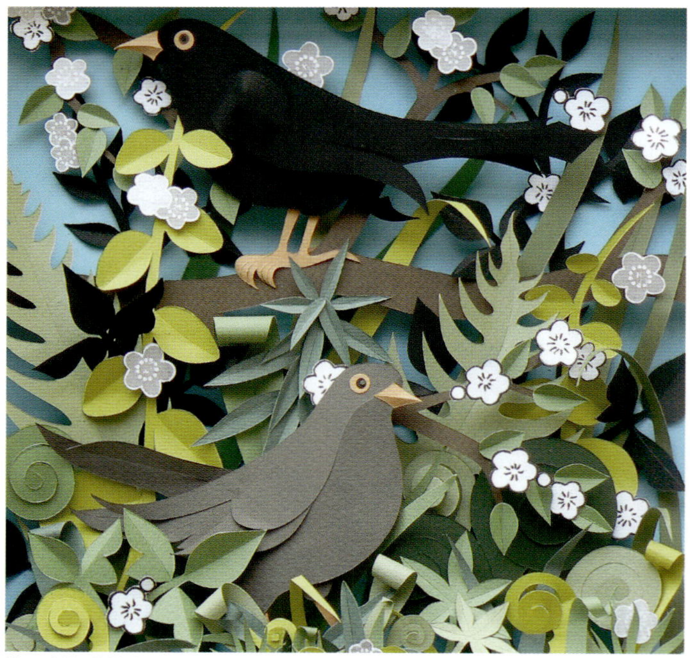

**Mr and Mrs B Bird**
Framed paper sculpture 255mmsq x 45mm
Private commission 2009

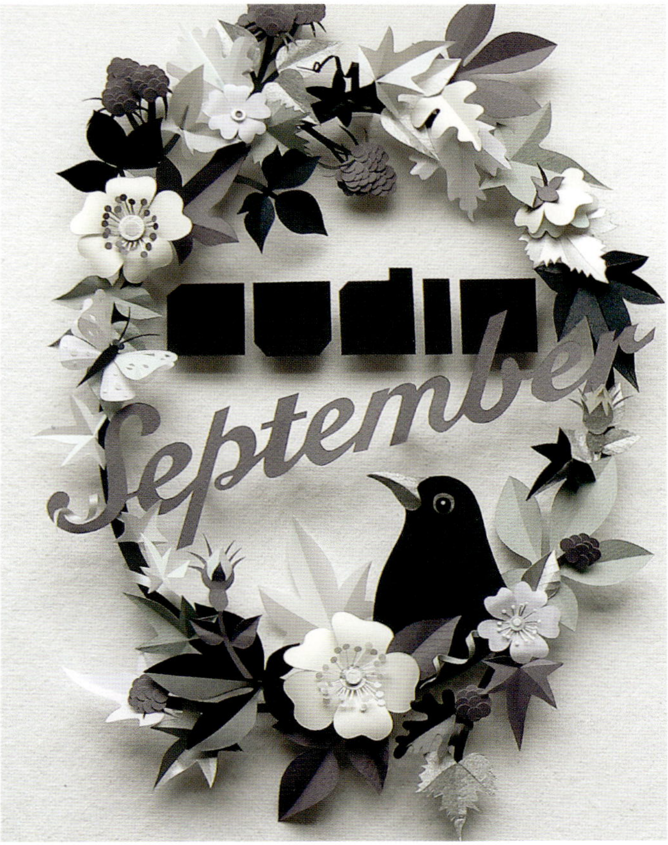


**September**
Paper sculpture 420mmx 290mm x 50mm
Audio Brighton 2009

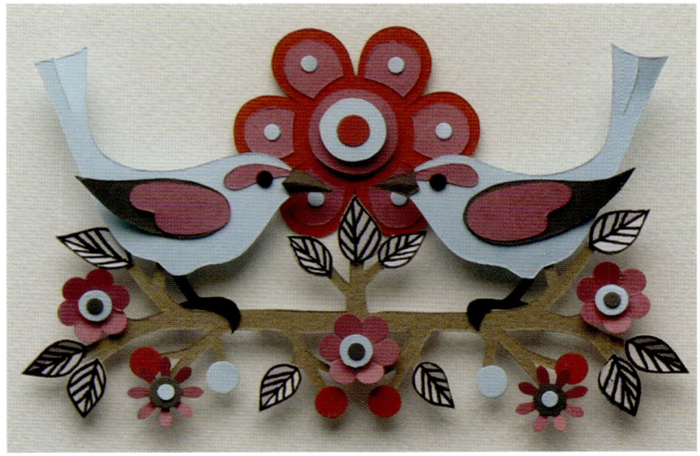

**Bluebirds**
Framed paper sculpture 200mm x 20mm
Private commission 2009

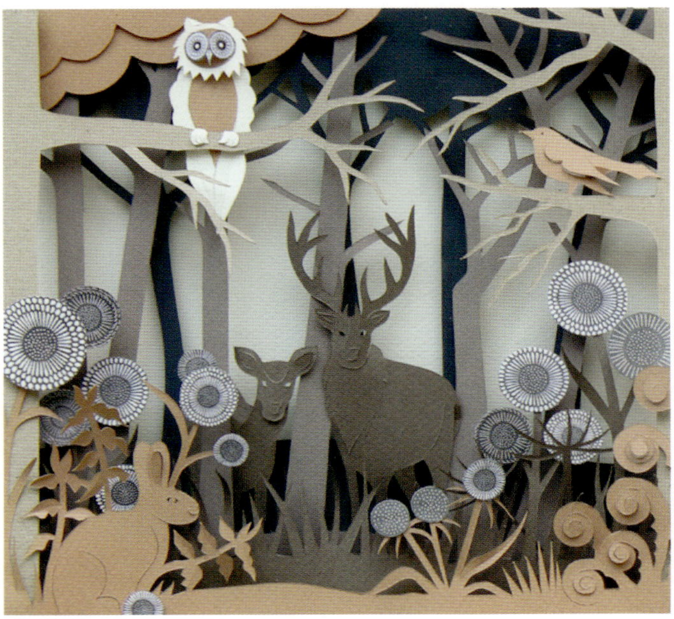

**Autumn Wood**
Framed paper sculpture 255mmsq x 45mm
Private commission 2009

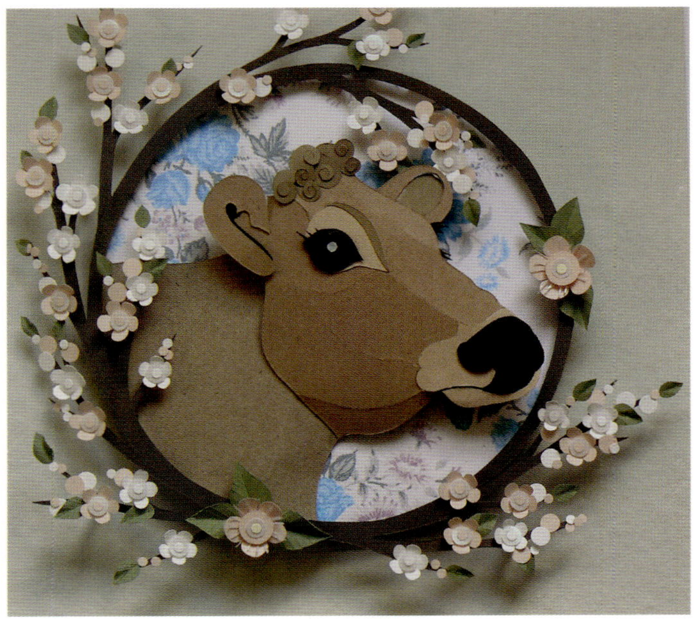

**Blossom**
Framed paper sculpture 255mmsq x 45mm
2009

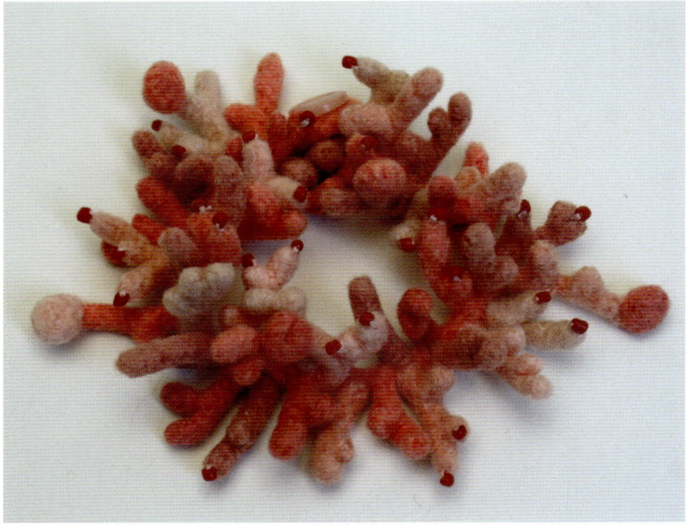

**Coral Bracelet**, 2008.
Preloved tapestry wool. 12cm

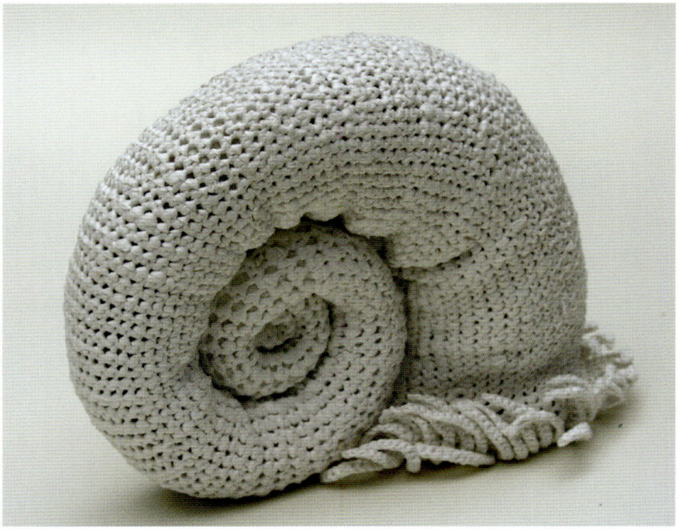

**Cephalopod**, 2007.
Discarded Plastic Bags. 25x25x8cm.

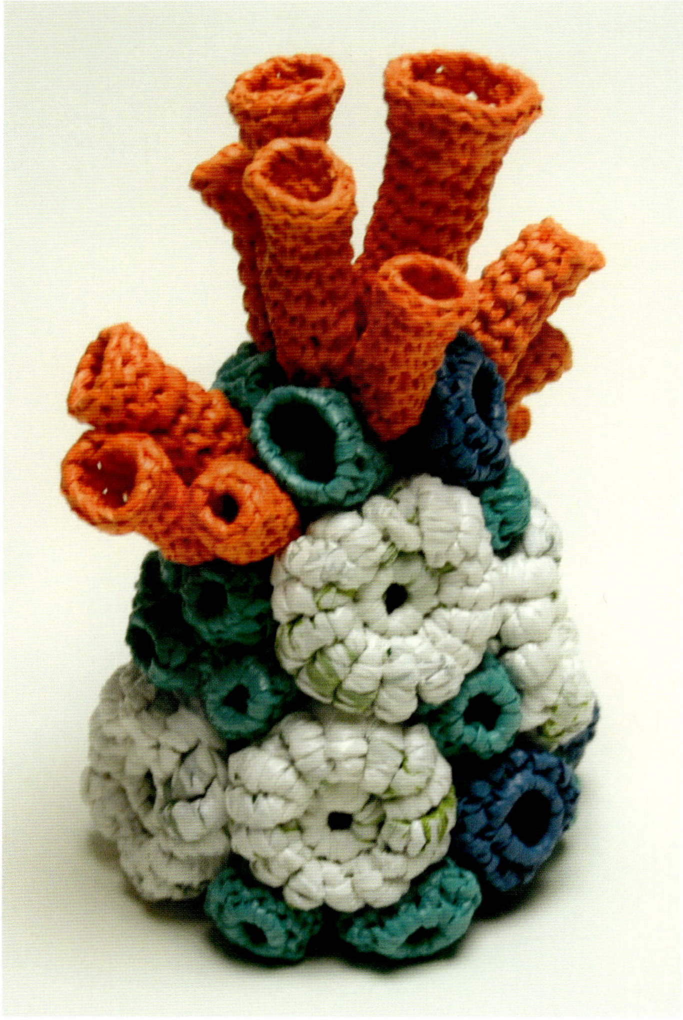

**Infant Barnacle Garden**, 2008.
Discarded Plastic Bags. 14 x 10 x 9cm.

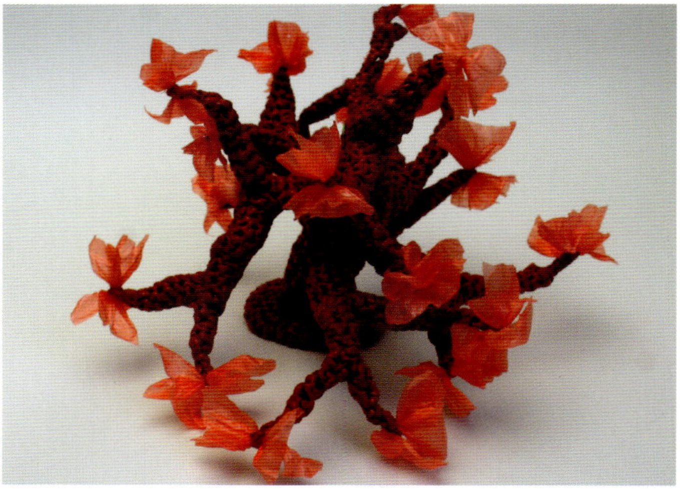

**Gorgonia, 2008.**
Discarded Plastic Bags. 16 x 23 x 20cm.

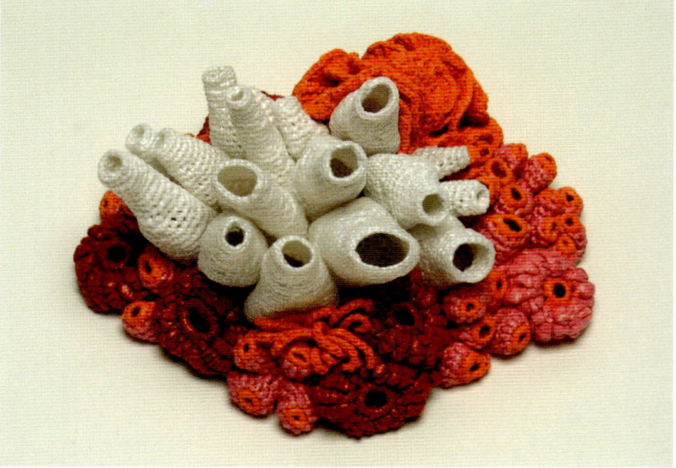

**Barnacle Garden**, 2008.
Discarded Plastic Bags. 10 x 21 x 17cm

# Helle Jorgensen

www.hellejorgensen.typepad.com

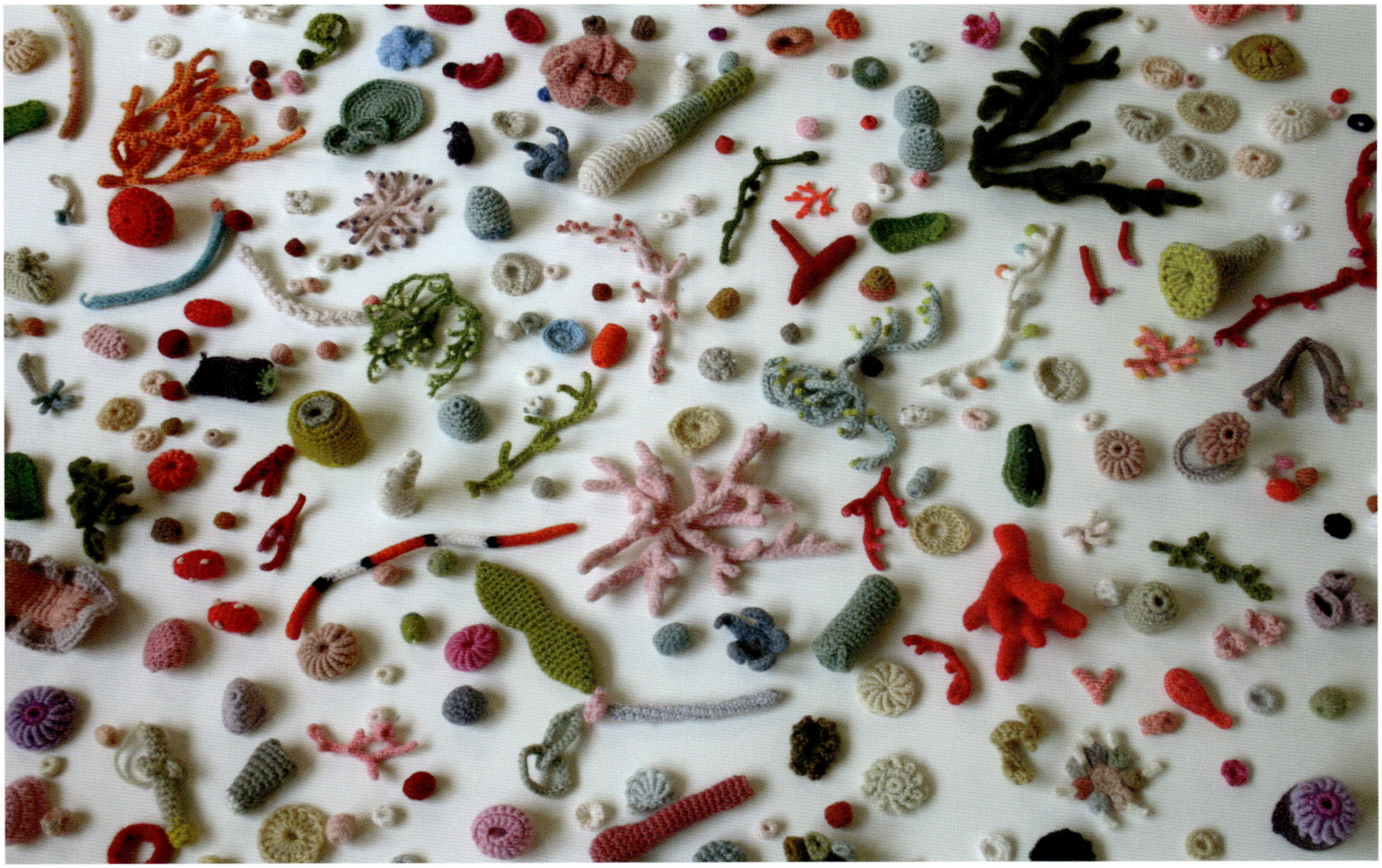

**Crochet Experiment**

My art is inspired by an evolving fascination with the natural world. This deep engagement has marked each of the three phases of my working life. Before becoming an artist, I completed a degree in biology and worked in research. Later, I trained in horticulture and worked in garden design while going on to study drawing and print making. By rediscovering free-form crochet as a sculptural technique, I am able to explore and express the mathematical basis of natural forms. Free-form crochet can mimic the mathematical process by which nature creates itself. Natural forms such as corals grow using mathematical principles such as hyperbolic geometry and the Fibonacci sequence. Scientific illustrations such as those of Ernst Haeckel frequently depict particularly elegant examples of the mathematical basis of natural forms and provide some inspiration for my crochet sea creatures and coral gardens. My choice of techniques and materials has an embedded message on two levels: the use of plastic yarn and the re-invention of the tradition of crochet. Plastic bags are notorious polluters, and recycling them into the yarn that forms the raw material for my art is an active response to climate change and pollution. Traditionally, crochet was a formulaic skill restricted to the domestic sphere, but by rediscovering this technique, I connect my art with the nurturing handiwork of generations of women.

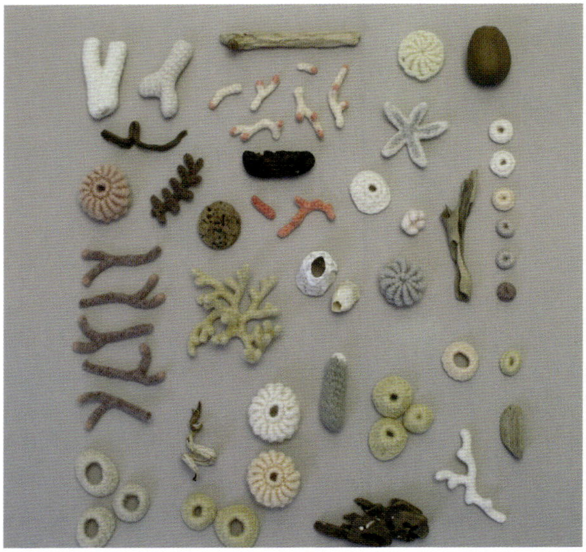

**Beach Collection I**, 2009.
Preloved tapestry wool. 37x32x3cm

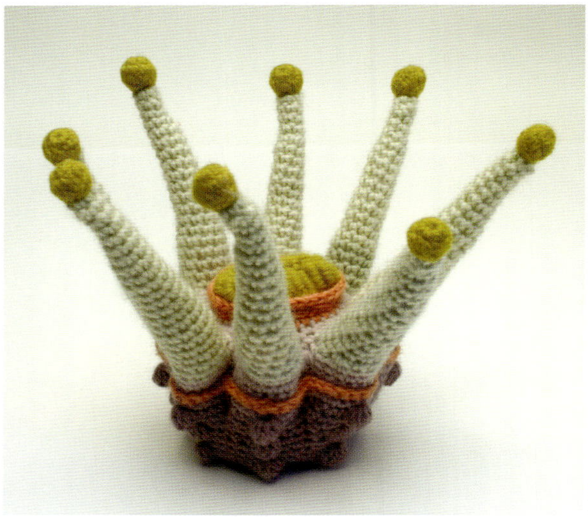

**Regina**, 2008.
Preloved tapestry wool. 18x15x12cm

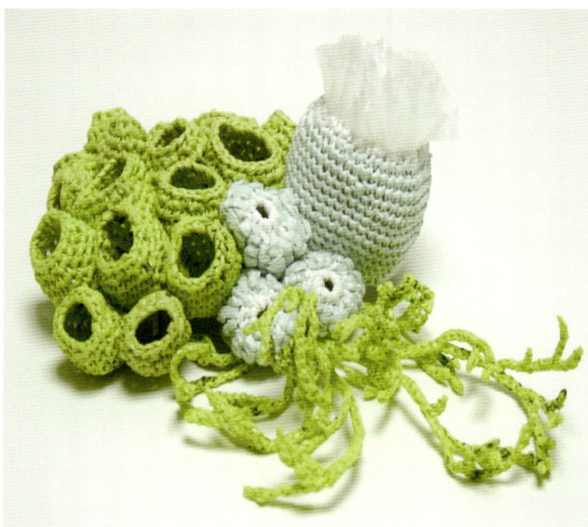

**Sagartia**, 2008.
Discarded Plastic Bags. 6x22x15cm

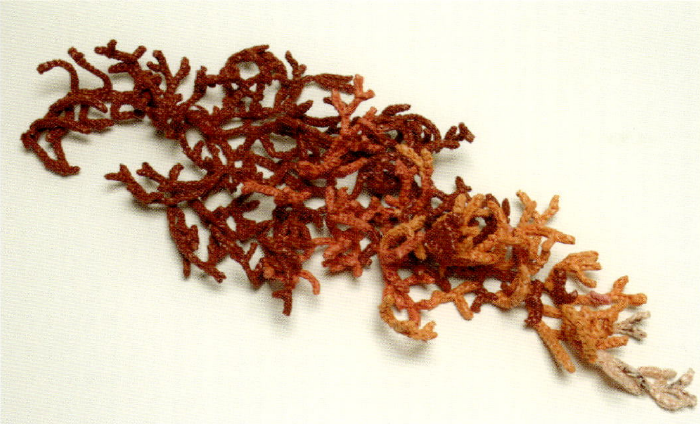

**Milliepora**, 2008.
Dicarded Plastic Bags. 8x40x12cm

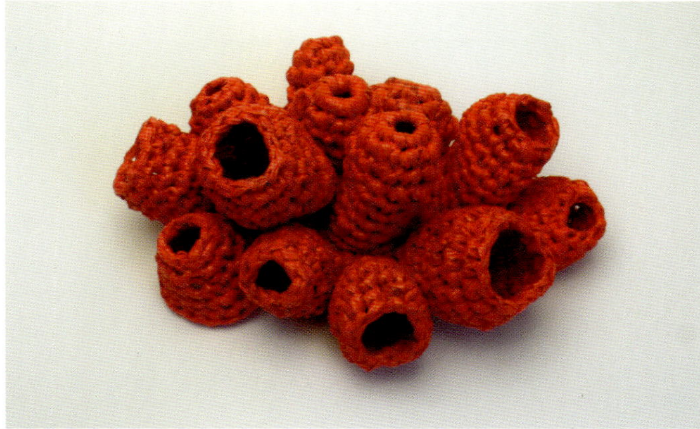

**Profera**, 2008.
Discarded Plastic Bags. 6x17x12cm

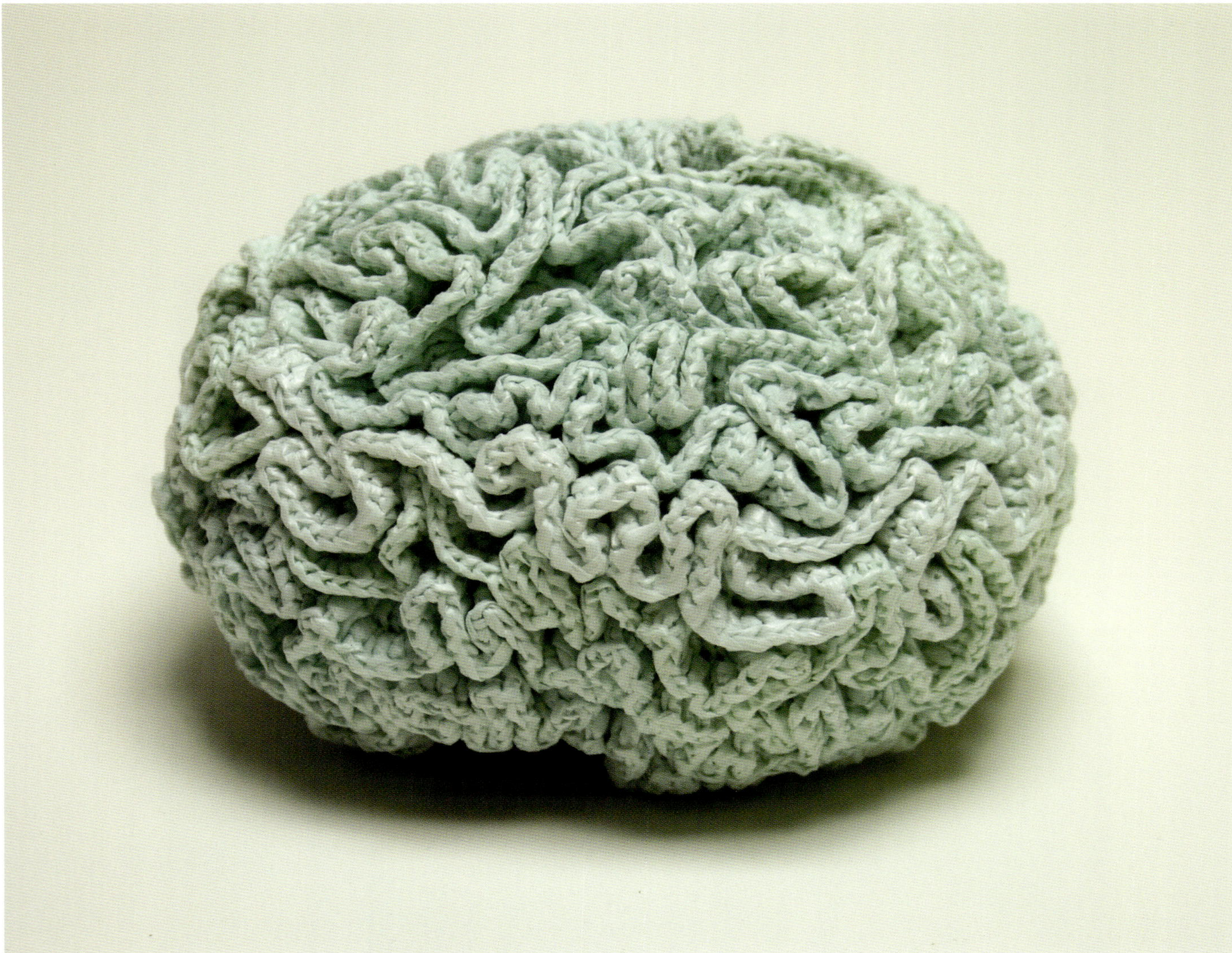

**Sargatia**, 2008.
Discarded Plastic Bags.

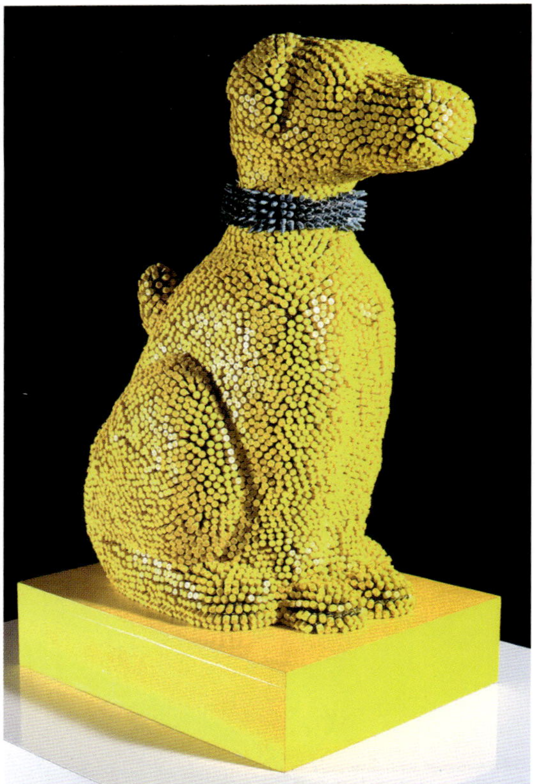

**Yellow Dog.** Crayons and mixed media, 42" x 28" x 19", 2004, collection of Ridley & Betsy Wills

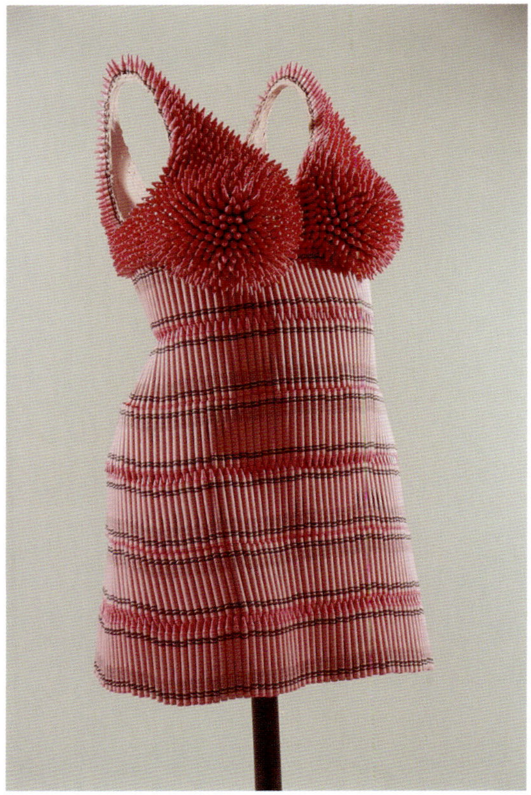

**Pink Slip.** Crayons and mixed media, 68" x 18" x 18", 2007, collection of Hotel Preston

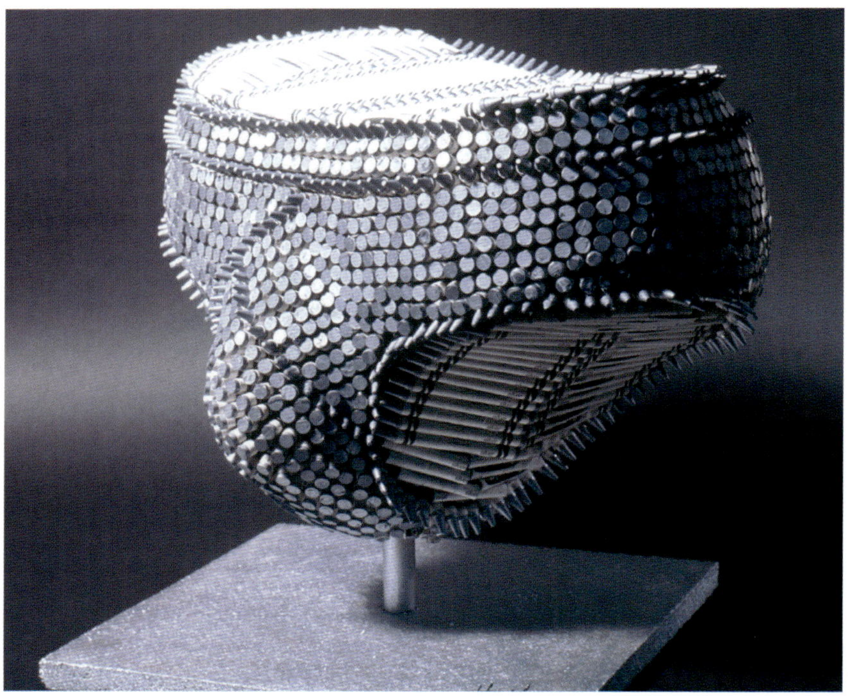

**Silverware.** Crayons and mixed media, 8" x 18" x 17", 2002, collection of Hotel Lucia.

# Herb Williams

www.herbwilliamsart.com

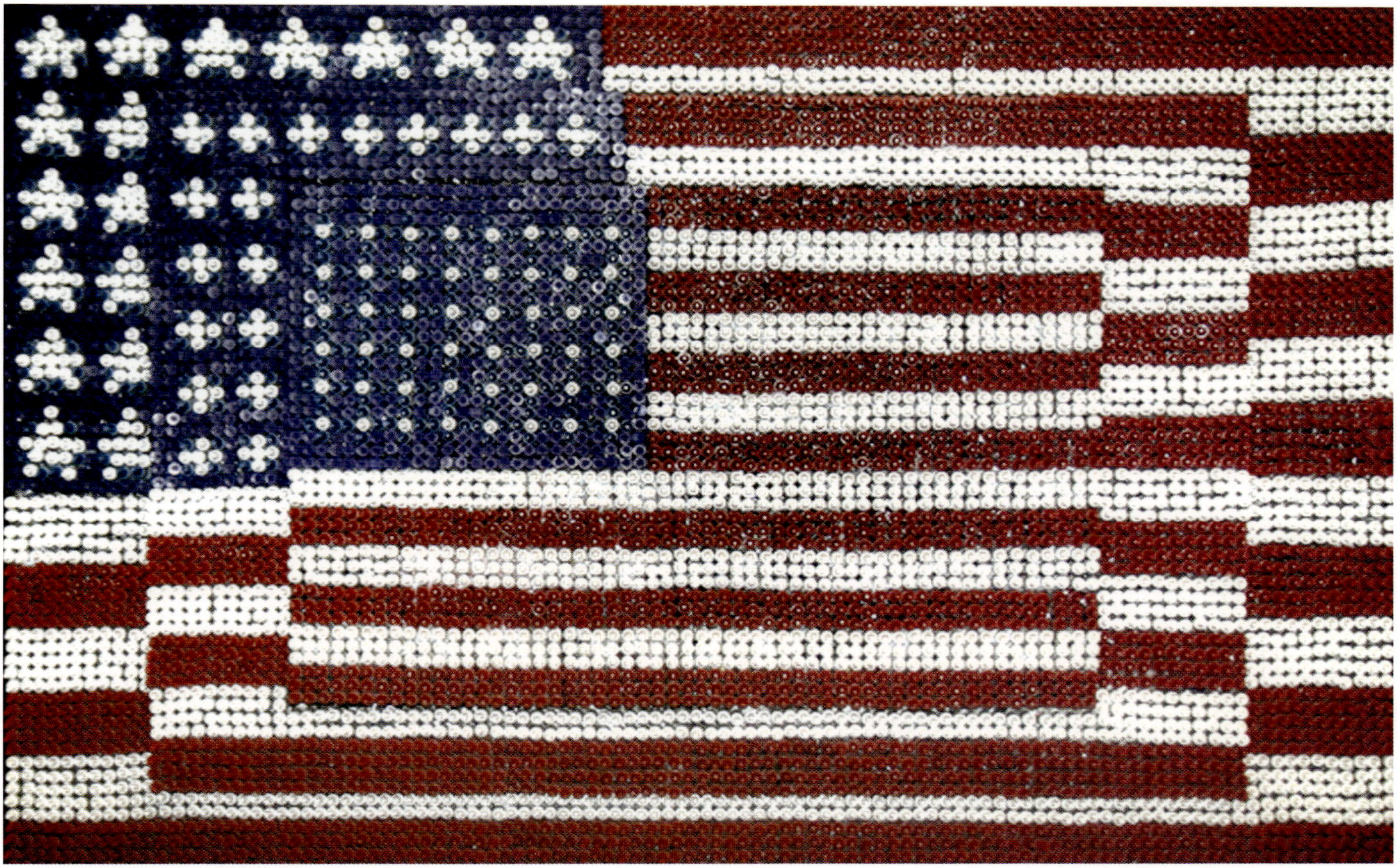

Herb Williams was born in Montgomery, AL, in 1973. Every summer from the age of twelve to graduating from high school at eighteen, he worked in construction, which gave him a deep understanding of form and materials. He received a BFA in sculpture from Birmingham-Southern College, and there apprenticed under two professional sculptors off-campus, Cordray Parker, and Branko Medenica. Upon graduation Herb immediately went to work at a bronze foundry in West Palm Beach, FL. There he helped cast hundreds of sculptures with the atelier Popliteo and the last piece of work by photo realist Duane Hanson, "Man on Riding Lawnmower." He then moved to Nashville, TN, where he has lived and created art since 1998. He has two beautiful children, Clay and Maggie, with his wife (and first model), Amy. Herb received The Joan Mitchell Foundation Museum Purchase Grant in 2004 and the Next Star Artist Award in 2008. Herb is one of the only individuals in the world with an account with Crayola. He creates original sculptures out of individual crayons that may require as many as hundreds of thousands. He will also cast the completed crayon sculptures in a silicone jacket mold with a two-part epoxy resin and then paint the resin sculpture to look like the original, occasionally producing a small edition. The cast sculptures have been placed in public arenas, such as children's hospitals, corporate lobbies, and museum walls. Crayons are a gateway drug. To most adults, the sight and smell of crayons produce specific memories of childhood. The twist in the road to nostalgia is the creation of a new object, from a medium in which it was not intended. This element of unexpected interaction and play had me at hello. Because I am in pursuit of larger ideas, the playful aspect of my medium is integral to the works of art I'm creating. I can subversively insert a concept that may bloom well after the initial recognition of the form as a familiar children's implement. To create my work I need to produce sculpture on a grand scale (which takes thousands and thousands of crayons), so I order each color individually packed (3000 to a case) and cut the sticks down to the length I need. I then bond the paper - not the wax - to a form I have carved or cast, completely enveloping the form.

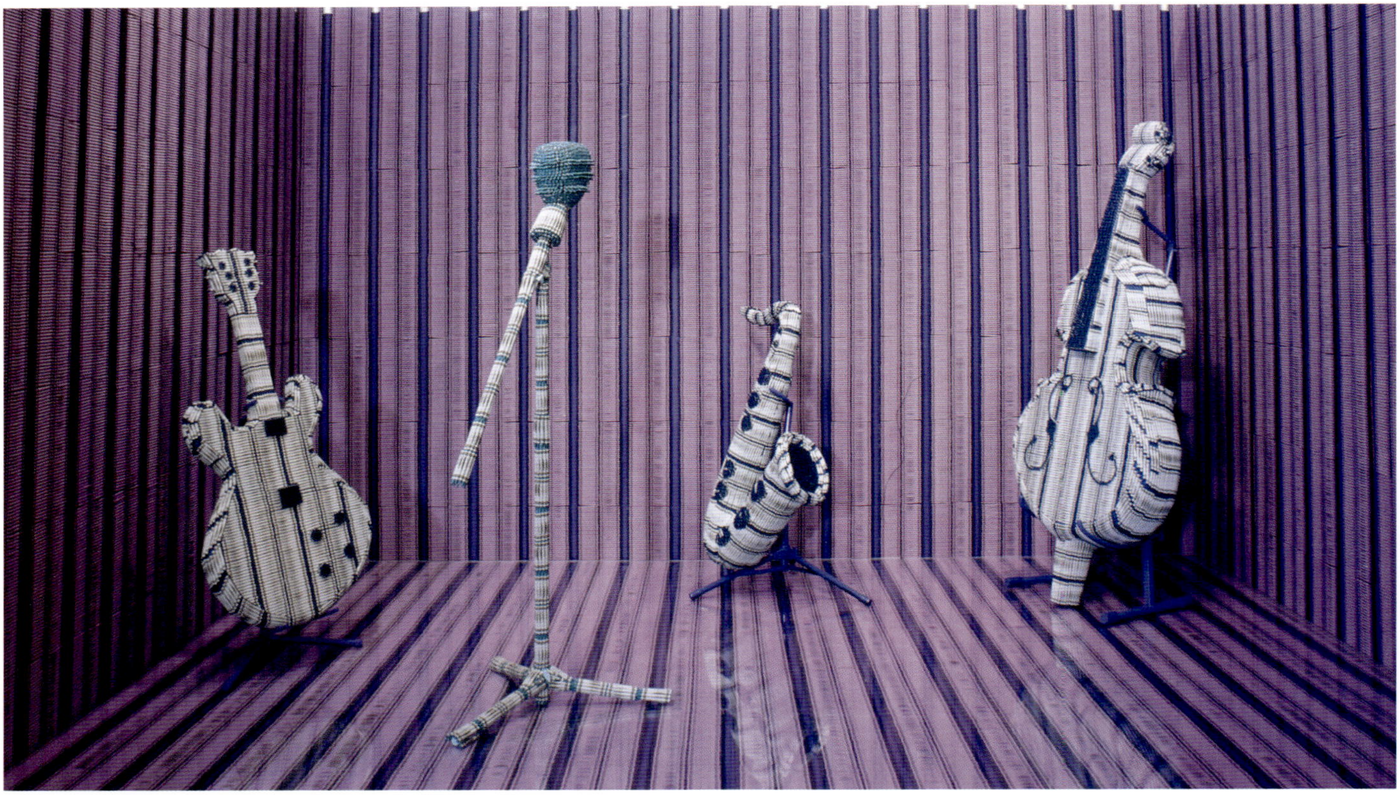

**The Blues Room.** Crayons and mixed media, 144" x 96" x 96", 2005, collection of The Gary Group

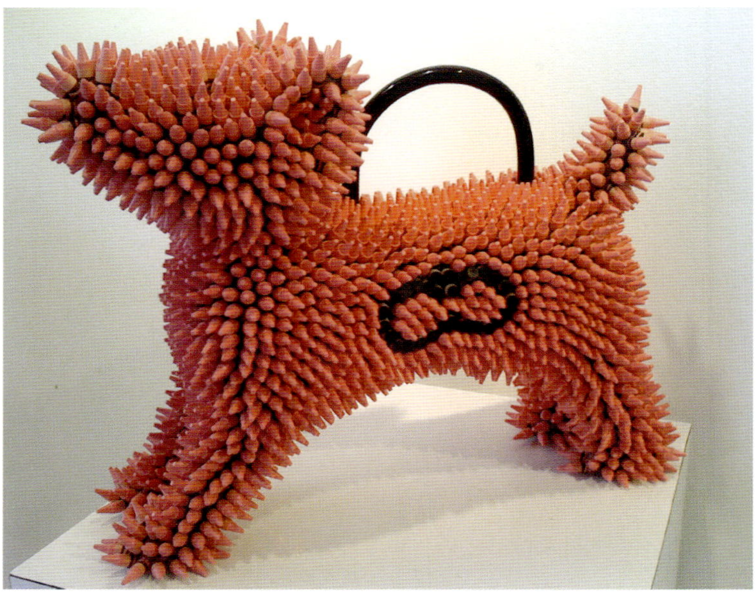

**Bitch Bag.** Crayons and mixed media, 13" x 17.5" x 6", 2009

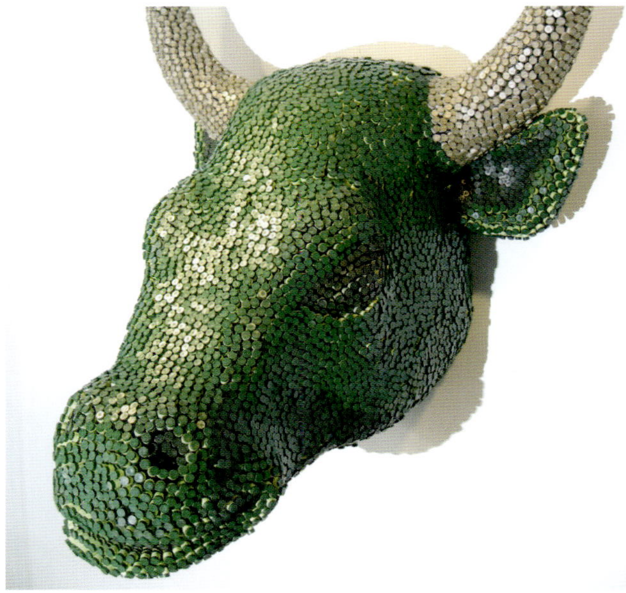

**Bull Market.** Crayons and mixed media, 36" x 28" x 26", 2007, collection of Gage Logan

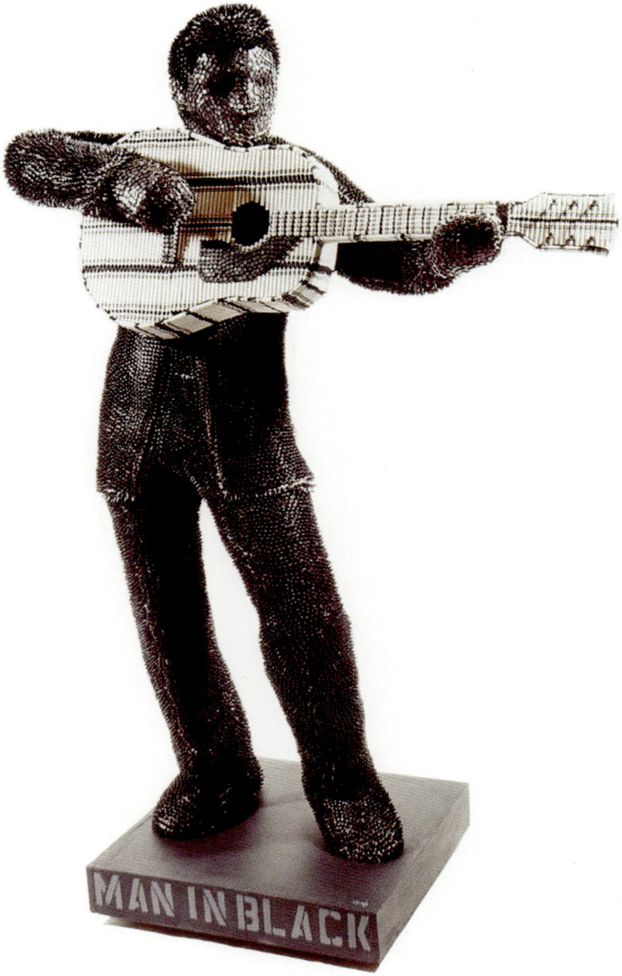


**The Man In Black.** Crayons and mixed media, 79" x 58" x 24", 2006, collection of Chancellor Gordon Gee4.

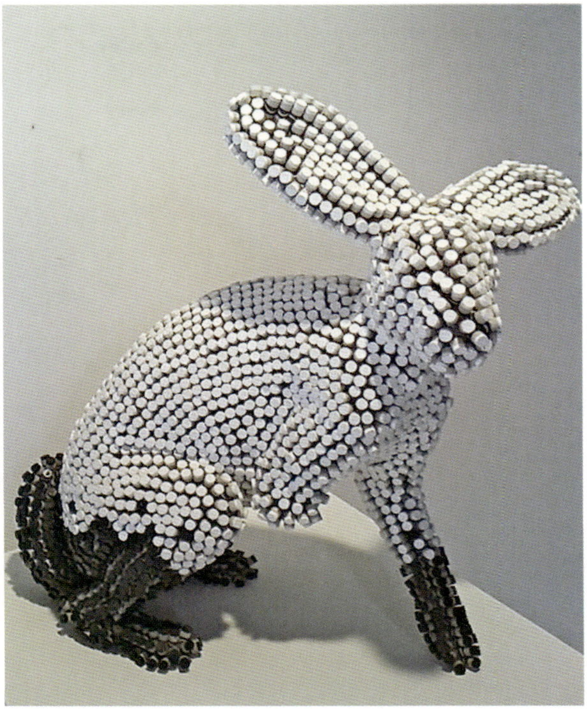

**White Rabbit.** Crayons and mixed media, 18" x 13" x 14", 20097.

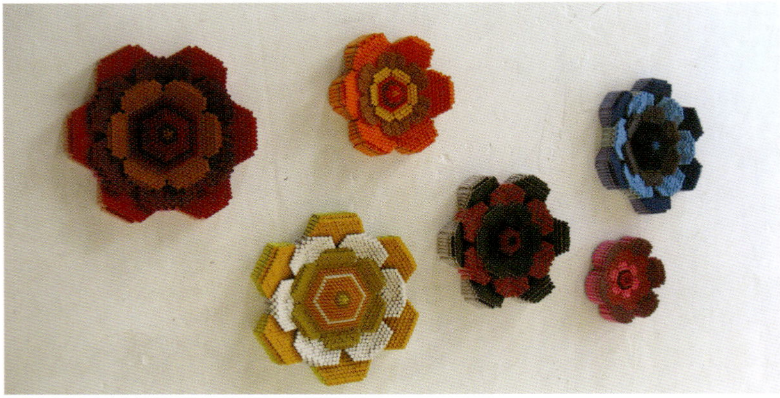

**Wall Flowers.** Crayons and mixed media, dimensions variable, 2008,

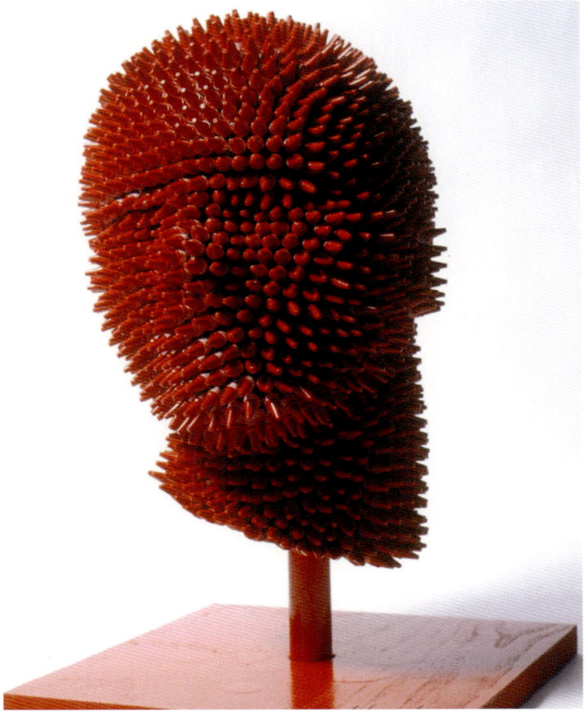

**Red Head.** Crayons and mixed media, 17" x 12" x 12", 2002, collection of The TN State Museum5.

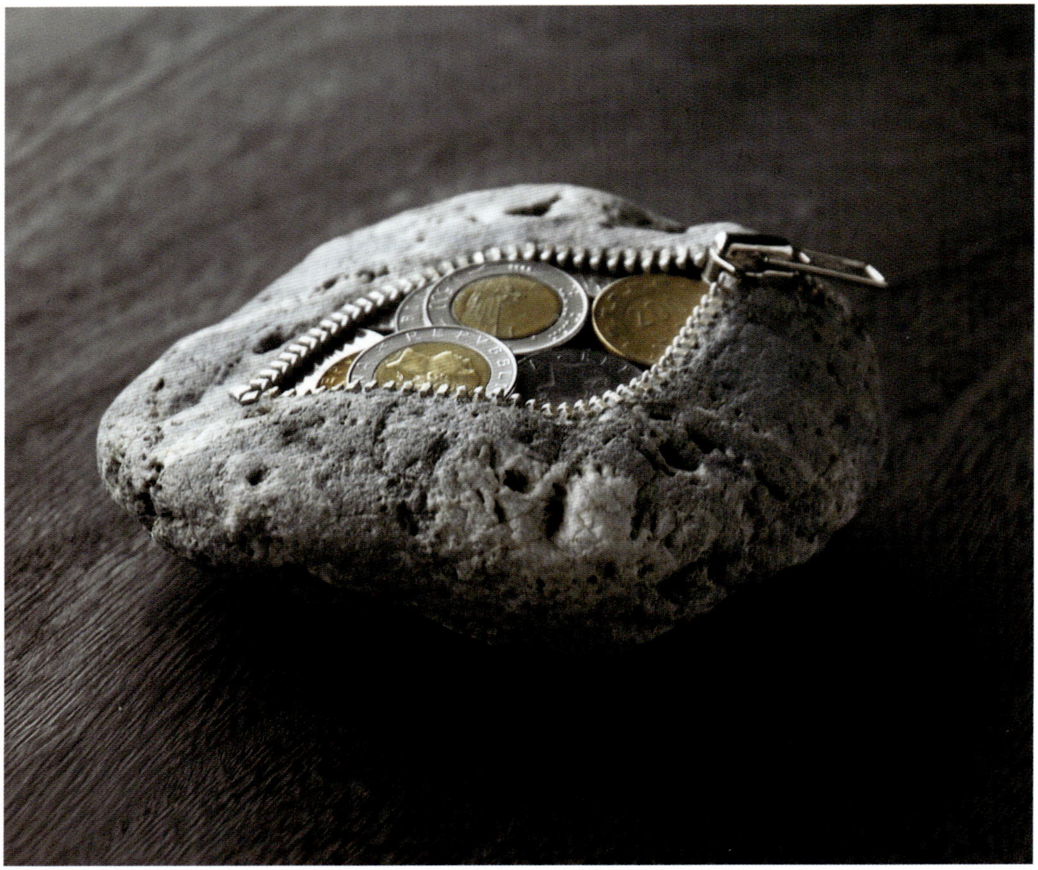

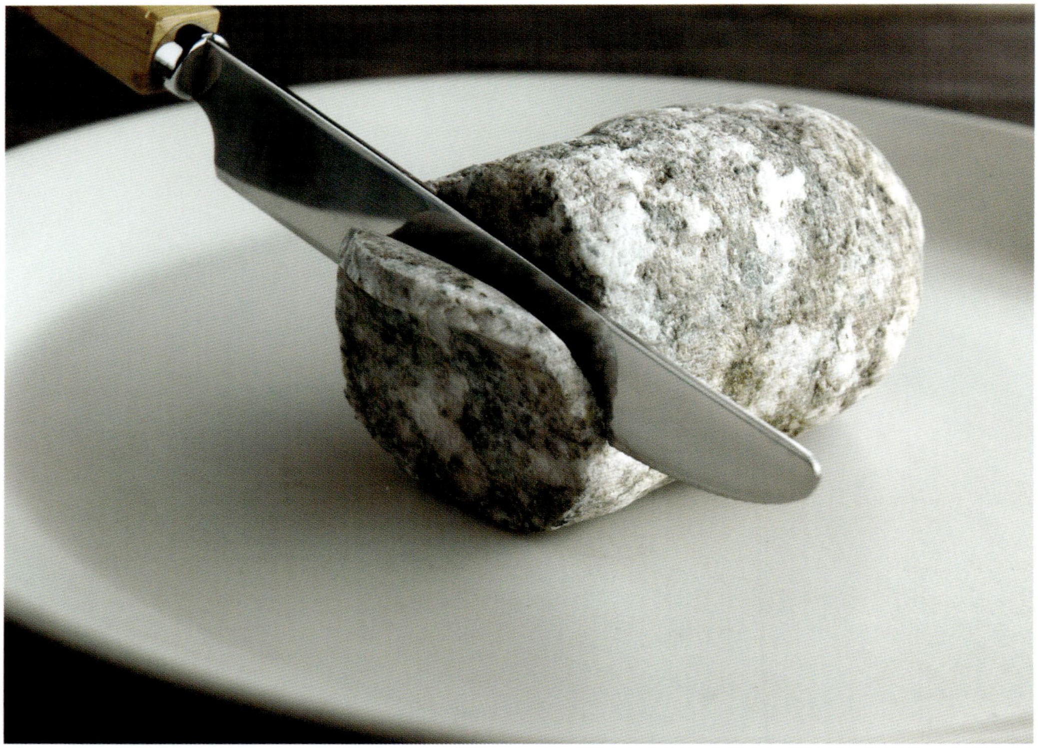

# Hirotoshi Ito

www.jiyuseki.com

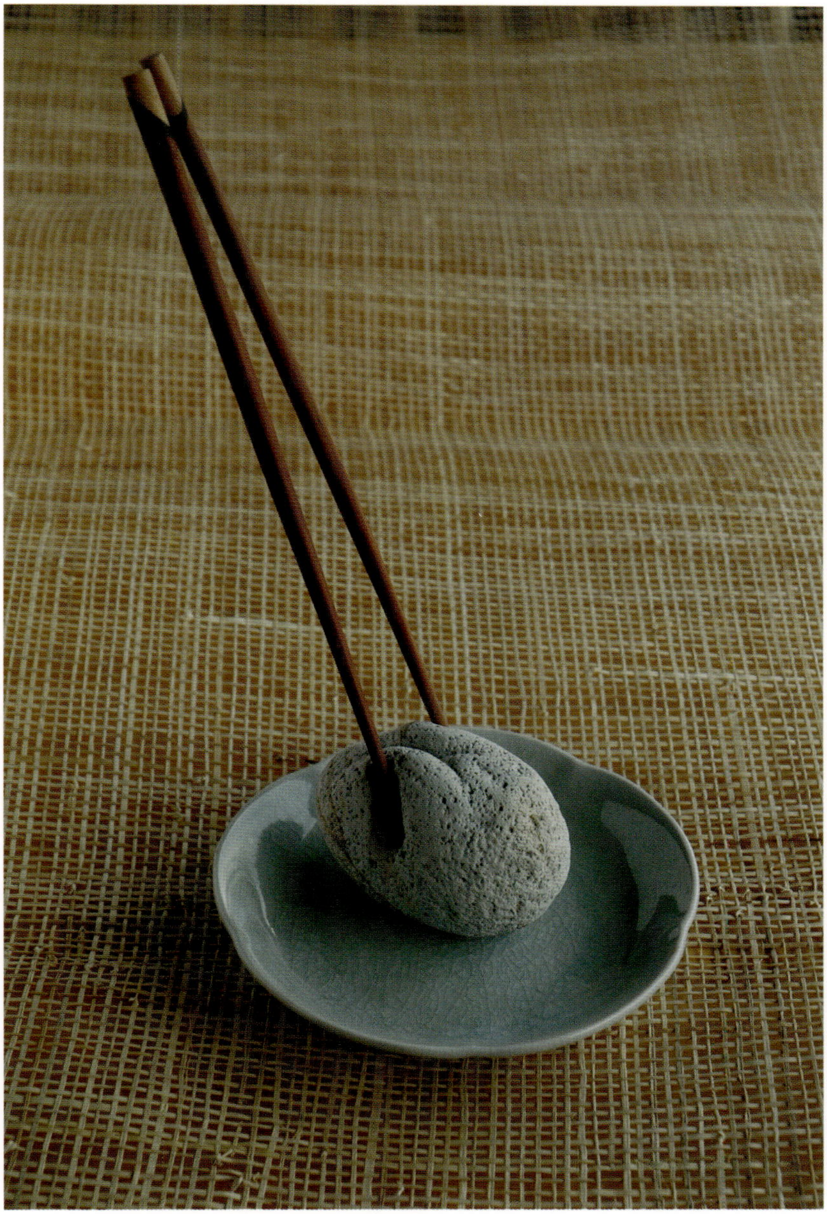

Hirotoshi Ito is a stone sculpture artist, whose work has been known for its unique structures with a sense of humor. After graduating from the distinguished Tokyo University of the Arts, Ito was destined to take over his father's masonry business in his hometown of Matsumoto City in Nagano Prefecture. He works out of his studio at home, creating his sculptures, while attending his family business. While taking metal work courses at the university, he became fascinated by his own search for finding new ways to transform the hard and cold images that the metals have, into something soft and warm. Although his metal work days are over, his search, now shifted to utilizing stones, continues. Ito collects his art supplies, the stones and rocks, along the river banks near by. Ito Hirotoshi continues to find new and original ways to create sculptures that people would touch and feel the unexpected softness and the warmth of them. He would be honored if his work would add laughs and smiles to people who come in contact with them. He is very active in promoting the growing contemporary craft traditions of Nagano area, and twenty years ago he and his friends initiated a grass roots project which has grown into an annual craft festival in Matsumoto City, for which he now serves as President.

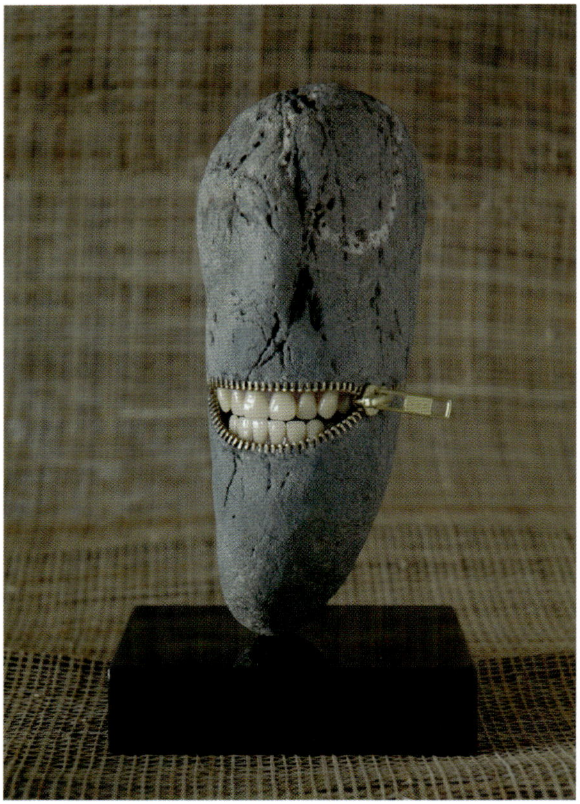

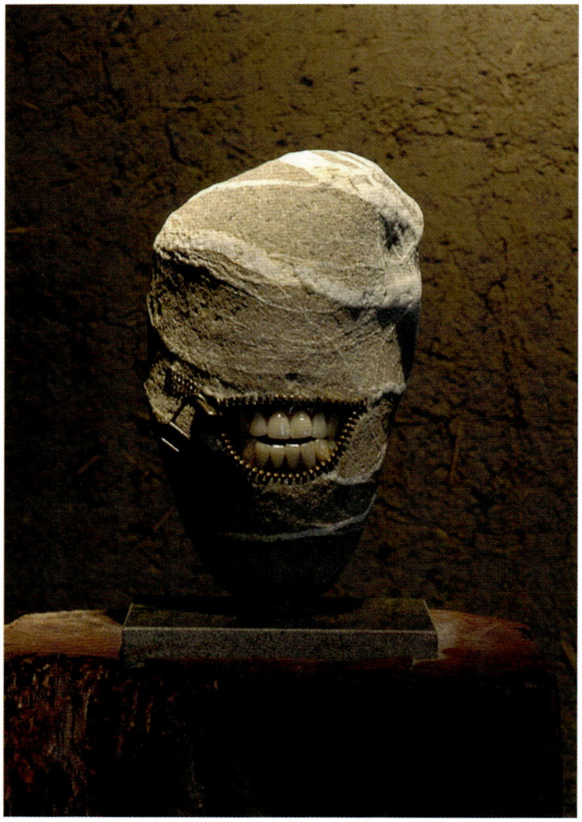

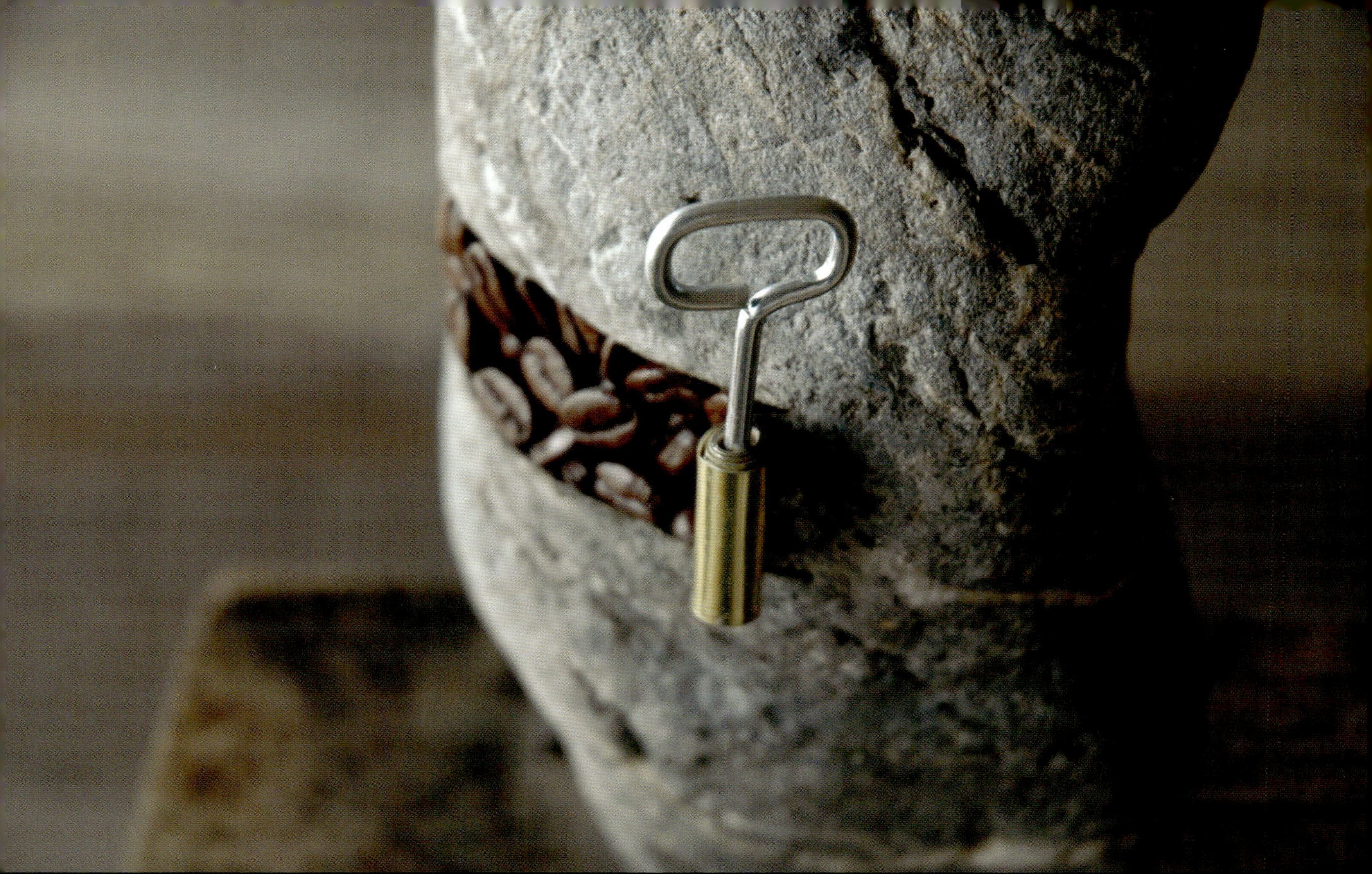
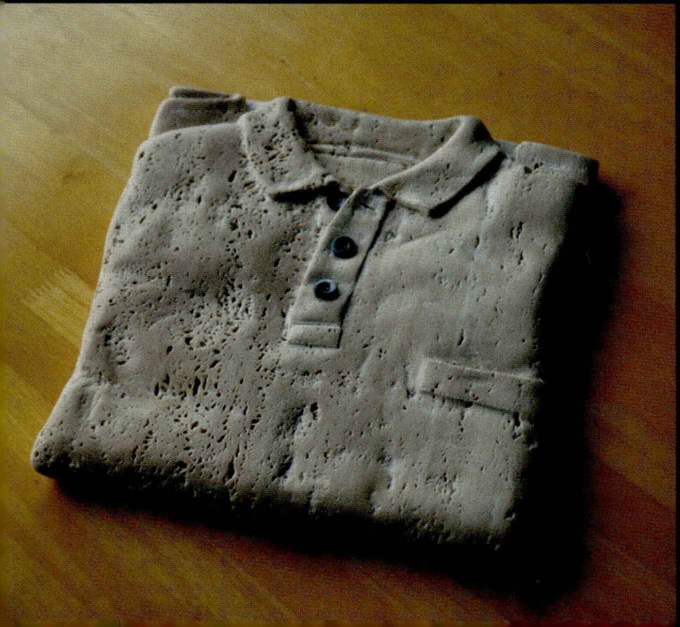
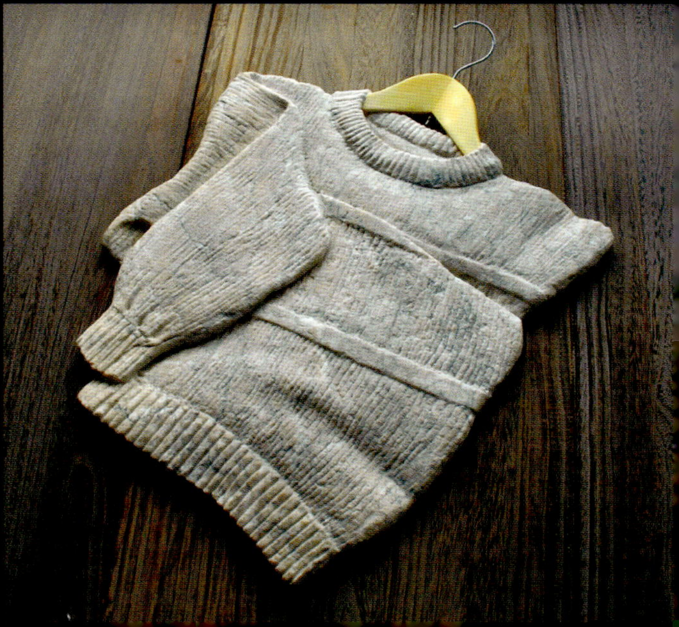

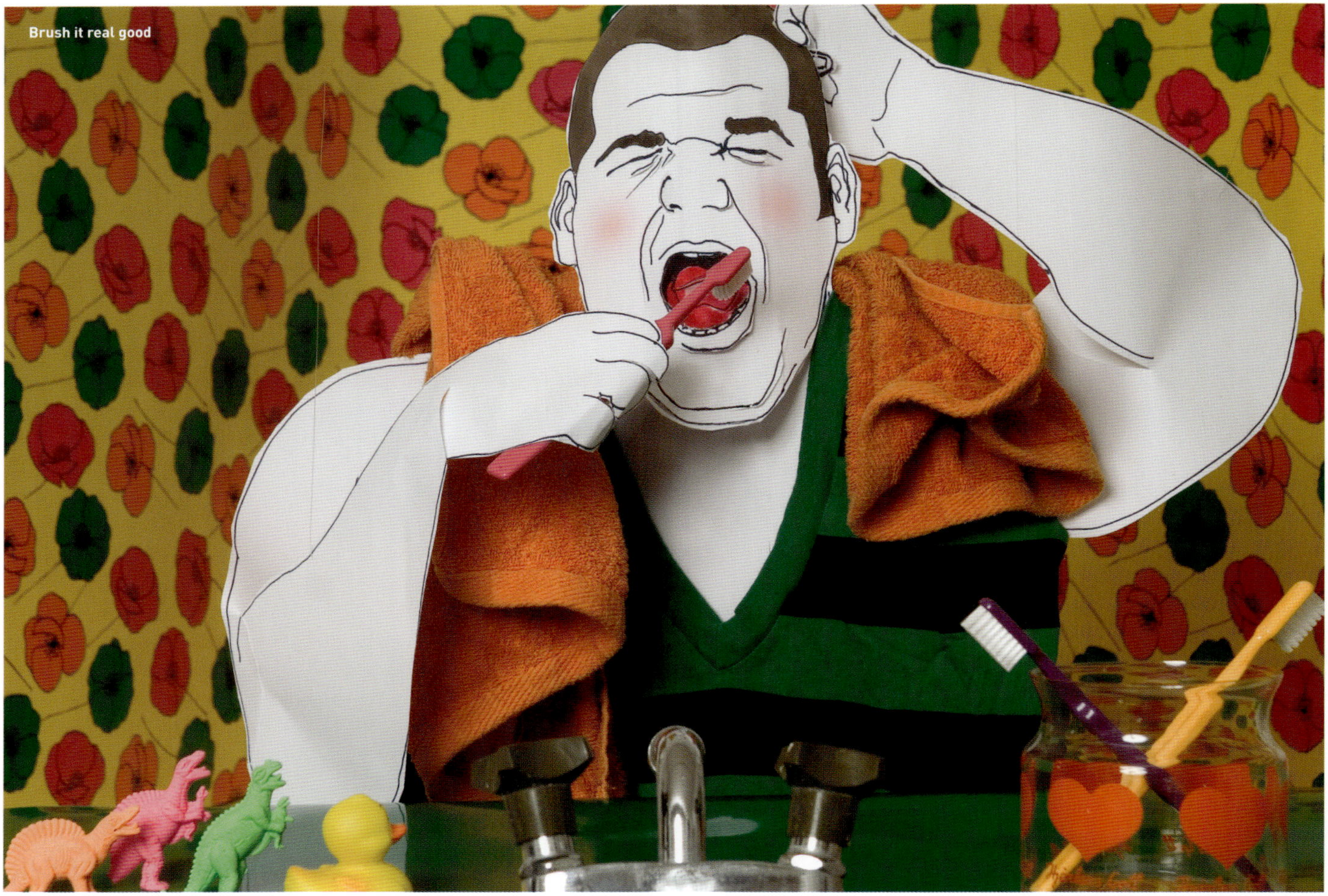
Brush it real good

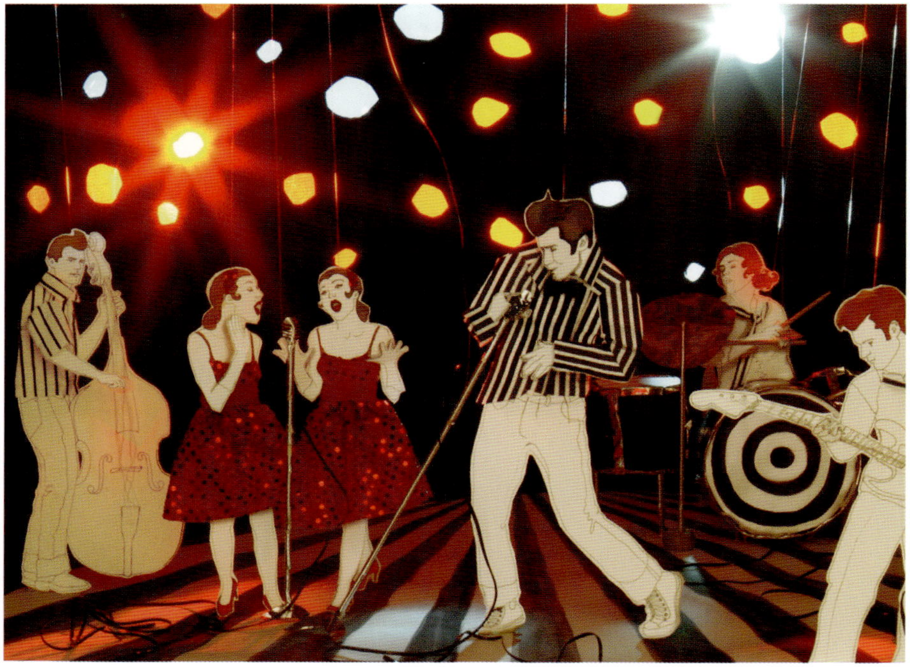

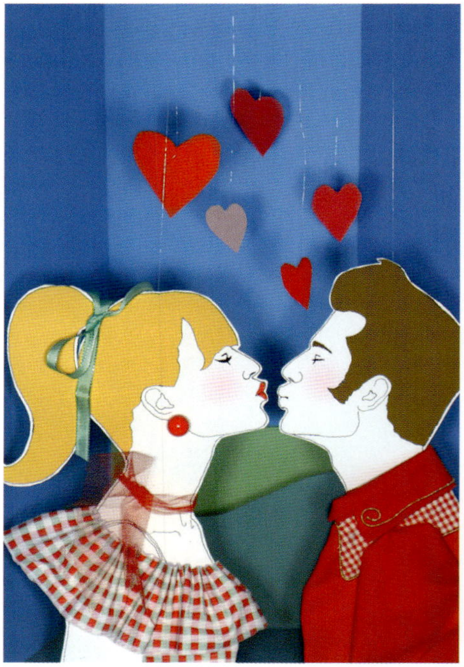

# Ingela/Och Vi

www.ingelaochvi.com

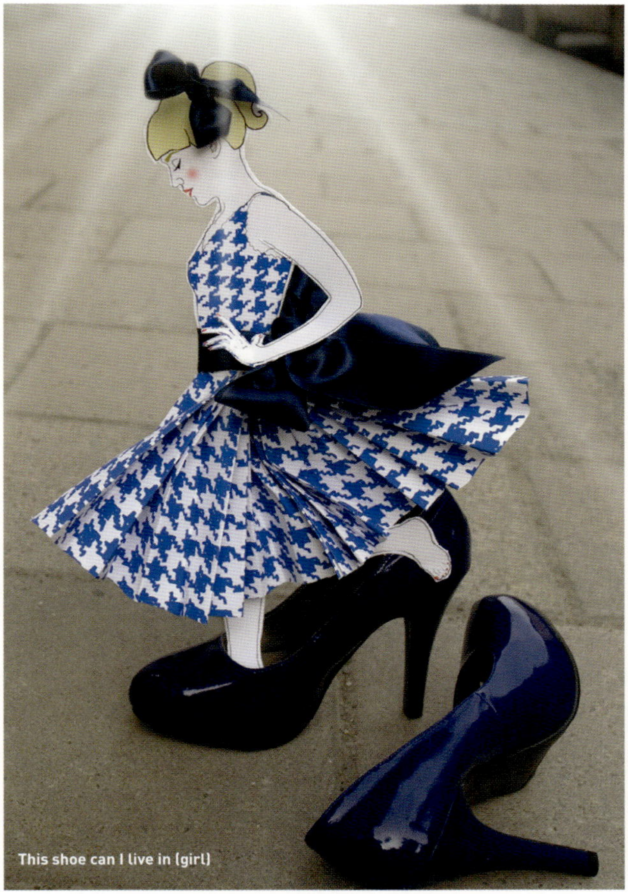

This shoe can I live in (girl)

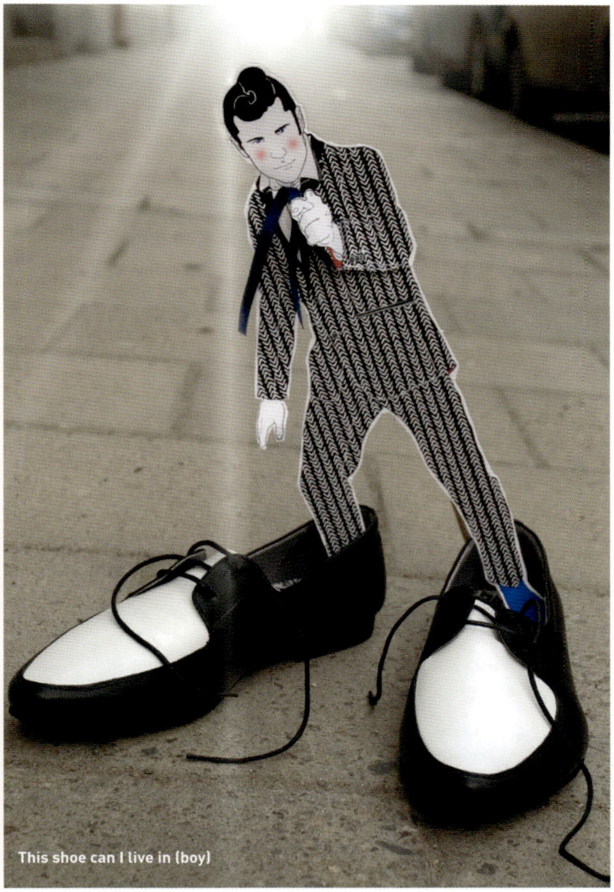

This shoe can I live in (boy)

The illustration duo, Ingela och Vi, started in January 2004 when Elisabeth Månsson (illustrator and graphic designer) and Peter Turkalj (photographer) first conceived of the idea of creating three-dimensional illustrations by combining illustration and photography. Elisabeth had just finished 5 years of studying visual communications at Denmarks Design School in Copenhagen and Peter was an assisting photographer working freelance. Early in her career, Elisabeth had been working on combining 3D techniques with two-dimensional objects, but then she began working with Peter and they realized that together it was possible to take their work to a whole new level. Since then they have been creating wildly original and intriguing work that has become their trademark style. Their illustration work has gained much applause, and they have won awards in Sweden including the award for Best Commercial Illustration in 2006 at the yearly Swedish illustration competition, Kolla! The graphic design magazine, CAP&Design pronounced them the future of Swedish illustration and design. Their influences range from early Walt Disney films to Chinese shadow play and origami, and they take much inspiration from classic cinema and their favorite bands. Most of our ideas we get from movies, music and just the daily life. To begin our process we plan the act for an example how the room shall look like and how the characters shall act. The work continues with the characters which are illustrated to their right and exact expression. Then their cut out in paper and dressed with textilies to increas the 3D expression. The characters are then placed in the scenorio as actors and to keep them in place we use fishing line which has become a sort of our trademark. To created the right mood of the scenorio lights are setup and the photographed to become the finished setdesign. Their clients include Elle Sweden, Residence interior magazine, Die Welt, Venue magazine, NK Department Stores, McDonald's (Sweden), Stranger magazine, 'Bea Szenfeld Fashion Team, Spendrups Brewery and Monsa Publishing.

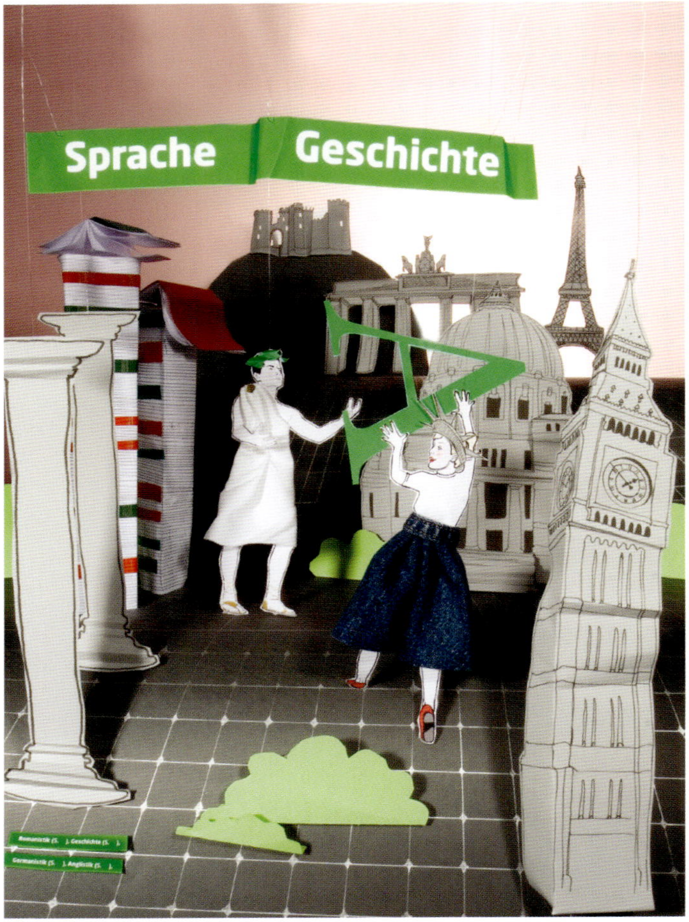

Die Zeit

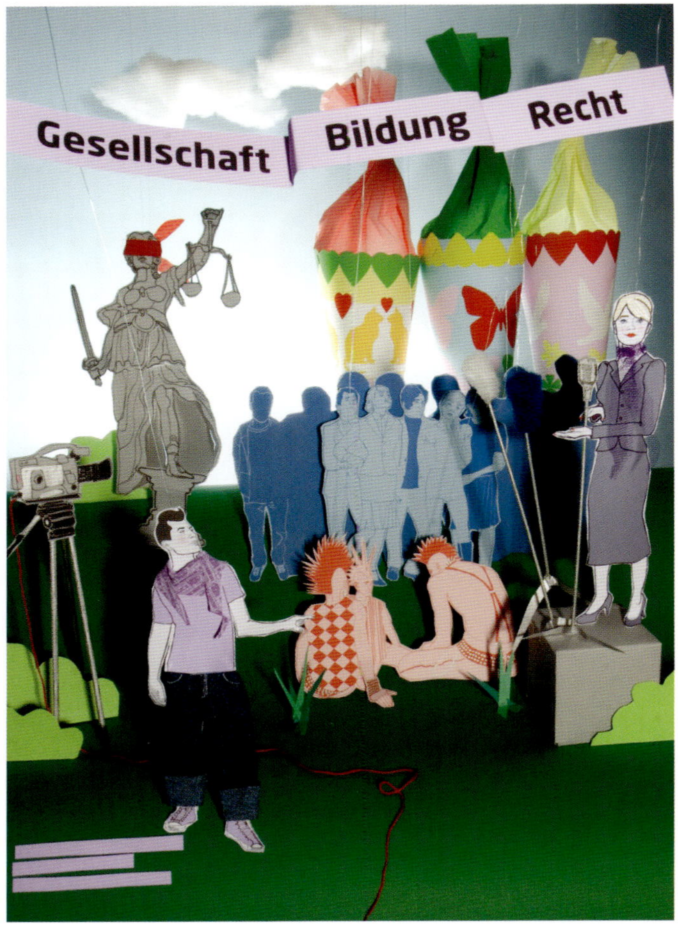

Die Zeit 2

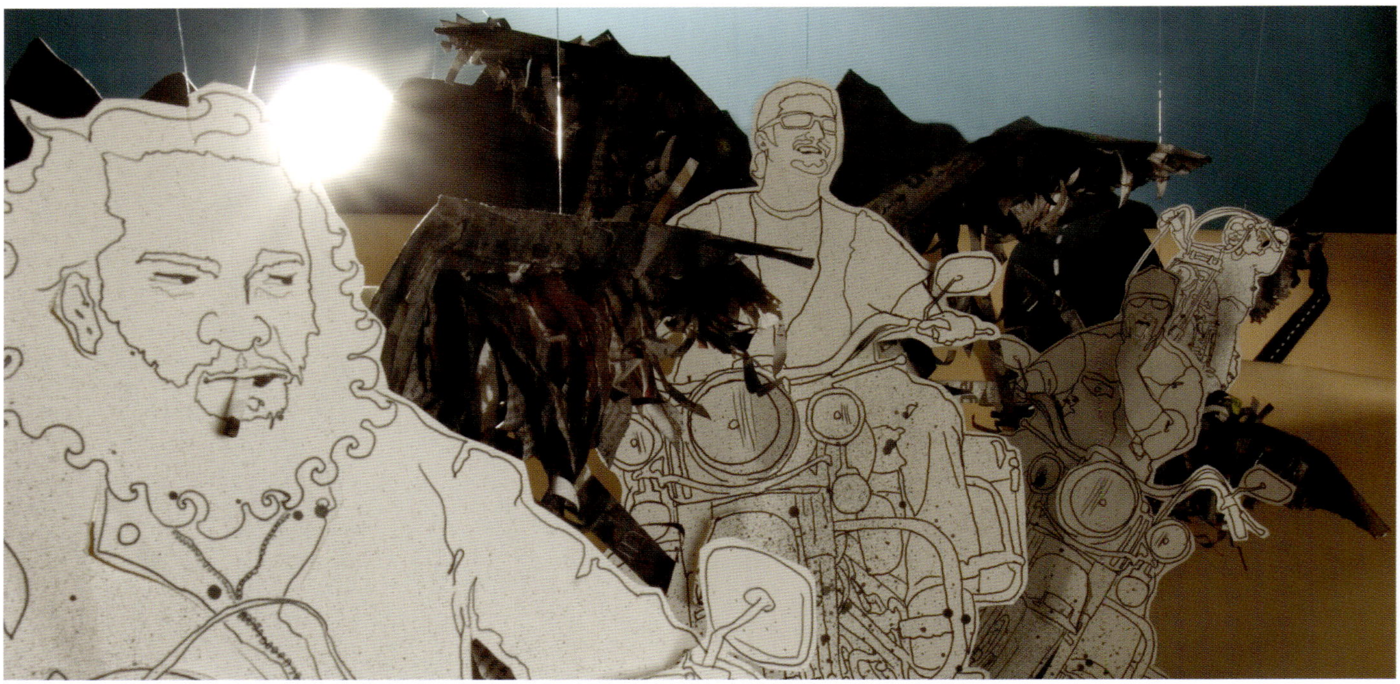
Hell angels - Booklet magazine

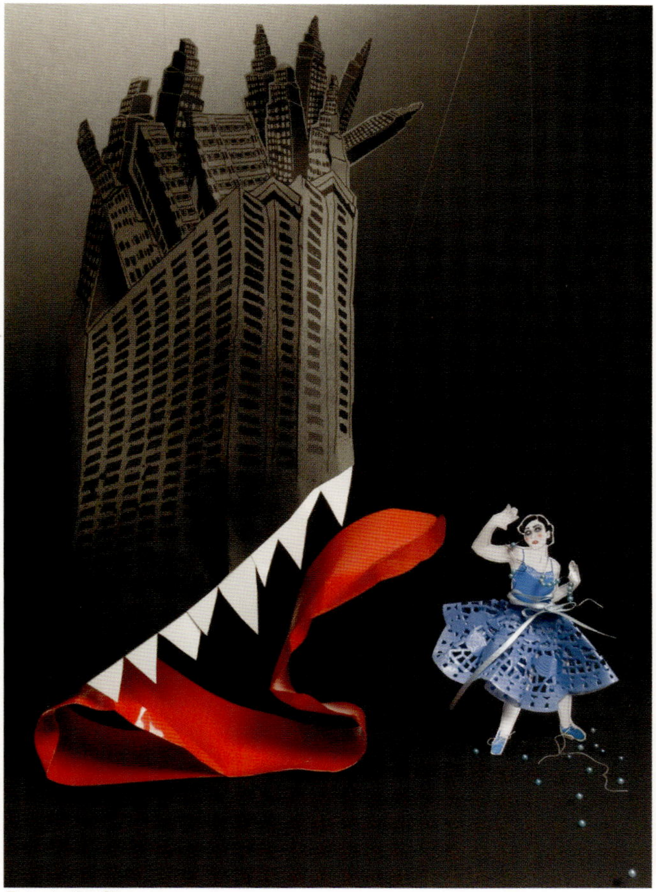

Eaten by the City

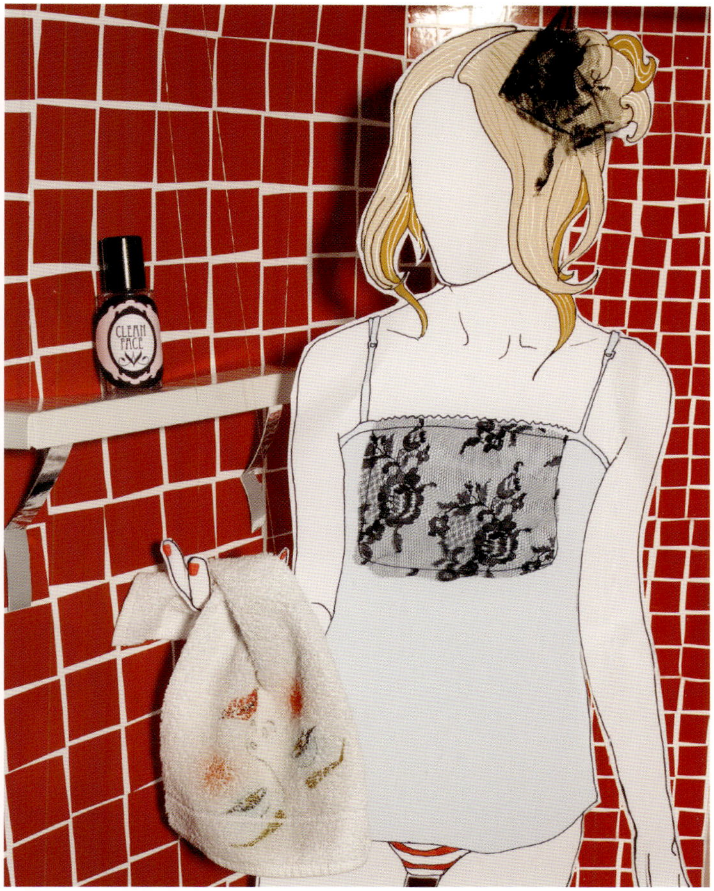


Face off

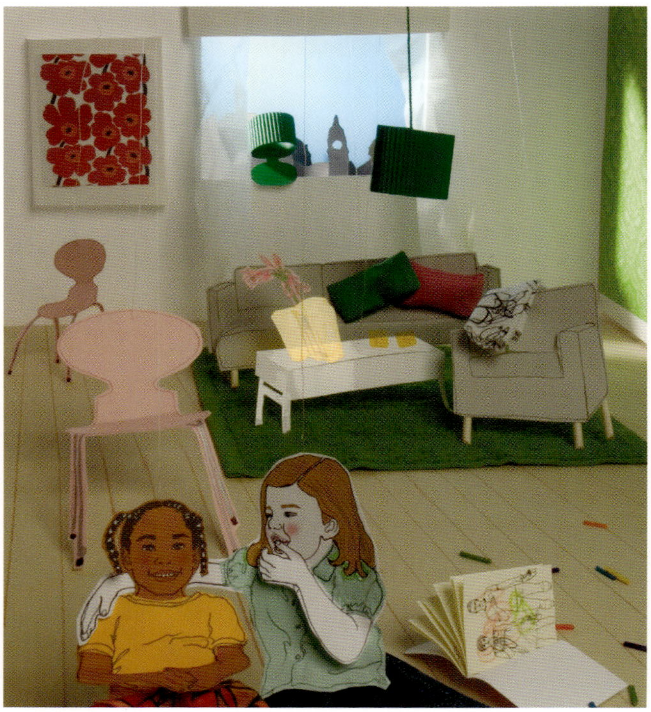

**Family living**

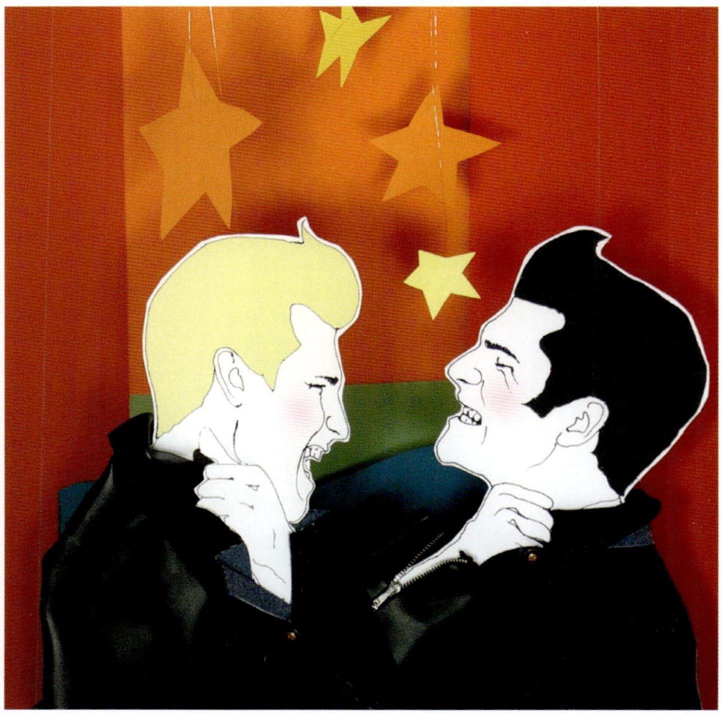

**Hate**

**8 pieces** 200x200 cm, embroidery on canvas + street events + courtyard exhibitions - As part of Instant Hutong, the Urban Carpet project consists in 8 carpets embroidered by hand and several temporary public events taking place in the Hutong alleys. Each carpet represents the map of a Hutong area with a size of approximately one square kilometer and a total population of about 30.000 people. These areas have been isolated and presented as autonomous towns within the much larger city. The process of obtaining such detailed maps of the old Beijing Hutong areas from the Chinese government has proven to be no easy matter. An extensive preliminary research work was crucial for the development of the task and it was followed by a meticulous work which consisted in manually remapping entire areas from scratch. These maps have been reinterpreted as spatial textures and have been embroidered by hand with the same technique once applied in the propaganda tapestries of the seventies. They were consequently further elaborated through the means of wool thread insertions.

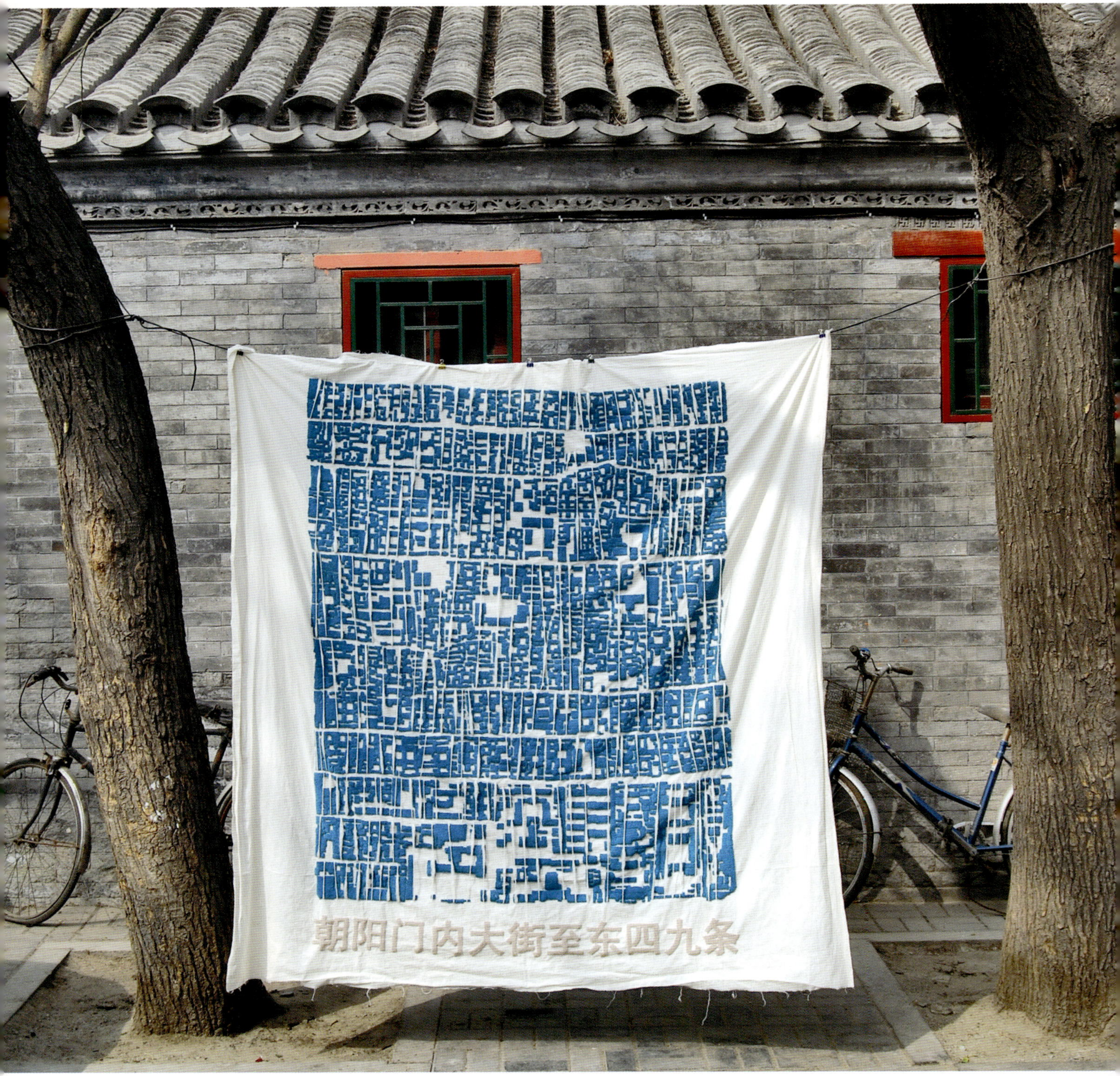

# Instant/Hutong

www.instanthutong.com

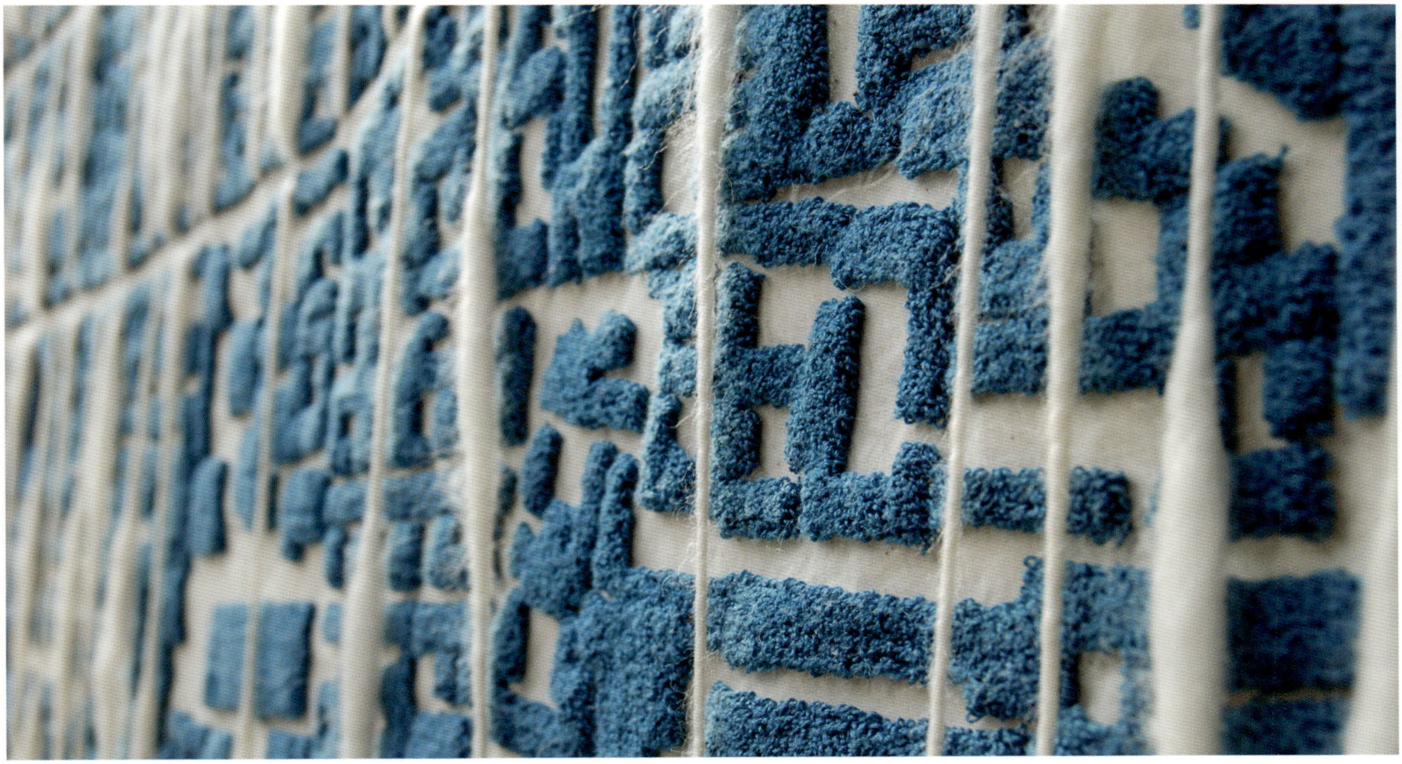

MARCELLA CAMPA and STEFANO AVESANI have been interested in the urban growth of Chinese cities and their transformation since 2003. In 2005 they co-edited the n.78 monographic issue of the international magazine AREA about Chinese contemporary visual art and architecture. They have been awarded with the international Archiprix prize in Glasgow for a double coordinated project for historical districts in downtown Beijing and Shanghai. They moved to China in October 2005 and started working on the Instant Hutong project. An art project created to record as well as draw people's attention onto traditional patterns of neighbourhoods, courtyards and lanes in Beijing, all of which are threatened by construction development. This work explores both spatial and social aspects of the traditional Hutong urban tissue and the community of people living in it. It is organized as a series of art pieces and installations on the border between art, social investigation and urban research with the aim of generating and stimulating an open debate. The work currently involves issues such as density, gentrification, human relationships and the concept of physical space, as well as property speculation and the fast pace disappearance of the sense of community and identity. These issues are expressed through merging the social sphere with the aesthetic one. The Hutong Districts in Beijing used to form a large continuous tissue built of one storey courtyard houses (Siheyuan) which filled the spaces in-between the alleys (Hutong in the local language). The buildings forming each Siheyuan are organized in a sequence of courts. The spaces of Siheyuan have proven very adaptable to changes during different historical periods. In the past 60 years, following the strategy of redistribution of dwellings, houses that had originally been occupied by one single family, were then assigned to several nuclei. Due to the changes in living conditions, a singular new concept of living has developed among the Hutong Districts, the distinctive traits of which are density, capability of adaptation, neighborhood relationships and a "street-oriented" lifestyle. Following the recent extensive demolitions, such Hutong culture is nowadays undergoing the risk of destruction. The Instant Hutong project aims at increasing the awareness of such distinctive culture, offering new ways of looking at the Hutong districts while actively involving its inhabitants to be part of the project and interact with it during the public events organized inside the courtyards and adjacent lanes. Since 2007 their work took part in several exhibitions in China and abroad. Marcella and Stefano currently live and work in Beijing.

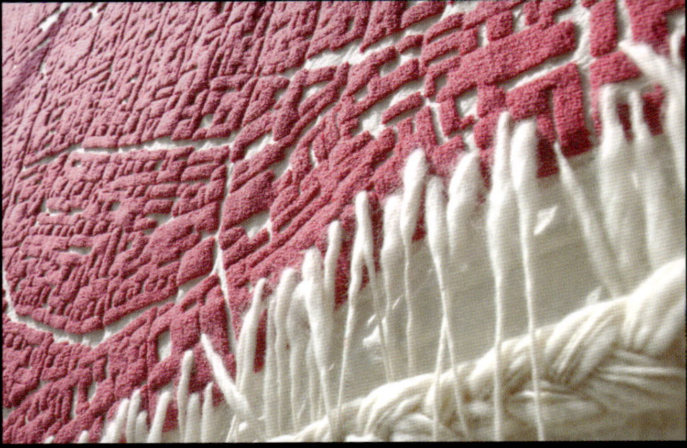

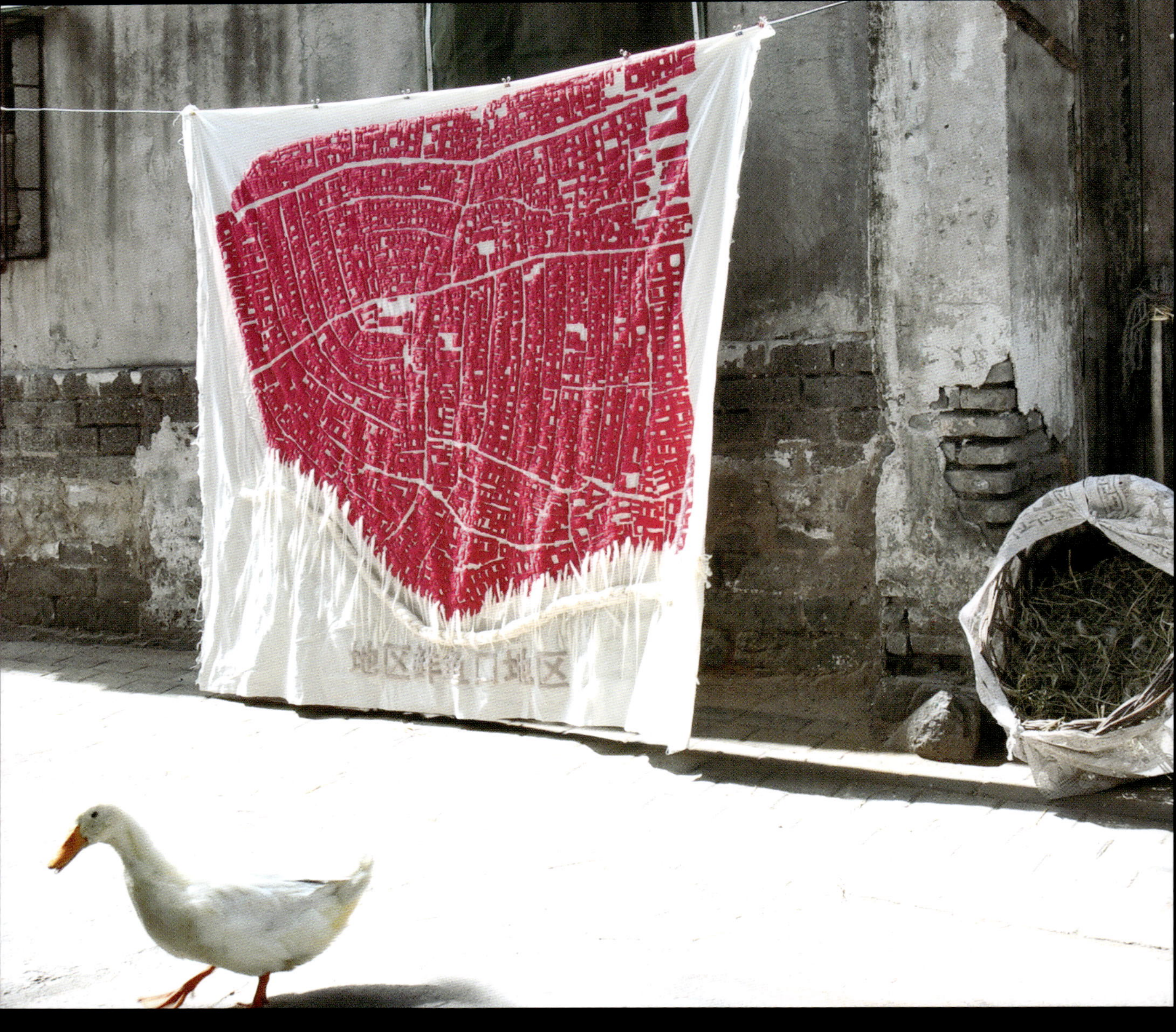

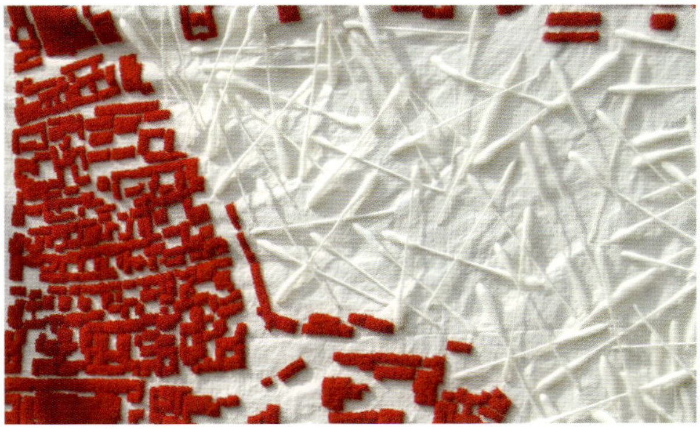

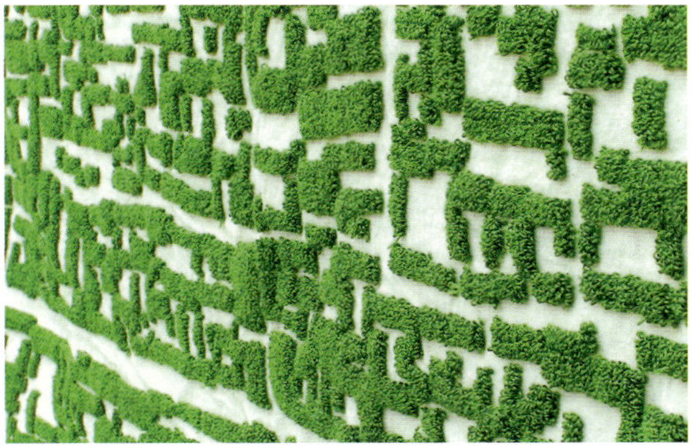

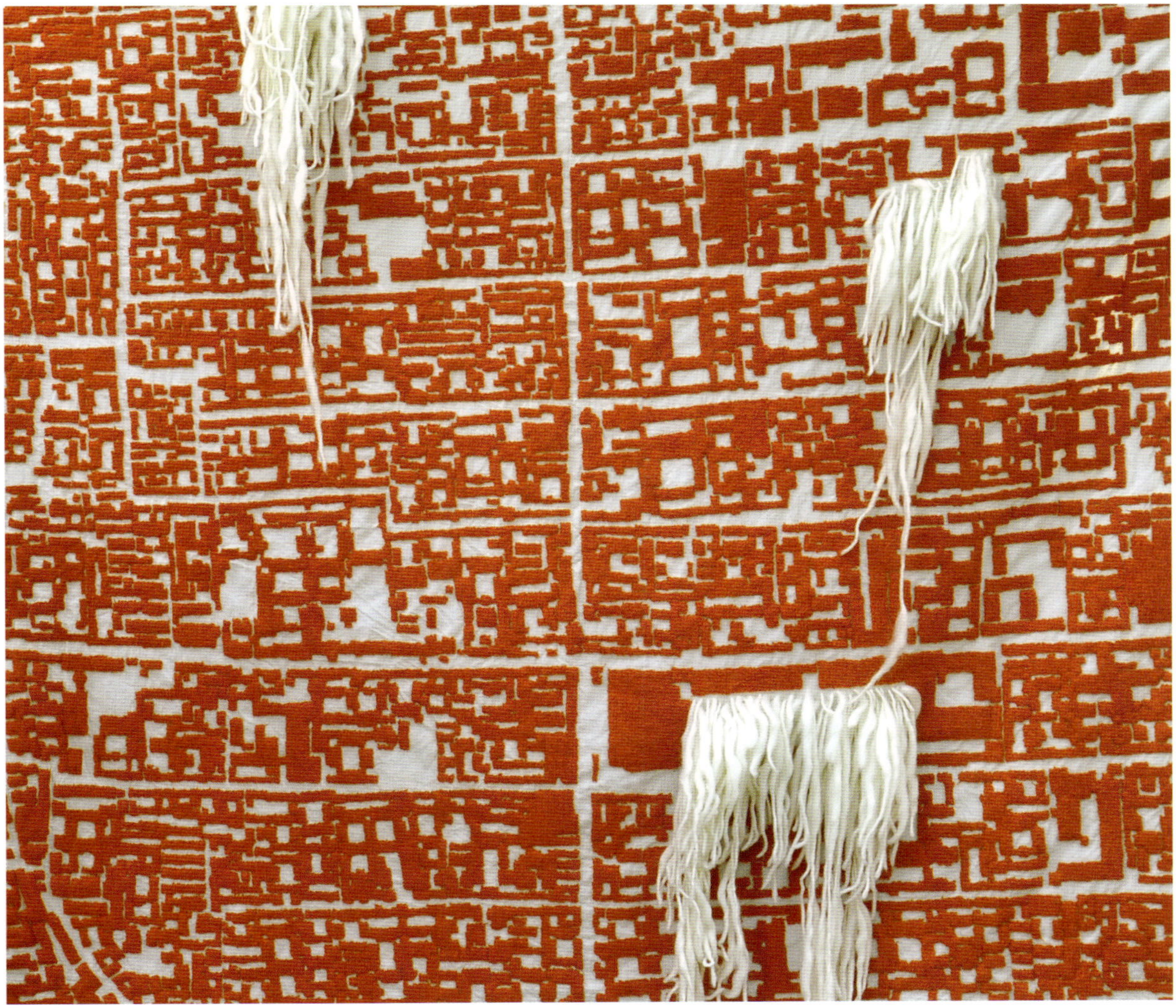

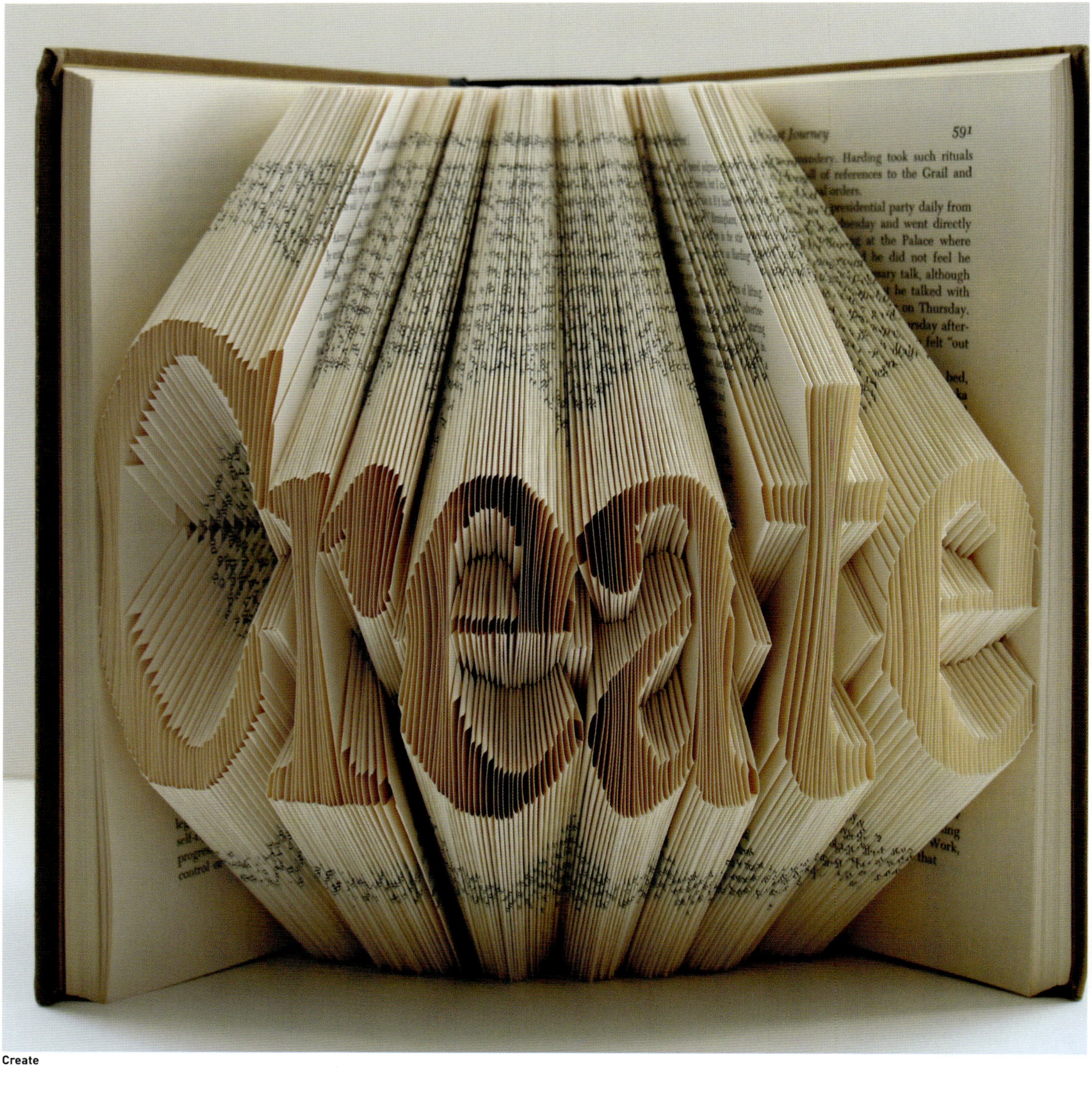


**Create**

# Isaac Salazar

www.flickr.com/photos/bookofart/

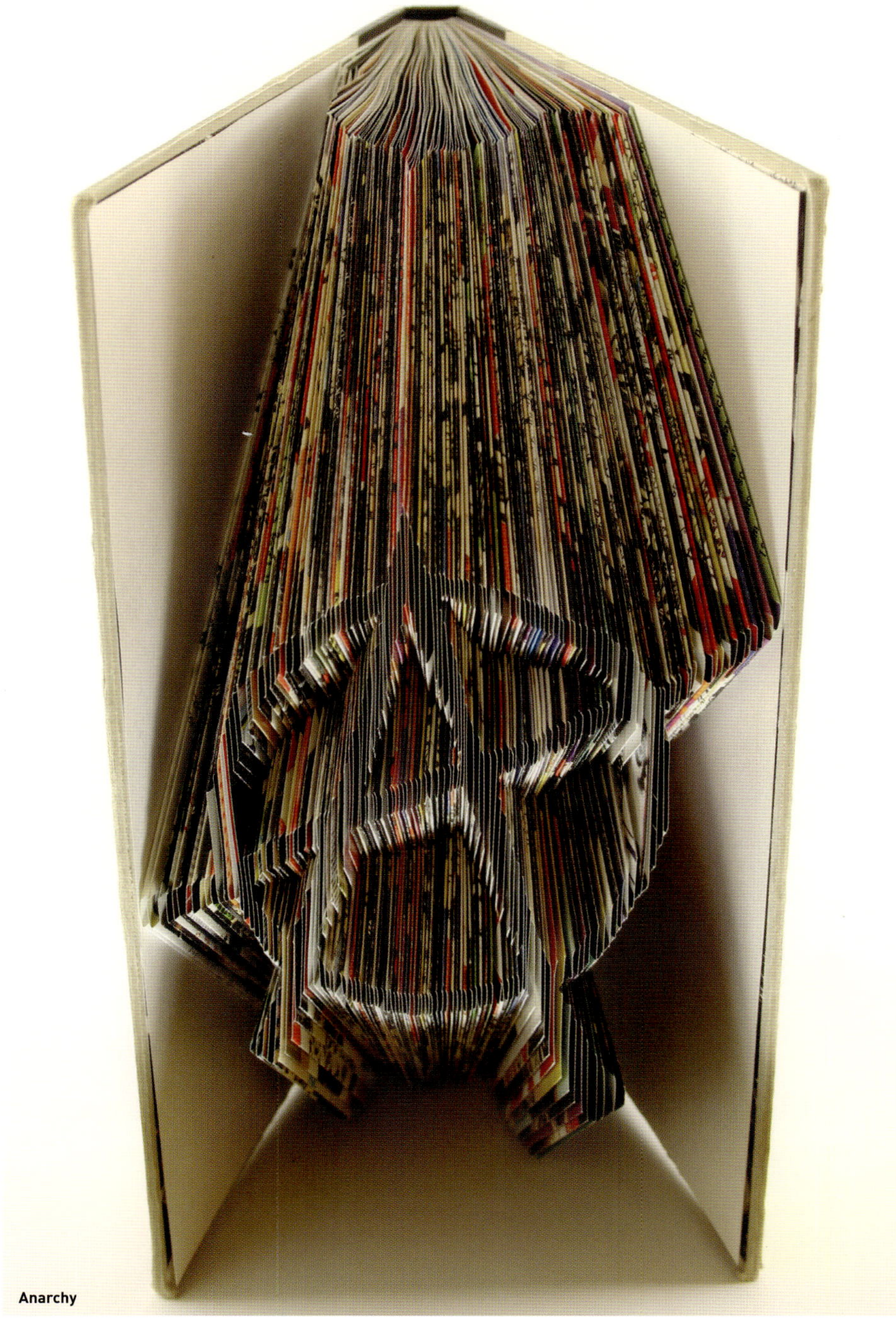

The artist is Isaac Salazar. Born in El Paso, TX on August 9, 1979. In July 2009, Isaac decided to venture into altered book art. He has taken altered book art into a whole new level. He has never taken an art class, nor has he thought of himself as an artist until recently. He begins by taking a book that has outlived its purpose on the shelf and folds each page precisely enough to display a letter, symbol or image in whole and repeats the process until he has completed his project. With the use of basic mathematics and the ability to foresee the end result, he is able to capture a unique way to read a book from a different perspective.

**Anarchy**

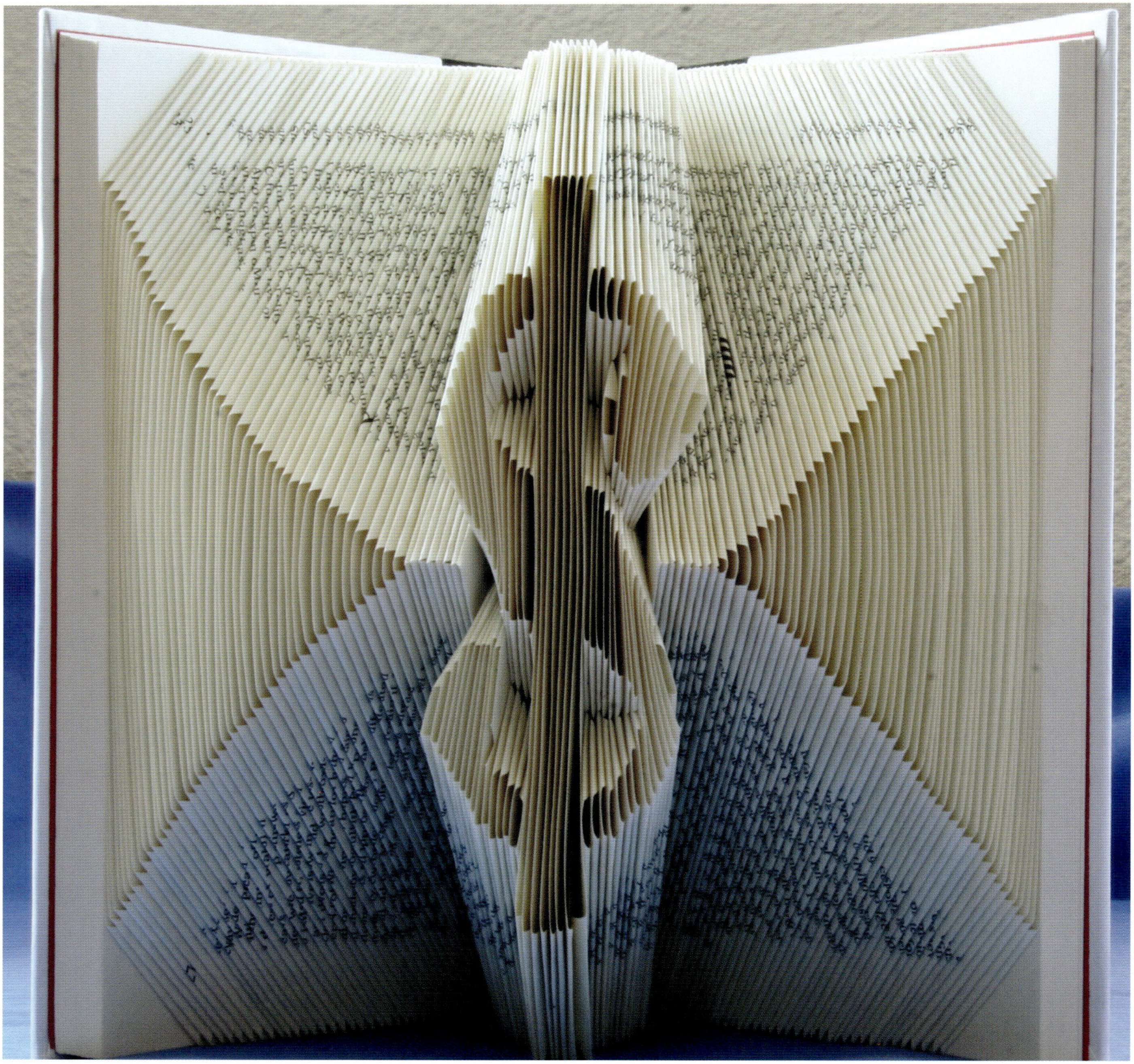

**Dollar Sign**

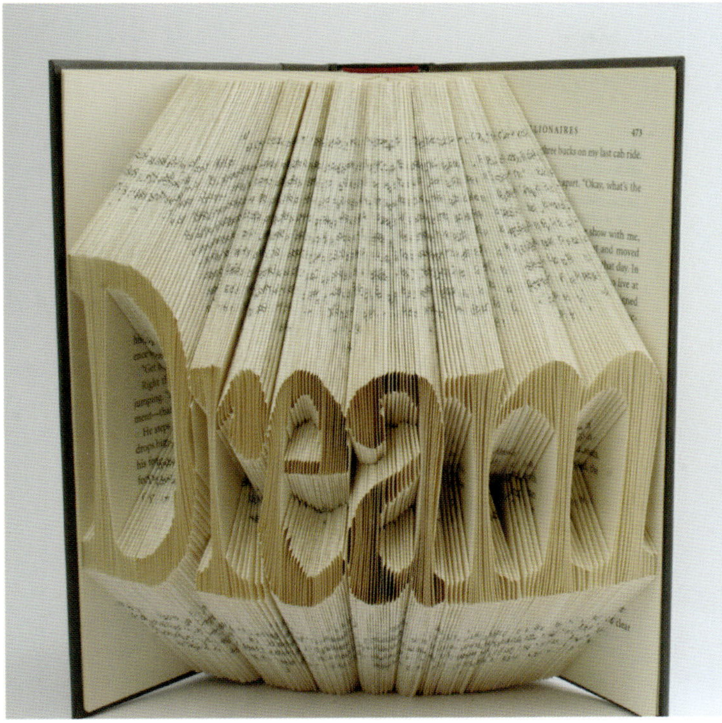
**Dream**

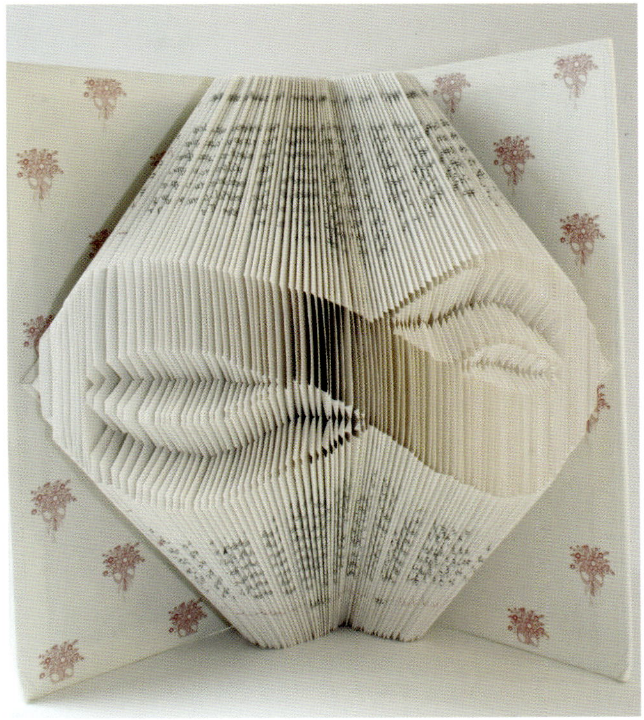
**Infinity**

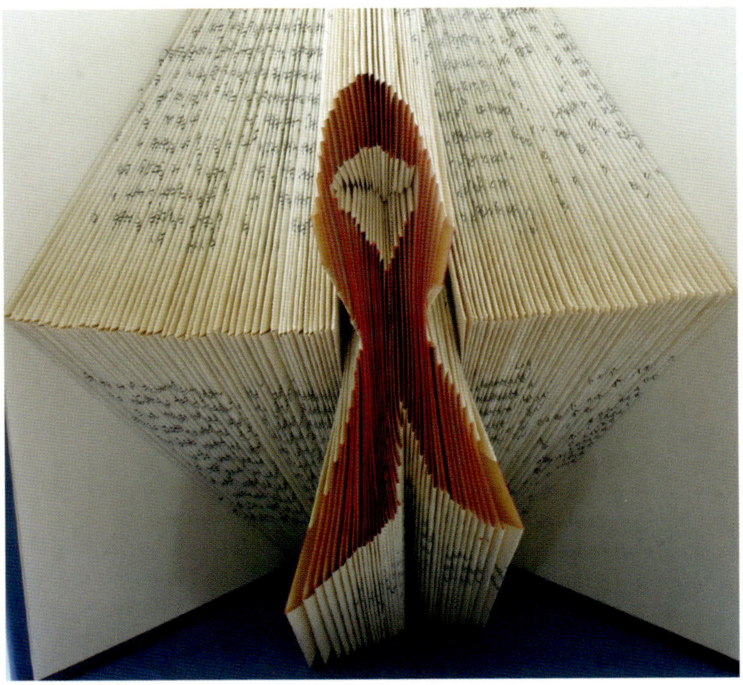
**Pink Ribbon**

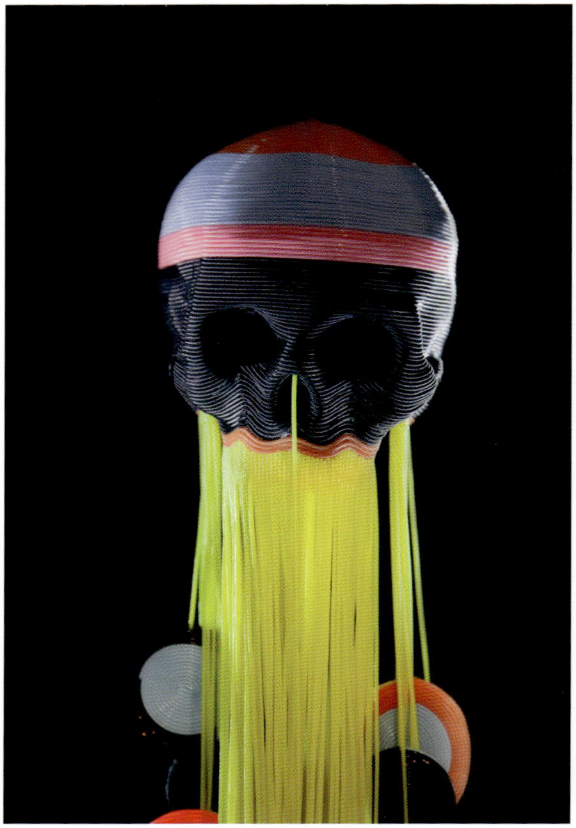

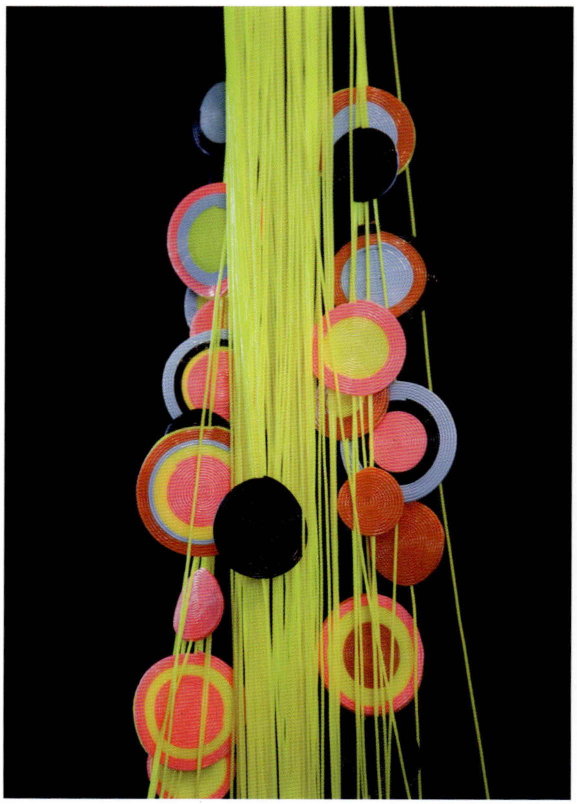

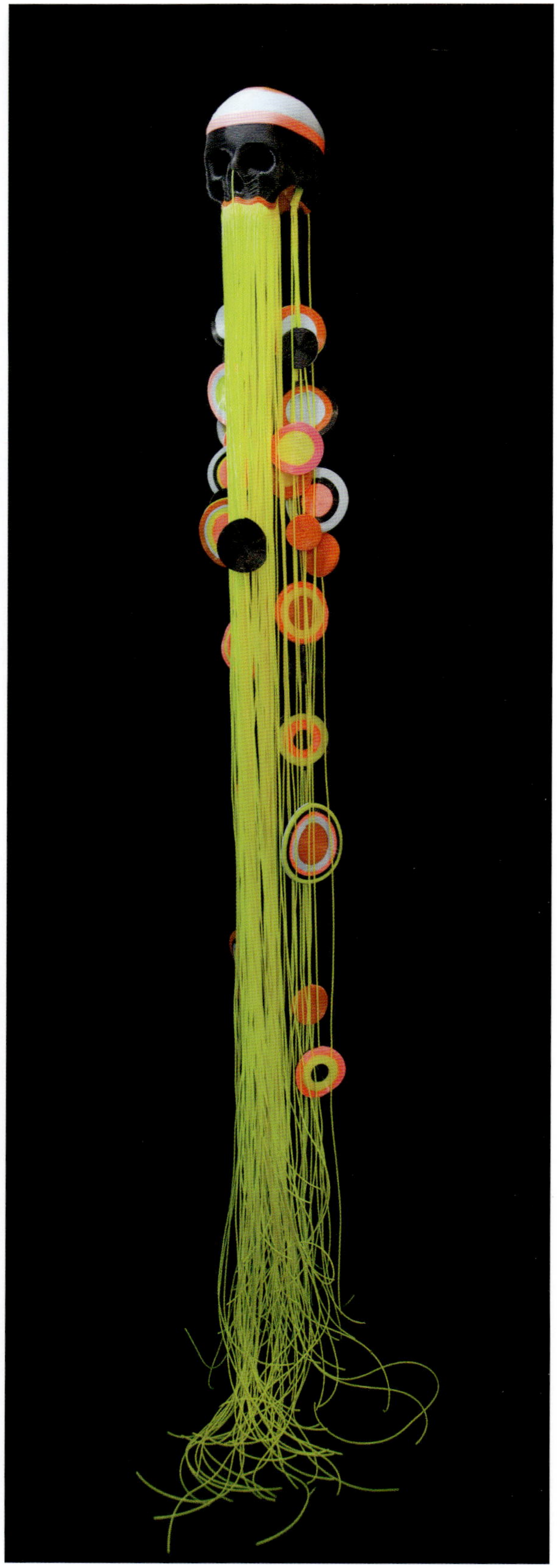

# Jim/Skull

www.jim-skullgallery.com

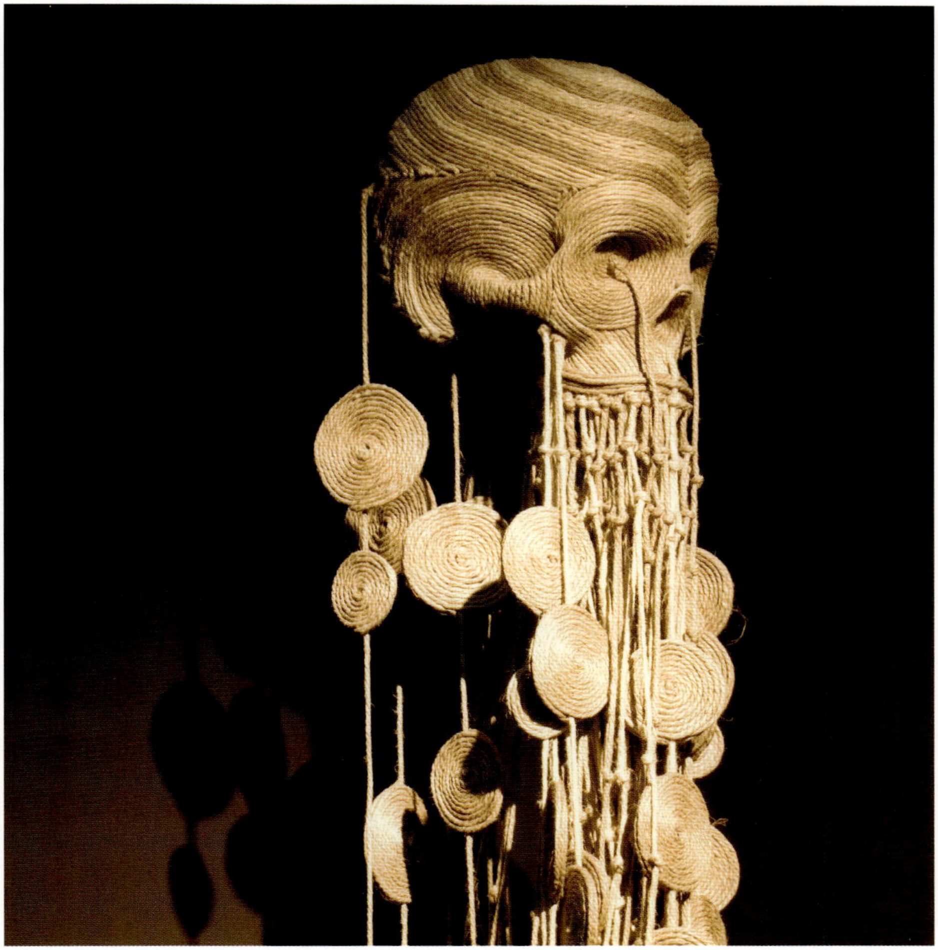

Sculpteur, France. October 7, 1959. We are in the Pacific. Lattitude 20°34' South. It is in Koumac in New Caledonia that the adventures of Jim, our skull artist, begin. It is also a gateway for Oceania and many other horizons. He goes to New Zealand, stops over New Hebrids, discovers Autralia, India, and lands in Hong-Kong. Human experiences, cultural, ritual, he is marked by his travels and encounters. Back to Paris, we are in 1979. He enters Estienne School, then the Applied Arts School Oliviers-de Serres. 1980, he creates his first skulls. His vocation is now revealed and will never leave him. He holds exhibitions in Parisian bars, takes part in the Salons d' Art, improves his technique creating the refined result we know of today. Contemporary art, African, Oceanian, Amerindian, popular, religious, multiple passions and a melting-pot of influences.

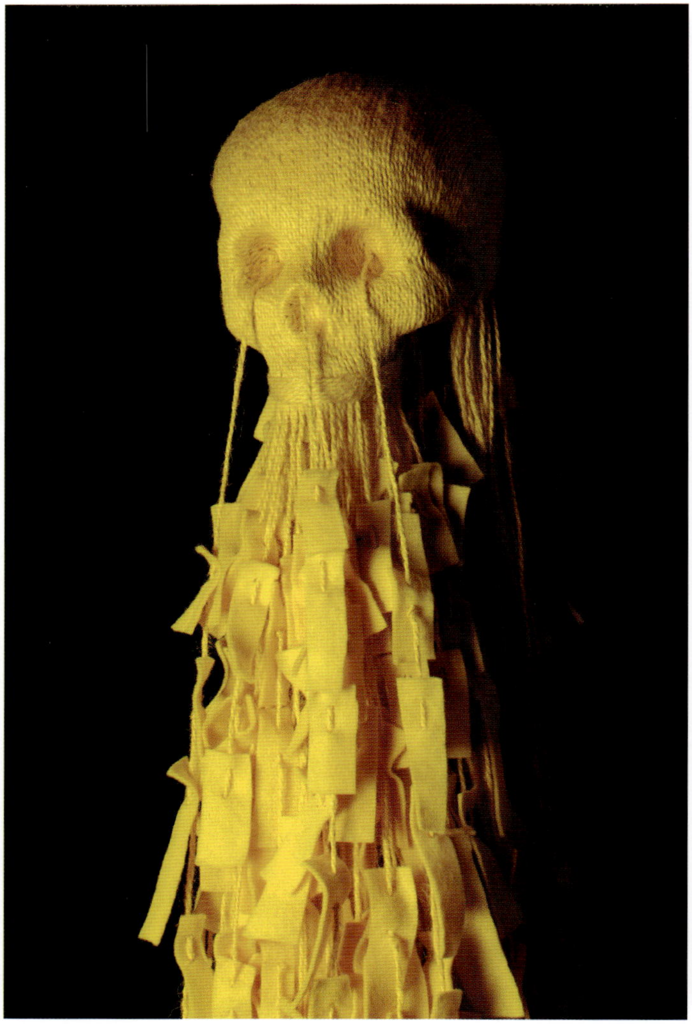

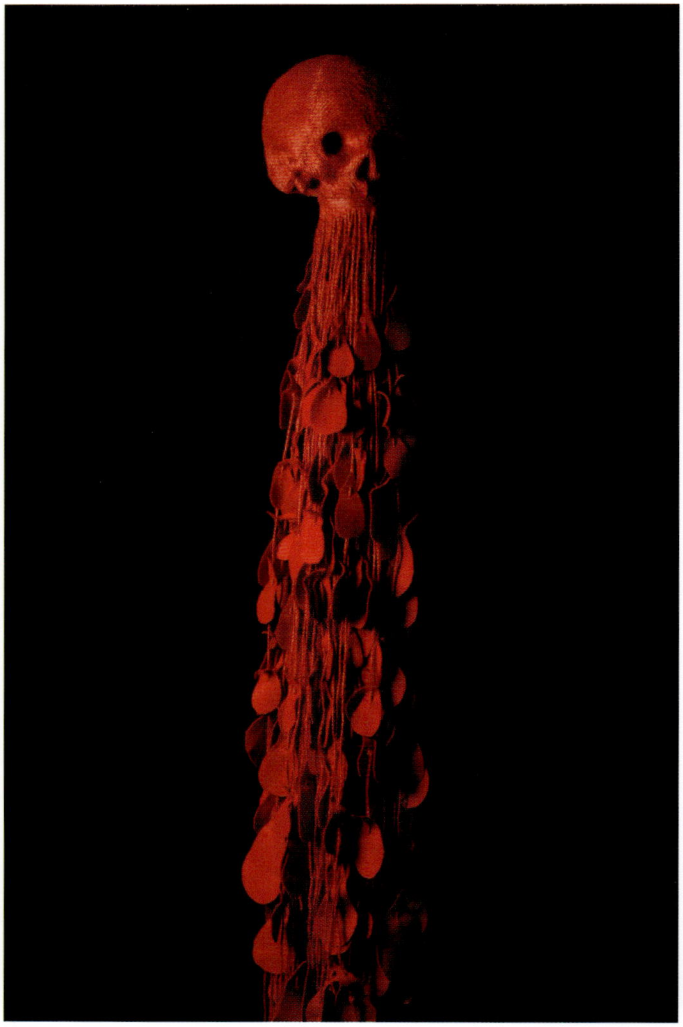

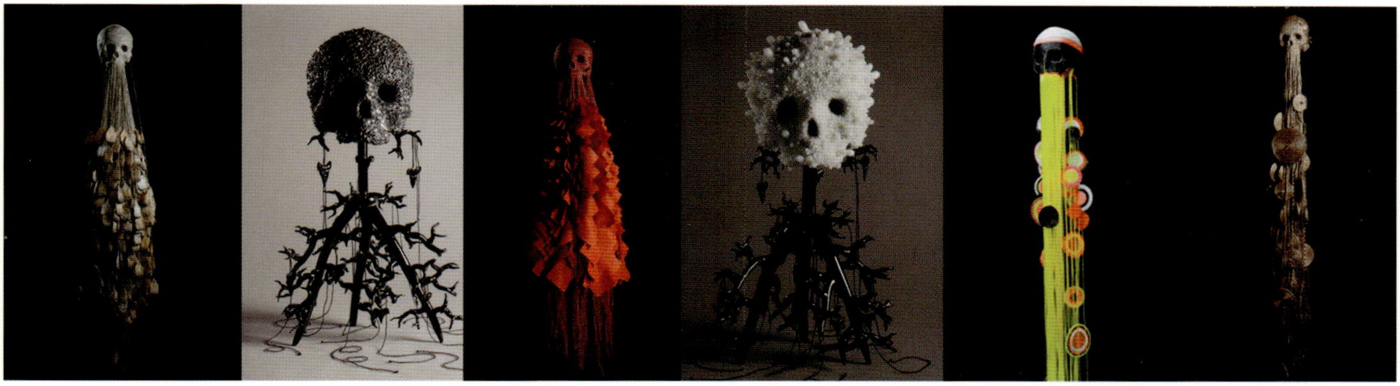

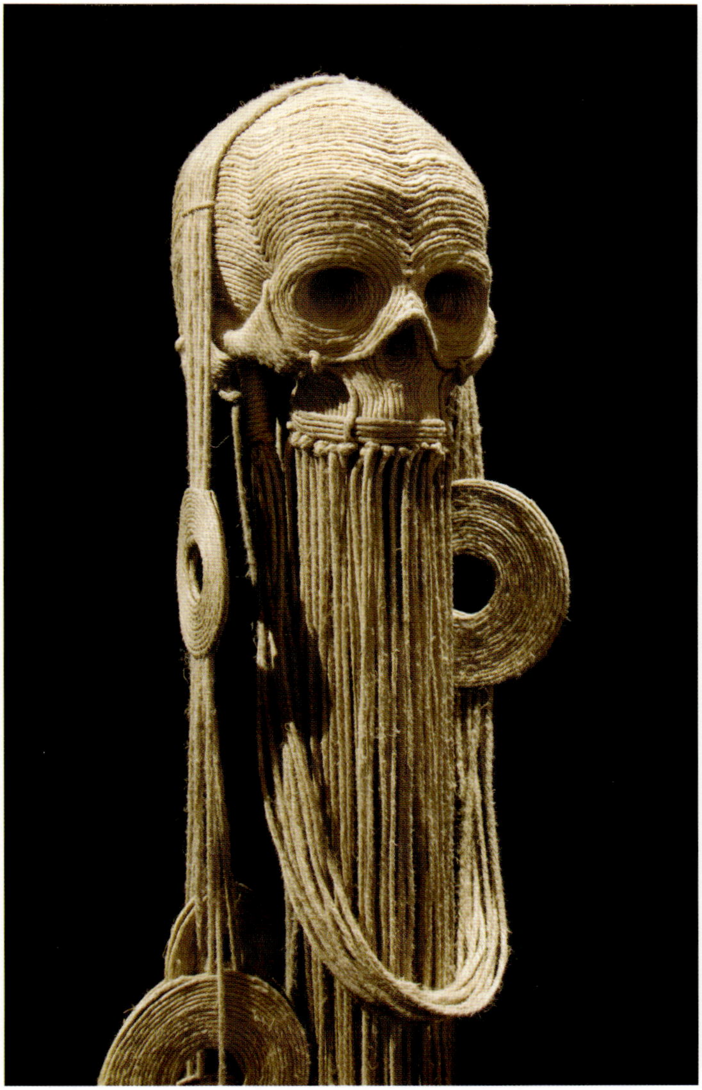

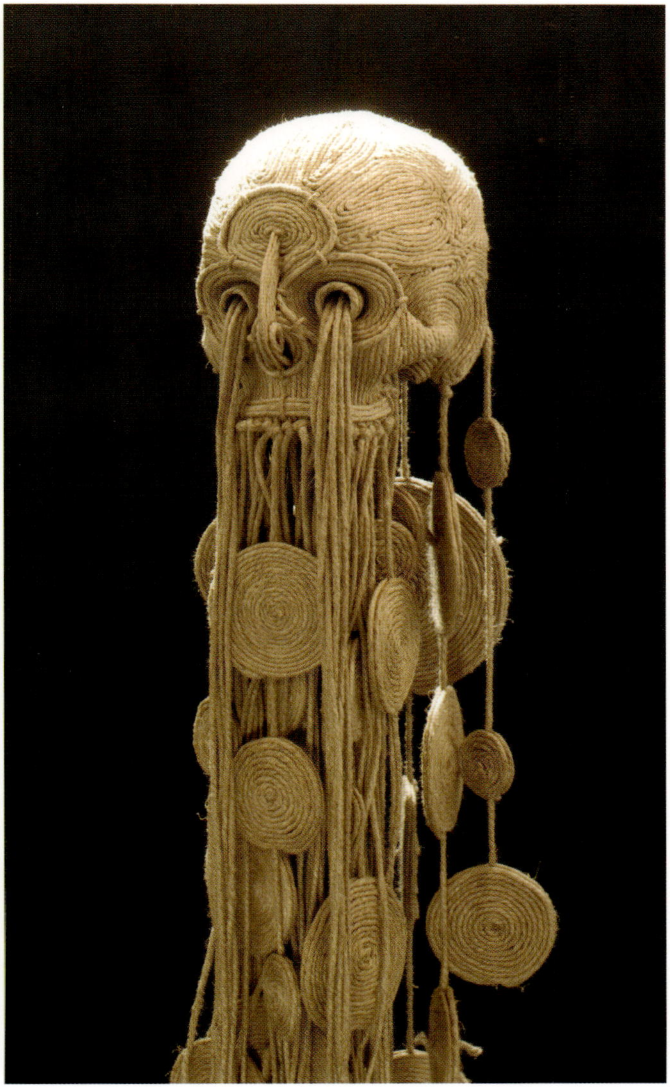

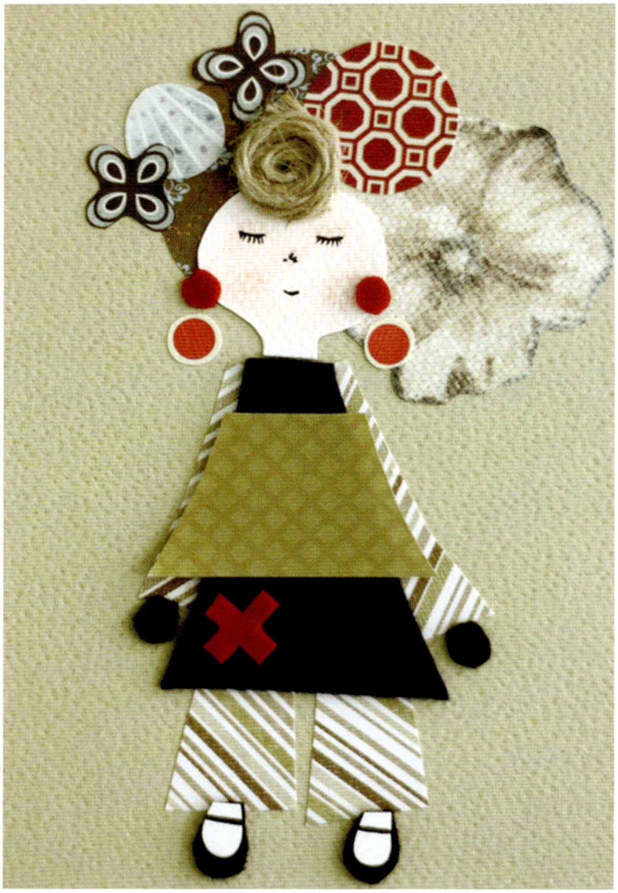
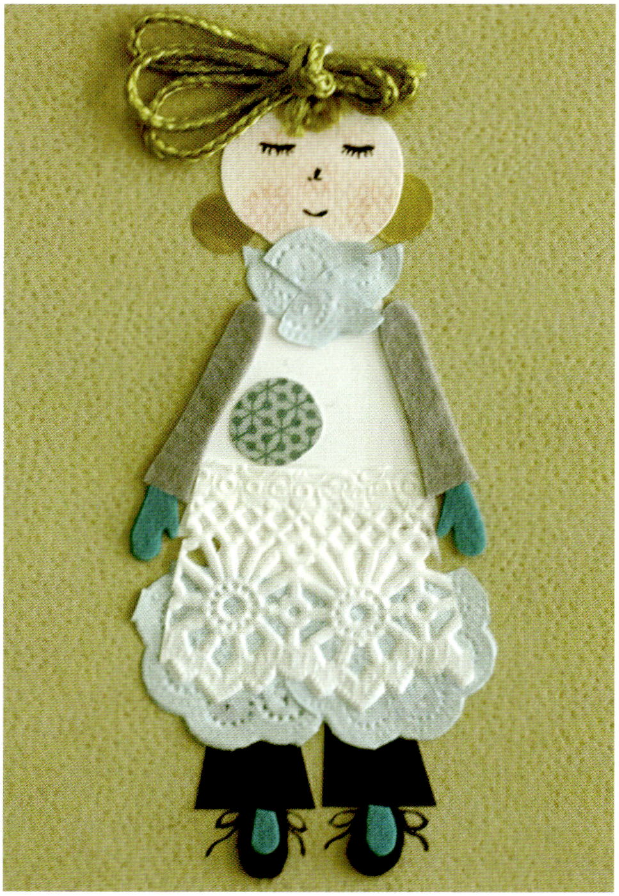
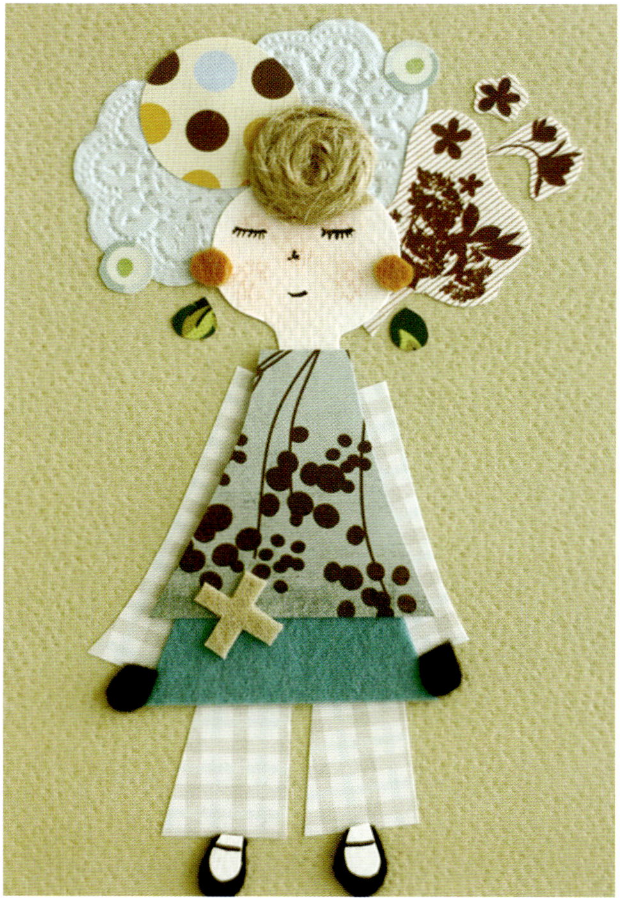
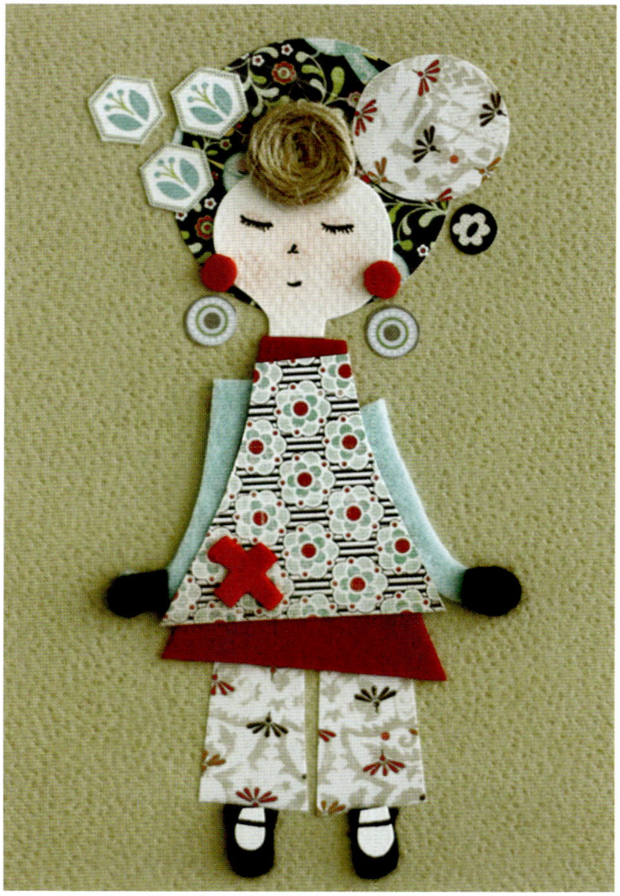

# Joaquima Casas

www.kupkup-land.blogspot.com

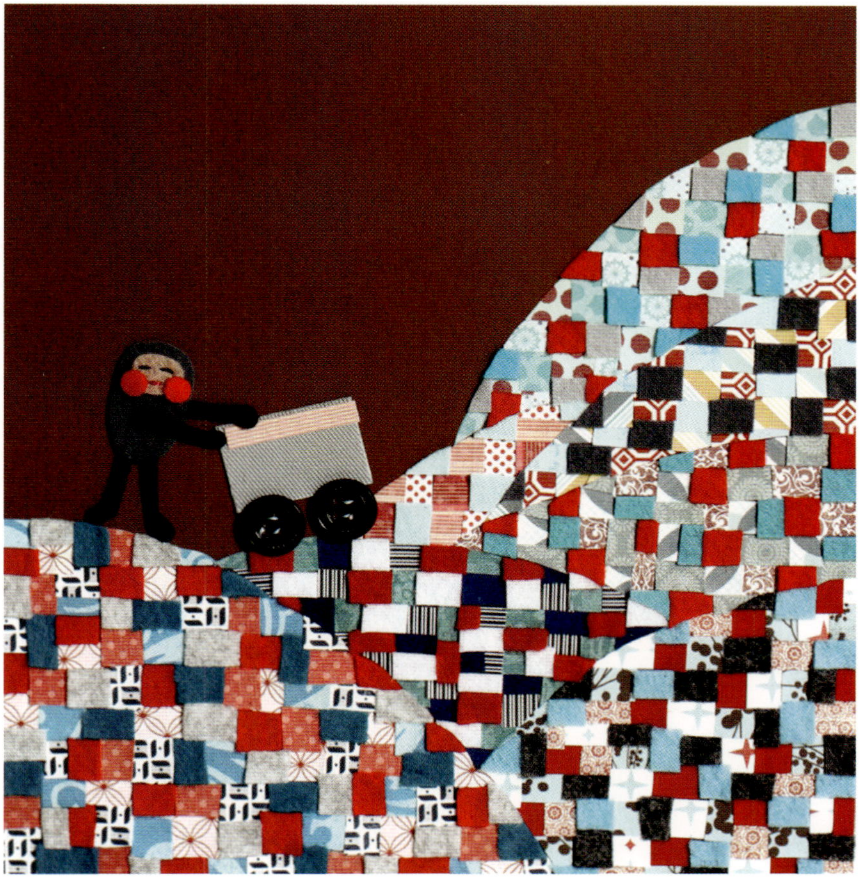

Hailing from Barcelona and currently living in Athens, Greece. I always loved to draw, paint, I have studied graphic design and illustration and two years ago I startet to play with fabrics, buttons, sewing and I Discovered felt! A fantastic material with you can create a lot of thinks from illustration to many interesting projects. My inspiration comes from the materials themselves, the fabrics, the colors, the drawings, the ornaments etc. The materials make me visualize the idea I have for a creation. I am fond of most japanese styles in craft making as i am of comics, illustration books for children, nature and life itself. I love cut and paste!! Sewing by hand and machine, embroidery, draw..I try to combine all these elements. I like to experiment with all sorts of materials but without doubt felt is my favourite one: i like to combine it with fabric and other materials paper, wool. My style is kind of pop and baroque at the same time, I love to use many diferents colors and elements together - at times i try to make things more minimal, I really thing that "less is more" but in my works the result never satisfied me so far- so i guess that's what defines me better.

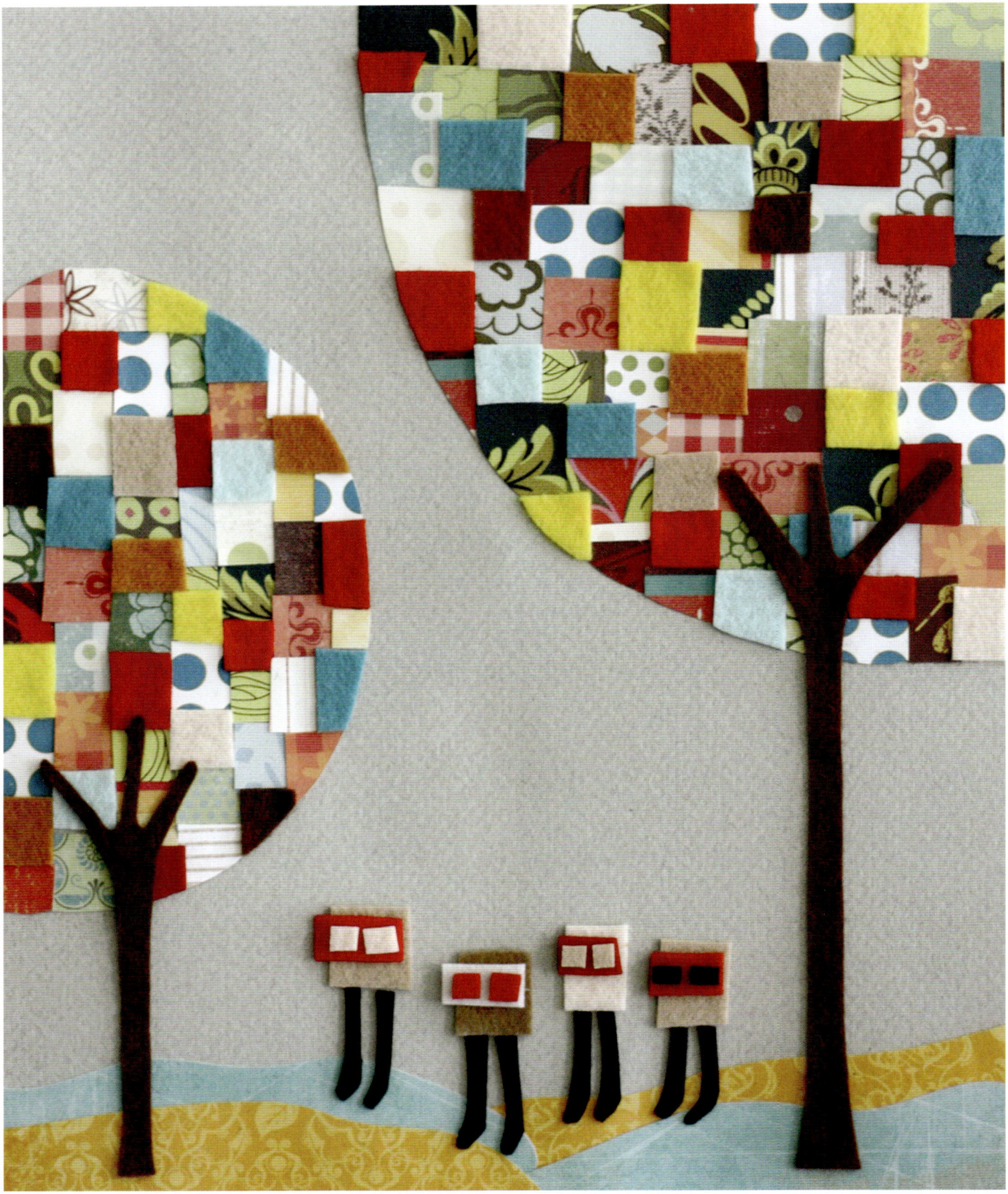

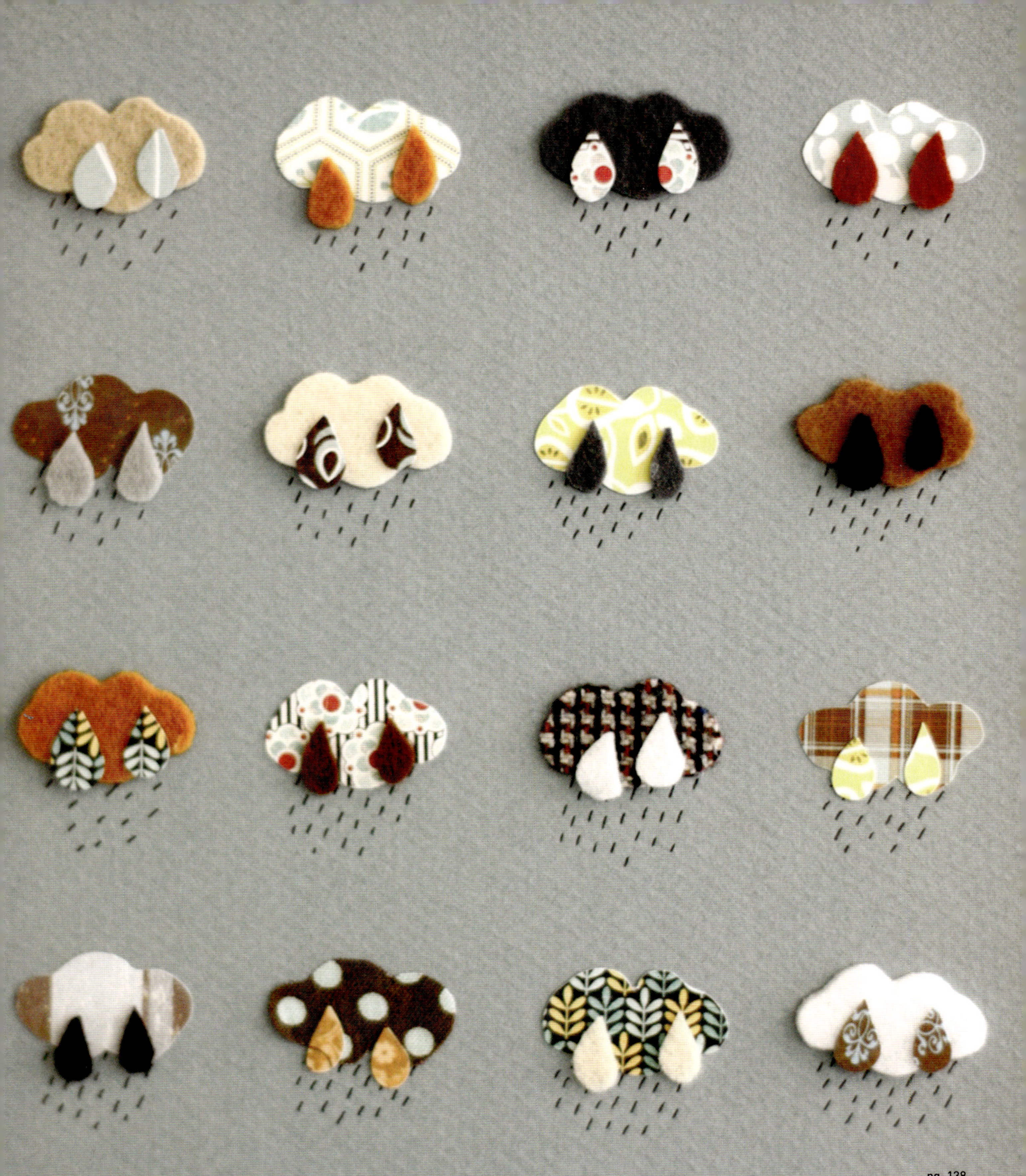

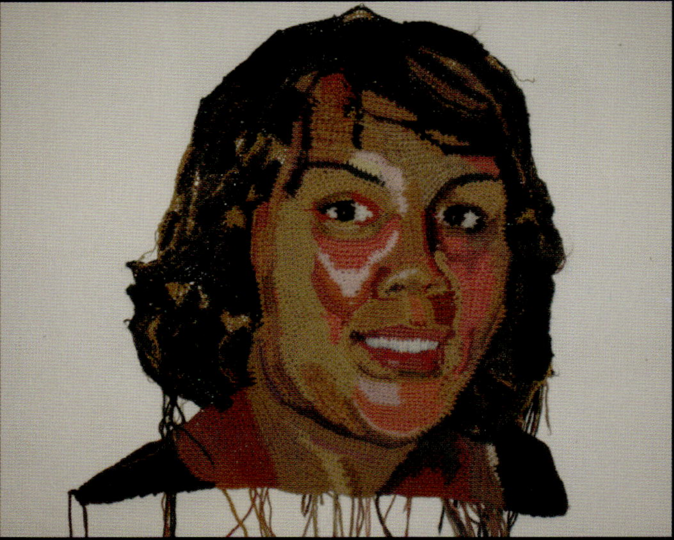

**Chevonne Ball** Mixed yarn, 22 x 27"

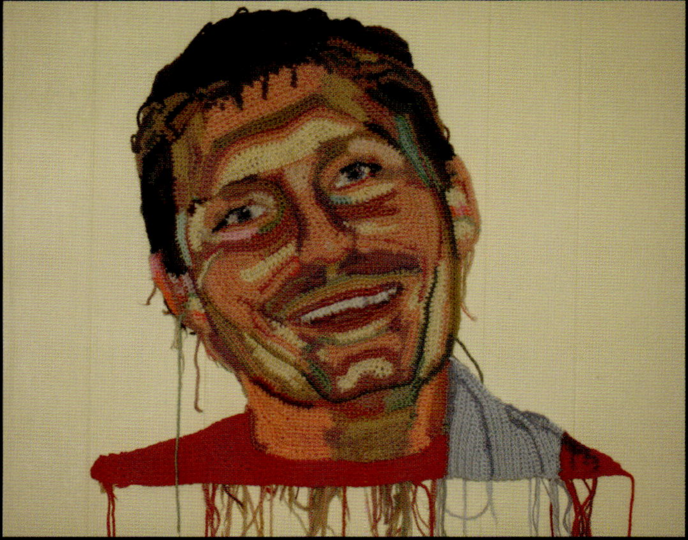

**Erik Van Kley** Mixed yarn, 23 x 21"

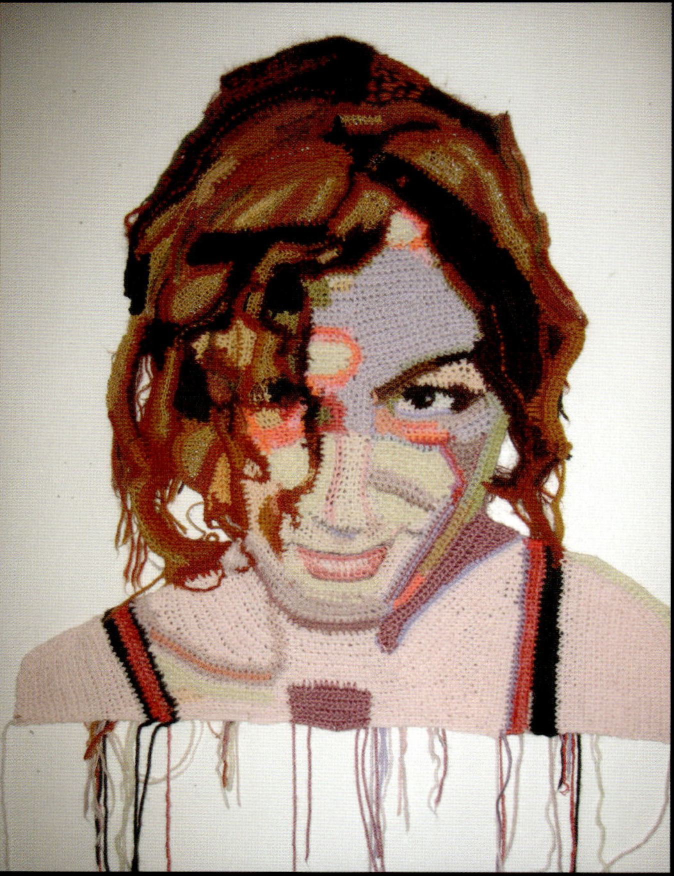

**Self-Portrait** Mixed yarn, 23 x 25"

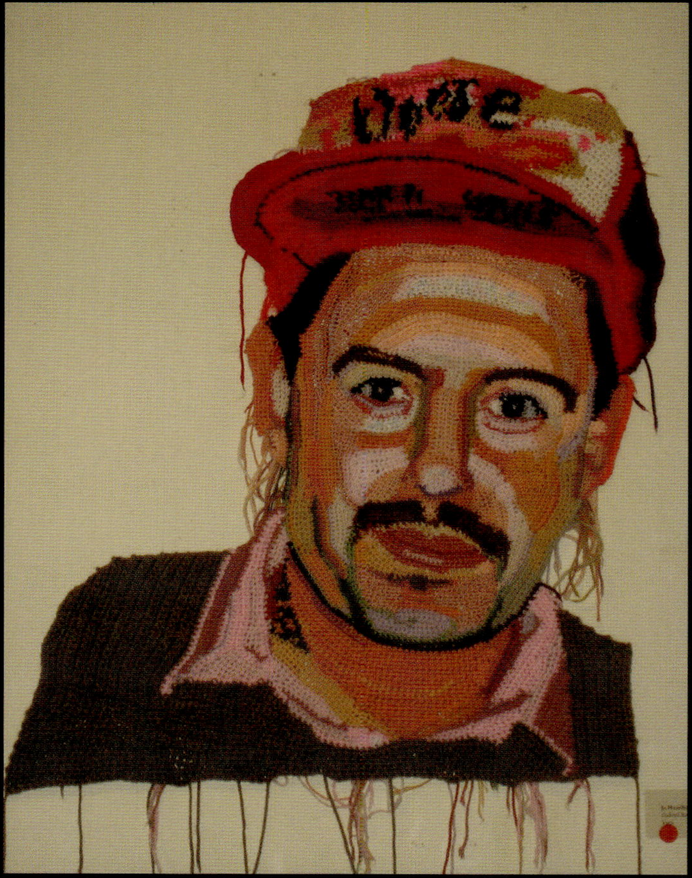

**Gabriel Rucker** Mixed yarn 31 x 25"

# Jo/Hamilton

www.johamiltonart.com

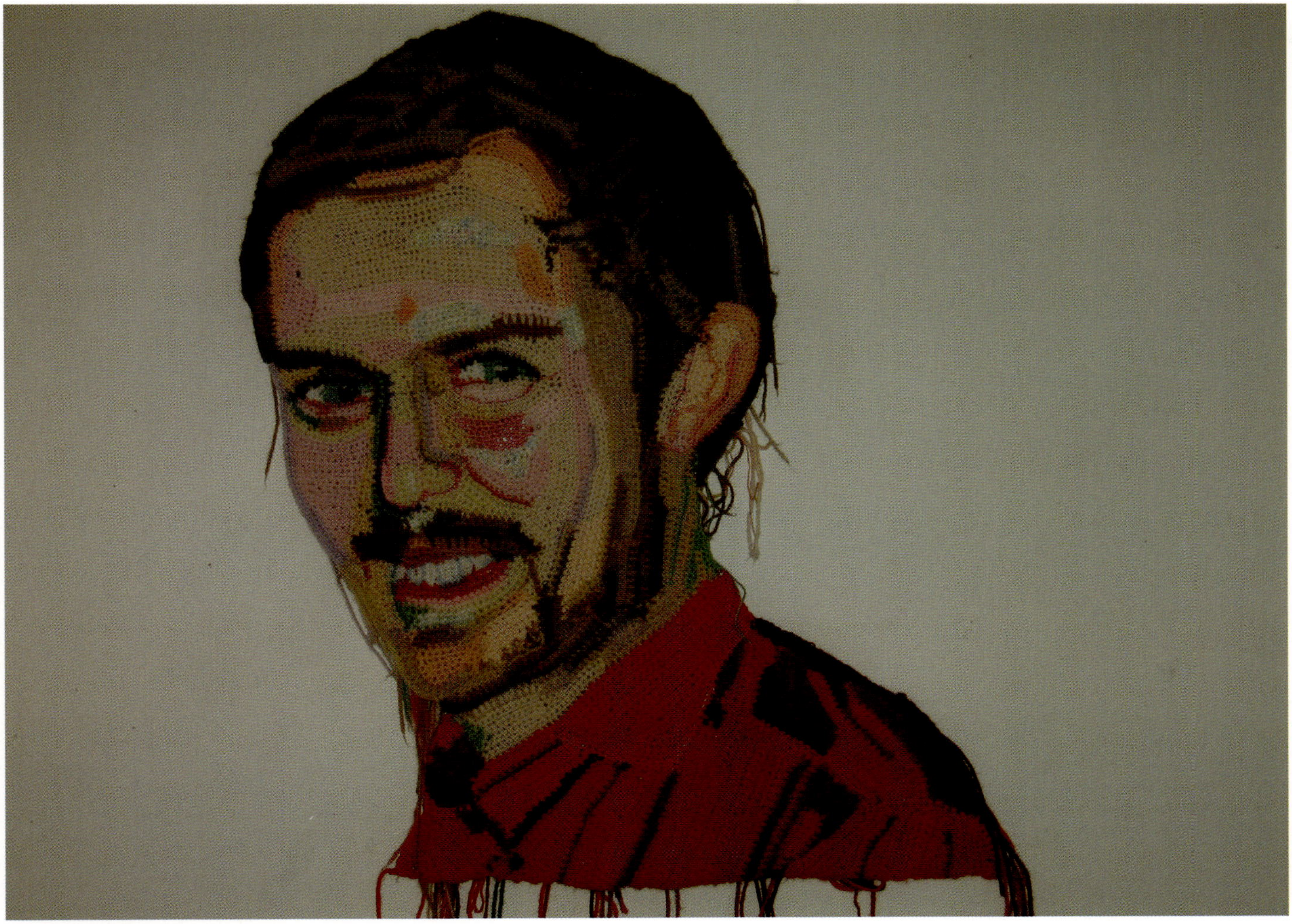

**Bryon Adams Harford** Mixed yarn, 22 x 27"

Jo Hamilton was born in Scotland and studied Drawing and Painting at the Glasgow School of Art. She relocated to Portland, Oregon in the mid-nineties, continuing to make art and show at a number of underground venues. She was inspired by a show at the local craft museum to attempt a 'crocheted painting' of sorts, and began the first six city blocks that would in three years become the massive 'I Crochet Portland' piece. It is based on a composite sketch of the city she loves. The portraits began as a dare to her coworkers at the restaurant where she works, and the resulting resemblances are as surprising to her as to their subjects. Jo takes photos of her friends, prints them out and crochets directly from them- there are no graphs, or patterns, or computer programmes involved, just her eyes, brain, and hands. She enjoys the simple, humble process of tying millions of knots to complete a larger whole. Her huge yarn collection comes mostly from second-hand stores. She enjoys playing with colour, plus the warmth, humor and friendliness of the completed pieces. She plans to continue her portraits of Portland people, commission pieces, and of the city itself.

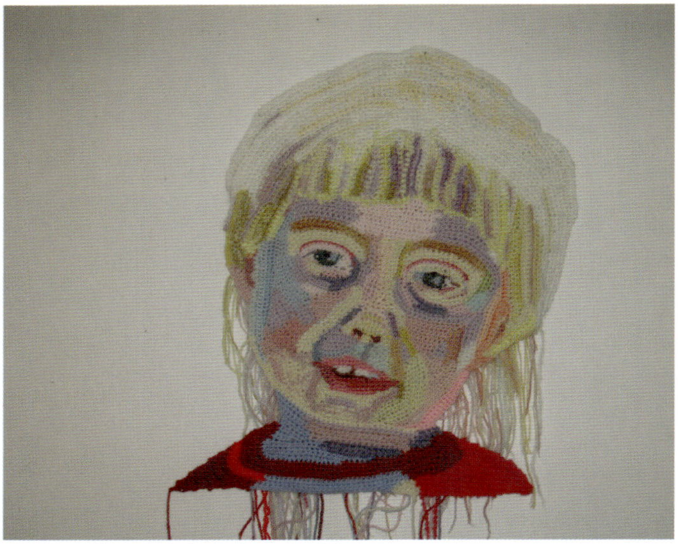

**Hugo Habetz** (commission) mixed yarn 25 x 25"

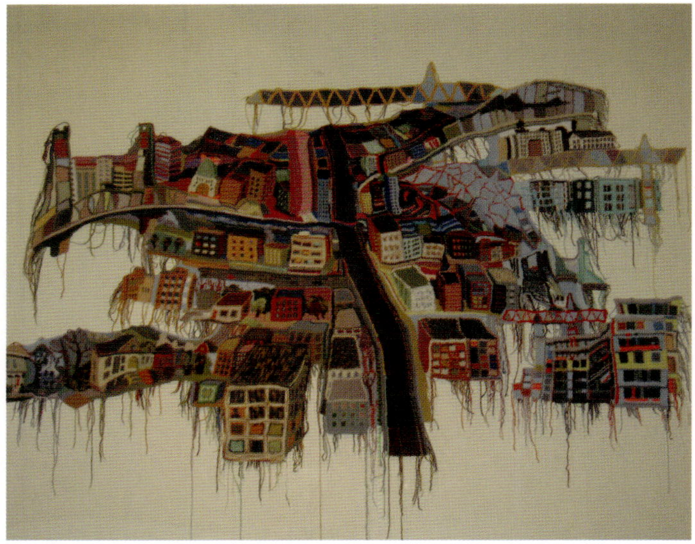

**I Crochet Portland** Mixed yarn, 9 x 4 feet, approx.

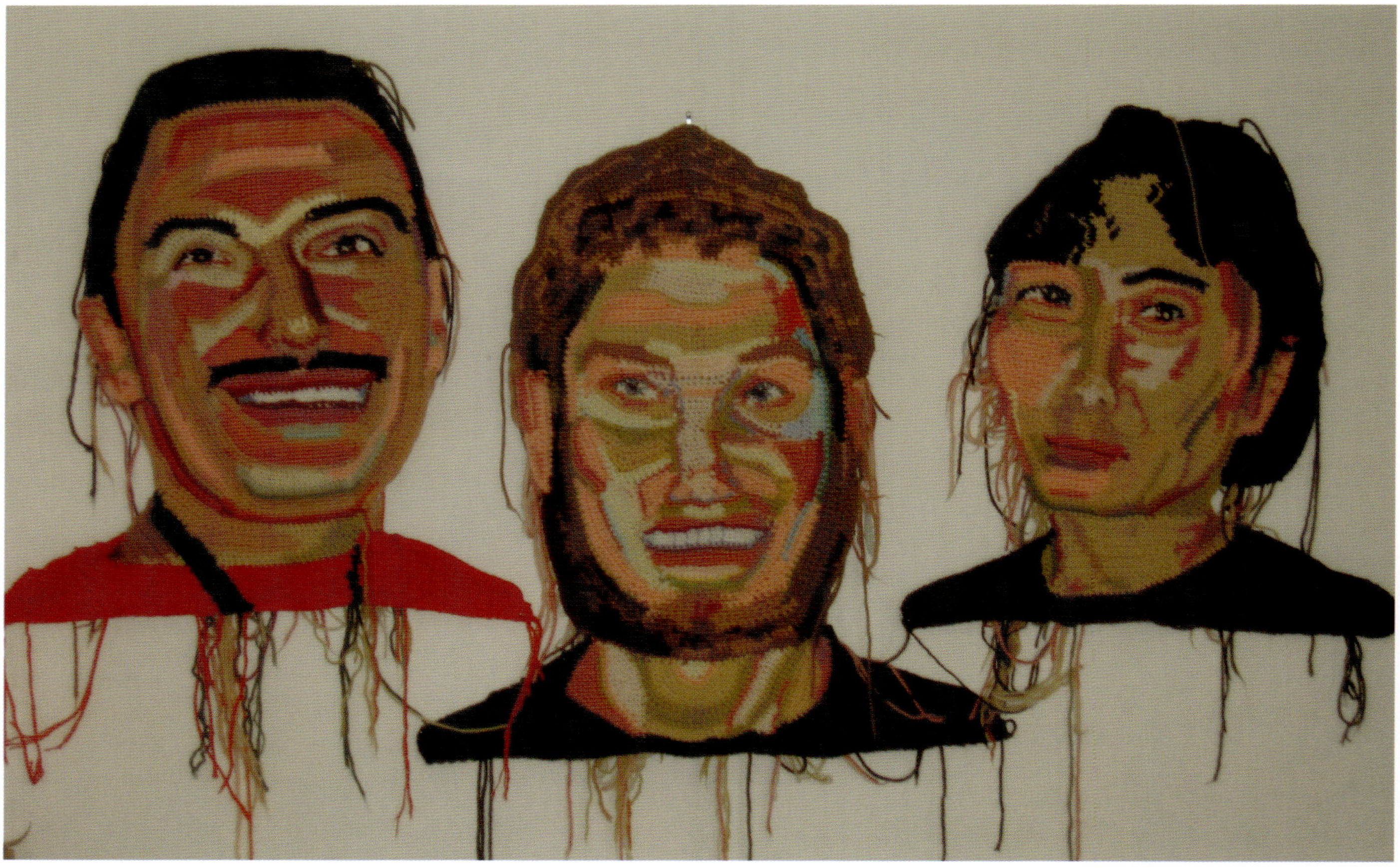

**Isaac Montalvo** (21 x 22) **The Amish Turk** (23 x 23) **Su-Lien Pinot** (19 x 20)

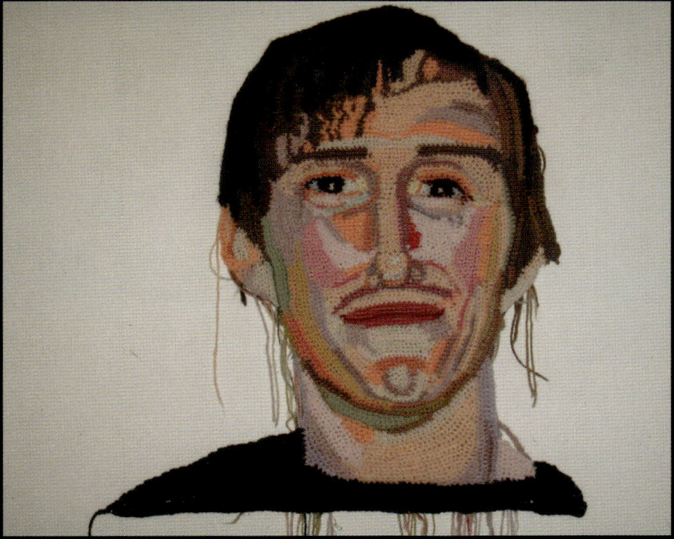

**Jon Anderson** Mixed yarn 22 x 25"

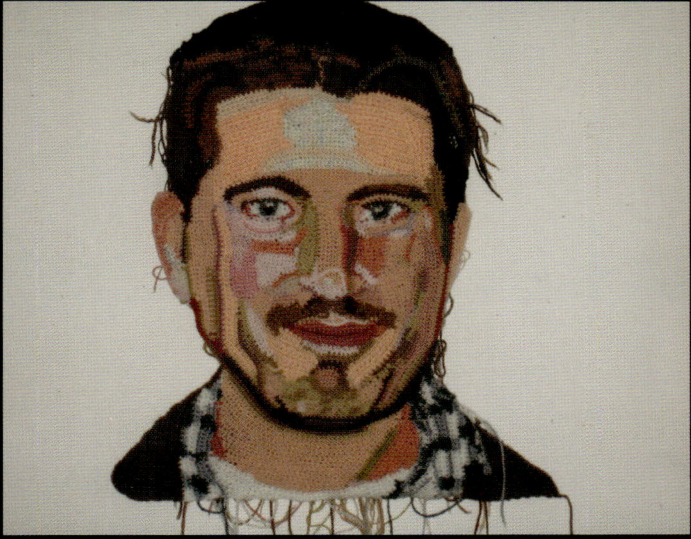

**Paul Brady** Mixed yarn, 21 x 25"

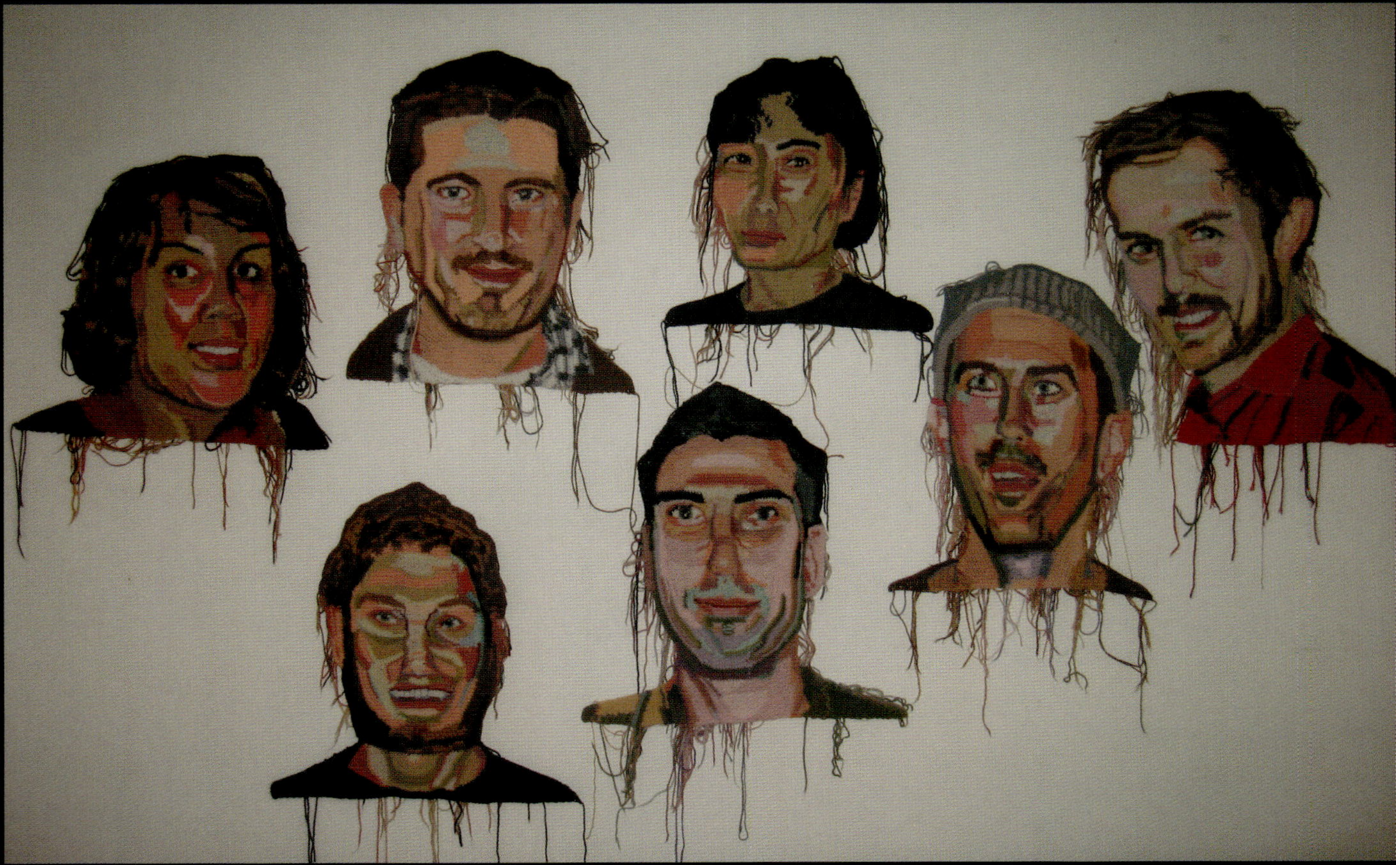

**Pigelife.**
Left to right: Chevonne, Amish, Paul, Grant Davis, Shreddy, Bryon

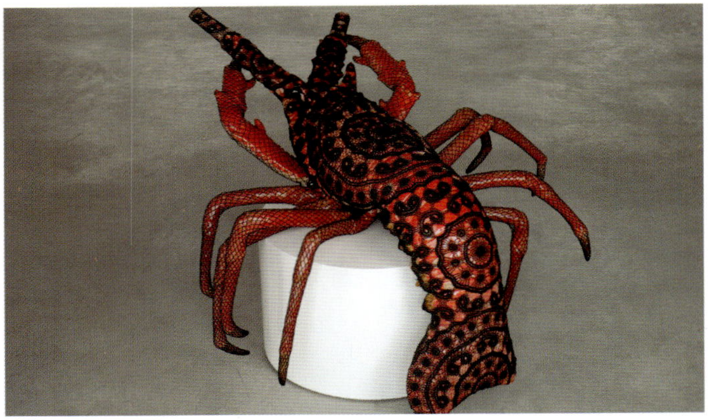

**Calypso, 2009**
Rafael Bordalo Pinheiro painted faience with
glazed ceramics and hand-made cotton crochet
84 x 125 x 140 cm Artist's collection

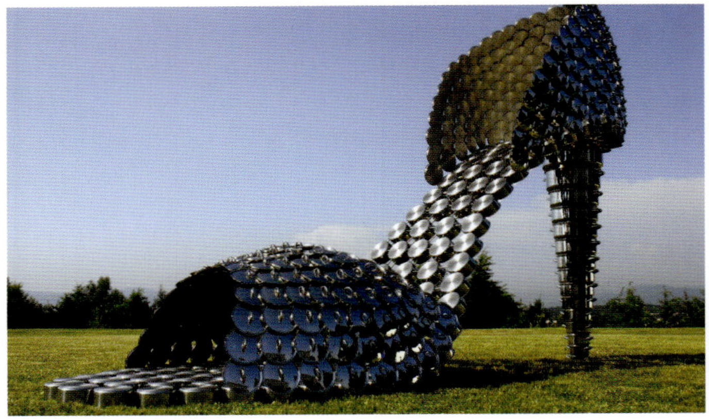

**Carmen Miranda, 2008**
Stainless steel pans and lids, cement
270 x 150 x 430 cm
Jorge Guimarães collection, Ponte de Lima

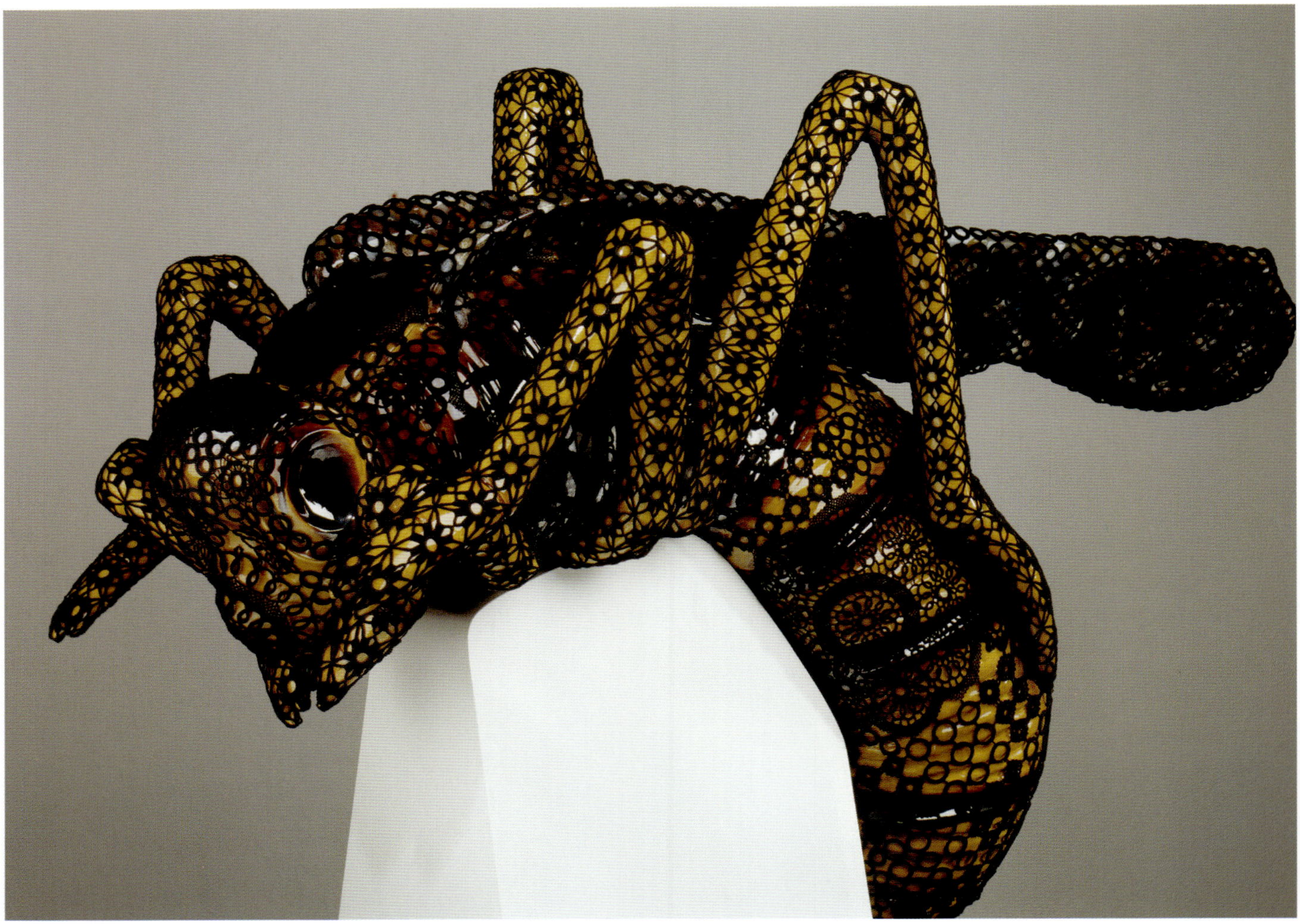

**Cléopatra, 2009**
Rafael Bordalo Pinheiro painted faience with glazed
ceramics and hand-made cotton crochet.
100 x 70 x 135 cm. Artist's collection

# Joana Vasconcelos

www.joanavasconcelos.com

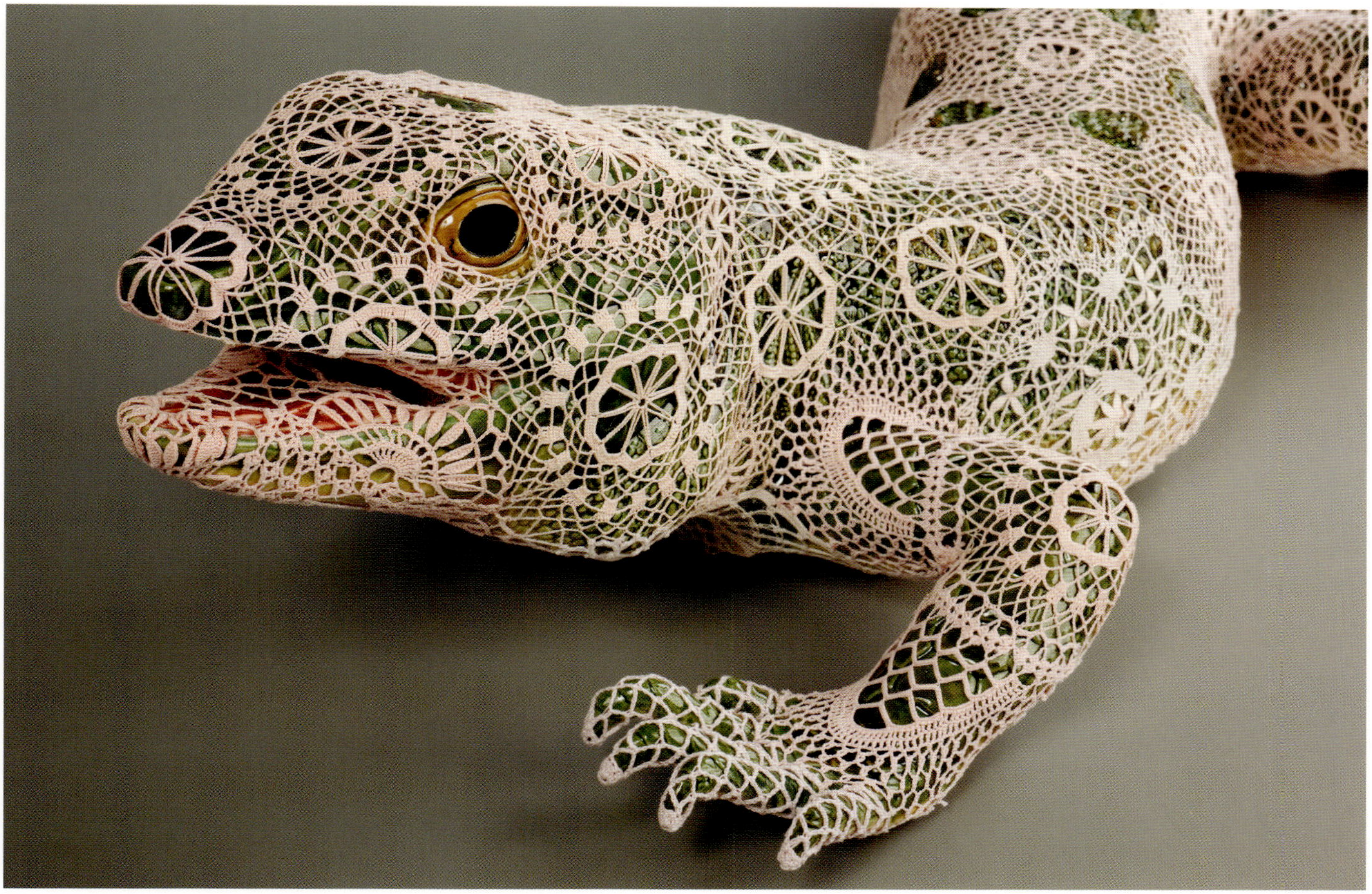

**Ali Baba, 2008**
**Rafael Bordalo Pinheiro painted faience with glazed ceramics and hand-made cotton crochet 25 x 55 x 125 cm**
**Private collection, Lisbon**

The nature of Joana Vasconcelos' creative process is based on the appropriation, decontextualisation and subversion of pre-existent objects and everyday realities. Sculptures and installations, which are revealing of an acute sense of scale and mastery of colour, as well as the recourse to performances and video or photographic records, all combine in the materialisation of concepts which challenge the pre-arranged routines of the quotidian. Starting out from ingenious operations of displacement, a reminiscence of the Ready-Made and the grammars of Nouveau Réalisme and Pop, the artist offers us a complicit vision, but one which is at the same time critical of contemporary society and the several features which serve the enunciations of collective identity, especially those that concern the status of women, class distinction or national identity. From this process there derives a speech which is attentive to contemporary idiosyncrasies, where the usual dichotomies of hand-crafted/industrial, private/public, tradition/modernity and popular culture/erudite culture are imbued with affinities that are apt to renovate the usual fluxes of signification which are characteristic of contemporaneity.

Photo by: DMF, Lisboa, Ana Paula Carvalho, Clovis Franca- Pinacoteca do Estado de Sao Paulo, Isabella Matheus, Bertrand Huet, Tutti-Galerie Nathalie Obadia Paris, Luis Vasconcelos, Joao Miranda, Atelier Joana Vasconcelos.

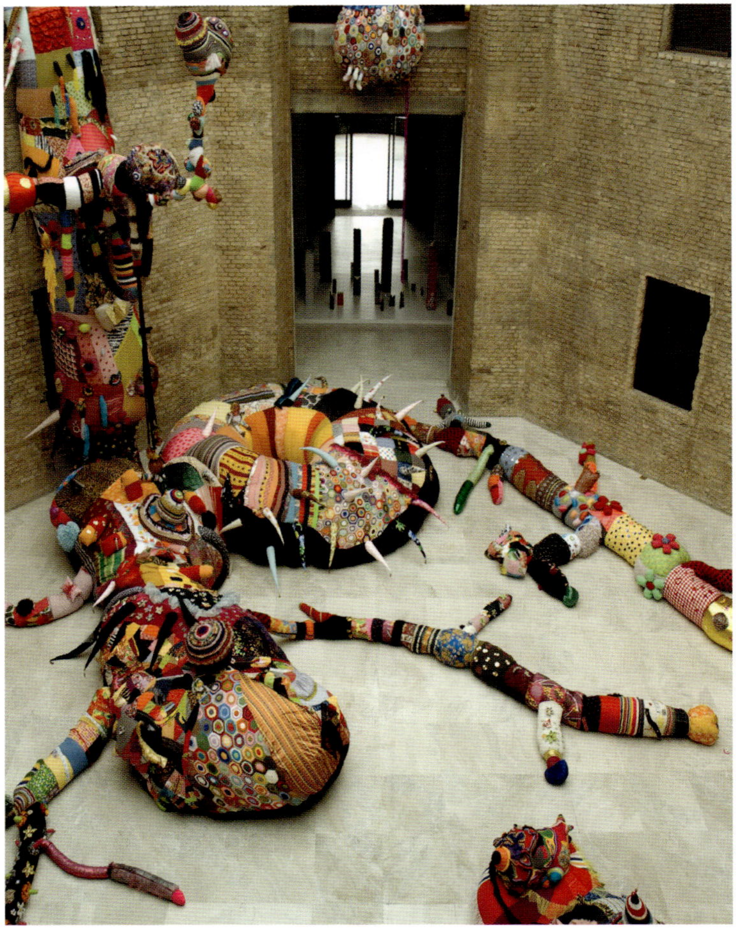

**Contamination, 2008**
Installation at Pinacoteca do Estado de São Paulo. Hand-knitted and hand-made woollen crochet, industrial acrylic fabric, fabrics, ornaments, polystyrene, polyester, steel cables variables dimensions
Artist's collection

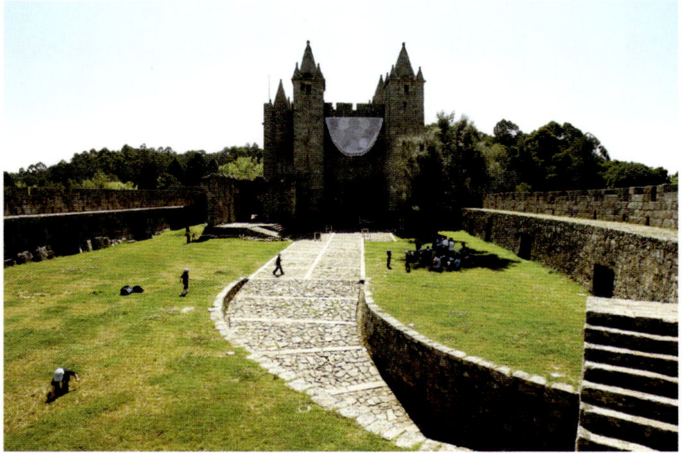

**Donzela, 2007**
Municipal Council of Santa Maria da Feira collection
Hand-made cotton crochet, aluminium, steel cables
455 x 780 cm

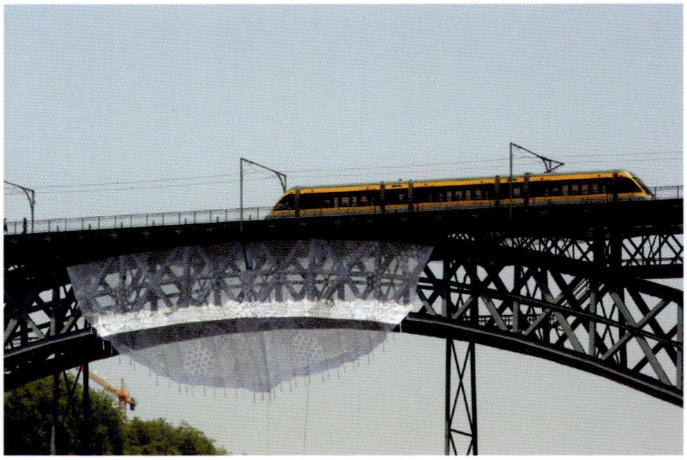

**Varina, 2008**
Installation at D.Luis I Brigde, Porto, 2008
Hand-made cotton crochet, steel cables
1500 x 3500 cm Artist's collection

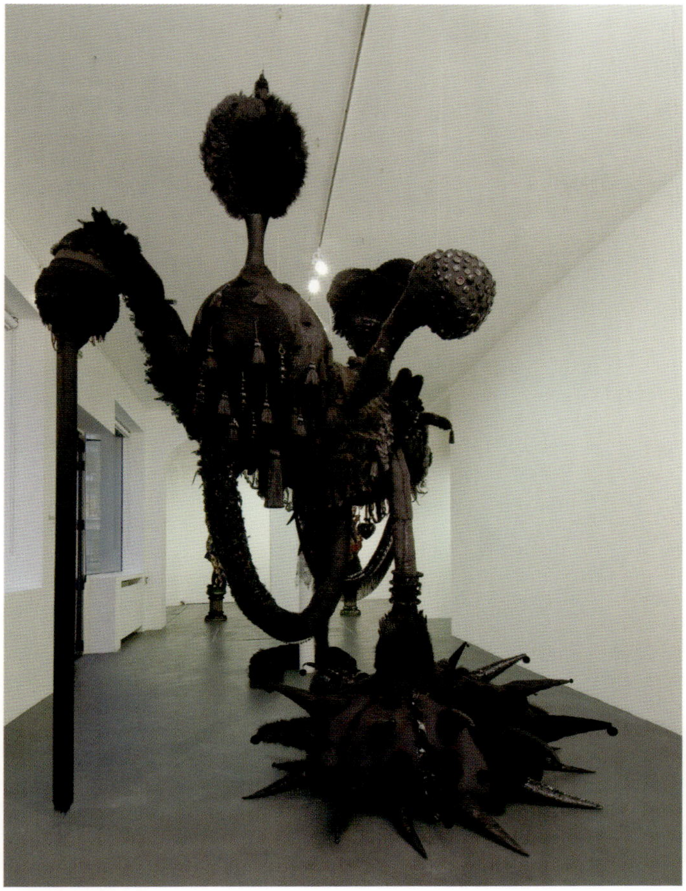

**Victoria, 2008**
Hand-knitted and hand-made woollen crochet, industrial acrylic fabric, fabrics, ornaments, polyester, steel cables
400 x 300 x 350 cm. Artist's collection

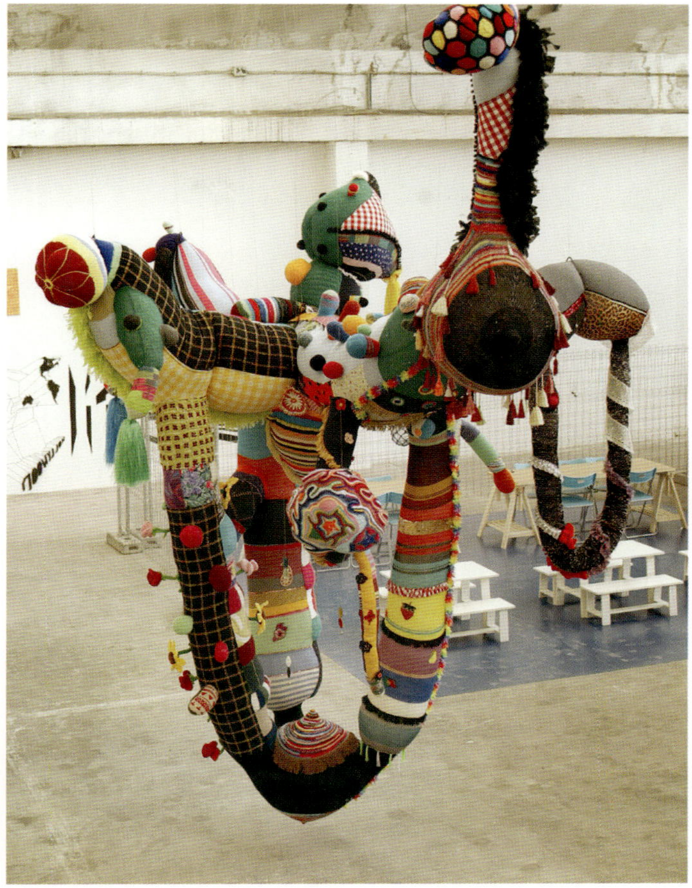

**Valkyrie Excesso, 2005**
Hand-knitted and hand-made woollen crochet, industrial acrylic fabric, fabrics, ornaments, polyester, steel cables
600 x 550 x 550 cm. Artist's collection

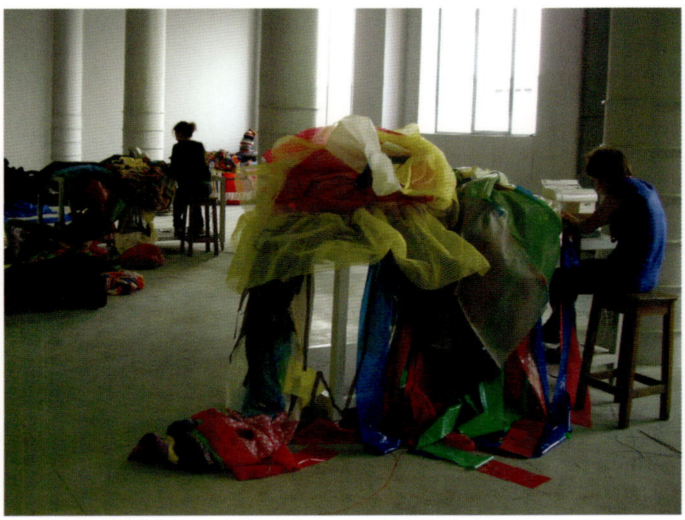

**Vitrine, 2008**

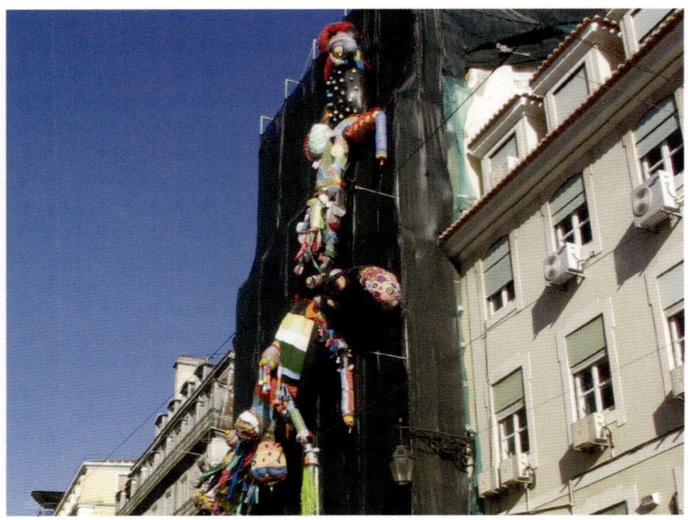

**Vitrine, 2008**

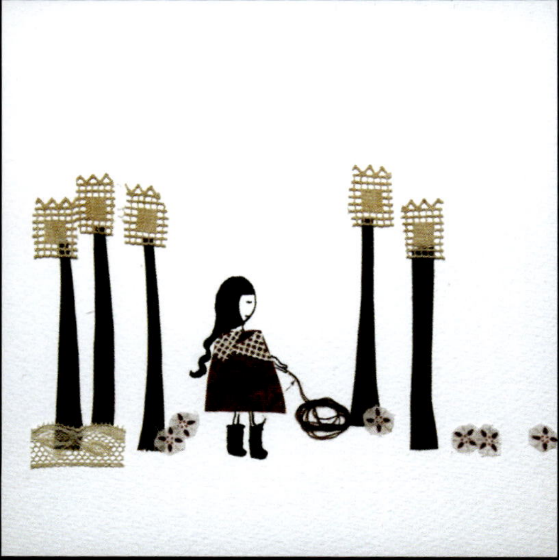

**Little Red Maiden Hood**. Self Promotion work, 2009
Ink, fabric, lace and thread collage on paper

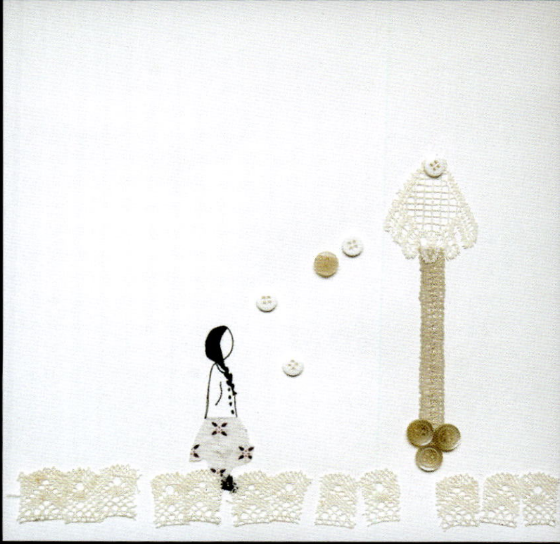

**Flower from Passing on**. Self published book, 2009
Ink, fabric, buttons and lace collage on paper

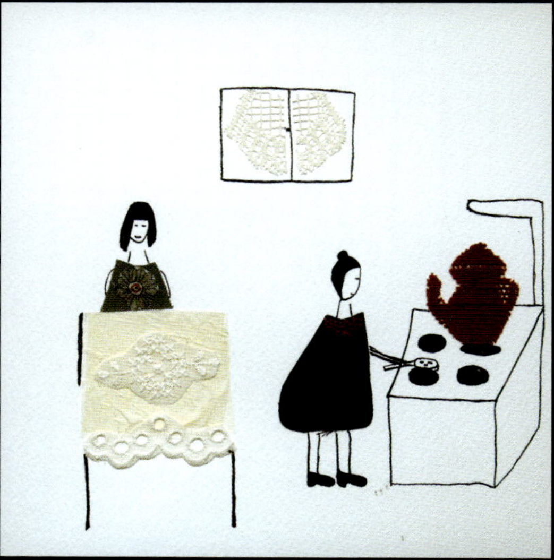

**Kitchen from Passing on**. Self published book, 2009
Ink, fabric, buttons and lace collage on paper

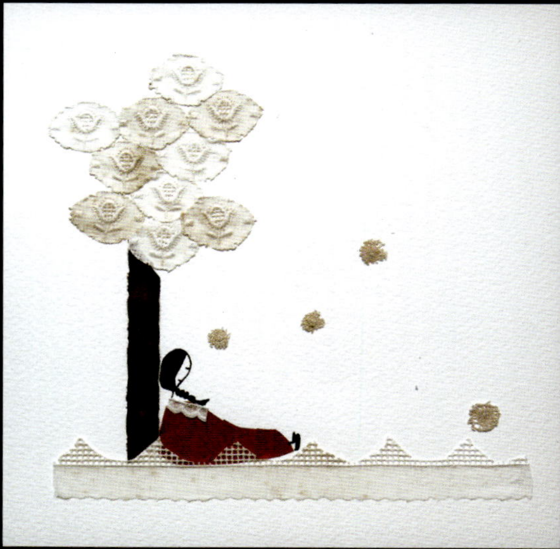

**Little Red woodland creature sitting**. Self Promotion work, 2009
Ink, lace and paper collage on paper.

# Julie Vermeille

www.julievermeille.com

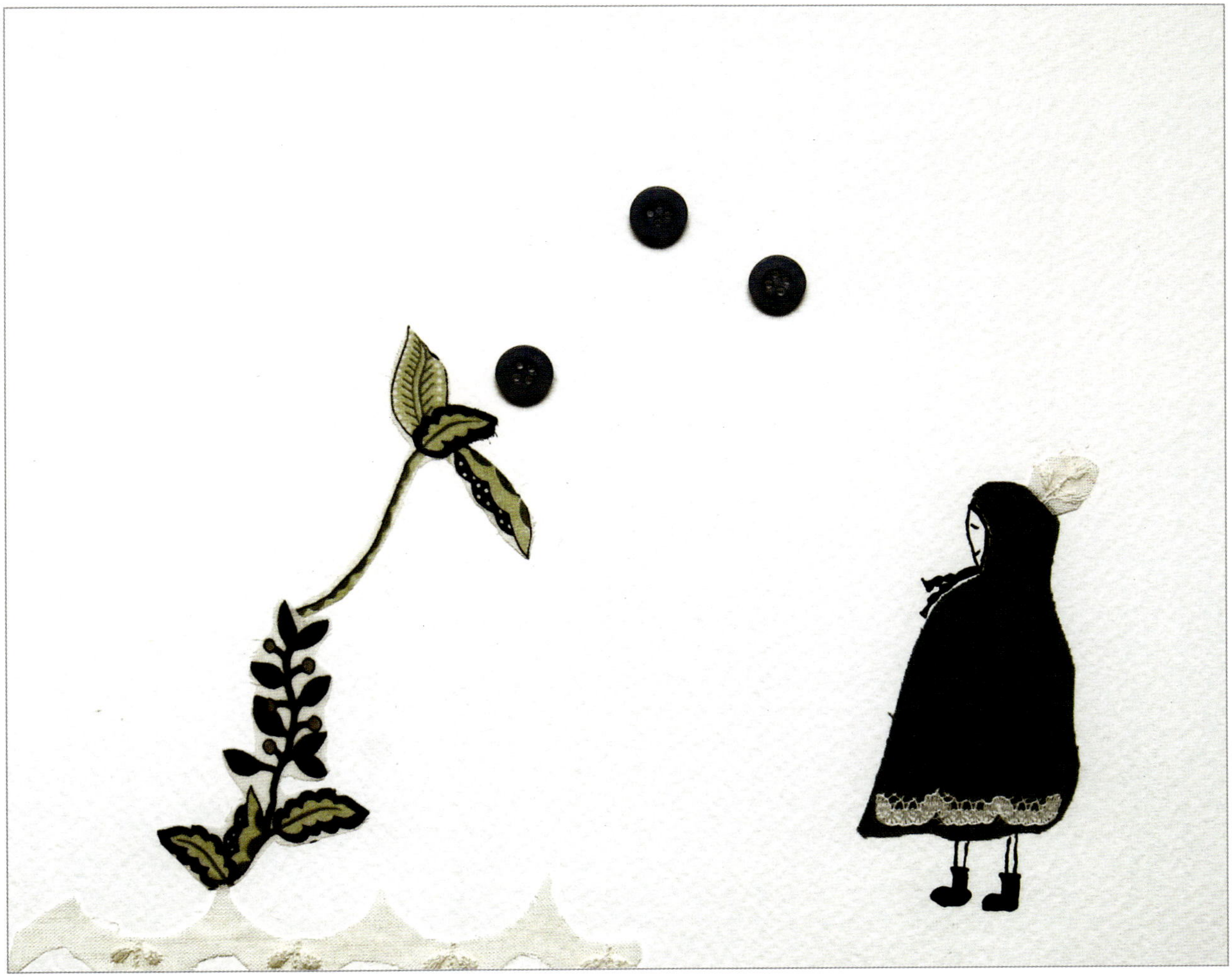

**Cherry Tree from Passing on.** Self published book, 2009
Ink, fabric and buttons collage on paper

Julie Vermeille is a French freelance illustrator based in london, Uk since 1999. She studied a BTEC Foundation Diploma in Art and Design at the London College of Printing and graduates in 2004 from a BA (hons) in Illustration in Camberwell College of Arts ( both in London). She has been part of the Craft Central Designer network since 2007 and as well as producing her own hand bound books, she works for commissions for private collections. She has been working collaboratively on the Chocolate Rain group exhibition in Hong Kong, in April 2009. She has also been designing and illustrating a concept album for children as well as working with writers on illustration for children stories. She illustrates and creates the promotional material for online arts and literature magazine, Creaturemag.com.

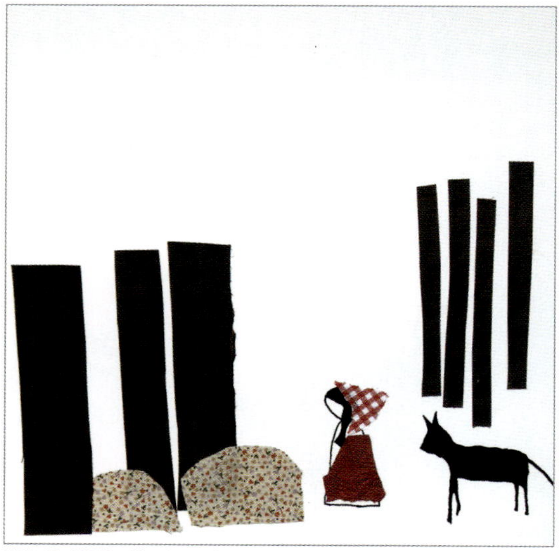

**Little Red Riding Hood meeting the wolf.**
Self published book, 2008
Ink, paper and fabric collage on paper

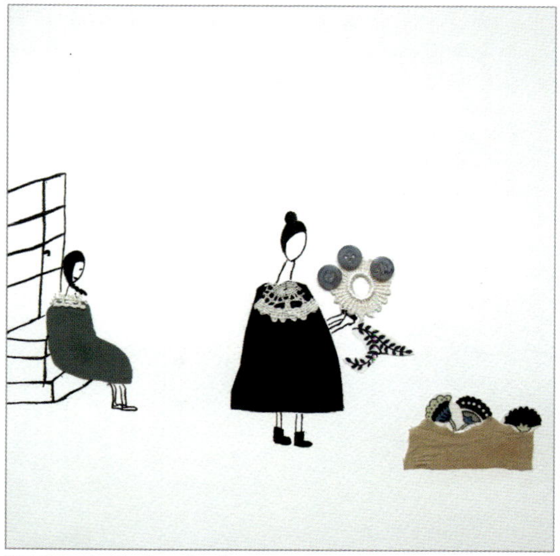

**Grandma planting from Passing on.**
Self published book, 2009
Ink, fabric, buttons and lace collage on paper

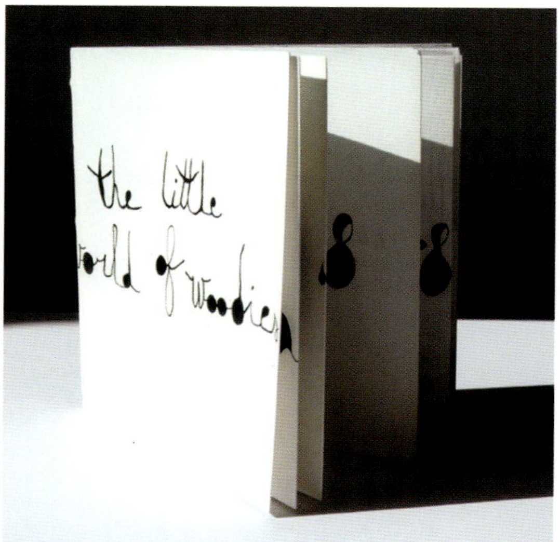


**The Little World of Woodies Book**
Hand bound and Self published
Ink drawings book (Edition of 20), 2008

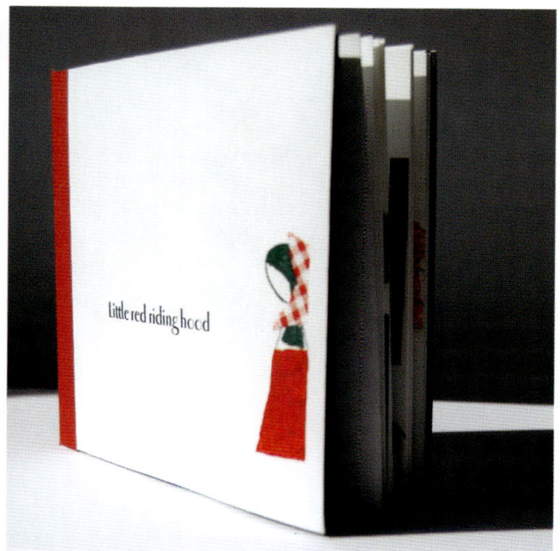


**Little Red Riding Hood Book**
Handbound, Self Published
(Edition of 20), 2008

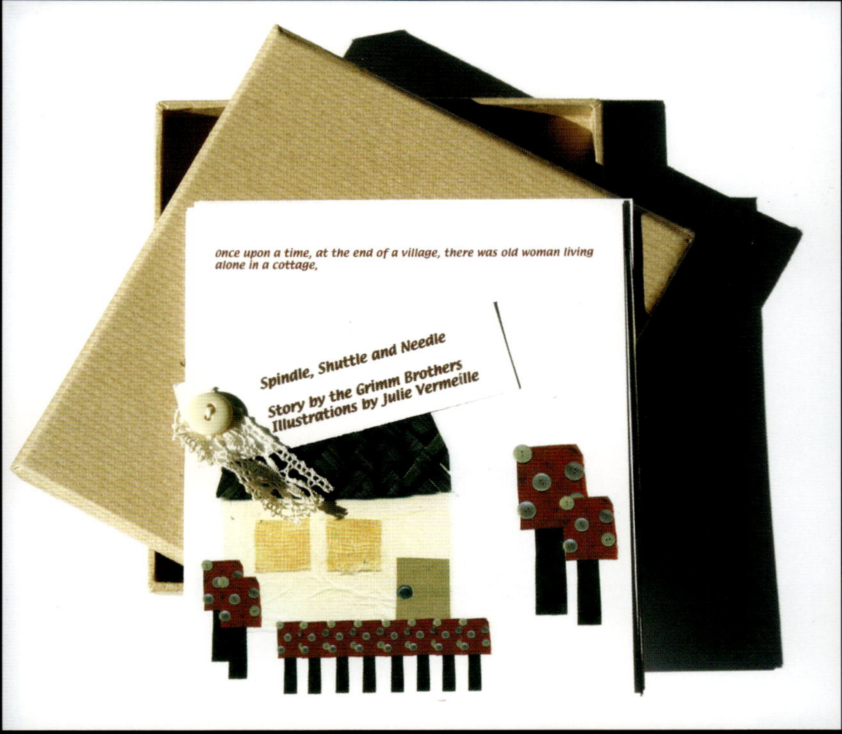


**The Little World of Woodies Book**
Hand bound and Self published
Ink drawings book (Edition of 20), 2008

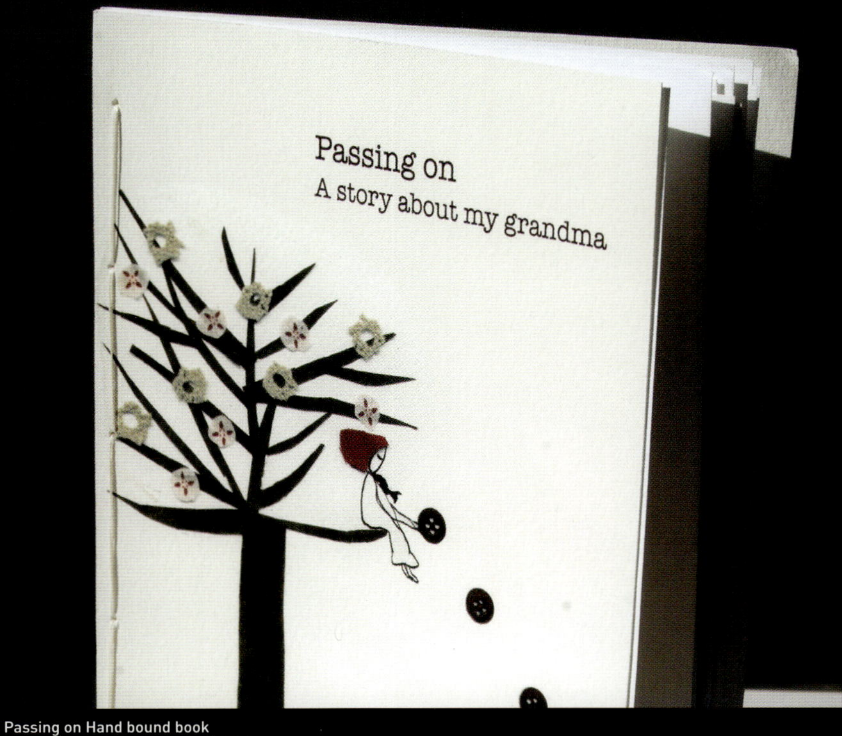


Passing on Hand bound book
Self published, (Rdition of 20), 2009

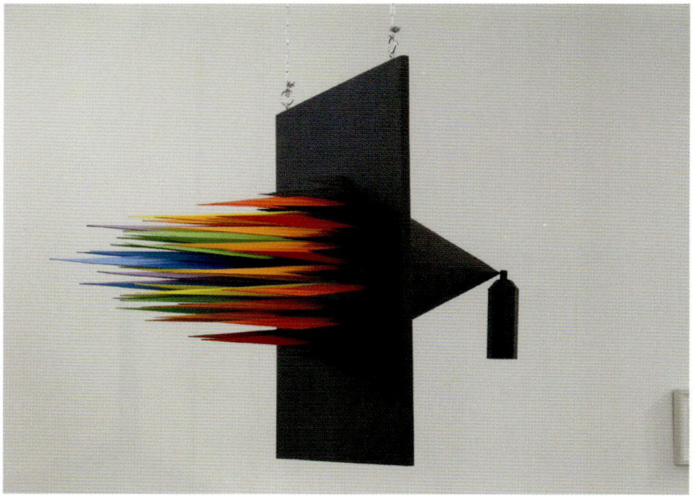

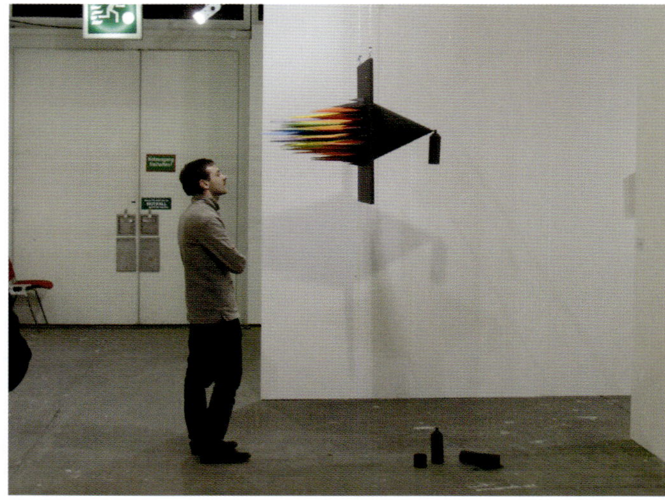

**Illustrative Zürich**

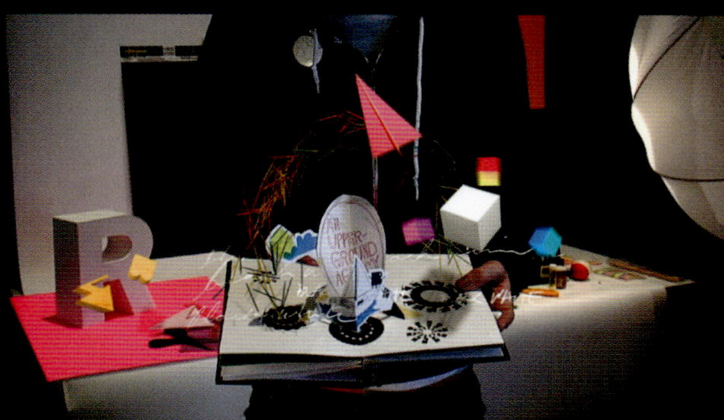

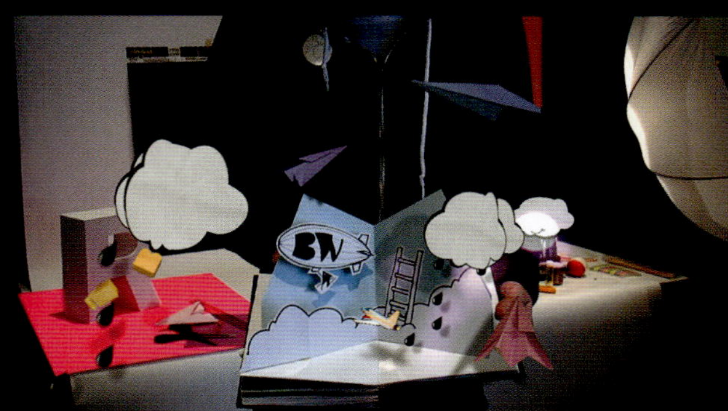


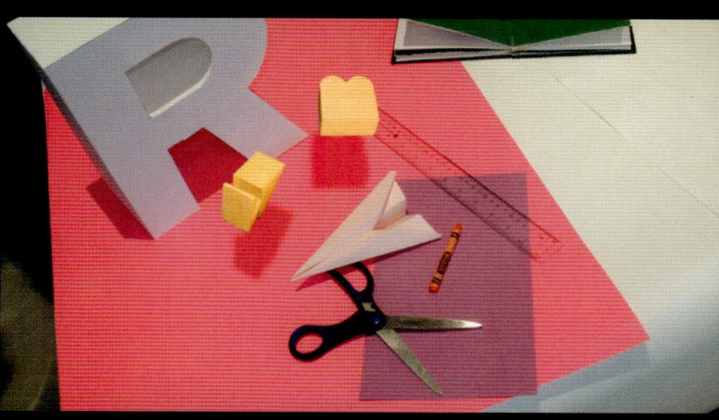

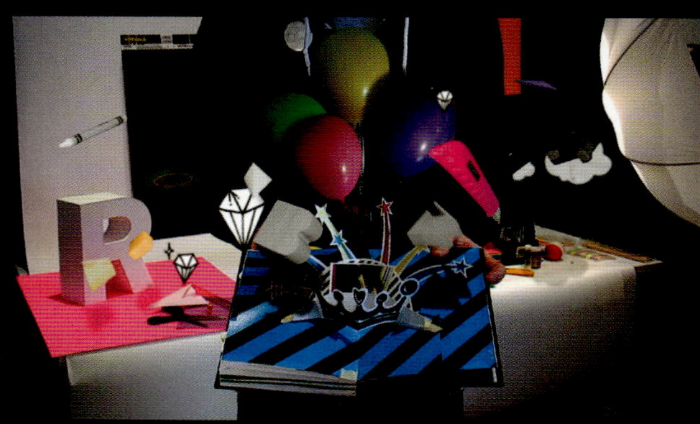

**Black & White Teaser**
The video was created for a division of Bleublancrouge Montreal's agency "Black and White". Objects popping out of the book's represent the tools that were used in the creation of the Black and White's products. http://vimeo.com/2543056
Credits: Art direction + Design + Animation: Julien Vallée & Bleublancrouge Client: Bleublancrouge Year : 2007
Music : René-Pierre Guérin 1590 x 893 px

# Julien Vallée

www.javallee.com

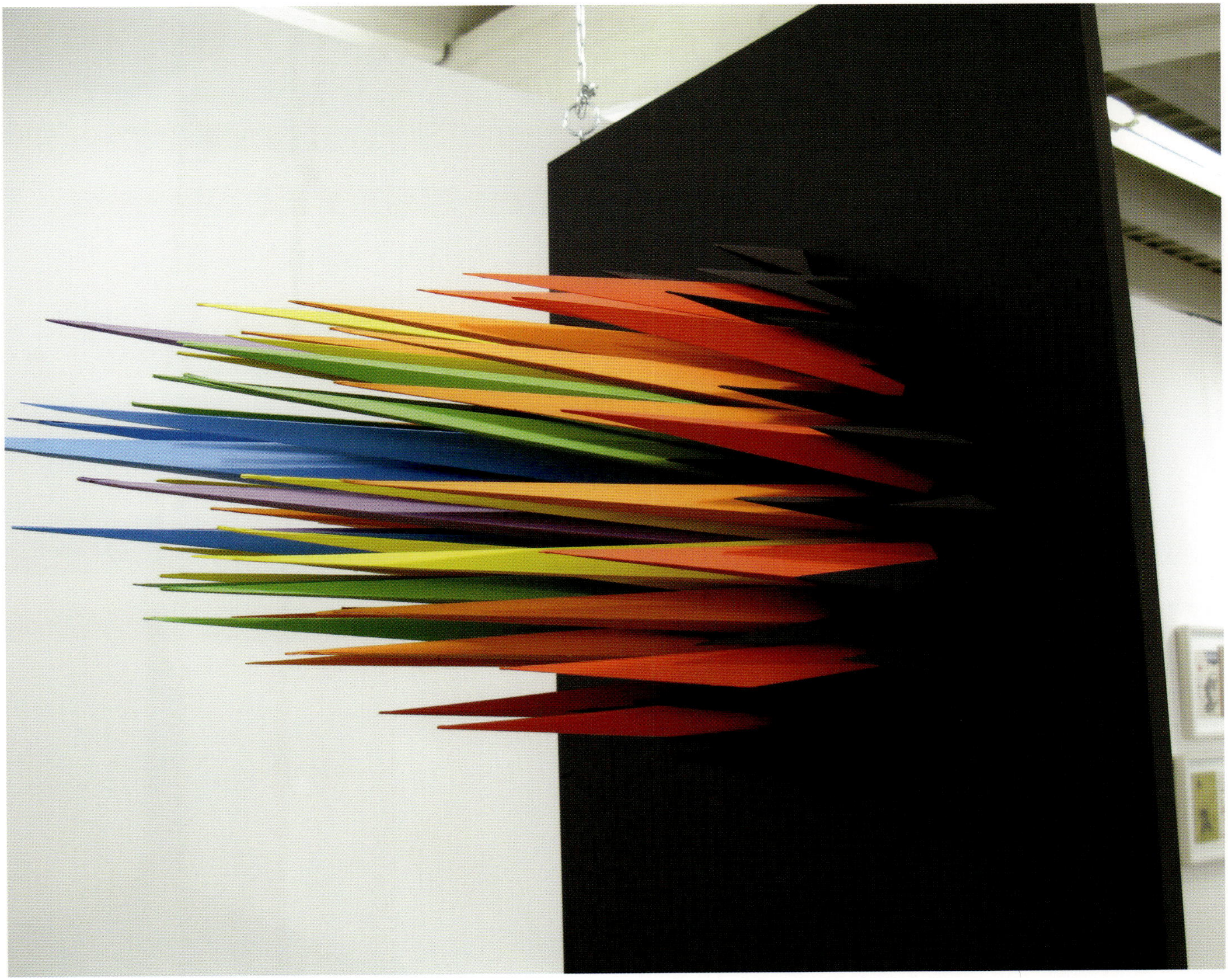

My name is Julien Vallée and I am a graphic designer based in Montréal, Canada. I am working on a range of projects including art direction, motion graphic, print design, art installation and video + design for the music industry. I try to get in touch with every aspect of the environnement. I like to use manual art well endorsed by the various technological tools available in order to make the bridge between manual and virtual art.

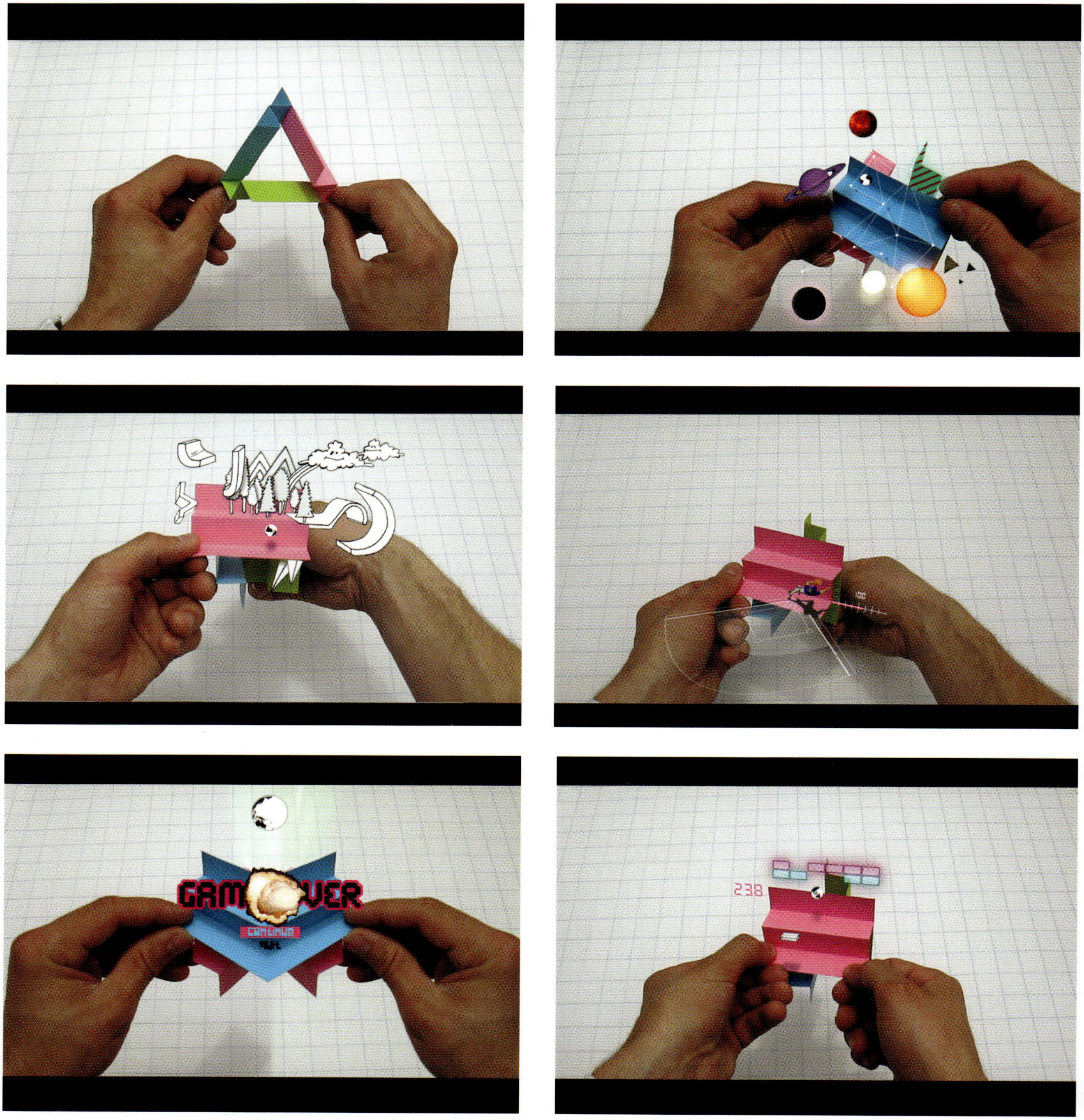

**Globo-Logos - "Oh oui, elle tourne"**
This video was created for the Earth Day. A ode to the work of Jacques Languirand. The video will take part of the Globo Logos event that will take place in differents festivalsfor diverse events all around the world. Globo Logos aims to bring purity and dignity back to the ideation process by creating a space where ideas can live and evolve, independent of those who would use them for political or commercial ends. http://vimeo.com/1150719 Credits: Art direction + Design + Animation: Julien Vallée Client: - Year : 2008 Music: René-Pierre Guérin
2133 x 1500 px / 7 x 5 in

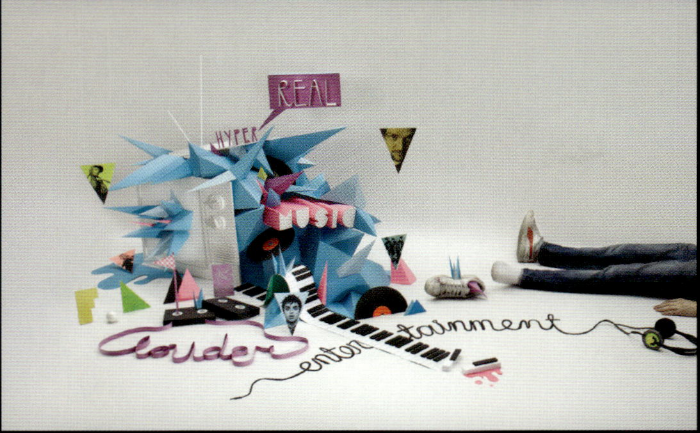


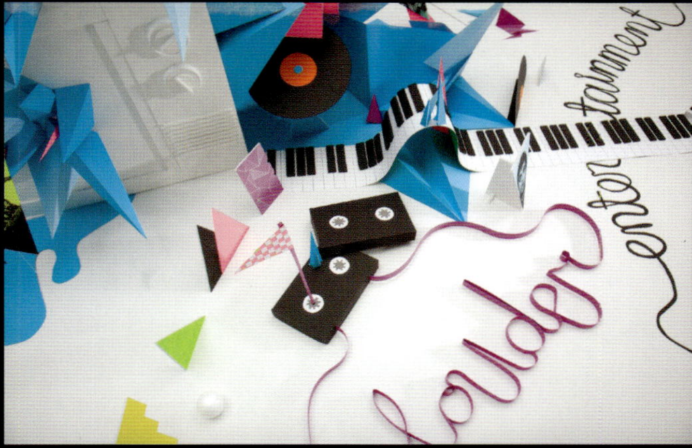


**MTV-One**
Image proposition for MTV-One in collaboration with Dixon-Baxi. Credits: Art direction: Julien Vallée + DixonBaxi Design: Julien Vallée Photographer: Simon Duhamel Client: MTV-One Year : 2008 Dimensions: 20 x 13 in

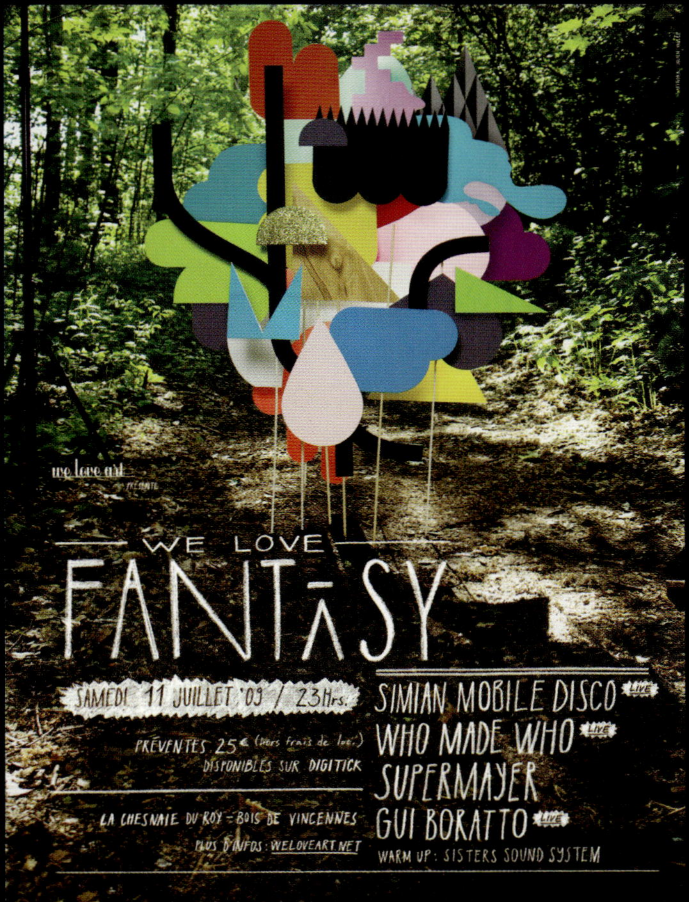


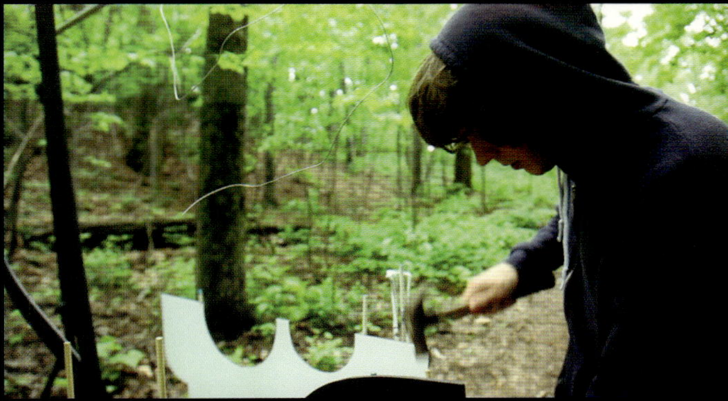

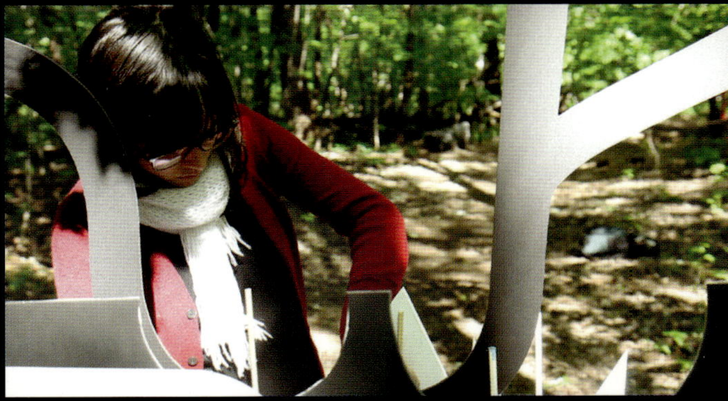

**We Love Fantasy**
Event poster for the music festival 'We Love Fantasy' Credits: Art direction : Julien Vallée Design: Julien Vallée Guillaume Vallée Eve Duhamel Year: 2009 Photographer: Simon Duhamel 16 x 24 in

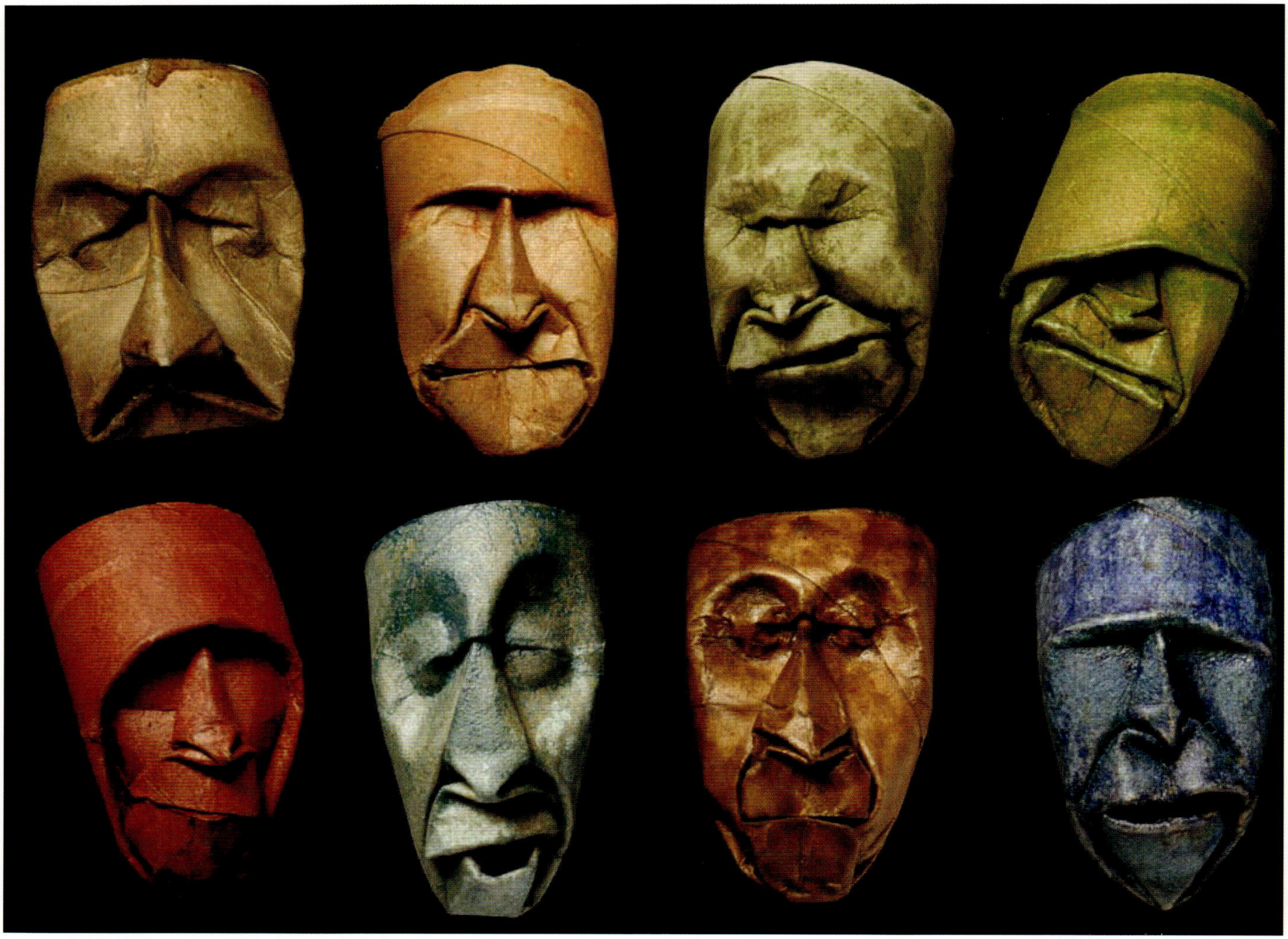

This diverse collection of masks, which consists of 40 unique pieces, presents unlimited and fascinating faces of fictional personalities. The creation process and development of the artist is as unique as it is astonishing. The masks are sculpted by hand out of toilet-paper rolls. The pieces are afterwards coated with shellac and different pigments. Each mask can be fixed on a flexible metal stalk, 10 to 100 cm long, and a black steel foot, 9x9 cm. Expressive and impressive, these big masks lead you off towards their stories and challenge your imagination. The pieces are about 30 to 40 cm height and folded with only one sheet of white or black Canson paper. These can be mounted on flexible metal threads and suspended on a white or black metal foot, 9x9 cm. The small masks are also available in high definition photos in 6 coloured prints, size 30 x 45 cm. Different formats are available on demand only.

# Junior Fritz Jacquet

www.juniorfritzjacquet.com

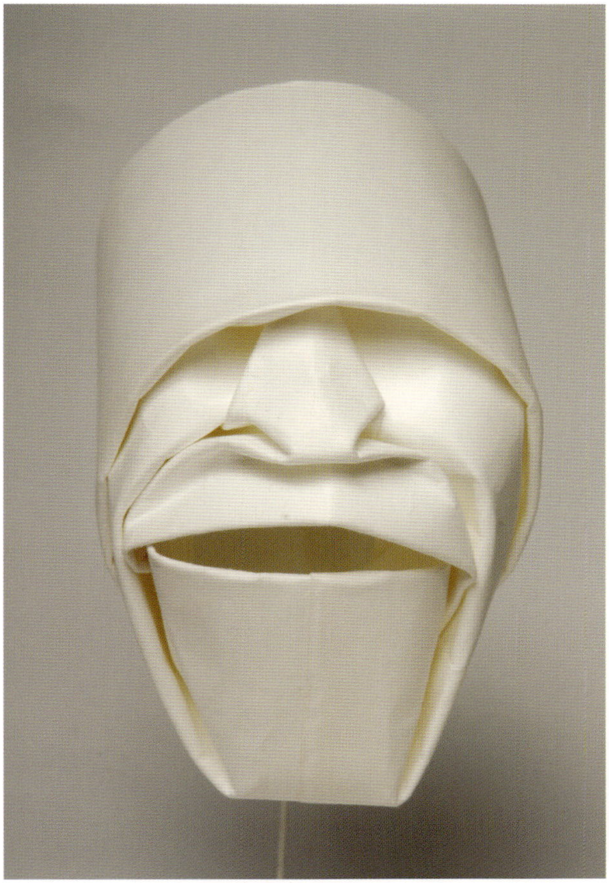

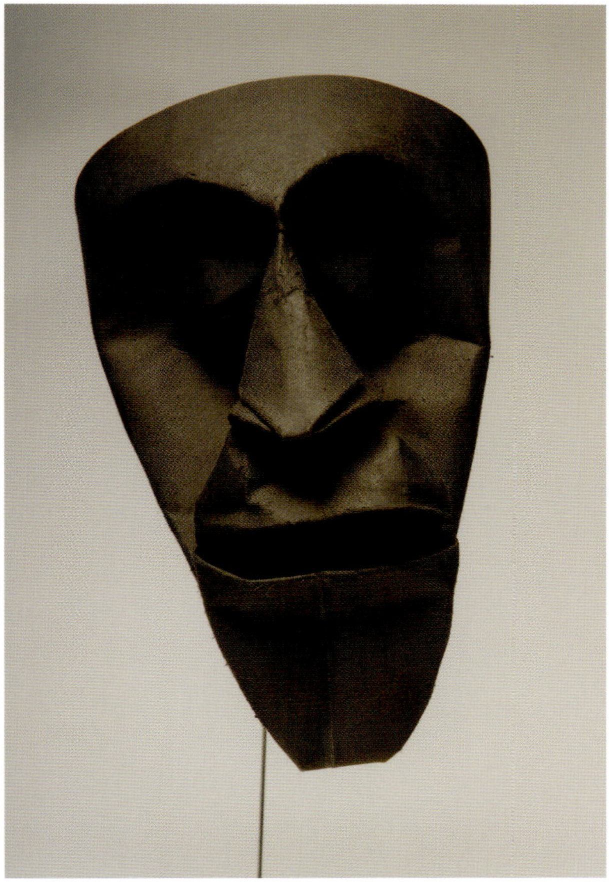

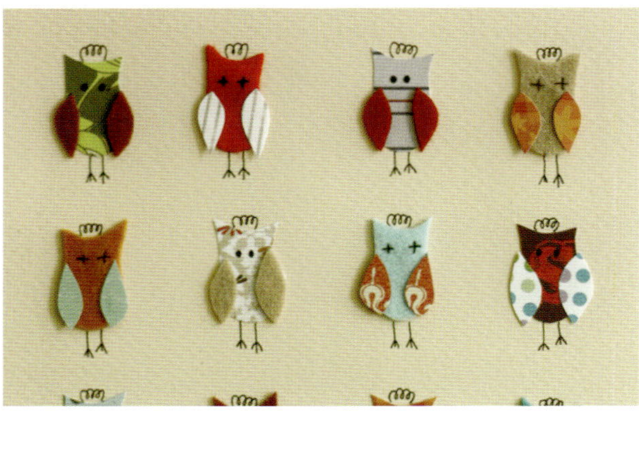

Fascinated by paper from a very young age, Junior Fritz Jacquet explores and experiments with folding and crumpling techniques, innovating with his fingers methods still undiscovered to create forms and craft poetic objects, that visually enhance any surrounding. The origins of his unique technique are still heavily inspired by the traditional art of origami, using only one sheet of paper.

Photos by Dan Marquès, Matthieu Gauchet, Ted Tabor

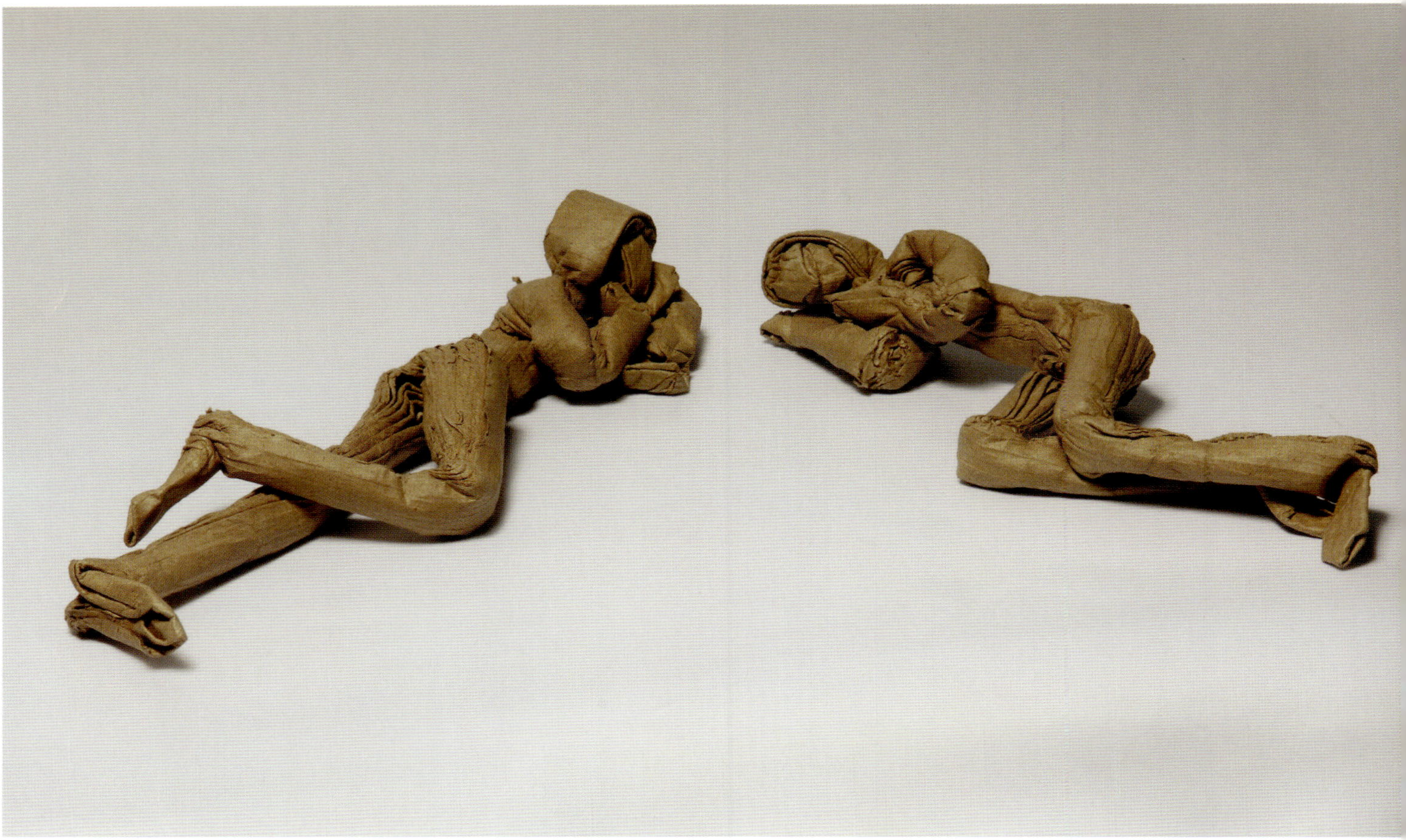

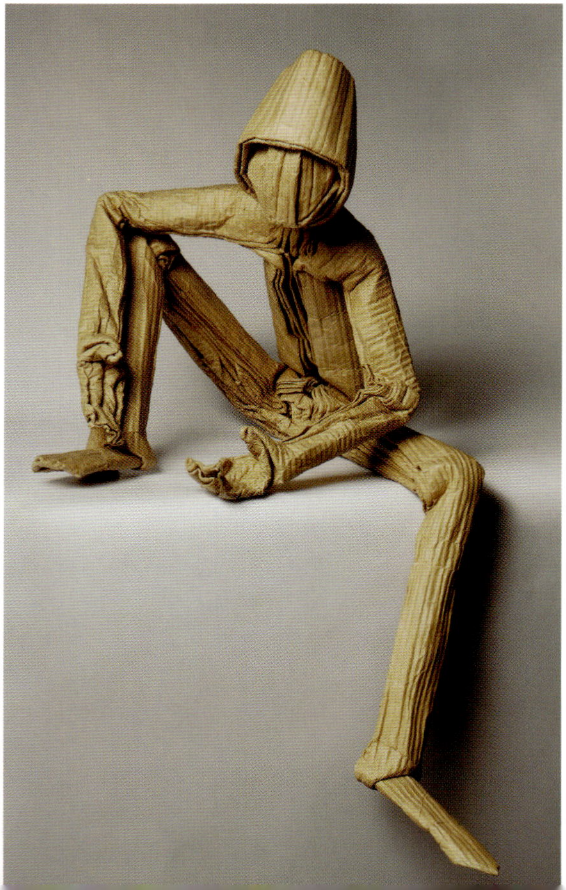

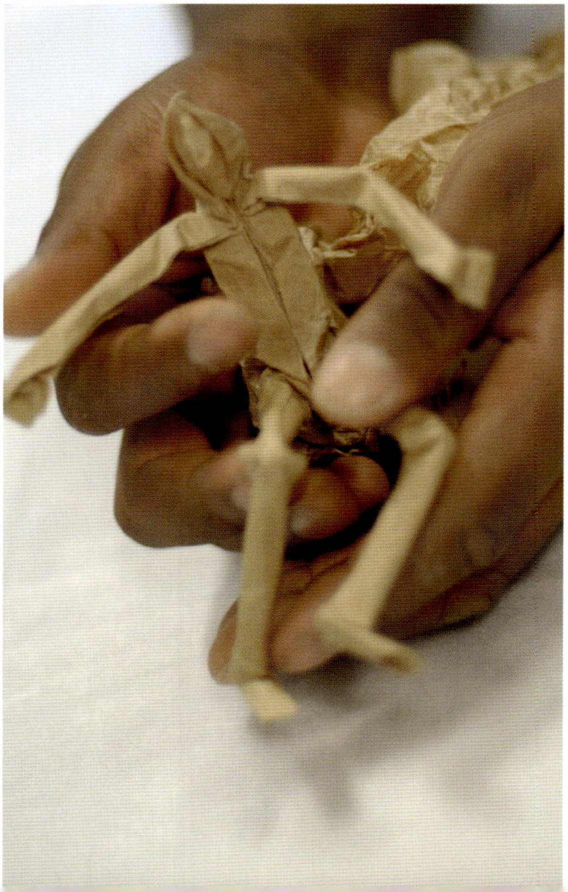

**Bonhomme Canelle**
This is an amusing little man, "Bonhomme Canelle", who appeals to the playful and spontaneous spirit in all of us. His body is like his spirit: sincere, funny, and glib. "Bonhomme Canelle" is a story on his own. Bursting with energy, he laughs loudly, always ready for action, sitting down breathlessly, tapping with his foot while he waits. Once he is tired he relaxes, chattering wit fully, and finally falling asleep. He is made out of one sheet of cardboard and stands upright on a wooden support. He also sits, lies down and feels at ease almost anywhere.

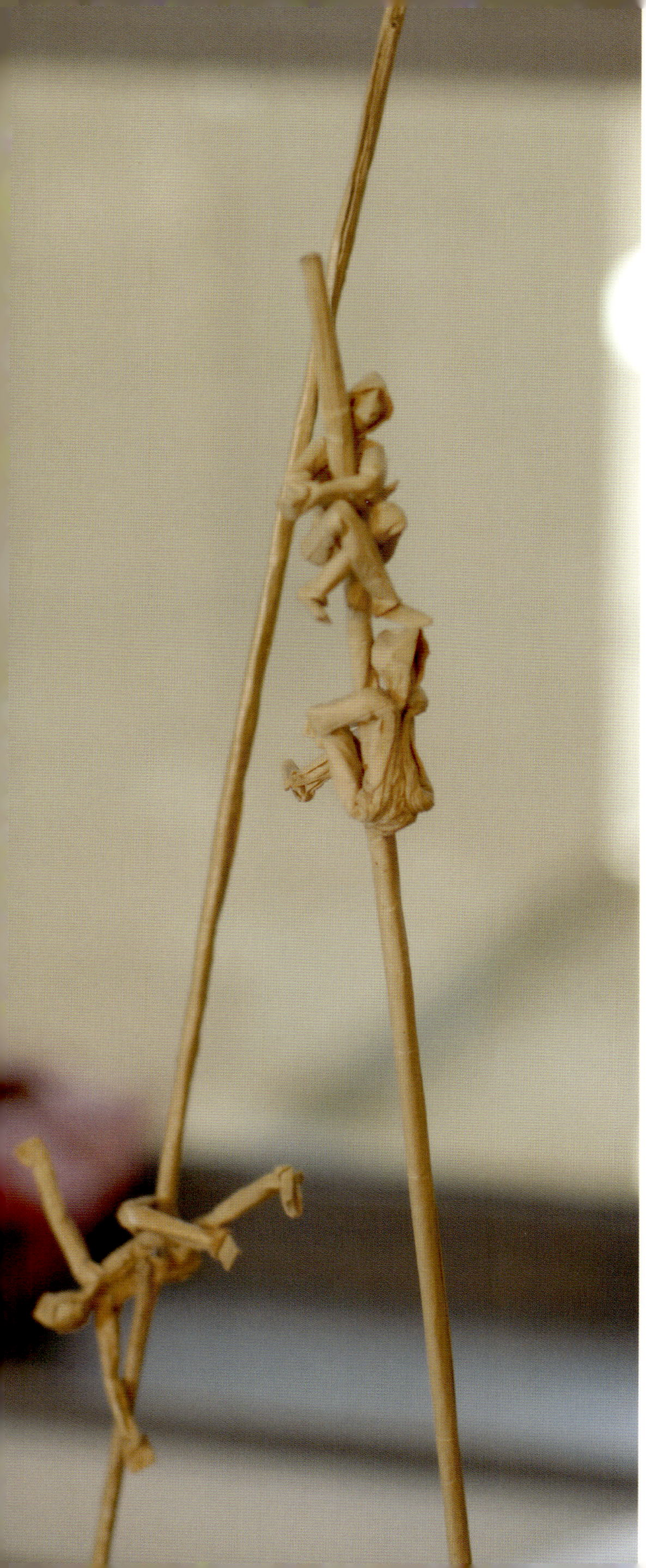

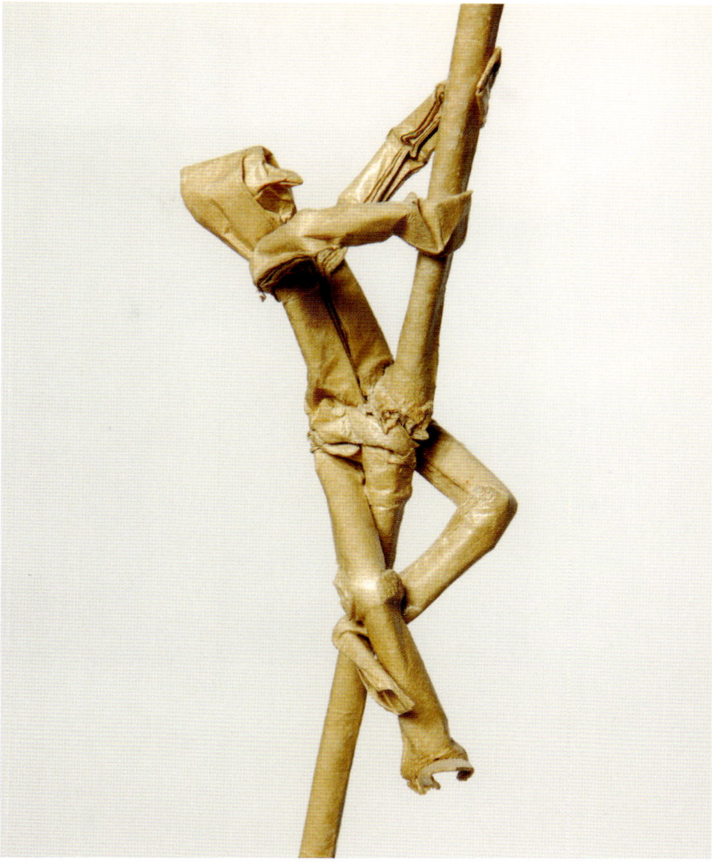

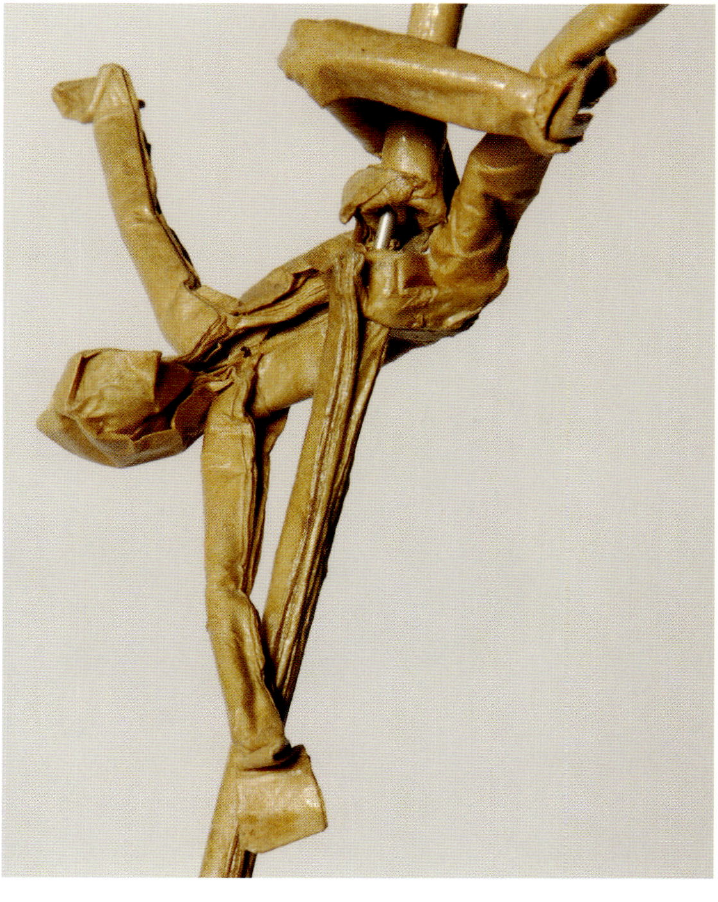

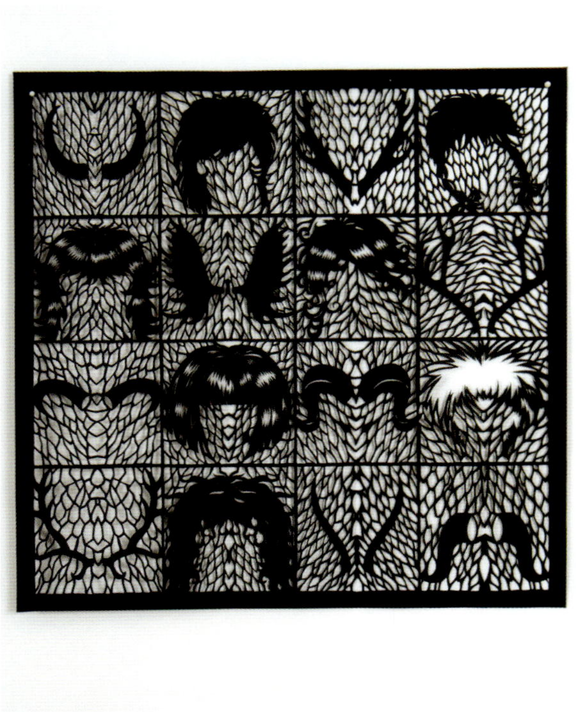

**Horns and Wings,** 2005
Hand cut black paper
17 x 17 inches

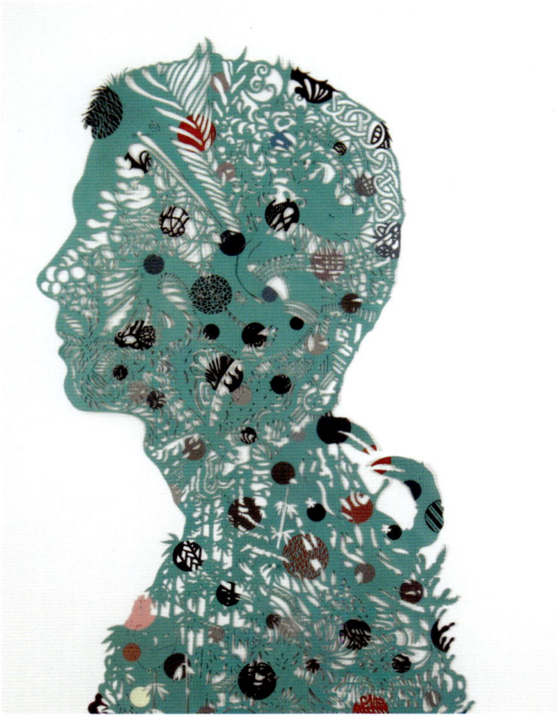

**PJS (portrait series I),** 2006
Hand cut paper with acrylic
28 x 18 inches

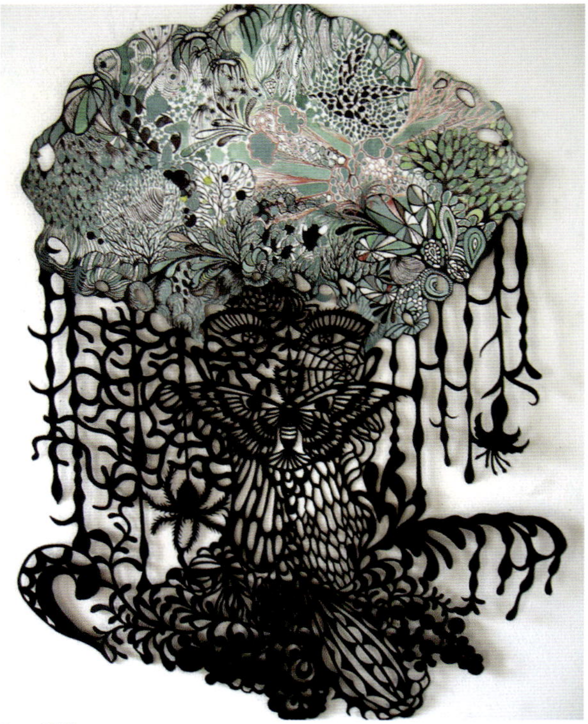

**Gaze,** 2005
Watercolor on hand cut black paper
20 x 14 inches

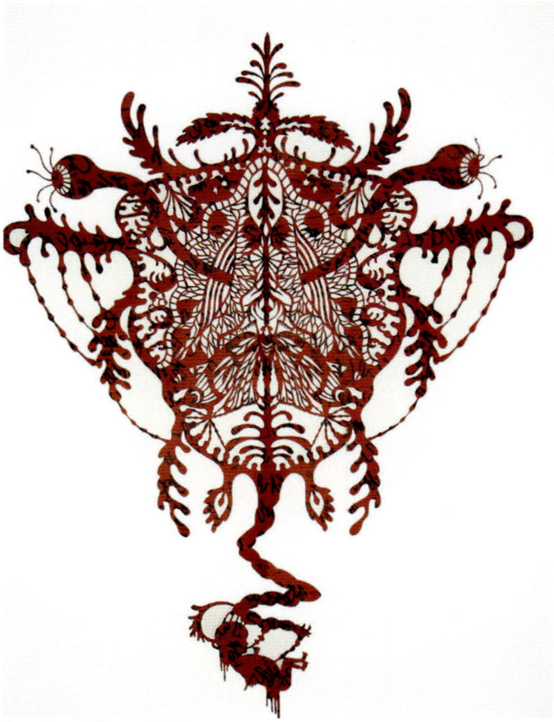

**Dreaming of Foetus,** 2007
Hand cut washi paper
35 x 26 inches

# Kako Ueda

www.kakoueda.com

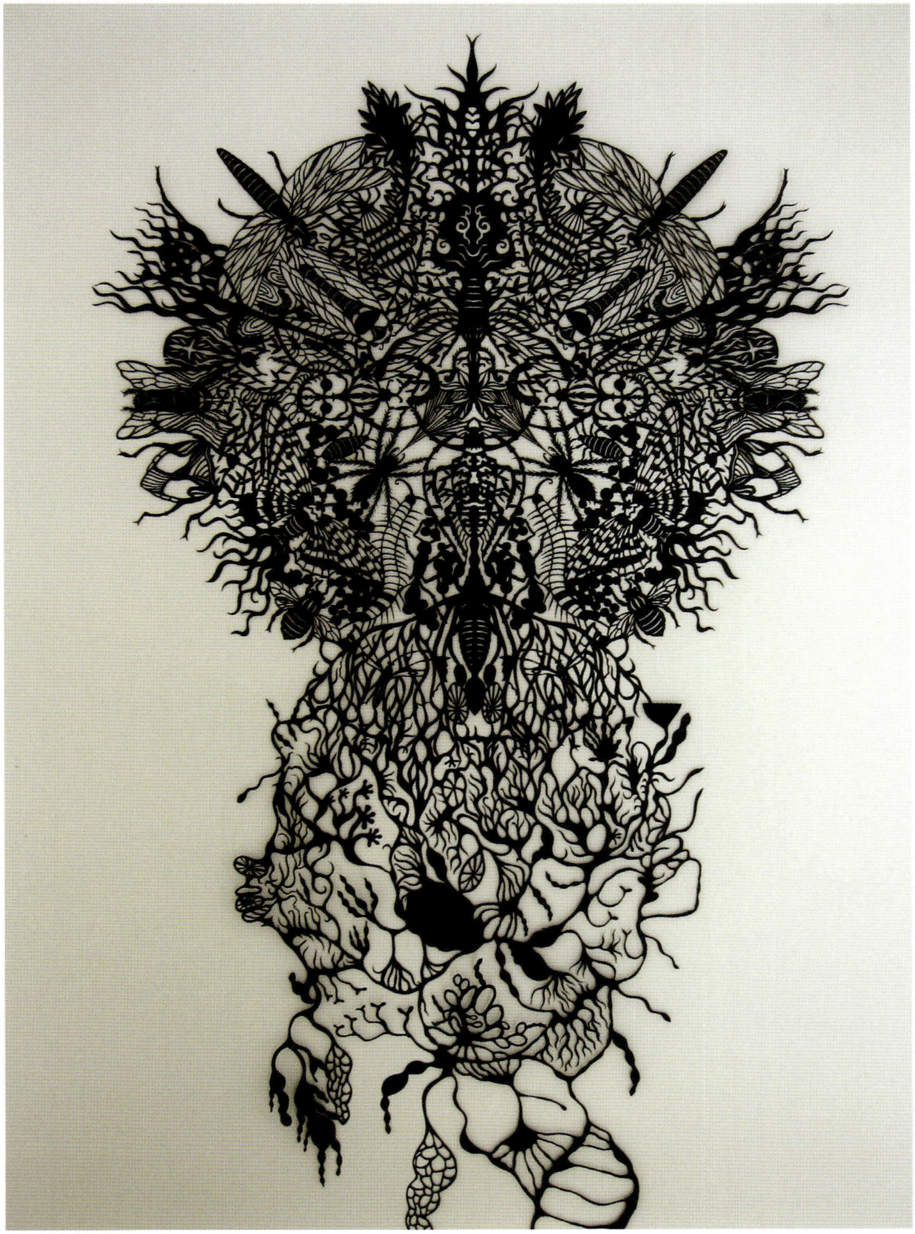

Allure, 2004-04
Hand cut black paper 50 x 28 inches
Private collection.

Paper has been my primary medium of choice for a long time. It is an everyday material yet has potential to manifest itself in surprisingly diverse ways. I have drawn and painted on paper, printed images on paper (photography), then in graduate school (Pratt 99') folded paper. And for the past 7 years, I've mainly been cutting paper besides making other types of art. Cut paper exists in many cultures and is normally perceived as a craft medium, however as we witness these days more and more contemporary artists have been actively utilizing this medium as their way of expression. In Japan where I was born, this medium is used for stencil making--a way to make patterns for kimono wear. I became attracted to the medium because of its history as well as its process of cutting to make images. Cut paper piece has a look of a drawing at the same time has its own physicality. It is a "2 and a half" dimensional medium, so to speak. I am interested in organic beings - insects, animals, and human bodies--how they are born out of nature but constantly being influenced and modified by culture. And the line between culture and nature is always shifting and not so clear. At the beginning, I focused on the notion of body as environment/ecosystem based on the philosophy of ancient Chinese medicine (holistic approach) and Greek philosophy of macro/microcosm idea.

**Images courtesy of George Adams Gallery.**
**Photos: Adam Reich.**

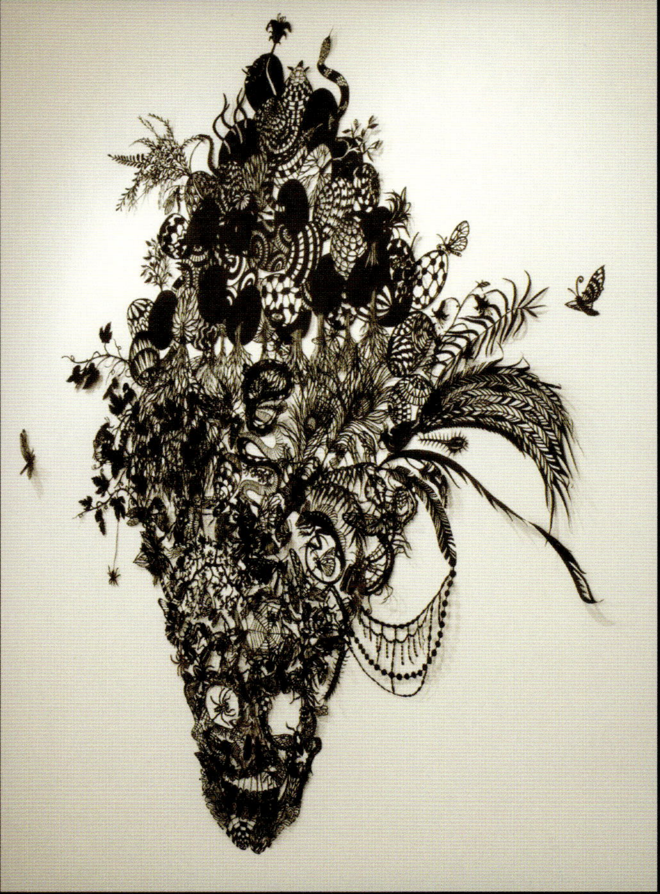

**Eros & Thanatos**, 2007
Hand cut black paper
78 x 69 (Variable: site specific wall relief)

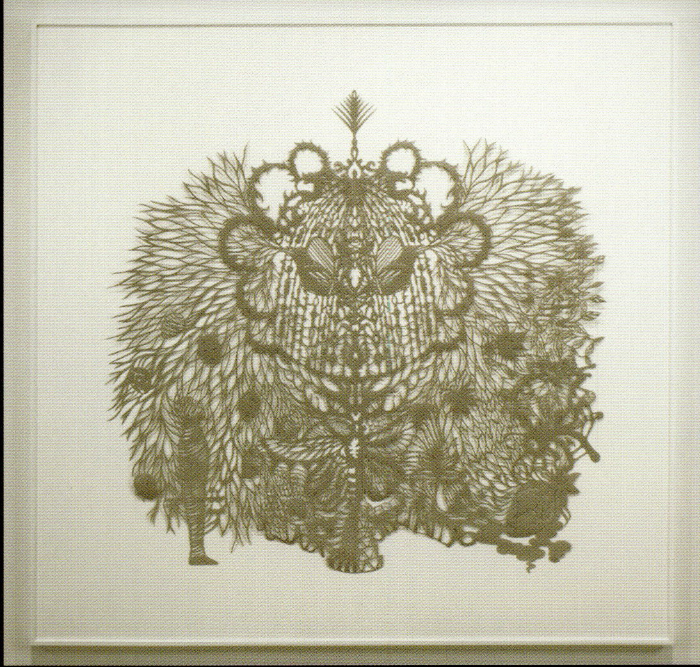

**Oracle**, 2008
Hand cut paper
36 x 36 inches

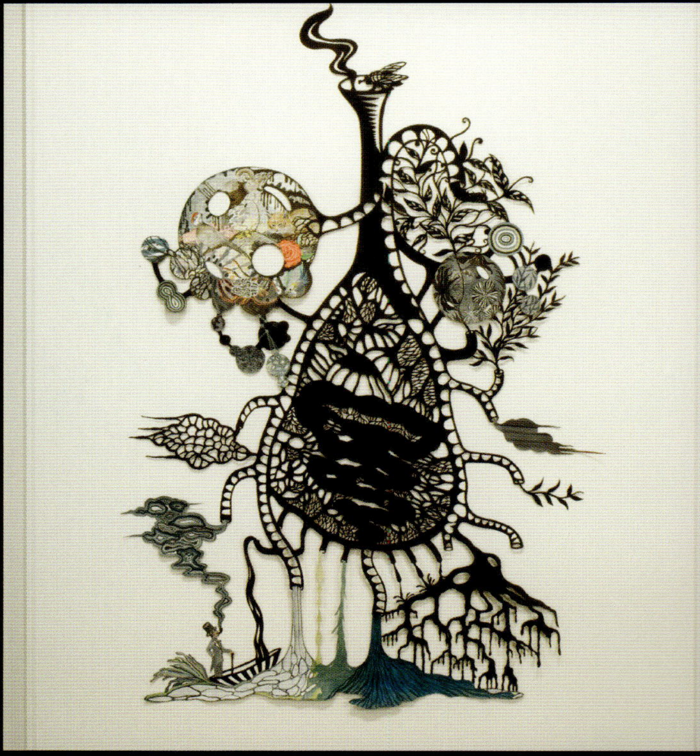

**Contemplation**, 2008

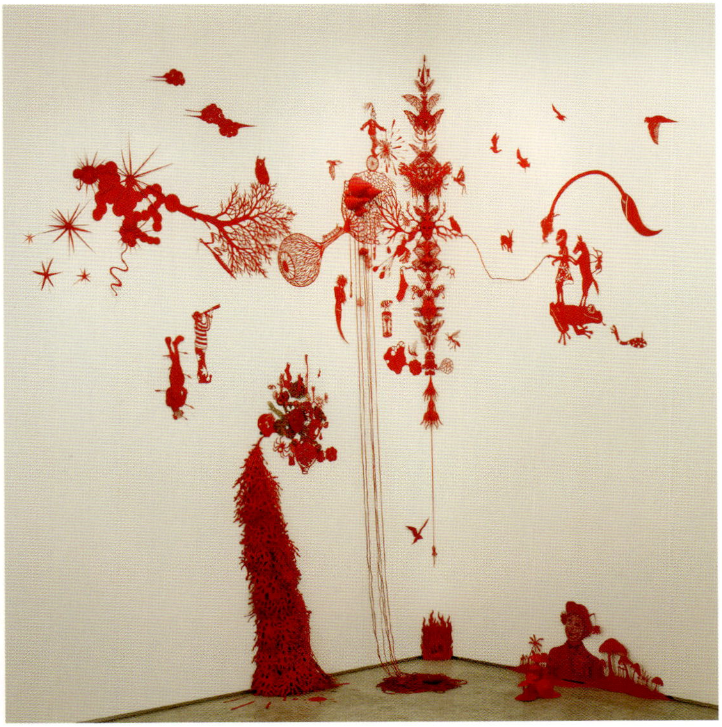

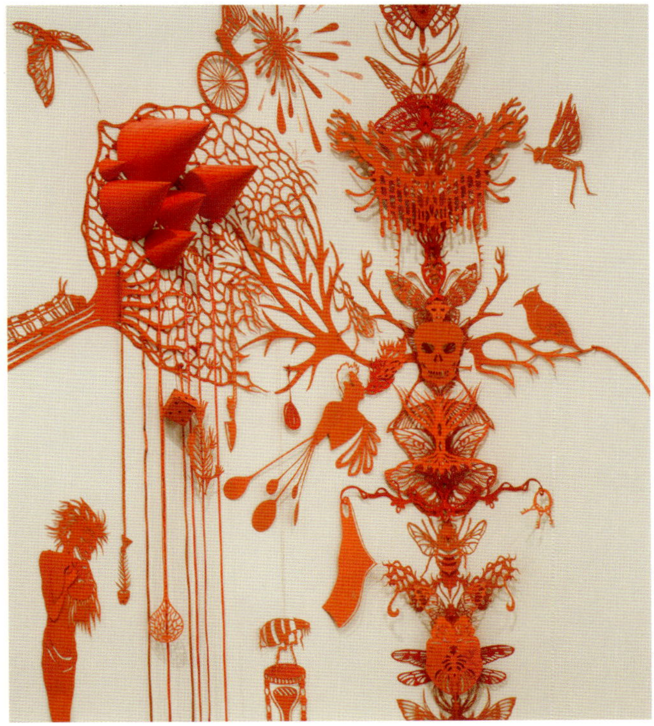

**Totem,** 2008
Hand cut paper, collage, string
9'2" x 84" x 58' x 30" (Variable wall and floor installation)

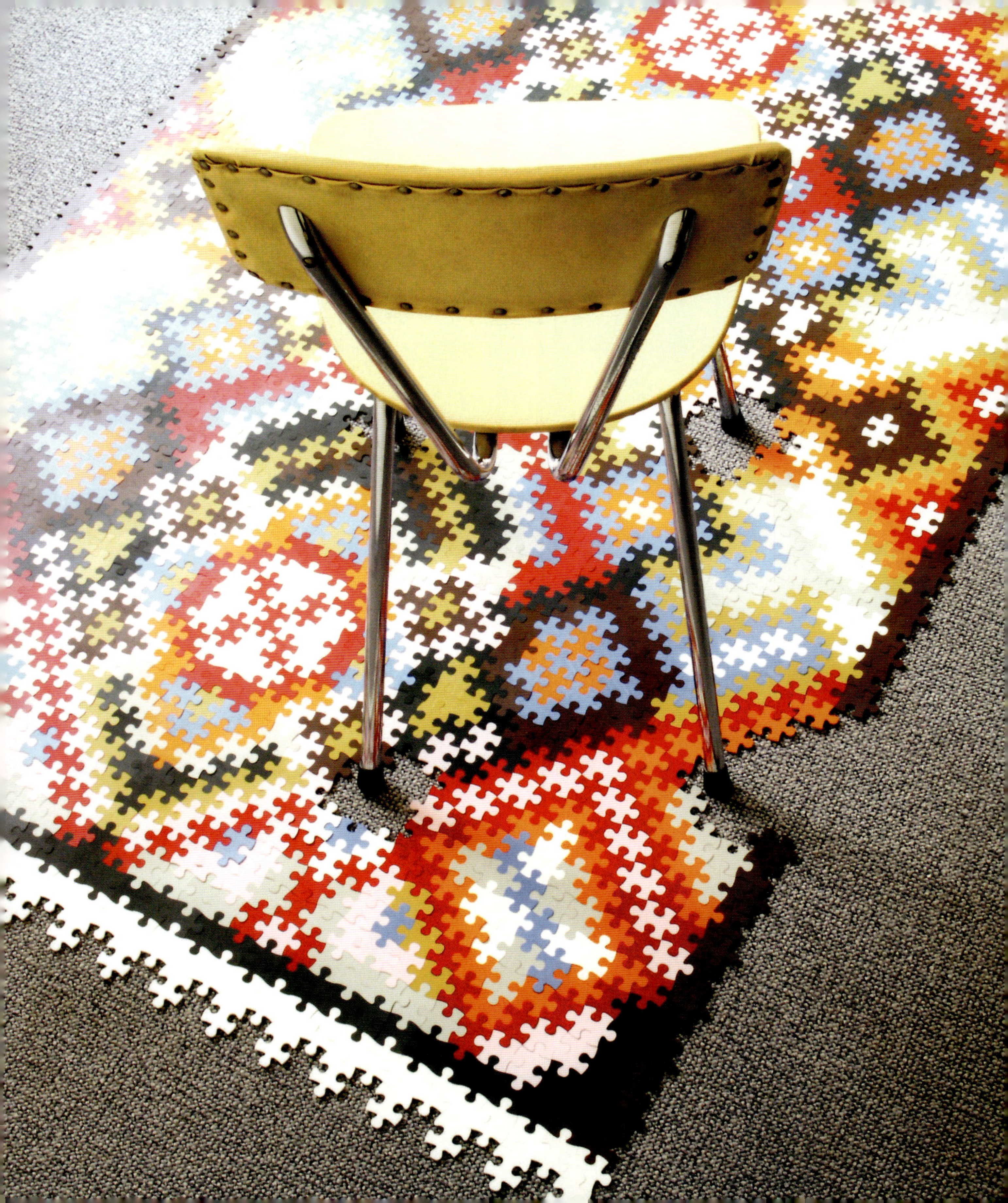

# Katrin Sonnleitner

www.katirn-sonnleitner.com

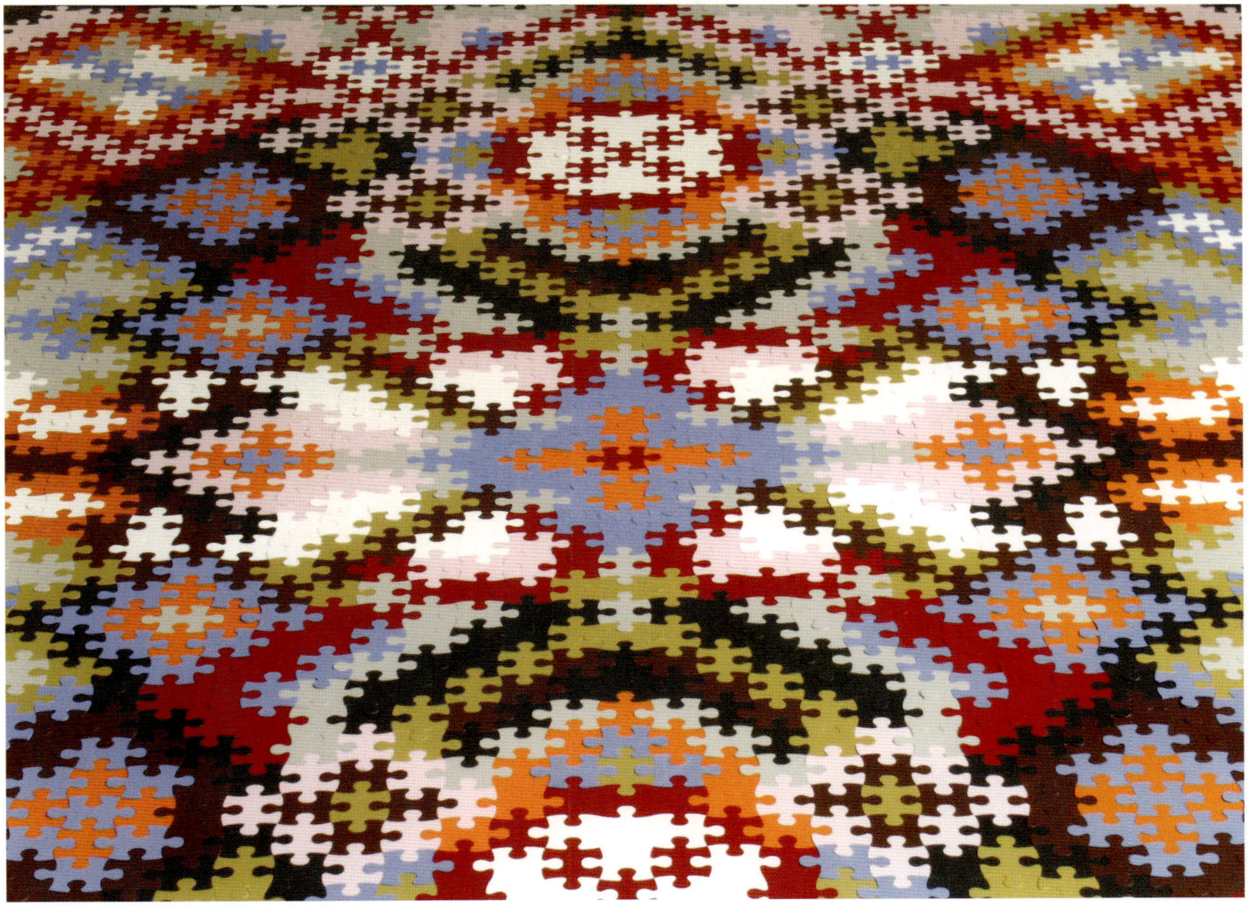

Persian rugs have been hand-knotted for hundreds of years. The arrangement of the knots in different colours forms the ornamental pattern of the rug. The Persian Puzzle Rug is made to be an individual floor and wall covering for the home. Putting the pieces together everybody may create their own floor ornaments whereever they desire. We also offer the service of design of a special colour and pattern concept for business premises or public spaces. Resolution - Single piece 35 x 35 mm. Whole carpet: endless. Material: recyclable mix of natural and synthetic rubber in 30 colors imm cologne 2008: PuzzlePerser is awarded with the 3rd prize in d3 contest – interior innovation award. 2009: Katrin Sonnleitner designs a limited edition PuzzlePerser for the new brand kkaarrlls

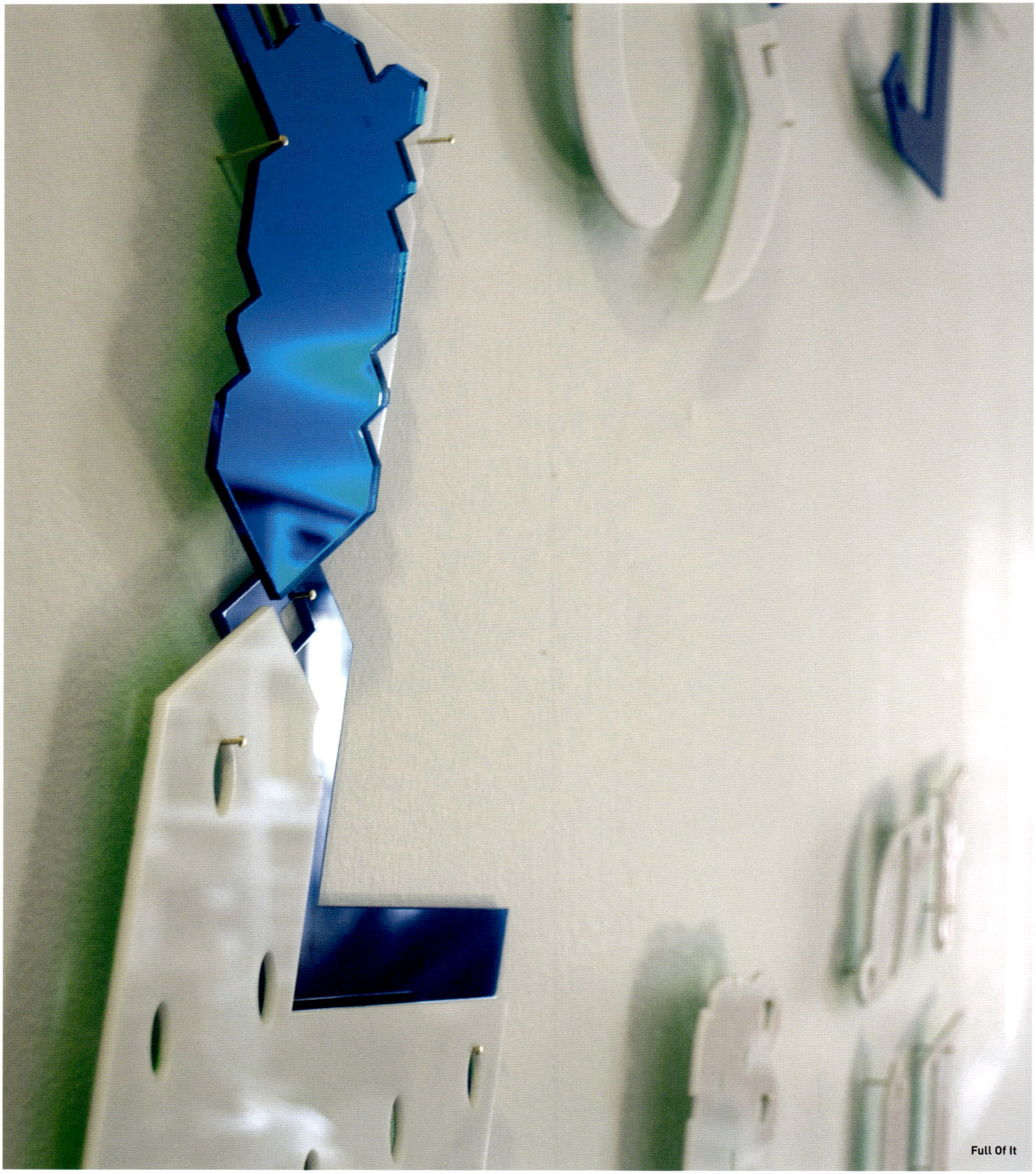
Full Of It

# Keetra Dean Dixon

www.fromkeetra.com

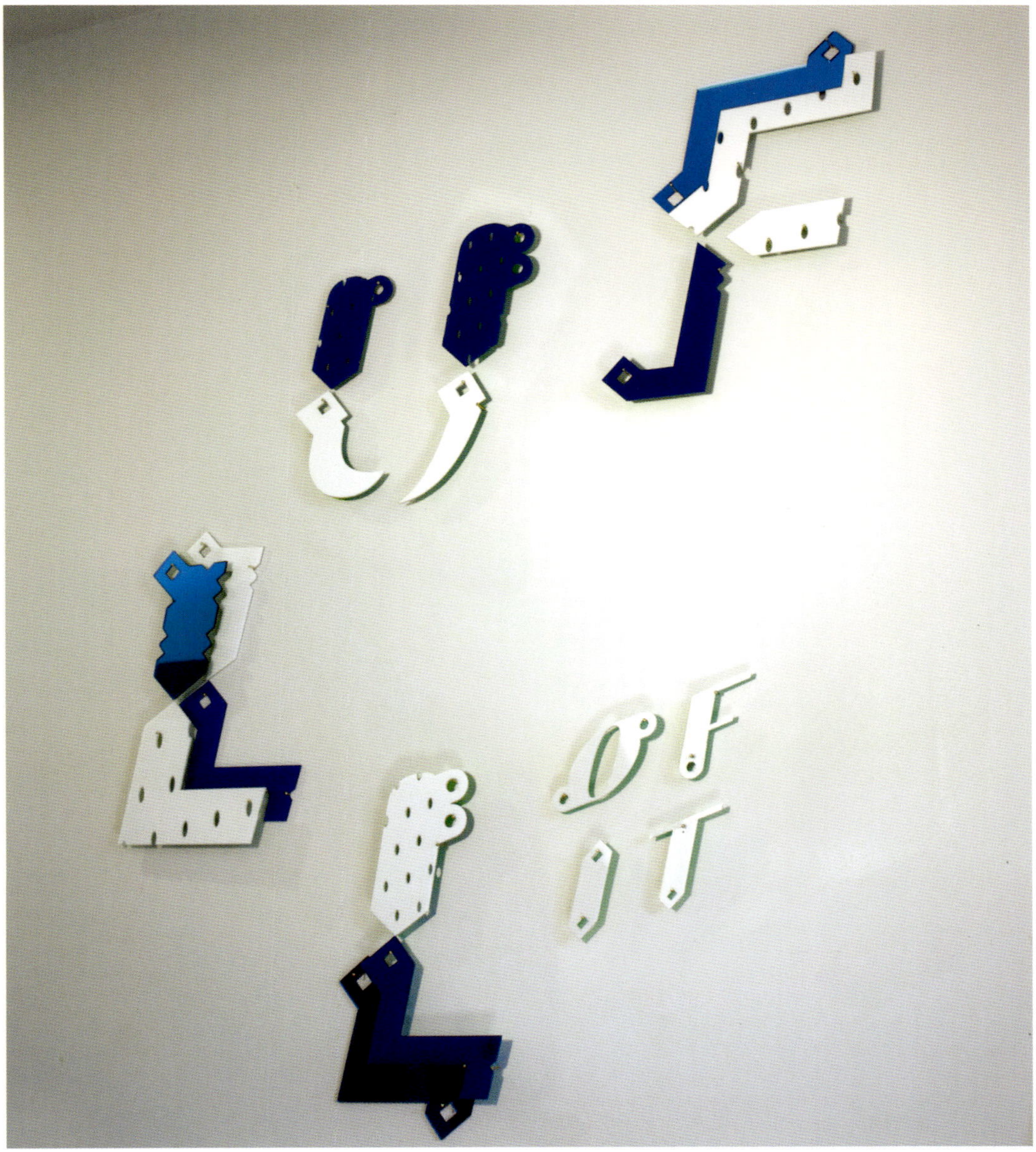


Keetra Dean Dixon graduated with a BFA from the Minneapolis College of Art and Design and an MFA from the Cranbrook Academy of Arts.

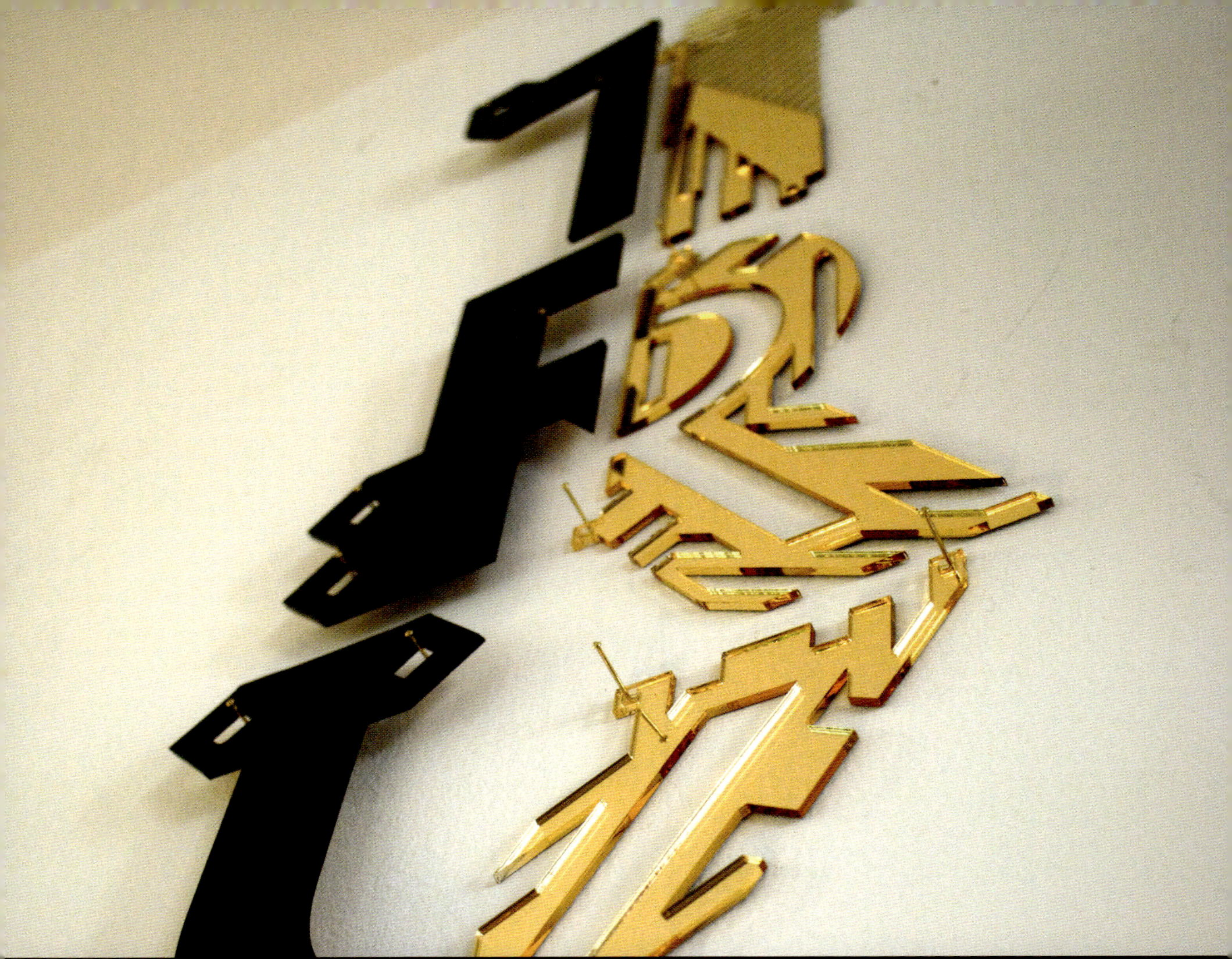

**Half Truthing, Half Trying**

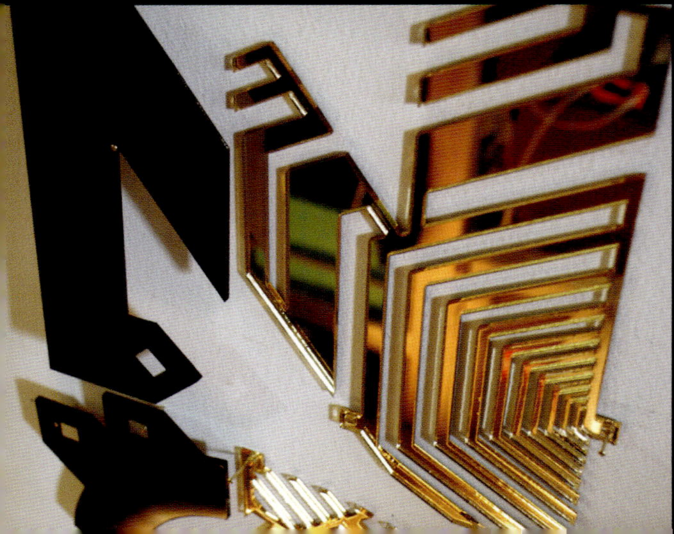

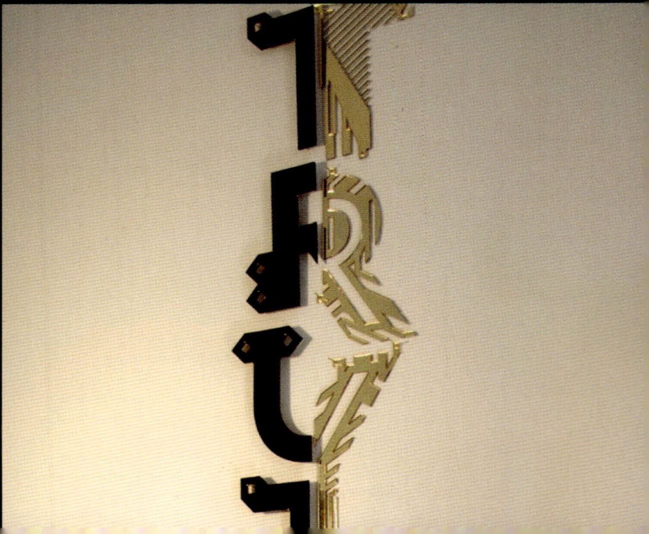

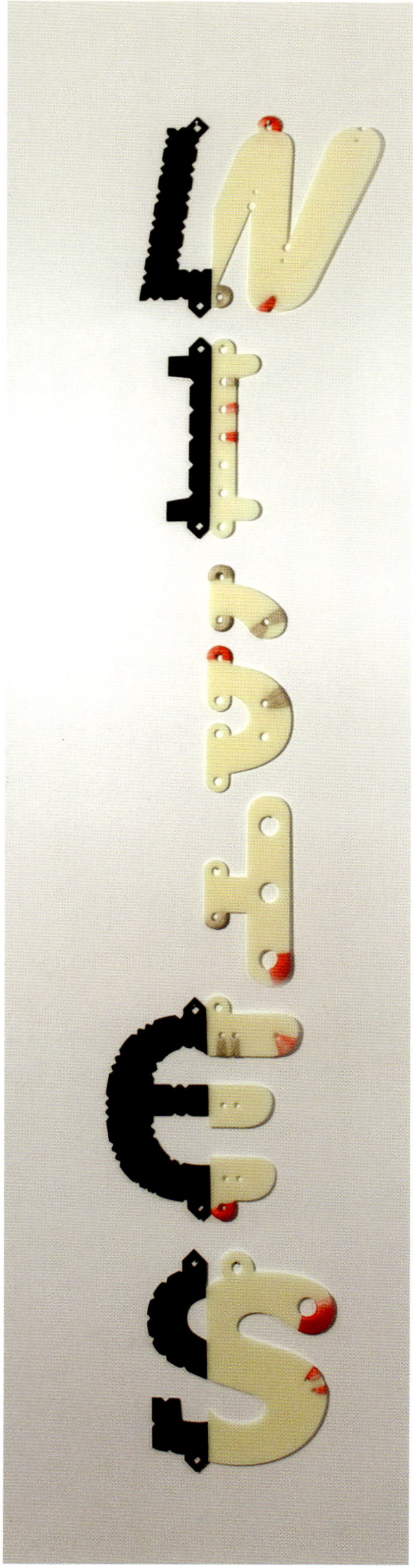

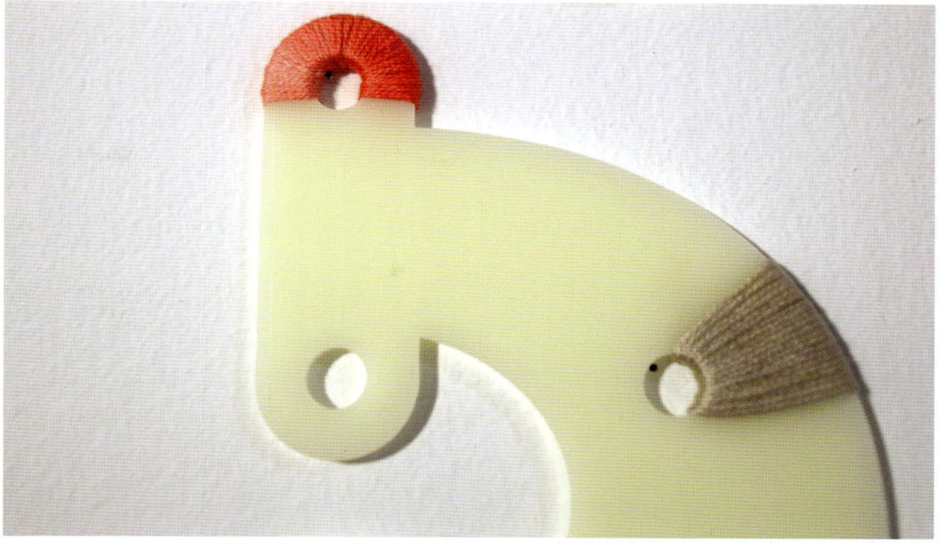

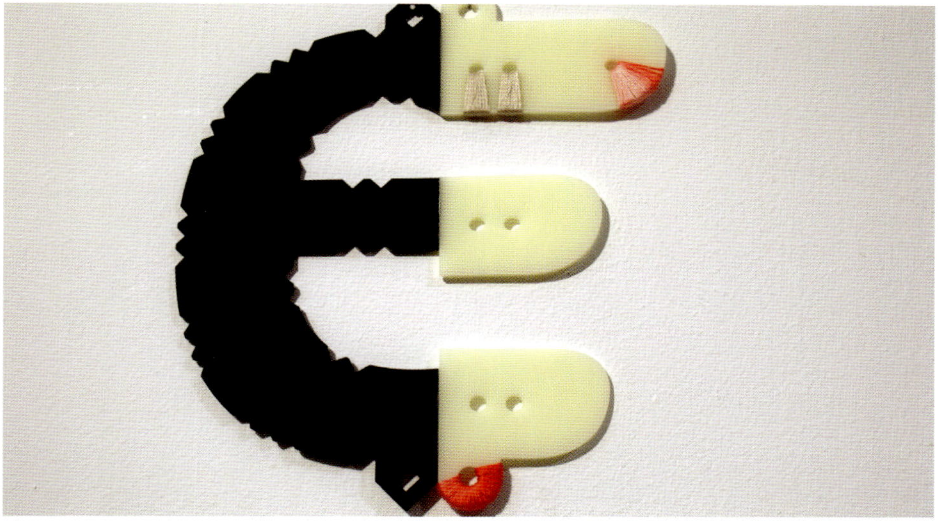

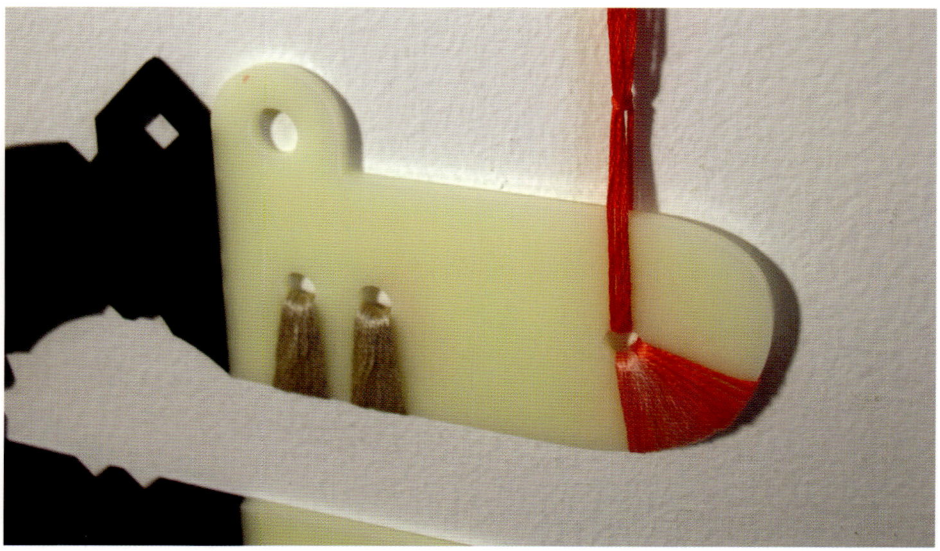

Half Wishing, Half Lying

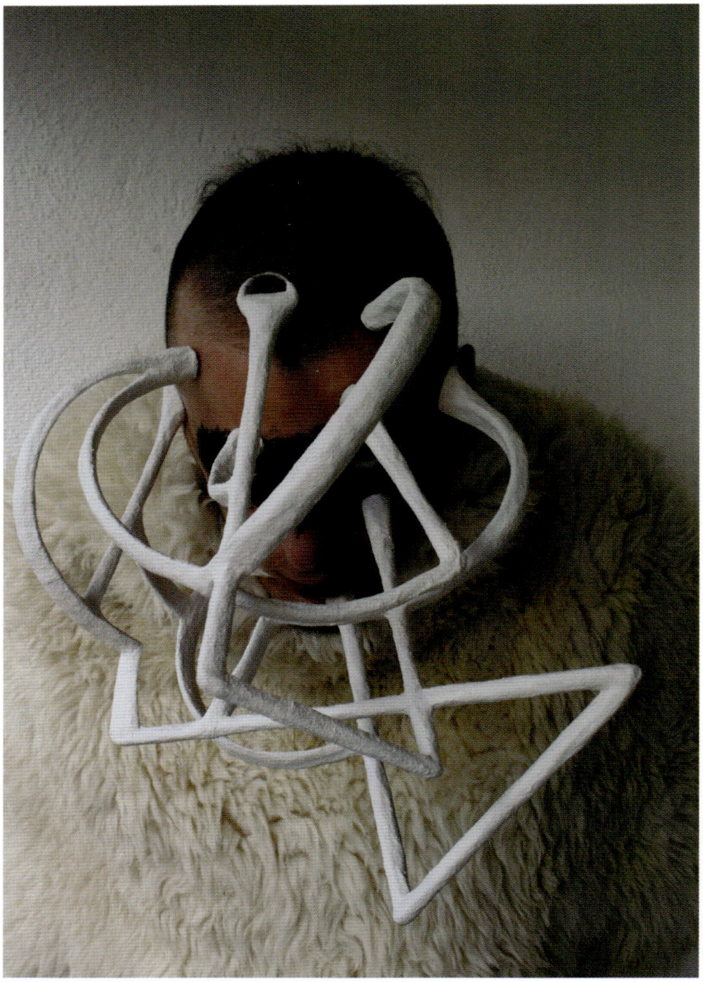

Photo: Olivia Mortimer

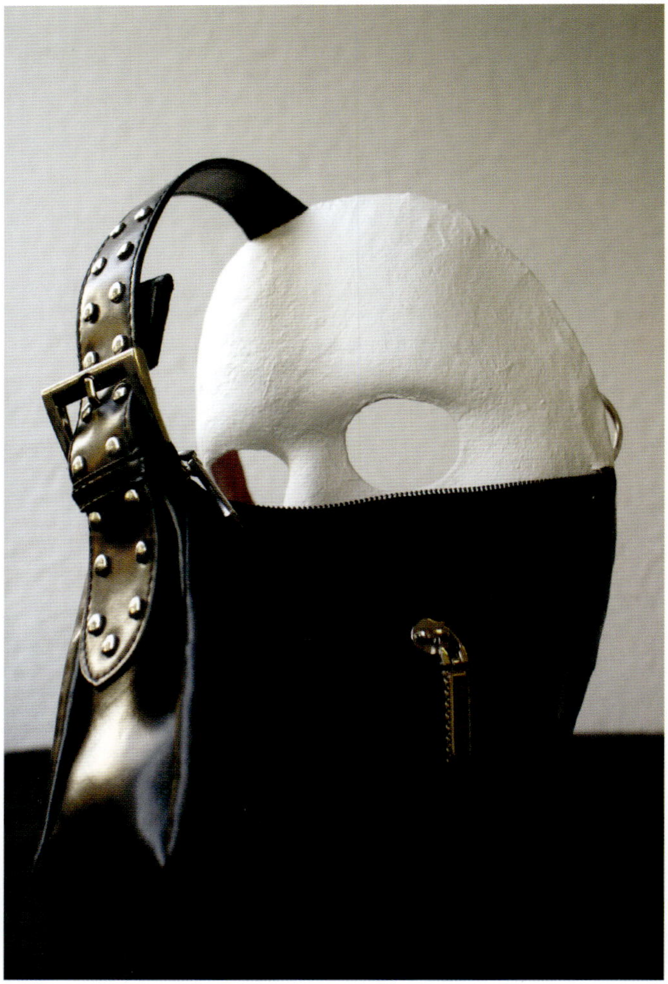

# Kepa/Rasmussen

www.kepa.co.uk

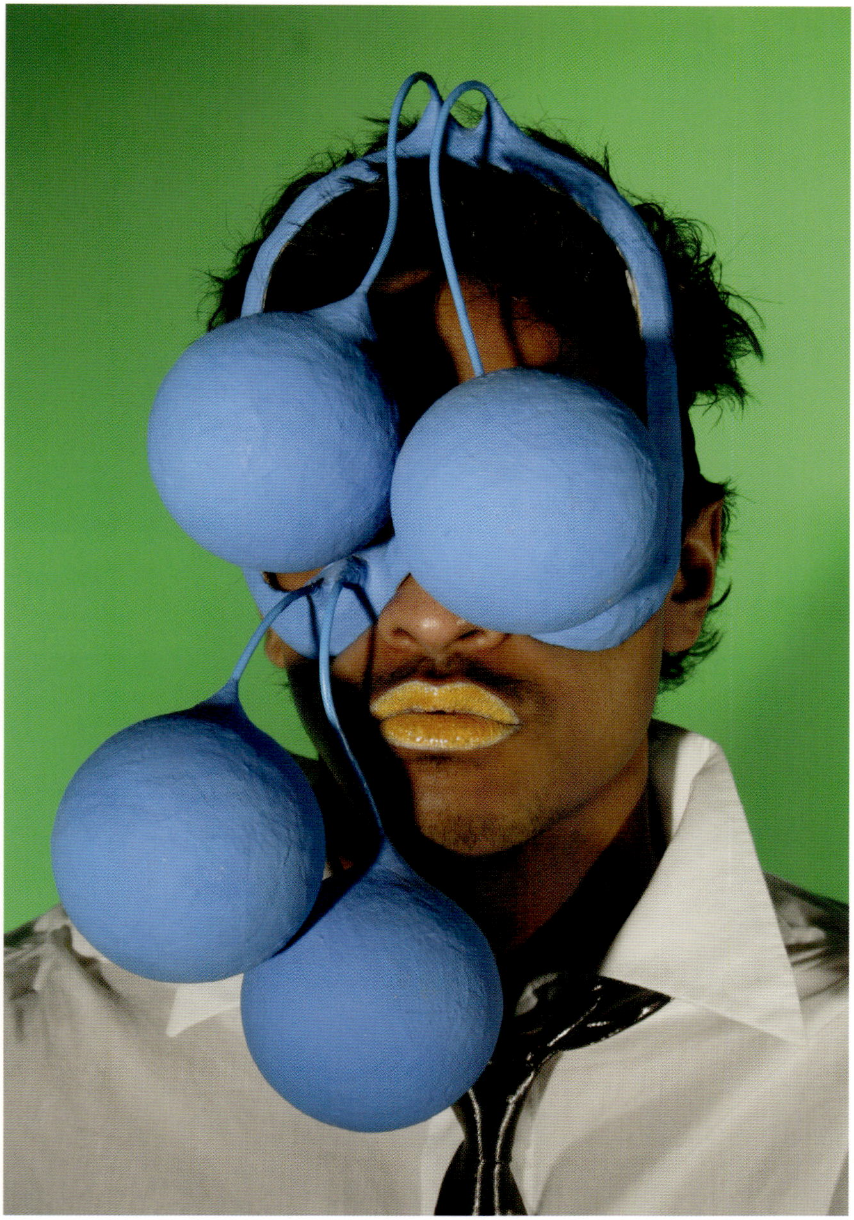

Photo: Niall Walker
Make-up: Anna Mackenzie
Shirt: Florence To
Model: Bill
@ Checamille

Kepa Rasmussen, is an artist living in Glasgow Scotland, with Spanish, Danish, Russian and Czech blood. Producing only original one of a kind designs, that transcend disciplines and boundaries, a body of work that centres on the human form and its abstraction. The work is hard style papier-mâché, a technique which in the past has been used for samurai armor, car bodies and bullet proof vests. The technique is very labor intensive, and involves the individual layering of thousands of pieces of paper on top of each other. Using different grades of paper at different stages. Materials: PVA glue, paper, paint, mixed media

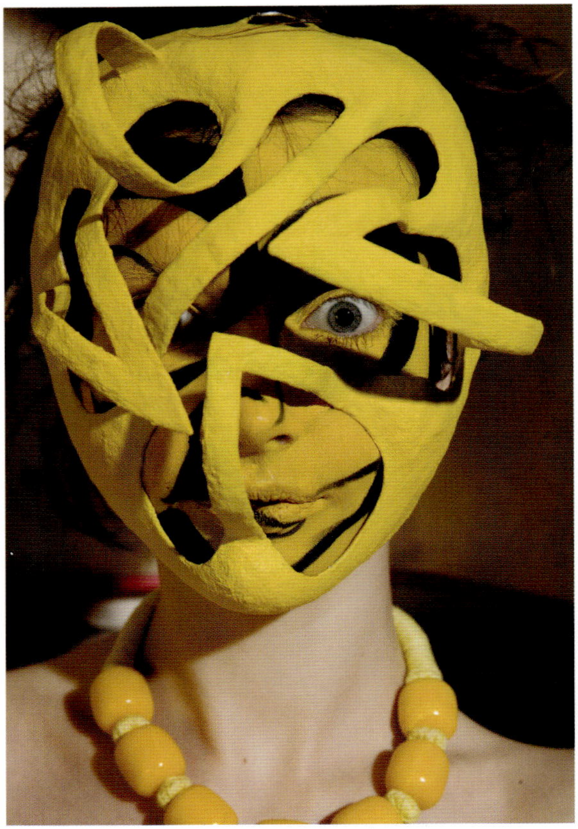

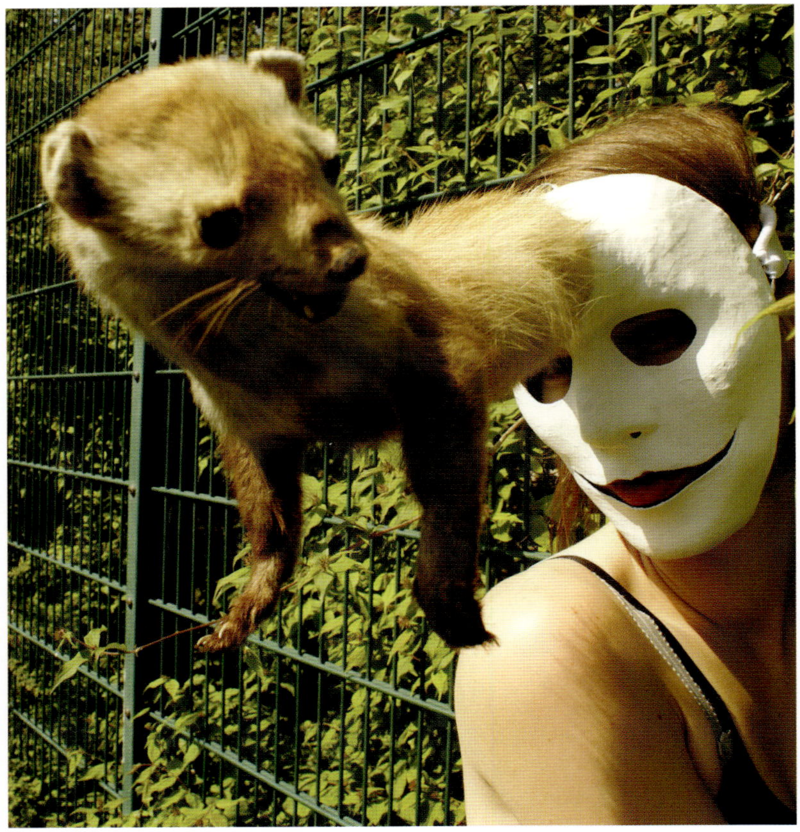

Photo: David Stanton
Make-up, hair & styling: Laura Mcnair
Model: Gemma Elise Gerber
@ The Chateau, Glasgow

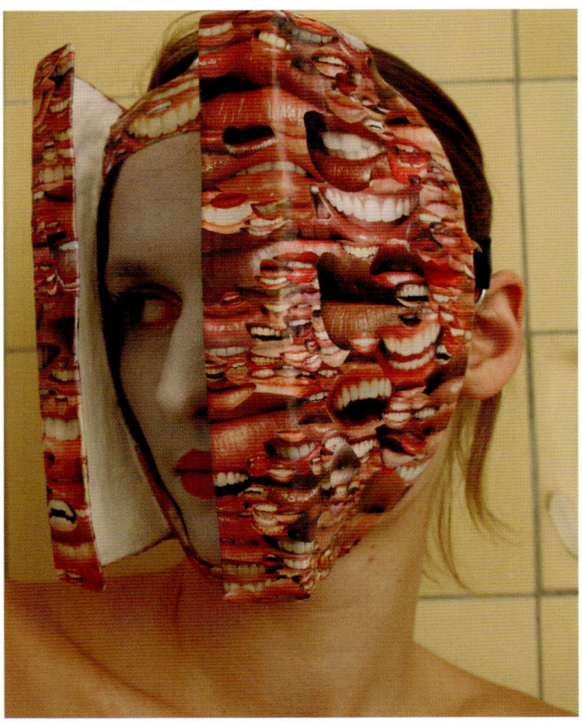

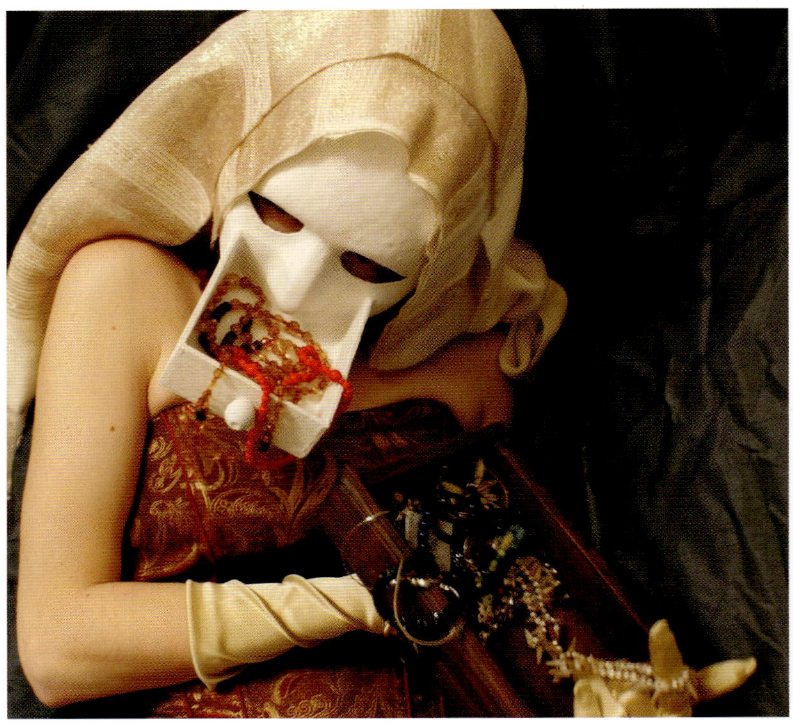

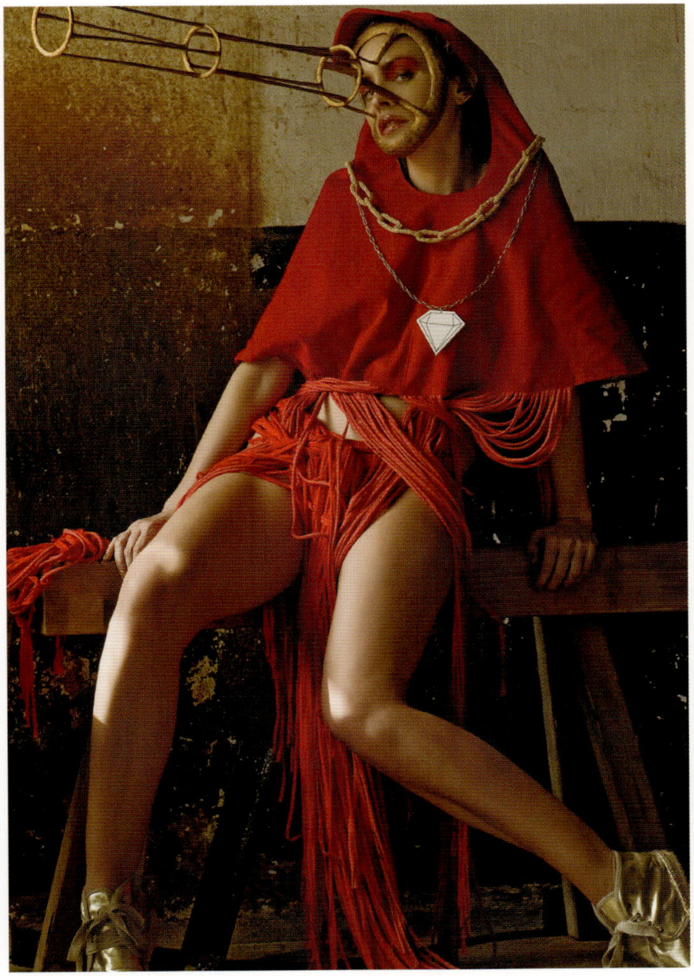

Photo: Marco Benedetti
Garments: Boycotletts
Jewellery: Anker Crew
Model: Sarah Nuenlist
Make-up: Nelly Staneva
Shoes: Apek

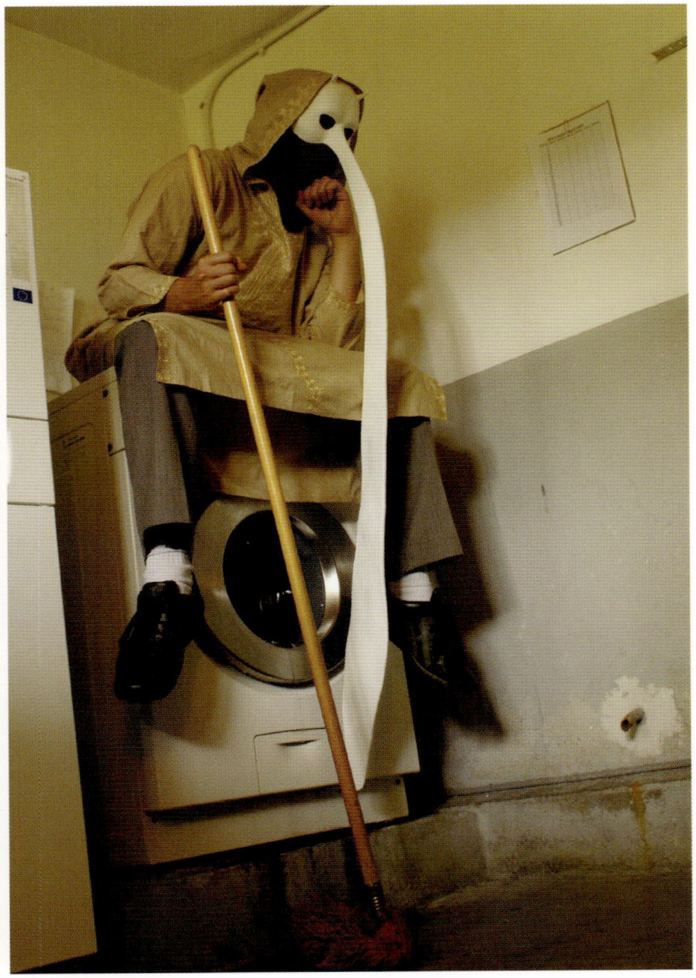

Photo: Olivia Mortimer

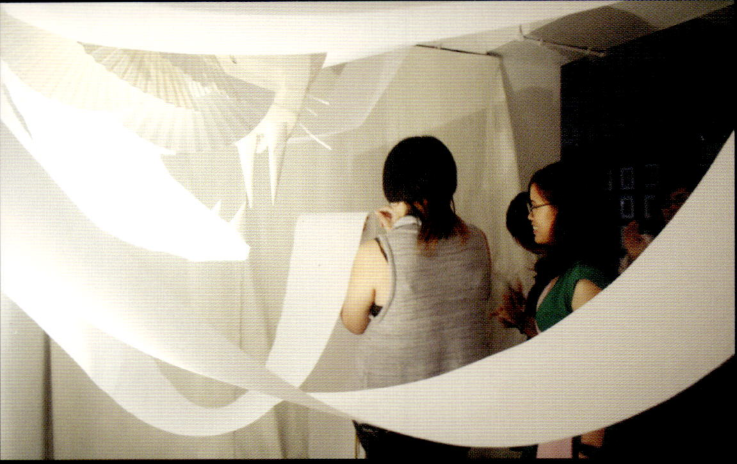

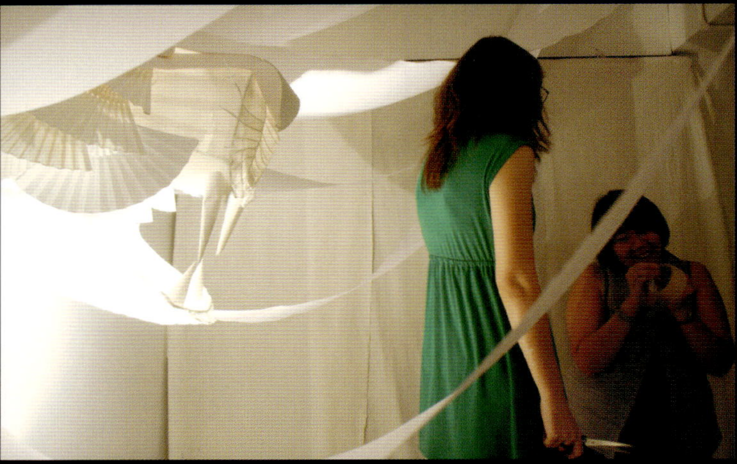

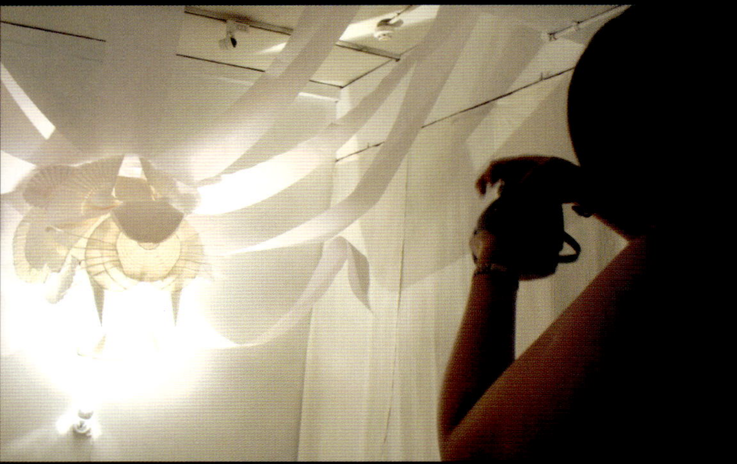

**MER.T.GER**

The 3D installation was commissioned by Tiger Beer to be part of an exclusive museum-on-the-streets happening in Singapore. Lim Si Ping was the only student who was invited to exhibit at the event, alongside other creative professionals working in the design industry. This project is based on the convergence of Singapore's Merlion and Tiger Beer's iconic feline. By combining the significance of our leading beer brewery with our locally-renowned mascot, it exemplifies the influential energy of the lion city's nightlife by placing it in the midst of night-goers' presence. The entire installation was created with paper fans from Chinatown, with strips of long cotton fabric that represent the Merlion's mane. A light casts the energy of the tiger by shining through the paper material, creating a lantern-inspired effect.

Photo: May Chiang (www.peace-and-quiet.net)

# Lim Si Ping

www.pixel-pastry.com

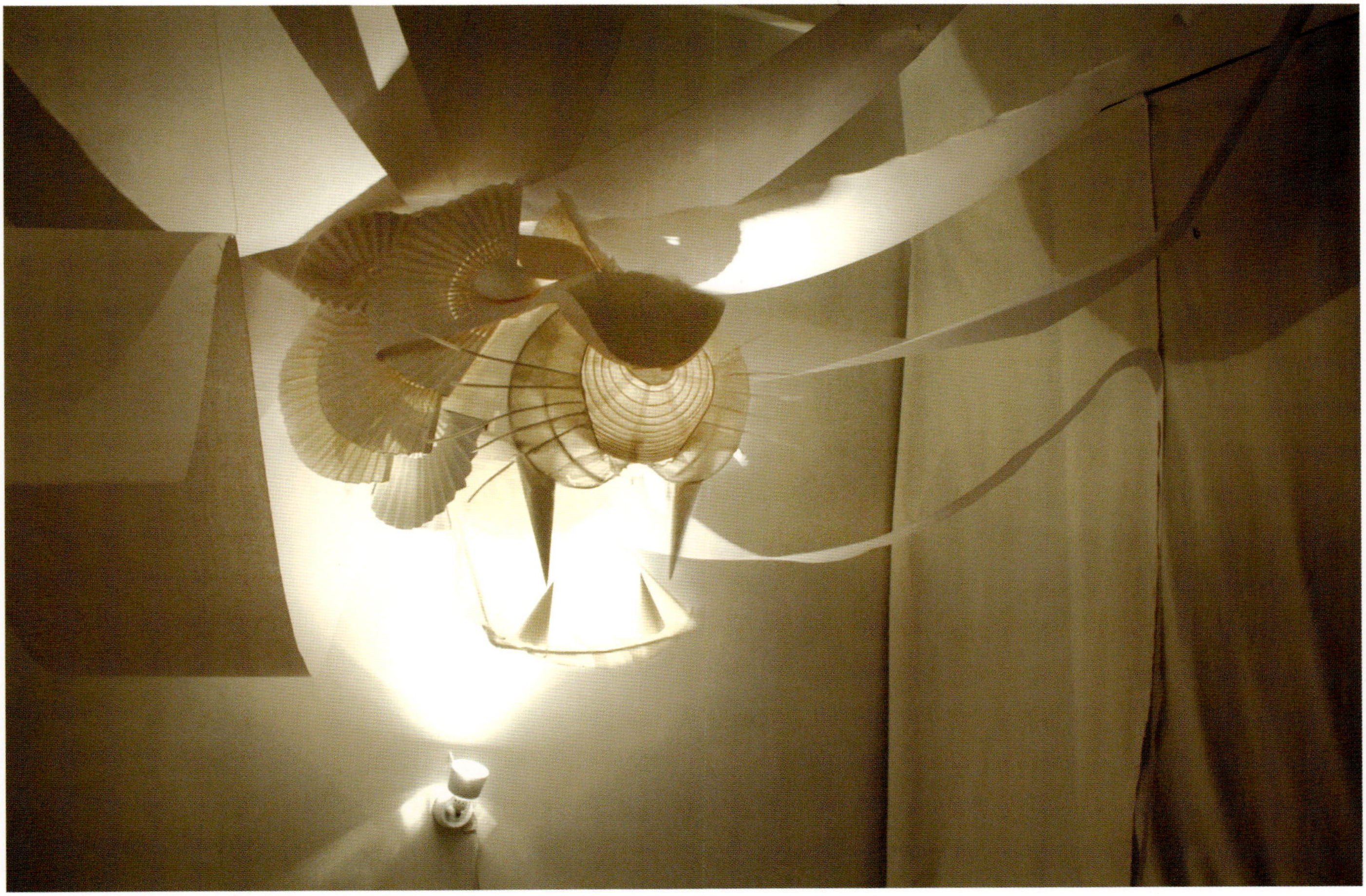

Lim Si Ping is a Singapore-based designer who first made her presence known in the design industry at the age of 18. Her portfolio is a spectrum of visionary work that first emerged from an established profession in digital illustration. In the span of her four-year career as a freelance artist, her work has gained her recognition in international media, which includes Territory Magazine (Asia), Lürzer's Archive (Austria), Computer Arts Magazine (UK), and The Art Directors' Club (Germany). In 2006, she was listed by Computer Arts Magazine as one of the 20-up-and-coming illustrators that will break new ground in the international industry. In 2007, she was invited by Tiger Beer to be part of a movement to support Asia's emerging generation of creative talents. She also made an appearance in a campaign video for the Nokia N-series as one of the four creative individuals in Singapore. Today, she is accredited by Lürzer's Archive as one of the 200 best illustrators worldwide. She has graduated from LASALLE College of the Arts with a BA (Hons) in Graphic Design. She has also represented her college at the D&AD New Blood 2009 in London.

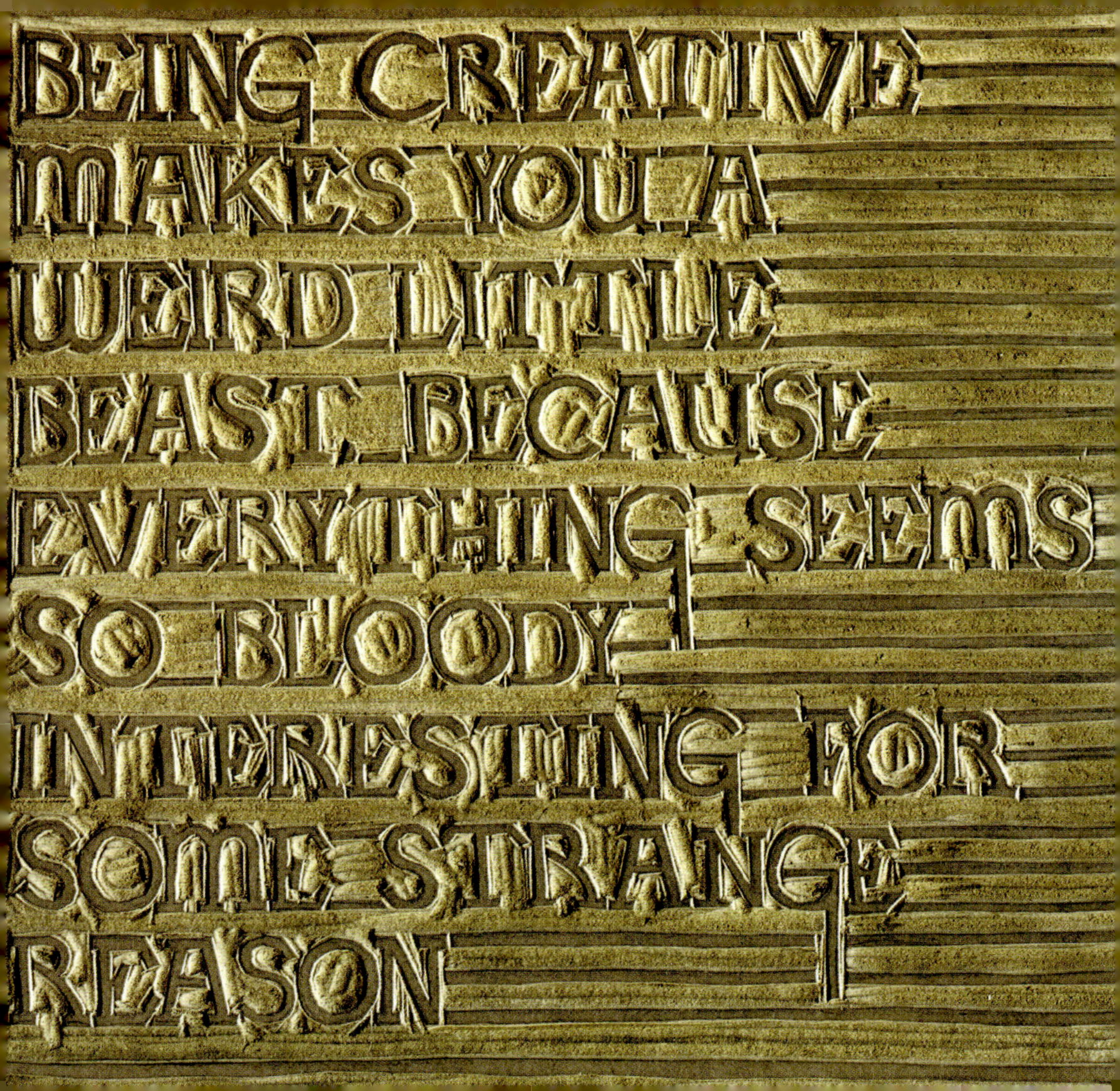
BEING CREATIVE
MAKES YOU A
WEIRD LITTLE
BEAST BECAUSE
EVERYTHING SEEMS
SO BLOODY
INTERESTING FOR
SOME STRANGE
REASON

# Mark Andrew Webber

www.markandrewwebber.com

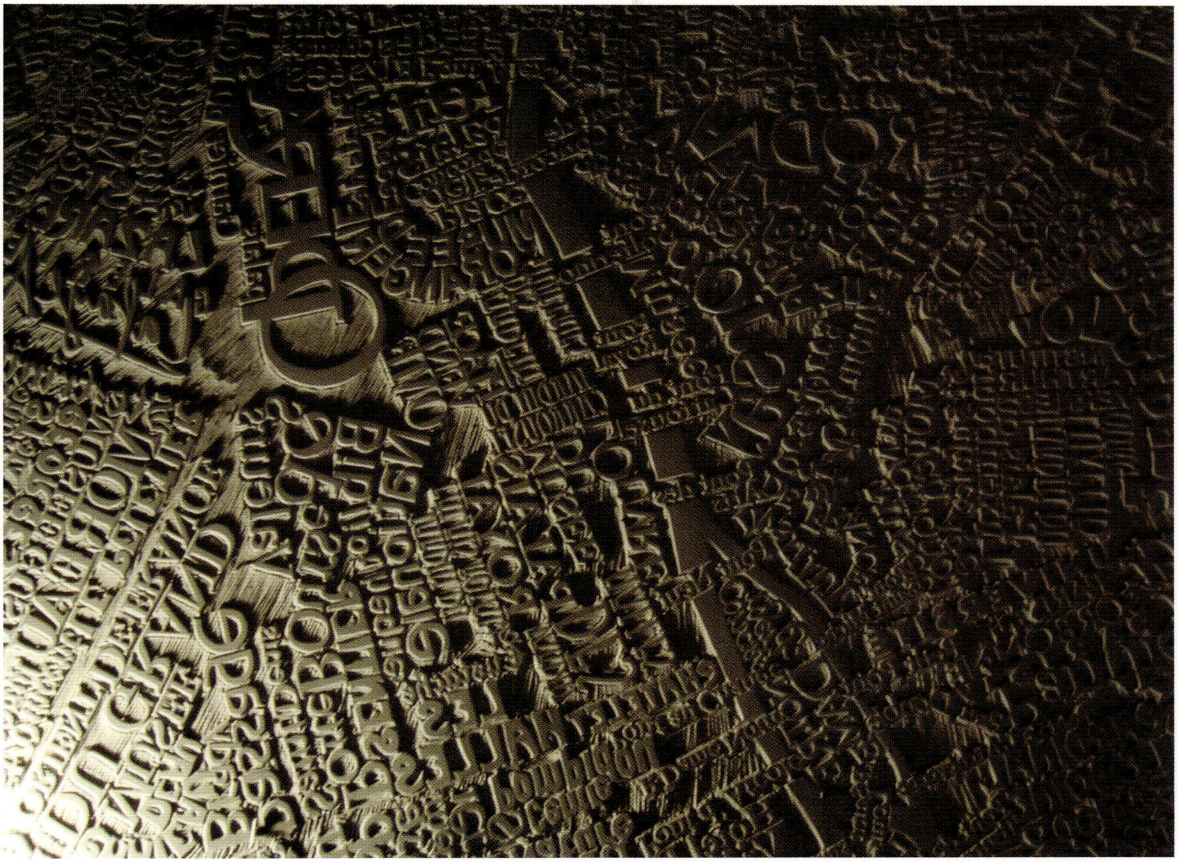

My name is Mark Andrew Webber, I am a graphic designer from Reading, England. I am a graduate of the Ba (hons) Graphic Design course at University College Falmouth. Though the main basis for my works started when I was studying at TVU - Reading, in which I studied graphic design at various levels for four years. This is where I was shown printmaking techniques and did a course in it, and was taught in a very open minded way. I started my "Where in the world city map series", in 2006 on the last year at TVU. I am a member of the international society of Typographic Designers (ISTD) and was commissioned by them to be involved with the 2006 London Design festival, ISTD exhibition which was named, my city, my London. I was able to show my work along side some amazing people and was thrilled to be amongst the works of, Alan Fletcher, Margaret Calvert, Ken Garland, and Derek Birdsall. The next point of my career was that same year in August, I was asked by the Arts council of England to design and lino carve the Front cover of their magazine, and use the actual lino carving inked up in various colours as the front cover of the magazine, which was then used as the Nov/Dec issue, and was distributed all over the UK and some to America and parts of Europe. My project which is titled Linocuts - traditional printmaking is a series of experiments with some different carvings I have made, being either rubber stamp illustrations, linocut prints, lino carved animation, or the actual lino carving itself. The series is based on city maps and the more well known areas of each city, i have been developing the maps, as these first three i have done, london, new york, and amsterdam, have been only slightly different, i am working on designs of other cities that will be more colorful and larger.

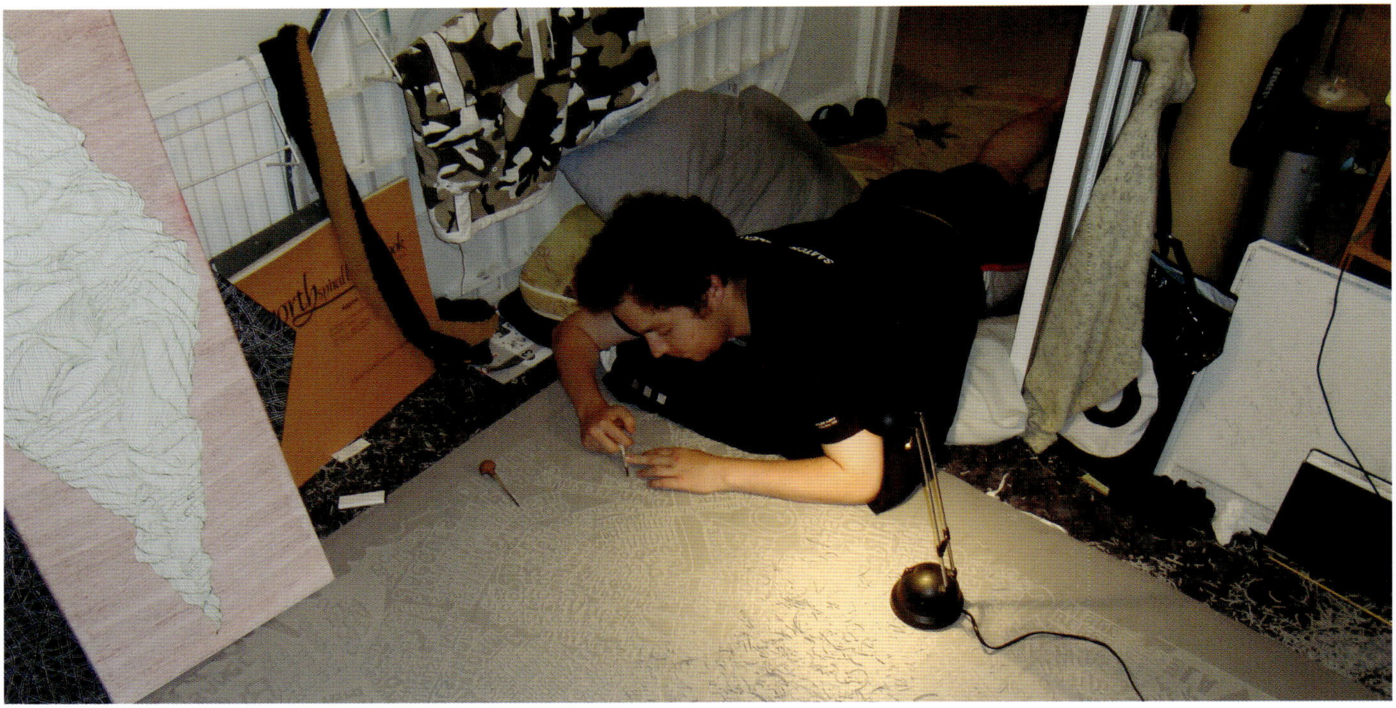

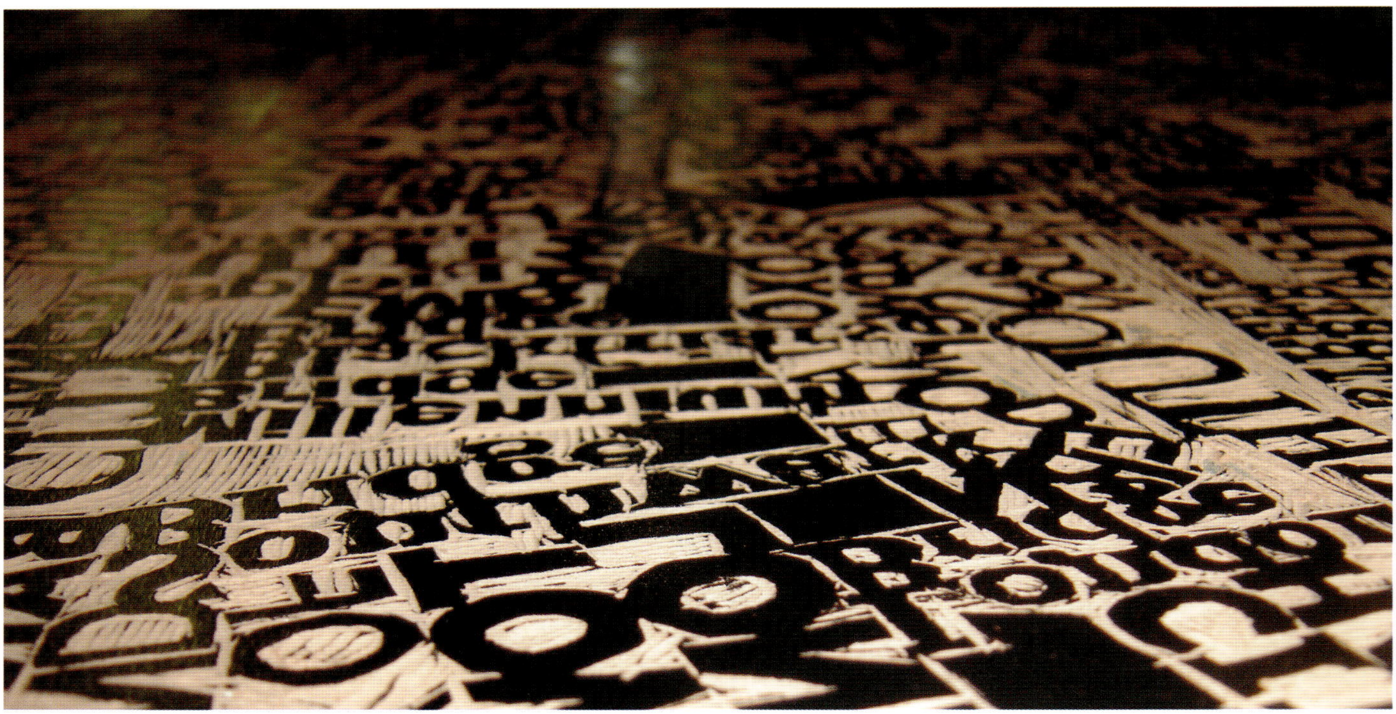

FEAR IS
THE THIEF
OF DREAMS

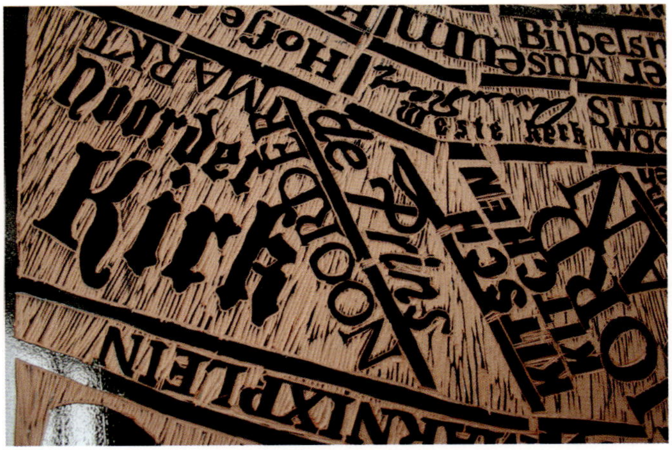
Noorder
Kirk
de Prins

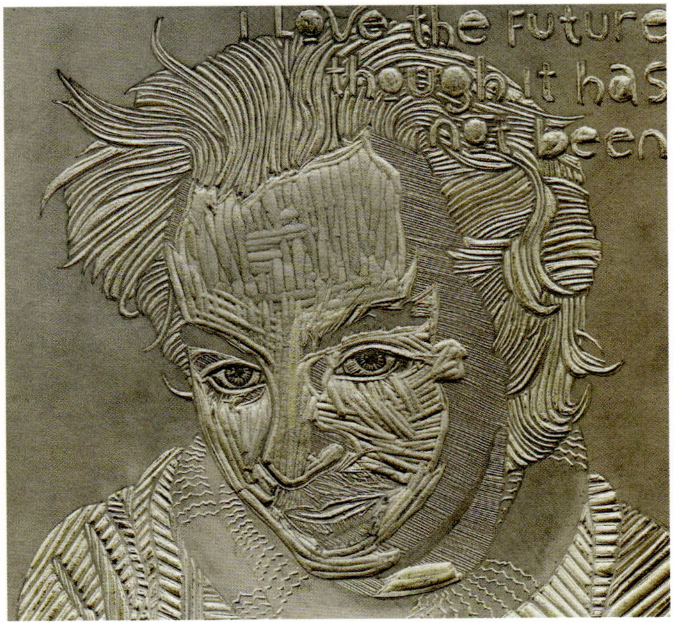
I Love the future
though it has
not been

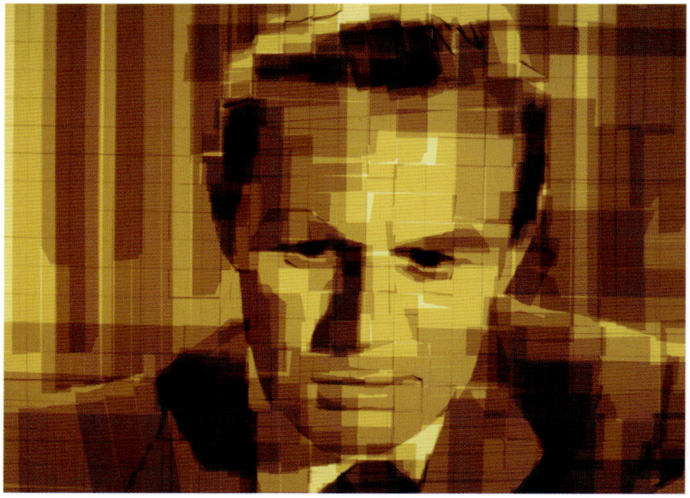
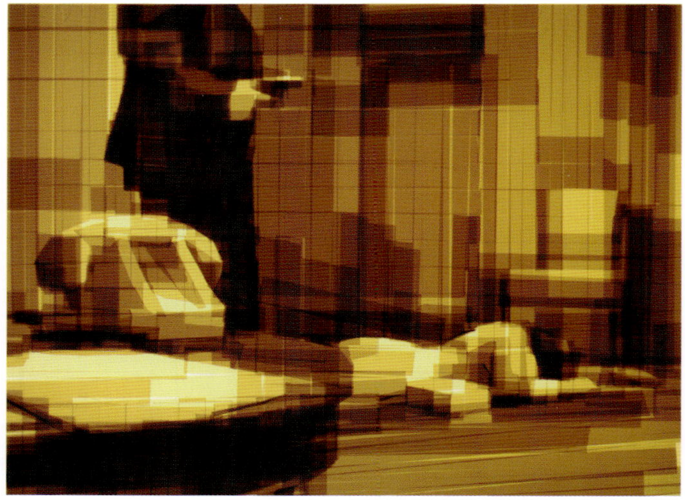
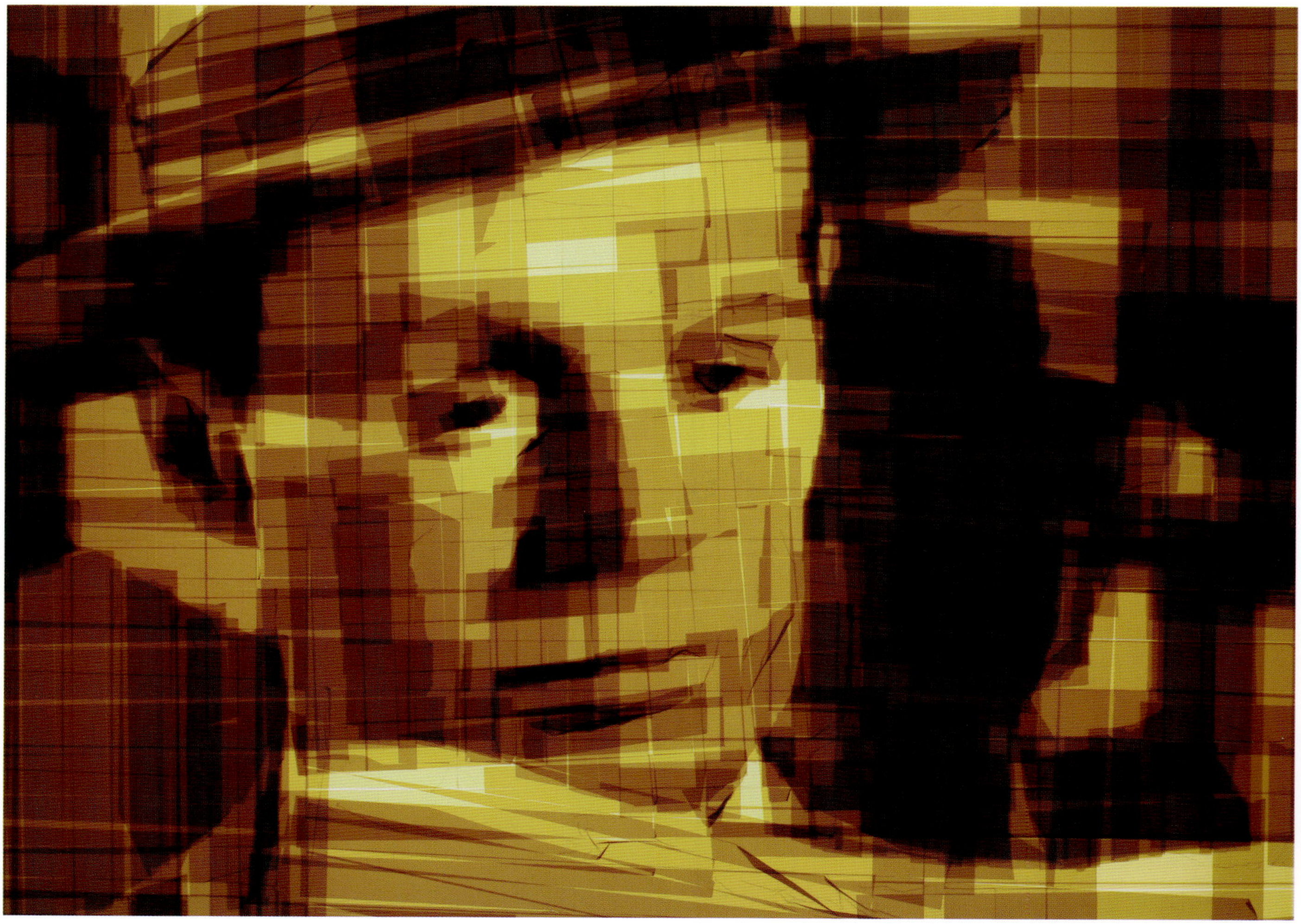

# Mark Khaisman

www.khaismanstudio.com

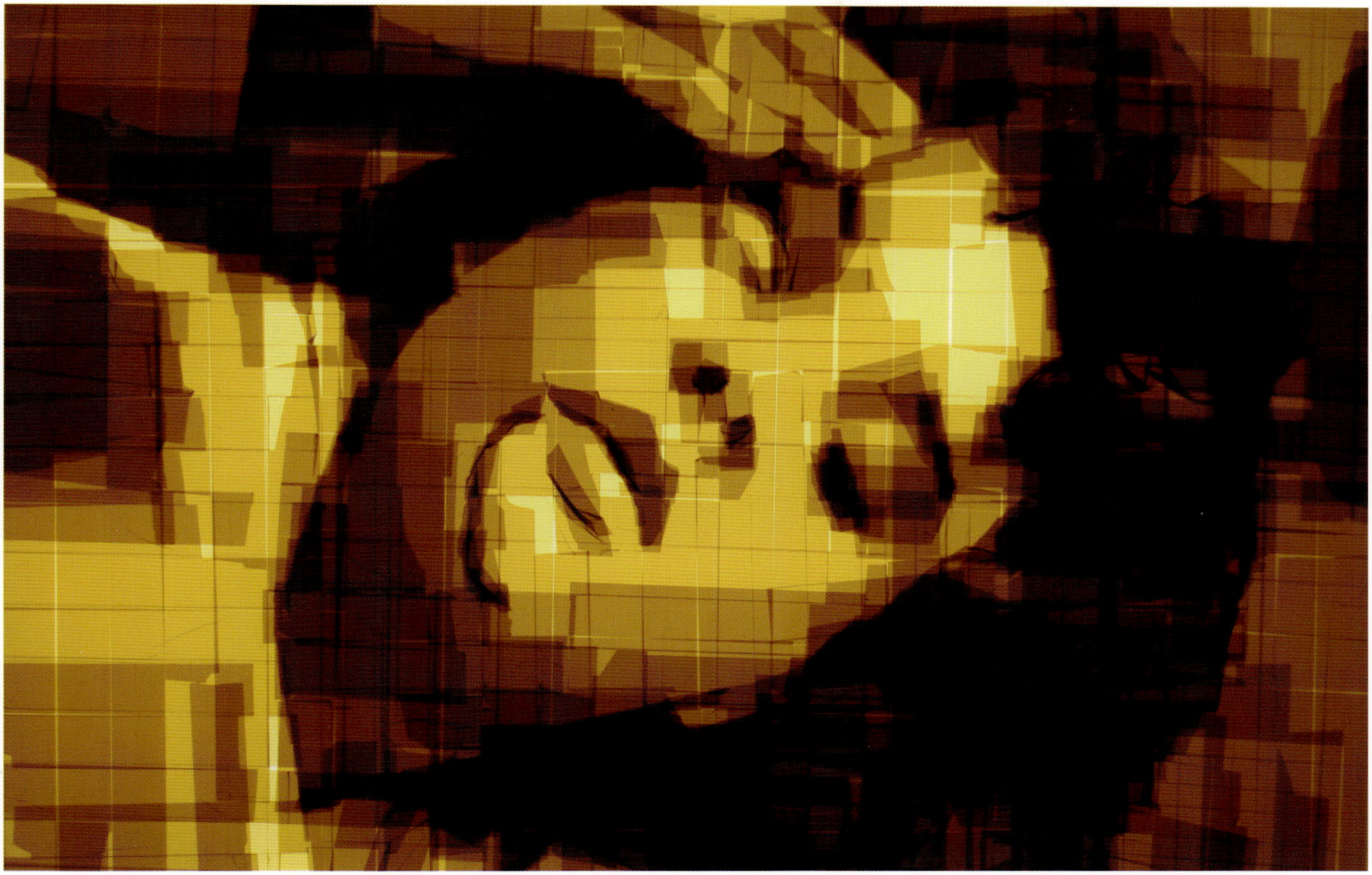

I work on the light easel, applying layers of translucent packing tape on clear Plexiglas panels. The tape is used as the most direct way of manipulating the light. I treasure the alchemy whereby a commonplace material is transformed into a fine art medium. My technique involves layering and intersecting; while doing it, I am contemplating on the layering and intersecting of universal and personal meanings and memories. People react to my tapes because it talks to them on many levels, starting from the very basic level of tactile feeling - almost everyone hold this tape in their hands, and is familiar with the sensation of striking a line with it. Many may almost feel it and hear the sound of adhesive being pulled off the roll. And then I build on it. I add the images, which are as familiar as the material itself. My tapes are about recognition: recognition of a tactile sensation, recognition of an image, recognition of a memory. They are very much play-it-again; it is the very essence of my work. When I work on the image, I try to keep it on that edge of almost falling apart, so that an eye of a viewer is given the challenge of assembling it in a recognizable shape. And after the first moment of visual recognition, the joy of a memory's recognition could come. At least that's how I want it to be. I am limiting my imagery to the highly recognizable cultural icons: I remake images, which have became classic in the context of various aspects of Western culture, and by doing so I highlight such issues as high and low culture, authorship and anonymity, different timescales as in timelessness of the original versus expediency of packing tape, and a phenomenon of presence as the inherence of prototypes within the tape images.

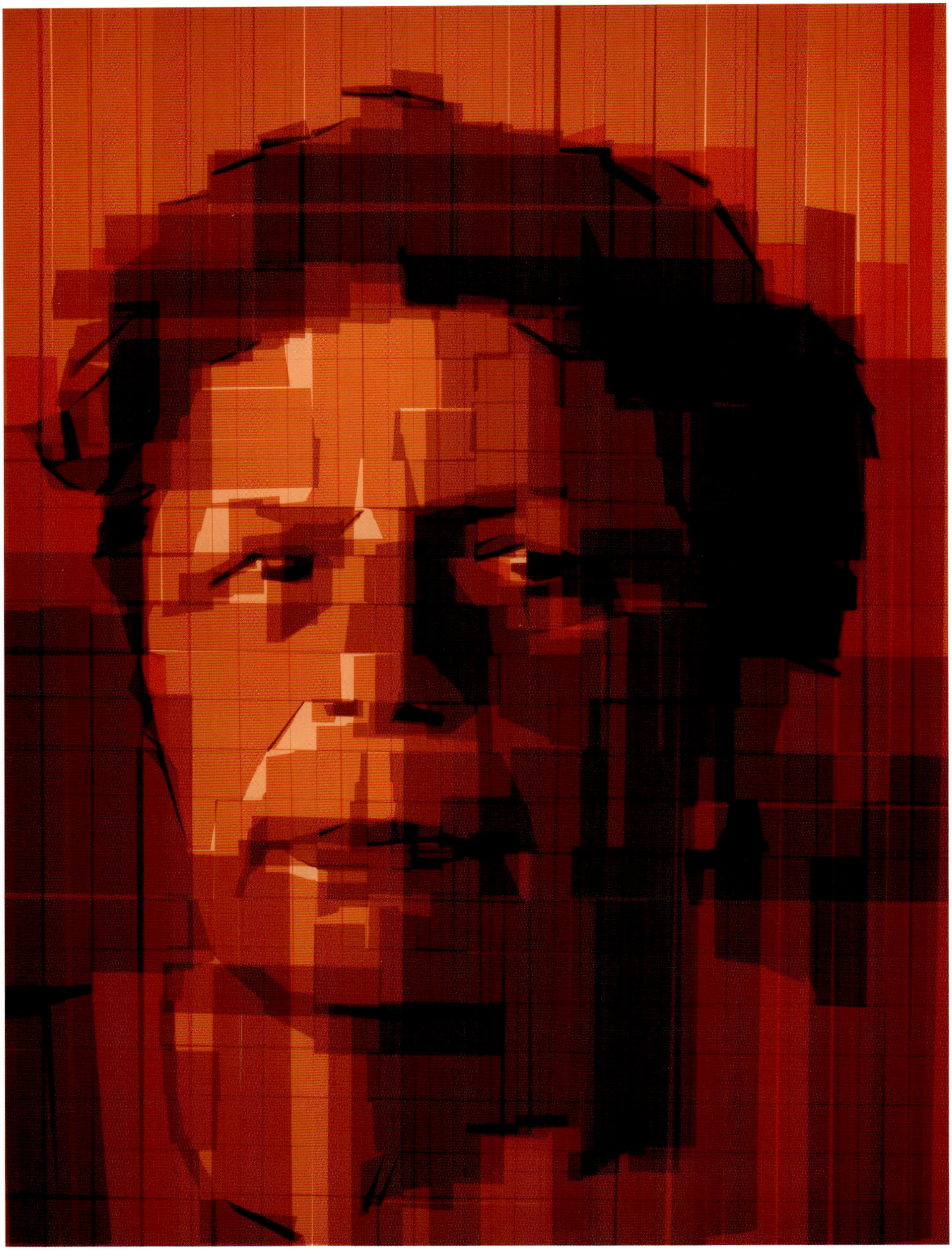

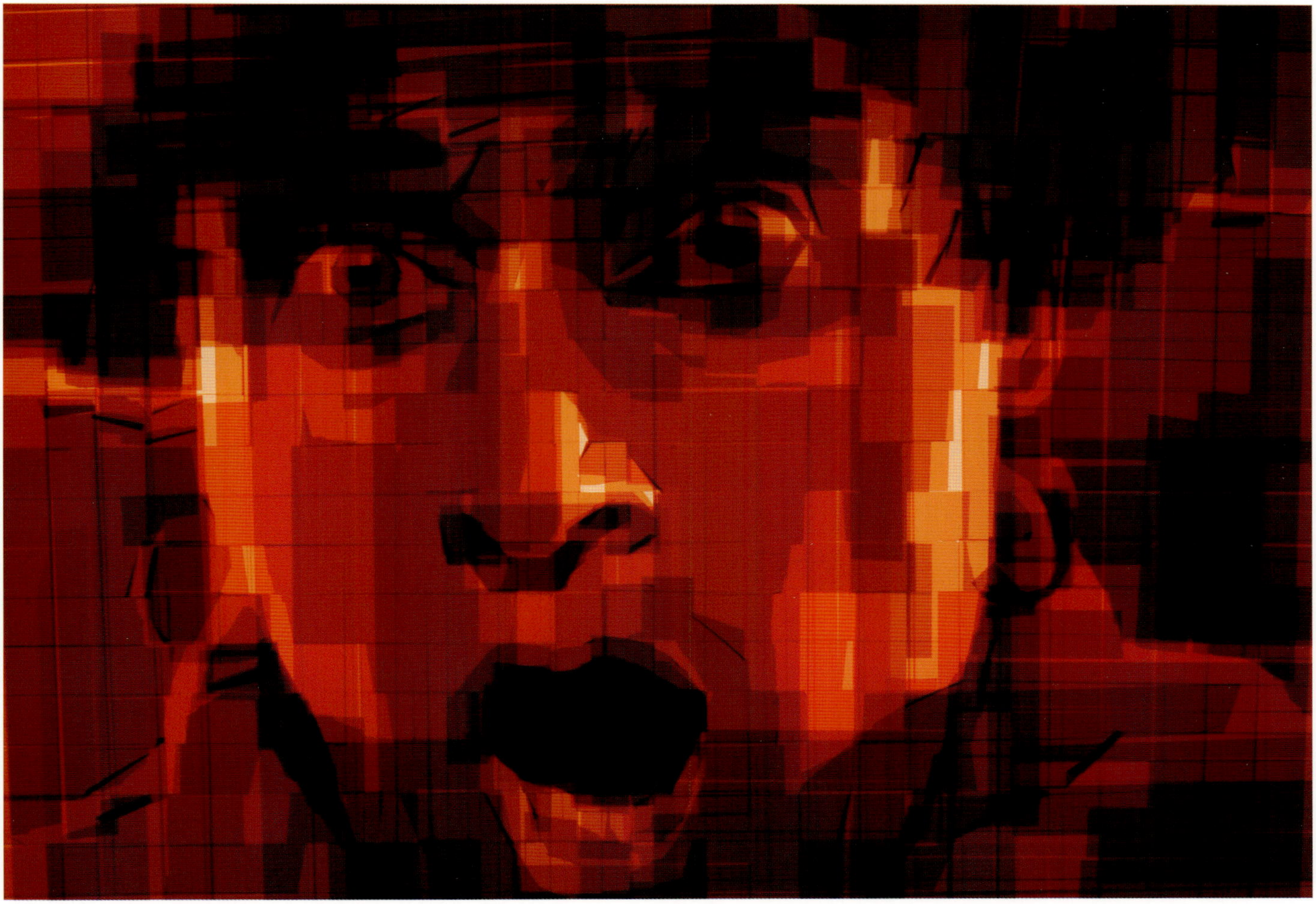

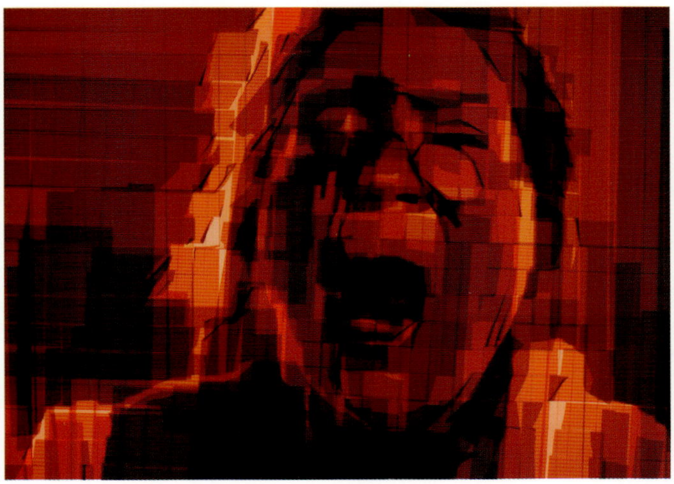

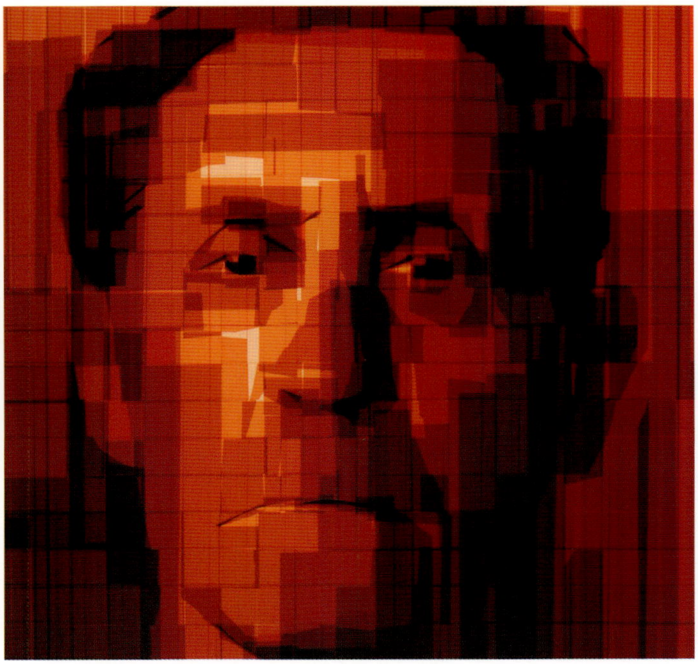

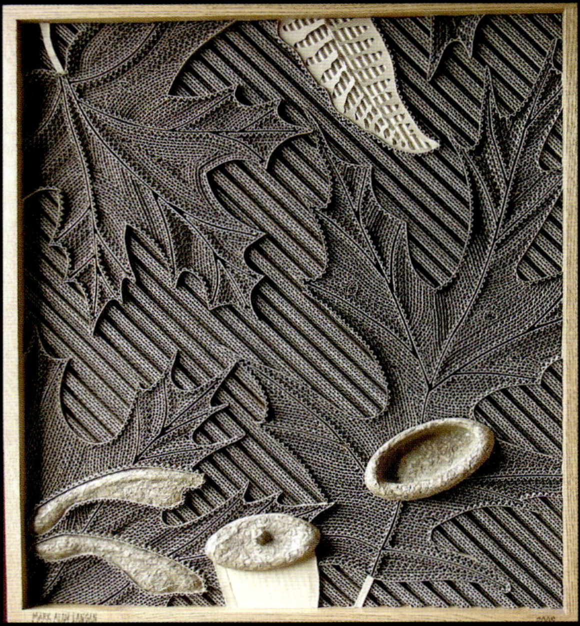

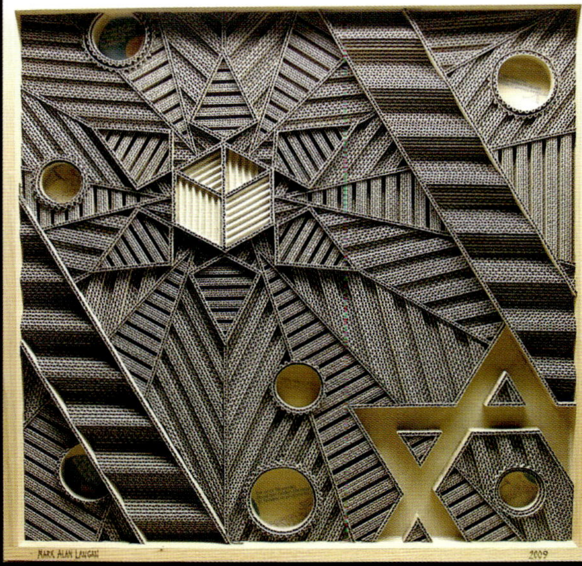

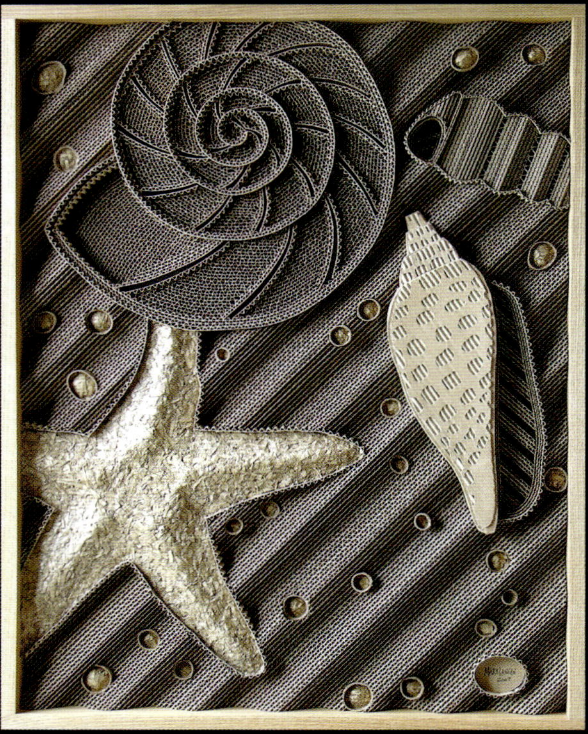

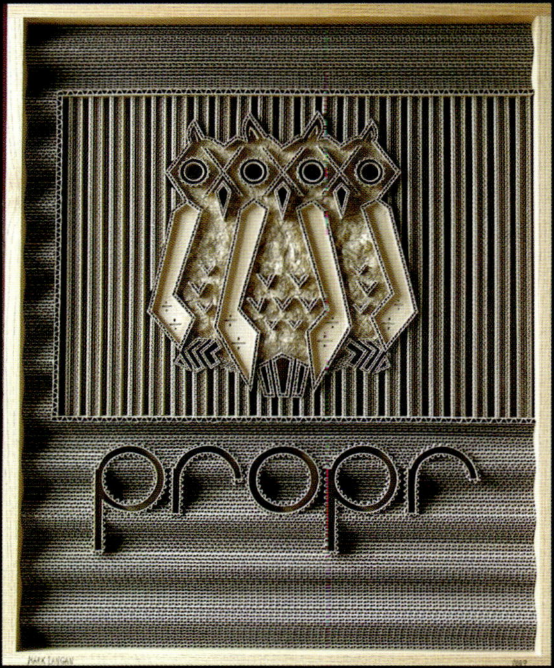


**v Propr**
Mr. David Arquette in his logo design for his newly launched clothing line called ©PROPR, developed the design in which 3 owls morph into one - this depicts the three principal owners of the business being himself, Ben Harper (Musician) and David Bedwell (Fashion Designer - former Penguin) and how the owl represents their shared vision and wisdom. My art being green and his clothing promoting the use of natural cotton fabrics, and focusing on sustainability practices.

# Mark Langan

www.langanart.com

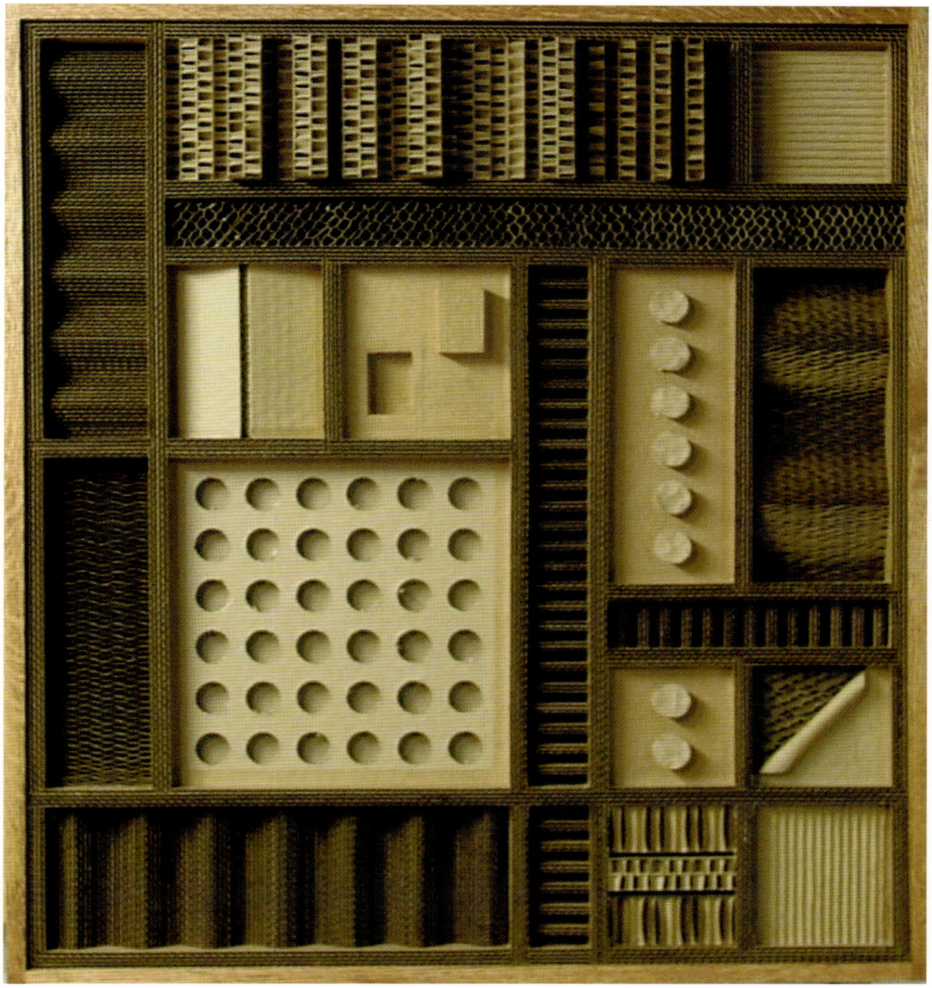

Mark Langan is an Artist who resides from the Cleveland, Ohio suburb of Brunswick Hills. Well versed and adept with numerous artistic mediums, he has concentrated his focus since the year 2004 by working strictly with a reclaimed material. A rather unlikely choice for which he creates fantastic sculptural works using nothing more than mere corrugated boxes, non-toxic glue, a razor knife, a cutting edge and mat. Artwork that is intriguing and unique because of its composition but also cries out making the visual statement...reduce, reuse, recycle! Langan sometimes shies away and dislikes using the terms "green" but none-the-less, it is a term well suited by standards today. He's been creating this Art using reclaimed materials before the fashionable buzz words of "green" and "sustainability" became commonplace. It would be naïve' for him to claim that he's making a huge dent in reducing waste material going into landfills but as he states, "It is something rather than nothing." His sincere hope that his Art displayed on this site contributes to the recycling movement by inspiring others to ask of themselves, "What can I do to help?" Mark has had a successful campaign by marketing and targeting his Art to many diverse venues unlike your typical Sculptor. Those facets include artwork commissioned by paper, corrugated manufacturers, packaging companies, recycling firms, green industries, organizations and related events. His artwork currently adorns the boardrooms and lobbies from small to prominent firms throughout the U.S. Art that he is obviously passionate about and proudly states... "If you like this just wait, the best is yet to come!"

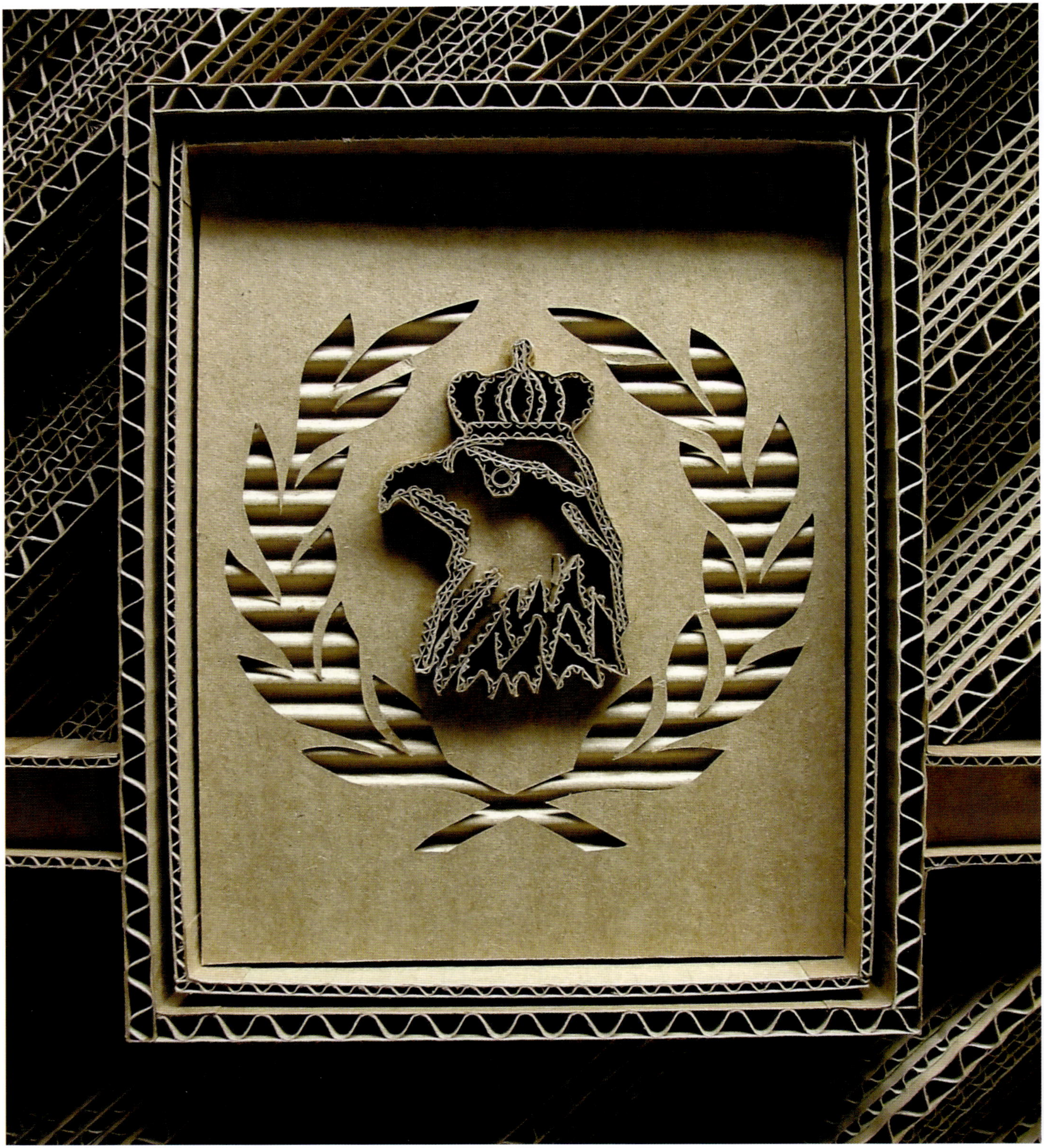

**Joh Clouth**
This is an artwork that I recently created for Timco Clouth in Marysville, Ohio - a USA Sister company of Joh. Clouth in Germany. This artwork was presented to the CEO of Joh.Clouth as a gift from Timco. Clouth's business is the sales of blades used for the manufacture of corrugated. In recreating the Eagle head motif of their logo it was rather small and conventional corrugated I couldn't work with. I wound up using the corrugated sleeve from a Starbuck's coffee that is a micro flute to get the results I needed.

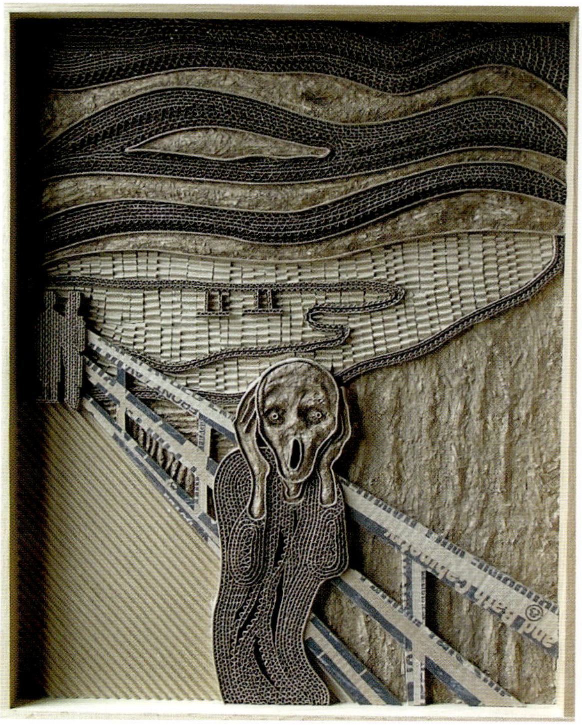

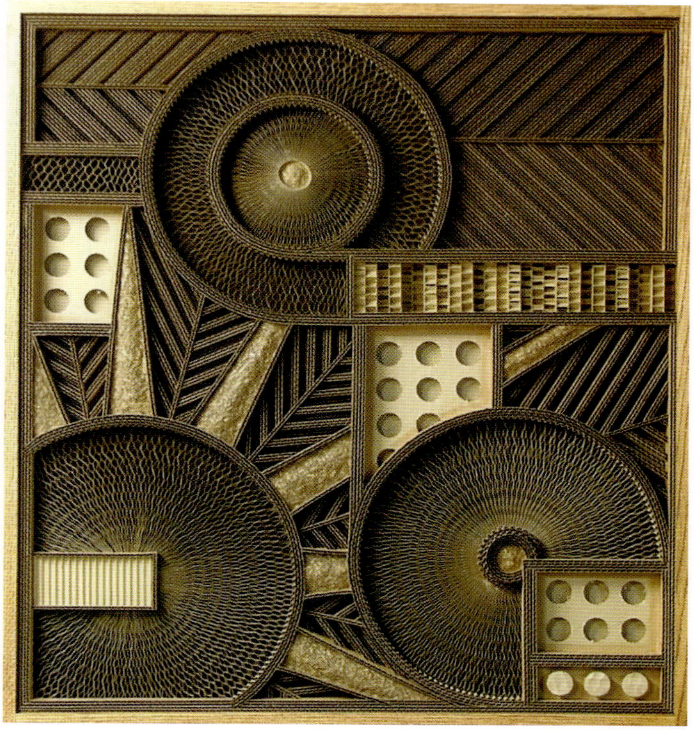

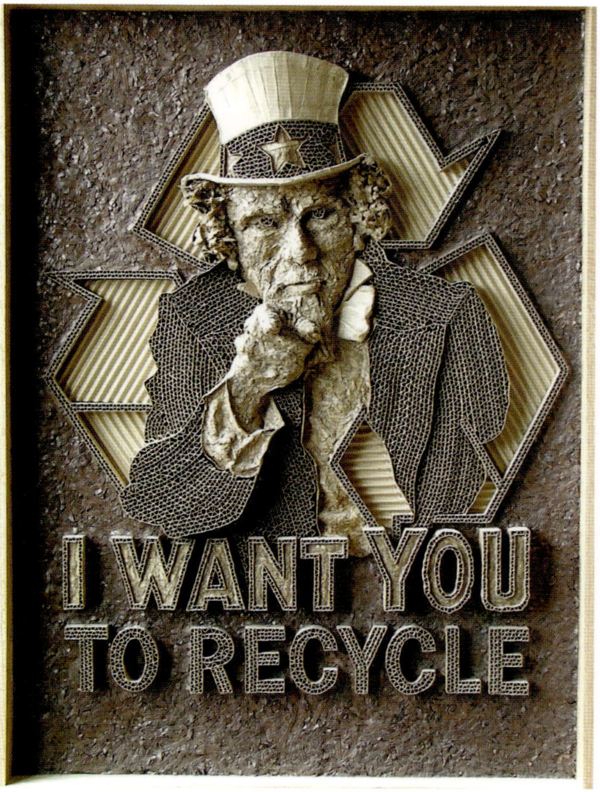



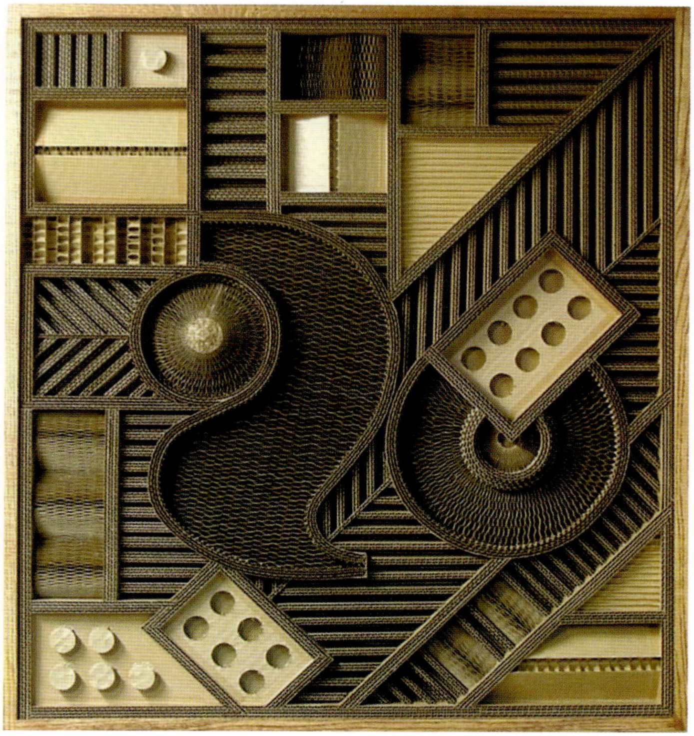

**Mid-States**
Mid-States Packaging in Lewistown, Ohio manufactures a unique medium that is very similar to corrugated being called honey comb. They commissioned me to create artwork for their boardroom which was quite long and the space the art needed to fit measured 10 linear feet. So a triptych (3 panels) was created to fit the space. My ideas for the art were to create visually appealing sculpture with lots of movement at the same time to also focus on what they manufacture by using a combination both of corrugated and honeycomb in the project.

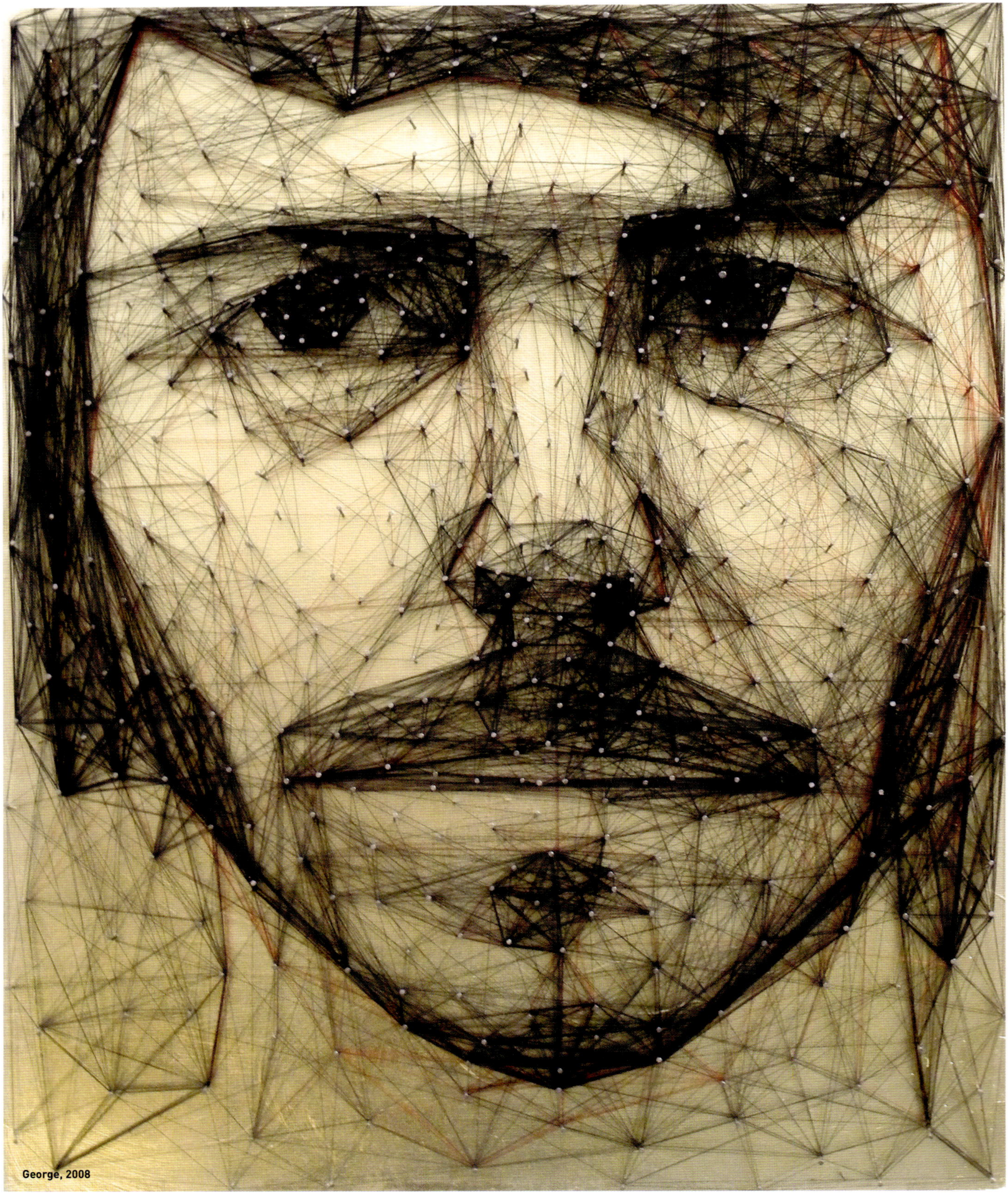
George, 2008

# Miriam Maselkowski

www.myspace.com/mmaselkowski

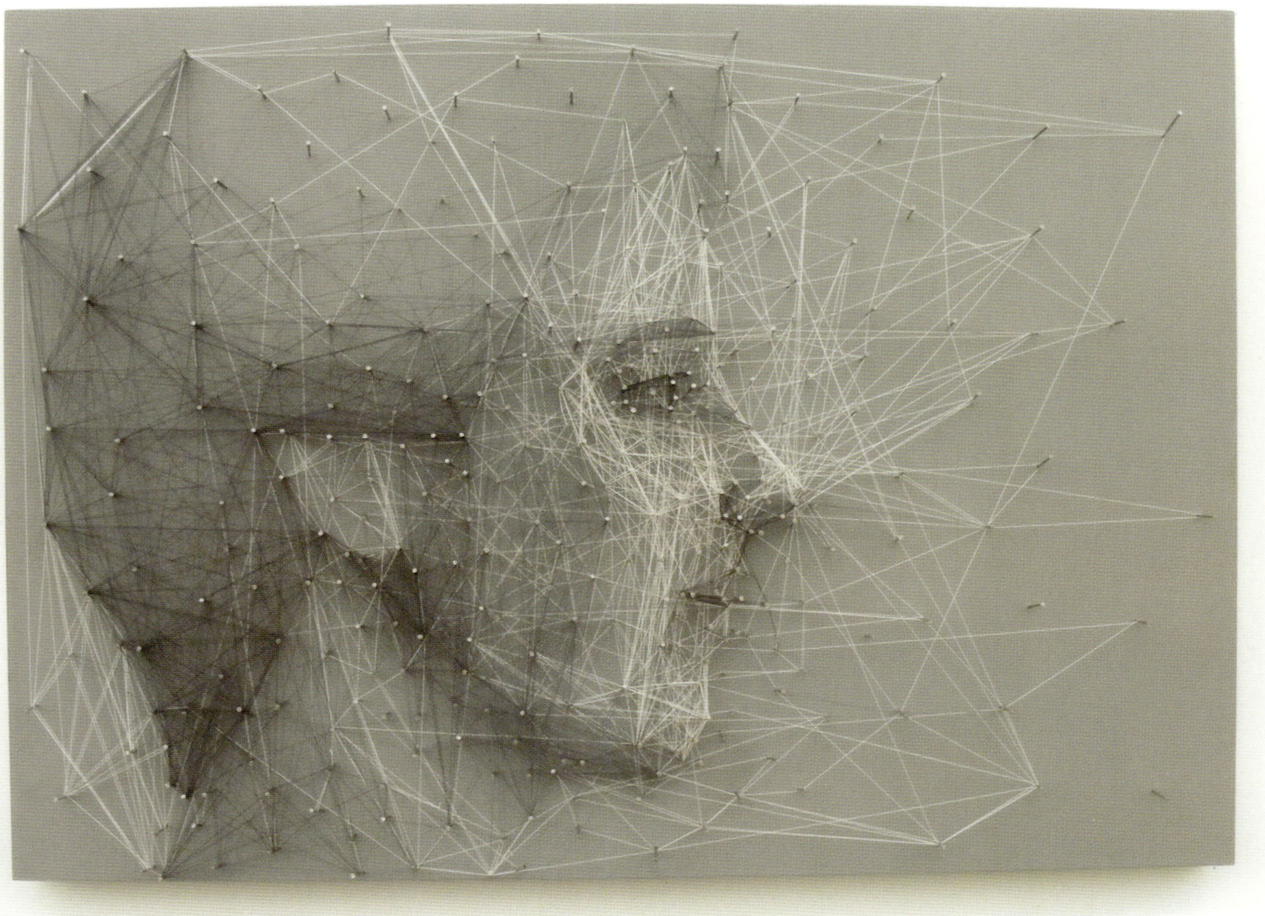

**Luke Profile**

With my current work I am exploring my interest in textile and stitch and feeding it into the painterly practices of portraiture and still life. With my still lifes I am exploring ideas of representation, opting, as opposed to the traditional still life, to create playful, 3-D, fabric doppelgangers of everyday objects. My portraits are made using nails and thread to draw out a likeness from a dense cloud, a network of lines

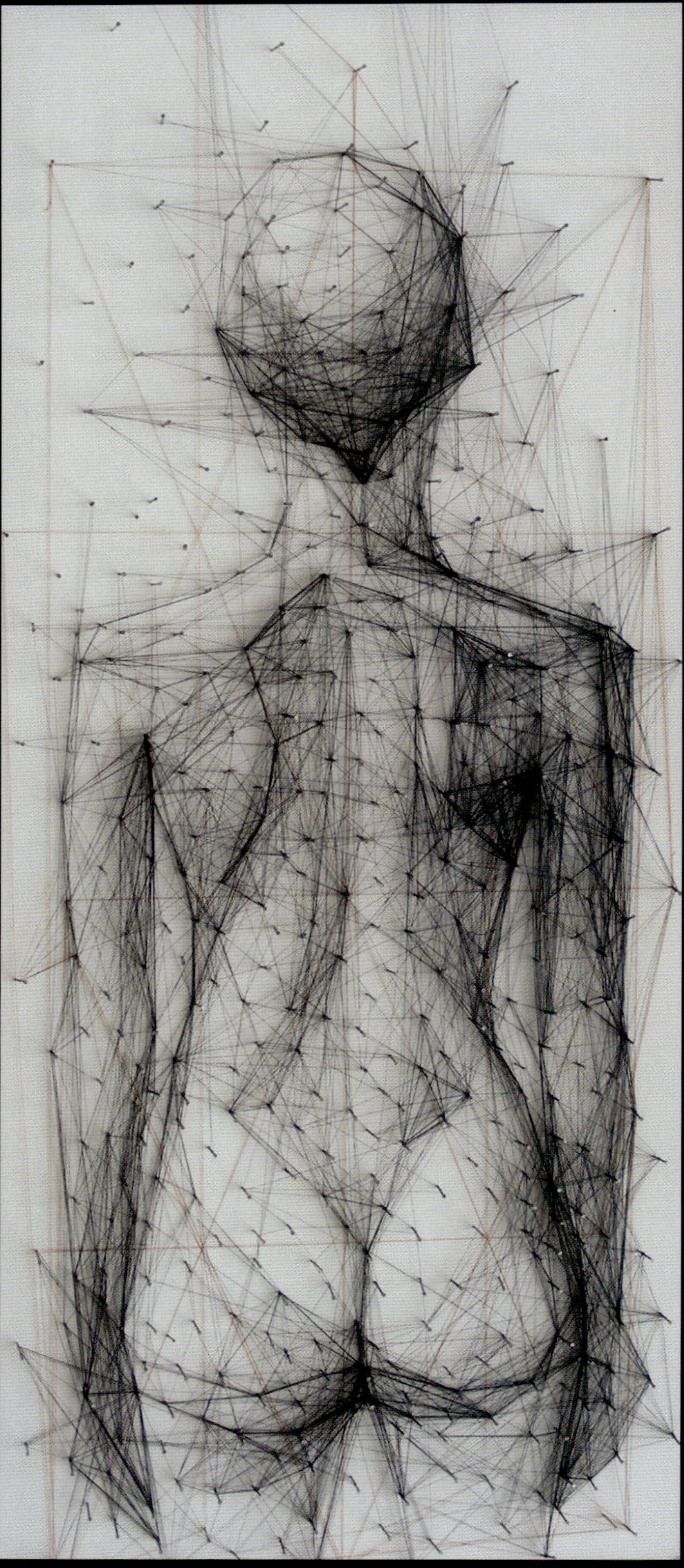

Nude 1

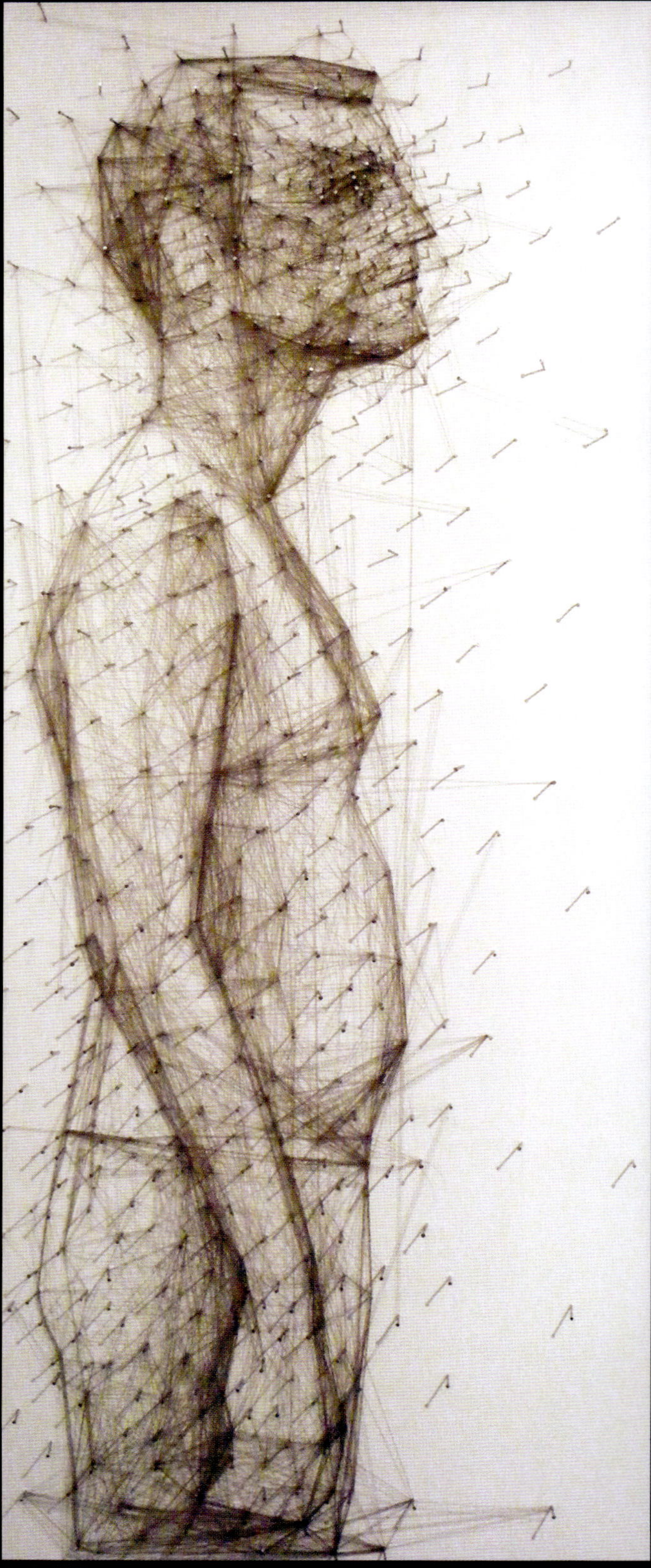

Justin, 2008

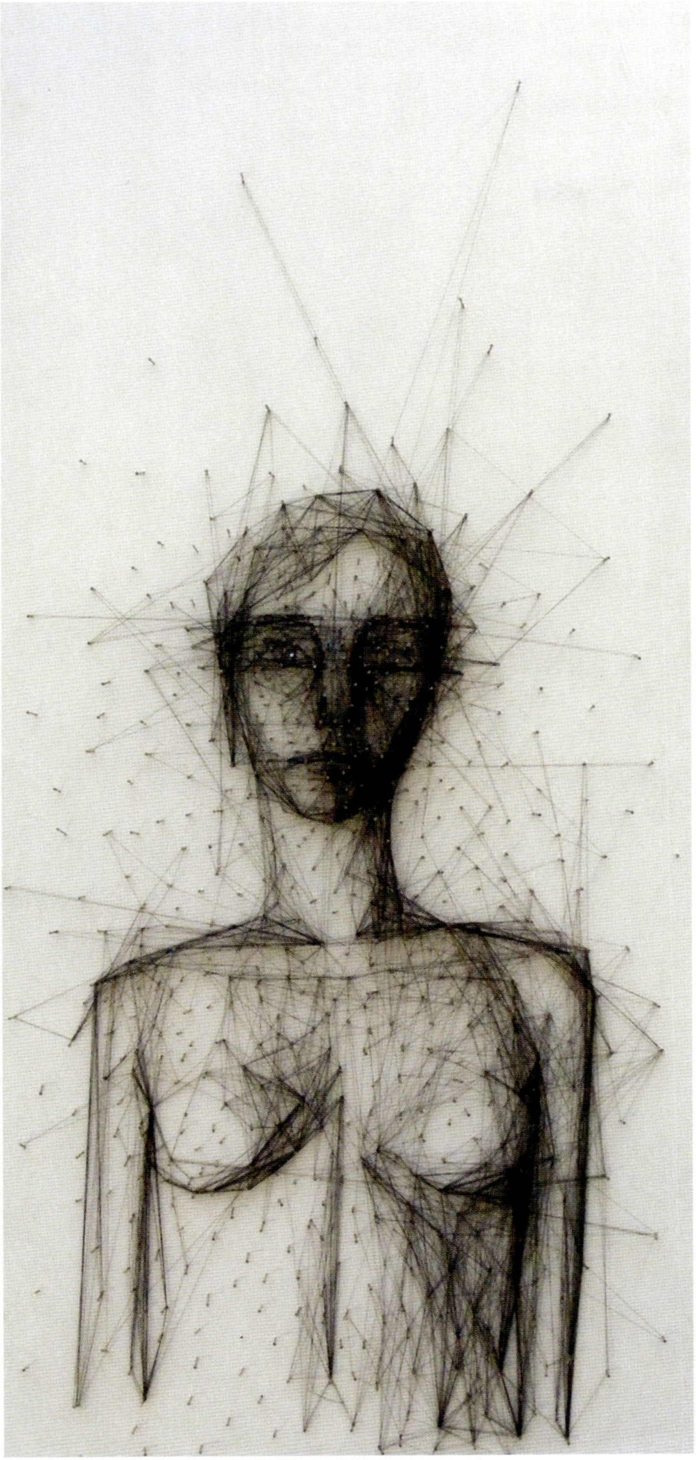

Self Portrait II, 2008

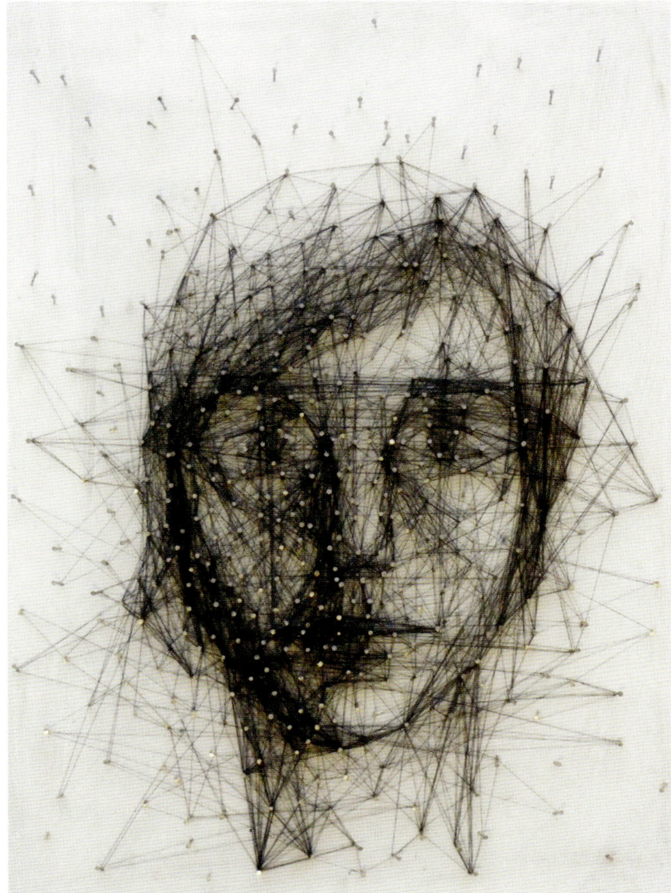

Self Portrait I, 2008

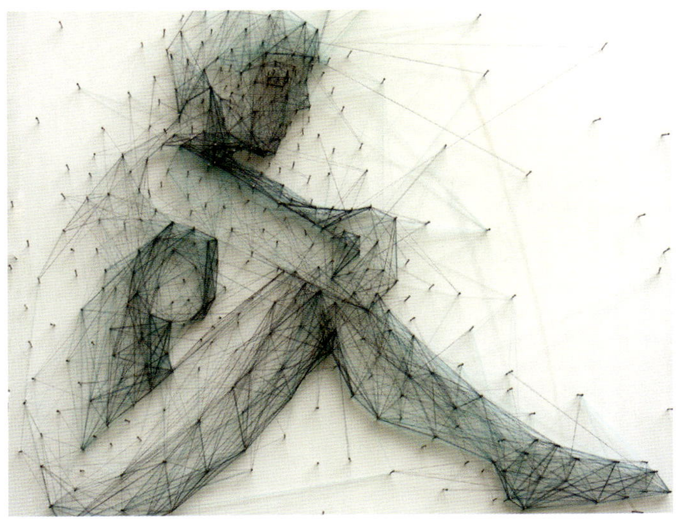

Nude 2

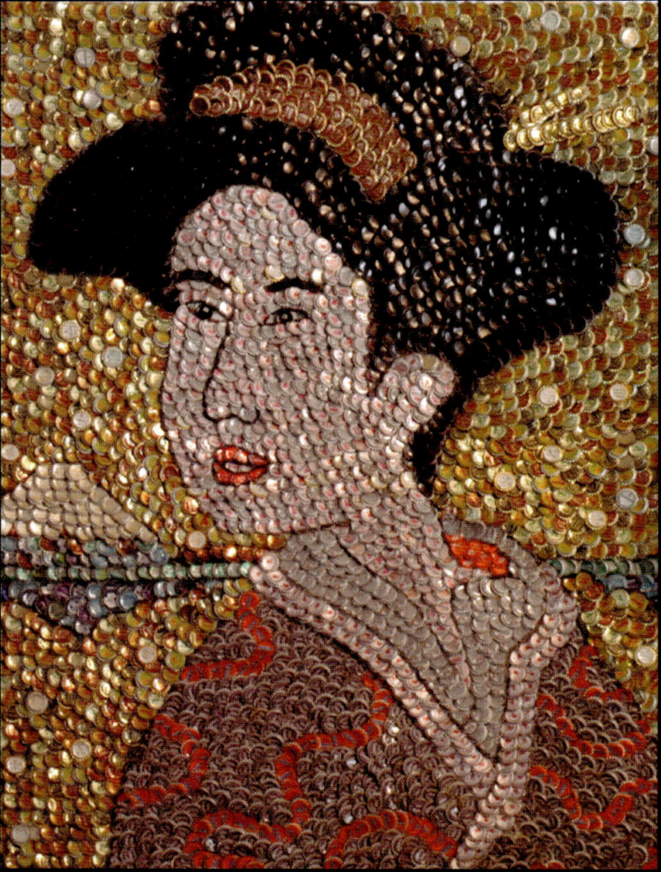

**Geisha Mt Fuji**

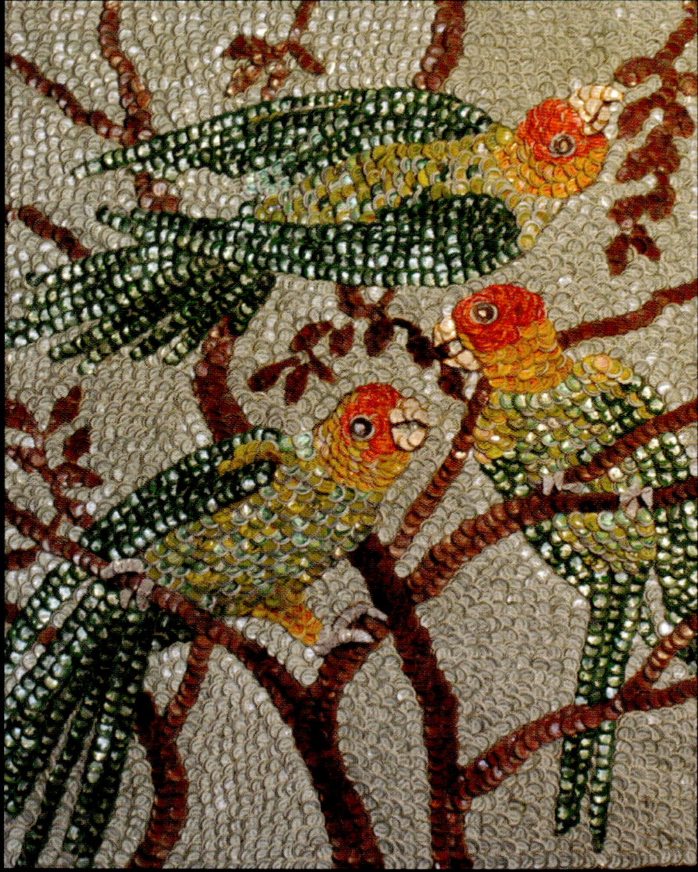

**Carolina Parakeets**

The bottle cap portraits begin with a painted portrait, on a piece of sheet metal. The caps are then glued to the painting, in such a way that they overlap, like the scales of a snake. The bottle caps date from the 30's to the 70's and are considered collectable on their own. Particular attention is given to the craftsmanship, so that no traces of glue are visible. Transparent washes of glaze are often used to further define the image. Most of the portraits are 4' x 5' and weigh 60-70 pounds.

# Molly/B Right

www.mollybright.com

Right was born in 1963, in Greensboro, NC. She has lived in Charleston SC since 1969. She began painting in 1993, and is self taught. Right's subject matter has ranged from vignettes of her childhood to minimalist figurative works. More recently, her focus has been on questioning religious imagery most often painted on wood panel or metal surfaces bearing the theme "Jesus Saves". These provocative theistic works turned the fertile ground from which Molly B. Right's bottle cap works would eventually emerge. The super-sized imaages which began with Jesus and his mother Mary now include a host of iconic women who evoke at once an ethereal presence and an earthy grit.

This series of bottle cap pieces evolved from musings about the phrase "Jesus Saves". Saves what? Does he just save souls? If he had the time or inclination, would he save string? Rubber bands? Would Jesus save bottle caps? Yeah. Somehow that became a full size bottle cap portrait of Jesus. Funny how one notion morphs into another. Now I'm doing bottle cap portraits of archetypal women that don't have anything to do with Jesus saving anything. Now I'm the one who is saving bottle caps.

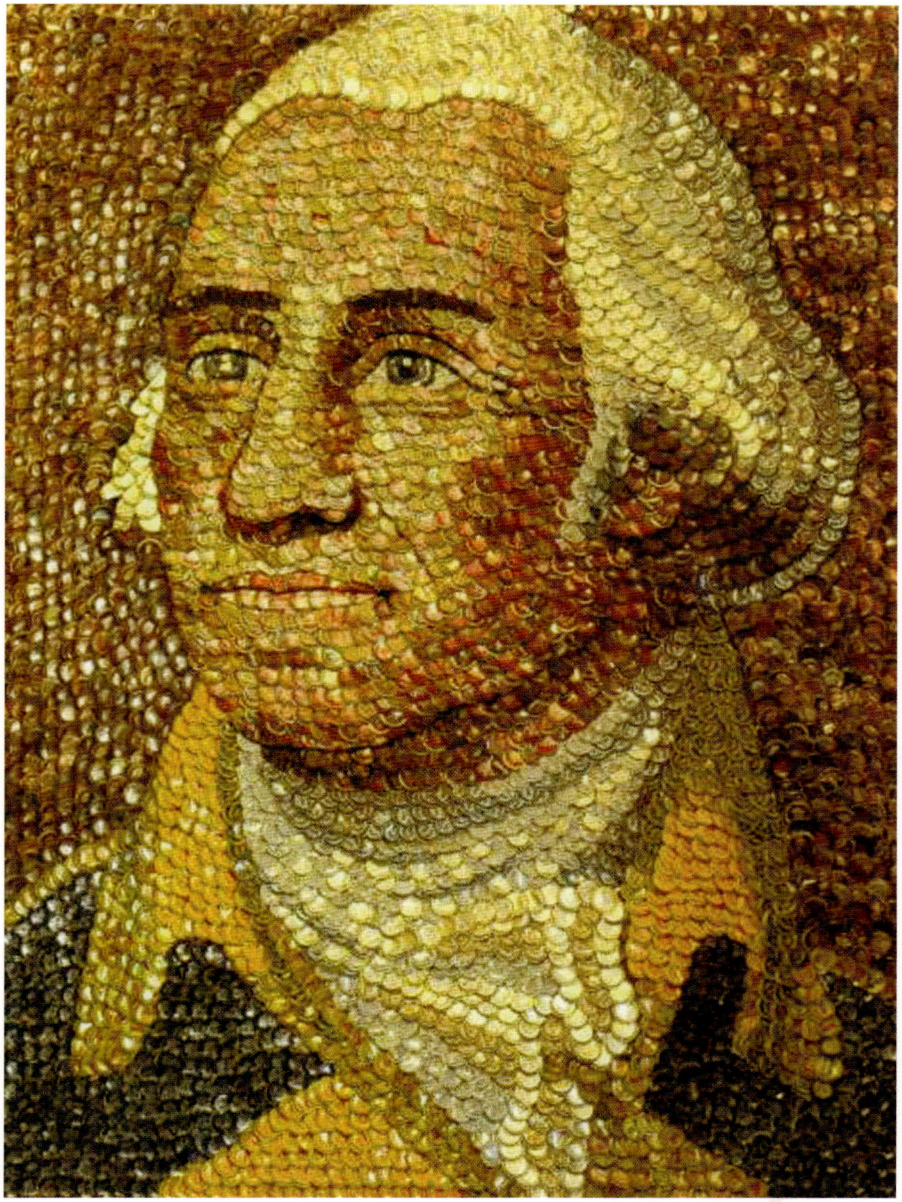

**George Washington**

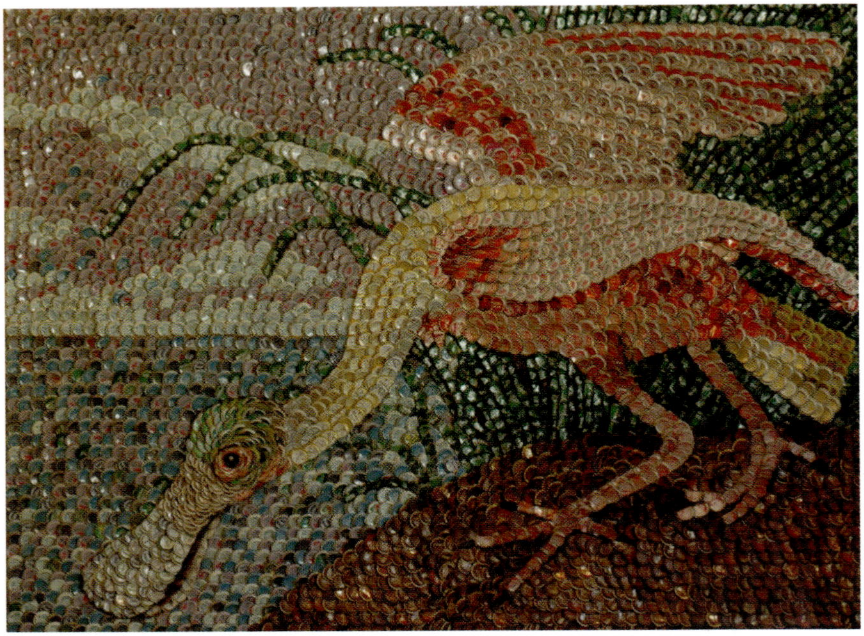

Great Blue Heron

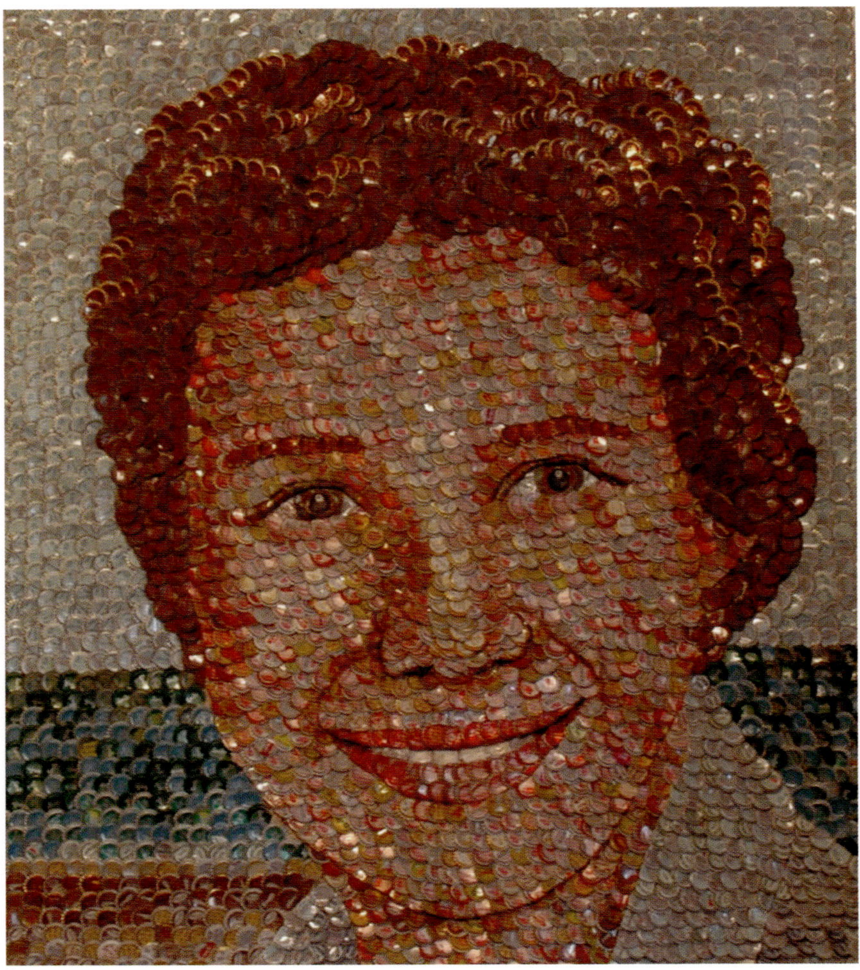

Grace

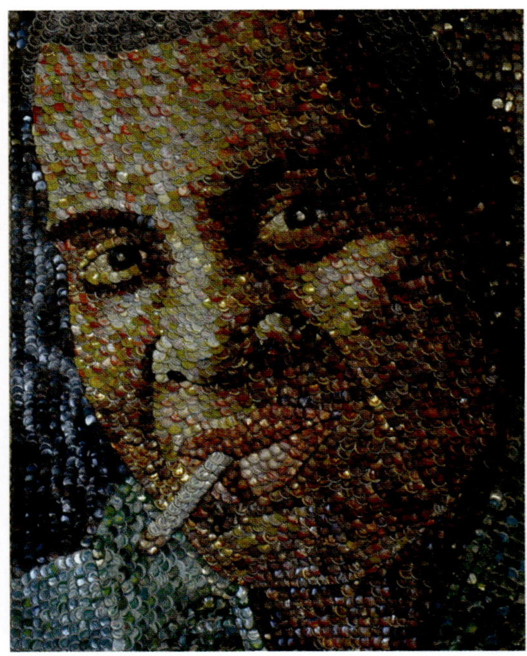

Howlin Wolf

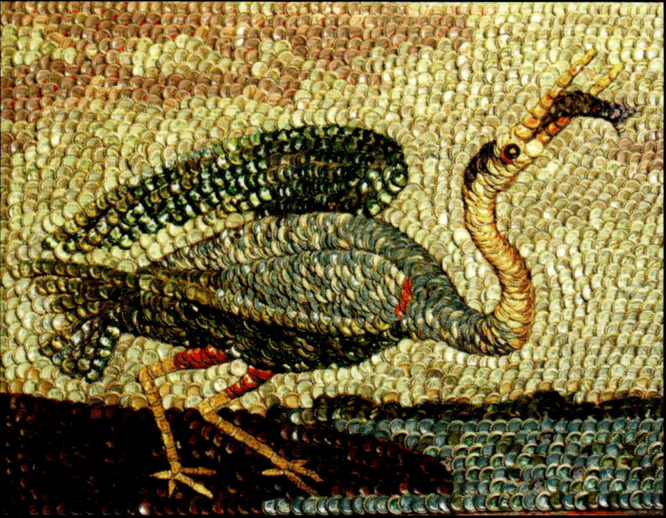

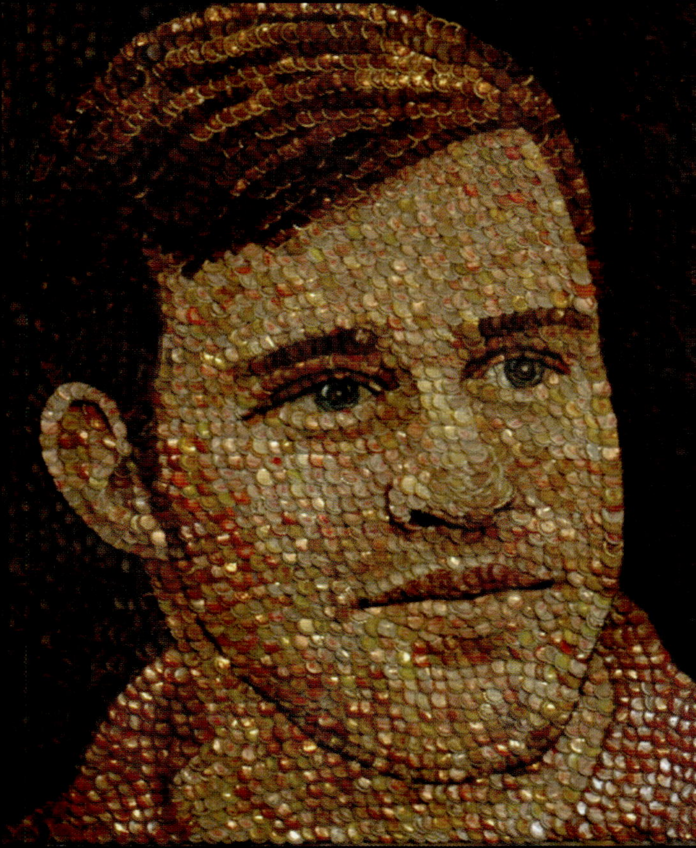

Harrison

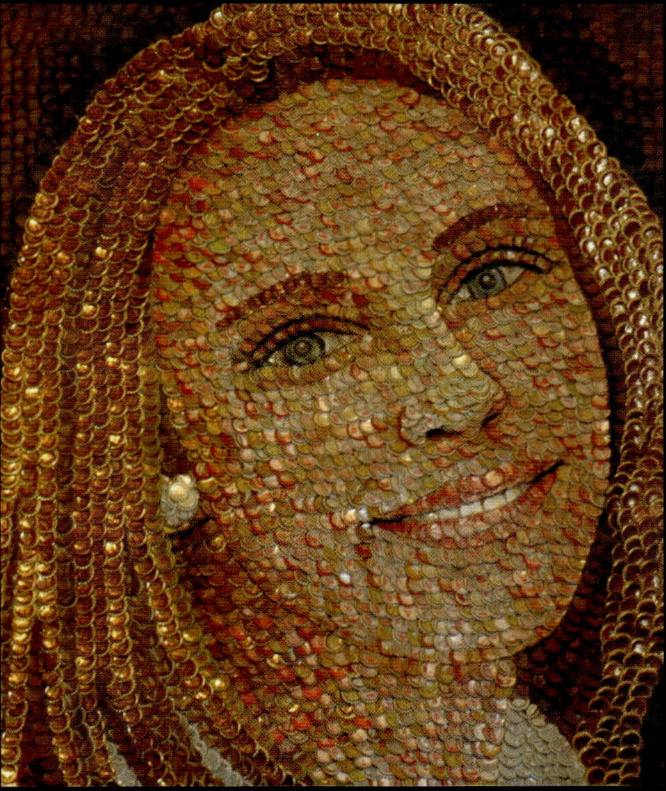

Lauren, Lauren close up

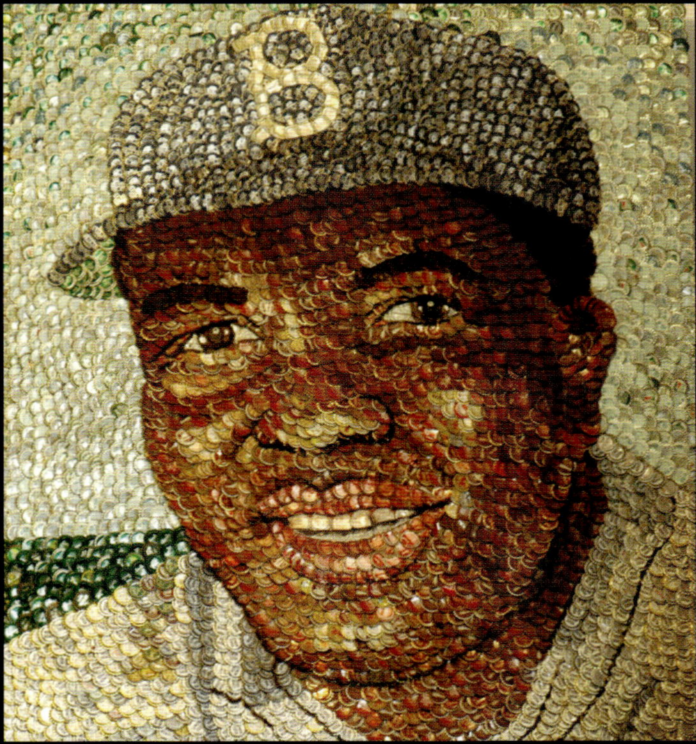



Jackie Robinson

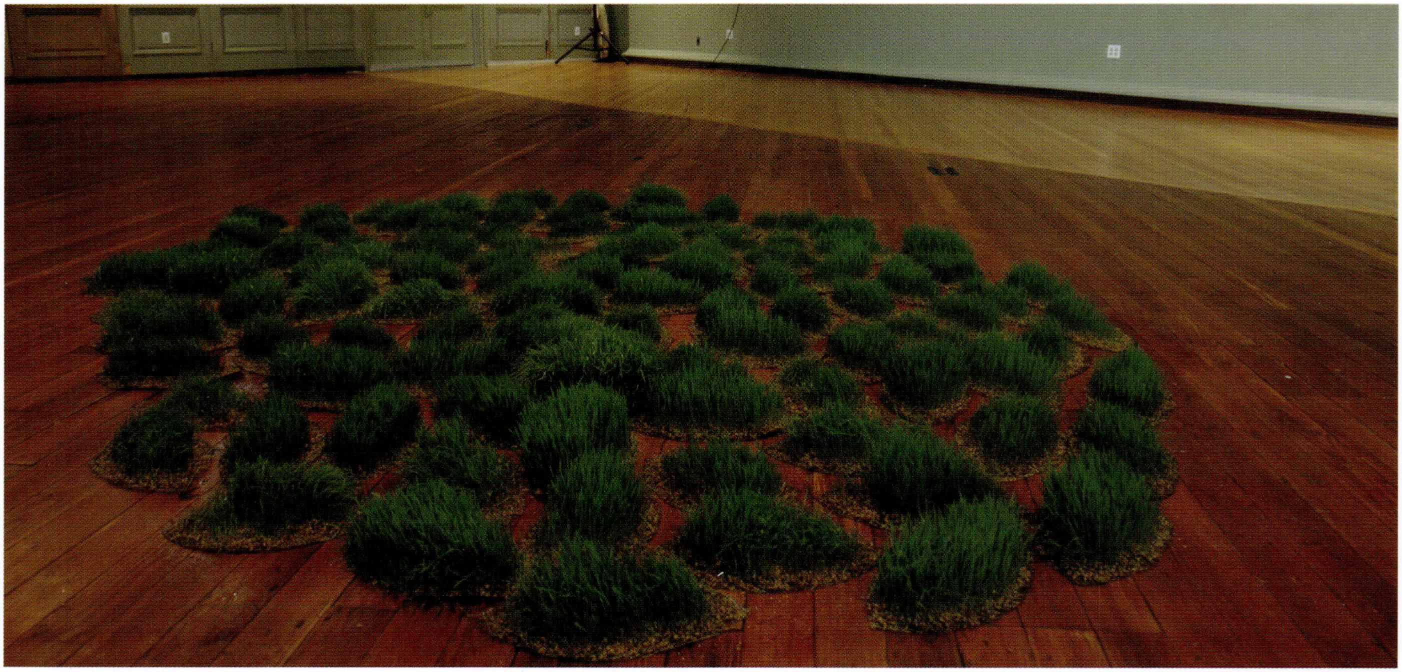

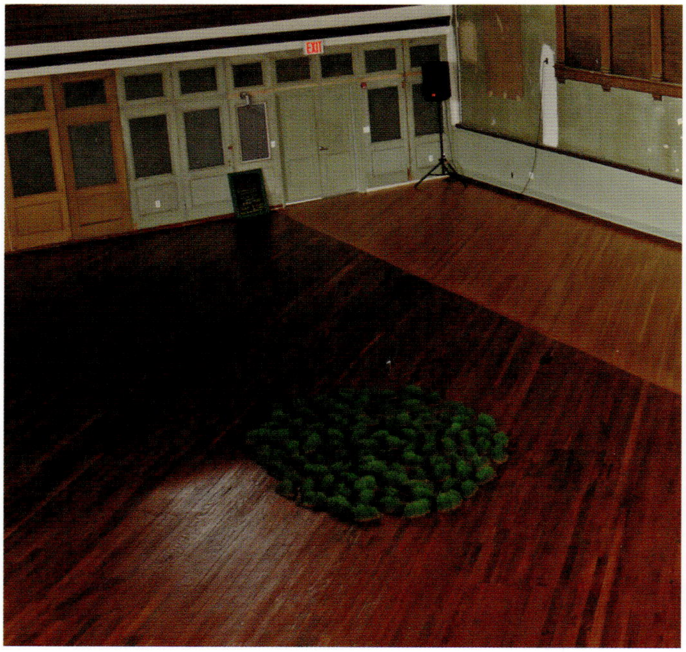

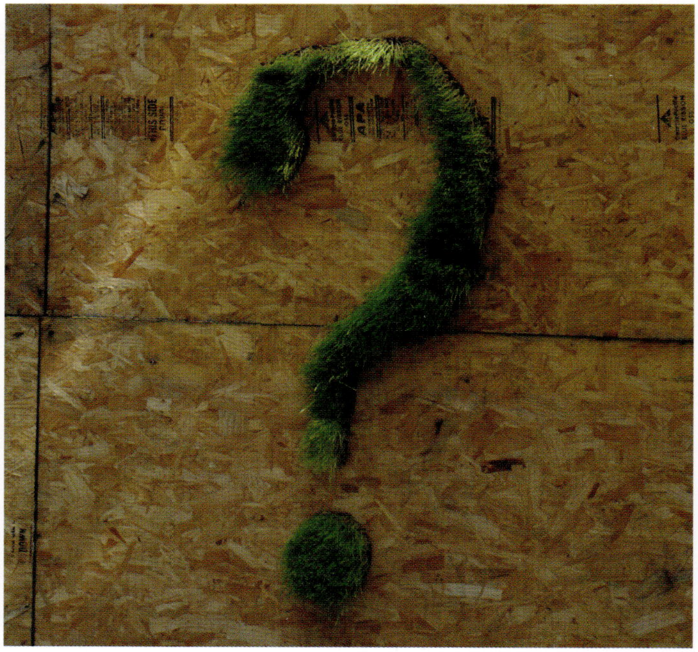

**Grass Mark, Brooklyn, 2008**

# Mosstika

www.mosstika.com

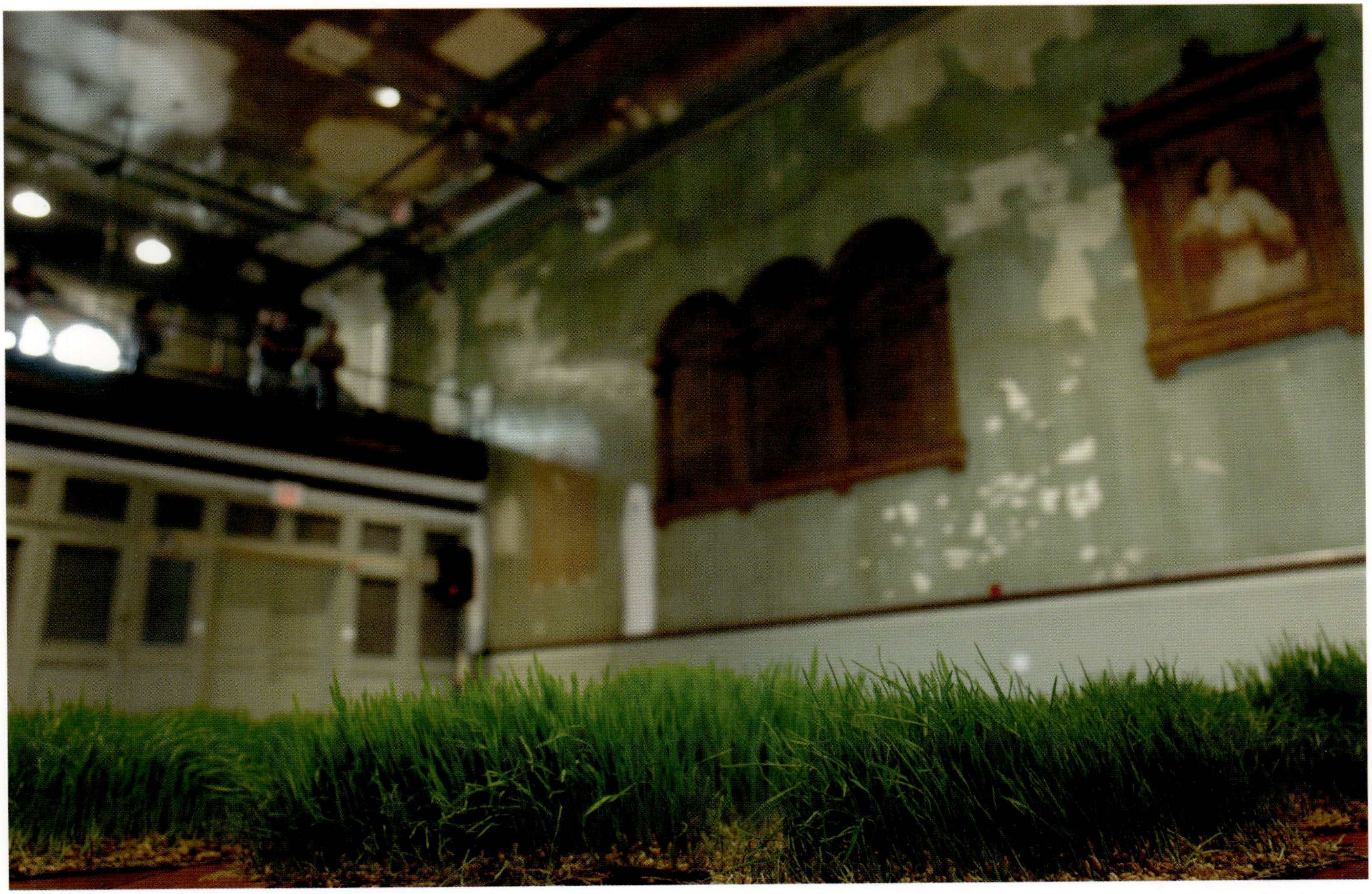

Irondale, Brooklyn, 2009

"Mosstika" group was formed by Edina Tokodi and Jozsef Valyi-Toth in Brooklyn 2006. Our actions contain this kind of critical view of our attitude towards living in and with nature as well as our passion for it. As a public artist I feel a sense of duty to draw attention to this deficiency in our daily life. I intend my moss installations to function as exclamation marks aall around the city. This is my personal way of 'going green'. My greatest ambition is to create even more complex works that allow me to explore the diversity of and possible intricate connections between (organic) materials while still remaining close to nature. Most of them were independent (temporary) street artworks but I've made pieces for a green campaign in Philadelphia as well as permanent living installations here in Brooklyn, NY. The street art works has been made from moss or wheat grass, the living installation is made completely out of succulent plants for the recent Fort Green Garden Walk in Brooklyn. The project was also made as a public art piece which will last as long as they continue to tend to it.

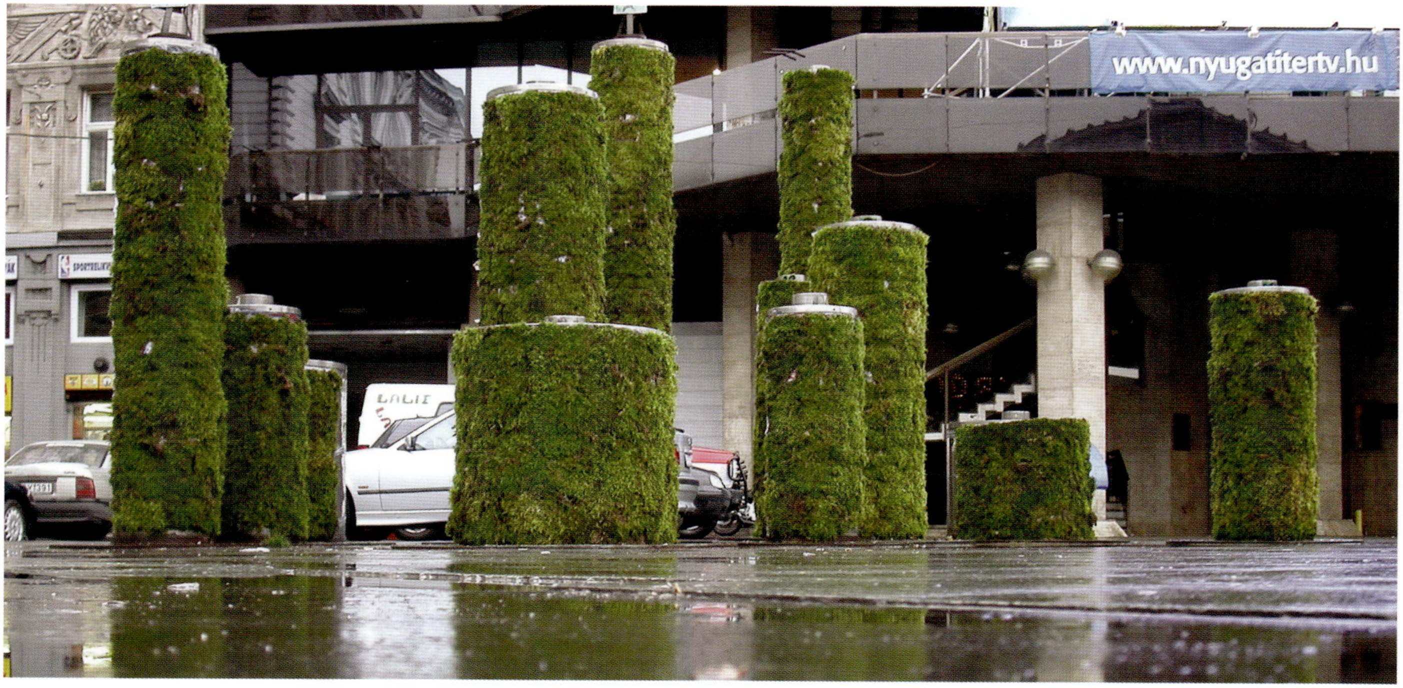


Budapest, 2004

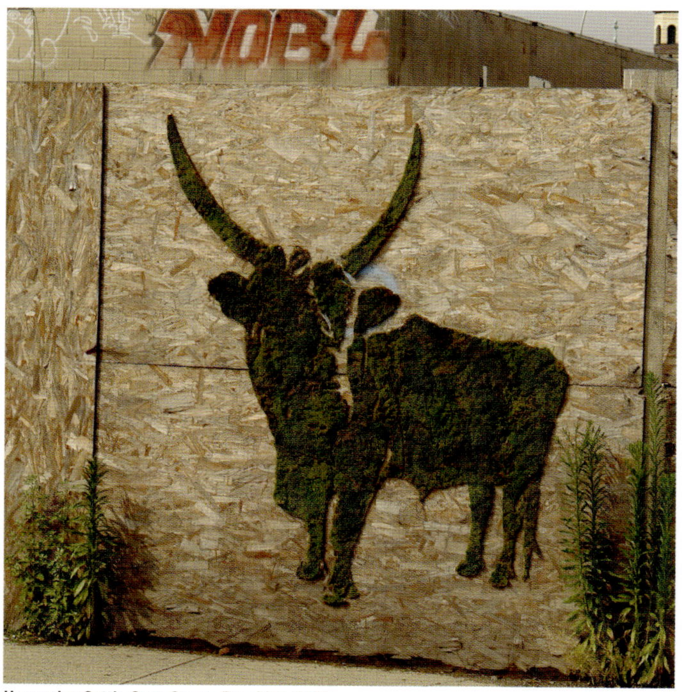

Hungarian Cattle Goes Green, Brooklyn, 2008

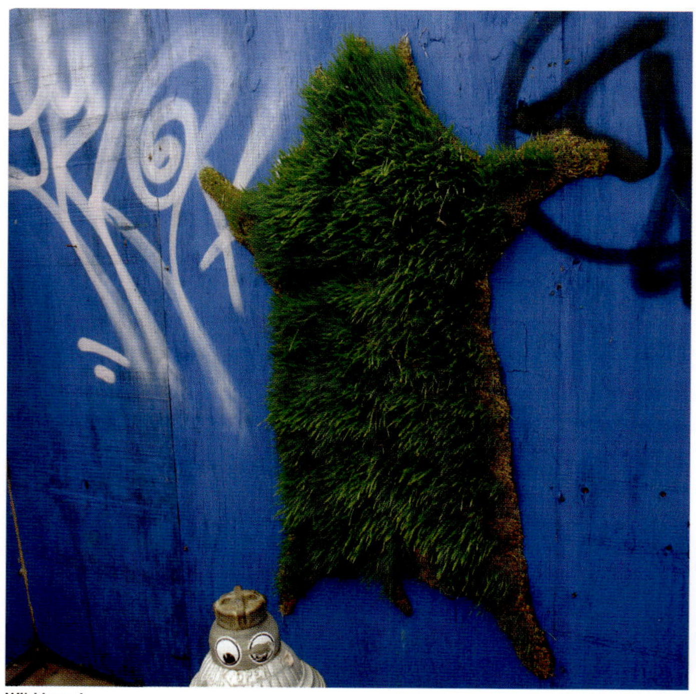

Wild board

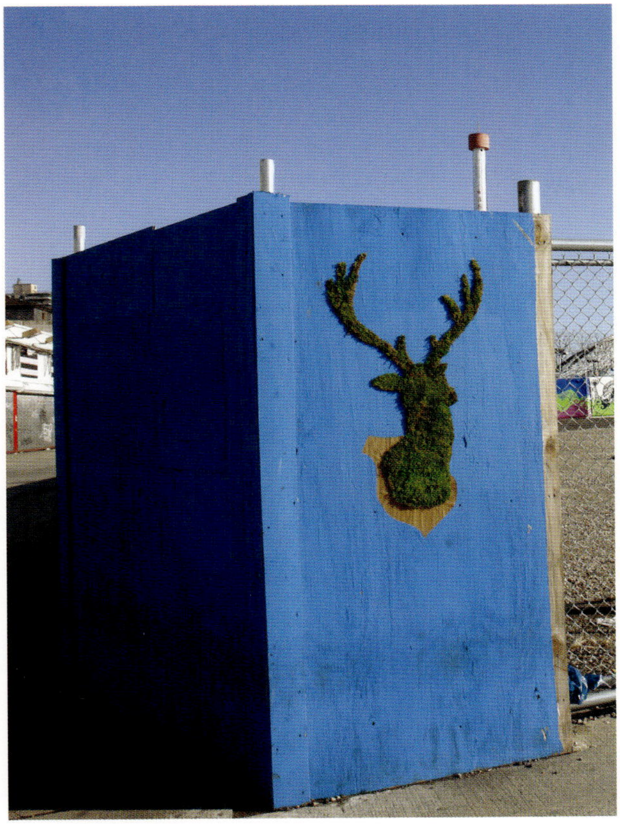

Coney Island Moss, 2008

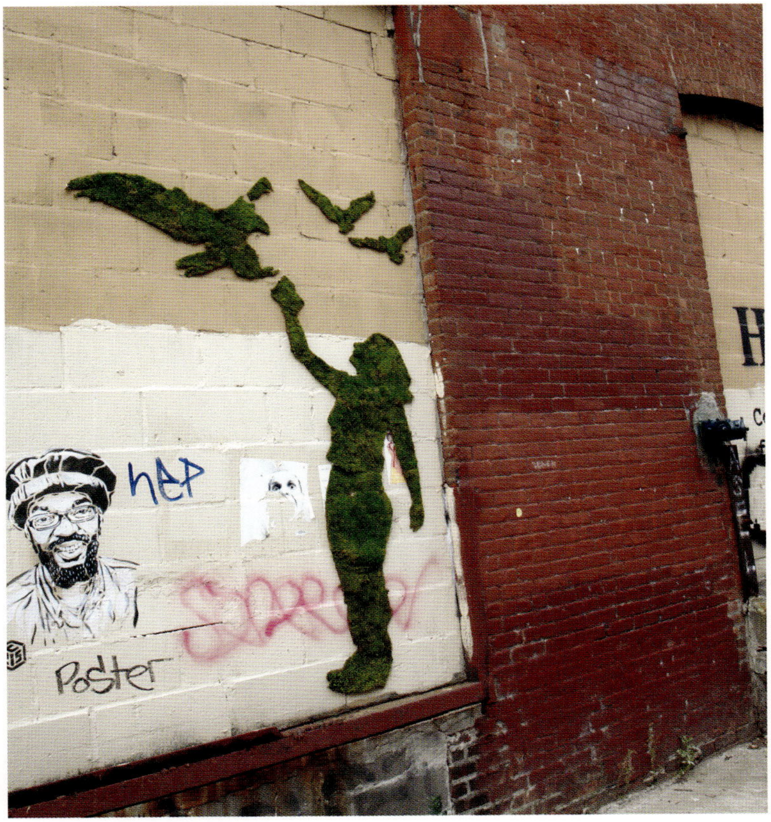


Moss Stencil Dumbo, Brooklyn, 2008

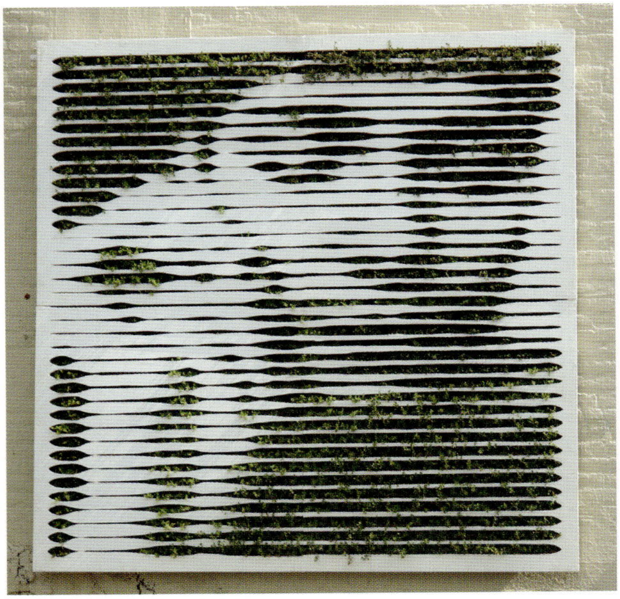

Living Wall Installation, Brooklyn, 2009

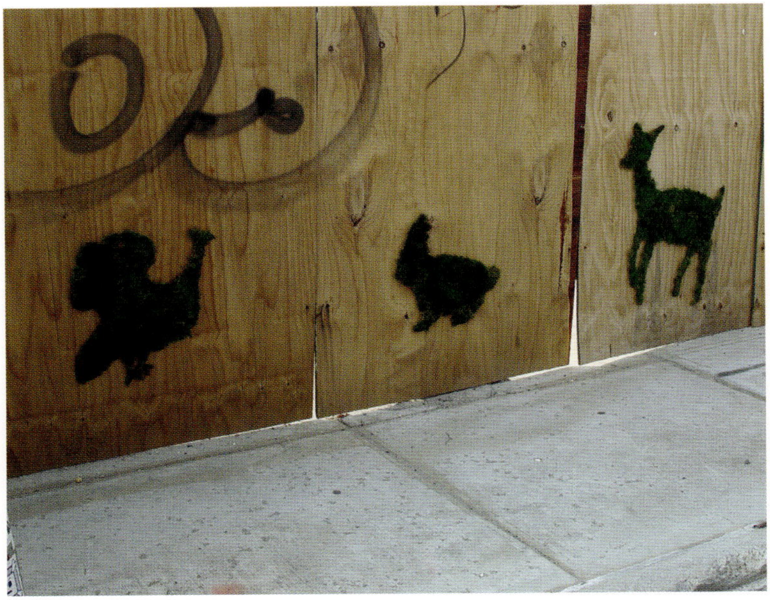

Moss Animals, Brooklyn, 2006

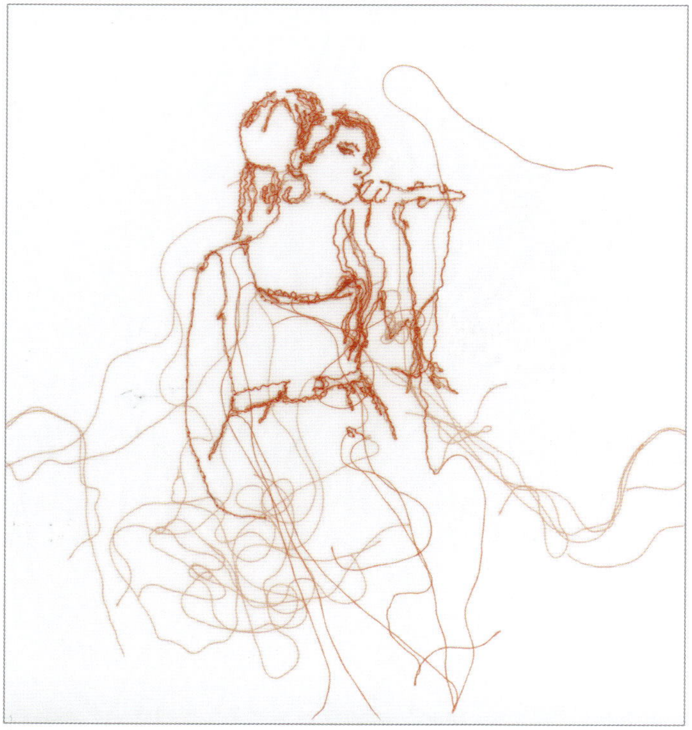

**Amy** - This again is a detail of one motif from an embroidered curtain this time on silk chiffon. This piece incorporated many aspects of a festival from the crowd to the acts. The embroidery is freehand machine embroidery.

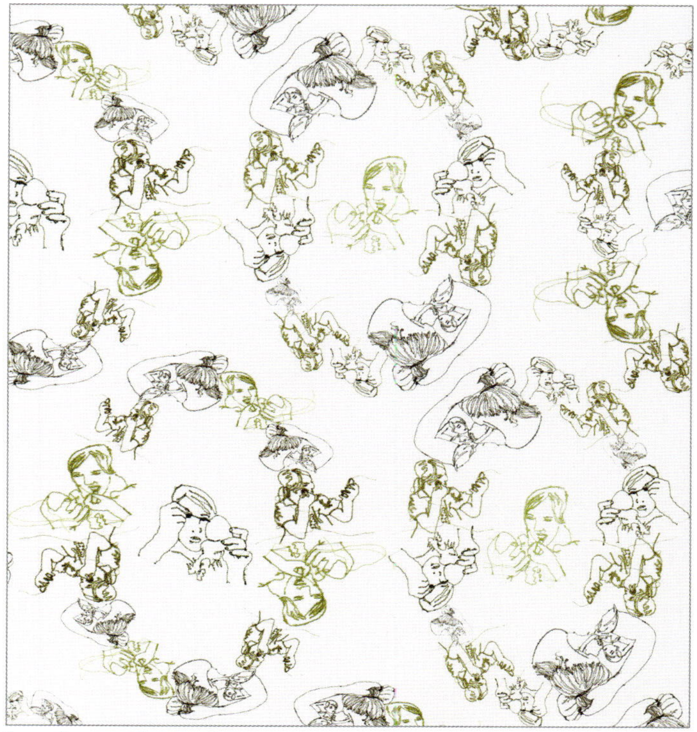

**Cameo Pattern** - These motifs were taken from the silk chiffon curtain above. I take each embroidered piece and tidy it and make patterns from them in Photoshop. In this piaece I concentrated on Katherine putting on her make up and wanted this piece to be like old cameo wallpaper.

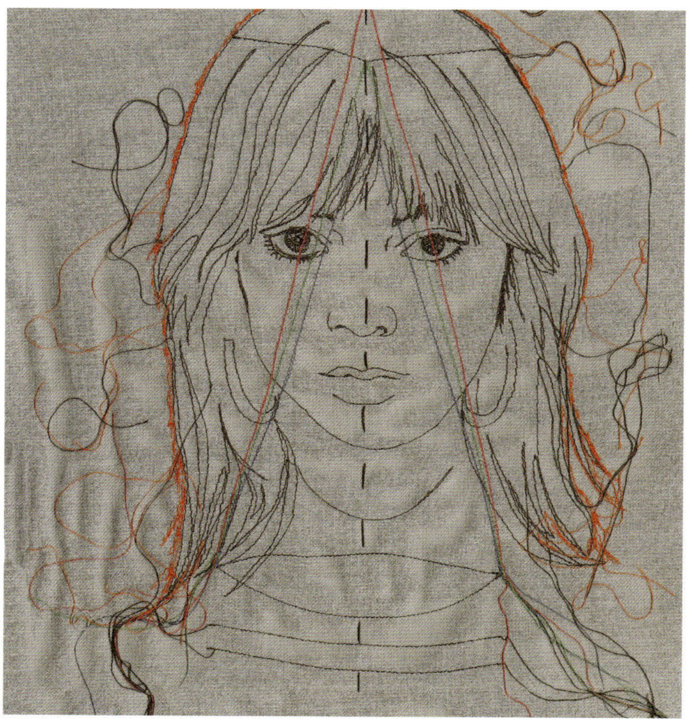

**Chromatics** - An embroidered piece on naturally dyed fabric. This was for a poster for the band Chromatics. Chromatic in photography causes a red glow around a person so that's what I was trying to create.

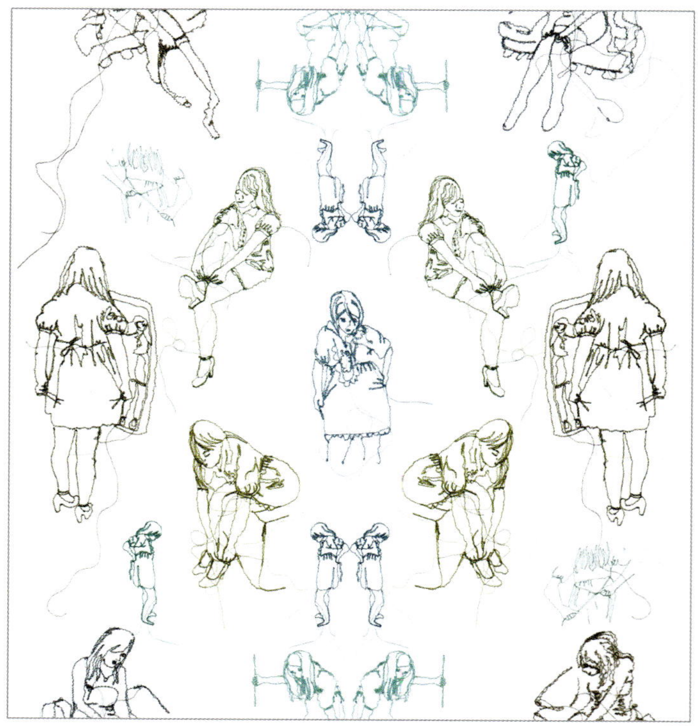

**Kath Puts Her Clothes On** - This is another pattern taken from the 40 illustrations but this piece focuses on Katherine getting up and putting her clothes on.

# Naomi Ryder

www.naomiryder.co.uk

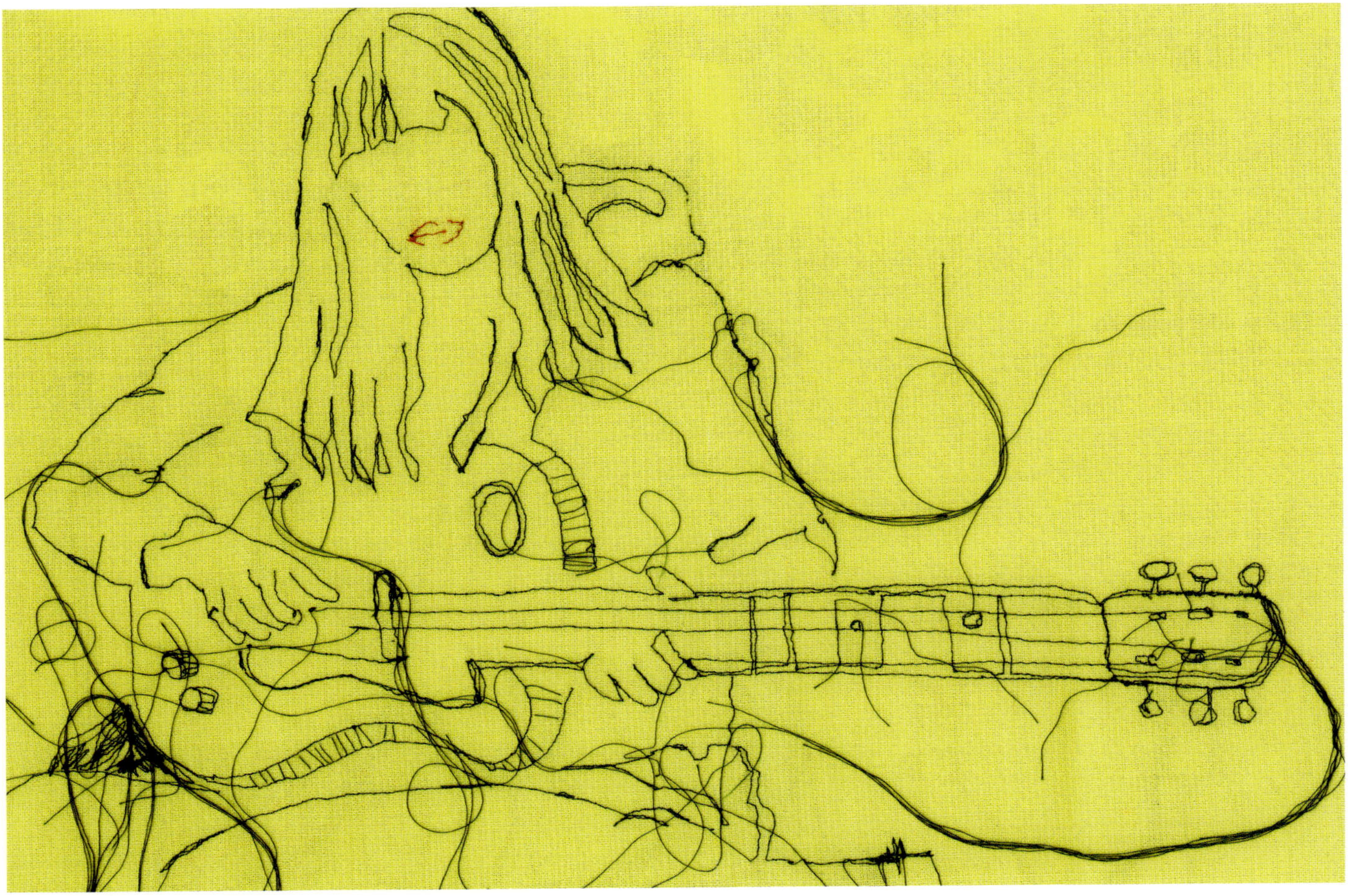

**Cat Power Portrait** - This piece was made for and Irish magazine called foggy notions of cat power and has become one of my signature pieces. This again is freehand machine embroidery on acid yellow fabric.

Naomi Ryder is an extraordinary textile designer and illustrator specialising in embroidery, drawing with stitch to create beautiful images of the everyday. Naomi's proficiency in illustration led to her combining her love of drawing with textile work using both hand and machine embroidery and occasionally using print. Naomi's main source of inspiration is the beauty and humour found in day-to-day culture and mundane routine tasks that make up our daily lives. She has recently explored this theme by stitching people brushing their teeth, getting out of bed and talking on the telephone. She is able to capture the moment rarely noticed, yet is an essential part of living. She presents such moments using delicate and luxury materials that create an interesting contrast between essential and superfluous, beauty and ordinary. Naomi's range of products includes a collection of embroidered hand made cushions, throws, duvets, pillows, she is in the process of developing the range further to include curtains and home ware. Naomi has worked on many commissions for Domino records, Habitat and the Queen Elizabeth hall, Southbank as well as illustrations for magazines such as Plan B. She has worked with fashion designers including John Rocha, Ali Malek and Lainey Keogh in Dublin. All commissions are unique, individually designed and hand made to the client's specification.

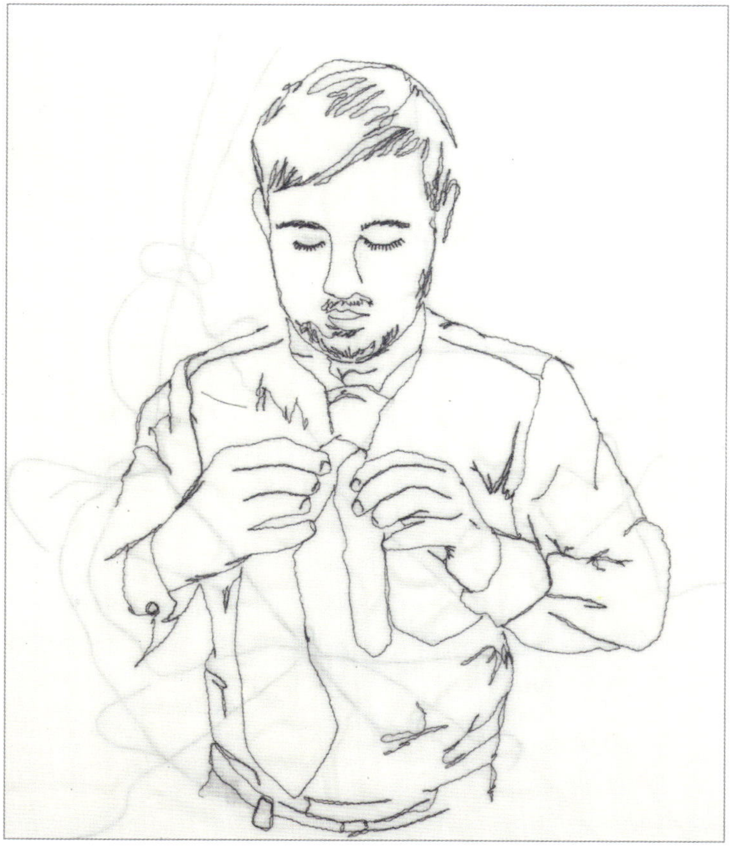

**Mark Ties His Tie** - These two illustrations are details on a curtain with 17 embroidered illustrations. Every day I see my flatmate mark getting ready for work. He looks incredibly smart and I wanted to capture the daily routine and process that he goes through to get there. They are embroidery on fine cream wool fabric. Size of the whole piece is 3m x 1m.

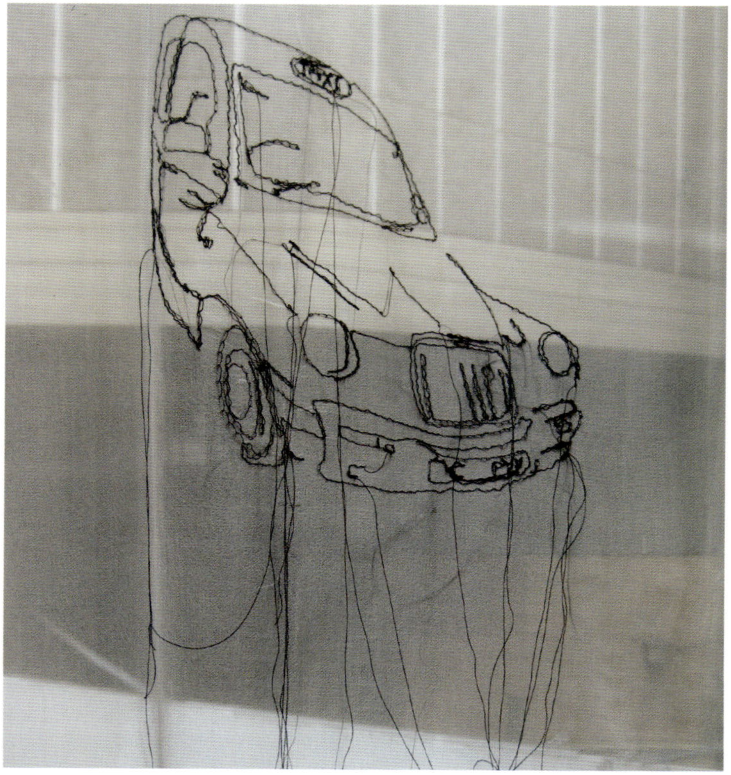


**Taxi** - This piece was an embroidered detail on a silk chiffon curtain with forms of London transport.

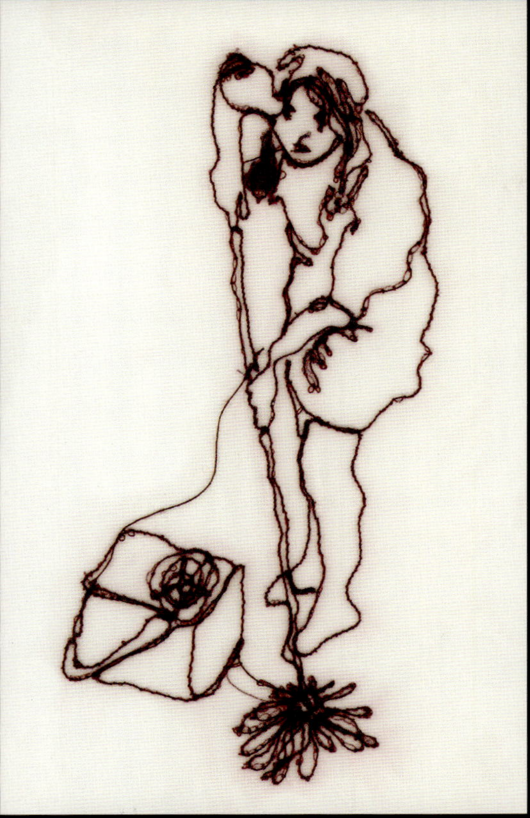

**Mopping** - One of 40 illustrations embroidered onto silk chiffon. This is the day in the life of my friend Katherine. I followed her around for a day sketching her doing ordinary things and tried to make them into something beautiful.

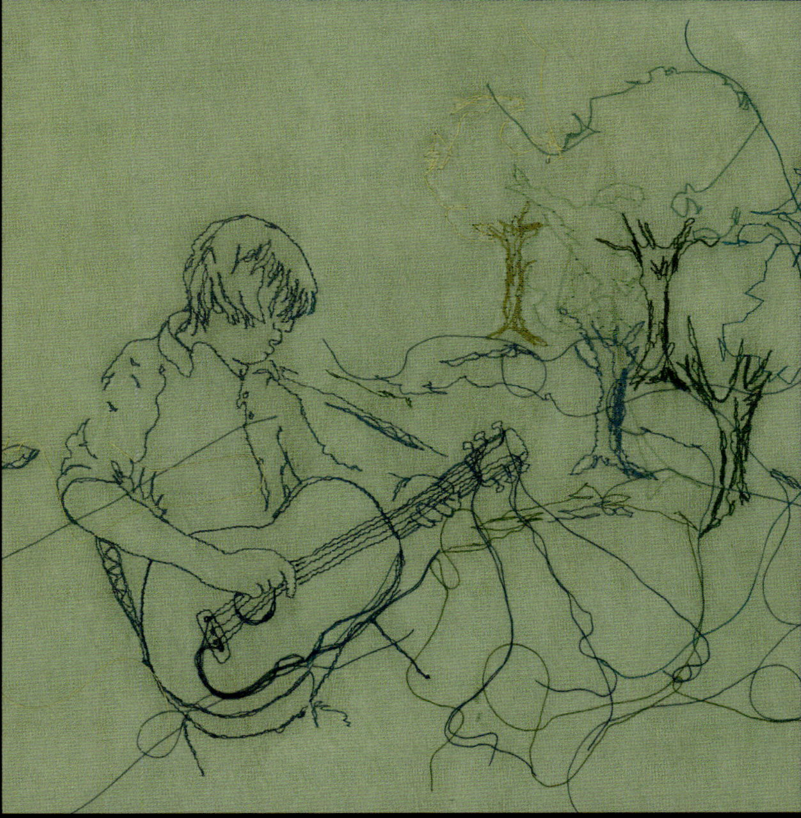

**Thurston** - The drawing was for a music magazine called Plan B. Embroidered again onto naturally dyed silk.

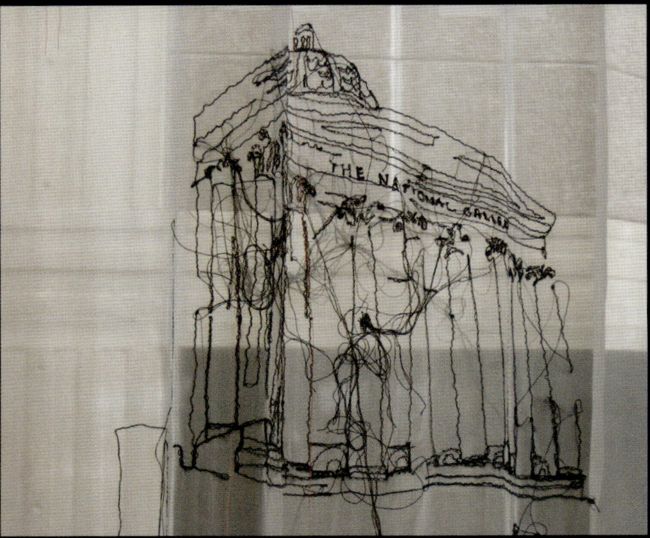


**National Gallery** - Silk chiffon curtains were embroidered with 10 galleries of London for the Queen Elizabeth hall in the south bank.

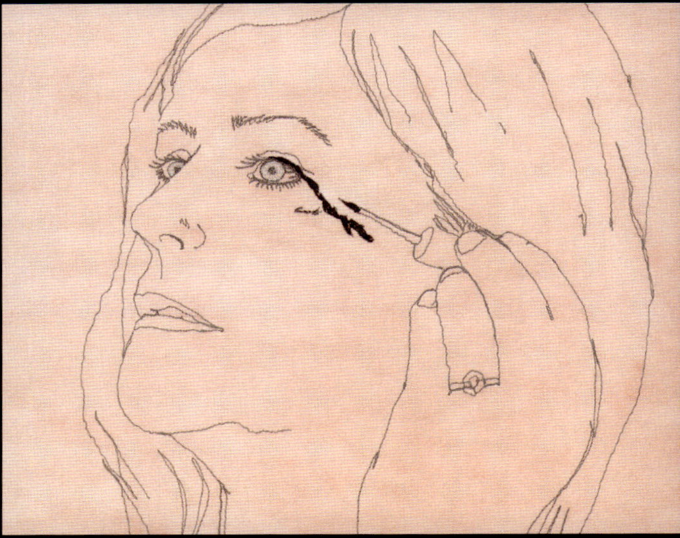

**Slipped Eyeliner** - This is in a series of three. Unfortunate incidents. This one is called don't apply your eyeliner on the train.

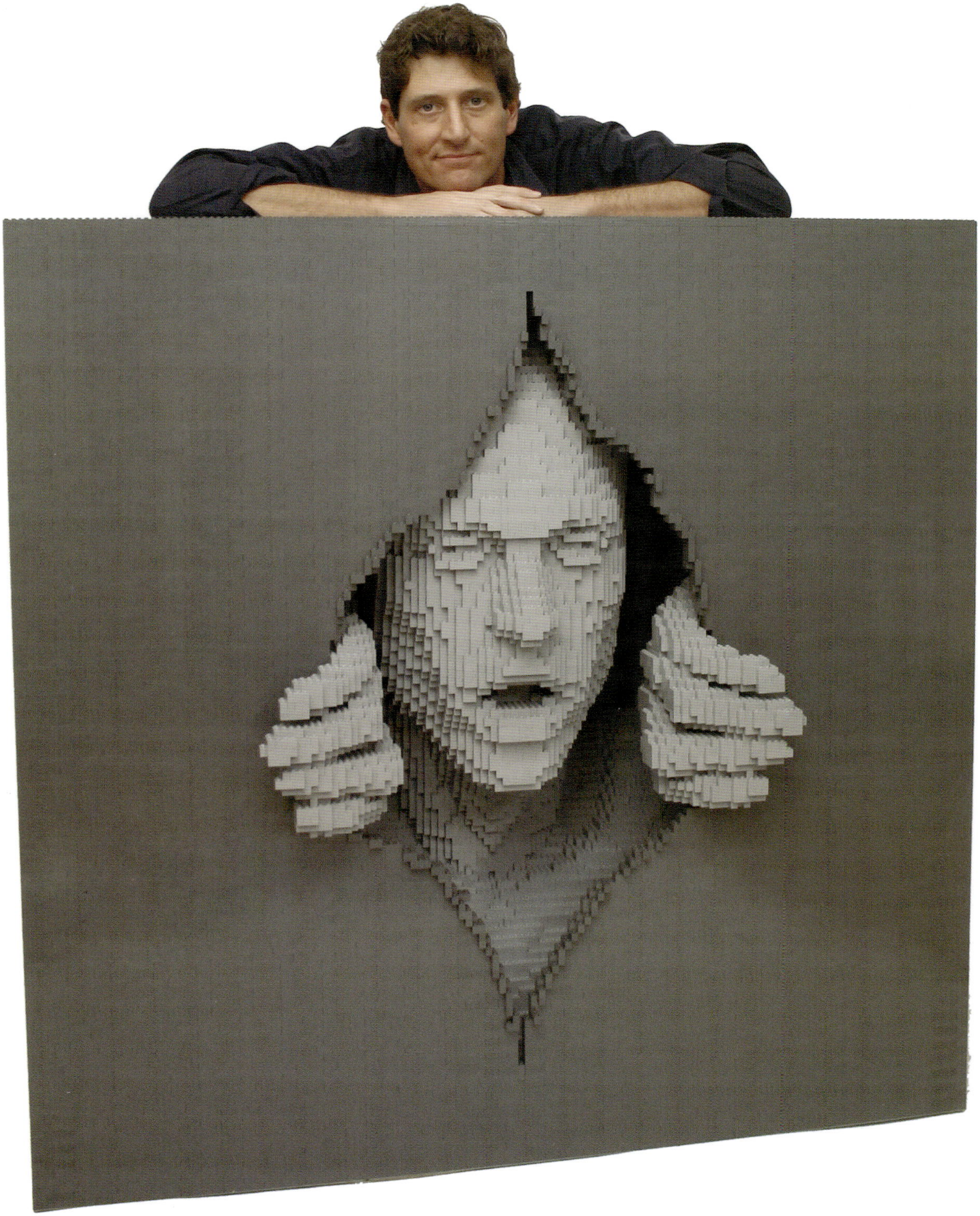

**Gray** was created by artist Nathan Sawaya out of nearly 50,000 LEGO bricks. Built over the course of a month, Gray is an oversized figure emerging from a dark gray box. The box represents depression with the illuminated emerging figure suggesting escape or release from the despair.
45 x 45 x 15"

# Nathan Sawaya

www.brickartist.com

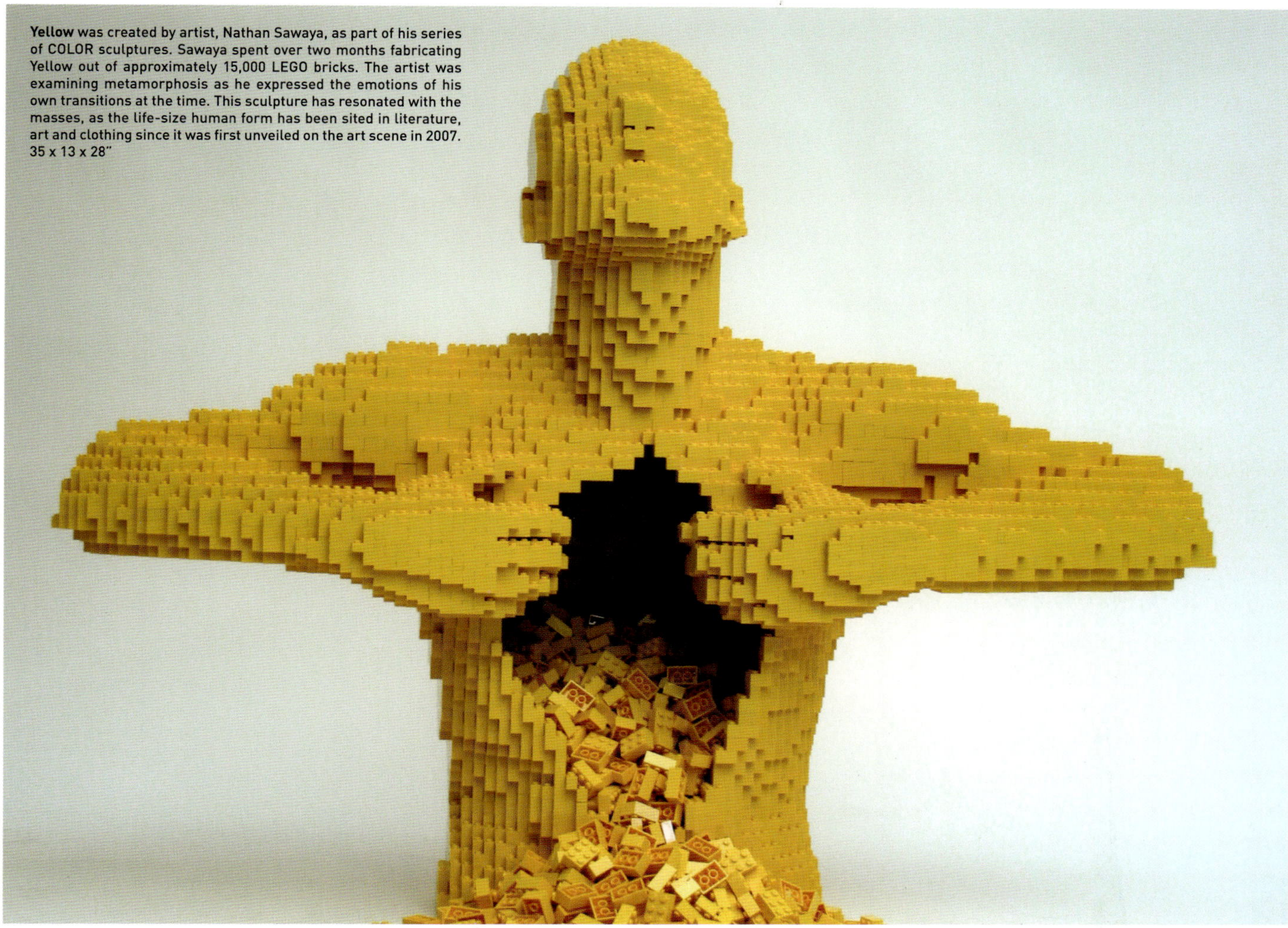

**Yellow** was created by artist, Nathan Sawaya, as part of his series of COLOR sculptures. Sawaya spent over two months fabricating Yellow out of approximately 15,000 LEGO bricks. The artist was examining metamorphosis as he expressed the emotions of his own transitions at the time. This sculpture has resonated with the masses, as the life-size human form has been sited in literature, art and clothing since it was first unveiled on the art scene in 2007. 35 x 13 x 28"

Nathan Sawaya is a New York-based artist who creates awe-inspiring works out of some of the most unlikely things. His recent North American museum tours feature large-scale sculptures using only toy building blocks. LEGO® bricks to be exact. Sawaya's art is currently touring North American museums in a show titled, The Art of the Brick. It's the only exhibition focusing exclusively on LEGO as an art medium. The creations, constructed from nearly one million pieces, were built from standard bricks beginning as early as 2000. Born in Colville, Washington and raised in Veneta, Oregon, Sawaya's childhood dreams were always fun. He drew cartoons, wrote stories, perfected magic tricks and also played with LEGO. Sawaya attended NYU. After college he rediscovered LEGO but not as a toy, but rather as a medium. Today Sawaya has more than 1.5 million colored bricks in his New York art studio. His work is obsessively and painstakingly crafted and is both beautiful and playful. Sawaya's ability to transform LEGO bricks into something new, his devotion to scale and color perfection, the way he conceptualizes the action of the subject matter, enables him to elevate an ordinary toy to the status of fine art. According to journalist Scott Jones, "Sawaya is a surrealist mash-up of forms and artists. Imagine Frank Lloyd Wright crossed with Ray Harryhausen, or Auguste Rodin crossed with Shigeru Miyamoto, and you start to get a sense of where Sawaya is coming from." Sawaya's art form takes shape primarily in 3-dimensional sculptures and oversized portraits. He continues to create daily while accepting commission work from around the world.

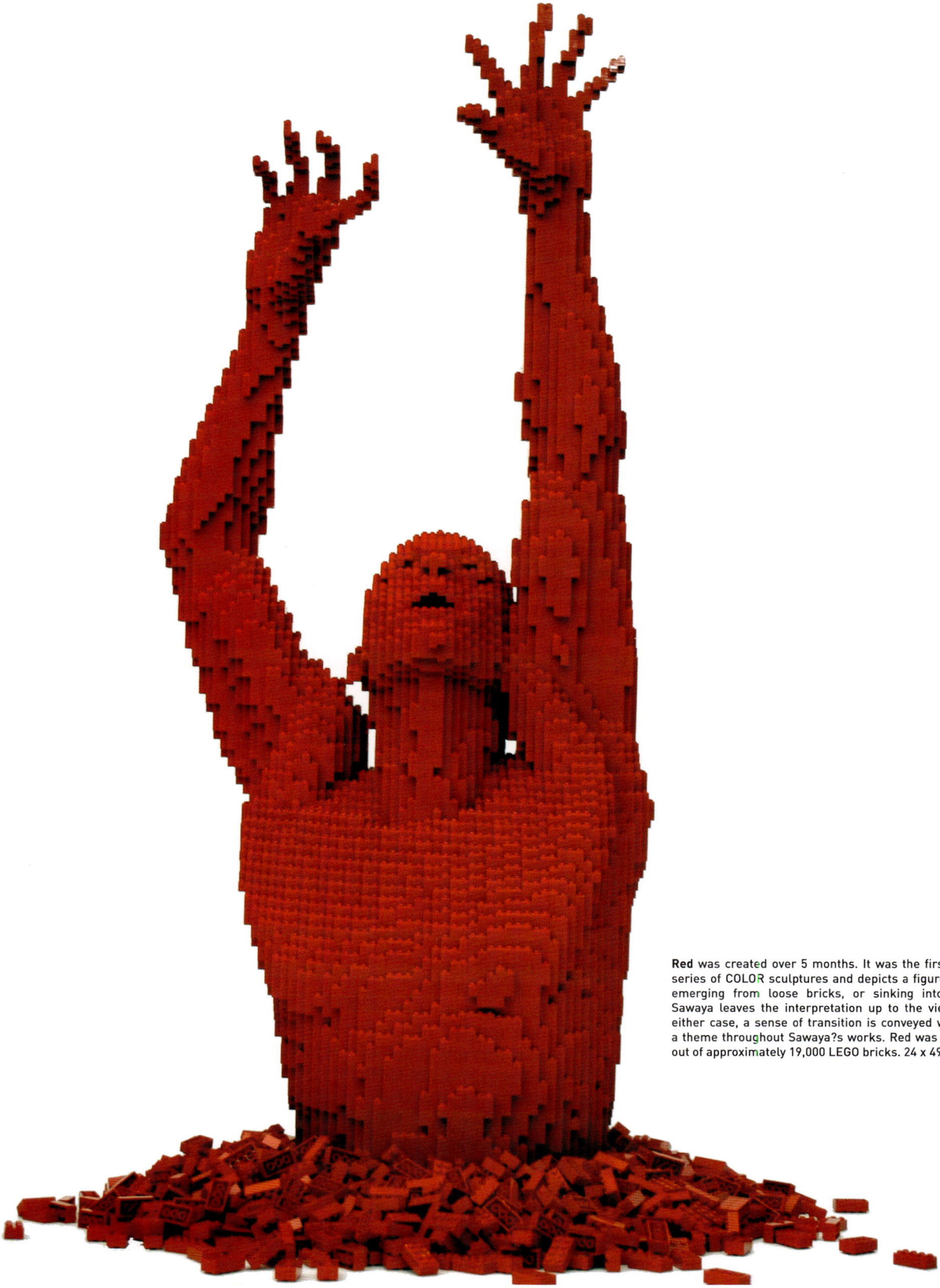

**Red** was created over 5 months. It was the first in his series of COLOR sculptures and depicts a figure either emerging from loose bricks, or sinking into them. Sawaya leaves the interpretation up to the viewer. In either case, a sense of transition is conveyed which is a theme throughout Sawaya?s works. Red was created out of approximately 19,000 LEGO bricks. 24 x 49 x 26"

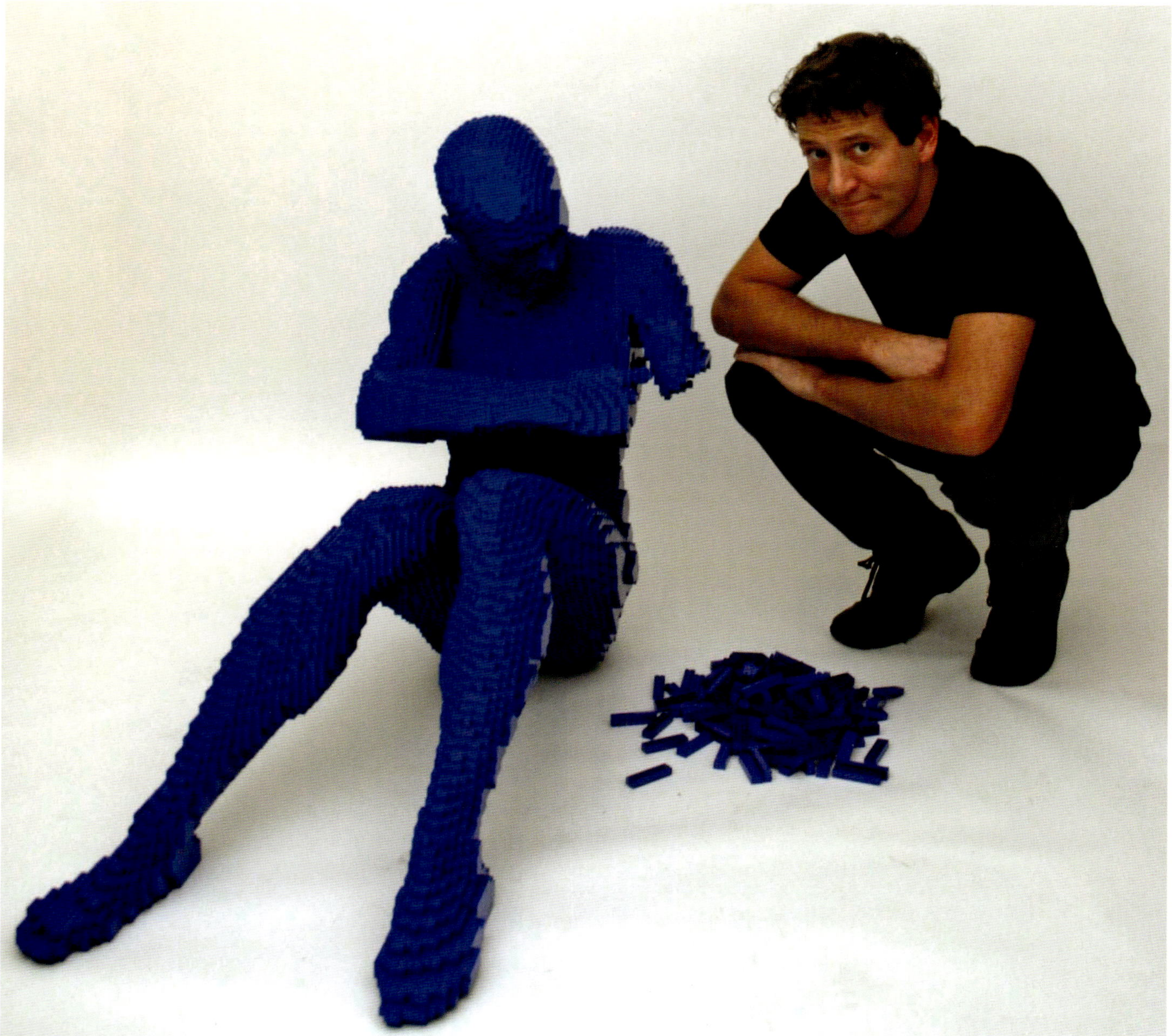

**Blue** was created over four months by artist Nathan Sawaya. Blue was built out of approximately 26,000 individual LEGO bricks. Blue suggests the struggle one has with putting themselves back together after a devastating loss. Blue, as well as Sawaya's popular COLOR series of sculptures, continue to tour museums and other public venues across North America.
42 x 34 x 18"

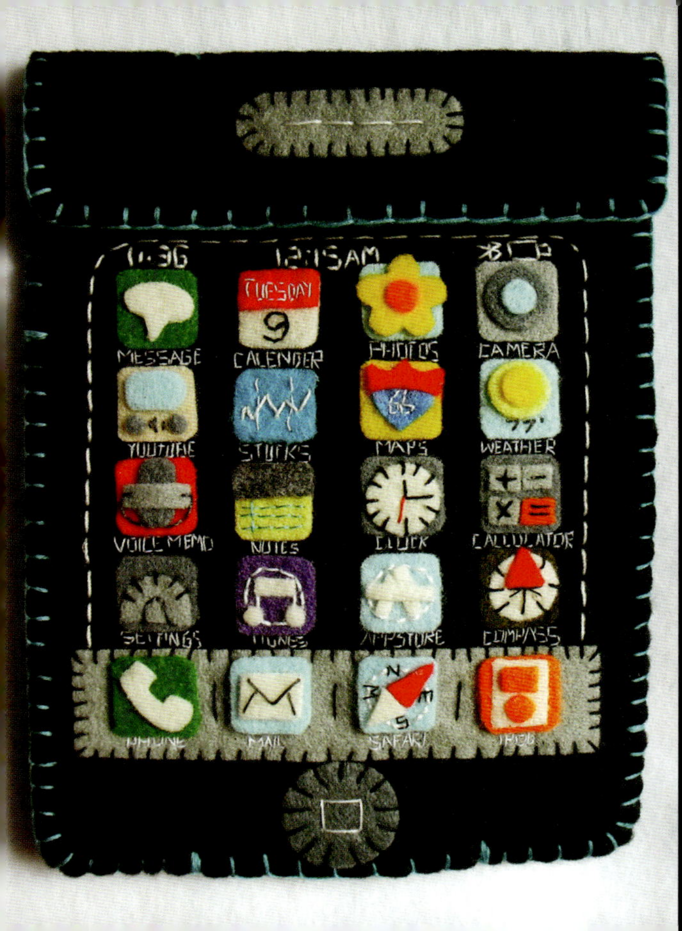
12:15AM
TUESDAY
9
MESSAGE
CALENDER
CAMERA
MAPS
WEATHER
VOICE MEMO
NOTES
CALCULATOR
SAFARI

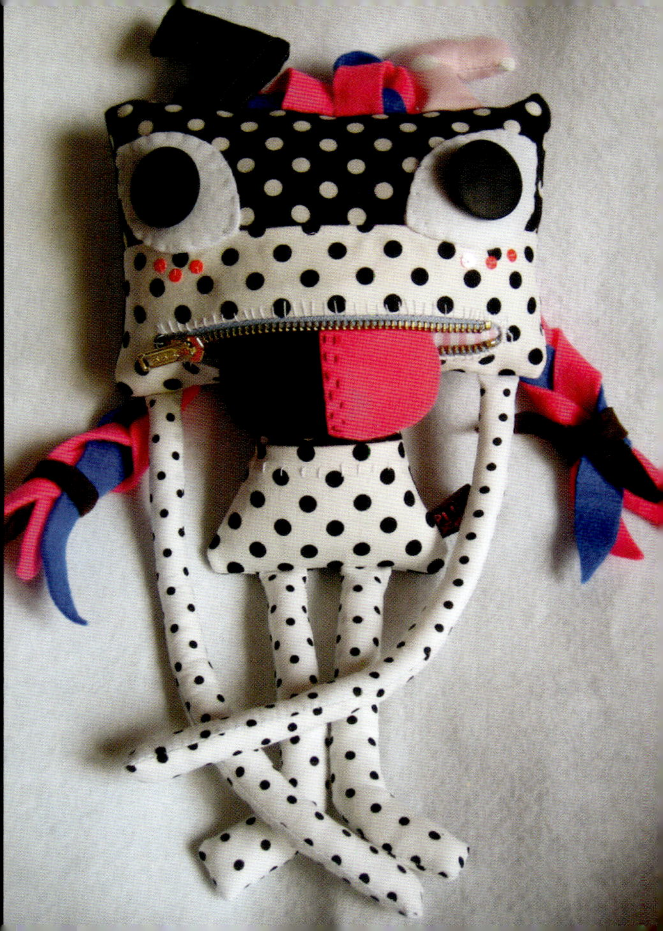

# Nico

www.plushism.blogspot.com

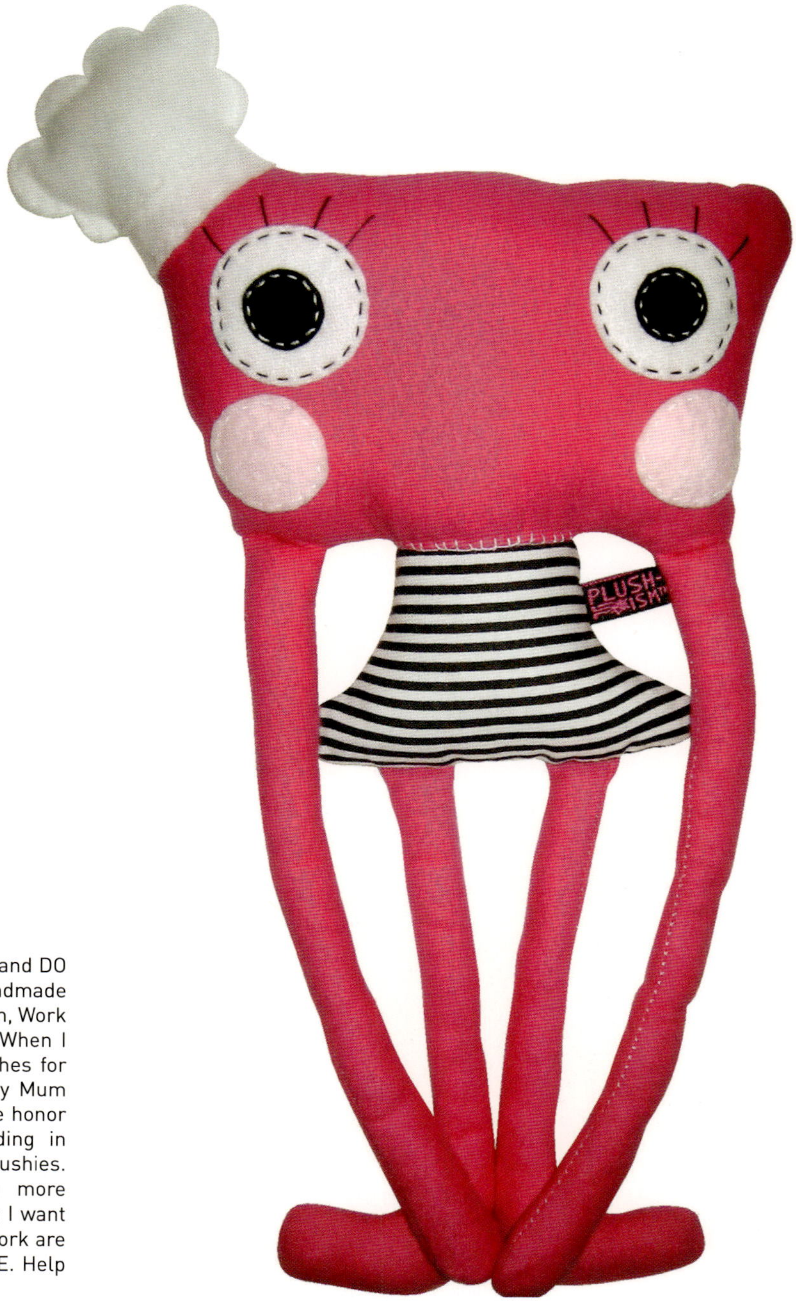


I DARE TO DREAM to LOVE what I DO and DO what I LOVE. All my products are handmade by me. I am a ONE-GIRL-SHOW! Dream, Work and Play hard are what I love to do. When I am a little girl, I started making clothes for my Barbie doll and cute soft toys. My Mum is a seamstress which let me have the honor of learning how to sew. After landing in Plushism land of all my huggable plushies. My passion became wilder! Doing more functional artwork became something I want to pursue further. Every piece of my work are individually made with LOVE and CARE. Help me SPREAD MY HANDMADE LOVE.

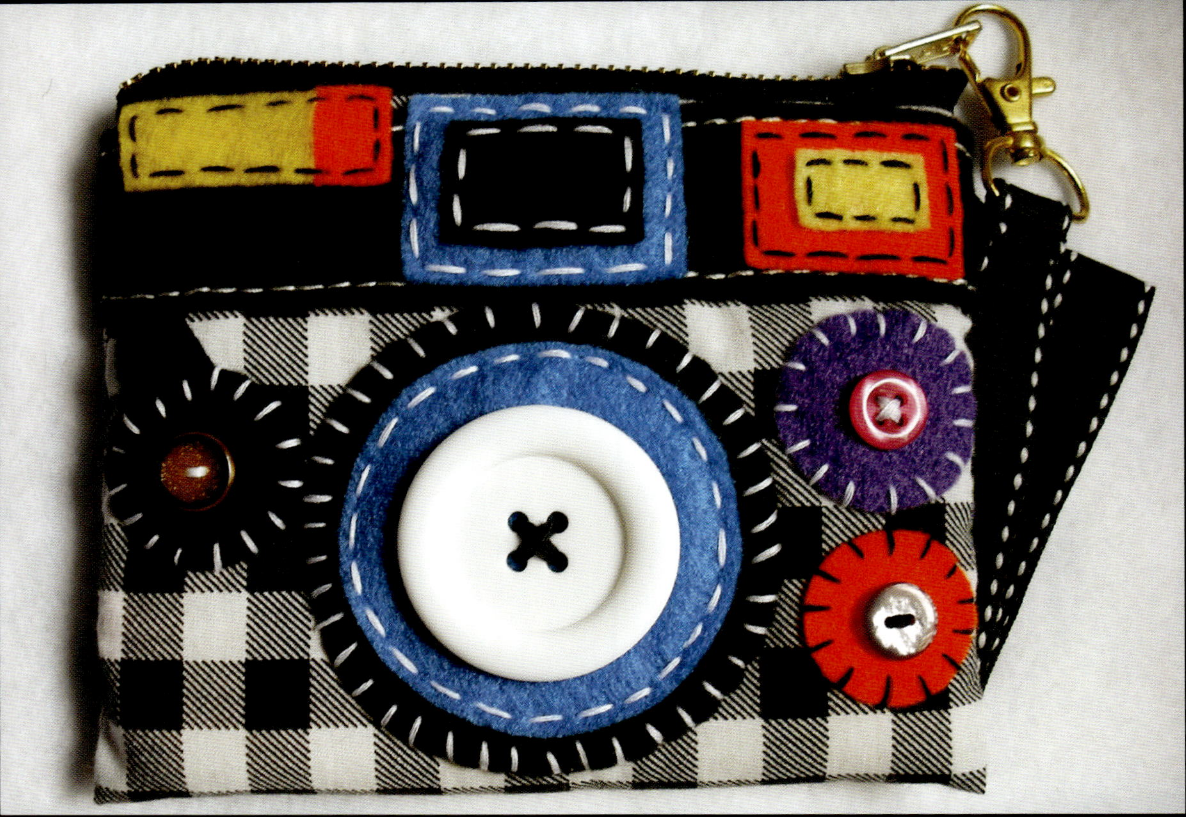

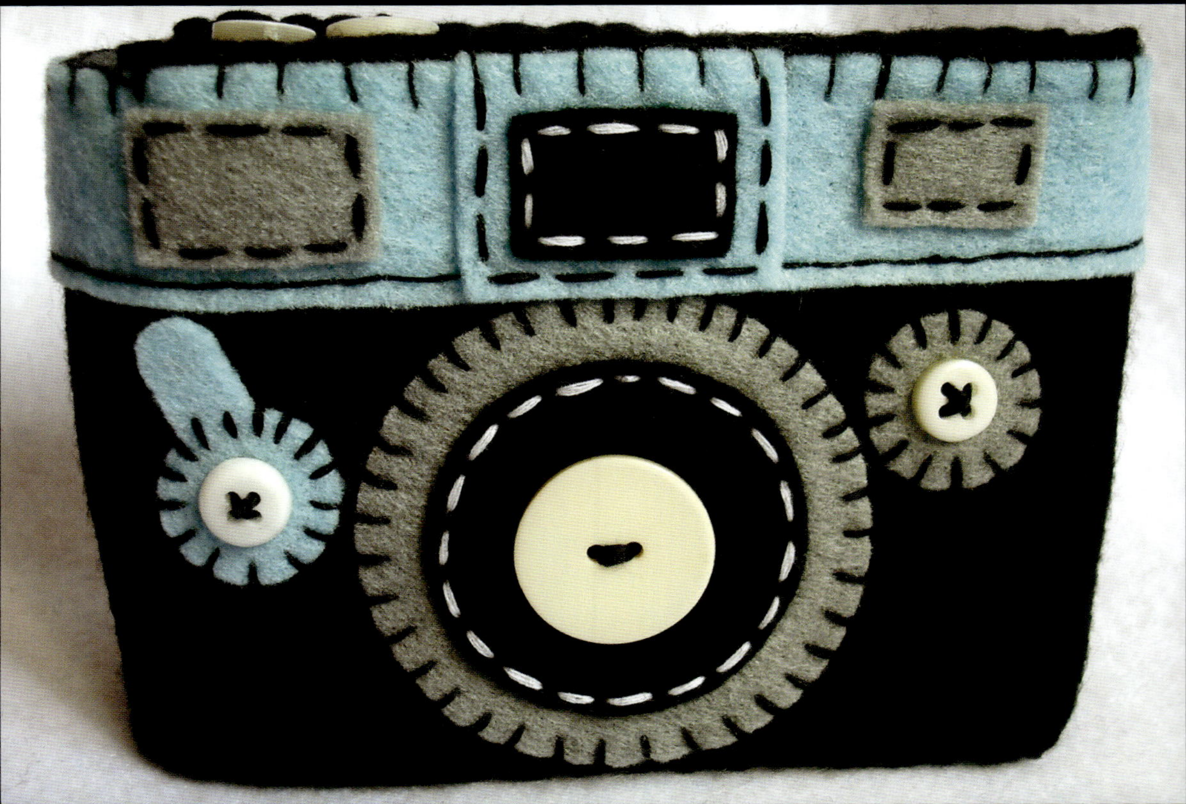

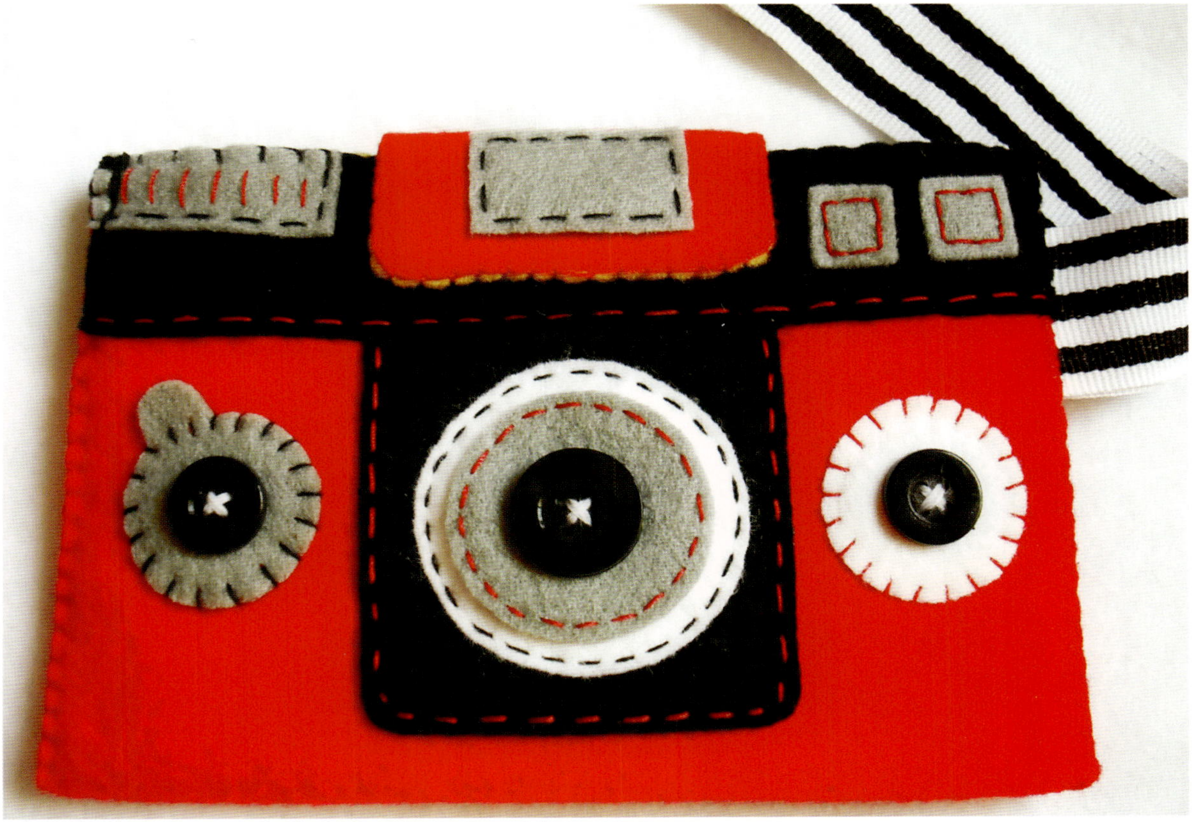

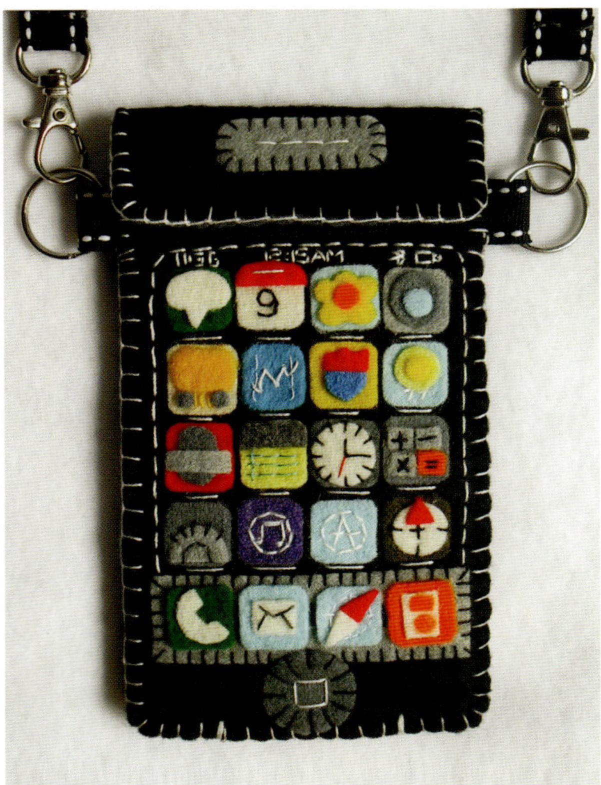

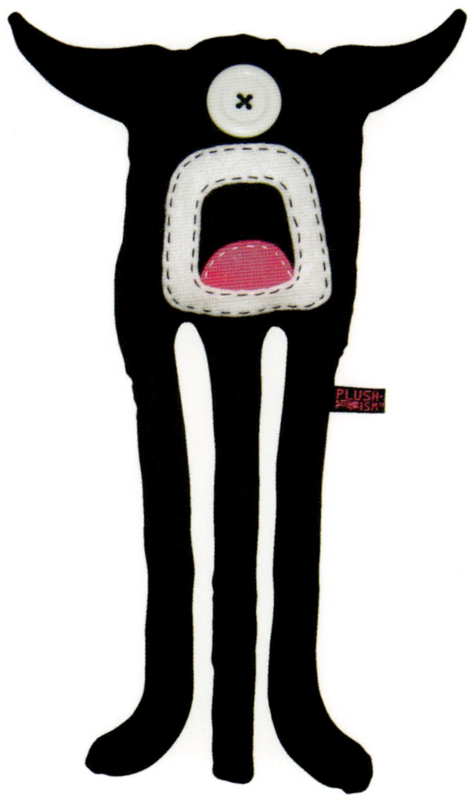

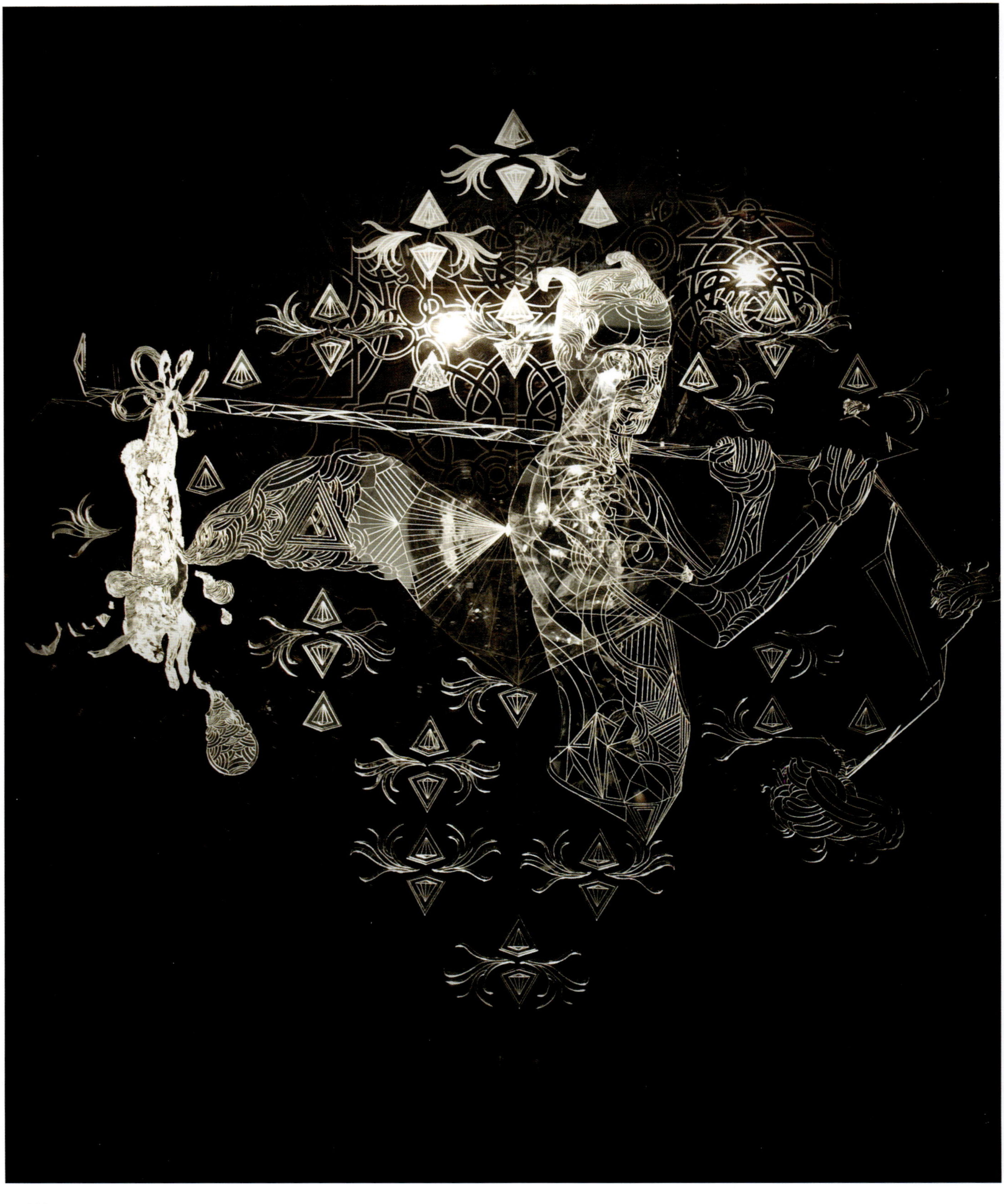

# Nicolás Cuestas

www.nicolascuestas.com

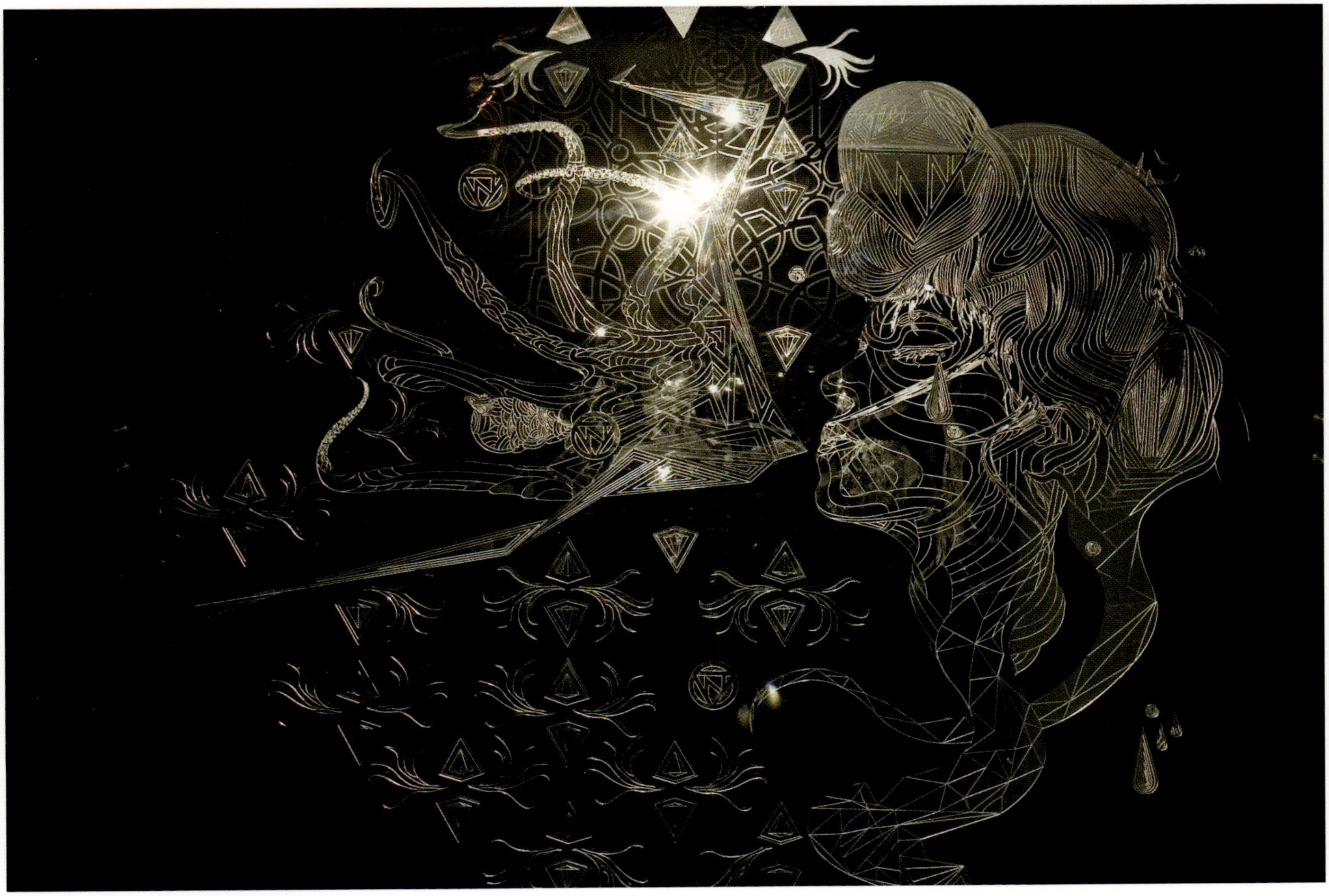

**Equilibrio Precario Precarious Balance**

Cuestas® is a multidisciplinary artist who lives and works between Brooklyn and Bogota. He studied Visual Arts back in La Universidad de Los Andes where he started a Visual and Design collective called Makinola®, developing art projects, curatorial proposals and designing exhibitions-paraphernalia and clothes. Based in Colombia, Cuestas® went to Tokyo in 2002, where he worked as a greeting card designer and animator, an experience that changed his perspective of the world. He started moving around, capturing realities, cultural-shocks, and learning gestures and words to summarize emotions and sensations. Later on Cuestas® continued traveling around Barcelona, Tel Aviv, Beijing, and so on. He made a stop in Peru-Lima's dunes where he worked with children living under precarious conditions and created a project to support their community and promote fashion designers from Perú and Colombia.

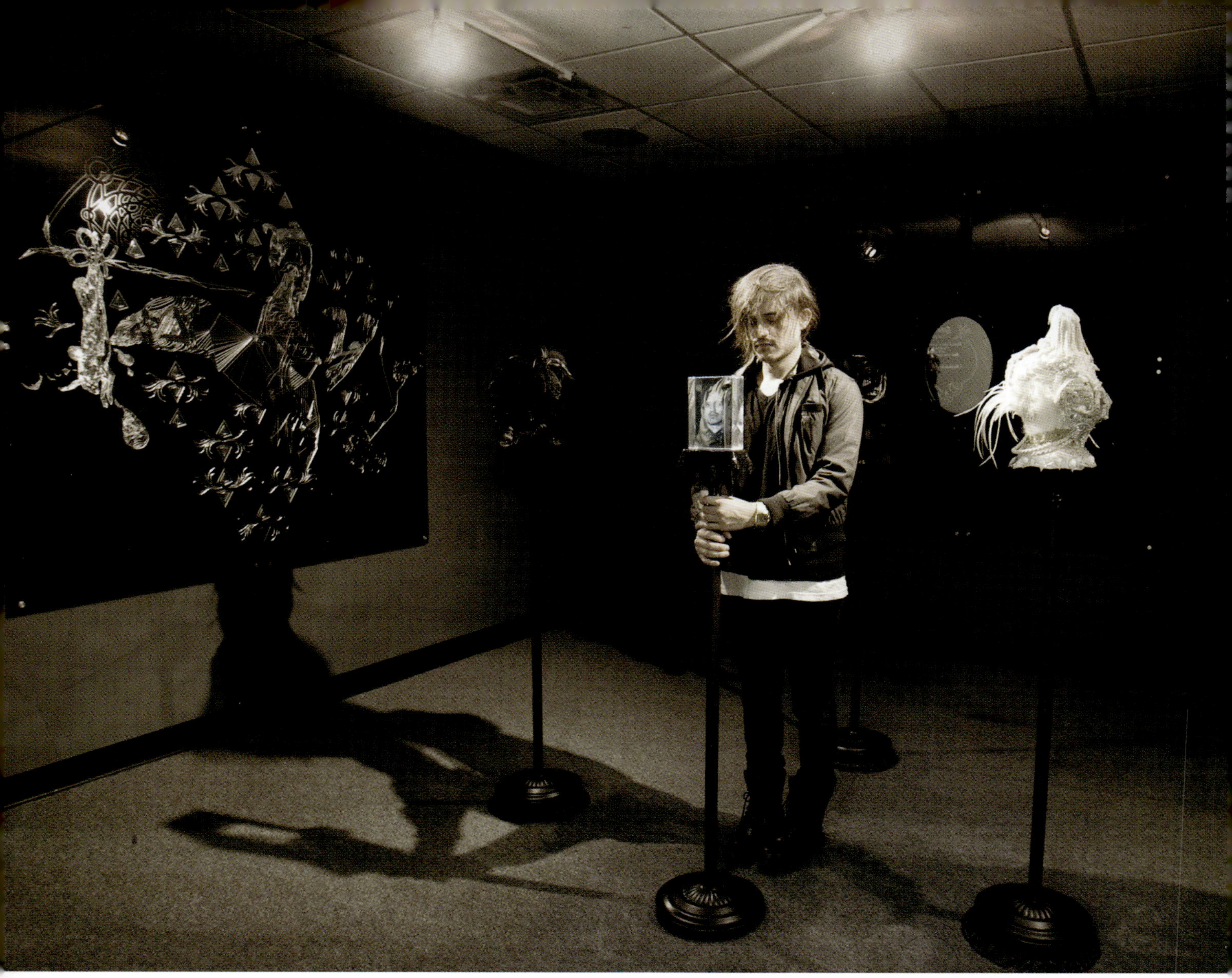

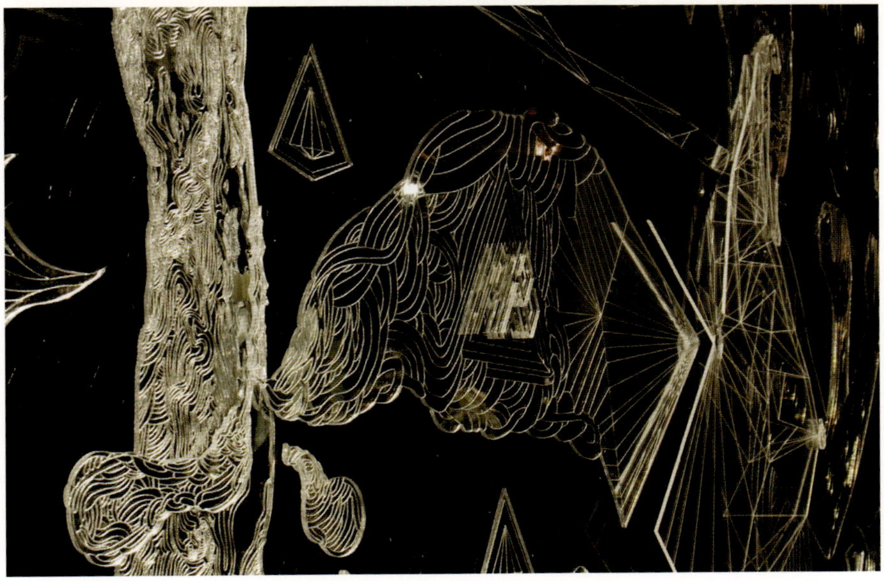

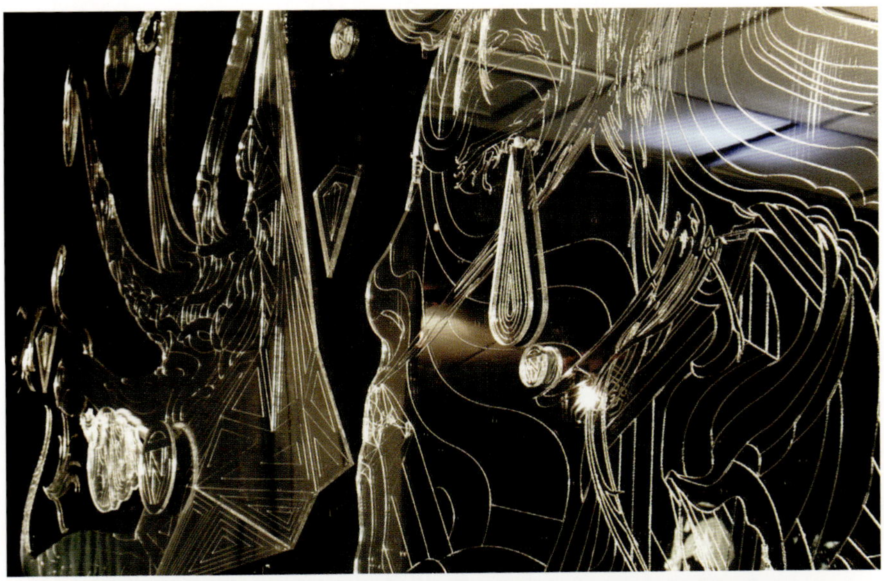

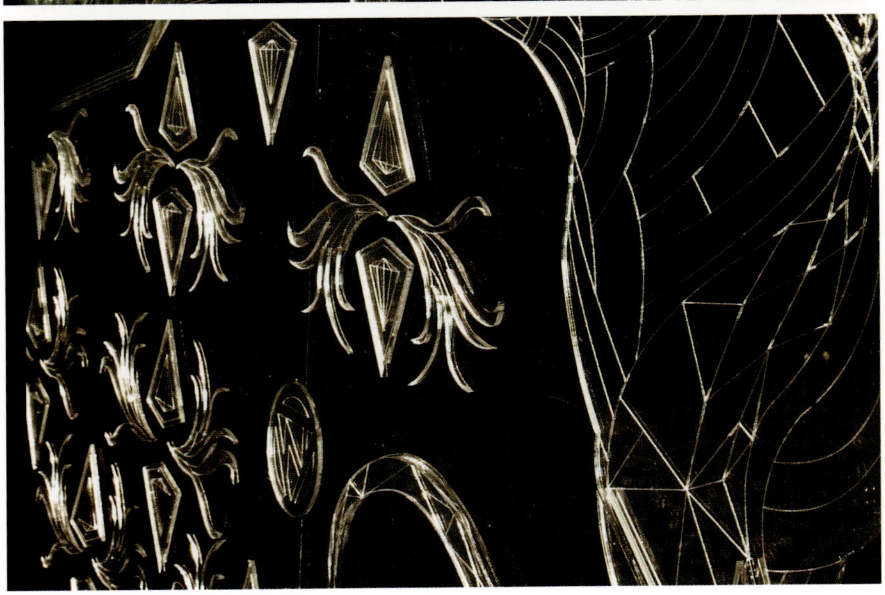

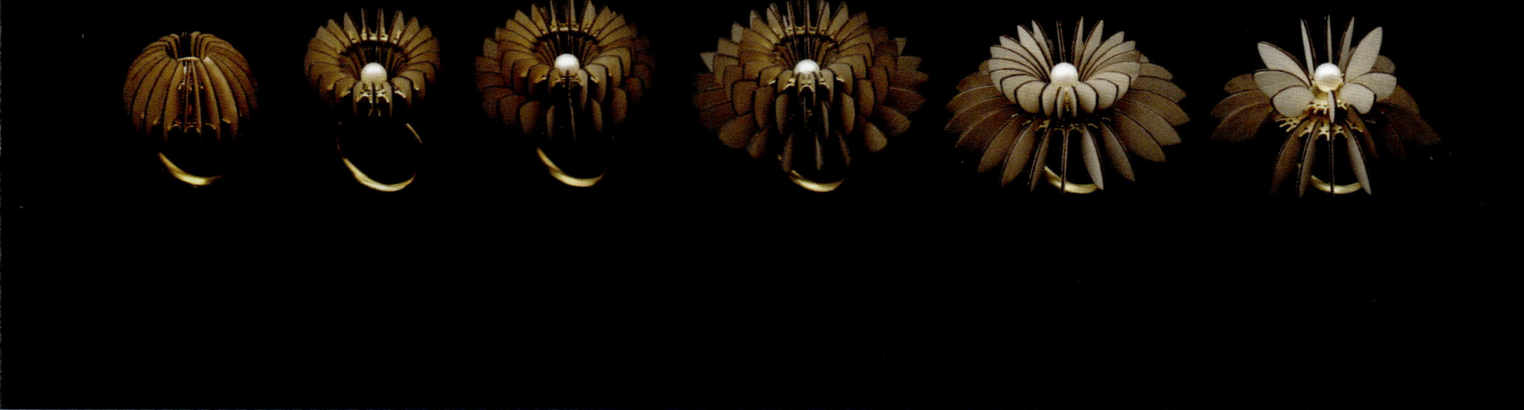

**Blossoming** series compose of 7 rings, demonstrates a lifetime of a blossoming flower. Each ring illustrates each state of blossoming, from close to full blossom until wilt, die and ready to rebirth. This collection was chosen to be one of the permanent ring collections in Victoria and Albert Museum, London.

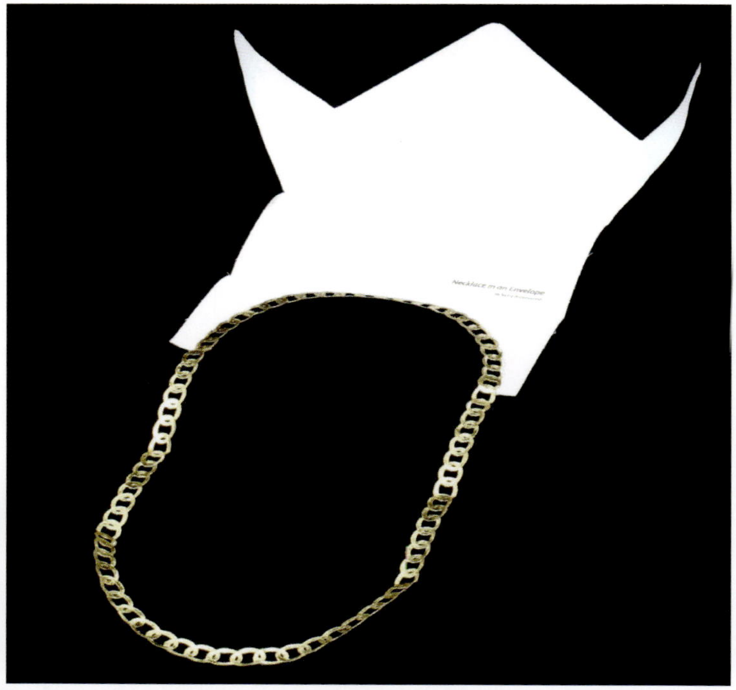

**Necklace in an Envelope** is recommended when a letter is not enough to tell someone how much you love her. A classic gold necklace made of fine canvas, applying with 22CT goldleaf, attached with a love letter. Writing the message and give to your love one, then let her cut and enjoy!

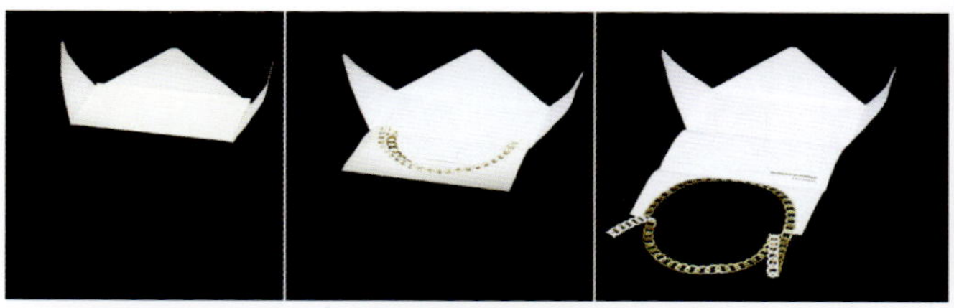

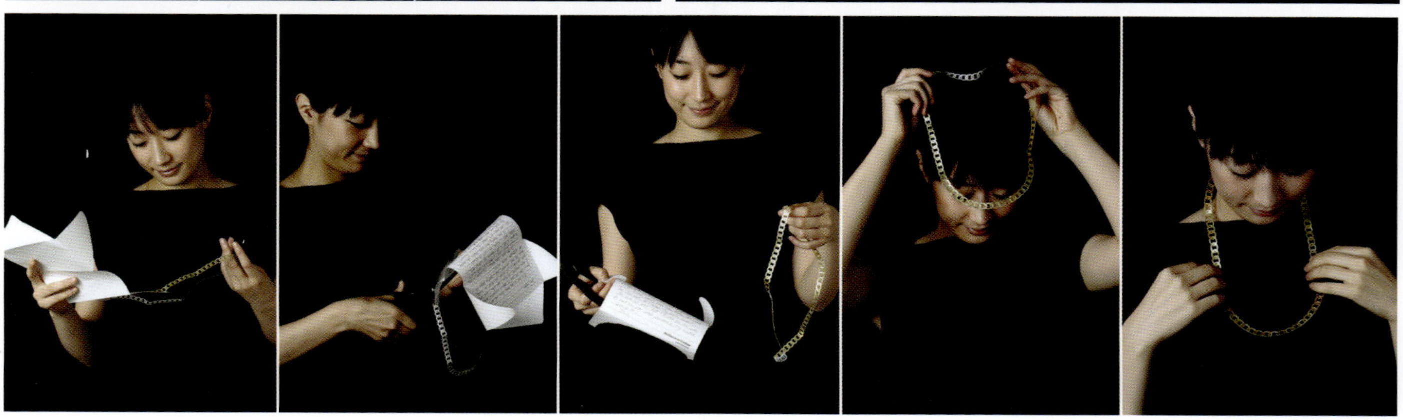

# Nutre Arayavanish

www.nutrejeweller.com

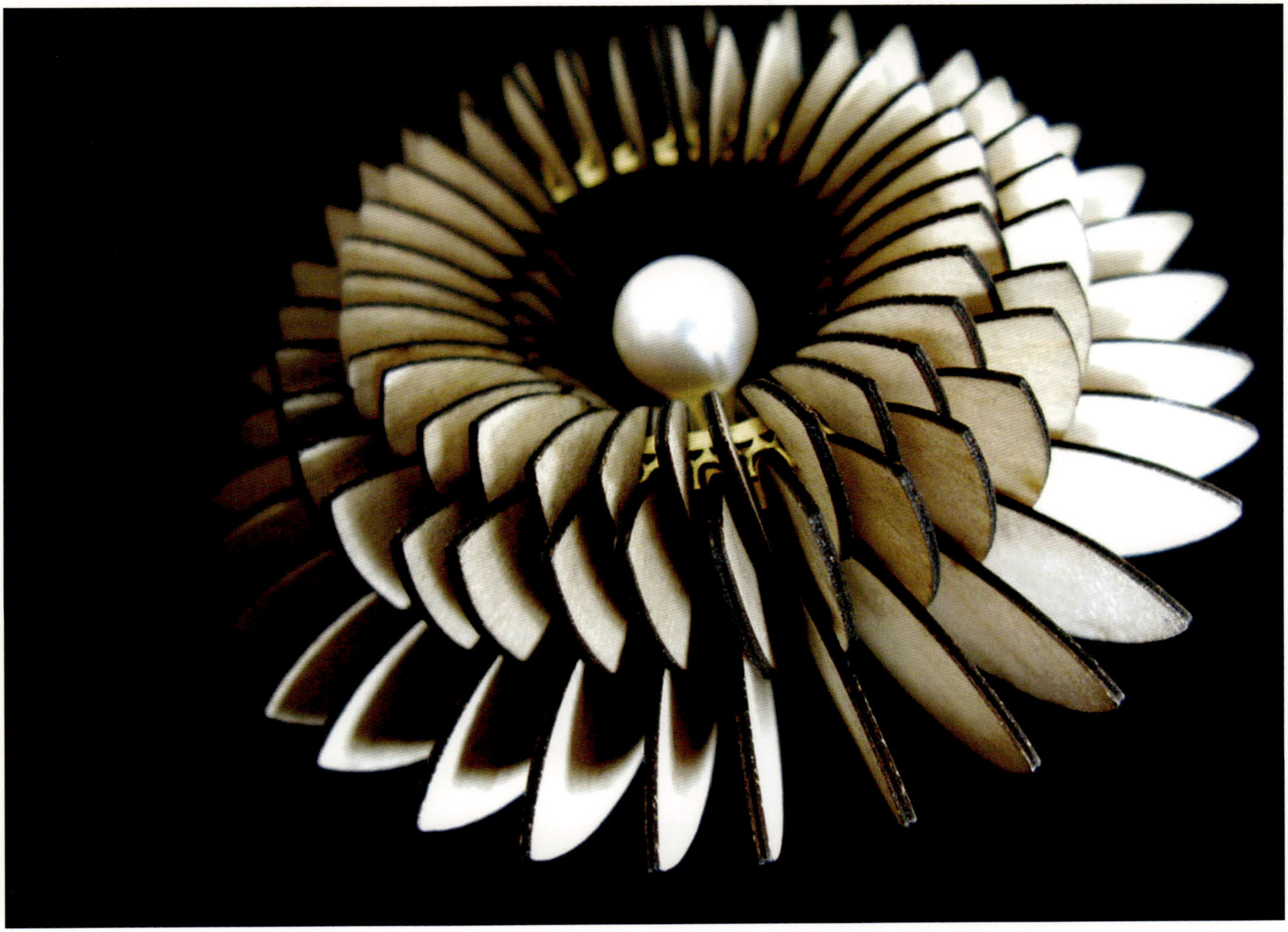

Born in Bangkok. Trained in jewellery design and making it at Silpakorn University then completed her master degree in goldsmithing, silversmithing, metalwork and jewellery at the Royal College of Art in London. She has won a number of prestigious awards, including New Designer of the Year from London Business Design Center and Jewellery Designer of the Year from British Jewellers' Association (BJA) in 2007. Using both traditional techniques and new technologies, her pieces are delicate and refine. She explores the relationship between maker, jewellery and wearers in order to encourage the wearer to engage more with the piece apart from wearing them. The public perception or reaction to the jewellery when presented to them in different states of existence and brings new experience to wearers or viewers, and a new level of jewellery wearing.

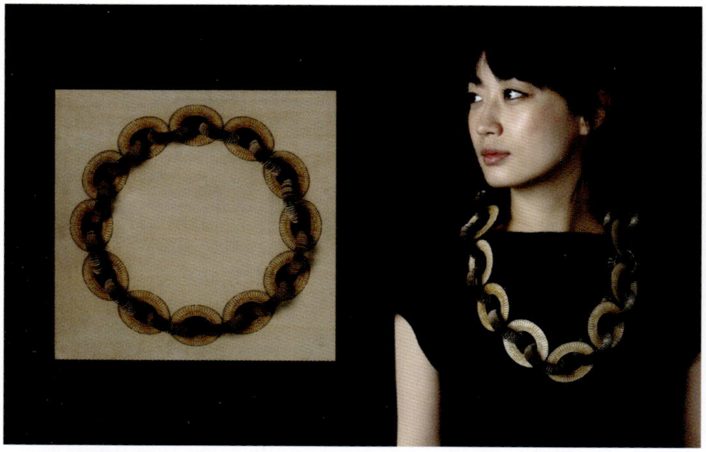

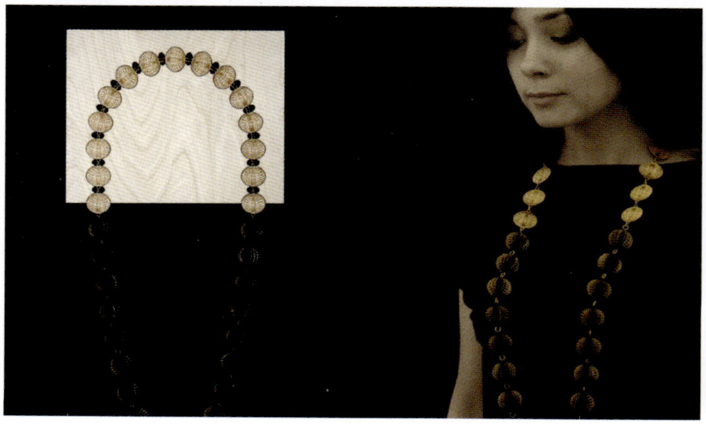

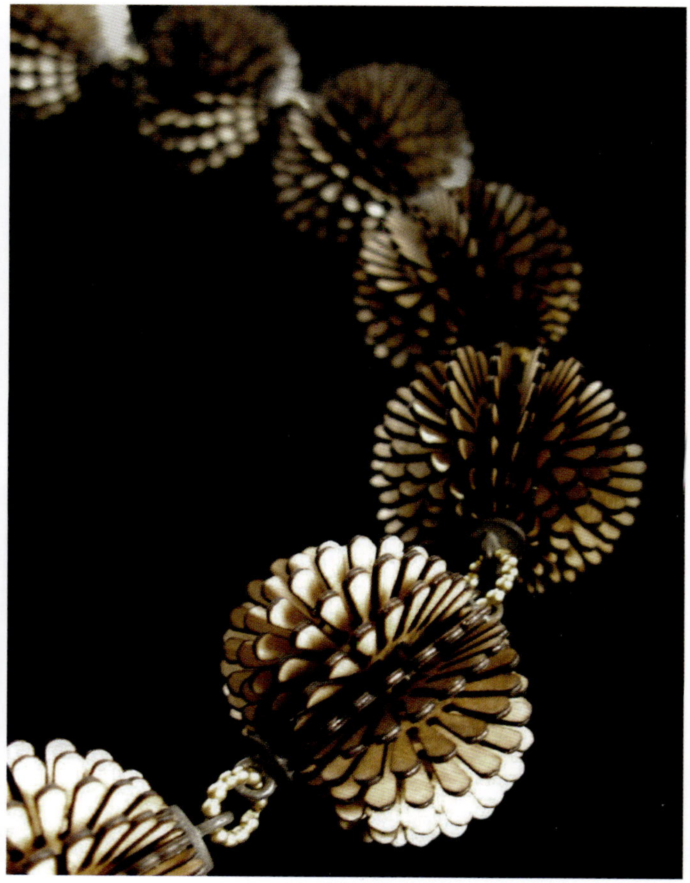

**Petal Wreath** series compose of 3 necklaces presented as hanging pictures await for the wearer to pop them out to wear from the pre-cut wooden sheet. All beads in the necklance were constructed by petal-shaped components.

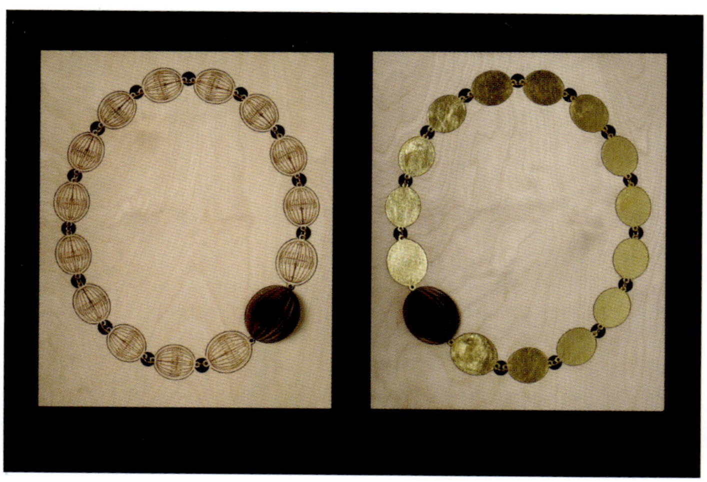

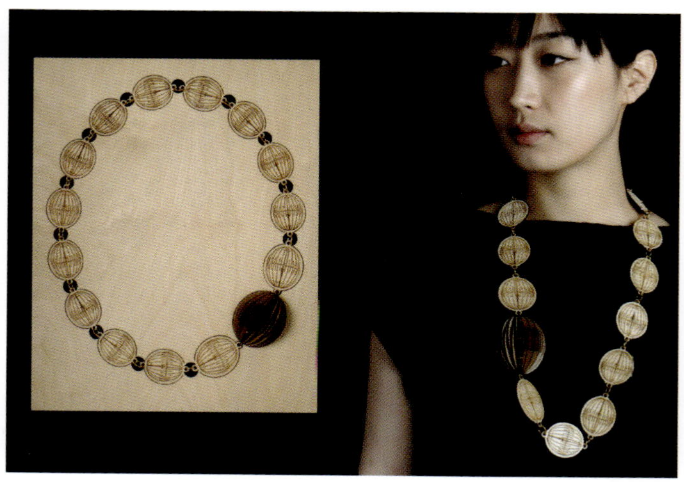

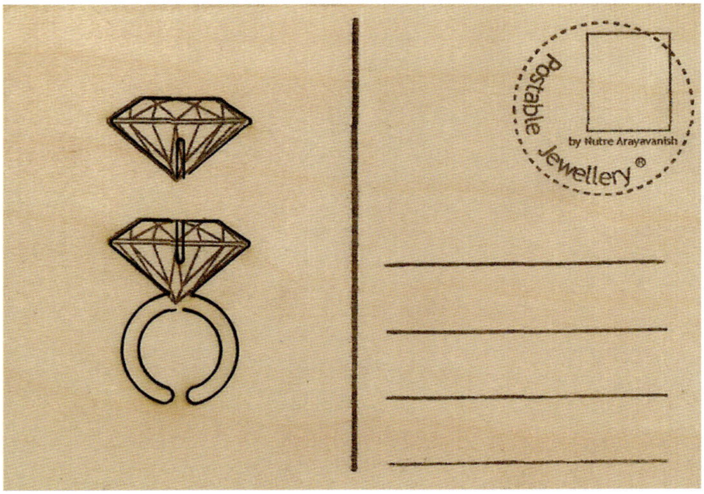


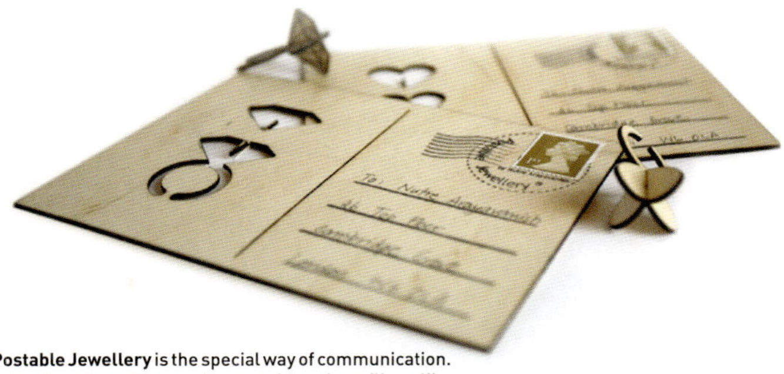

**Postable Jewellery** is the special way of communication. It is a jewellery that can be sent through mailbox, like a postcard. Postable jewellery bears the evidence of journey, marks, stamps, stains, adding to the romance and uniqueness of it. Assemble by slotting each component together, postable jewellery can be a perfect present for any occasions.

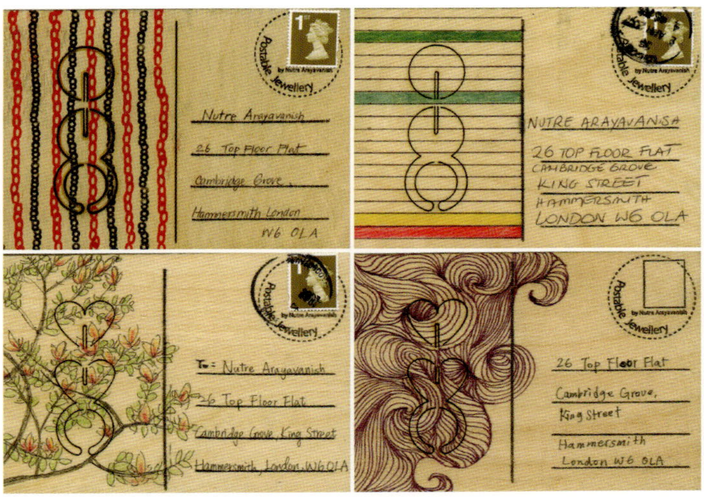


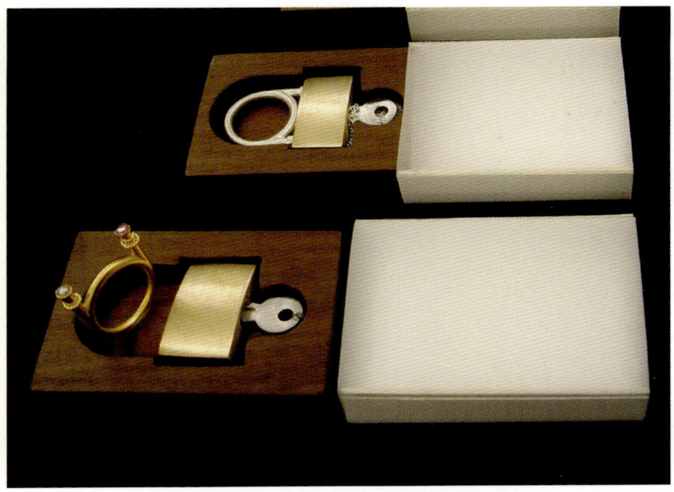

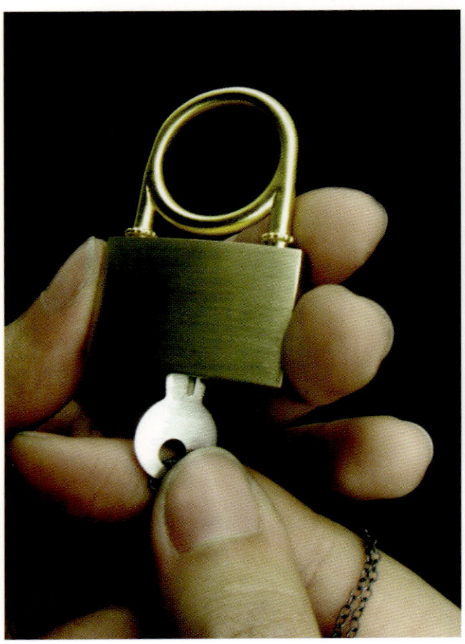

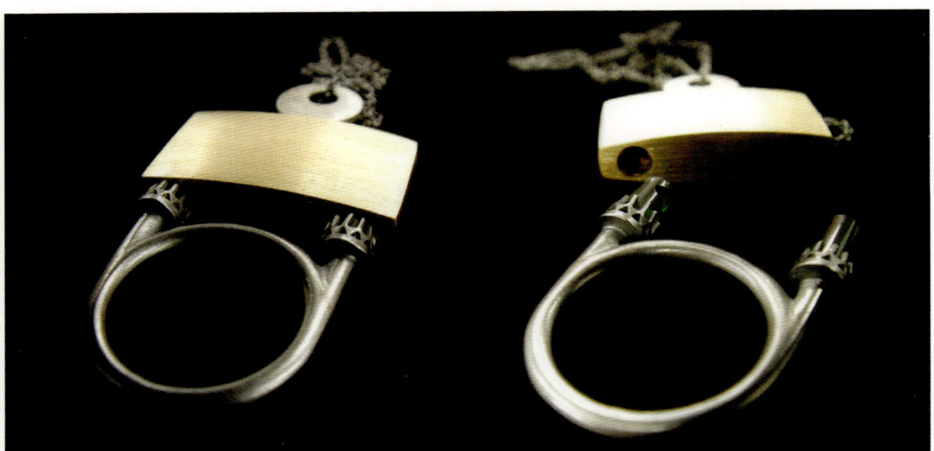

**Treasure Lock** is the collection made for a creative currency exhibition in collabration with Bank of America. The project compose of 5 rings which are locked in the brass padlocks. The idea is about locking precious gemstones inside when they are not worn. The rings are released to wear by the key provided.

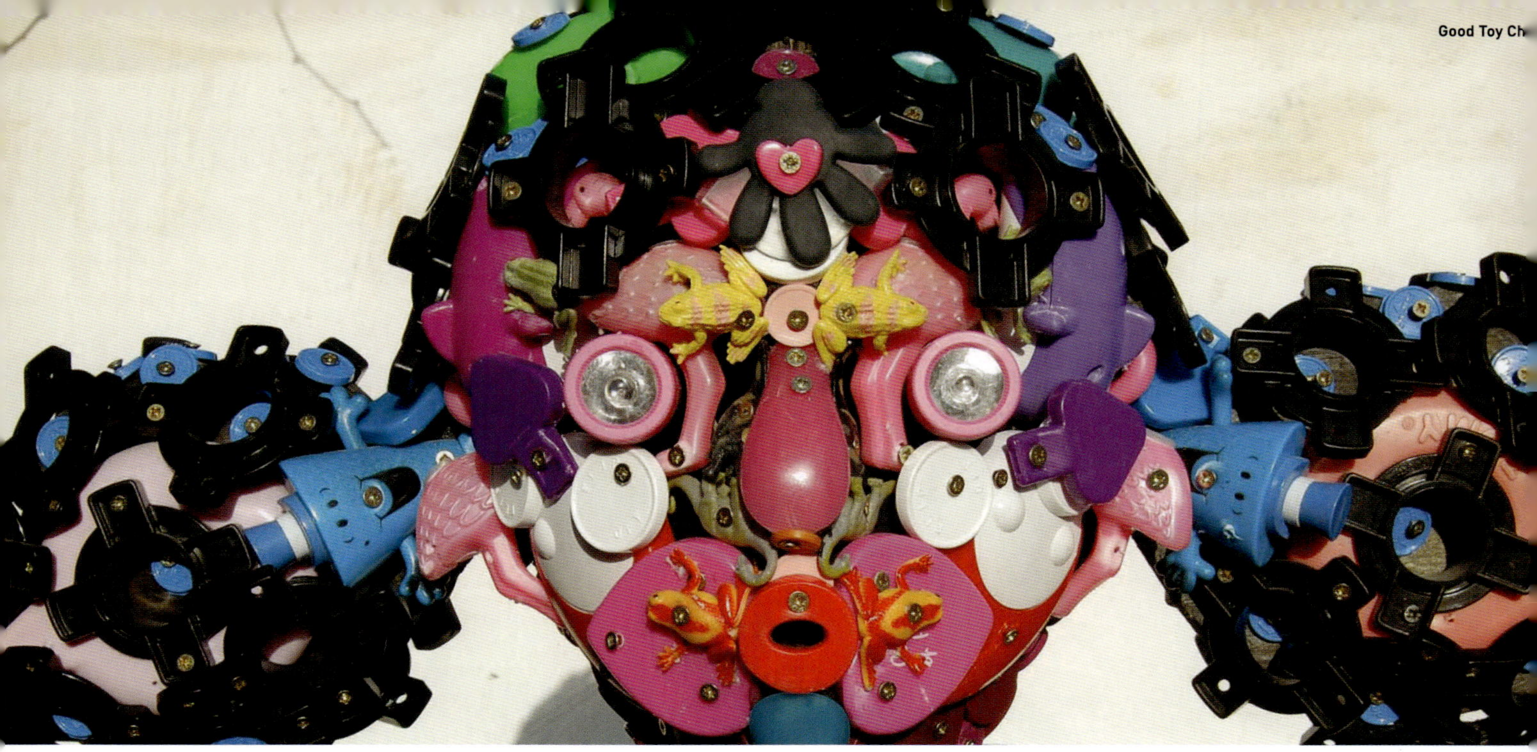

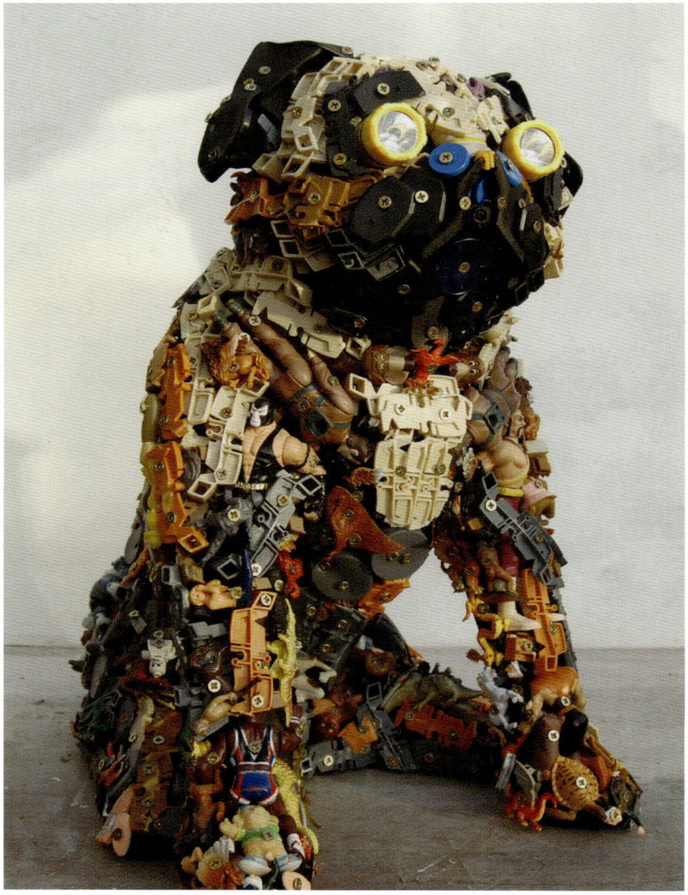

**Pug One**
Commissioned by Envie D'art

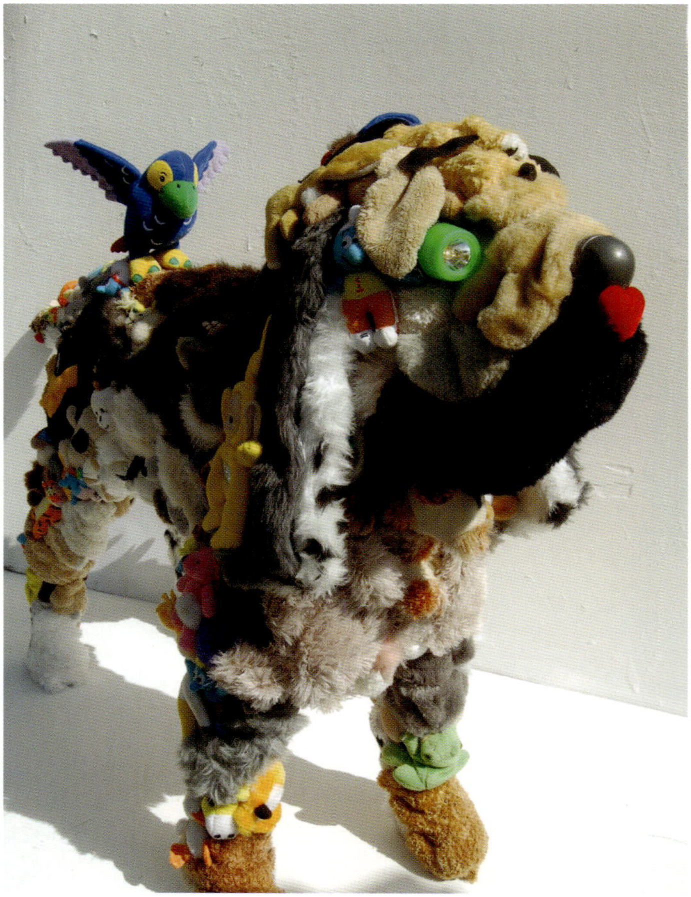

**New Dog, New York**

# Robert Bradford

www.robertbradford.co.uk

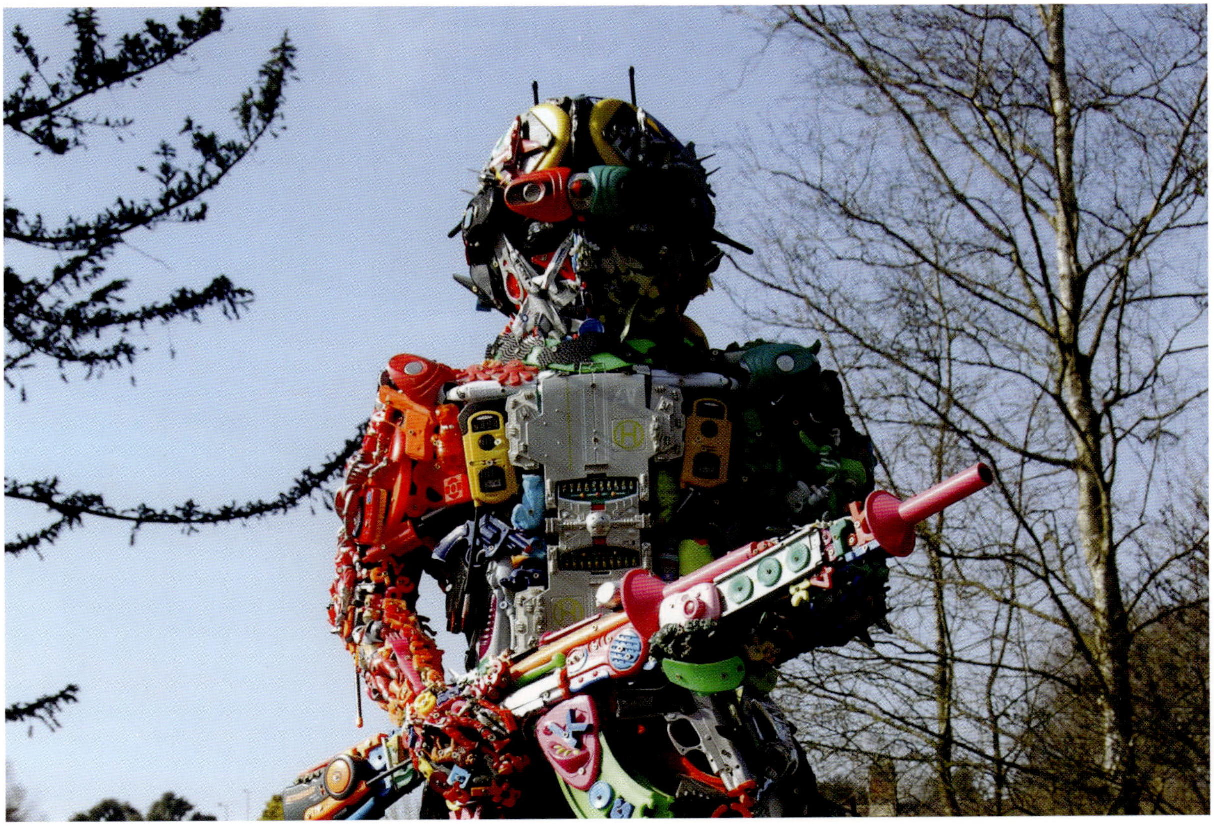

**Toy Soldier at Quenington**

PLASTIC TOY SCULPTURE SERIES - For a long time now I have preferred to use materials that are not bland i.e. have some kind of history of weathering or use. One day about four years ago out in the studio I was looking into my childrens box of outgrown / discarded toys which happened to be stored in the same building and responded to the random collection of colours shapes and forms they made. I figured that if I could find a way of putting them together to constitute a larger form they would have great potential as larger scale sculpture. Over the next while I experimented with two other construction methods (which both had their downsides) - in frustration I tried putting a screw through one toy and then many others, to my surprise most didn't crack or shatter and the new series has been largely based around and developed from that fact. Ideally the pieces will work on many levels. The toys themselves interest me in their own right as mini sculptures by unknown and uncredited artists. Mostly I use the toys abstractly as forms with which to build muscle bone or internal or external organs but all types of human pursuits can be referred to and represented through them - things loved or hated - things used and carried as tools etc etc. They provide interest in surface detail whilst making their contribution to the totalities. The toys also provide a moving history of fads and fashions as they pass through the media and our awareness temporarily significant and then forgotten. Public reaction to the sculptures has been largely very positive (in some cases gleeful)- often children drag their parents to come and look at the pieces and then a whole sequence of recognition and recollection usually begins, naming the various toys and recalling the times and circumstances of their use. There is usually some fascination with the sculptures, the individual toys used and with the process of their acquisition and construction. Sometimes there is outright laughter. There is usually a whole process of going back and forth between looking at the sculptures as a totality and the individual parts from which they are made (which of course is my intention). Some people of course just say they are rubbish which of course is perfectly true! There is also often talk about consumerism waste and recycling, which whilst not being my central concern is also in my view positive when it occurs. Some find the sculptures beautiful/ curious/ scary/ weird/ emotional and etc. (which considering all they are really are , is bits of what is usually seen as trash) is great. In a way the sculptures are also history pieces in the sense that you could date any one of them roughly speaking from the time that the last toy screwed on to the structure was produced.

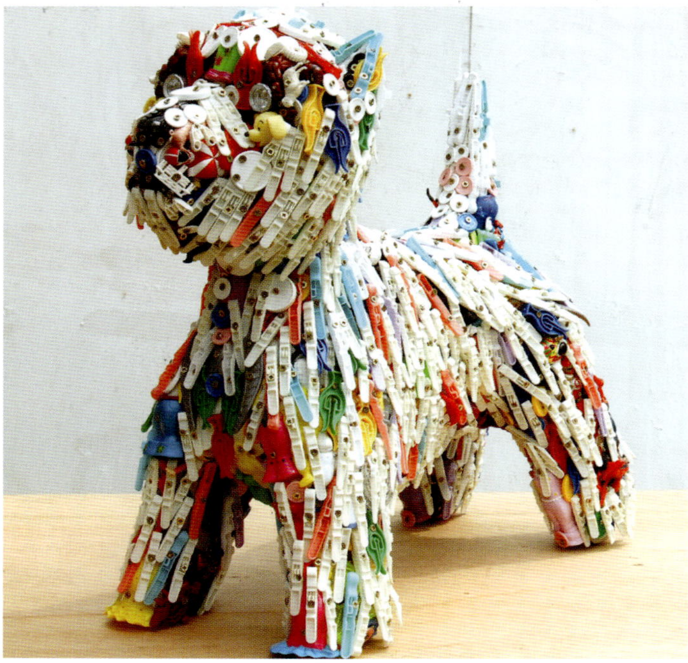

Terrierist

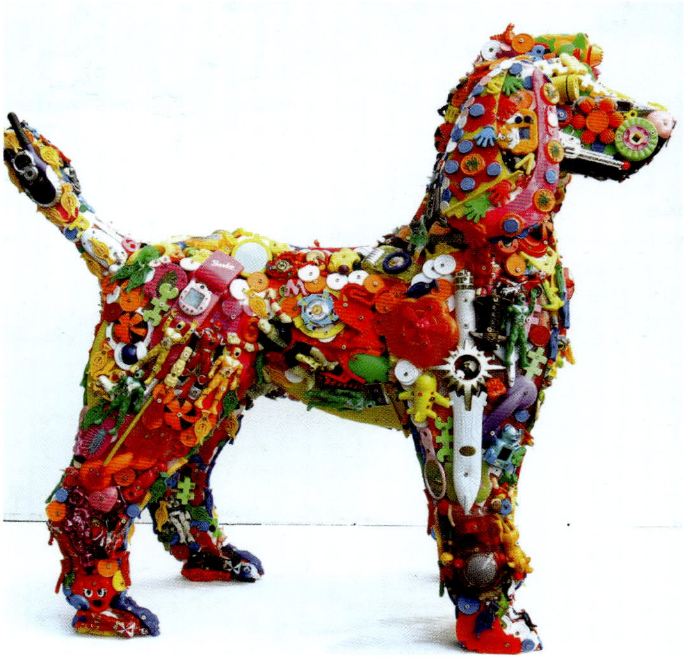

Foo Foo

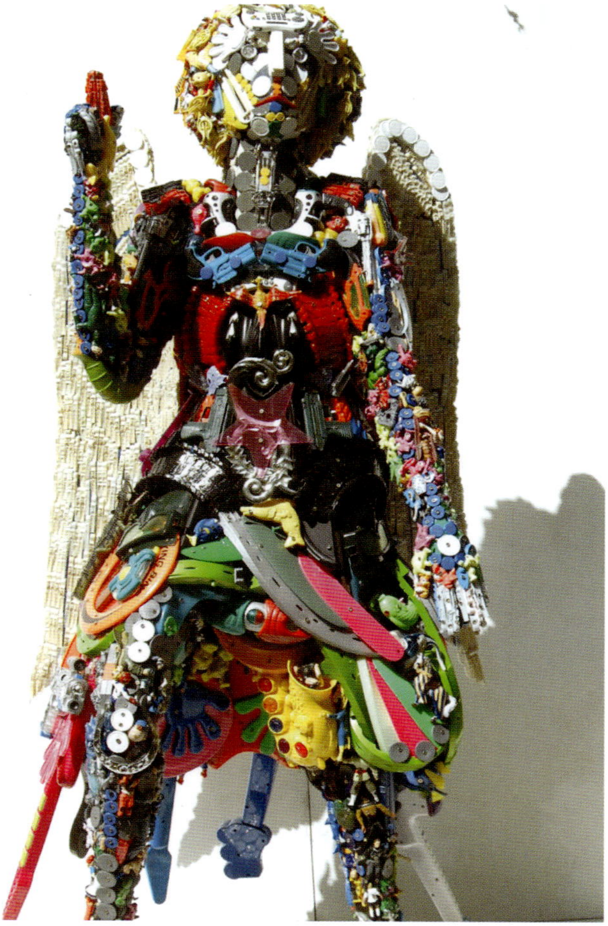

Angel for Ripleys

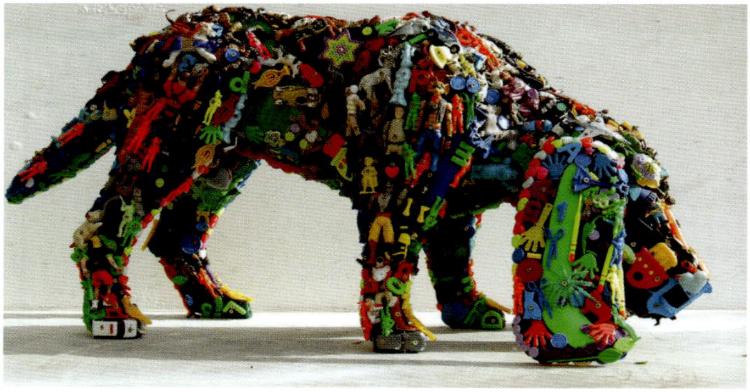

Sniff Miami

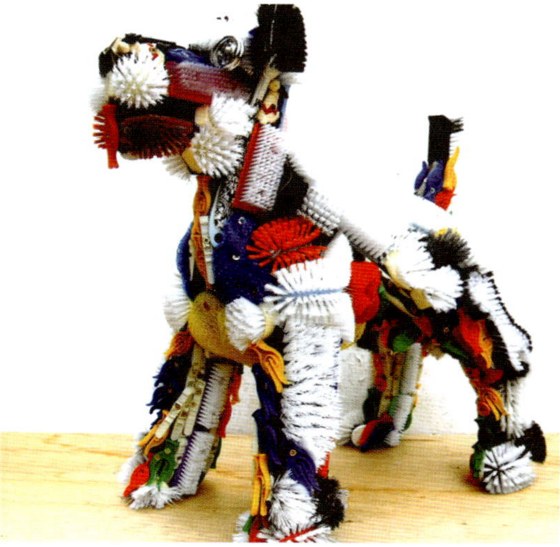

Domesticated Animal

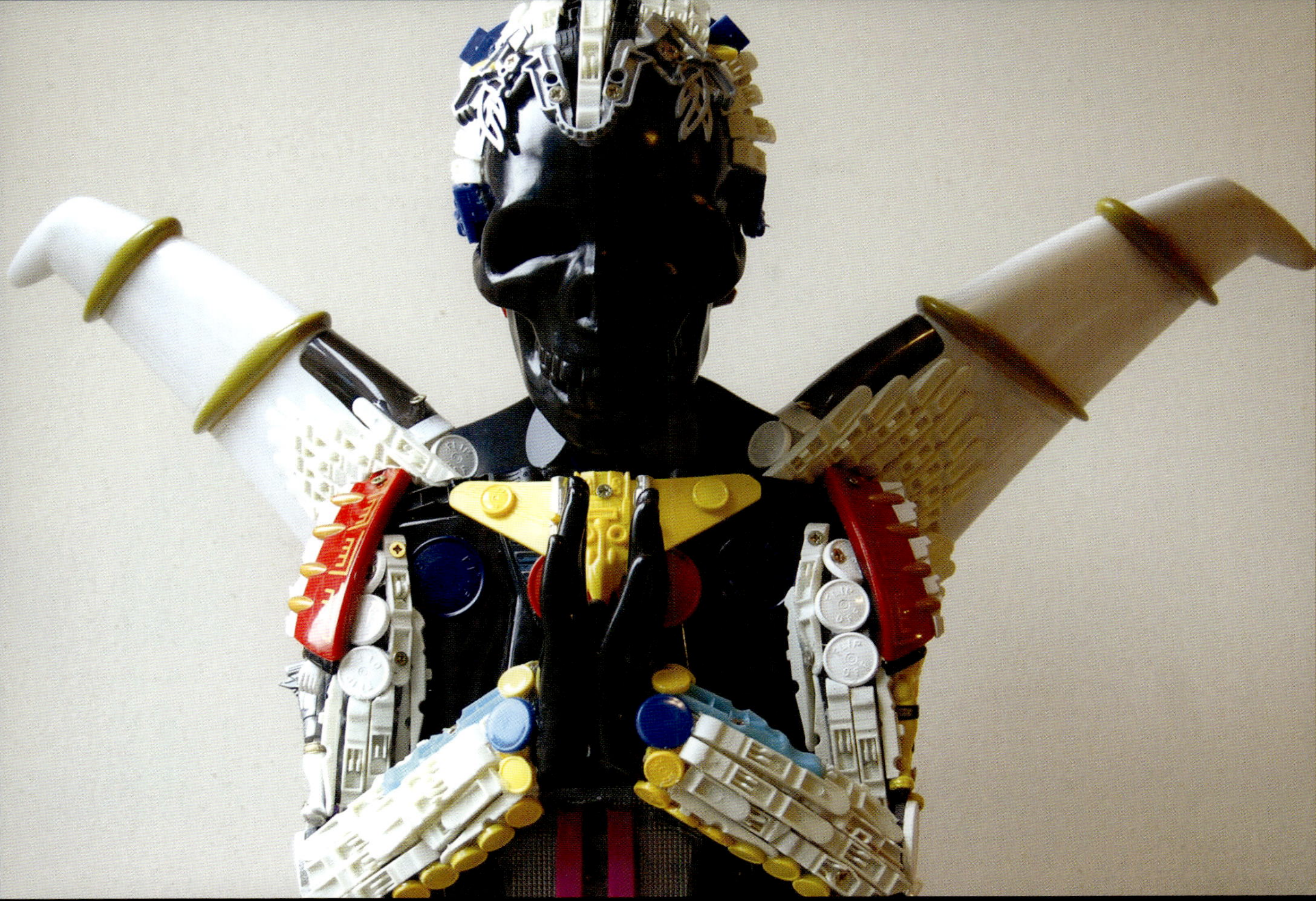

Power Angel of Death

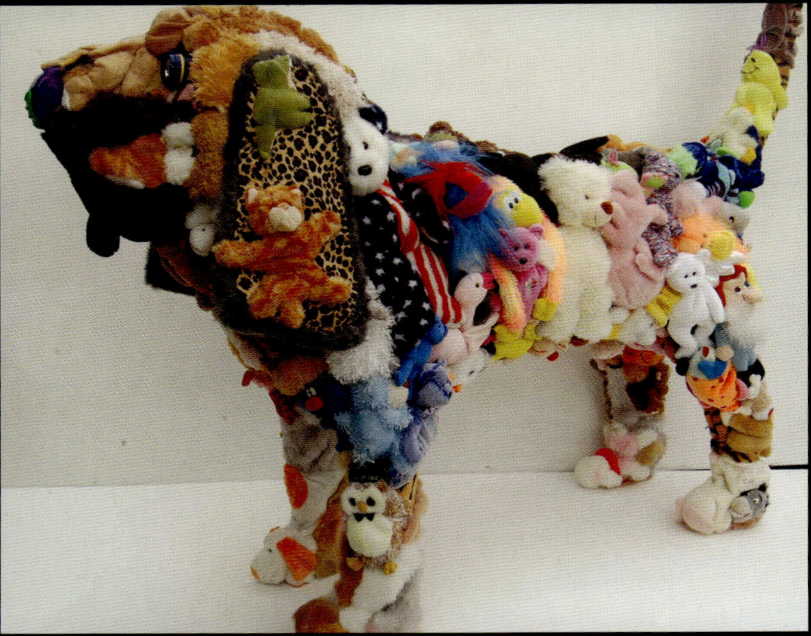

Soft Dog

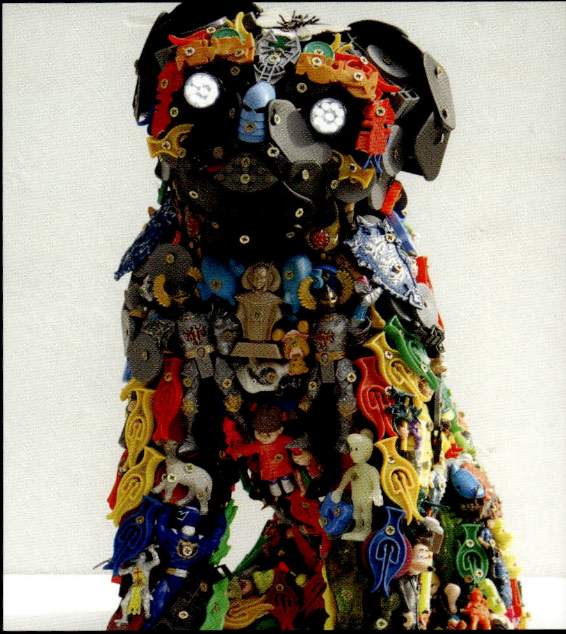

Pug Two

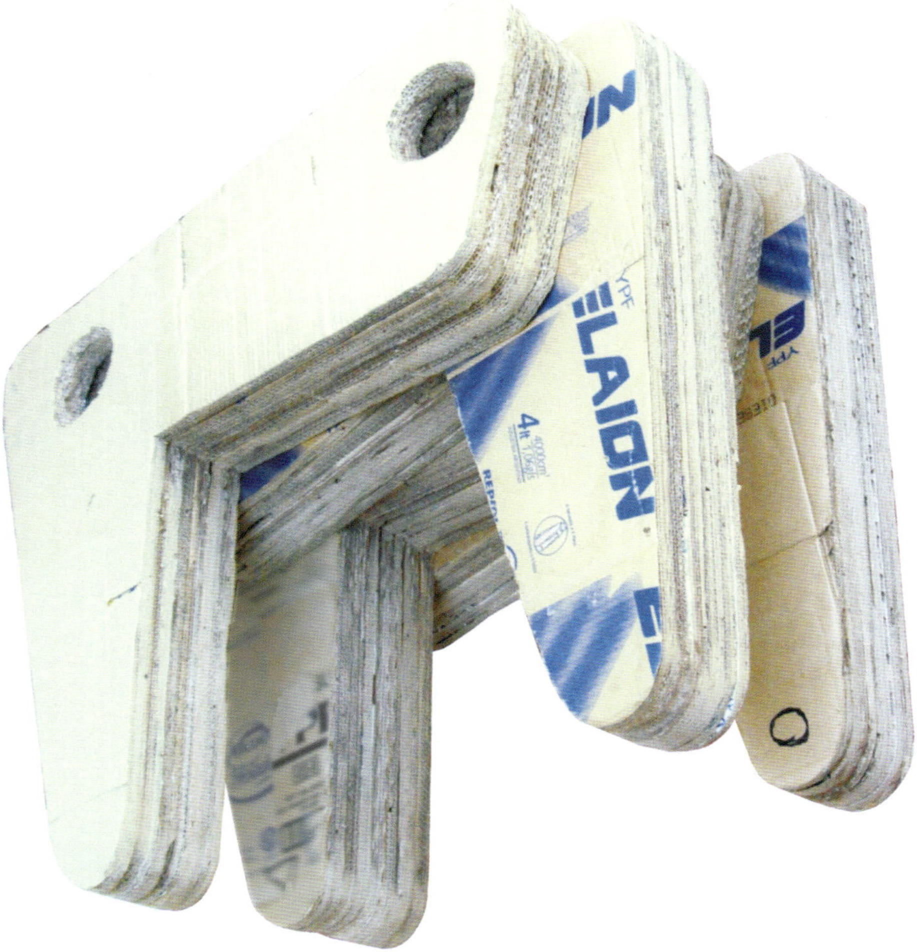
YPF
ELAION

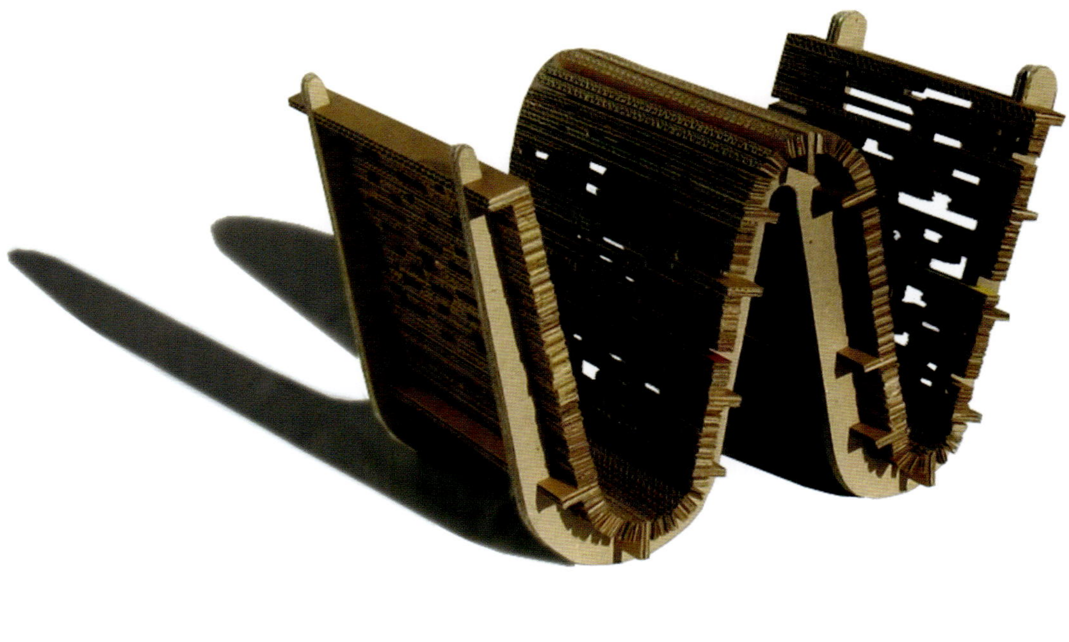

# Santiago / **Morahan**

www.disenocartonero.blogspot.com

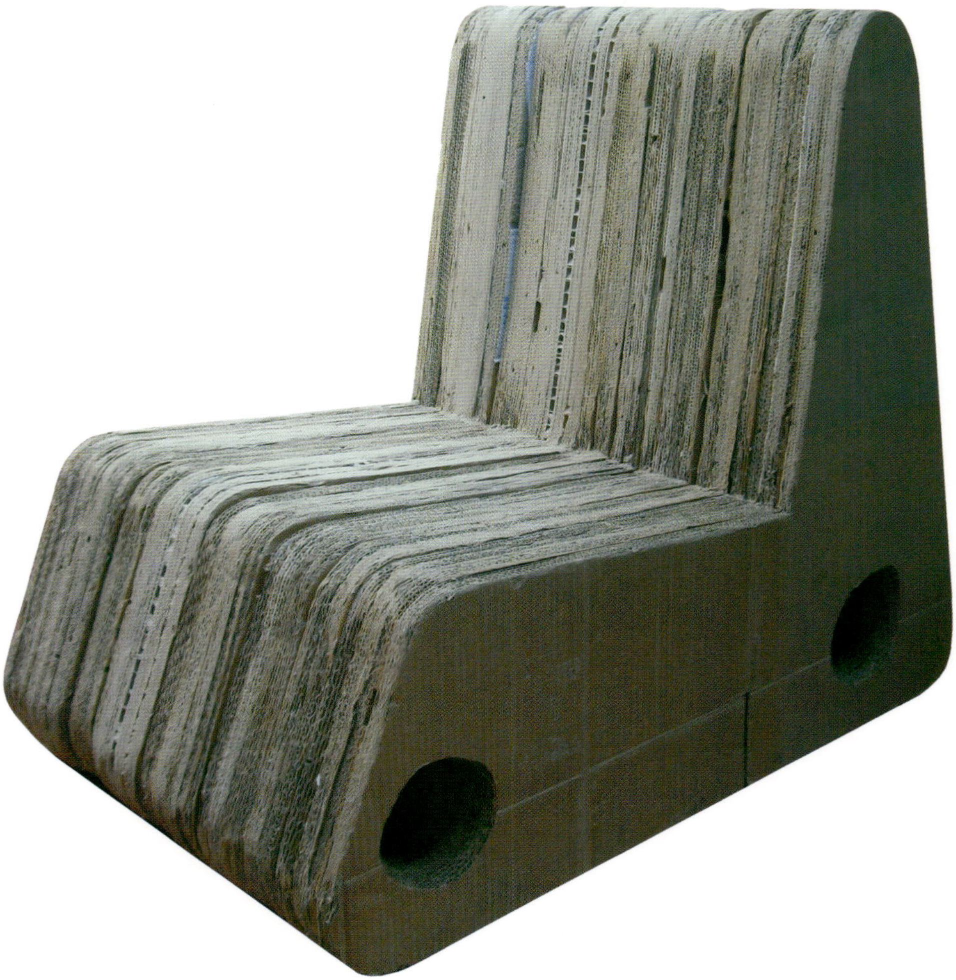

Diseño Cartonero (Spanish for Rubbish Collector Design) started in early 2007 as a solo project by Santiago Morahan from Paraná, Entre Ríos, Argentina, an independent designer and artisan, an amateur kayaker and a full time nature lover, the latter being my strongest motivation for my work. There was a need of creating a freelance design job for myself, in a workshop in which I could feel free to make my own design process and research. My primary medium is making cardboard furniture, lamps, toys, office accesories and scale models within sustainable design, reusing corrugated cardboard especially, but occasionally reusing plastic and metal as well. I pick the materials myself, and I also make my very own version of fair trade by purchasing the materials from street rubbish collectors at a higher price than they would receive at a recycling facility. Diseño Cartonero's products are eco-friendly, made entirely with recycled materials, and seek to fulfill a utilitarian need without relegating aesthetics. In addition, every single detail is considered in the fully-craft making process. Every product made is unique and not repeated, with its creator's impressions on each and every one of them, which therefore makes every object not only a design one, but artistic as well. Since all materials reused have different dimensions, textures and printings, working on them constantly challenges my creativity, for it makes me not to repeat and standardize procedures and forms. I also seek to deal with serious environmental issues, like what to do with materials that we supposedly don't use anymore. That's how I intend to give a second life to them. The consequent conservation of natural resources and saving of the energy required to process them, leads to create and integrate sustainability as the currently unavoidable fourth component of design, along form, function and technology.

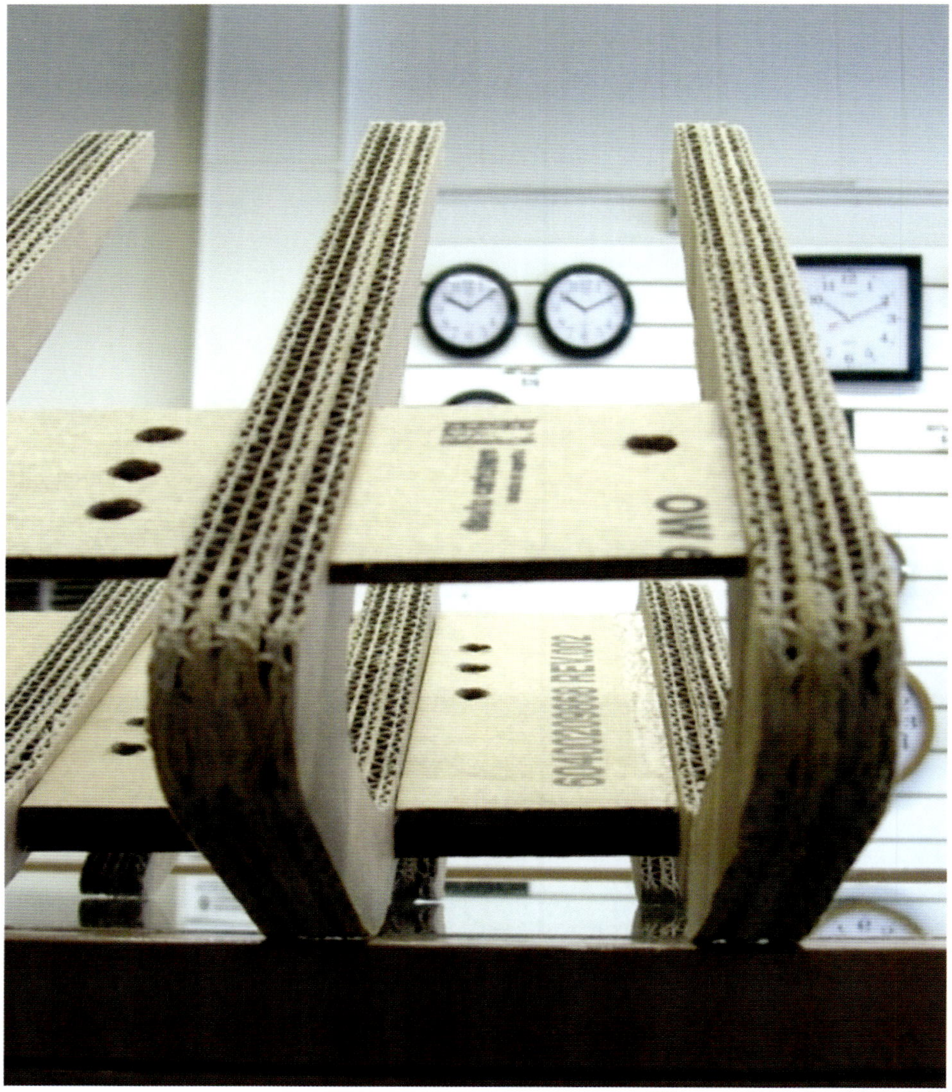

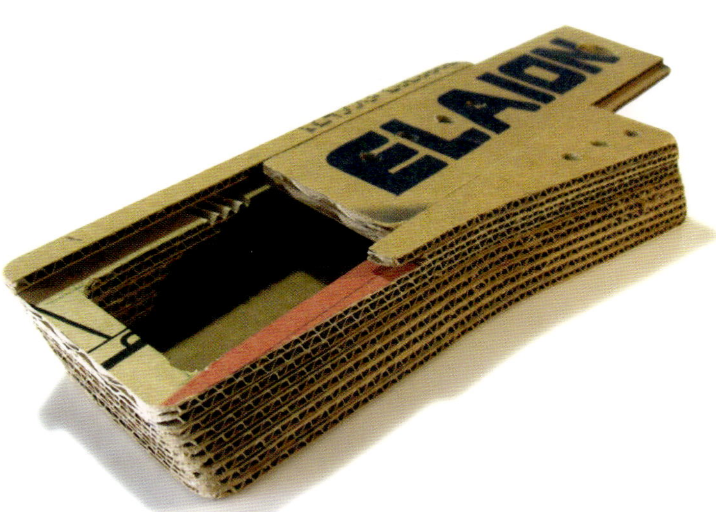
ELAION
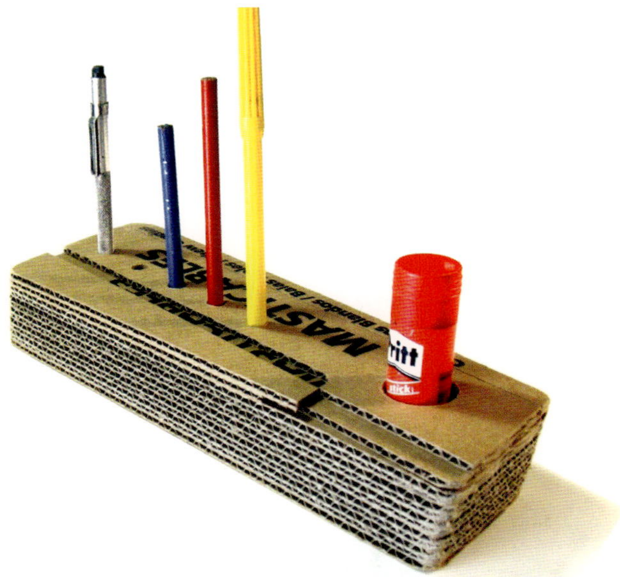
MASTICABLES
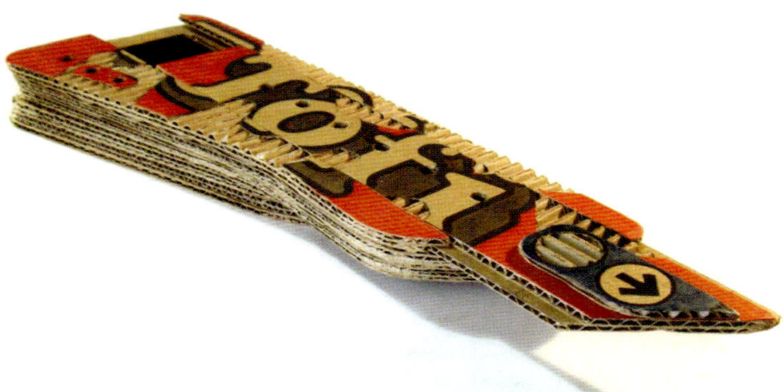
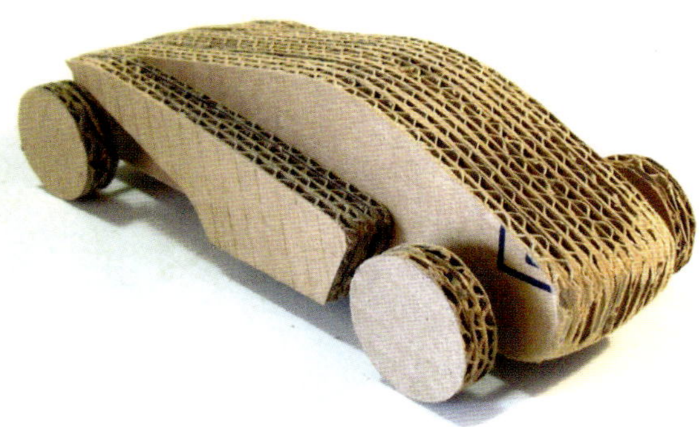
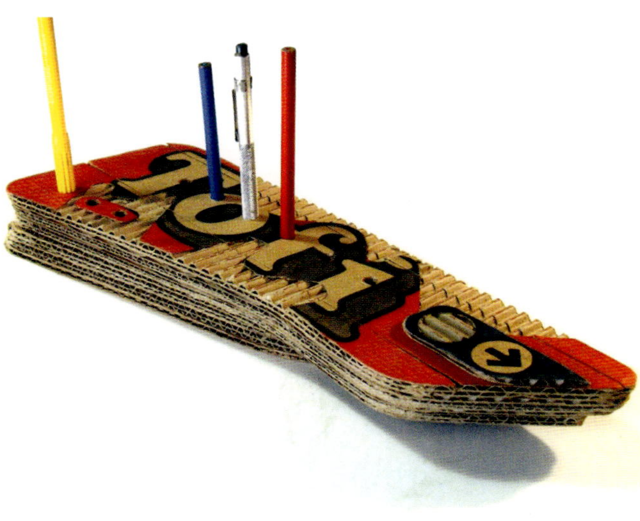
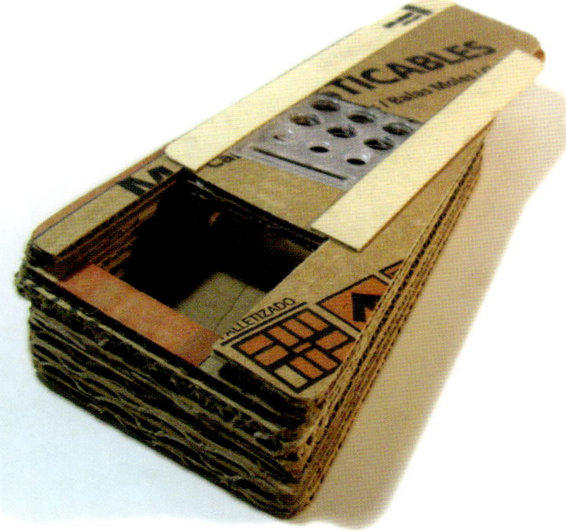
TICABLES

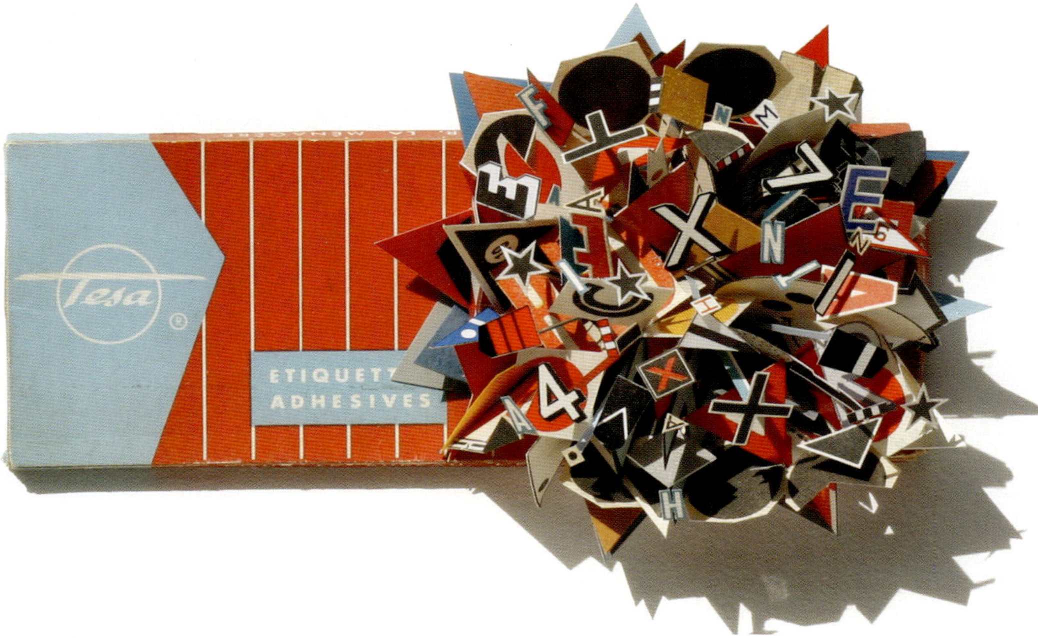


**Etiquettes Adhesives**

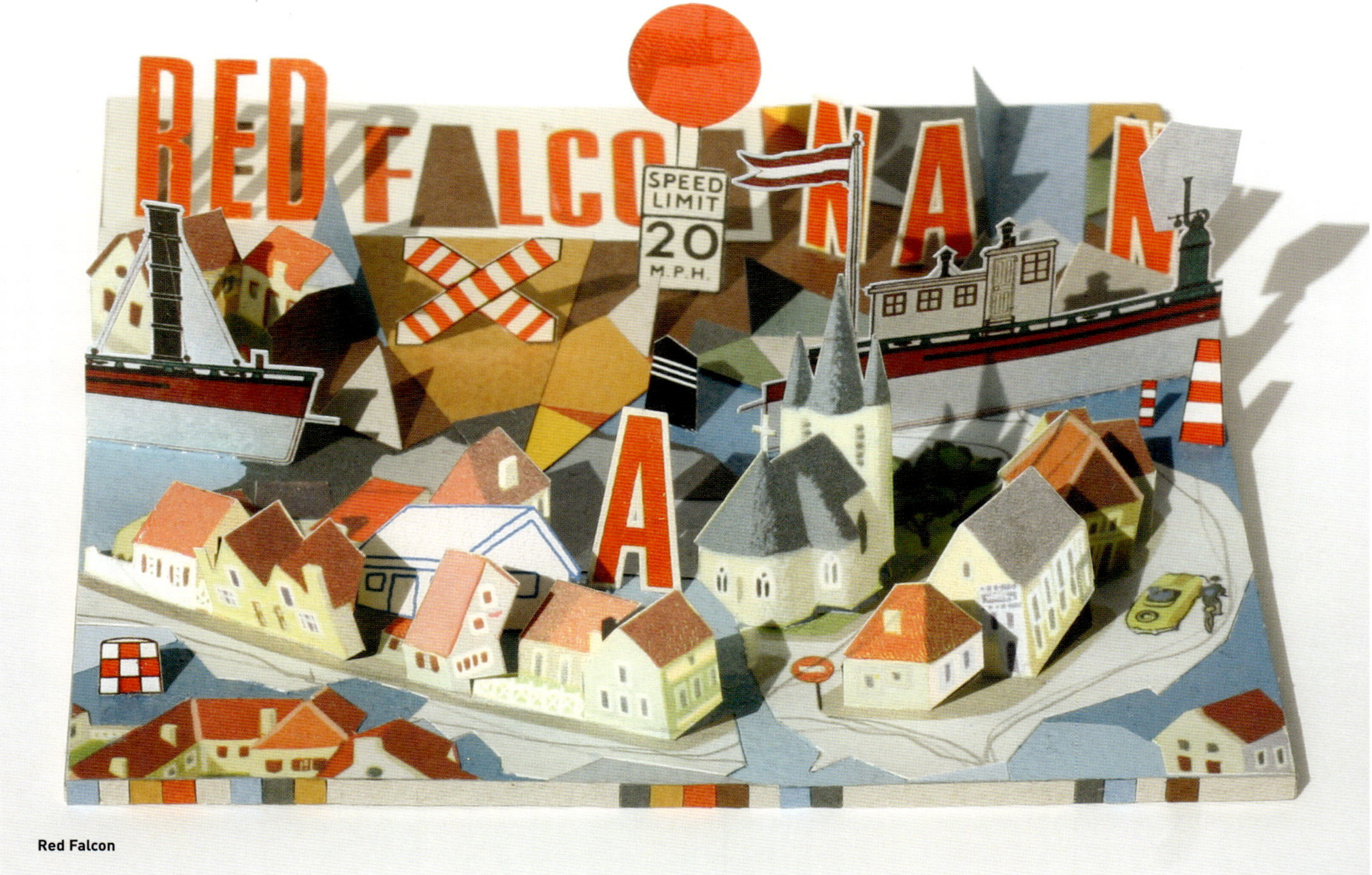


**Red Falcon**

# Sarah Bridgland

www.sarahbridgland.com

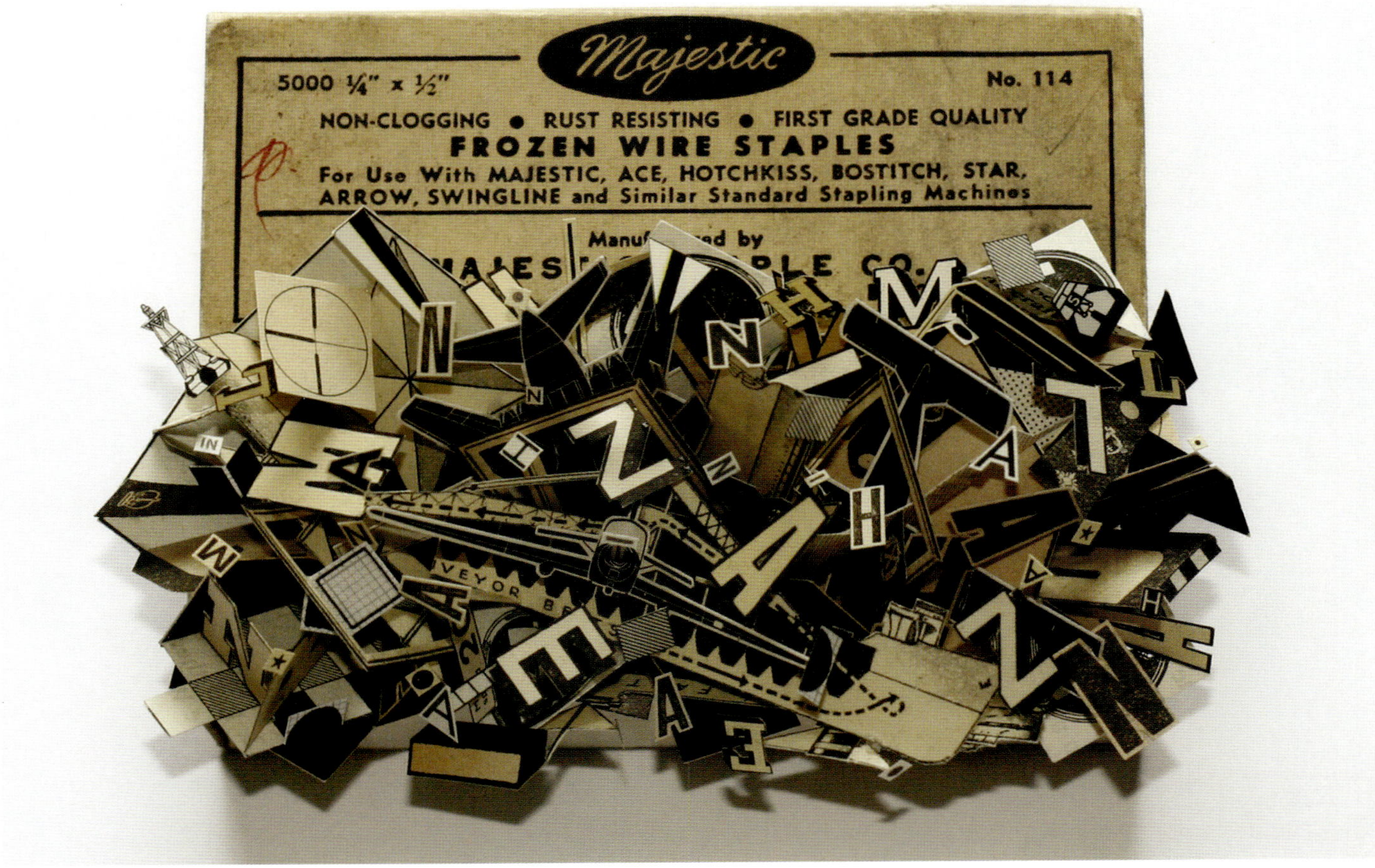


**Cut-Out Collection (Black And White)**

Sarah Bridgland's diminutive paper creations inhabit the territory between sculpture and collage. Delicately fashioned out of second-hand ephemera collected from junk shops and fragments of Bridgland's own printed media, they create spaces where the real and the imagined co-exist, where fact and fiction collide. Each piece is a myriad of textures, shapes and lettering, reflecting Bridgland's interest in the formal concerns of the Russian avant-garde and Constructivism. Bridgland is fascinated by the marriage of forms and her work celebrates this. Playful in approach, it explores the endless permutations of the cut out as a miniature type of reality. Recalling the mobile paper engineering of children's pop-up books and toy theatres it exploits the cut-out's potential to create a narrative, make-believe world, where Bridgland employs each piece as if it were an actor or a prop in a play. Rather than writing a story, though, Bridgland is interested in the way chance narratives are invoked through the arrangement of the cut-up material. Adopting a formal language, Bridgland organizes space by balancing the effects of different typefaces and graphics, textures and colours, to create a kind of three-dimensional drawing in which snippets of imagery and information invite the viewer to make their own associations, imaginary conversations between the juxtaposed forms. Exploring the intimate link between object and memory, there is a simultaneous sense of both loss and preservation in Bridgland's work. A desire to hold on to the past contends with a process that necessarily destroys it. Using forms and materials that are explicitly nostalgic, each element becomes part of a constructed history as time is re-arranged and the viewer is invited to re-experience the past in an entirely new way – half real, half imagined. The intimate scale of the work encourages daydream and reverie, heightened by wonder at its meticulous craftsmanship. Bridgland plays upon our desire to dream, creating miniature worlds made all the more enchanting by the comforting ordinariness of the their constituent parts before they spring collectively to life.

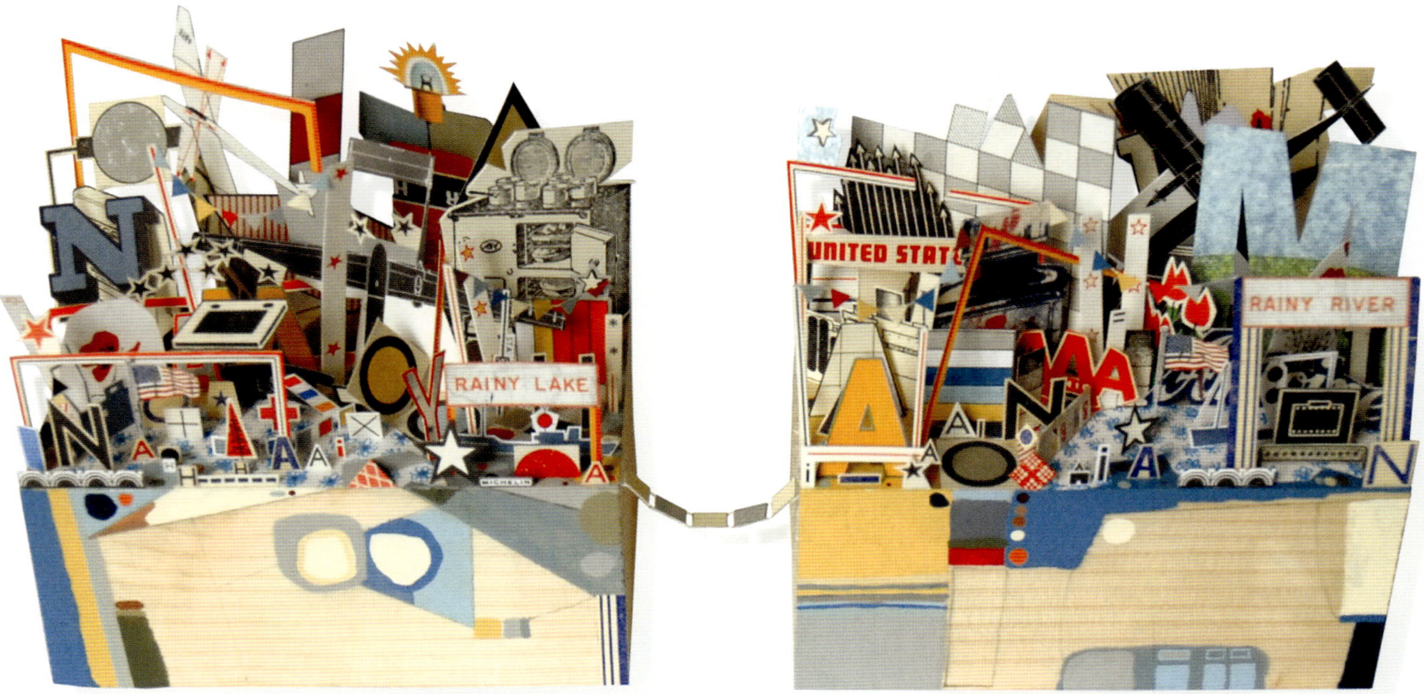


Rainy Lake

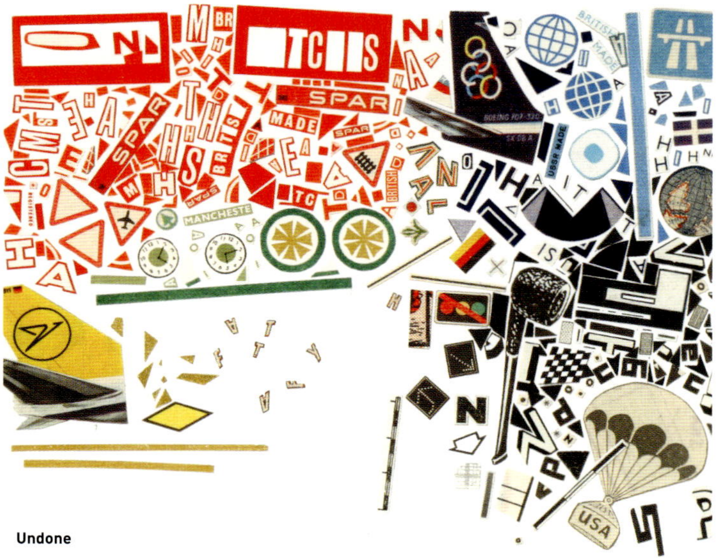


Undone

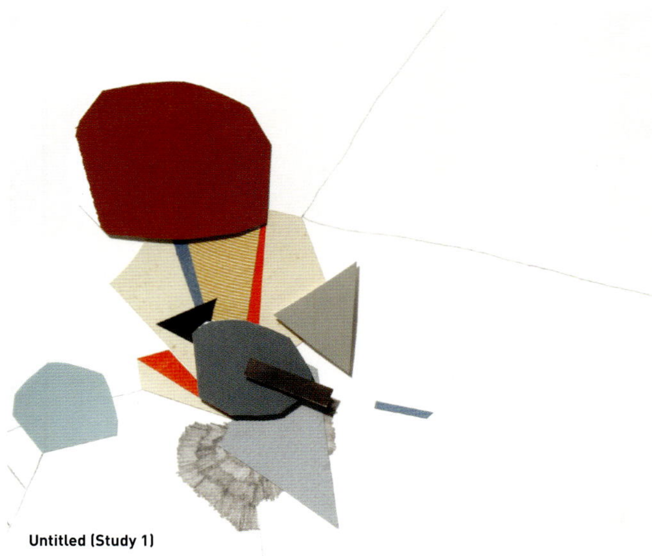

Untitled (Study 1)

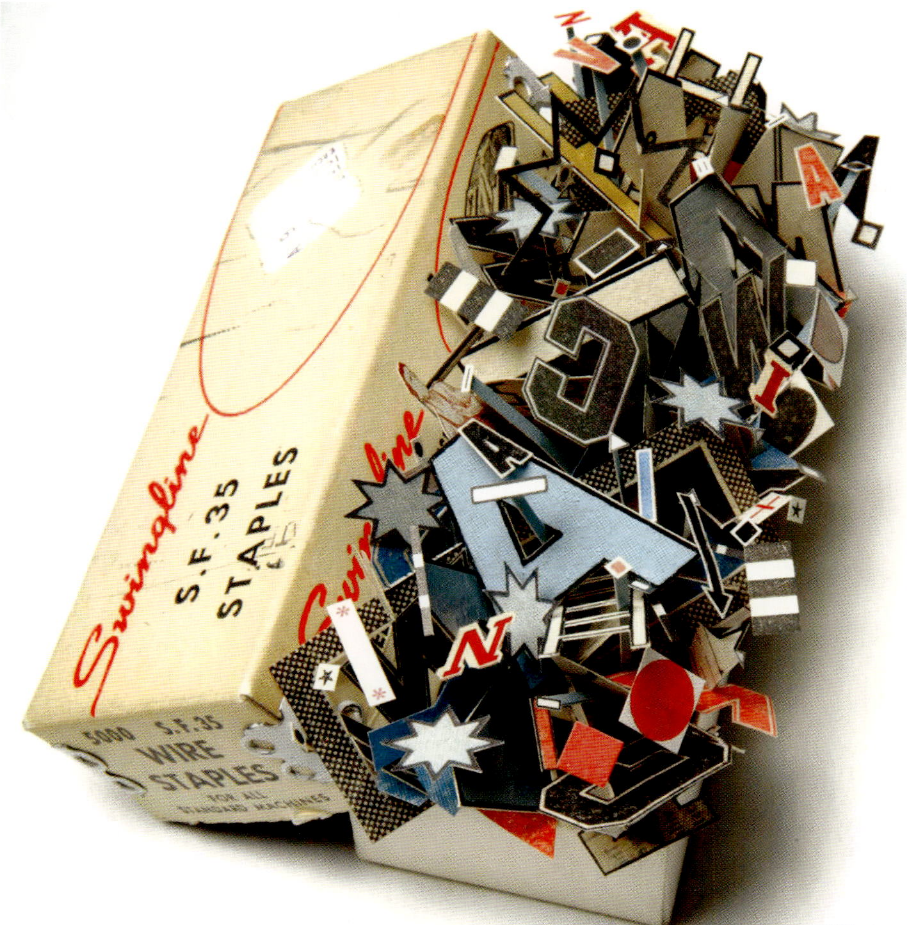


Swingline S.F.35 Staples

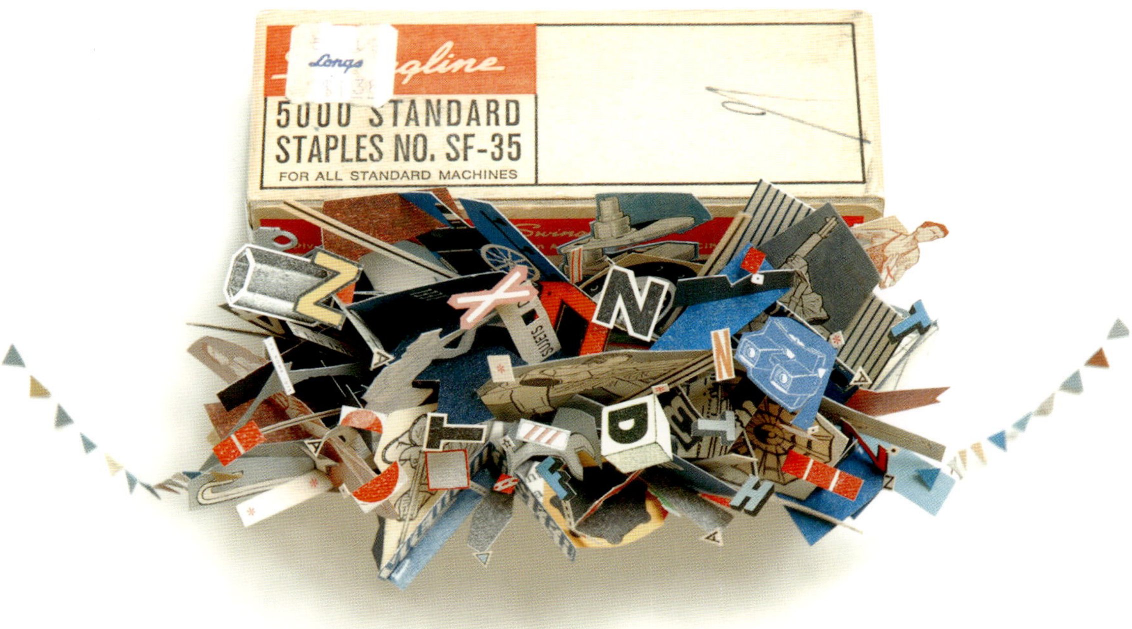


Taken It All

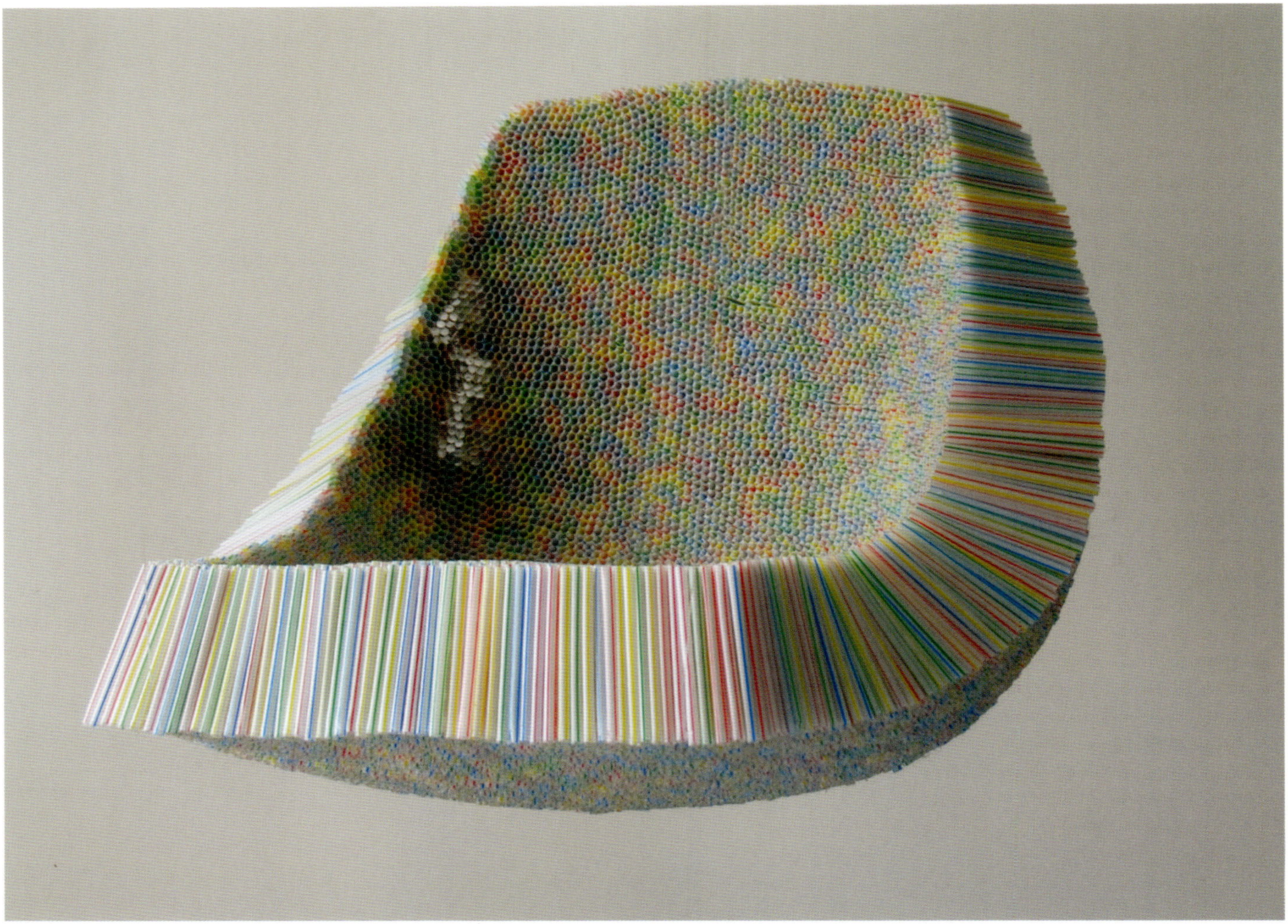

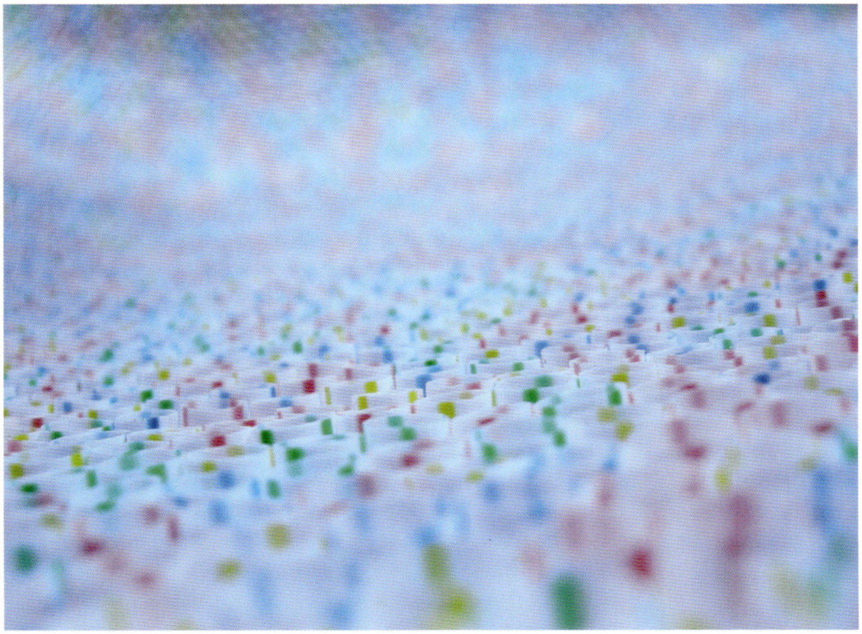

**The Clutch Chair**

Made from 10,000 drinking straws, the Clutch Chair is an exploratory research piece that passes comment on our disposable culture. The development process of this piece also informed that of the Clutch Light, both of which were developed from an observation of the structural characteristics of trees. This piece was selected by Zaha Hadid as her Curators Choice at Noise Festeval 2008. The Clutch Project began as a microscopic observation of the structural composition of trees and the directional properties of Capillary tubes (xylem). Details of the seating surface of the Clutch Chair - Ubiquitous drinking straws are grouped and transformed into a primitive spot light. The reflective inner surface of the straw transmits the light in a directional manner creating a jewelesque effect.

# Scott Jarvie

www.scottjarvie.co.uk

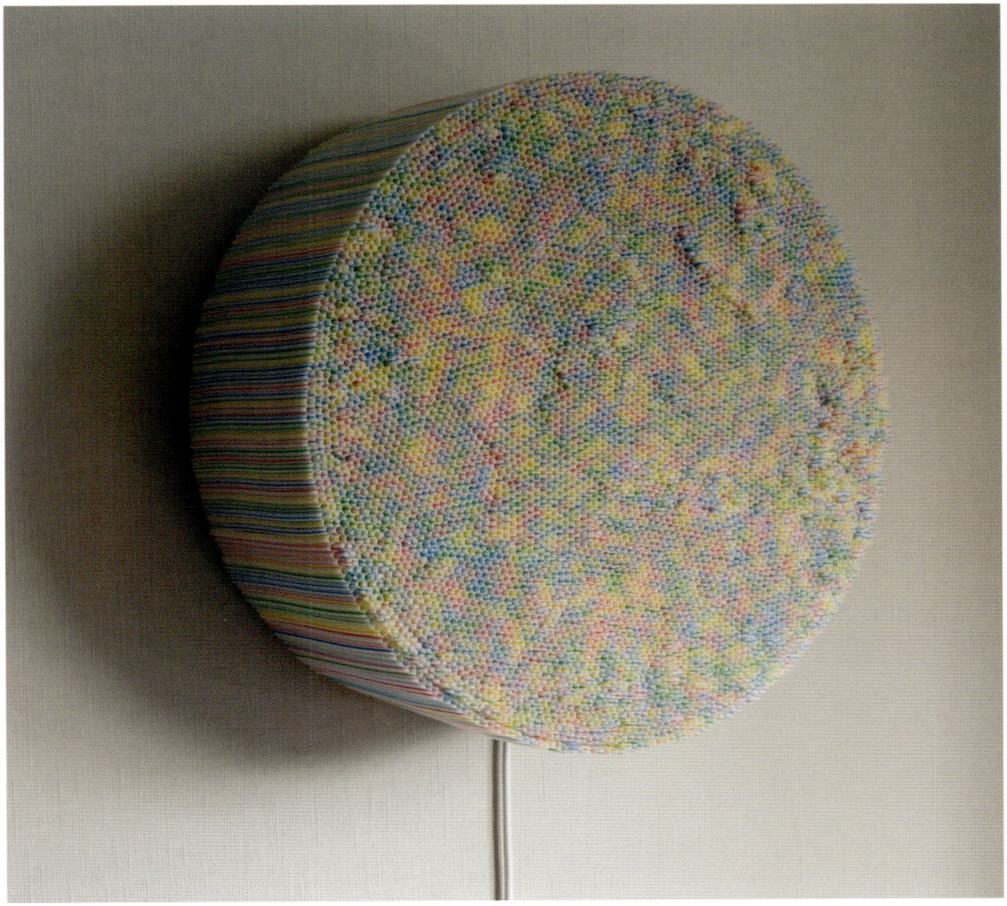

Scott Jarvie runs a multi-disciplinary design consultancy that engages in product, furniture, spatial and graphic design projects. Jarvie believes that the solution to any design problem can be assimilated by creative interrogation, research and thought. It is this thinking process that equips Jarvie with the necessary apparatus to create works that are attuned to the project requirements whilst creating proposals that are not marred by preconception. It is this free thinking process that invites solutions to present themselves, regardless of the restrictions traditionally associated with the narrow definitions of the various disciplines. The son of a graphic designer and an automotive engineer, Scott Jarvie was born in Glasgow, Scotland in 1983.

Having studied at Glasgow's College of Building and Printing, Jarvie proceeded to study Product Design at Napier University's School of Design and Media Arts. Scott graduated with first class honors and was awarded the University Medal. Jarvie is a vigorous artist and designer who is constantly generating and pursuing ideas that span all creative disciplines. He holds the firm belief that creativity is the transferable application that facilitates all progressions, both tangible and cerebral.

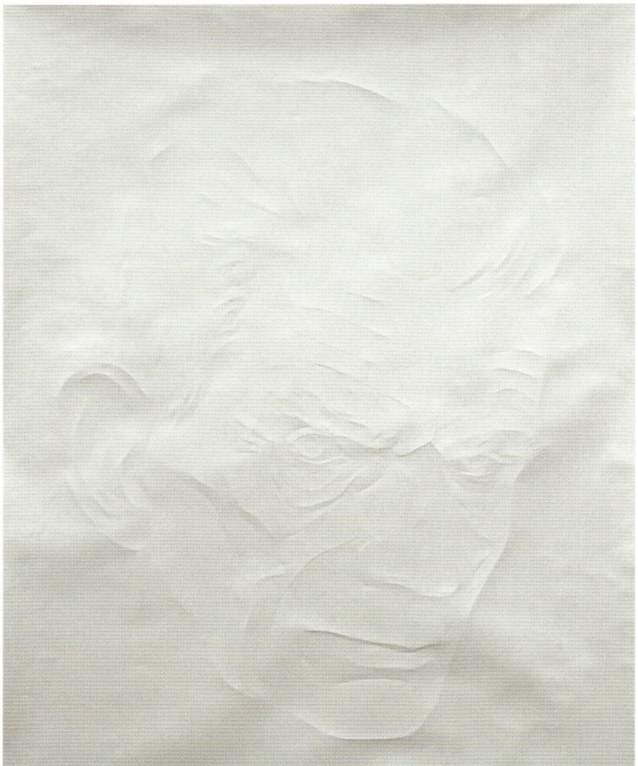

o.T. (Samuel Beckett), 2008
Paper, 100 x 75 cm | 39.4 x 29.5 "

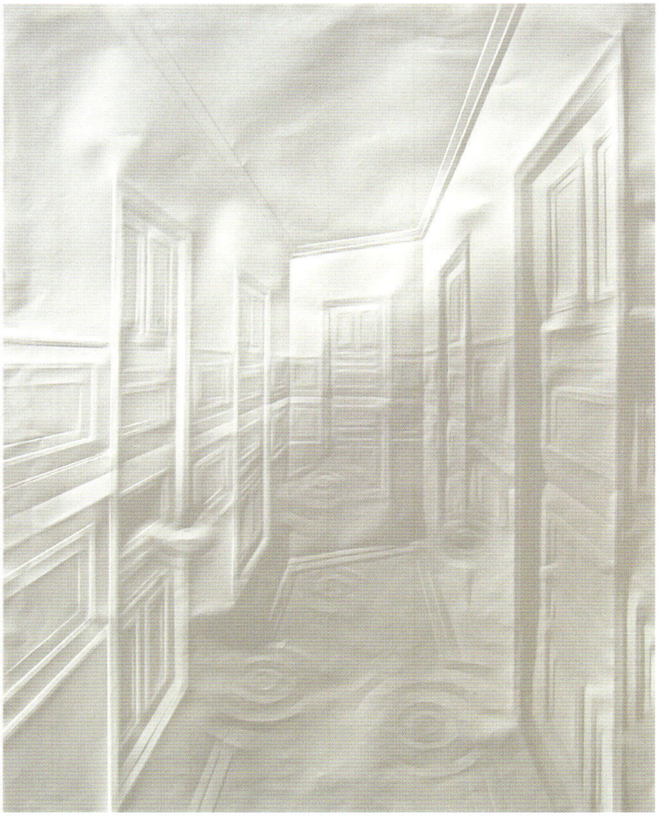

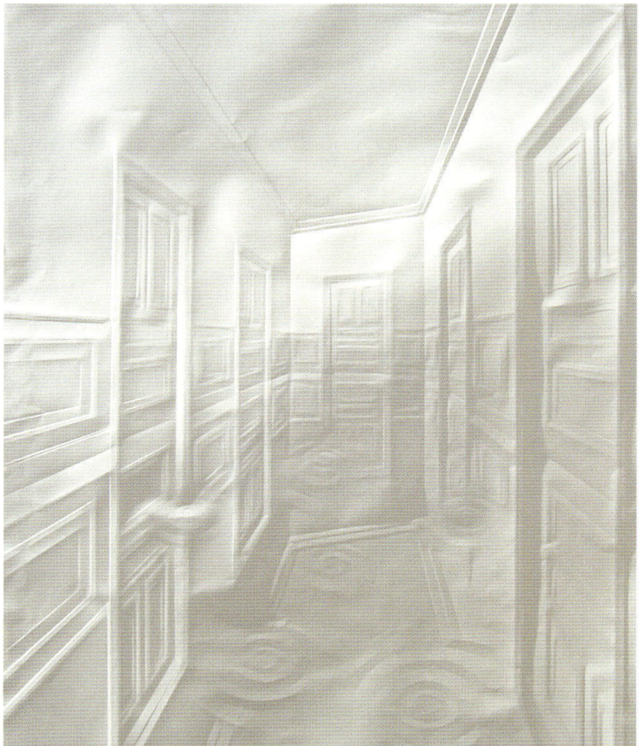

o.T. (verzerrter Flur gespiegelt), 2009
Paper, 100 x 75 cm | 39.4 x 29.5 "

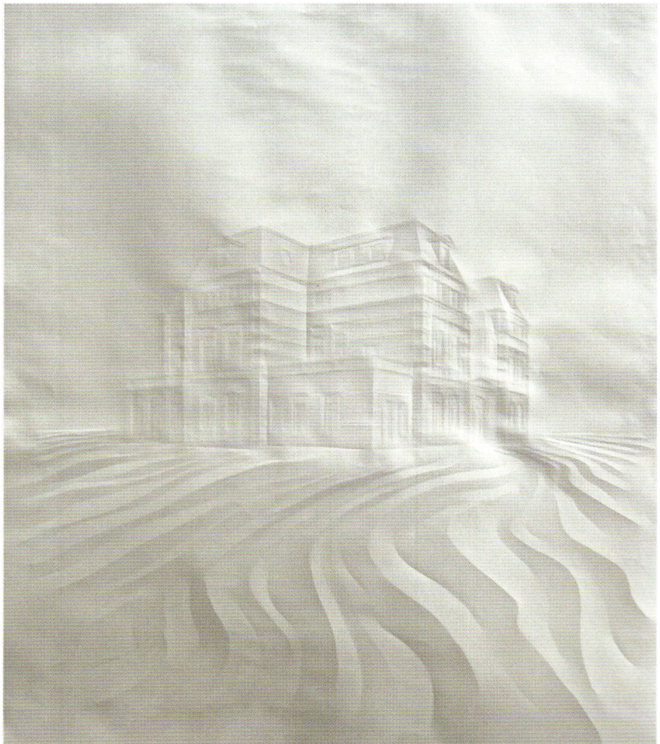

o.T.(Villa Z.), 2009
Paper, 100 x 75 cm | 39.4 x 29.5 "

# Simon Schubert

www.simonshubert.de

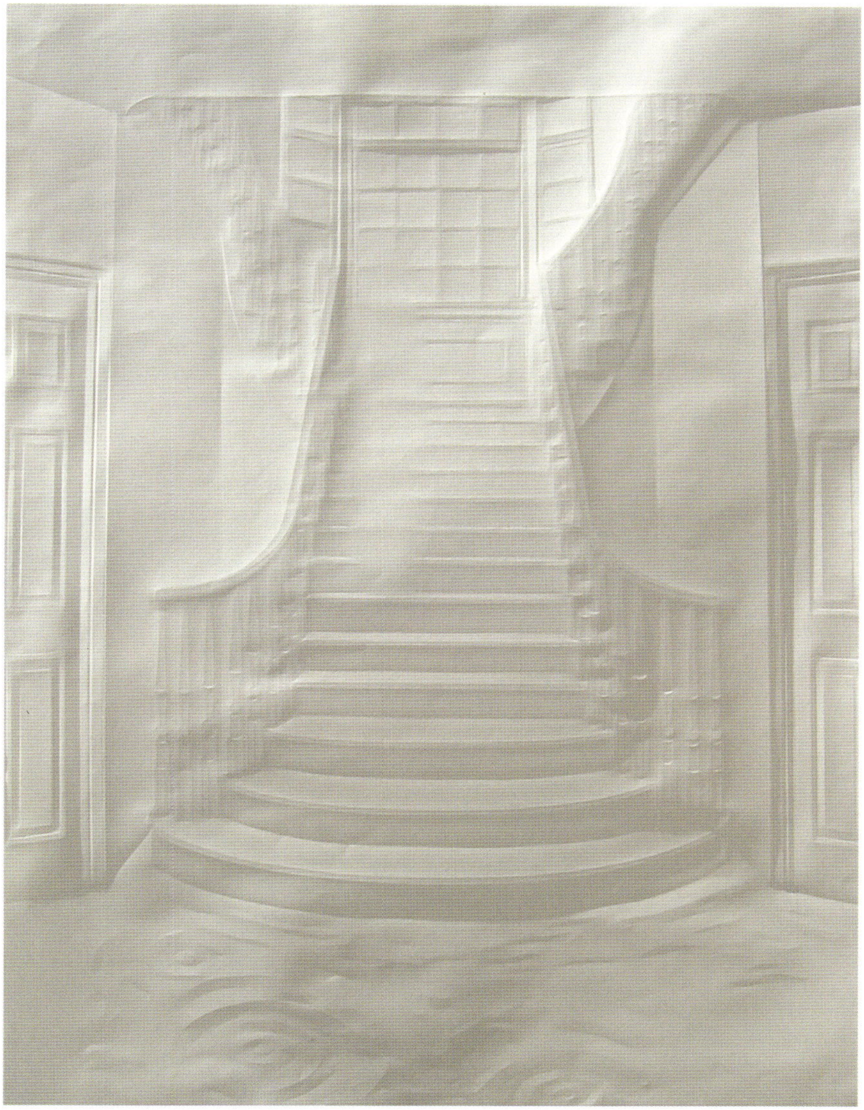

o.T. (Treppe aus dem Wasser), 2009
Paper, 100 x 75 cm | 39.4 x 29.5 "

The artist Simon Schubert (born 1976) graduated in 2004 from Duesseldorf Art Academy, where he was a post graduate in the master class of Professor Irmin Kamp. He was awarded the ZVAB Phoenix Art Prize for his work in 2008. Schubert, who mentions authors Samuel Beckett and Edgar Allan Poe as his main influences, deals with the most existential and fundamental questions. Loneliness, isolation, loss and disappearance are the recurring issues in his paper works and sculptures. The mysterious and unsettling atmosphere in his works confronts the viewer with subconscious fears and anxieties. Simon Schubert folds and creases sheets of paper in an extraordinary technique, adding a three dimensional quality to it without any graphical aid. In a complex process of folding the German artist creates lines, angles and even circles raised several millimetres. In the play of light they suddenly appear as views of stately homes with coffered ceilings, long corridors, staircases and halls with mirrors. The rooms are inhabited by hidden human figures whose ghost-like shadows seem to enter or leave the scene.

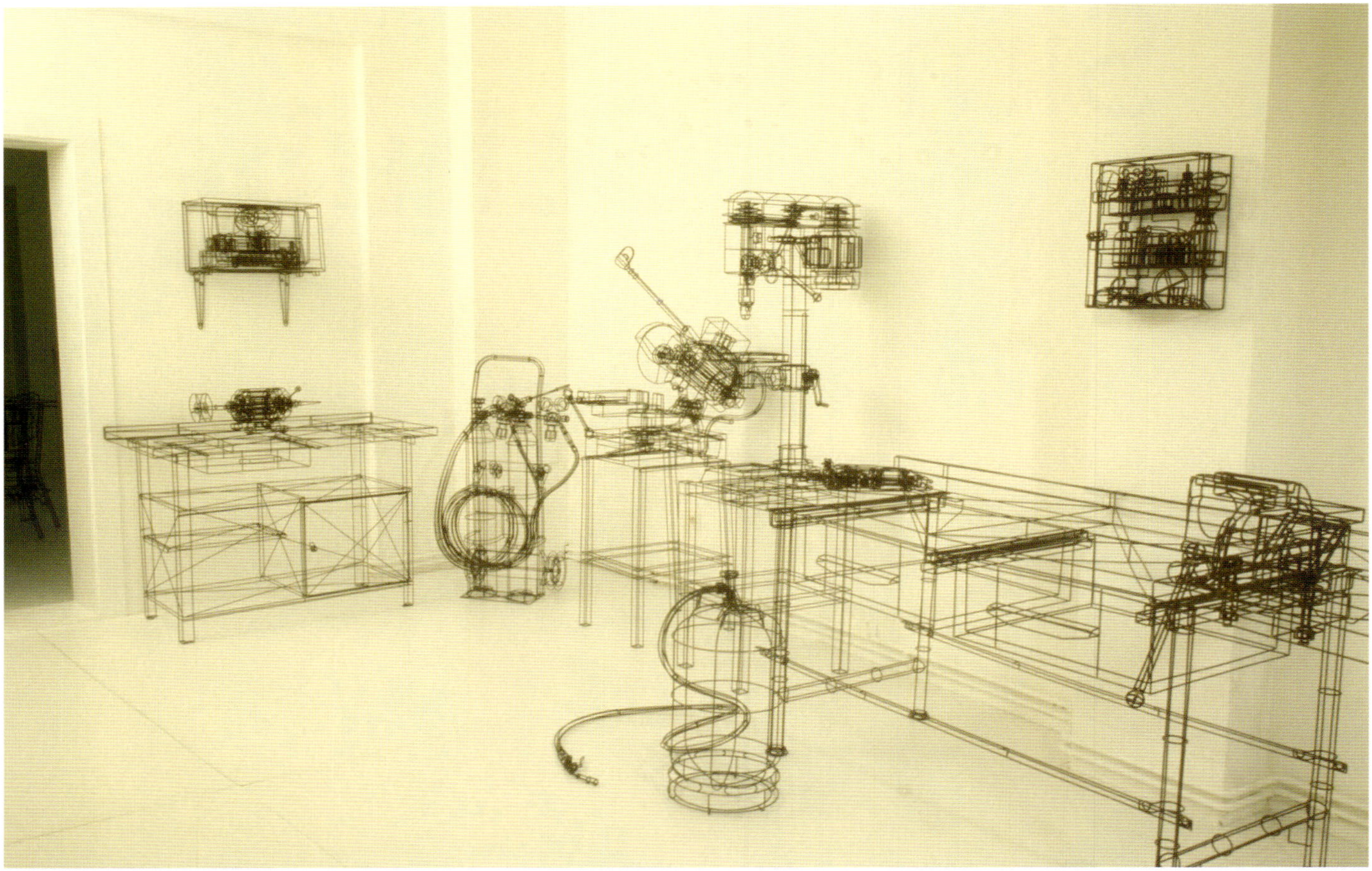

Lastwagen 2001 Eisendraht, gelötet 12 x 31 x 13

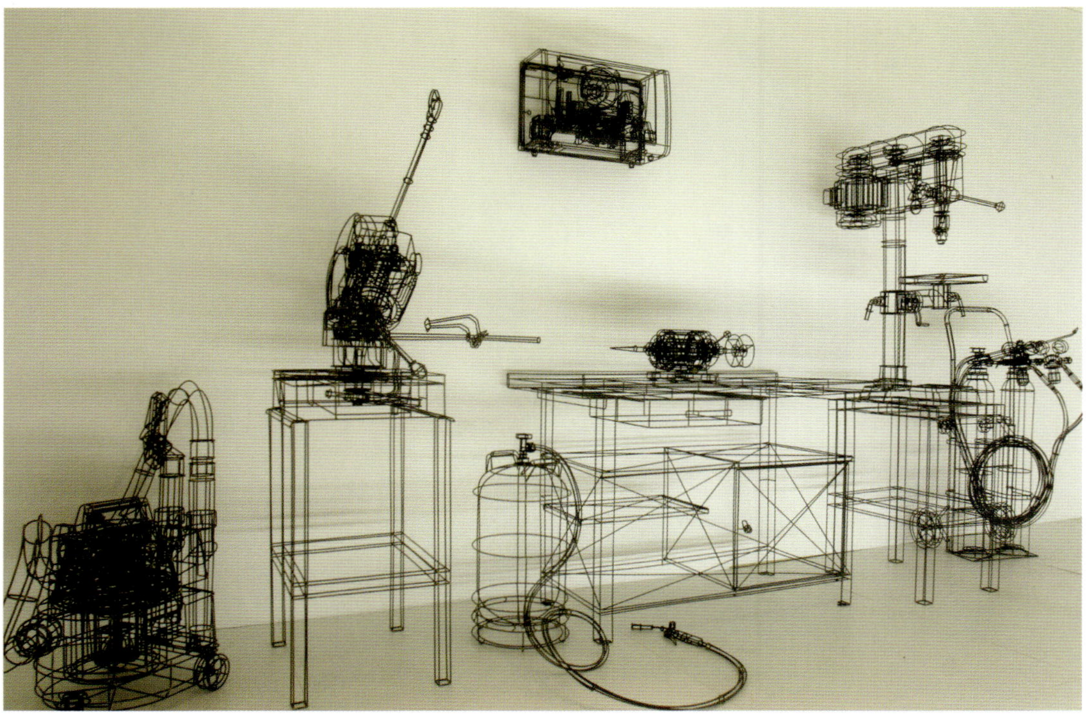

# Thomas / Raschke

www.thomasraschke.de

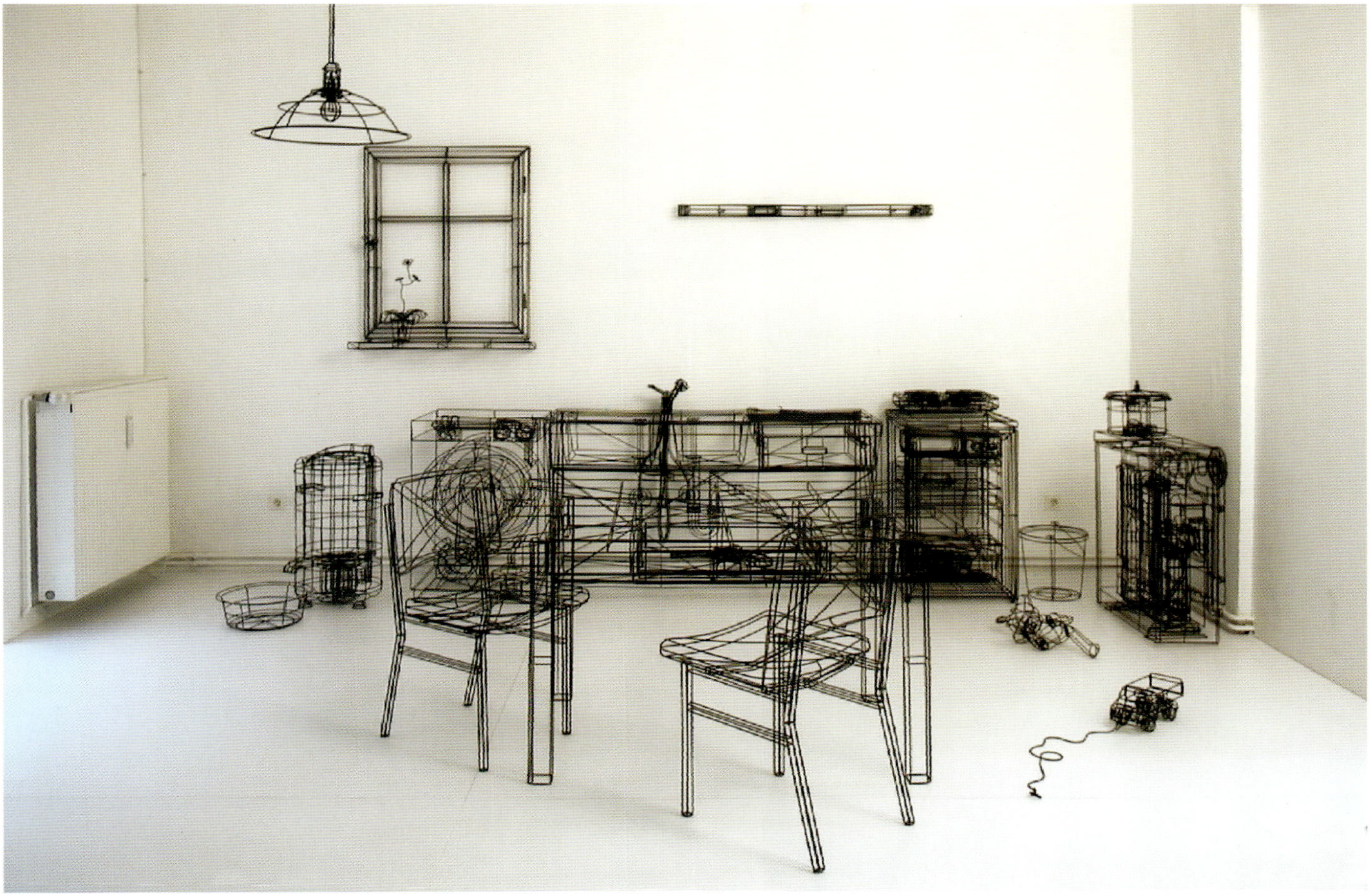

**Kalaschnikow 2002 Eisendraht, gelötet 34 x 6 x 96**

What is it? A kitchen made from wire-frame sculptures. Listen up: this is real. Thomas Raschke doesn't fool around with computer renderings. What's more, the whole idea is to mystify and confuse observers with wire sculptures that visitors are encouraged to touch. Raschke and wire have been inseparable for a couple of decades now. He recalls seeing his first wire frame at the age of 18 - on the screen of a CNC machine - as if it were yesterday. 'A screen filled with nothing but rotating lines.' It took him more than 20 years to answer the question he asked himself at that moment. 'Can I do what the computer is doing?' The answer was yes. For Thomas Raschke, a native of Berlin currently living in Stockholm, art is a question of unremitting labour, of bending and welding and endless patience. 'A table and chair take me about six weeks to complete'. His work has nothing to do with special 3D software. As he begins a project, there's not even a sketchbook in sight, because Raschke makes everything full scale and true to life the first time around. Like the refrigerator that the artist approached with a ruler, taking care to get the measurements exactly right, looking, contemplating, absorbing every angle and opening in preparation for copying the appliance in wire as precisely as possible. The accompanying sketch is the final step, like an afterthought, made when the piece has been completed. It's totally opposite to the process you'd expect him to follow. Raschke loves throwing us off balance. The wire sculptures are his way of flirting with reality. 'I look at it as a bet with the computer. And you know what? I'm the winner. I've done it!' We're not the first to be confronted with Raschke as the crazed creative – a euphoric sculptor who abandoned a career as a goldsmith in his search for more artistic freedom.

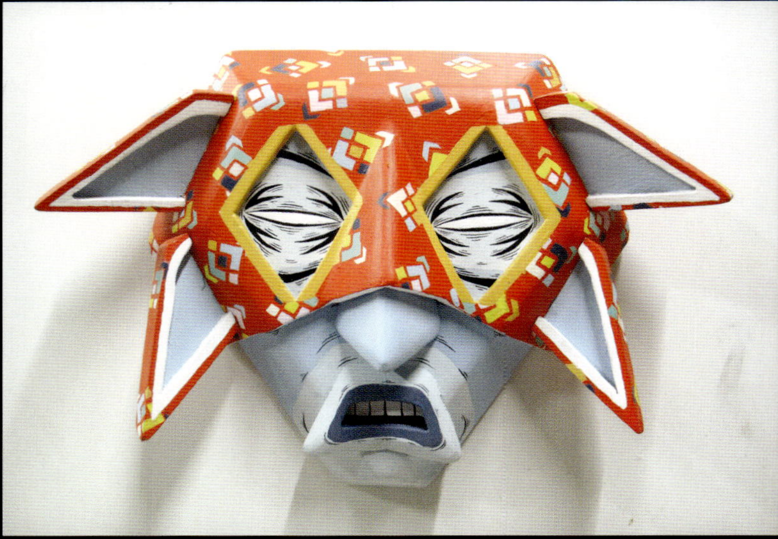

**Bad Brains #2**
and ink on Wooden sculptured mask
26cm x 28cm – 2009

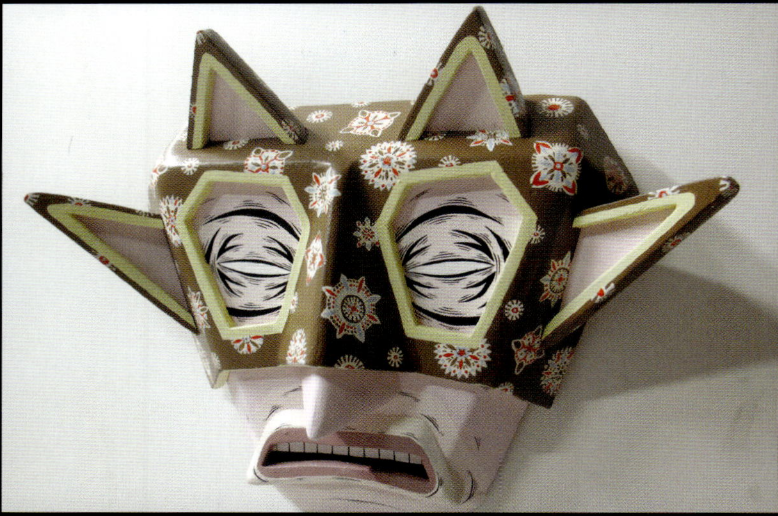

**Bad Brains #3**
and ink on Wooden sculptured mask
26cm x 28cm – 2009

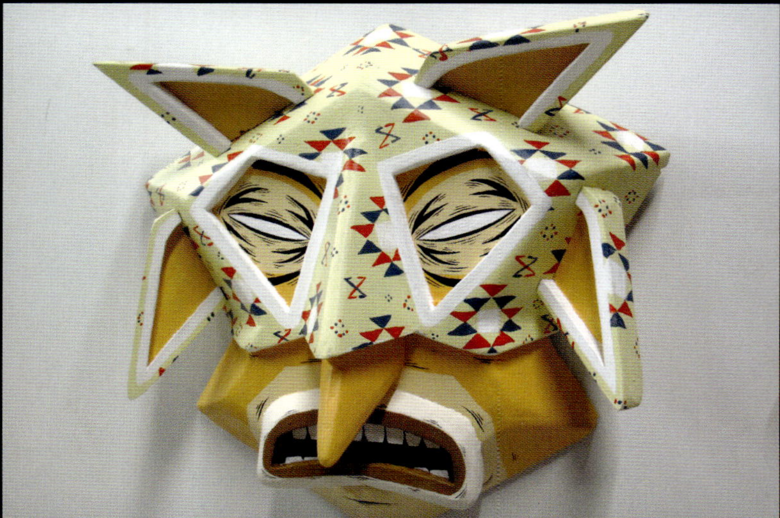

**Bad Brains #4**
and ink on Wooden sculptured mask
26cm x 28cm – 2009

# Trent Whitehead

www.trentwhitehead.com

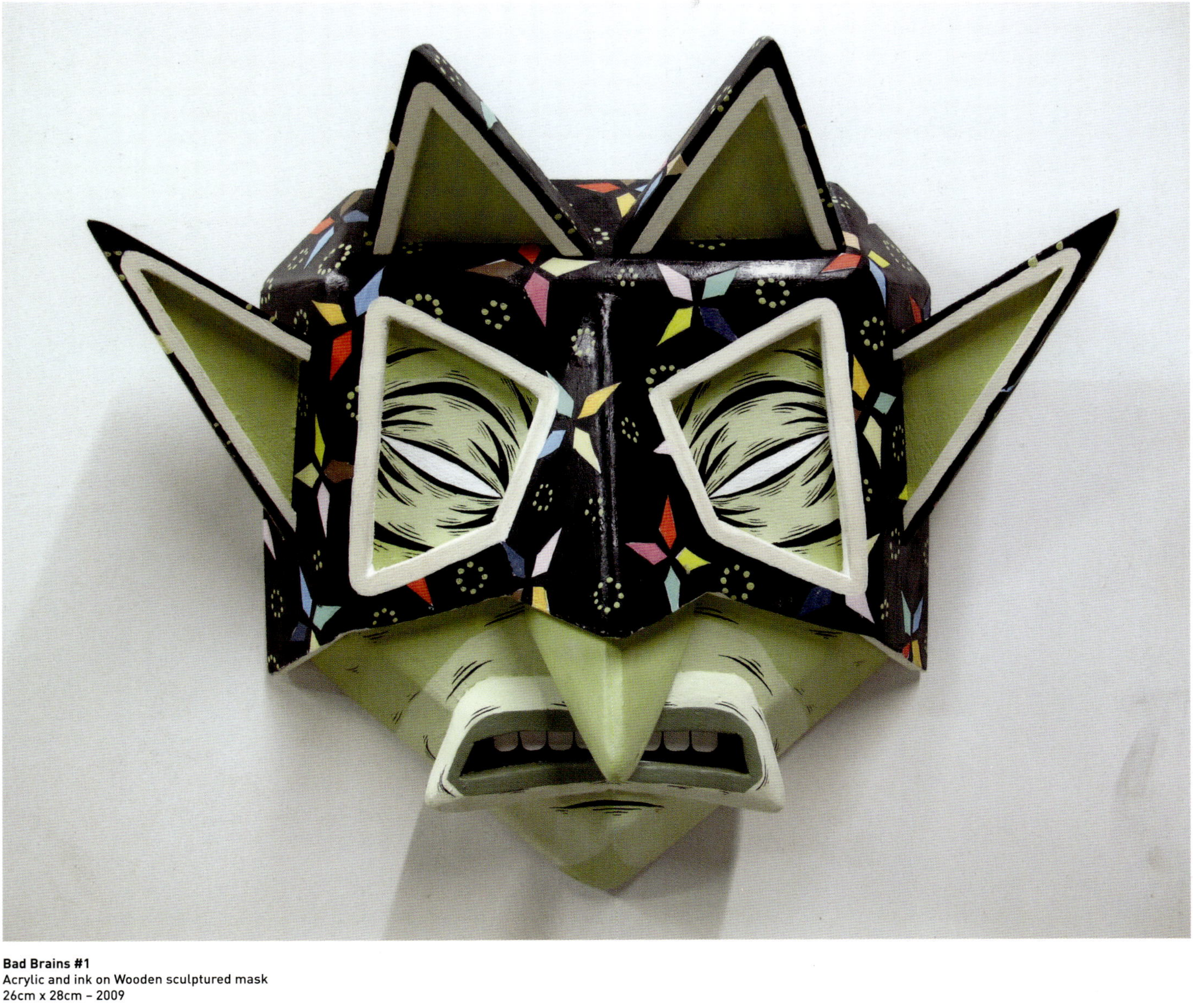

**Bad Brains #1**
Acrylic and ink on Wooden sculptured mask
26cm x 28cm – 2009

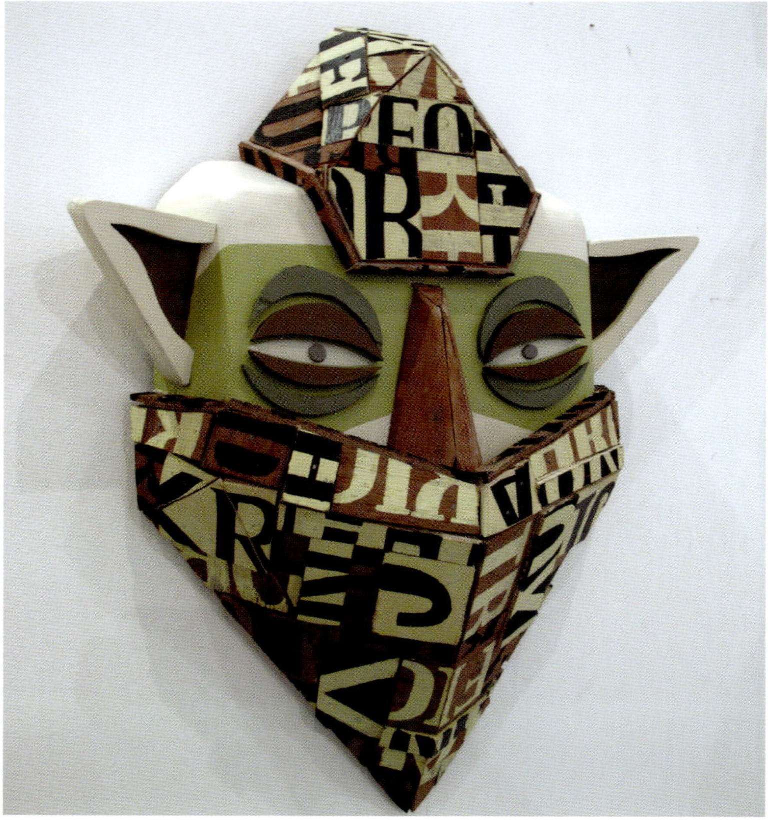

**Banditos #1**
Acrylic and ink on Wooden sculptured mask
42cm x 34cm – 2009

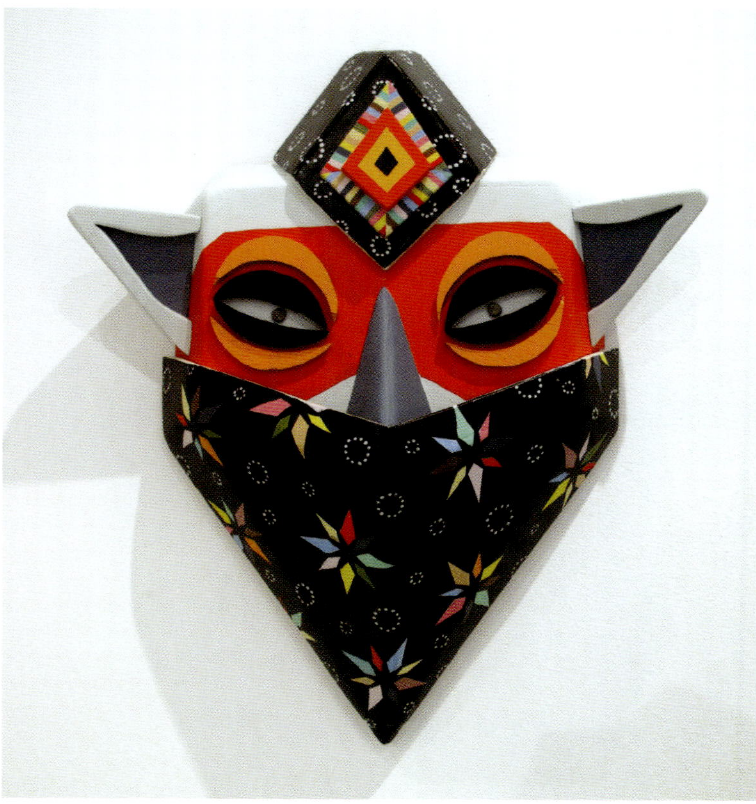

**Banditos #2**
Acrylic and ink on Wooden sculptured mask
42cm x 34cm – 2009

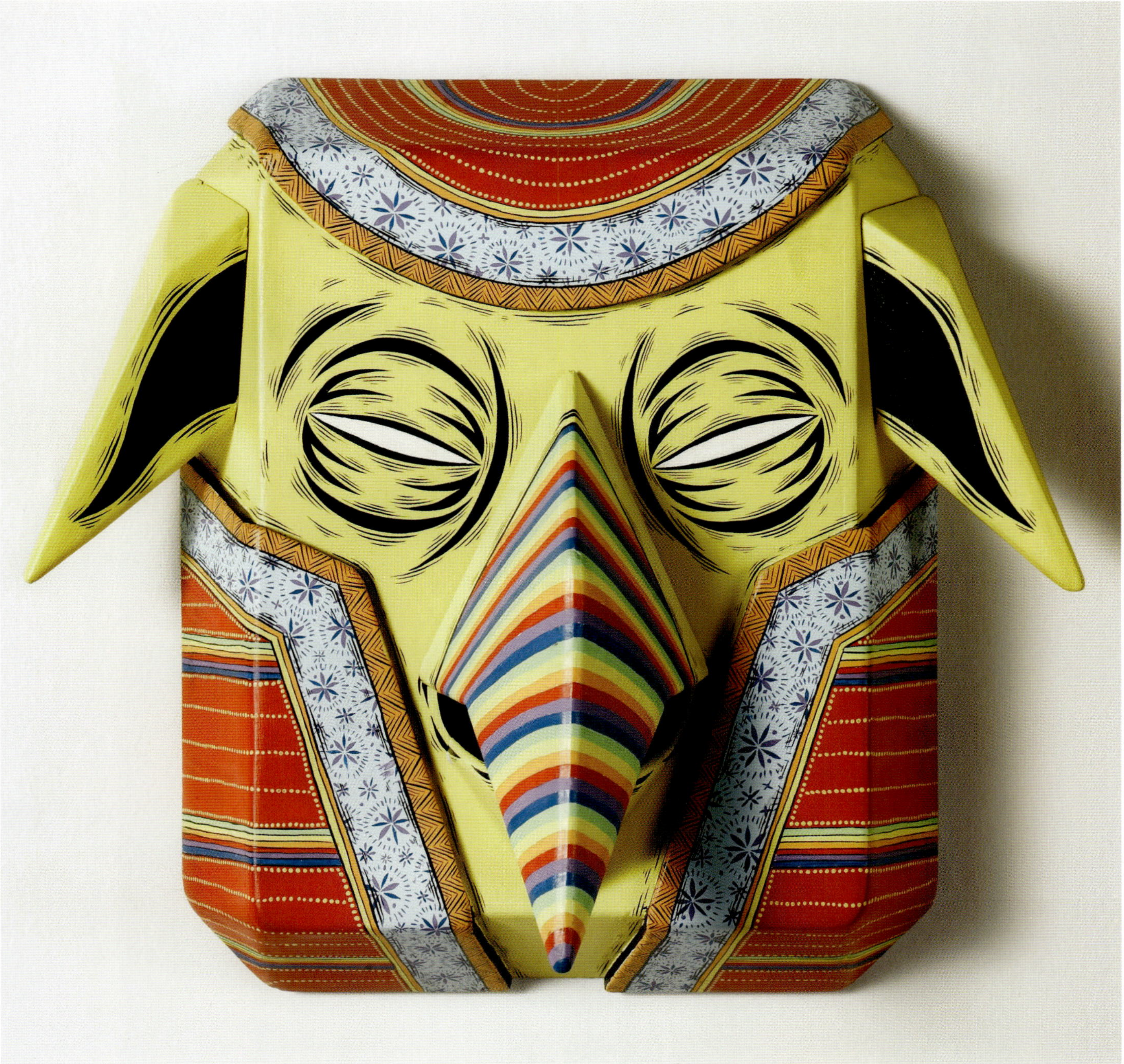

**Yellow**
Acrylic and ink on Wooden sculptured mask – 2008

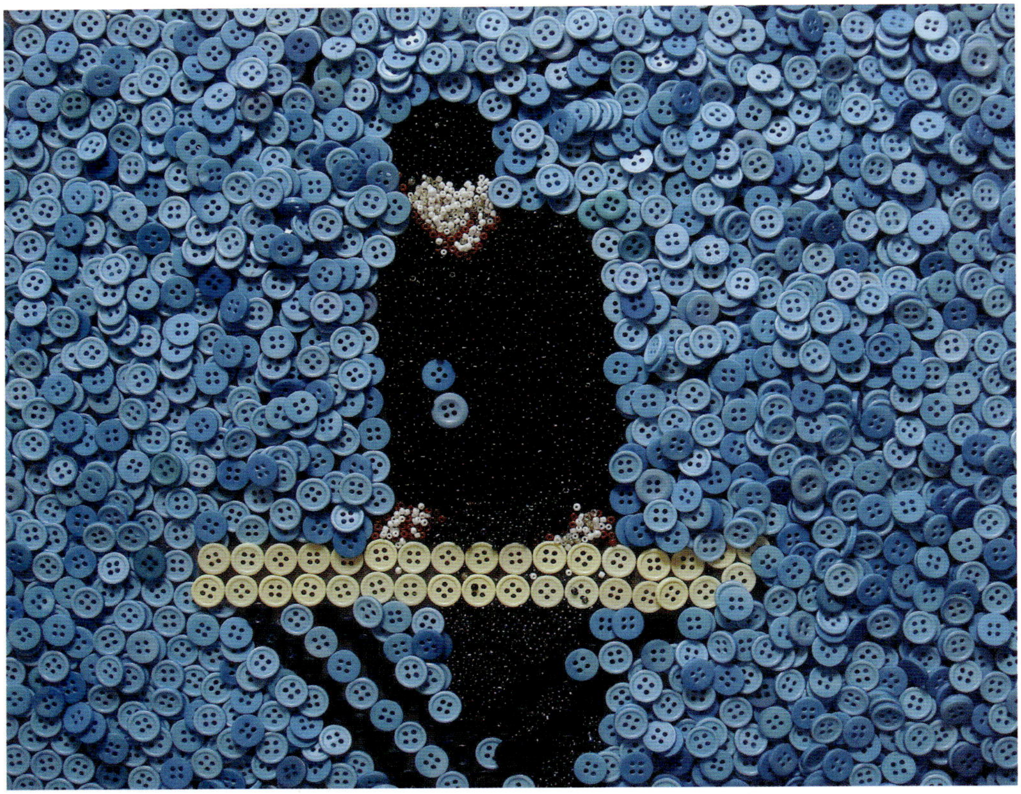

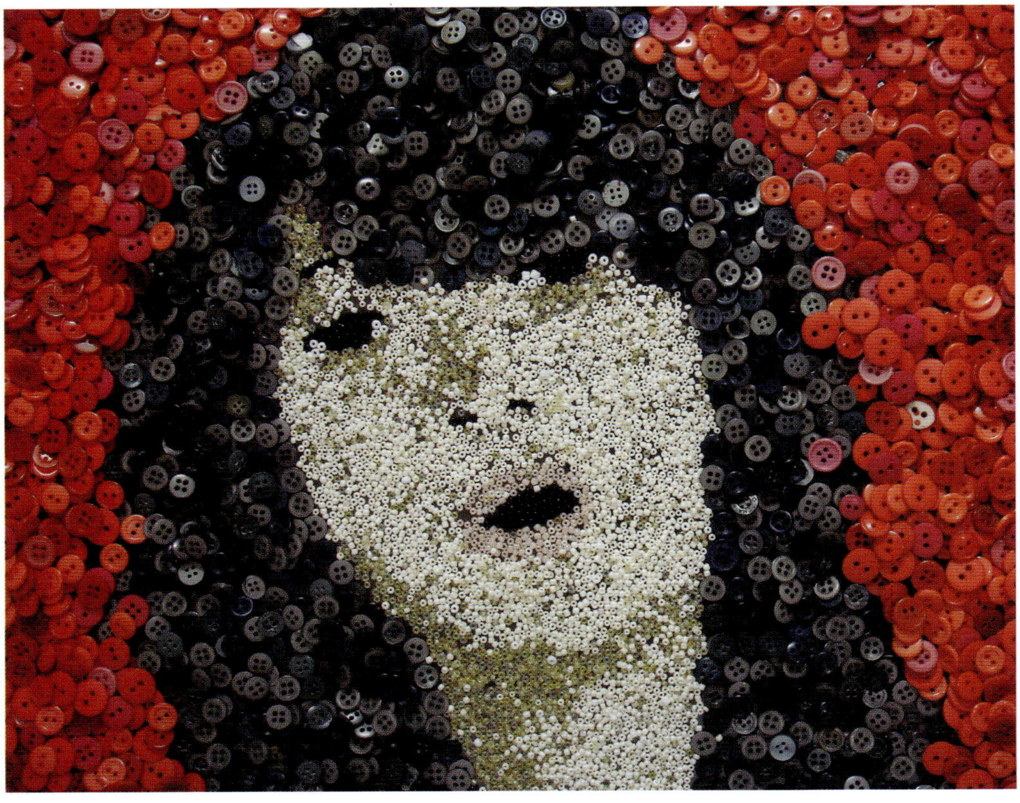

**Zsa Zsa Zsu,** 2007
Stop motion animation with buttons and beads
Duration: 00:04:52

# Tromarama

http://tromaram.blogspot.com

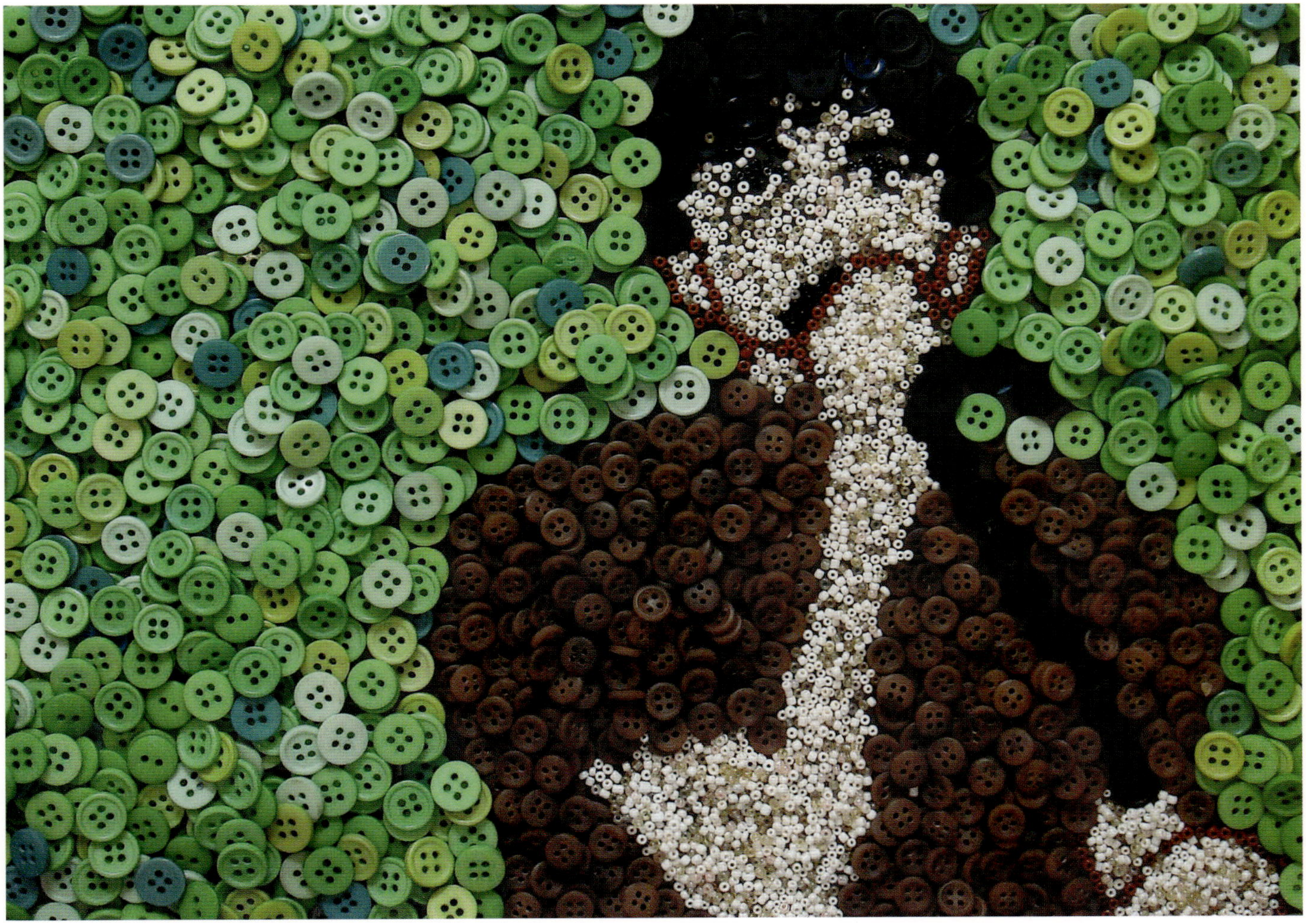

**Zsa Zsa Zsu**, 2007
Stop motion animation with buttons and beads
Duration: 00:04:52

A video art group, founded in Bandung, Indonesia at 2004 by the three members: Febie Babyrose, Herbert Hans Maruli and Ruddy Hatumena. We started our career, doing music video clips commissioned by our musician friends. Using a simple, yet laborious technique of stop-motion video editing, with plywood board in woodcut technique. We tried to combine our imageries made out of woodcuts, buttons, color paper collage, or even mugs, plates and bowls. Trying to push music video clips into an independent stand alone video art piece, and hope to bring video art closer into a popular culture environment. For Tromarama, art is a playground--a place where we're free to imagine what inside our minds. We love to imagine our daily things moving as if they're alive ( that's why we loved using stop-motion technique). It's like everything got a second chance being something they're not meant to be, even the tinniest part of this world and unnoticed things have a story. Febie Babyrose: Jakarta, 5 February 1985, Graduated from Faculty of Visual Arts and Design,Bandung Institute of Technology, Printmaking Studio (2008) Herbert Hans Maruli: Jakarta, 28 April 1984, Graduated from Faculty of Visual Arts and Design, Bandung Institute of Technology, Visual Communication Design (2008) Ruddy Alexander Hatumena: Bahrain, 14 September 1984, Graduated from Faculty of Visual Arts and Design, Bandung Institute of Technology, Visual Communication Design (2007)

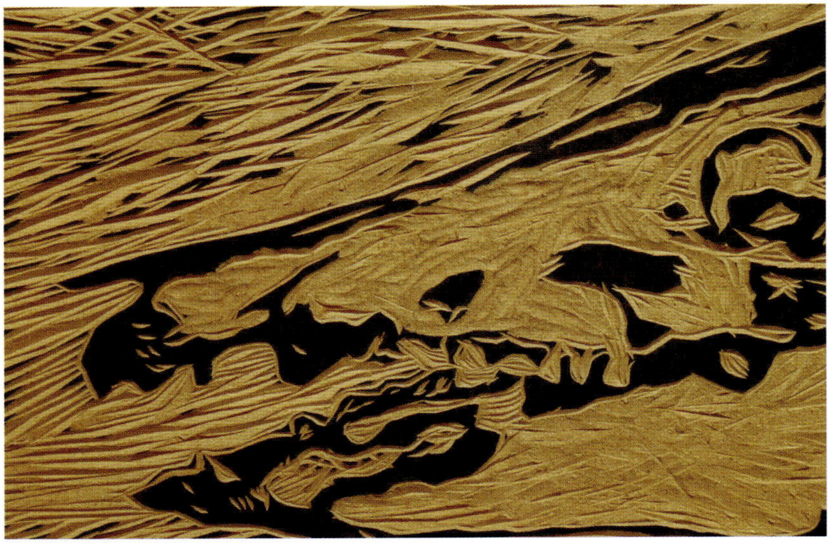

**Serigala Militia**, 2006
Stop motion animation with wood cut plywood
Duration: 00:04:32

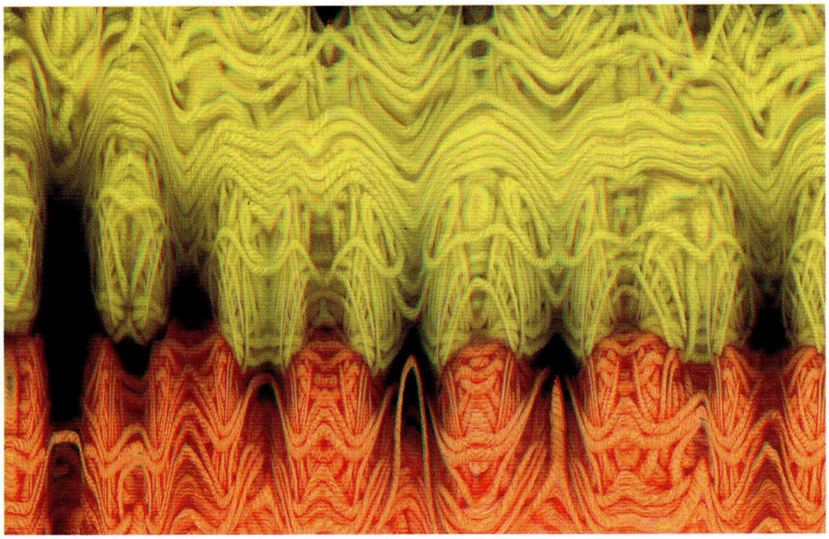

**3000ex**, 2009
Stop motion animation with
wool thread
Duration: 00:01:41

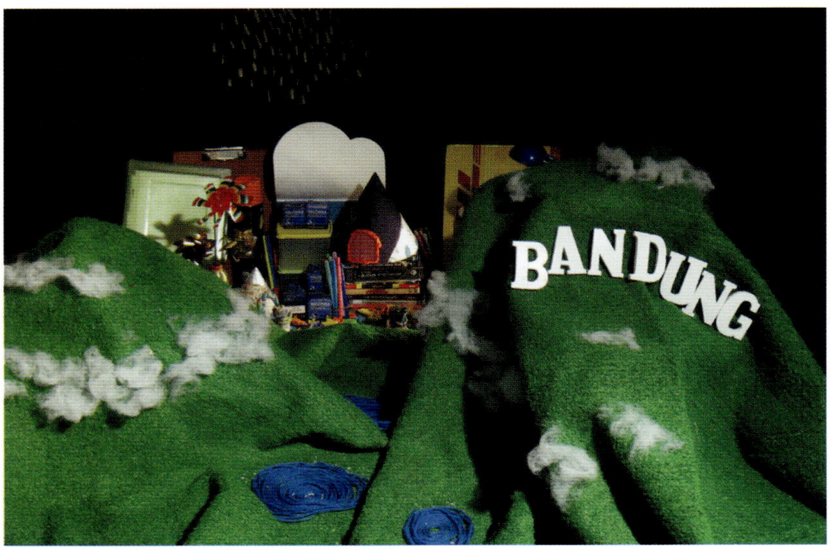


**BDG ART NOW**, 2009
Stop motion animation with various media
Duration: 00:05:15

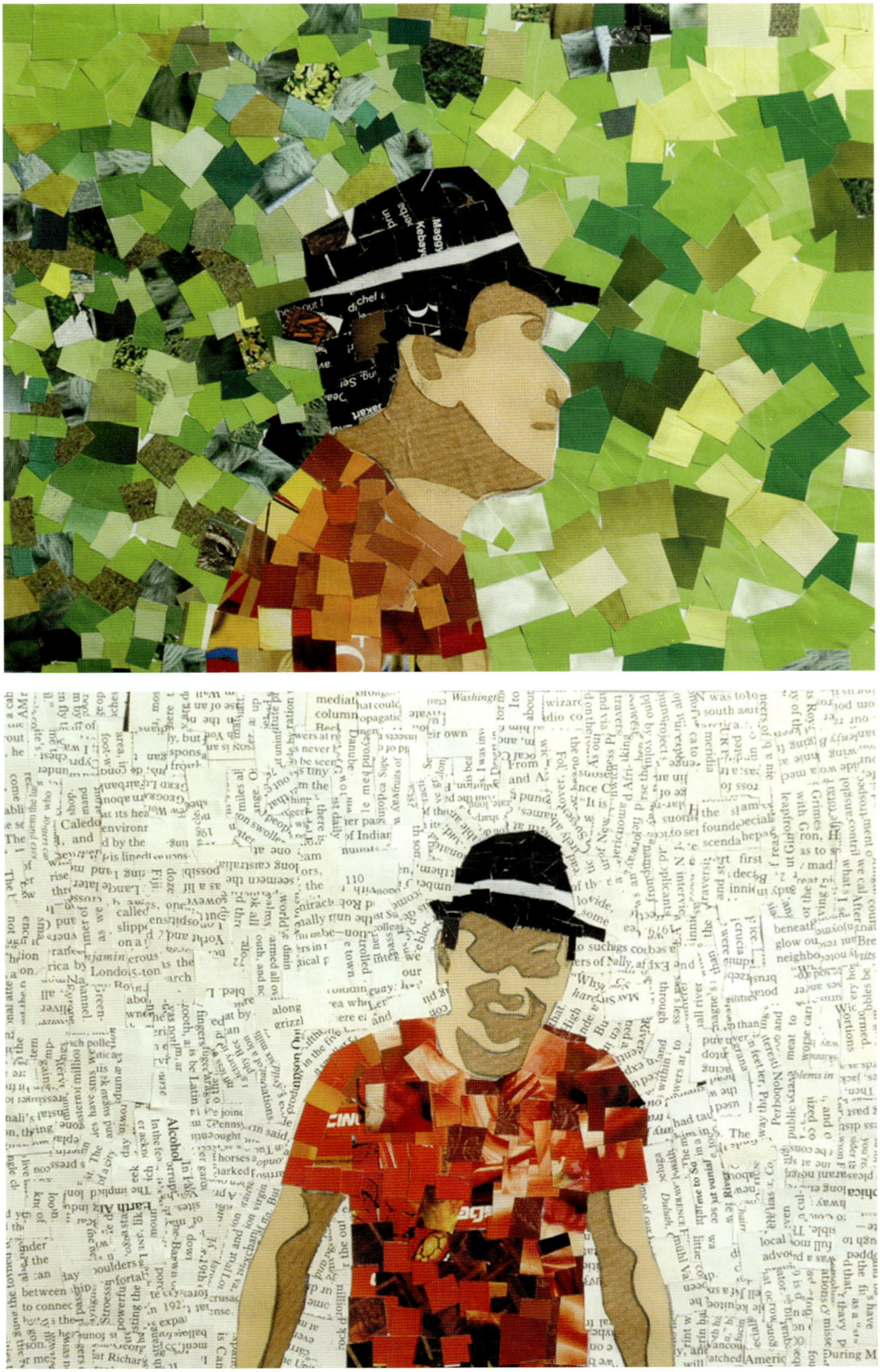

**Balonku,** 2007
Stop motion animation with paper collage.
Duration: 00:01:26

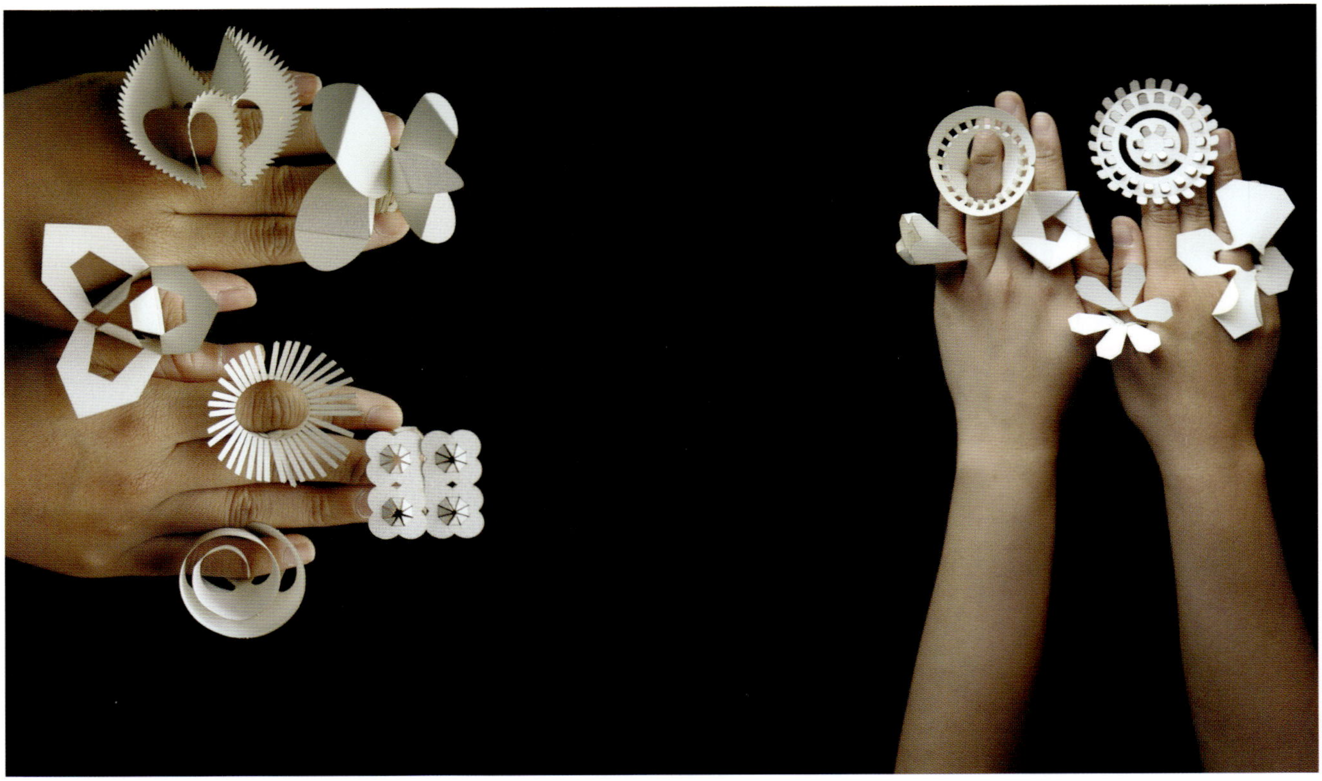

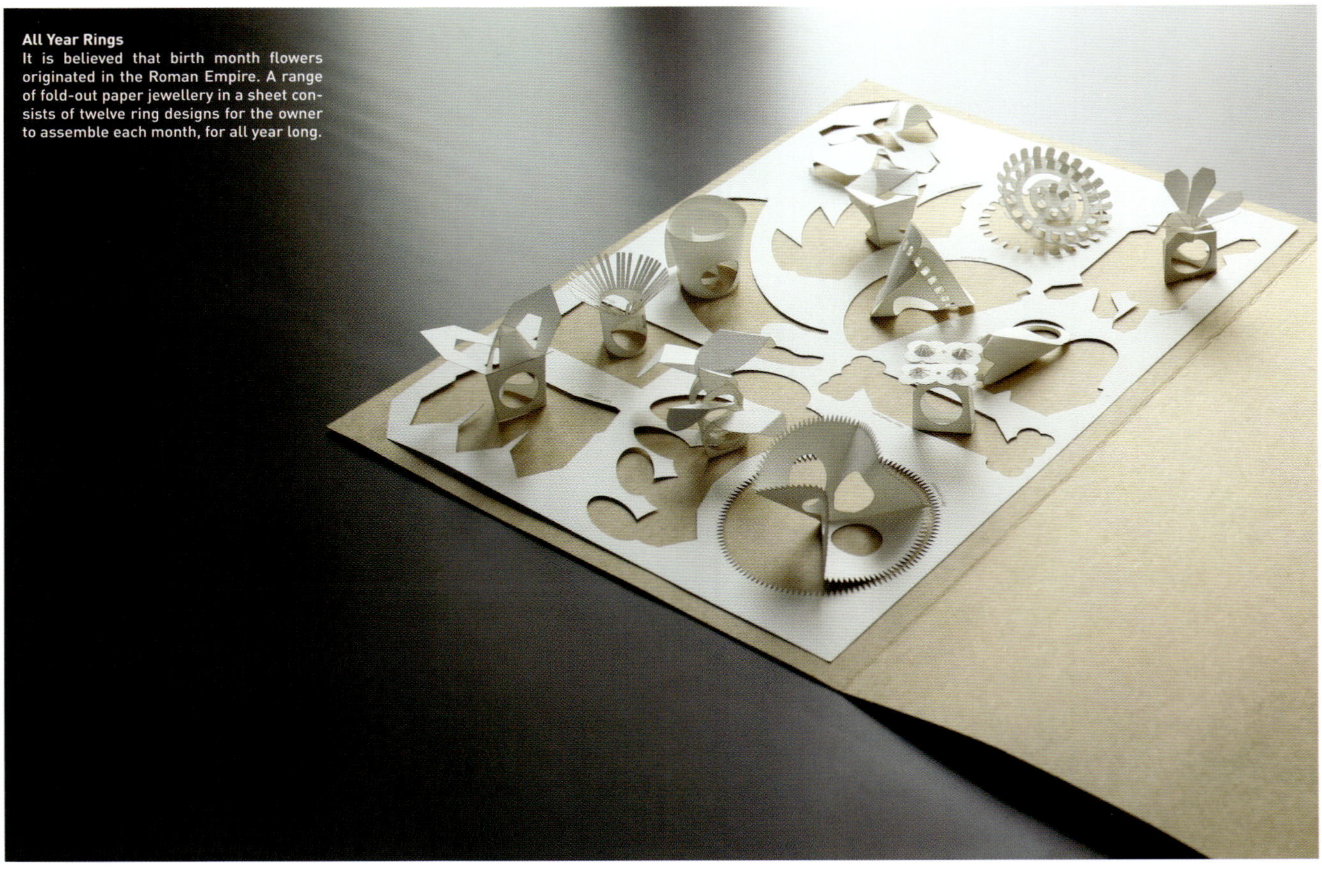

**All Year Rings**
It is believed that birth month flowers originated in the Roman Empire. A range of fold-out paper jewellery in a sheet consists of twelve ring designs for the owner to assemble each month, for all year long.

# TT:NT

www.tt-nt.info

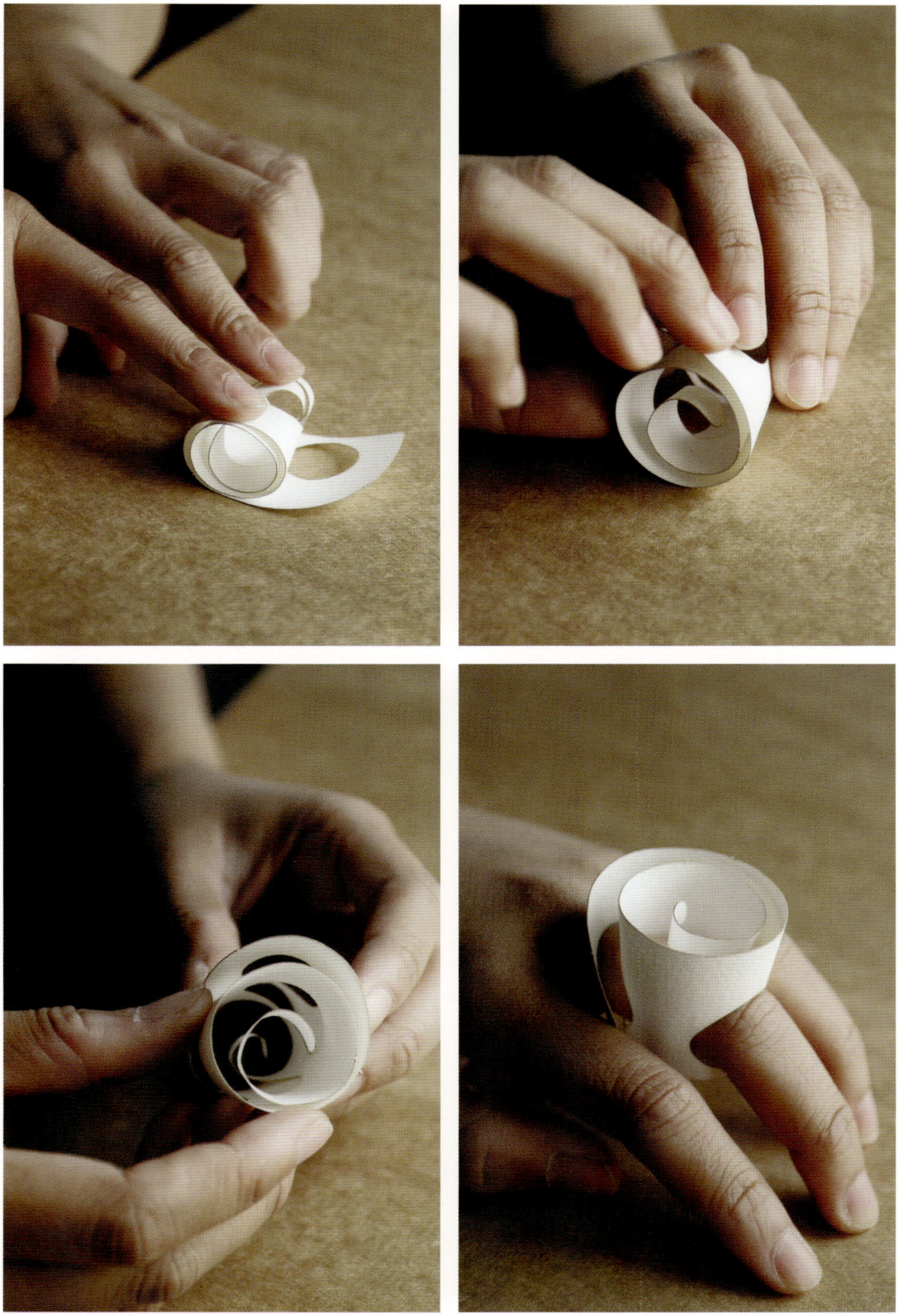

Established by the collaboration projects between us, Tithi and Nutre. We both graduated from Royal College of Art in 2007, one who graduated in product design and the other one in jewellery design and making, one who develops ideas in her dreaming head and the other who develops by her hand, one who do things in one piece and the other who put hundreds pieces in one, one who would go for the most basic stuff and the other who would look for the most detailing work. We our difference and insanity in the projects we've created under the name of TT:NT, seeking to design the product that response both design and craft needs, good concept and fine quality along with our uniqueness and of course, happiness.

**Photos by ©Suratchai C**

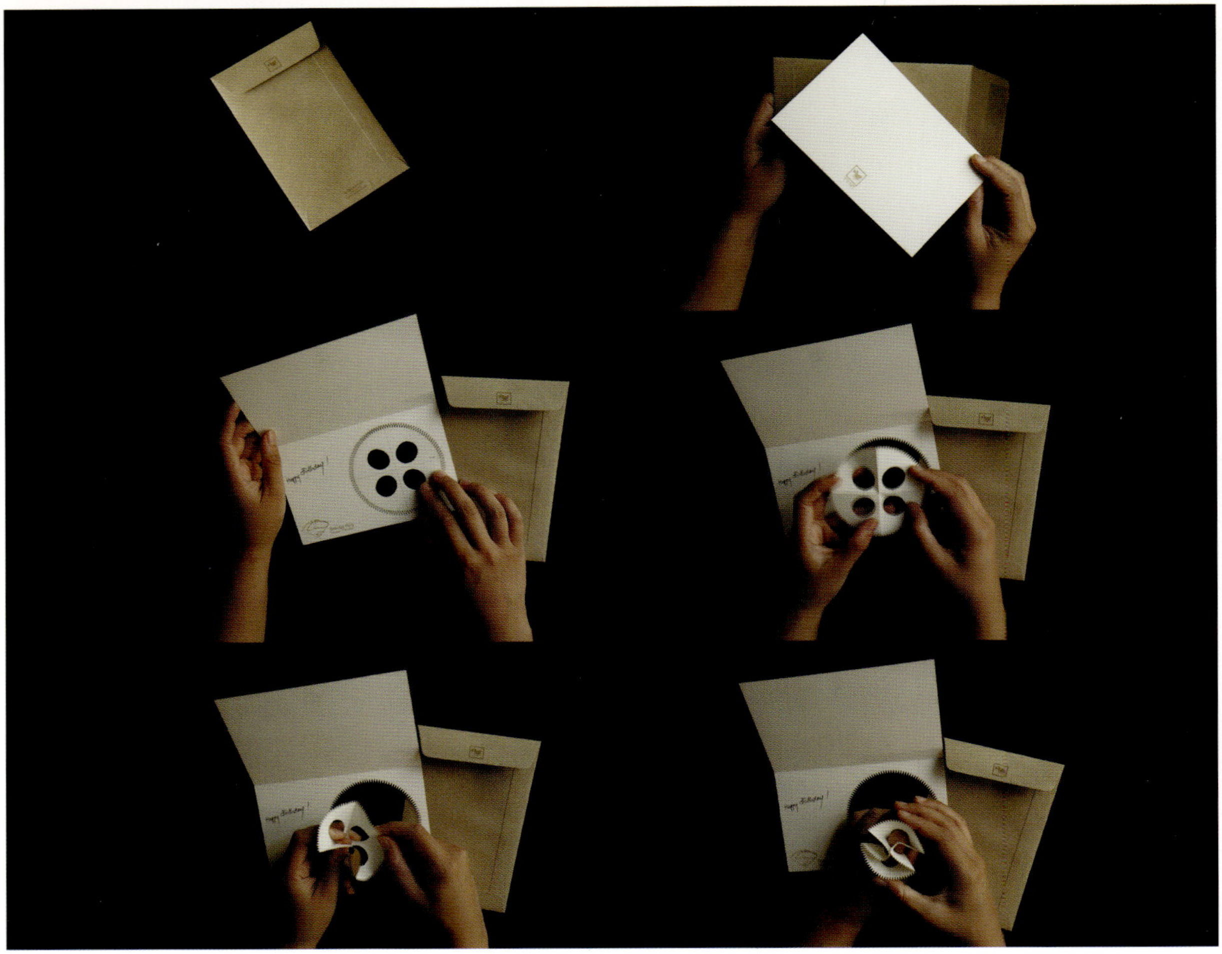

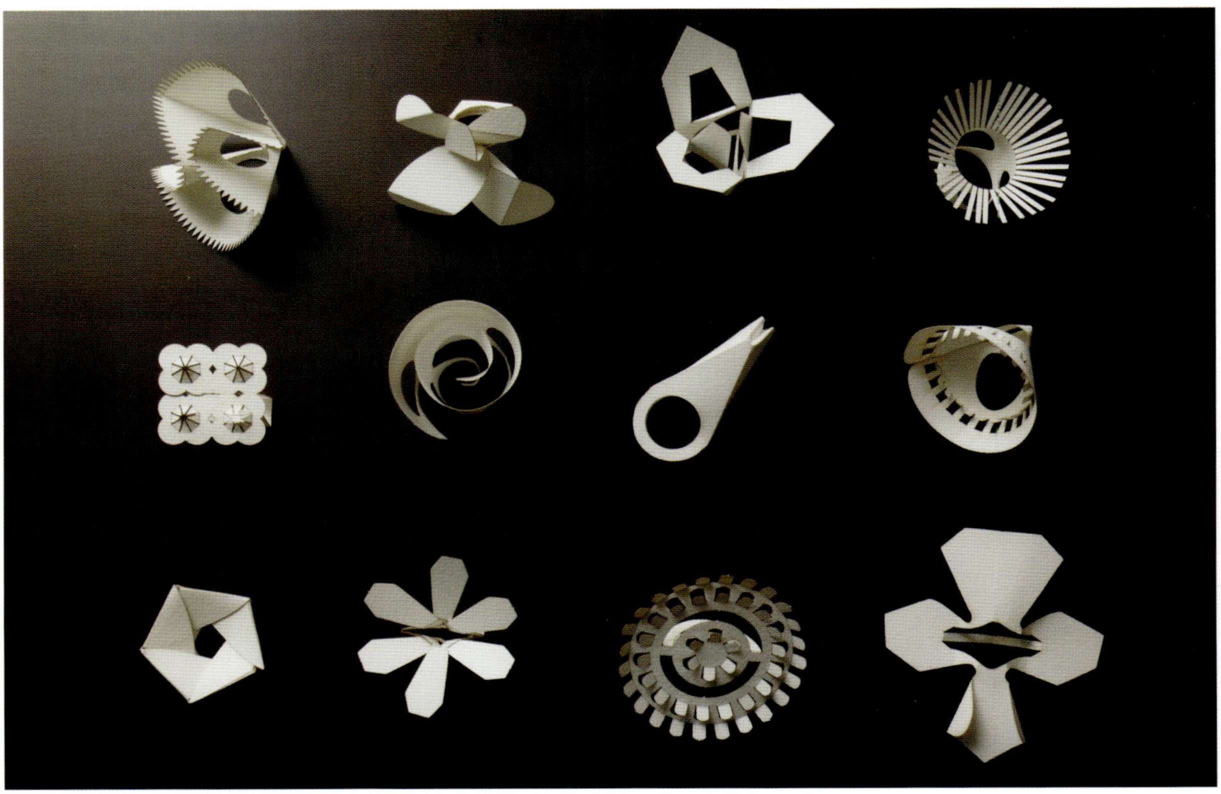

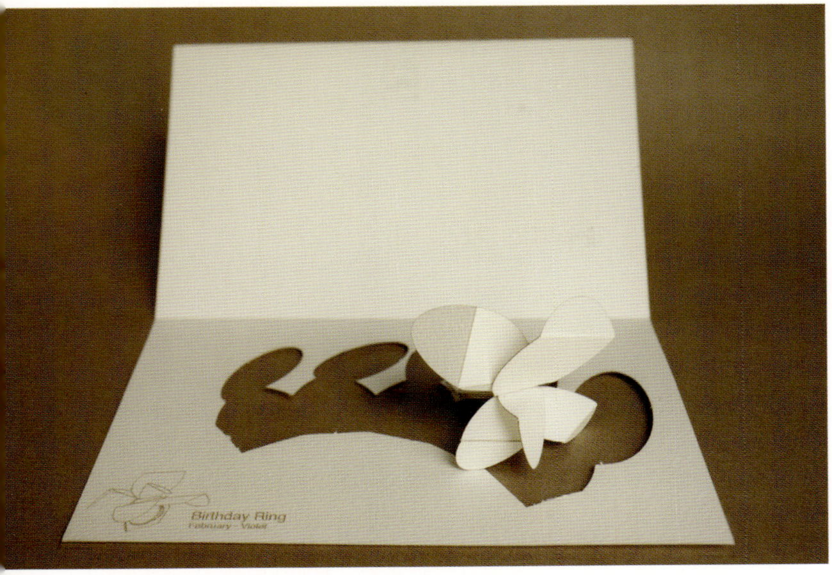


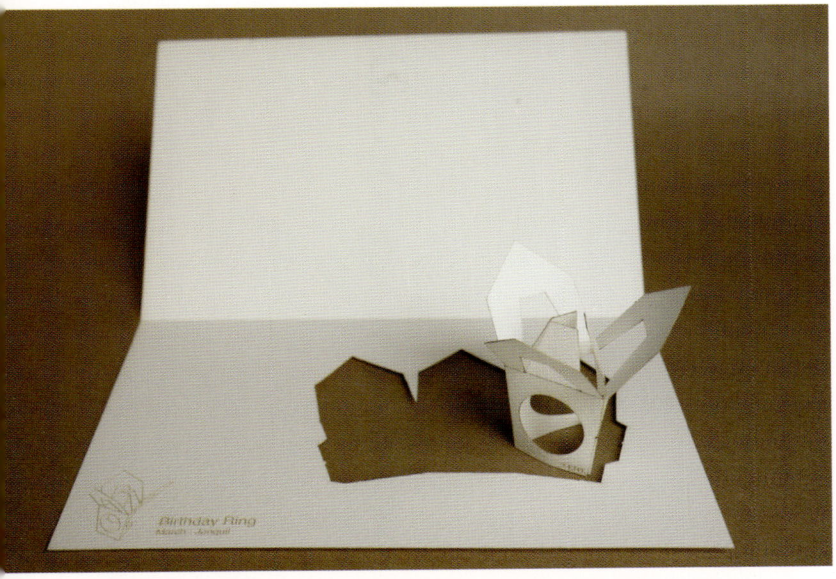


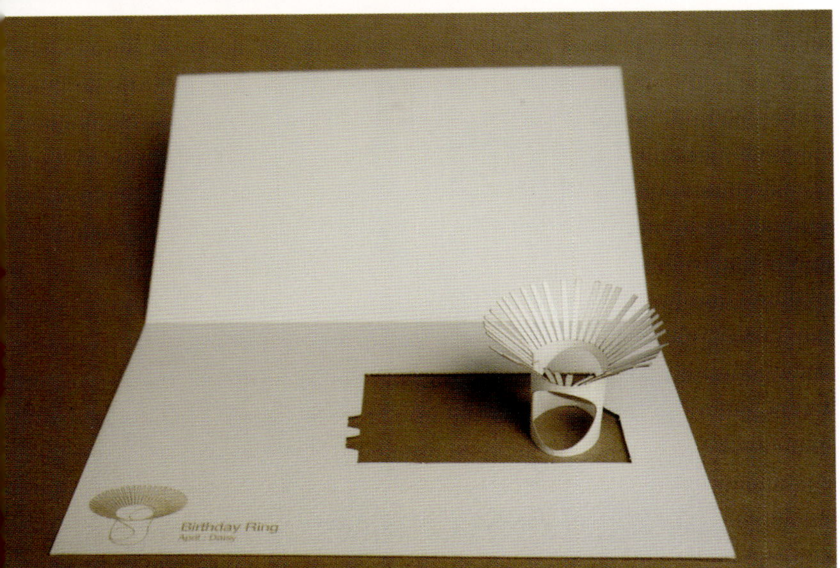


'**Birthday Ring**' collection is a paper card that folds into a flower-shaped ring resembling the birth flower for each calendar month. They are special birthday presents for the special person.

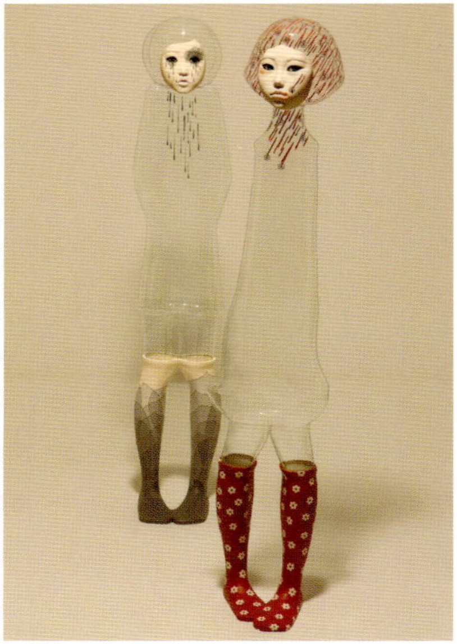

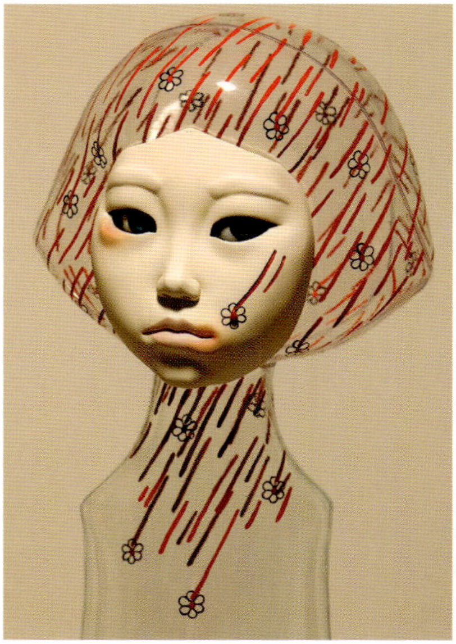

**The Disguised**, mixed media 130(h)cm, 2009

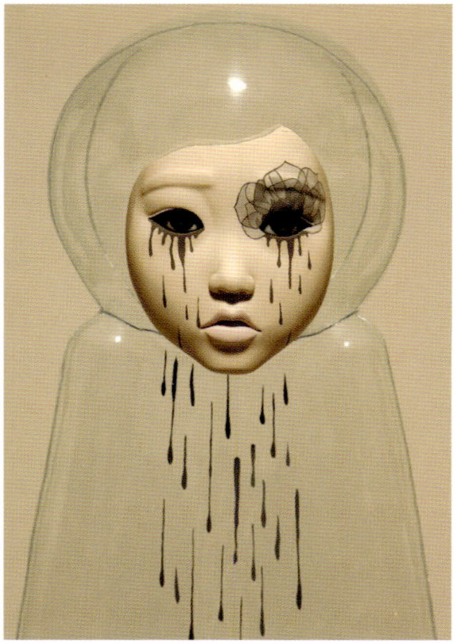

**The Disguised**, mixed media 127(h)cm, 2009

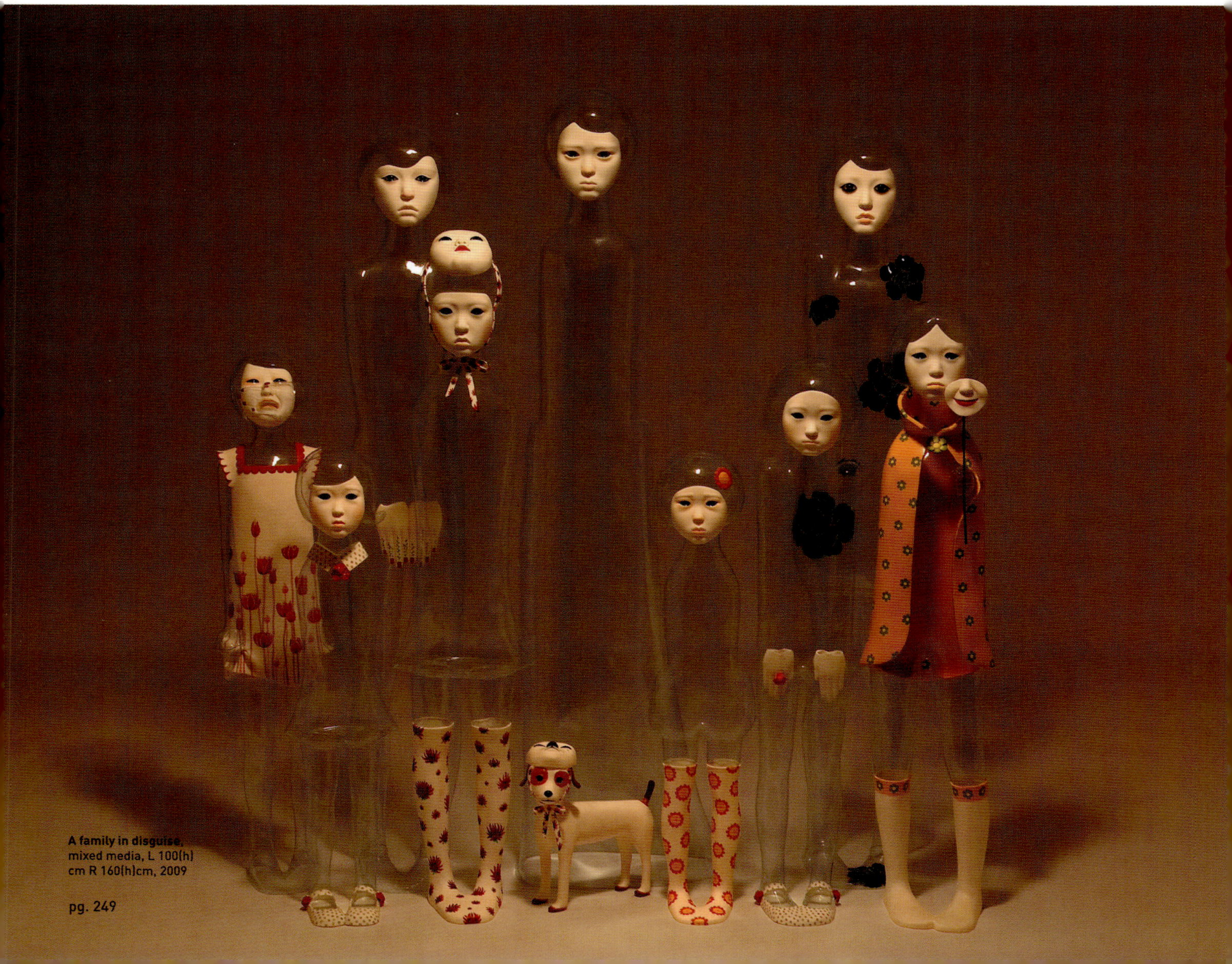

**A family in disguise**, mixed media, L 100(h) cm R 160(h)cm, 2009

# Yu Jin Young

http://blog.naver.com/u_jin0

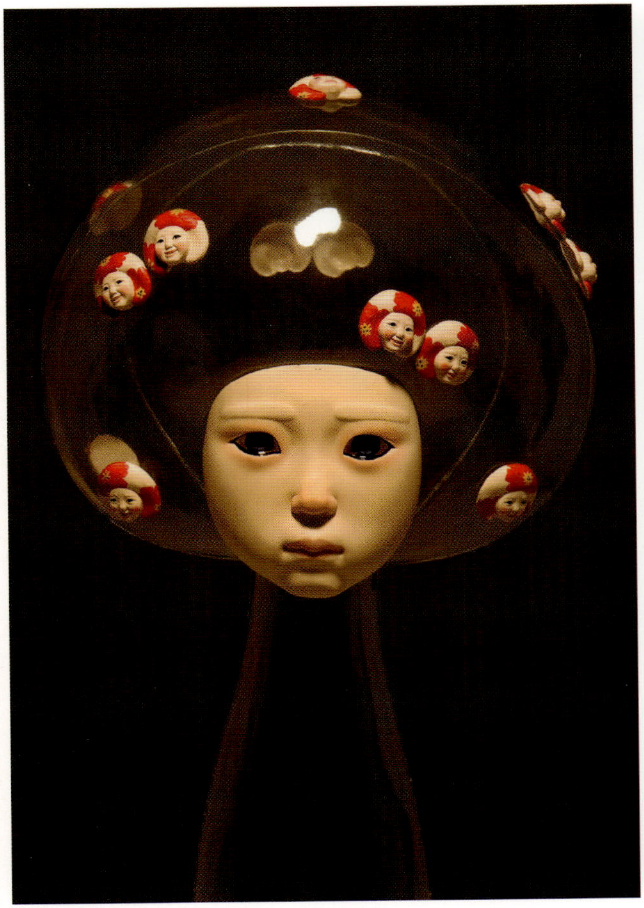

**A family in disguise.** Mixed media 130(h)cm/ 2008

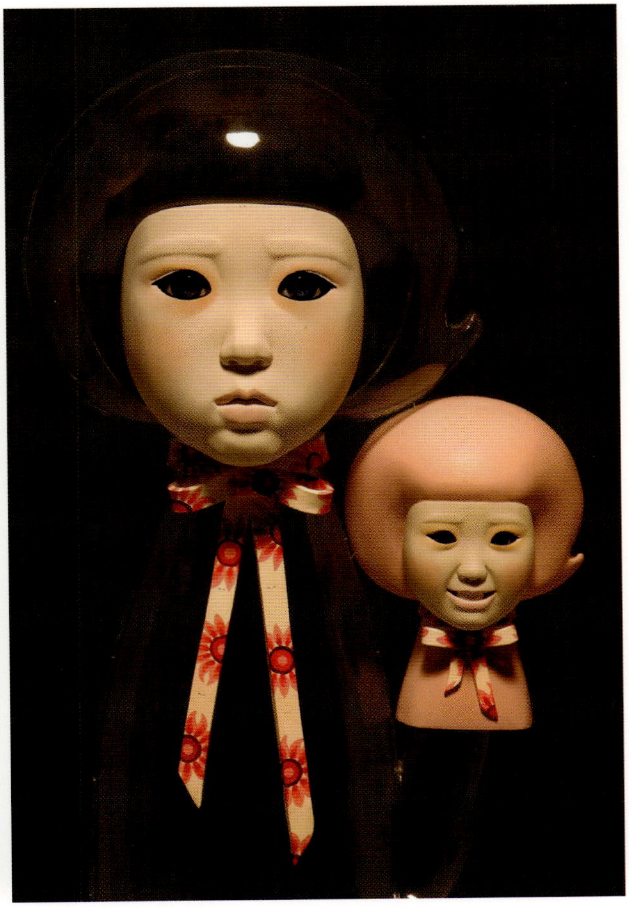

**A family in disguise.** Mixed media 110(h)cm/ 2008

My works feigning expressionless and loneliness faces. They are holding their tears back and swallowing them, or they try to put on a cool face despite the traces of tears on their faces. Or simply they seem to have something hiding behind the hurried pretense of expressionless faces. The transparent body means a perfect shield that makes it possible to hide itself anywhere, while the crying face has a meaning of warning as 'Don't come to me!' My figures defend themselves through their crying faces because they make it uneasy for others to come closer. It seems that if others come and say something to comfort them, they might burst out crying. But it is also true people cannot pass them by when they see their faces once. The pieces warn the gallery, 'Come to me, if you could comfort me with all your heart!' In other words, it's like a sign of warning and refusal to the people who try to give help not having fully understood their situations.

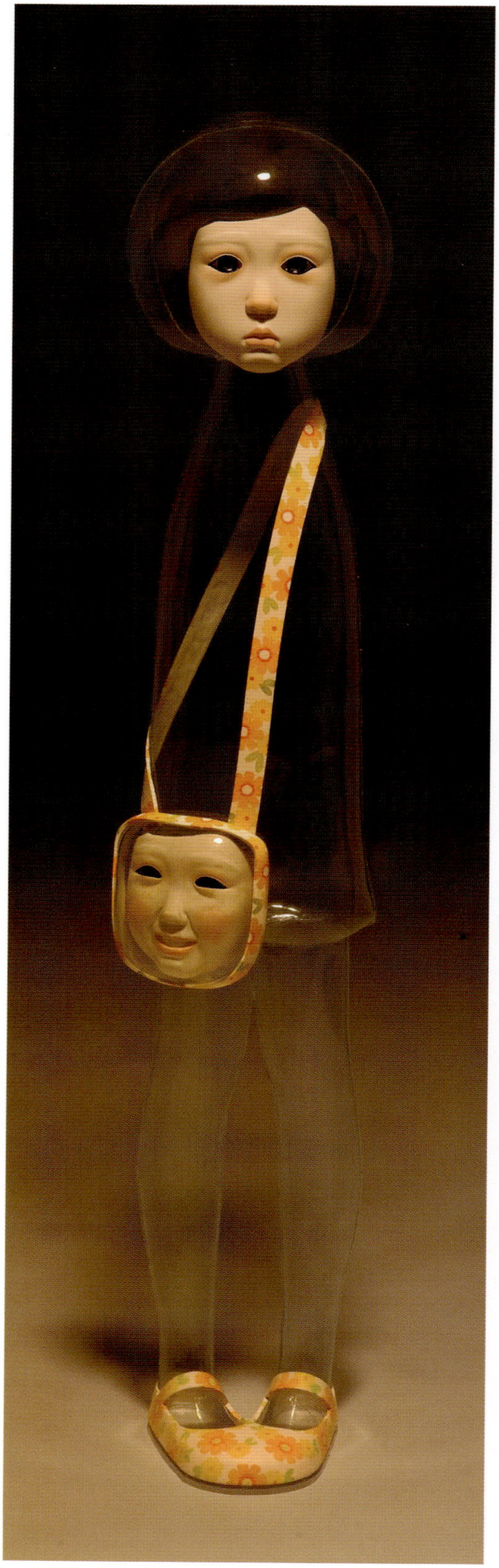

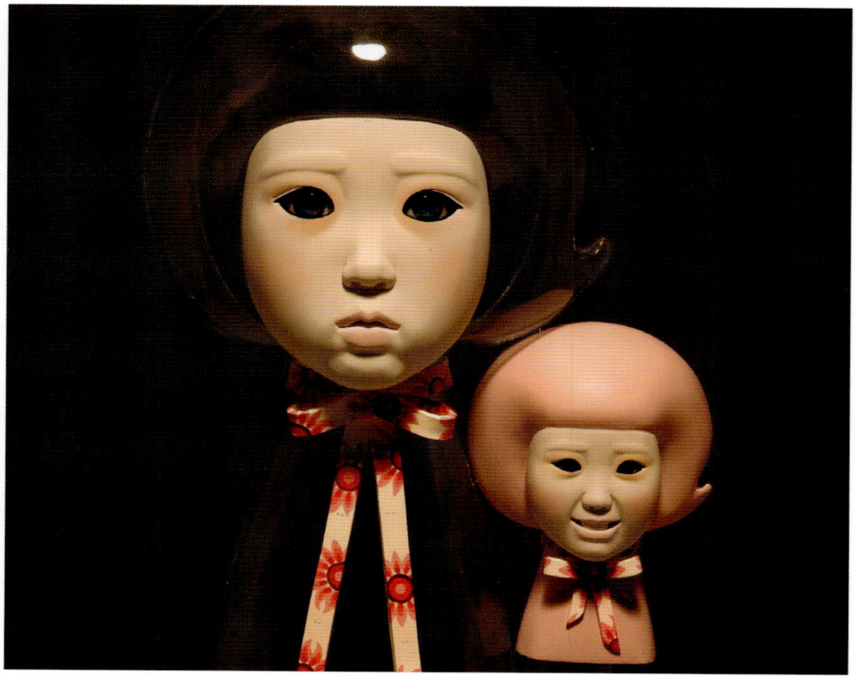

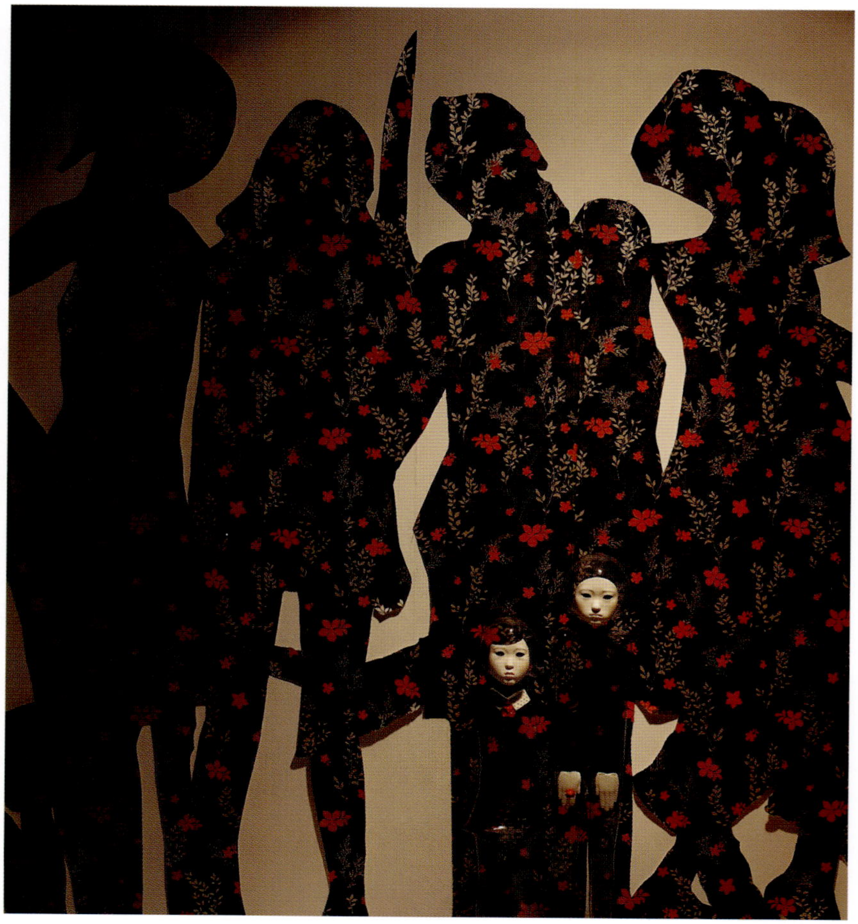

**Welcome - The guests**, mixed media, L 92(h)cm, R 111(h)cm , 2007

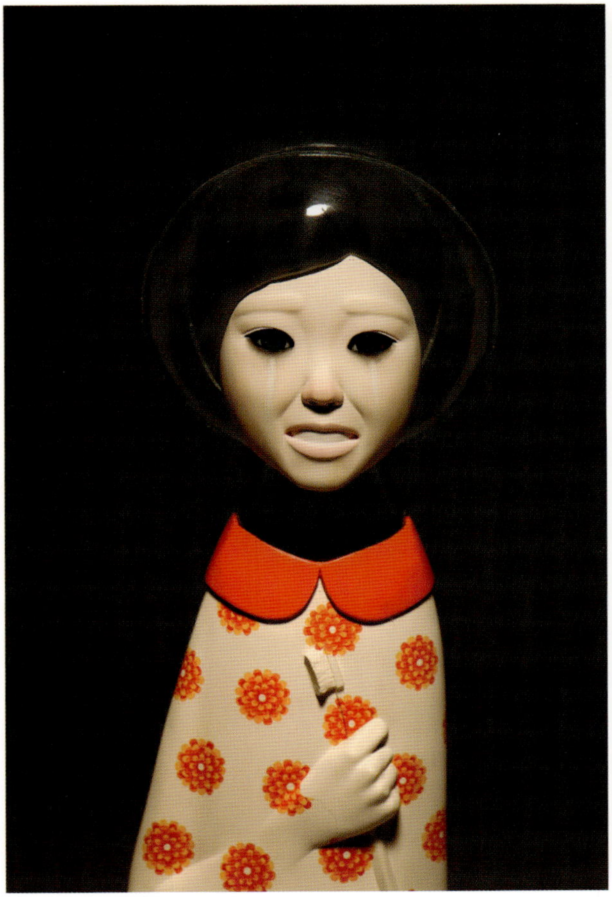

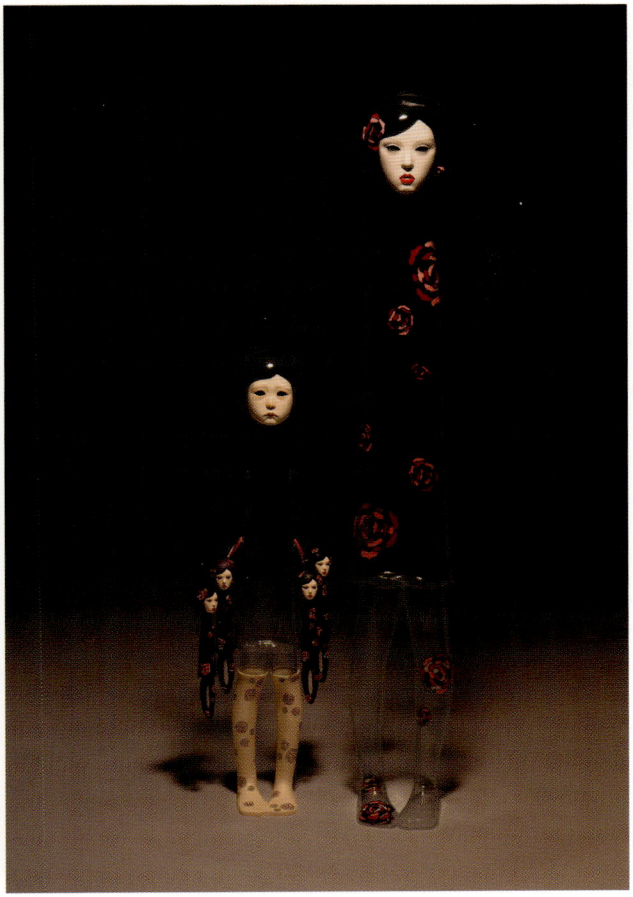

**A family in disguise**. mixed media 110(h)cm/ 2008

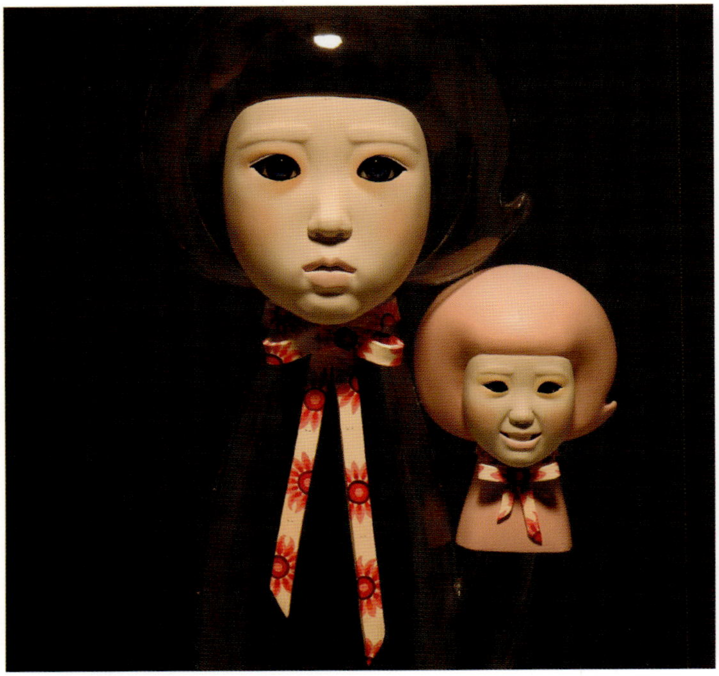

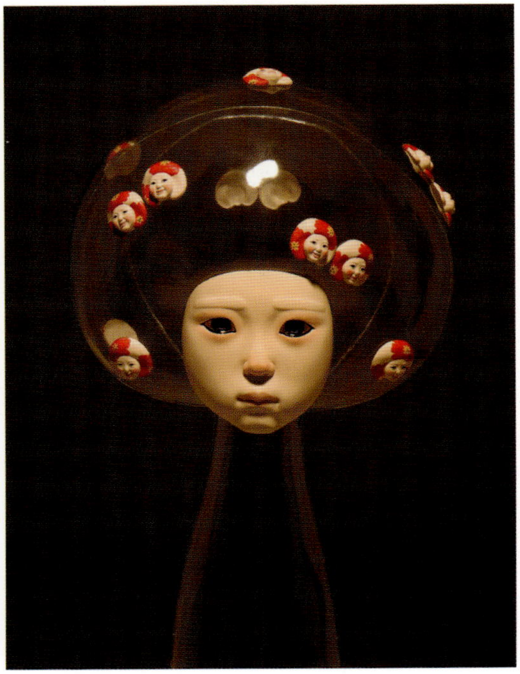

**A family in disguise**. mixed media 130(h)cm 2008

# Index

| | |
|---|---|
| ALTHEA CROME | www.bugknits.com |
| AMY SARKISIAN | www.asark.com |
| ANTHEA BUSH | www.antheabush.com |
| AOYAMA HINA | www.hinaaoyama.com |
| ARTYARN | www.artyarn.org |
| ATELIER PARIRI | www.pariri.com |
| BEATRICE DE DOMENICO | www.myspace.com/beadedomenico |
| BENJAMIN SHINE | www.benjaminshine.com |
| BRIAN DETTMER | www.briandettmer.com |
| BUBBLESBINSBURRY | www.bubblesbinburry.com |
| CARSON FOX | www.carsonfox.com |
| CATHERINE HAMMERTON | www.catherinehammerton.com |
| CHRISTIAN TAGLIAVINI | www.christiantagliavini.com |
| DEBBIE SMYTH | www.debbiesmyth.blogspot.com |
| DOMINIC WILCOX | www.dominicwilcox.com |
| DOROTHEE VAN BIESEN | www.broderoll.wordpress.com |
| ELISA STROZYK | www.elisastrozyk.de |
| ERIC KU | www.ericku.org |
| ERIKA IRIS SIMMONS | www.iri5.com |
| FURNISH | www.furnish.jp |
| GABRIEL DISHAW | www.gabrieldishaw.com |
| GAVIN LIAO | www.cuber34.blogspot.com |
| GEHARD DEMETZ | www.geharddemetz.com |
| GHOSTPATROL | www.ghostpatrol.com |
| GWON OSANG | www.eosang.net |
| HAPPYCENTRO | www.happycentro.it |
| HELEN MUSSLEWHITE | www.helenmusselwhite.com |
| HELLE JORGENSEN | www.hellejorgensen.typepad.com |
| HERB WILLIAMS | www.herbwilliamsart.com |
| HIROTOSHI ITO | www.jiyuseki.com |
| INGELA OCH VI | www.ingelaochvi.com |
| INSTANT HUTONG | www.instanthutong.com |
| ISAAC SALAZAR | www.flickr.com/photos/bookofart/ |
| JIM SKULL | www.jim-skullgallery.com |
| JOAQUIMA CASAS | www.kupkup-land.blogspot.com |
| JO HAMILTON | www.johamilton.com |
| JOANA VASCONCELOS | www.joanavasconcelos.com |
| JULIE VERMEILLE | www.julievermeillie.com |
| JULIEN VALLÈE | www.javallee.com |
| JUNIOR FRITZ JACQUET | www.juniorfritzjacquet.com |
| KAKO UEDA | www.kakoueda.com |
| KATRIN SONNLEITNER | www.katirn-sonnleitner.com |
| KEETRA DEAN DIXON | www.fromkeetra.com |
| KEPA RASMUSSEN | www.kepa.co.uk |
| LIM SI PING | www.pixel-pastry.com |
| MARK ANDREW WEBBER | www.markandrewwebber.com |
| MARK KHAISMAN | www.khaismanstudio.com |
| MARK LANGAN | www.langanart.com |

| | |
|---|---|
| MIRIAM MASELKOWSKI | www.myspace.com/mmaselkowski |
| MOLLY B RIGHT | www.mollybright.com |
| MOSSTIKA | www.mosstika.com |
| NAOMI RYDER | www.naomiryder.co.uk |
| NATHAN SAWAYA | www.brickartist.com |
| NICO | www.plushism.blogspot.com |
| NICOLÁS CUESTAS | www.nicolascuestas.com |
| NUTRE ARAYAVANISH | www.nutrejeweller.com |
| ROBERT BRADFORD | www.robertbradford.co.uk |
| SANTIAGO MORAHAN | www.disenocartonero.blogspot.com |
| SARAH BRIDGLAND | www.sarahbridgland.com |
| SCOTT JARVIE | www.scottjarvie.co.uk |
| SIMON SCHUBERT | www.simonshubert.de |
| THOMAS RASCHKE | www.thomasraschke.de |
| TRENT WHITEHEAD | www.trentwhitehead.com |
| TROMARAMA | www.tromaram.blogspot.com |
| TT:NT | www.tt-nt.info |
| YU JIN YOUNG | blog.naver.com/u_jin0 |

MERGE; Art x Craft x Design


Publisher: Abdul Nasser

Published in 2012 by :
Gingko Press, Inc.
1321 Fifth Street
Berkeley, CA 94710
T: (510) 898-1195
F: (510) 898-1196

First Published in 2012 by
BASHEER Graphic Books
Block 231, Bain Street, #04-19
Bras Basah Complex
Singapore 180 231
T: (65) 6336 0810
F: (65) 6334 1950
E: abdul@basheergraphic.com
W: www.basheergraphic.com

Concept: Abdul Nasser
Curator: Euphemia Toong
Designed by: Big Bros Workshop
Cover artwork by: Joaquima Casas
Printed by: Tiger Printing (Hong Kong) Co. Ltd

ISBN: 978-1-58423-398-5



-------

ACKNOWLEDGEMENTS

BASHEER Graphic Books would like to thank all the artists, designers or studios for their kind consent to publish their works and the photographers who have generously granted the permission to use their images. Also to being so patient with us right from the start till now when the book is published. This project would not have been possible without your complete trust and understanding towards us. Also to those who has made significant contribution to the compilation of this book, you are definitely much appreciated and loved. We are also very grateful to the many others whose names do not appear on the credits but have made specific input and continuous support the whole time. We cannot stress how thankful we are to each and individual one of you - you know who you are, without you there wouldn't be MERGE; Art x Craft x Design.